War and Peace
in the
Nuclear Age

WAR
AND
PEACE
IN THE
NUCLEAR
AGE

John Newhouse

 Alfred A. Knopf, New York | 1989

THIS IS A BORZOI BOOK
PUBLISHED BY
ALFRED A. KNOPF, INC.

Copyright © 1988 by John Newhouse and WGBH Educational Foundation
All rights reserved under International and Pan-
American Copyright Conventions. Published in
the United States by Alfred A. Knopf, Inc., New York, and
simultaneously in Canada by Random House of Canada
Limited, Toronto. Distributed by Random House, Inc.,
New York.

Library of Congress Catalog Card Number: 88-45324
ISBN: 0-394-56217-8

Manufactured in the United States of America
First Edition

TO

Symmie, Elizabeth

and John

"WE HAD THE EXPERIENCE BUT
MISSED THE MEANING."

—T. S. Eliot, *Four Quartets*

Contents

Acknowledgments

Writing is a learning experience, and I am indebted to the people who enriched my knowledge and understanding of the nuclear age. They were a large number. This book covers a lot of ground—from the stirrings of the "new physics" early in the century to events of June 1988, notably the last meeting between Ronald Reagan and Mikhail Gorbachev, and Mr. Gorbachev's special conference of the Soviet Communist party some days later. In between came crises, confrontations, negotiations and even a few arguments. I have tried to relate much of that and to describe the historic effect of nuclear weapons on relations between adversaries, as well as the singular effects of these weapons on relations between allies.

Quite apart from the pyramiding material on nuclear-related issues that is now available, the writer of this kind of history must rely heavily on the willingness of those who were directly involved in the events of interest to speak frankly of what they know and remember. Much of this book draws upon information obtained in innumerable interviews, and since some of the people concerned cannot be identified, perhaps none should be identified. Still, I wish to note that the background and many of the insights I acquired from Hans Bethe, General Andrew Goodpaster, John Manley, Richard Neustadt, the late I. I. Rabi, Benjamin Read, Dean Rusk, and Joseph Volpe were especially useful and could not, in my view, have been supplied by others. I am, of course, indebted to all who helped—current and former officials, civilian and military, current and former staff aides, and current and former diplomats of several countries.

I enjoyed and benefited from my exposure to the gifted people from WGBH, Boston's public television station, who put together the series of thirteen programs, also called "War and Peace in the Nuclear Age," for the Public Broadcasting System. I would like to express appreciation to them, starting with Zvi Dor-Ner, the Executive Producer, and Elizabeth Deane, the Senior Producer. Other producers who deserve mention include: David Espar, Sue Crowther, Austin Hoyt, Jonathan Holmes, Carol Lynn Dornbrand, Ben Shepherd, Graham Chedd, Christopher Koch, Peter Raymont, Alice Markowitz, and Chana Gazit. A special word of thanks is due Peter McGhee, Program Manager for National Production at WGBH, and another to Deborah Paddock.

My appreciation also extends to the coproducers: Central Independent Television, Great Britain; and Nippon Hoso Kyokai (Japan Broadcasting Corporation), Japan.

Further appreciation goes to the underwriters: The Annenberg/CPB Project; the Chubb Group of Insurance Agencies; W. Alton Jones Foundation; Andrew W. Mellon Foundation; the Rockefeller Brothers Fund; the Corporation for Public Broadcasting; the Alfred P. Sloan Foundation; and the John D. and Catherine T. MacArthur Foundation.

I feel a deep sense of gratitude to the following organizations: the Brookings Institution of which I have been a guest scholar over the past several years; the Florence and John Schumann Foundation for its support of the research on the book and specifically to William Mullins, its President; and the Alfred P. Sloan Foundation for its support.

Arthur Singer of the Sloan Foundation was a catalyst for the entire project, and one who encouraged me to undertake the book. I would like to thank him. I am indebted to Philip Farley, Raymond Garthoff, and Leon Sigal, each of whom read chapters.

The people who have been named in the acknowledgments bear no responsibility for the book's conclusions or point of view. That is mine alone.

I was temporarily helped with the research by first Lydia Howarth and then Jana Belsky. I am indebted to them. With the arrival of Sidney Brown, I had continuing and splendid assistance. Apart from research assistant, a role in which she excelled, Sidney was largely responsible for finding and selecting the pictures that accompany the text; I am deeply grateful to her.

A final note of thanks is owed to Ashbel Green, my editor at Knopf, who also encouraged me to take on this book and then, as before, provided considerable and expert help.

War and Peace
in the
Nuclear Age

I

The Rivals

Nuclear physics was a lively though still obscure subject in November 1933, when Maxim Litvinov, the Soviet People's Commissar for Foreign Affairs, arrived in Washington to restore diplomatic relations; the United States had broken them off after the Bolshevik Revolution in 1917. Establishing relations was strenuously opposed within some American political circles and by much of the clergy. Godless communism, it was said, would now be able to exploit the discontent among American working people and the host of the unemployed. Stalin's ministers had been hinting that American exports would again find their way into the controlled Soviet market if relations were restored. Herbert Hoover never took the bait, but the incoming administration of Franklin D. Roosevelt—intent on being innovative about the Depression—was interested. The pressure from commercial interests, which saw Russia as a huge untapped market, may have tipped the balance. "We could lick Soviet propaganda by sending over a couple of boatloads of Sears Roebuck catalogues"[1] was a fancy shared by many businessmen.

Actually, the dispute was obscured by more robust events, the foremost of which was the return of legal liquor; Prohibition ended less than three weeks after Litvinov's arrival in the United States. America's interest in the big world, such as it was, seemed then to be trained on the conquest by men and women of the airspace above them. Wiley Post's record-breaking flight around the world in the *Winny Mae*, a high-wing monoplane, was probably the second most exciting event of 1933.

Neither of today's superpowers was a major figure on the world stage in the 1930s, although Russia, unlike America, was arming vigorously. The

United States had turned a generally blind eye to the disorder and anarchy into which relations between the European powers were drifting. In 1935, Congress passed the Neutrality Act, an evenhanded statue which obliged the President to deny arms to any aggressor or to any victim of aggression. The act didn't cover the conflict in Spain, but Roosevelt adopted the nonintervention policies of Britain and France and imposed a "moral" embargo on military assistance to all nations. In 1937, Congress stiffened the Neutrality Act and made it permanent. Isolationism was ascendant, sailing under a banner which proclaimed, "No Foreign Wars."

Joseph Stalin worried about threats from the East and West. Japan's seizure of Manchuria in 1931 sharpened his interest in moderating relations with the Western democracies. Hitler's aggressive diplomacy and military buildup were launched while Stalin was still engaged in extending his authority over eternal Russia—a legion of nationality groups spread across twenty million square miles and eleven time zones. He was liquidating opposition, real or imagined, to the colossal task of herding a feudal peasant society into the machine age. The terrible purges occurring between 1936 and 1938 depleted most institutions, destroyed a million or more lives, and caused eight million to be imprisoned in labor camps. Stalin was at least as insular as the American isolationists; he routinely invoked the threat to world socialism from decaying but still aggressive capitalist societies to justify a tyranny that drew its authority from the secret police and other so-called organs of suppression. The purges pointed up the regime's phobic insecurity, which could be explained by the large numbers of people in western Russia who welcomed Hitler's panzer units as liberators in 1941.

In vain did Henry Stimson, who would become Secretary of War in 1940, and a few other clearheaded Americans try to alert their society to the threat from abroad. Abruptly, most of the world's military power had been gathered by Germany, Japan, and the Soviet Union. No one knew against whom Stalin was arming, or which side he would take if shooting started between the blocs. Stalin probably didn't know himself. Bolshevism wasn't rash; it would encourage revolution elsewhere but not take part in making it happen. Stalin's diplomacy was aimed at discouraging any power from breaching Russia's frontiers. Still, an alliance of convenience between the three totalitarian states couldn't be excluded, and quite clearly would overwhelm the defenses of the lightly armed democracies. The world balance of power had turned dramatically against them. Stimson, having worried aloud about "Japanese militarism" since 1931, began arguing in 1935 against neutrality and isolationism. Soon, he and the other Cassandras were stressing the threat to Britain and France—hence to America—from German fascism.[2]

It may have been too late for Britain and France to have done much about Hitler after acquiescing in his reoccupation of the Rhineland provinces in 1936 and his seizure of Austria in 1938. The victors of World War I shrank from the prospect of another great bloodletting. France was bound by treaty to help the Czechs defend themselves, and Britain was bound to aid France. But alliances weren't being taken seriously. It was as puerile a patch of diplomatic history as any Europe had known. In 1938, British Prime Minister Neville Chamberlain described the threat from Hitler to Czechoslovakia as "a quarrel in a faraway country between people of whom we know nothing."[3] Britain, as always, worried about maintaining a balance of power in Europe, and was reluctant to back France against Germany. The only leaders who seemed to know what they were doing were Hitler and Stalin. Hitler wanted calm in Eastern Europe while he pursued his ends in Western Europe. Once these were attained, he would attack the Soviet Union. Stalin needed to buy time to prepare for that moment, or if possible to head it off. In August 1939, he and Hitler turned the anti-Comintern pact between Germany, Italy, and Japan on its head by signing a nonaggression agreement. He, too, misread Hitler by trying to appease him with ill-advised moves such as aiding the German war effort with Soviet exports. "Stalin and I are the only ones who see the future," said Hitler to his General Staff, "so I shall shake hands with Stalin within a few weeks . . . and undertake with him a new distribution of the world." But later, he added, "We shall crush the Soviet Union."[4]

Both the Nazis and the Soviets damaged their prospects by abusing many of their best natural scientists. Stalinism's intolerance of abstraction, and its aversion to truths that couldn't be easily squared with doctrine, guaranteed a conflict. The effect of the Nazis on German science, by comparison, was more immediate, more clear-cut, and broader. The illustrious names in German and world physics were by and large Jewish or partly Jewish. A month or so after Hitler took full possession of the government in 1933, a campaign to rid the laboratories of non-Aryan figures began. Some were abruptly retired or dismissed; others resigned to avoid being forced from their places. Most left Germany for laboratories in Copenhagen, Paris, Zurich, Cambridge, England, and elsewhere in Europe. Some went to America; among these was Albert Einstein, who in the fall of 1933 left Berlin to take a job at the newly created Institute for Advanced Study in Princeton, New Jersey. A French physicist, Paul Langevin, captured the reaction of his European colleagues, saying, "It's as important an event as would be the transfer of the Vatican from Rome to the New World. The Pope of Physics has moved and the United States will now become the center of the natural sciences."[5] (His comment was considerably more prophetic than Langevin probably intended it to be.)

By then, a change of Copernican scale in thinking about nature was under way in laboratories across Western and Central Europe. The classical physics of an earlier era was being pushed aside by two revolutionary ideas, one of them Max Planck's quantum theory. In 1900, he suggested that energy is discontinuous—discharged like bullets from a gun. Five years later, Einstein magisterially expanded Planck's concept by publishing his theory about the relativity of energy and mass. "Einstein's genius was panoramic," wrote one atomic physicist. "In one mind-boggling, super-novaesque . . . burst of creativity, Einstein had united matter, radiation, and energy by verifying the quantum theory and postulating the Theory of Relativity, from the submicroscopic dimensions of the atomic nucleus to the vast reaches of the cosmos."[6] The classical view of energy as being emitted in continuous waves receded. Einstein called the bullets of energy "quanta." His legatees—the first fiddles of the "new physics"—didn't imagine that they were going to affect history or tame natural forces. They were driven by a sense of arcane universal truths being nearer to hand and perhaps within reach. Some of the excitement arose from debate and disagreement between brilliant peers. Some were more skeptical and cautious than others, often questioning the meaning of their own work or misreading its implications. In 1919, Ernest Rutherford vindicated the alchemists by transmuting one element into another. He did this by smashing an atom, thereby causing a nucleus of nitrogen to become a nucleus of hydrogen. Eight years earlier, Rutherford had discovered the nucleus—the heart of the atom and twenty thousand times smaller. This atomic nucleus was shown to be a powerhouse, once it became apparent that radioactive energy originated there, as for many years Rutherford had been saying it did. (In 1913, Marie Curie, who discovered radium in 1898, described Rutherford as the "one man living who promises to confer some inestimable boon on mankind.")[7] For purposes of scientific inquiry, the structure of matter had become the structure of the atom.

Germany was the center of excitement throughout the 1920s—"the beautiful years," as Robert Jungk called them in his *Brighter than a Thousand Suns,* a vivid portrayal of the early period of the nuclear age. Laboratories and lecture halls in Berlin, Göttingen, Leipzig, and Munich were swept up in the transition from the classical to the new. Each had its luminaries. Max Planck lectured on theoretical physics in Berlin. (Sir Rudolf Peierls, a Berlin-born physicist who helped create the atomic bomb, was a student of Planck's and in a memoir called *Bird of Passage* says the lectures were "the worst I have ever attended. He would read verbatim from one of his books, and if you had a copy of the book, you could follow line by line.")[8] Foreign visitors streamed to these institutions, above all to the Georgia Augusta University in medieval Göttingen. Many of them came to learn from three of the new physics' brightest stars: Max Born, James Franck, and David Hilbert. Rutherford in Cambridge and Niels Bohr in Copenhagen were deservedly preeminent, but these three Germans, who began working together at Göttingen in 1921, were singularly gifted disciples. They interpreted the lengthening sequence of discovery and contributed to it.

Göttingen had a special glow then. Students welcomed one visiting physicist by marching to his house at twilight and chanting Planck's quantum formula.[9] Among the visitors was Robert Oppenheimer, who supervised the building of the first atomic bombs at Los Alamos. In Göttingen, "Oppy" was remembered not only as a budding physicist but also for the intensity of his interest in philosophy, philology, and literature. In a letter to a friend at Cambridge (England), written in 1926, he said: "You would like Göttingen, I think . . . The science is much better than at Cambridge, and on the whole, probably the best to be found. They are working very hard here and combining a fantastically impregnable metaphysical disingenuousness with the go-getting habits of a wall-paper manufacturer. The result is that the work done here has an almost demonic lack of plausibility to it and is highly successful."[10] Oppenheimer was just twenty-two then, but few of those at Göttingen were over twenty-five. Paul Dirac, an Anglo-Swiss mathematician who won a Nobel Prize ten years later but was then scarcely older than Oppenheimer, composed some lines for a student revue:

> *Age is of course a fever chill*
> *That every physicist must fear*
> *He's better dead than living still*
> *When once he's past his thirtieth year.*

The Jewish scientists, including Born and Franck, who left Germany in the spring of 1933, scattered widely, although none went to the Soviet Union. Many were attracted to Bohr's Institute for Theoretical Physics in Copenhagen, partly because Bohr sent notes to Germans involved in atomic research, saying, "Come and stay with us for a while, and think things over quietly until you decide where you would like to go."[11]

Bohr was one of those improbable figures whom everyone talked about endlessly but always approvingly. He was as admired as he was revered, the natural leader of others because, Einstein aside, they judged him the greatest among them and the noblest. (I. I. Rabi, the eminent American physicist and Nobel laureate, was asked about Bohr and whether he was indeed the foremost figure of his era. He was "second only to Einstein," said Rabi. "Einstein had a pipeline to God.") Einstein described Bohr as "like an extremely sensitive child who moves around the world in a sort of trance."[12] Peierls said, "One could usually recognize people who had spent some time in Copenhagen by their use of some of Bohr's phrases."[13]

The exodus spread beyond Germany as scholars in Budapest, Vienna, and many other places distanced themselves from racial laws. The list of those who went into exile and later took part in developing the atomic bomb is long and impressive. Leo Szilard, one of several illustrious Hungarian physicists, left Berlin for Vienna in 1933, but he glimpsed what lay ahead and six weeks later went to London. Szilard was more politically acute than his colleagues, and as early as 1935 he was advising some of them not to publish the results of their atomic research; unlike the others, Szilard was already thinking about a bomb—a German bomb.[14]

Enrico Fermi was a Catholic, as were his children. But his wife, Laura, was Jewish, and when Italy adopted anti-Semitic laws in 1938, the family left, first for Stockholm, where Fermi received a Nobel Prize, and then for New York and Columbia University.

In 1934, he had discovered that metal bombarded with neutrons was vastly more radioactive if the neutrons were slowed down by water or paraffin. He began bombarding uranium and decided that the effect of doing so was to create a new element or elements. He misunderstood. Almost surely, the main effect had been to split the uranium atom.[15] A few years later, Fermi, who in Rome had been called "the Pope" by younger colleagues, would contribute as much and probably more than any other physicist to the work that led to the atomic bomb.

Edward Teller, the best known of the expatriate Hungarian scientists, left Budapest in the late 1920s because local laws denied higher education to most Jews. Only eighteen, he, too, became a bird of passage, making stops at Karlsruhe, Munich, Leipzig, and then Göttingen to work under Max Born. At Los Alamos, Teller made little, if any, contribution to the creation of the atomic bomb, but he was a driving force behind the fusion, or hydrogen, bomb, of which he became known, with some exaggeration, as "the father." As a student, Teller shared with Oppenheimer a passion for philosophy and literature. Both wrote poetry. Both were inordinately complex. Each made deep and lasting friendships, but each was abrasive, willful, and on occasion invited hostility from others. In 1954, Oppenheimer was stripped of his security clearance in a federal proceeding during which

Teller spoke against him, an event that shocked and embittered a great many of their colleagues, most of whom strongly supported Oppenheimer.

To travel and work outside the Soviet Union, a scientist needed the regime's trust, a tribute rarely bestowed. The most prominent of those who managed it was Pyotr L. Kapitza, a brilliant physicist and flamboyant character who left Russia in 1921 to join Rutherford at Cambridge. Kapitza became Rutherford's favorite. Peierls recalls a "Kapitza club" of young men who met once a week in the Russian's rooms at Trinity College to discuss the latest developments in the new physics. Peierls says that Kapitza once invited Nikolai Bukharin, then Soviet Minister for Education, to dinner at Trinity College, "mainly in order to be able to make the introduction, 'Comrade Bukharin—Lord Rutherford.' "[16] Rutherford arranged to have a special laboratory built for Kapitza's experiments, but in 1935, during a visit to Moscow, Kapitza's passport was canceled on the grounds that his services were needed at home "in view of the danger from Hitler."[17] In vain did Rutherford, the Royal Society, and Prime Minister Stanley Baldwin try to arrange Kapitza's return. In the end, his special equipment was sold to the Soviet Academy of Sciences so that he could continue his research. Kapitza was eventually placed under house arrest for seven years by Stalin for his refusal to work on the atomic bomb.

The people working in atomic physics were a far-flung international community, and although communication between them was very good, the romance and excitement lay within European laboratories during most of the 1930s. Numerous first-rate Americans were taking part, but most of them hadn't worked in Europe and felt somewhat cut off. "We read the literature and knew what the song said, but we had to go abroad to learn what the song was all about," recalls John Manley, a highly regarded experimental physicist who worked closely with Oppenheimer at Los Alamos. Rabi and Oppenheimer, who had studied abroad, were sought out and heard. Manley describes as "thrilling" summer sessions at Ann Arbor, Michigan, when he and other young American physicists were able to mingle freely with visitors like Bohr and Fermi and some of the eminent Germans. "We were especially impressed by the Germans," he says. The Americans "thought little and knew little about the Soviets. People had heard of Kapitza. That's all. No one was reading Russian literature."[18] The literature being read was in large part written in German by Germans. Still, American physics was maturing rapidly.

The chances of atomic energy becoming more than a fascinating abstraction were a lot higher by the end of the 1930s than at the beginning. In 1933, Rutherford said that people who envisaged the release of atomic energy on a large scale "were talking moonshine."[19] Even Einstein compared using atomic energy with "shooting in the dark at scarce birds."[20] In a brief memoir, Leo Szilard described how in 1933 he was walking in London and thinking about Rutherford's "moonshine" comment and a novel by H. G. Wells—*The World Set Free*—published in 1914, in which a fissionable atomic bomb is developed and used. Szilard said he was more impressed by Wells than by the skeptics among his colleagues. It seems that as he was waiting for a light to change, he suddenly began to envisage a chain reaction based on an element that, when split, would emit two neutrons as it absorbed one.[21] The next year, Fermi performed his seminal experiments on slow neutrons and the team of Frédéric and Irene Joliot-Curie created artificial radioactivity—by bombarding a target with alpha particles. On December 19, 1938, Otto Hahn and Fritz Strassman, who were nuclear chemists at the Kaiser Wilhelm Institute in Berlin, split the uranium atom into two nearly equal parts. Unlike Fermi in 1934, they drew the right conclusion from the experiment, realizing that a new kind of reaction—nuclear fission—had occurred.

A last big tumbler had fallen into place. Hahn sent word of the experiment to his partner, Lise Meitner, an involuntary exile living in Sweden. She and her nephew, the physicist Otto R. Frisch, who was working with Bohr at Copenhagen, told Bohr, who was about to leave for the United States to confer with Einstein and others. Shortly after arriving, Bohr received word from Frisch and Meitner that a laboratory experiment of their own showed large amounts of energy being released in the fission process. The remaining question was whether a chain reaction could be produced. Szilard, who by then had come to Columbia, quickly satisfied himself that an explosive chain reaction was indeed possible. And, once again, he urged colleagues not to publish their findings. In a cautionary letter to Joliot-Curie, Szilard wrote: "Obviously, if more than one neutron was liberated, a sort of chain reaction would be possible. In certain circumstances, this might lead to the construction of bombs which would be extremely dangerous in general and particularly in the hands of certain governments."[22] But it was really too late. The Hahn-Strassman breakthrough was the immediate focus of discussion within the international community of atomic physicists, and many of them began building experiments around it. Some did publish. In April 1939, the Joliot-Curies wrote in *Nature*, a British journal, that 3.5 neutrons are produced each time another neutron splits an atom of uranium. (They were off just a bit, the real number is 2.5. One of the neutrons goes on to create the next fission, thus sustaining the chain reaction.) In *Nature* alone there were twenty contributions on the subject of uranium between January and June 1939.[23]

Some of the experiments were, of course, being conducted in Germany, as the Hahn-Strassman had been. Anxieties of the kind expressed by Szilard and a few others slowly began to register in London and in Washington.

The expatriate Europeans overestimated the reach of German atomic physics, as did the American and British governments—at least until midway in the war. It was an understandable mistake. The Nazis headed the list of powers which would turn atomic power to destructive purposes if that could be done. A large body of German physicists who remained at Hitler's disposal were as accomplished as any. They included Carl von Weizsäcker, the older brother of West Germany's President in the mid-1980s, Richard von Weizsäcker. Von Weizsäcker studied under Bohr at Copenhagen, where he became a close friend of Edward Teller's. Everyone considered von Weizsäcker highly gifted, but his German colleague Werner Heisenberg, the son of a professor of ecclesiastical history, was truly awesome—at least as bright as any of the brightest lights in the field and the likely heir to Bohr's mantle. Conversations with Bohr when he was nineteen years old had persuaded Heisenberg to study physics. The atomic theories of the ancient Greeks, as described by Plato, already fascinated him. At age twenty-three, Heisenberg became Max Born's assistant. At twenty-six, he was a full professor at Leipzig, having in the meantime lectured on theoretical physics in Copenhagen. At thirty-two, he received the Nobel Prize for theoretical studies that he had actually carried out several years before.[24]*

Their expatriate colleagues always liked von Weizsäcker and Heisenberg but became wary of them as another European war drew near. Neither of them was an admirer of Hitler, but both were authentic Germans and judged unlikely, whatever happened, to become disloyal or seriously disaffected. Whether the quest to exploit the atom's energy would blind them to the implications of doing so on behalf of the Third Reich was a deeply disturbing imponderable. Expect the worst was the prudent prevailing view.

Actually, Germany's uranium fission program never moved much beyond the talking stage. German researchers couldn't determine whether an explosive chain reaction was even possible, nor did they ever acquire the means or material to build a bomb. (At the war's end, they didn't even have a working reactor.) The style of the Third Reich discouraged much that was novel. Hitler, wrote Albert Speer, "was filled with a fundamental distrust of all innovations which, as in the case of jet aircraft or atom bombs,

---

*In 1927, Heisenberg concluded that the movement of subatomic particles could not be predicted—that ultimately the universe is unknowable. Einstein rejected this "Uncertainty Principle," claiming that "God does not throw dice."

went beyond the technical experience of the First World War generation . . ."[25] With familiars, he referred to both nuclear physics and the
relativity theory as "Jewish physics." Speer said that Hitler mentioned the
subject to him only once in twenty-two hundred recorded passages of
conversations they had, and then "with extreme brevity." The precise
attitude of the physicists isn't clear. "On [their] suggestion," Speer says,
"we scuttled the project to develop an atom bomb by the autumn of 1942."
And as to whether a bomb could be made, Heisenberg, he wrote, "was by
no means encouraging."[26] That a few German scientists dragged their feet
does seem fairly clear from the record. That the technical obstacles to
creating a bomb seemed insurmountable to most of them is clearer still and
more important.

The cycle of scientific revelation had made the eccentric notions of
H. G. Wells and other visionaries into a looming presence. President
Roosevelt made the decision to build an atomic bomb, or try to, on October
9, 1941, two months before Japan attacked Pearl Harbor. The war in Europe
and, of course, the concern about Germany's fission program left him no
alternative. The move was the first in a series that made the Roosevelt-
Truman years the most momentous of the nuclear age. They influenced
events as nothing had before and may continue to do so for as long as the
mind can imagine. Harry S Truman was dealt the harsher choices. His
decision to use the bomb against Japan—as unavoidable as was Roosevelt's
to build it—was taken under odd and disturbing circumstances, among
them a near lack of presidential involvement in crucial parts of the episode.
And Truman's decision nearly five years later to develop a fusion bomb was
probably the most significant taken by any recent President. It, too, was
probably unavoidable, given the pressure on him to approve the project, but
again he took the step in rather dubious circumstances and with little
forethought. It set a precedent for moves that lay ahead which were to
guarantee a fateful competition in weapons of mass destruction between
America and Russia, the countries that had emerged from the wreckage of
the war as world powers.

Washington underestimated Soviet nuclear potential as badly as it had
overestimated the Third Reich's. Truman's approval of a fusion bomb—a
device of incomparably more destructive potential than even the atomic
bomb—was provoked by the Soviet Union's abrupt entry into the nuclear
domain in August 1949. Neither Truman nor most of those around him

expected a Soviet nuclear weapon. America's security in the atomic era was supposed to be assured by a monopoly, the world's by an American *pax atomica*. Only the scientists who had developed the American bomb were not shocked by a Soviet atomic device. Probably without exception, they expected to see one not very long after the first American test, which was ambiguously called Trinity and conducted near Alamogordo in the New Mexican desert on July 16, 1945. "After all, we did the test for them," says I. I. Rabi. He and many other American initiates reckoned that their Soviet colleagues would test an atomic weapon within four to five years of Trinity. "The Soviets were in the business early—as early as we were," says Rabi, "and they were better positioned to approach top management [leadership] than we were. Soviet scientists made direct approaches to Stalin. No one here had access to Roosevelt or Truman."[27]

At first, Truman and a few of his senior advisers refused to believe the Soviets had tested an actual atomic bomb. Experts who said otherwise were thought to have exaggerated the effects of an accident—a Soviet reactor explosion perhaps. A few skeptics had convinced themselves that no one else could do it without American help—least of all the Russians, who were thought to be all thumbs. With a little help, the British could manage it, but Washington had decided against assisting anyone, including the British, even though wartime agreements between Roosevelt and Winston Churchill committed the United States to close collaboration with Britain on nuclear matters.

A few other skeptics didn't believe the evidence of the test, simply because they didn't want to believe it—to see demolished the sanguine assumptions about America's monopoly. Then, as the truth sank in and Truman approved the fusion bomb, there began the cycle of action-reaction that has strongly influenced the nuclear age. The wartime allies were now adversaries, and the Soviet bomb threw them into a situation for which history offered neither precedent nor guidance. Two societies with radically different backgrounds, outlooks, and attributes have since groped uncertainly as they tried to meet the demands of their adversary relationship while also avoiding steps that could lead to nuclear war.

Ordinary people also reacted to the bomb. America's created unease and some anxiety. The Soviet test, as it ushered in a time of rival nuclear powers, broadened first impressions into a deep and abiding sense of vulnerability and insecurity that had normally lain beneath the surface, but not far beneath. Societies sensed that the nuclear era was, indeed, a sharp break with the past, at least in relations between big powers. Nuclear weapons, not traditional considerations, set the tone of these relations and put the history of our time on its curious course—a course that has avoided another

great war only because of the common fear of crossing the nuclear threshold. Still, there has been uncertainty about the reliability of the course, let
alone the ability of leaders to hold to it down through the corridors of time.

Just before the war formally ended, the British Embassy in Washington sent a long and prescient message to London, most of which was
devoted to America's reaction to the weapon that had persuaded Japan to
surrender on August 11, 1945: "Politically, it is clear that the bomb is doing
more than Pearl Harbor or the war to obliterate the last vestiges of the
isolationist dream, and in this sense it is a new weapon of the international-
ists. At the same time, nationalists are insisting that if America can only
keep the secret she will be powerfully placed to make other nations, not
least the Soviet Union, behave."[28]

The Soviet Union's atomic test occurred at a time when the cold war
had reached the peak of its intensity. The prospect of hot war seemed
alarmingly serious; in the past, differences of a similar, or even lesser scope
had led invariably to war. But war between nuclear powers was gradually
becoming all but excluded by the nature of the weapons and their peculiar
ironies. They confer immense power but in a form so destructive as to make
their employment madly irrational. They are less useful politically than
more primitive, less destructive weapons, especially against smaller countries; each of the nuclear superpowers is necessarily influenced by the
other's weapons; but smaller countries, because they pose no threat to the
superpowers, do not feel threatened by their weaponry. However, they can
and do threaten one another, and the superpowers normally discourage
regional conflicts that could lead to their own involvement and a possible
confrontation. Briefly, nuclear weapons can and often do affect the behavior of nations. Between 1870 and 1939—less than the space of a lifetime—
Europe engulfed itself in three wars. But the last one ended almost half a
century ago, a long time for the old continent to have avoided war. The
inhibiting effect of nuclear weapons has been the main difference.

Since the end of World War II, well over a half million Americans
have been killed or wounded in battle. During this time, no American
President ever seriously considered using nuclear weapons to shorten a
war or settle a political crisis in which the interests of the United States
seemed to be directly threatened. (The memoirs of some presidents describe their experiences with the nuclear option in more dramatic terms
than the record can support.) Harry Truman never contemplated using
nuclear weapons against the Soviet Union, or even threatening to use
them, during the Berlin Blockade in 1948 and '49. The question of em-
ploying them against China during the Korean War was more acute, but
the only pressure for doing so then appears to have come from General

Douglas MacArthur, who commanded American and allied forces in Korea. The record on Eisenhower, the only President to confront serious pressure for nuclear bombing from within his administration, is cloudier, mainly because he routinely concealed his intentions by spreading confusion about them. But Eisenhower, the least understood of modern presidents, was always determined to neutralize the pressure and keep the crises he dealt with well below the nuclear threshold. The confusion he spread was often aimed at keeping the hawks around him at arm's length and his own options open.

The danger of nuclear war may have been most acute during the Cuban missile crisis, a traumatic moment for most, probably all, of those involved with it on both sides. The crisis, however, was never as threatening to peace and stability as the frightening, uniquely volatile situation in Berlin during the summer and fall of 1961, perhaps the time of greatest peril in the nuclear age. Cuba aside, every other period of tension between East and West since then has been tame by comparison.

The Soviet leadership, by all accounts, has never considered using a nuclear weapon and only once seemed even to pause over the option. The moment was the summer of 1969. Clashes with China along the frontier caused the Kremlin to take steps signaling the possibility of a surgical strike against China's modest nuclear facilities. Very probably, these steps amounted to nothing more than unsuccessful nuclear blackmail and at no point reflected intent within the Soviet leadership to attack China. To have done so would have triggered a nonnuclear war with China, among the nastiest of prospects for Soviet leaders.

The Soviet Union, like the United States, has been ruled by cautious and careful men in the nuclear era. The only exception was Nikita Khrushchev, who was abruptly pushed aside in October 1964 for adventurism and initiatives described as "hare-brained." The most dangerous moments of the cold war occurred on his watch. Yet at various times Khrushchev, too, showed a sense of restraint and, for hardheaded reasons of his own, interest in accommodation. Soviet prudence is partly historical. Lacking frontiers, the land has been overrun many times, and, in deciding how much military power they need, Russians are conditioned by suffering and the accumulated humiliations of their history. Their word for security—*bezopasnost*, the B in KGB—conveys a broader meaning than the English equivalent. It means lack of danger—total safety. The most scarifying of the society's formative experiences was its most recent, World War II, when twenty million people were killed. Thinking about the Soviet attitude toward another war too often ignores or fails to give this national memory the overriding importance it warrants. The war has a far less vivid place in America's memory, because most Americans didn't suffer as Russians did.

Anxious and endlessly suspicious, Soviet leaders value consistency and predictability most highly in relations with the West, especially with the United States. Like other governments, Soviet leadership deplores the volatility of American positions, which sometimes change with administrations as do the diplomats who transact the business that ought to be transacted despite the adversarial nature of the relations. Like America's European allies, the Soviets complain that everything in Washington must be reinvented each time the government changes hands. There is, they say, no institutional memory. (The complaint, although not unfair, is a trifle clearer than the truth. Between the early days of the cold war and the start of the Reagan era, the basis of American foreign policy changed relatively little and slowly at that.) Moscow has usually been more comfortable dealing with pragmatic American conservatives, regarding them as more reliable than most liberals.

In any case, Soviet thinking has been conditioned by Leninist doctrine that argues that time is on the side of the revolution. At least since Khrushchev's day, however, this cherished notion has had to be tempered by reality; communism is universally seen as a failed experiment. And before Gorbachev took charge, Soviet diplomacy—often ham-fisted—had done little to redeem failures at home. The effort to improve relations with the West was aimed largely at the political confinement of China and acquiring access to advanced Western technology. The returns on this policy have been negligible, as the improvement in China's relations with Japan and the Western bloc suggests. So does the large technology gap between the Soviet Union and the West, a disturbing continuity; catching up with, if not surpassing, the capitalists has always been essential to the Soviet drive for status. Another grim continuity is the country's world position: It has lacked reliably good relations with any of the major governments of the world, excepting perhaps India. "Better the French as enemies than the Russians as friends" was a comment that took hold during the Congress of Vienna. Soviet problems are traditional Russian problems—timeless and all but intractable.

After the Soviet test in 1949, confident American notions about no other nation being able to build the bomb yielded to an overly pessimistic but less unrealistic sentiment that almost anyone could do it; that a world of proliferating nuclear weapons and club members lay ahead. Traditional powers such as Britain, France, and China were determined to have a place at what Tory British leaders liked to call the "top table." For Washington, resisting pressure to help its allies was difficult, especially in the case of the British, who had collaborated on the first bomb. The Soviets had a similar problem vis-à-vis China, its ally in the postwar years and the Marxist church's other apostle. In the late 1950s, Moscow did provide some technical help to the Chinese, but less than they sought. Moreover, the Soviets used assistance of this and other kinds, including high-performance military weapons, as a means of keeping China dependent on them and a compliant ally. It all ended in tears in 1959, when the Soviets, according to a Chinese interpretation of the episode, tore up a secret agreement made two years earlier in which they were to have provided China a sample atom bomb, but clearly didn't.[29]

Parts of the U.S. government have always supported helping Britain and France, but others had different views and could usually rely on Congress's aversion to assisting anyone. Britain wanted to revive the close wartime collaboration on nuclear matters, but for many years the congressional obstacle was too great. London's cause was harmed by the raft of Britons who were found to be Soviet spies; these included diplomats and major intelligence figures, plus Klaus Fuchs, a physicist who had been closely involved with both the fission and fusion programs at Los Alamos. Eventually, Britain got the aid it needed; France did not but managed on its own to obtain a place at the top table. In resisting pressure to help smaller countries acquire the means to develop nuclear weapons, both the Americans and the Russians have shown restraint and prudence. The Soviets have at least as strong an incentive as the Americans to discourage the spread of nuclear weapons. They deplore unstable situations which they cannot influence, let alone control. Perhaps more significant is the "Russianness" of their thinking about a spread of nuclear weapons. Russians always feel encircled by eternally hostile peoples. Each of the other members of the nuclear club, they know, targets its weapons against them.

II

Falls the Shadow

For most people, the nuclear age, like the universe, began with a bang—with the ravaging of two Japanese cities with atomic bombs. The universal ignorance of the story behind the fission bomb's creation was unavoidable; it was among the best kept and most improbable secrets of the war. Once the weapon was used, how it came about didn't seem to be very important. What mattered was its stunning performance and sober meaning. But most of the story's bits and pieces are coming to light, and what they tell is instructive, provided the chronicle of uncommon achievement is seen in relation to the decision-making process in Washington. Among the lessons of the story is the danger of entrusting political decisions, above all those made in the nuclear age, to politically unaccountable officials and bureaucrats; their goals—often narrow and reflecting limited insight—may collide with large, longer-term national interests.

In the early days of the war, Europe's atomic physicists, a great many of whom were refugees, divided into groups that could be loosely called optimists and pessimists. They knew by then that nuclear fission could be made to occur under laboratory conditions. They didn't know whether the process could be extended to produce a chain reaction and, in turn, a large explosion. Given the worry about what German scientists might be doing, optimists tended to be those who felt that a nuclear explosion wasn't possible. The pessimists, among whom Leo Szilard was the most conspicuous, took the dark view. There were more optimists than pessimists at this time. Niels Bohr provided reassurance; in 1939, he and one of his American students, John Wheeler, discovered that a chain reaction required the separation of uranium 235 from the rest of the uranium atom (U-238). Since

U-235, the significantly fissionable isotope, was known to amount to only seven tenths of U-238, a staggering obstacle to a nuclear bomb had emerged, or so it seemed. Moreover, Sir James Chadwick, who in 1932 discovered the neutron, calculated that an explosion would require from one to thirty tons of the U-235 isotope. This caused Lord Hankey, a minister without portfolio in Britain's war cabinet, to say, "I gather that we may sleep fairly comfortably in our beds."[1] The optimists persuaded Winston Churchill, who said, "As soon as the energy develops it will explode with a mild detonation before any really violent effects can be reproduced. Hence," he added, "the fear that this new discovery has provided the Nazis with some sinister, new, secret explosive with which to destroy their enemies is clearly without foundation."[2]

Otto Frisch, the Austrian physicist who had worked closely with Bohr in Copenhagen, improved the case for optimism in a paper he wrote at Birmingham University in Britain in 1940. Even by enriching uranium with ten times the normal amount of U-235, he wrote, a chain reaction of a kind that a "superbomb" would require was unlikely. "Fortunately," he wrote, "our progressing knowledge of the fission process has tended to dissipate these fears and there are now a number of strong arguments to the effect that construction of such a superbomb would be, if not impossible, then at least prohibitively expensive and that furthermore the bomb would not be so effective as was first thought."[3] However, the process of writing the article caused Frisch to reconsider the issue and to question his own judgment.[4] He was then living temporarily with Rudolf Peierls and the latter's Russian wife, Genia—birds of passage all. He began to think that instead of trying to increase the amount of U-235 simply by increasing the amount of natural uranium, a better approach would be to separate the U-235 from the U-238. The two isotopes are chemically similar but, like milk and cream, differ in weight.[5] In his memoirs, Peierls recalls that "one day, in February or March 1940, Frisch said, 'Suppose someone gave you a quantity of pure 235 isotope of uranium—what would happen?' We started working out the consequences."[6] In doing so, they alarmed themselves by concluding that a pound or two of U-235, not tons of it, would be enough for an explosion which, as Peierls wrote, "would be the equivalent of thousands of tons of ordinary explosive. We were quite staggered by these results: an atomic bomb was possible, after all, at least in principle! As a weapon, it would be so devastating that, from a military point of view, it would be worth the effort of setting up a plant to separate the isotopes. In a classical understatement, we said to ourselves, 'Even if this plant costs as much as a battleship, it would be worth having.' "[7]

Peierls and Frisch worried that what they had learned, or thought they had learned, was already known to colleagues who were busily developing weapons in Germany. They wrote a memorandum setting forth their analysis and conclusions, and maneuvered it into an official channel. An atom bomb's destructive nature, they suggested, "may make it unsuitable as a weapon for use by this country."[8] Just the radioactive effect, they said, would be fatal to living things long after an explosion. Peierls and Frisch were told that "the authorities were grateful for [their] memorandum, but that we would have to understand that henceforth the work would be continued by others; as actual or former 'enemy aliens' we would not be told any more about it."[9]

A committee was formed to look into the possibilities outlined by Peierls and Frisch. It was called M.A.U.D., and many of those involved wrongly believed the name to be a coinage for Military Applications of Uranium Disintegration. The real story of how this pivotally important group acquired its name is both beguiling and revealing. On behalf of Niels Bohr, Lise Meitner, who lived in Stockholm, sent a telegram to Frisch, her nephew, assuring him Bohr and his family had come to no harm from the German seizure of Denmark. "Tell Cockcroft and Maud Ray Kent," it said. The message was presumed to have a hidden meaning. Clearly, the Cockcroft was John D. Cockcroft (later Sir John), an eminent colleague at Cambridge, but the "Maud Ray Kent" reference was puzzling; it was "decoded" as signifying uranium disintegration. Not until after the war could Lise Meitner explain that Maud Ray was actually a woman who lived in Kent and before the war had been a governess to Bohr's children. In 1940, however, the committee was officially named M.A.U.D. and thereafter was always known as the Maud Committee.[10]

Although British subjects supervised its work, the Maud Committee depended heavily on the foreign scientists, virtually none of whom had at first been cleared by security; they could work on atomic fission, because it was not then considered as essential to the war effort.[11] Frisch and Peierls were joined in the technical activity by two French subjects who had been associates of Joliot-Curie—Hans von Halban, an Austrian, and Lev Kowarski, a Russian. (Joliot-Curie had elected to stay behind in Paris.) Halban and Kowarski worked closely, if not always happily, as a team and in a gesture described by Peierls, as "typical" of them, applied for patents on fissionable power at a very early stage.[12] (Just before they escaped from Bordeaux, Halban and Kowarski were instructed by Joliot-Curie to look after French interests, which could explain their action.)[13] The best known of the refugee physicists was Max Born, who was teaching in Edinburgh but refused to take part in war work.[14] The one who was to become better known than any of them, however, was Klaus Fuchs, a German parson's son, who played a role in calculating the size of the first atomic bomb. In 1950, Fuchs was found to be a Soviet informant, probably the only one who could have significantly aided the Soviet fission program. Fuchs, another refugee physicist, was recruited by Peierls, who says he "needed some regular help— someone with whom I would be able to discuss the theoretical technicalities . . . In due course he got a full clearance, and he started to work in May 1941 . . . Fuchs became a lodger in our house, and he was a pleasant person to have around. He was courteous and even-tempered. He was rather silent, unless one asked him a question, when he would give a full and articulate answer; for this Genia called him 'Penny-in-the-slot.' "[15] Fuchs later became a popular and well regarded member of the closed community at Los Alamos, New Mexico, where the first bombs were developed.

Finding some good way of separating the fugitive U-235 isotope from U-238 was perhaps the major concern of the Maud Committee. Isolating quantities of it would be a monumental task for which industrial technology offered neither precedent nor guidance. After looking at various methods, Peierls and Frisch concluded that a process of separating mixed gases by diffusing them through ultrafine membranes was probably best.[16] In America, George B. Kistiakowsky, the Ukrainian-born chemist who in 1918 fought in the White Army against the Reds and later became Eisenhower's science adviser, reached the same conclusion about gaseous diffusion, as the process is known, at about the same time. Another big problem was deciding on the best method of slowing down neutrons. For a chain reaction to be kept going, the turbulent neutrons must be throttled down by a so-called moderator; the leading contenders for this role were heavy water and graphite. In Britain, Halban and Kowarski were experimenting with heavy water, as well they might have been; most of the world's supply of heavy water, a product nearly as difficult to separate from ordinary water as U-235 is from U-238, had been produced by a company in Norway. On March 9, 1940, one month before the German invasion of Norway, French military intelligence was given all the heavy water for the duration of the hostilities. Three months later, Halban and Kowarski left in a cargo boat for Britain— one jump ahead of the Gestapo—with all twenty-six cans of Product Z, the code name for heavy water.[17] The effort to control the heavy water supply and, more important, deny it to Germany is an epic tale, with spies and commandos in the leading roles. In the end, the effort didn't mean much. The German fission program, as noted, never got beyond square one, and heavy water itself was never important. In New York, Szilard and Fermi were experimenting with graphite as a moderator. It was nearly as efficient a throttle as heavy water and available in unlimited quantity, whereas accumulating large amounts of heavy water would be a daunting problem. Graphite was eventually chosen as the moderator.

The big decisions lay well ahead, however—further than they had to. Even with the war under way, optimism remained the fashion within the community of physicists living in America. Aside from Szilard and Eugene Wigner, his Princeton-based Hungarian friend and colleague, most of them saw the atomic bomb as notional. Uranium fission, they felt, would not liberate energy in sufficient quantities to create a large chain reaction. At Columbia, Enrico Fermi told his colleague I. I. Rabi that the chance of an explosive chain reaction occurring was remote—perhaps 10 percent. "Ten percent is not a remote possibility if it means that we may die of it," said Rabi.[18]

America's somewhat tentative initial survey of the bomb as a possibility was the first example of bureaucracy's limitations in dealing with the new technology and with weapons of mass destruction. These early days were rich in anecdote, many of which are embedded now in folklore. There was the "Hungarian conspiracy," as some amused onlookers characterized the persistent efforts of Szilard and Wigner to impose their view of the danger on high authority and obtain funding for research. One of Szilard's ideas was to have his old friend Einstein alert the Queen of Belgium with whom he was known to correspond. Einstein wasn't drawn to this approach, but Alexander Sachs, a Russian-born banker-scholar, who was then vice president of the Lehman Corporation, a large investment company, told Szilard that he would take up the matter with Roosevelt, whom he knew well. Sachs, they agreed, would deliver a letter from Einstein to Roosevelt, in which the anxieties of the atomic scientists would be explained. In mid-summer 1939, Szilard took drafts of such a letter to Peconic, Long Island, where Einstein was summering. Szilard didn't know how to operate a car and was driven there by Edward Teller, who was also at Columbia. "I entered history as Szilard's chauffeur," says Teller.[19]

Not until October 11 did Sachs manage to see Roosevelt. Accounts of the meeting vary, but not on its conclusion. "Alex," said F.D.R. to Sachs, "what you are after is to see that the Nazis don't blow us up." "Precisely," said Sachs.[20]

Roosevelt then summoned an aide, General Edwin M. "Pa" Watson. "This requires action," he told Watson. The conversation between F.D.R. and Sachs had been a long one but had never dwelt on just what sort of action might be taken. So Watson set up the Advisory Committee on Uranium to act as liaison between the physicists and the administration. Lyman J. Briggs, the Director of the Bureau of Standards, was named director. He was then sixty-five and had been a government scientist for forty-three years; he was a Hoover appointee, and his specialty was soil physics.

Ten days after the meeting in the White House, the Uranium Committee (as it became known) met. The army and navy were represented by relatively junior officers—Lieutenant Colonel Keith F. Adamson for the army and Commander Gilbert C. Hoover for the navy. The Hungarian activists—Szilard, Wigner, and Teller—attended, along with Sachs. Adamson and a scientist named Richard Roberts, who was there representing the Carnegie Institution, expressed doubt that a chain reaction could be made to occur. And, Adamson cautioned, it was troops, not weapons, that win wars. It usually takes two wars before one can know whether the weapon is any good or not, he added. "In Aberdeen," he said, "we have a goat tethered to a stick with a ten-foot rope, and we have promised a big prize to anyone who can kill the goat with a death ray. Nobody has claimed the prize yet."[21] As for huge explosions of vast force, Adamson volunteered that he had happened once to be standing outside an ordnance depot when it blew up and hadn't even been knocked down.[22]

For the next several months, nothing happened. Washington lagged far behind London in coming to terms with the sobering message of the Peierls-Frisch report. Such dynamism as there was on the American side was supplied by the Hungarians, who impressed the stalwarts of the Uranium Committee as an odd bunch of visionary aliens, with an equally odd patron, the eager Sachs.

Washington in 1940 was very much a city within a capital, not a capital within a city, as in the case of London, Paris, and Berlin. Unlike them, it was a provincial place absorbed by its internal politics, as distinct from the politics and issues of the world beyond. Scientists, as McGeorge Bundy has written, "did not look to it for leadership; its political leaders did not easily look beyond the government for counsel."[23] The Hungarian conspiracy didn't understand Washington or its ways. Sachs had access to F.D.R. but was poorly cast as the key player; he struck most people, including Roosevelt, who enjoyed teasing him, as verbose and tedious. What the situation really needed was a small group of prestigious American born scientists, backed by one or two movers and shakers from the financial community. "Szilard and those other [politically] simpleminded Hungarians who went to Einstein and got that poor old man to write that letter didn't understand," says Rabi. "They should have gone to an American—Lawrence, for example." (He was referring to Ernest O. Lawrence, who in 1930 had invented the cyclotron, or atom smasher, and in 1940 was the Director of the Radiation Laboratory at the University of California, Berkeley.) Rabi thinks that from the outset Roosevelt should have focused on a plan of action involving people who knew how to work the political system and who had the President's confidence. "When you only try to influence the President, what can the poor fellow do?" he asks. "Roosevelt naturally called in the head of the Bureau of Standards, Briggs, who was out of his depth. And that held things up for a year."[24]

John Manley, who came to Los Alamos with Oppenheimer and is now retired and still living there, says he agrees with Rabi that another, more conventional approach should have been tried—organized by someone "who would have known, as all the Americans knew, that Lyman Briggs was weak, and the wrong man for the initiative."[25] At the time, however, no one other than Szilard seems to have had any appetite for the role of catalyst. The anxiety that drove him and assorted others wasn't widely shared. His great confederate, Fermi, impatient with lack of movement on the fission project, left Columbia temporarily for Ann Arbor to conduct cosmic ray experiments.

Not until June 1940 did there seem to be any sign of change. Vannevar Bush, who was Director of the Carnegie Institution and a resourceful insider, persuaded Roosevelt, whom he knew well, to set up a new committee—the National Defense Research Committee—which would absorb the Uranium Committee and "search for new opportunities to apply science to the needs of war." Roosevelt put Bush in charge of the NDRC, and James B. Conant, a chemist, who was then president of Harvard University and had helped Bush devise the committee, became chairman of the Explosives Division. For a time, Bush and Conant were more concerned with demonstrating the impossibility of a nuclear weapon than in trying to build one.[26] In the late winter of 1941, Conant visited London to open a liaison office between the NDRC and the British. Curiously, he asked no questions about British work on a bomb project, and when, during a luncheon conversation in March 1941, he did hear something on the subject, he says, "This was the first I had heard about even the remote possibility of a bomb." He didn't follow up the conversation.[27] By then the Maud Committee was taking for granted the feasibility of an atomic bomb. In April, Bush was saying, "It would be possible to spend a very large amount of money, indeed, and yet there is certainly no clear-cut path to defense results of great importance lying open before us at the present time."[28] In June, he said, "This uranium business is a headache," and he restated his skepticism about creating an atomic explosion.[29] Ironically, by June 1941, the frightening course of the war strengthened the reluctance of some to commit sizable funds to a uranium bomb project, because these, after all, might be needed for more urgent military purposes. Actually, the program might well have been scrapped but for Britain's Maud Committee, which produced its report in mid-July; an informal version had already reached Bush two weeks earlier. The report confirmed the feasibility of an atomic bomb and recommended giving the necessary work, which it outlined, the highest possible priority in order to have the weapon as soon as possible and thereby decisively affect the outcome of the war.

"With the news from Great Britain unofficially in hand," recorded Conant, ". . . it became clear . . . that a major push along the lines outlined was in order."[30] Conant himself was still not wholly convinced; over the summer there was some more dithering. But by then other strong voices were urging action. One of them was Ernest Lawrence. A few months earlier, a young chemist named Glenn Seaborg, working at Berkeley with Lawrence's cyclotron, had shown that under neutron bombardment uranium 238 was transmuted into an intensely radioactive new element, which had never existed on earth. Seaborg found that the new element, which he named plutonium, was, like U-235, very fissile when bombarded and might thus be made to serve the same explosive purpose. The emergence of another source of weapons-grade material—one that might be less difficult to produce—encouraged advocates such as Lawrence, whose voice carried. Another advocate was Conant's Harvard colleague and fellow chemist George Kistiakowsky, who was one of the country's foremost explosives experts; he believed in the bomb's feasibility and persuaded Conant. Bush himself was convinced by the middle of the summer.

On October 9, Bush met with Roosevelt and Vice President Henry Wallace. He described the Maud Committee's conclusions, noting the amount of uranium a bomb would seem to require, the cost of building a U-235 production plant, and the time it might take to build a bomb. Roosevelt then decided to go forward with the new weapon. He ordered Bush to put the matter on a close hold. Other than himself and Wallace, he restricted the circle of those who would be kept fully involved to Bush, Conant, Henry L. Stimson, who by then was Secretary of War, and General George C. Marshall, Chief of Staff of the Army.[31] He knew each of them well and trusted them all. Bush had not been given authority to build the bomb but rather to find out whether it would be possible. An actual production decision would require Roosevelt's sanction.

For the activist scientists, October 9 marked the end of the beginning. With war probably lying just ahead, F.D.R. could have done little else. His decision was nonetheless epochal, transcending the war. It began a sea change in world politics, even if neither he nor anyone else knew it.

Eight weeks later, Europe's war had broadened into another world war and efforts to build on Roosevelt's decision acquired corresponding urgency. Instinctively, the Americans turned to the British—inventors of radar and the jet engine and well ahead in most of the work on uranium fission. Existing Anglo-American links in that area were informal and hadn't amounted to much, thanks in part to the skepticism and shortsightedness of the Americans. Now they proposed, in effect, a joint program. On October 11, two days after meeting with Bush, Roosevelt had written to Churchill, proposing an exchange of views between them "in order that any extended effort may be coordinated or even jointly conducted."[32] However, the British, aware of their lead, were reluctant to do much sharing. Two months elapsed before Churchill replied, rather austerely at that: "I need not assure you of our readiness to collaborate with the United States Administration in this matter."[33]

A changeless Anglo-American pattern had been set. The side with the most to give may cooperate and even help the side with the most to get— the *demandeur*—but within limits. In the early 1940s, the need for military cooperation did foster a fair degree of joint activity in nuclear matters. But it wasn't long before a role reversal developed; Britain became *demandeur*. Also, issues developed on nuclear matters that Roosevelt and Churchill had to settle themselves. One of these was what to do about producing enriched uranium (U-235) and where to locate a production plant. In June 1942, Churchill met Roosevelt at Hyde Park, New York, where they discussed "Tube Alloys," Britain's code name for its uranium program. (Relevant communications between London and Washington always referred to Tube Alloys, and German intelligence never did connect this vague term to its meaning. Nuclear matters generated very little paper; when Roosevelt died in April 1945, the entire Tube Alloys file contained no more than fifteen to twenty pages; a typical message was terse: "Mr. X will be arriving next week to discuss Tube Alloys.")

At Hyde Park, Churchill pushed hard for a partnership in which all information would be shared, all work would be collaborative, and all results shared equally. On the seemingly toughest issue—where to build the "research plant"—Churchill and his advisers had come prepared to concede. Putting the plant in Britain, where it could be bombed by the Germans and would divert scarce resources, seemed ill advised, even though everyone knew that whoever possessed an enrichment capability would begin the postwar era with a huge advantage. By then, the scientists had agreed that gaseous diffusion was probably the best of all the immensely difficult and expensive methods for enriching uranium (although research on other methods was to continue). Three weeks after the meeting, Roosevelt informed Bush that he and Churchill were in "complete accord." Still, since no record of that meeting was kept, no one could be sure of what the leaders had committed themselves to on topics of which they had little knowledge. Eight months later, Churchill recalled the meeting as having ended in agreement that the partners were to be equal and share fully in the results.[34] Roosevelt and Churchill persisted in seeing their joint arrangements in that light, even as these became steadily more one-sided. Britain had shown the early speed, but geography and resources abruptly shoved America into the dominant role.

By then, the senior figures in both programs—people like Bush and Conant—felt that an atomic bomb could become available in time for use in the war. This thinking didn't single out either adversary as a potential target, even though most Japanese still suspect that no such weapon would have been used against Europeans. They are wrong. Within the small circle of those in Washington and London who watched the bomb being developed, there was little, if any, doubt that had it been available in time to have shortened the war in Europe, it would have been used there—probably against Berlin. The scale of devastation wrought against cities such as Dresden and Hamburg pointed up the determination of Roosevelt and Churchill to do whatever it took to bring down the Third Reich as soon as possible.

In the summer of 1942, the American program acquired alternate code names; one was DSM, or Development of Substitute Materials. The other was Manhattan Engineer District, or MED. The name that stuck was Manhattan Project. Control of the program had been transferred from the scientists to a Military Policy Committee. Vannevar Bush, who was to serve as Roosevelt's chief scientific adviser, became chairman. Conant was his alternate. Three military members were appointed: General Wilhelm D. Styer for the army, Admiral William Purnell for the navy, and General Leslie Richard Groves, who would be project manager—a vice president for operations, as Bush envisioned his role.[35]

In September 1942, Groves was a portly, forty-six-year-old colonel who belonged to the Corps of Engineers and had supervised the building of the Pentagon. He wanted an overseas job close to the war. He didn't want to run the Manhattan Project but had little choice; his selection had been approved by Stimson and Roosevelt.[36] He was rewarded with an instant promotion to brigadier general. Bush had misgivings about Groves, as did others. Casting any one person in this unusual role was full of risk, and it is easy to see how an obscure army colonel might have been judged inadequate. The scale of the Manhattan Project defied comprehension; it was the most expensive single program ever financed by public funds.[37] It had somehow to be an instant colossus, yet supersecret. The $2 billion in federal funds it consumed would be largely hidden from congressional oversight. Bertrand Goldschmidt, a French chemist who worked with Seaborg, noted that in three years the project's array of factories and laboratories grew to be as large as America's entire automobile industry.[38] By the end of 1942, three nuclear centers—"atom cities"—were well under way. Everything about them, including their location, remained a secret, even though each created a new town. They were referred to only by their code names: W, X, and Y. Site W was Hanford, Washington, where plutonium, the other source of explosive material, would be produced. Site X was Oak Ridge, in the Tennessee Valley. Its function was to separate U-235 from natural uranium. Site Y was Los Alamos, New Mexico, where the bombs were developed. Nearly 150,000 people became involved in various parts of the Manhattan Project.[39]

"The Manhattan District bore no relation to the industrial or social life of our country," wrote Herbert Marks, a young lawyer who served as Dean Acheson's assistant on nuclear issues. "It was a separate state . . . with its thousands of secrets. It had a peculiar sovereignty, one that could bring about the end, peacefully or violently, of all other sovereignties."[40]

At Oak Ridge, the perimeter of the plant for enriching uranium by the gaseous diffusion method was about two miles long; internally it was labyrinthine and involved 4,000 diffusion stages—passages of a gaseous uranium compound through porous membranes.[41] At Hanford, a place for sheep grazing, the construction of the plant and other facilities was described as equivalent to building enough houses for a city of 400,000 people.[42] Connecting Hanford to the world involved putting down 158 miles of railway track and 386 miles of road.[43] Many of Groves's decisions struck people not directly involved with the project—meaning most people—as alarmingly peculiar. For example, building a road with eight lanes to the plutonium works at Hanford seemed a great waste of money. For Groves, however, eight lanes amounted to insurance against accident. Plutonium is highly radioactive, and, in the event of an explosion at Hanford, eight lanes might have been just enough for working people and their families to escape the fumes.[44]

Los Alamos was the larger curiosity. On a stunning but isolated mesa nearly 7,000 feet above the nearby Rio Grande in New Mexico's Jemez mountains came nearly one thousand scientists and their families, most of them confirmed city dwellers. The site was proposed by Oppenheimer, who had been asked by Groves to run the scientific laboratory. Oppenheimer had a summer home across the valley from Los Alamos, and he knew the mesas from having ridden over them on pack trips. "Isolation and inaccessibility were the main criteria for selecting the site. It also had to be a place where explosive work could be done the year around," says John Manley. Other criteria included housing for thirty scientists (a massive underestimate) and cleared land that was either government-owned or could be acquired in secrecy. Los Alamos (named for the cottonwoods on the mesa) seemed ideal. The site contained about 54,000 acres of largely public land. The rest belonged to a boys' boarding school. In November 1942, after Groves had approved Oppenheimer's recommendation, the Los Alamos Ranch School was notified by the War Department of the government's need for the land as "a demolition range." "My two great loves are physics and desert," Oppenheimer had once written to a friend. "It's a pity they can't be combined." Now they were.[45]

Within a few months, a procession of gifted people, including many of the most illustrious names in science, began arriving at Site Y, or Shangri-La, as some of them sardonically called it. "A Nobel Prize winners' concentration camp" was another description evoked by the heavily veiled style of the place and its isolation. Szilard and a few other notables didn't come, because they felt that no one could think clearly or work effectively in so remote a setting. And some judged other projects as more essential to winning the war. Rabi, for example, decided to continue developing radar at the Radiation Laboratory of the Massachusetts Institute of Technology.* Furthermore, living conditions at Los Alamos were awful. The housing, which never caught up to the demand, was a jumble of prefabs, trailers, and apartment units sandwiched onto the unpaved streets, which winter snows and summer rains covered with mud. There was for a time only one telephone line—supplied by the Forest Service—and one hand-cranked phone. Dry cleaning had to be sent to Santa Fe, about forty miles away, until sometime in 1944. Visually, Los Alamos resembled a frontier mining town surrounded by armed guards and high barbed-wire fences. Still, the people were mostly young—during the war, the average age was twenty-seven—and many fell upon the rich outdoor life afforded by the mountains and desert. More important was the shared sense of high adventure. One of the wives wrote, "I felt akin to the pioneer women accompanying their husbands across uncharted plains west-

---

*Rabi has often said that the war could have been won without the atomic bomb but would have been lost without radar.

ward, alert to dangers, resigned to the fact that they journeyed, for weal or woe, into the Unknown."[46]

By then, everyone involved in the Manhattan Project—physicists, chemists, engineers, and technicians—was designated "scientific personnel" and had to comply with exceedingly strict secrecy rules. "It was a miracle that the secret was kept," says John Manley. "The self-imposed secrecy was not so hard to understand, because scientists understood the stakes—the race to the death with the Germans. But technicians and others might have talked." Edward Teller at some point composed a rhyming alphabet for one of Fermi's children. For the letter "S" he wrote:

> *Stands for Secret: you can keep it forever*
> *Provided there's no one abroad who is clever.* [47]

Barely a dozen of the total number of persons working within the Manhattan Project were granted an overall view of the plan. In fact, very few of the staff even knew that their work was aimed at creating an atomic bomb. The wives of the insiders were supposed to be kept in the dark, and most were. "The Manhattan Project generated very little paper," recalls General Kenneth D. Nichols, who was Groves's military aide at the time. "It was all oral."[48] Nichols says there was never anything in writing between Groves and himself.

Top-secret data were carried from one site to another by army officers, who traveled on trains in locked compartments; they carried pistols in hidden shoulder holsters and the documents in rubberized pouches strapped to their chests. Anonymity was the rule, and famous names were disguised. Enrico Fermi became "Henry Farmer"; Niels Bohr was "Nicholas Baker." The word "physicist" was forbidden; everyone was an "engineer." Laboratory people were not allowed direct contact with relatives and couldn't travel more than 100 miles from Los Alamos. They could visit Santa Fe but were closely watched. "The bartenders at the La Fonda Hotel were army intelligence officers," recalls William (Willie) A. Higinbotham, a physicist who later became executive secretary of the Federation of American Scientists.[49] Not until 1948 did citizens of Los Alamos acquire such basic rights as suffrage and divorce. On August 6, 1945, the day the bomb was used against Hiroshima and the curtain lifted on Los Alamos, the Santa Fe *New Mexican* talked about the secret activity on the mesa about which there had been rumors but no knowledge: "A whole social world existed in nowhere in which people were married and babies were born nowhere. People died in a vacuum, autos and trucks crashed in a vacuum." And Laura Fermi commented in 1954:

I always felt sorry for the Army doctors at Los Alamos who provided the medical services for which we did not pay. They had prepared for emergencies on battlefields, and they found themselves faced instead with a high-strung bunch of men, women, and children—high-strung because the altitude affected us, because our men worked long hours under unrelenting pressure; high-strung because we were too many of a kind, too close to one another, too unavoidable even during relaxation hours; high-strung because we felt powerless under strange circumstances, irked by minor annoyances that we blamed on the Army and that drove us to unreasonable and pointless rebellion. Our Army doctors were kept busy treating the minor ailments of a healthy population . . . In [the] hospital, an unbelievable number of babies came to life, at the standard price of fourteen dollars apiece—the cost of food for the mother. To the world at large, all those babies were born in Post Office Box 1663, Santa Fé.[50]

A successful bureaucrat may have his way by aligning other players with his goals, or he may overpower them with single-minded determination, backed by the authority he projects. Groves, a black-belt bureaucrat, fell into the second category. He lost no time making himself overlord of atomic policy in all of its parts. The project gained from his brusque, high-handed style, but it did produce conflicts with the scientists, most of whom he viewed with suspicion. "Your job won't be easy," he told his assembled staff when they first gathered at Los Alamos. "At great expense we have gathered here the largest collection of crackpots ever seen."[51] He worried Bush from the start: "Having seen Groves briefly, I doubt whether he has sufficient tact for the job," he warned Stimson. "I fear we are in the soup."[52] Groves was, as McGeorge Bundy has written, "a driving executive who understood more about getting the job done than about its meaning."[53]

To Groves, the secrecy of the project dictated compartmentalizing it. Access was supposed to be granted on a strict need-to-know basis so that most people wouldn't discover the nature of the program. But scientists require unconstrained access to information and to the work of colleagues. On most matters, Groves got his way. On the issue that arose over compartmentalization, he prevailed at Oak Ridge and Hanford but not at Los Alamos. There the scientists, led by Oppenheimer, insisted on being able to work as they were used to working—by exchanging ideas. Weekly colloquia (Oppenheimer's idea) promoted the free flow of knowledge and insight. Most of those who developed the bomb say they could not have done so—not in time to have affected the war—if Groves had had his way. Groves reacted by barring exchanges of information between Los Alamos and the rest of the project. Only Oppenheimer could visit other sites. Groves's decision irritated the scientists at Los Alamos.[54] A lot of information left the laboratory, but very little came in.

In another of the early struggles with Los Alamos, Groves had Oppenheimer on his side but not the others. Only by organizing the place on military lines, Groves felt, could it be made to function with the urgency demanded by the times. The notion of putting the scientists, many of them Nobel laureates, in army uniforms and under military discipline didn't bother Bush and Conant. Somewhat surprisingly, Oppenheimer was not at all displeased by the prospect of becoming a lieutenant colonel and wearing the uniform (which he had selected). However, the two physicists he most wanted to bring to Los Alamos strongly opposed militarizing the laboratory. One was I. I. Rabi and the other Robert F. Bacher, who was working with Rabi at MIT's Radiation Laboratory. Nothing useful, they argued, could be done in a place where scientists lacked autonomy. "We stopped that," Rabi says. "Bob Bacher and I explained how it wouldn't work—making it a military thing. The military would have had Robert by the short hairs." Rabi, who was as close to Oppenheimer as any scientist, was asked why Oppenheimer had gone along with the idea. "He had some mystical sense of it putting him at one with the American people," Rabi replied with a shrug. John Manley, who worked as long and closely with Oppenheimer as anyone, thinks the uniform and related attributes might have constituted "ego satisfaction for Robert."

Rabi and Bacher won the larger part of the argument. The scientists were promised a civilian laboratory for ten months but not more. Bacher wrote a letter of acceptance which included his resignation, effective on the day Los Alamos became a military operation. It never did. Rabi chose to be a consultant rather than a member. His colleagues at Los Alamos welcomed his visits, partly because they had a beneficial effect on Oppenheimer. Unlike most of the others, Rabi could often, though not invariably, influence Oppenheimer. "Rabi was father confessor to Oppy," says Manley. "He gave Robert a lot of help on personnel and organizational matters. He coached him on relations with Washington. Rabi, Conant, and Bush weren't there, but they were very important to the work of the place."

Oppenheimer could be hard on others, including the most illustrious. "[He] would give [Ernest] Lawrence a feeling that he didn't know physics."[55] He was arrogant, and at times abusive, as even his friends and supporters will say. Had he been less so, they also say, he'd have helped himself by making fewer enemies. "He was very vain and didn't care for fools," Rabi said. "He couldn't suppress a bon mot, and could do them so well. He had an unparalleled command of language." Some colleagues were put off by what seemed a disingenuous tendency. "He played many roles," says Rabi. "He was an actor. I enjoyed it. I played along with him."[56]

In a *New Yorker* profile of Rabi that appeared in 1977, Jeremy Bernstein asked him how he got along with Oppenheimer. " 'We got along very well,' " came the reply. " 'We were friends until his last day. I enjoyed the things about him that some people disliked. It's true that you carried on a charade with him. He lived a charade, and you went along with it. It was fine—matching wits and so on. Oppenheimer was great fun, and I took him for what he was. I understood his problem.' "

" 'What was his problem?' I asked."

" 'Identity,' Rabi answered. 'He reminded me very much of a boyhood friend about whom someone said that he couldn't make up his mind whether to be president of the B'nai B'rith or the Knights of Columbus. Perhaps he really wanted to be both, simultaneously. Oppenheimer wanted every experience. In that sense, he never focussed.' "[57]

Most people who worked at Los Alamos then doubt that anyone else could have done what Oppenheimer did there—produced the bomb in two years' time. Even his harshest critics respected him and admired his multiple gifts. Many were awed. "He was a great man," says Rabi. "Just those two years established that."

He was also an odd choice for the Los Alamos job, odder by far than Groves was for his. And it was Groves who picked Oppenheimer, although why he did so isn't clear. Oppenheimer hadn't administered anything; unlike many of the scientists already involved with the Manhattan Project, he was not well known. Norris Bradbury, who succeeded him at Los Alamos, says he took a course or two from Oppenheimer at Berkeley. "He wasn't known for his administrative ability. I can't imagine what it was about him that appealed to Groves."

"Groves had a fatal weakness for good men," Oppenheimer once said.[58] They could not have been more different: Groves was a no-nonsense engineer; Oppenheimer was reflective, as absorbed by psychology, poetry, and languages as he was by science. His intellectual versatility was dazzling. In a memoir called *Now It Can Be Told,* Groves states the case against selecting Oppenheimer, citing as major disadvantages his lack of managerial experience and the "strong feeling" among most of the scientific people, many of whom were Nobel laureates, that "the head of Project Y should also be one." Oppenheimer's work, Groves adds, "had been purely theoretical and had not taken him much beyond the point of being able to make an educated guess at the force an atomic fission bomb could exert. Nothing had been done on such down-to-earth problems as how to detonate the bomb, or how to design it so that it could be detonated. Adding to my cause for doubt, no one with whom I talked showed any great enthusiasm about Oppenheimer as a possible director of the project." Groves seems to have chosen Oppenheimer *faute de mieux*. "It became apparent," he says, "that we were not going to find a better man . . ."[59]

Curiously, Oppenheimer's real problem—links to Communists and former Communists—was put aside in 1943, whereas in 1954, after years of outstanding service to his country, these early associations were used against him in the proceedings which removed his security clearance. "His background included much that was not to our liking," said Groves. Yet Groves overrode the objections of army counterintelligence and cleared Oppenheimer himself. They were an odd couple and could never have been close; yet they respected each other. "We will never know whether anyone else could have done [the Los Alamos job] better or even as well," writes Groves. "I do not think so . . ."[60]

Edward Teller, whose testimony in 1954 gravely injured Oppenheimer, says, "Oppenheimer was probably the best lab director I have ever seen, because of the great mobility of his mind, because of his successful effort to know about practically everything important invented in the laboratory, and also because of his unusual psychological insight into other people . . ."[61]

Hans Bethe, the first head of the Theoretical Division, agrees. "He knew and understood everything that went on in the laboratory, whether it was chemistry or theoretical physics, or machine shop. He could keep it all in his head and coordinate it. It was clear also at Los Alamos that he was intellectually superior to us."[62]

What made the immaculate secrecy surrounding the bomb so bizarre was the abundance of discussion about nuclear fission from 1939 until the curtain dropped in the early forties. Journals in America and Britain which had teemed with articles about the uranium atom fell strangely silent on the subject then. The silence was noted by scientists in other countries. In 1940, a team of Soviet physicists discovered spontaneous fission, an exploit for which they were later awarded the Stalin Prize. They sent an account of the discovery to the American scientific journal *Physical Review* and their letter was printed, but its failure to arouse any response from

American scientists was taken to mean that a large and secret program was under way in the United States.

The Soviet team had been working under the direction of Igor Kurchatov, who, like other great figures in the field, was a prodigy; Kurchatov had been running a major laboratory since his late twenties.[63] These were years when the regime viewed modern physics as "dangerous idealism"— as allowing the individual too much influence over natural phenomena.[64] But after 1939, when Kurchatov and others began alerting the government to the possibility of nuclear fission leading to a bomb, and warning that Heisenberg and other German scientists might be creating one, the official attitude changed. In February 1943, Kurchatov was chosen to manage the development of a Soviet bomb. He wasn't selected because he was the most illustrious of his country's nuclear physicists; that distinction belonged to Kapitza. He was chosen because he impressed an advisory committee, which included Kapitza, as the man best equipped to coordinate so vast and challenging a program. (Kapitza, a Nobel laureate, but a born soloist, would have been miscast as impresario.)

Kurchatov was a burly, pensive-looking man, known to colleagues as "the beard."[65] Like Oppenheimer, he dazzled those around him with his multiple gifts and insight into all parts of the work. But his first task, a heavy one, was restoring laboratories that had been abandoned after the German invasion. But for the war's disruptive effects, a Soviet bomb might have been tested before 1949, according to many Western scientists who judged Soviet physics as more than equal to the task. Other experts demur, however, arguing that the Russian scientists would have moved less rapidly if Klaus Fuchs hadn't kept them in touch with what was being done at Los Alamos. "All things were available to Fuchs," says General Nichols. "He sat in on all the policy meetings on the fission bomb with people like Fermi, Bacher, and Rabi. It was a colloquium. There was no compartmentalization. Knowing what worked and what didn't was very useful to the Soviets."

Carson Mark, who replaced Bethe as head of the Theoretical Division, disagrees. "I don't think Fuchs was of any use to them at all," he said. "They were probably fascinated but not dependent on him. They didn't need him or other spies. They'd have come out at the same place at the same time if he had sent them nothing."

Rabi doubts that Fuchs mattered except in one critical sense. "For him to tell the Soviets the Americans were working on this was of immense help," said Rabi, adding that he used to ask a Soviet scientist whom he had gotten to know how he obtained money for research. "It is very simple," he would say. "I go to the Politburo and say, 'This is what the Americans are doing.'"

John Manley thinks Fuchs did matter. "Whenever you know not just that something is being worked on, but that it is feasible, it removes any number of hurdles," he says. Asked about Rabi's skepticism regarding Fuchs's technical help to the Soviets, Manley says, "Rabi, like Oppy, was clumsy in a laboratory. The how-to is often what is important."

If the scientific import of Fuchs's duplicity is unclear, its political effects are not. Just telling Moscow that its American ally was working in total secrecy on an atomic bomb—indeed, doing so with help from the other ally, Britain—reinforced the regime's paranoia and sense of isolation. Conversely, Fuchs's real affiliation, when it came to light in 1950, reinforced America's sense of betrayal by a recent ally now become a minatory foe.

Among those who felt that Russian science would fashion an atomic bomb in little more time than Anglo-American efforts would require was Niels Bohr, who had escaped to Britain (via Sweden) in 1943. Bohr instantly began looking beyond the war and worrying about the prospect of a nuclear arms race between competing power blocs. As before, he took on the role of the conscience of modern physics. Early in 1944, Bohr visited Los Alamos. His presence was a tonic and morale builder, but as he later told a friend, "They didn't need my help in making the atom bomb."[66] In February, Bohr arrived in Washington and lunched with Justice Felix Frankfurter in the Supreme Court chambers; Frankfurter was an old friend and close to Roosevelt. The Soviet Union, Bohr urged, should be told about the bomb well before it was used; in turn, the confidence that such a disclosure might create would increase chances for negotiations down the road on controlling nuclear arms. At Los Alamos, Bohr had for the first time heard talk about a hydrogen bomb possibly following the fission bomb.

Roosevelt was not pleased to find that Frankfurter knew about the project, but he agreed to see Bohr. Very little is known about Roosevelt's reaction to Bohr's views, because he rarely took anyone into his confidence on this matter (not even Stimson, Bush, or Conant). Some believe that Bohr obtained a mandate from F.D.R. to take up with Churchill the idea of sharing the secret and looking ahead to international control of the atom. Bush and Conant were themselves warning that security in the future wouldn't lie in secrecy.

A good guess is that Roosevelt, although impressed by what he was hearing, was uncertain. Churchill, he knew, saw security as anchored to secrecy, above all, from that other totalitarian host, the Soviet Union. Churchill was more relaxed about the Nazi nuclear program, because his secret service had been reporting since sometime in 1942 that it was laboring. (Not much of this intelligence was being shared then with Washington.) An Anglo-American partnership—a monopoly really—was Churchill's prescription for the near, middle, and long term. Roosevelt didn't share his great confederate's anxiety about imperial Soviet aims, but he does seem to have felt, on balance, that the knowledge of the atomic bomb probably should be confined to Anglo-American custody. In any case, he and Churchill had already decided as much, or thought they had, at Quebec in August 1943. Britain and the United States, they agreed, would never use the weapon against each other, and neither would use it against a third party without the other's consent. Neither would provide information about Tube Alloys to a third party except by mutual consent. Also, because the United States was bearing the entire burden of producing the bomb, the "British government recognize that any post-war advantages of an industrial or commercial character shall be dealt with as between the United States and Great Britain on terms to be specified by the President of the United States to the Prime Minister of Great Britain."[67]

In May, two months after his conversations in Washington, Bohr did see Churchill in a meeting he had hoped would be a turning point. It went badly. Concision was not among Bohr's strengths; the great statesman wrote off Europe's greatest scientist as a woolly-head.

The meeting probably reinforced Churchill's commitment to secrecy. "One of the blackest comedies of the war," said C. P. Snow of the meeting. "We did not speak the same language," Bohr said later.[68] Still, as the Americans were yet to discover, the strictly Anglo-American approach agreed to at Quebec was somewhat illusory. Britain had already made some concealed arrangements with Halban and Kowarski, whose political ties lay with the Free French provisional government of Charles de Gaulle in Algiers. And in Paris, Juliot-Curie was kept informed of the bomb's progress by his former associates and by the British. In effect, the British were holding back information from the Americans and then were surprised themselves to discover how little Roosevelt was telling his closest advisers about the understandings with Churchill. "I do not know whether Roosevelt consulted any Americans at Quebec on atomic energy," wrote Groves in his memoir. "I doubt very much that he did. All we were able to learn of the proceedings there was that, on August 17, the President signed the Quebec Agreement . . ."[69] Nichols now says, "Roosevelt did the Quebec accord on his own—without advice or advisers. Bush and Conant felt he didn't have the authority to do this under the War Powers Act. And Groves was opposed to any agreement with the British on the grounds that by then we didn't need help from anyone. He wanted to go it alone."

Roosevelt and Churchill discussed Tube Alloys again at a meeting in

Hyde Park in September 1944. A few weeks before, Bohr had seen Roosevelt, who seemed genuinely responsive to his concern about a Russian
bomb and the prospect of a nuclear arms race. Roosevelt agreed that an
approach to Russia must be tried, saying it would open a new era of human
history. Bohr felt encouraged enough to hold himself in readiness to go to
Moscow.[70] But Churchill got Roosevelt back on track at Hyde Park. There
he drafted a secret aide-mémoire for his and Roosevelt's signatures that
rejected and also misrepresented Bohr's position: "The suggestion that the
world should be informed regarding tube alloys, with a view to an international agreement regarding its control and use, is not accepted." Incredibly,
it added a baseless slur: "Enquiries should be made regarding the activities
of Professor Bohr and steps taken to ensure that he is responsible for no
leakage of information particularly to the Russians." Roosevelt's advisers
would have been distressed had they known about the document, especially
an undertaking in which "full collaboration between the United States and
the British government in developing tube alloys for military and commercial purposes should continue after the defeat of Japan unless and until
terminated by joint agreement."[71]

In short, Roosevelt, without telling anyone, had agreed that security
in the postwar era would rely on an Anglo-American partnership. "It was
a strange situation," says Joseph Volpe, then an army captain on Groves's
staff. "FDR and Churchill would get together and agree on total collaboration. Then it would come down to Groves who was opposed to all of it.
So was Stimson."[72] Roosevelt's aides, as soon as they learned about his
agreements with Churchill, would set about watering them down in talks
with the British. The partnership to which the two freewheeling statesmen
kept committing themselves was never feasible. Gradually, America's vast
Manhattan Project absorbed Britain's modest program. The British would
be allowed to help with the work at Los Alamos but with little else.

Britrish scientists and technicians began arriving at the mesa in November 1943. "Welcome to Los Alamos, and who the devil are you?" said
Oppenheimer when he saw them.[73] Peierls was the nominal leader of the
group, which also included Frisch and Fuchs. On both sides it was later said
that the work by the British team significantly shortened the time it took
to make the first bombs. Estimates of how much time was saved have ranged
from two months to the extreme of a year. But the immediate effect of the
British presence was to help Oppenheimer solve a serious problem involv-

ing two of his luminaries—Teller and Bethe. Teller appeared to have felt that he, not Bethe, should have been selected by Oppenheimer to run the Theoretical Division. Bethe said, "That I was named to head the division was a severe blow to Teller, who had worked on the bomb project almost from the day of its inception and considered himself, quite rightly, as having seniority over everyone then at Los Alamos, including Oppenheimer."[74] Even then, Teller's main interest was the fusion bomb, not the fission bomb to which the work of the laboratory was devoted. "[Bethe] wanted me to work on calculational details at which I am not particularly good," said Teller, "while I wanted to continue not only on the hydrogen bomb, but on other novel subjects."[75]

Teller's real problem lay not with Bethe but with Oppenheimer. "One could feel a certain tension between Teller and Oppenheimer," wrote Peierls. "Perhaps the reason was that Teller was anxious to earn Oppenheimer's respect, not only as a physicist—which he undoubtedly had—but as a person."[76] It was Peierls whom Oppenheimer chose to replace Teller at the helm of the group that was supposed to find a way to detonate the plutonium bomb, later known as "Fat Man" (for Winston Churchill). This was easily the toughest of the lab's various tasks. Work on "Little Boy," the enriched uranium bomb, was proceeding smoothly; it would be detonated by a so-called gun method—shooting one subcritical mass of U-235 into another so that the two together would become supercritical and explode. This straightforward method didn't work with plutonium. The only way to produce an adequate detonation of Fat Man, it seemed, was by implosion—turning a blast of conventional high explosive inward toward a quantity of fissile plutonium; the force of the explosion squeezes the material until it becomes supercritical and explodes. Implosion posed very difficult problems of physical theory and technique and was to use up a large part of the laboratory's energies during much of 1944 and early 1945.[77]

Teller was another soloist, and Oppenheimer, it seems, did want someone else managing the implosion group. But why Teller insisted on devoting himself to the hydrogen bomb, which was clearly several years away, and would, in any case, require a fission bomb as trigger, mystified many of his colleagues. "While his [Teller's] ideas are always original and often brilliant, they are not always practical or timely," wrote Peierls. "He pursues his ideas with great insistence, and this makes him act at times like a prima donna. But, just as only an outstanding singer can afford to behave like a prima donna, he is an outstanding physicist."[78]

"Teller was disruptive," says Rabi. "But Oppy let the work on fusion go on. Teller wanted Oppy to recruit people to work for him. Actually, he wanted Oppy to work for him." Rabi adds, "I first met him [Teller] when he was a student of Heisenberg's at Leipzig. He was a tremendous Ping-Pong player, but the best player there was a Chinese physicist who was opposite in temperament. Teller would slam and slash the ball, and the Chinese would just stand there hitting them all back."

Oppenheimer understood Teller better than most of the others did, mainly because they were alike. "They were both spurred on by a similar burning ambition," wrote Robert Jungk. "They both felt themselves to be immeasurably superior to their fellow men. They were both, as Bethe . . . remarked, 'almost more like artists than scientists.' "[79]

Their stylistic opposite was Fermi, who took an uncomplicated approach to most things, including his work, which prospered whether he was soloing or being a team player. "He always had a low profile," recalls Willie Higinbotham. "He was too famous to get involved, or so he thought. He rarely knew what he felt about issues. Fermi thought of government as being made up of responsible people. If they wanted his help, he would provide it. He was unlike his European colleagues who had learned to mistrust the judgment of governments. He was shy about talking politics." "Not a philosopher," said Oppenheimer of him. "Passion for clarity. He was simply unable to let things be foggy. Since they always are, this kept him pretty active."[80] Peierls wrote, "In Fermi's hands, problems that had been terrifyingly complicated for others often became very simple."[81] Colleagues often wondered how he managed to do what he did. Occasionally, said his most renowned student, physicist Emilio Segré, "Fermi would tell you things, then you asked him, 'But really, how? Show me.' And then he would say, 'Oh, well, I know this on c.i.f.' He spoke Italian. 'C.i.f.' meant *con intuito formidable.* 'With formidable intuition.' So how he did it, I don't know."[82] According to Manley, "Fermi was the supreme champ at Los Alamos for Twenty Questions. He never could be beaten. Once a few people thought they had him. The topic was Moses' staff. He got it on about question fourteen."

His several exploits are legendary, but Fermi is best known for one experiment that had to succeed before an atomic explosion could be judged feasible. In late 1942, while Oppenheimer was trying to recruit the best and the brightest for Los Alamos, Fermi was building a graphite "pile," as the first crude reactor was known, in a squash court on the University of Chicago campus. Workmen on two twelve-hour shifts stacked layers of graphite on a wooden frame, with slots built in for the cadmium rods which absorbed neutrons and would be withdrawn slowly until a critical mass of neutrons was reached, thus allowing a self-sustaining chain reaction to begin. On December 2, a subfreezing day, in an unheated building, men for the first time produced a controlled chain reaction. American physicist

Arthur Compton watched the successful procedure and then made his famous phone call to Conant: "Jim, you'll be interested to know that the Italian navigator has just landed in the new world."

Szilard didn't share the enthusiasm of the others who watched. "I shook hands with Fermi and I said I thought this day would go down as a black day in the history of mankind," Szilard wrote.[83] That same evening, the Fermis gave a party for colleagues and wives. The wives had been told nothing, and Laura Fermi was puzzled to hear some of the scientists mutter congratulations to her husband. She took aside Leona Woods, the only woman physicist of the group, and asked why Enrico was being congratulated. "He's sunk a Japanese admiral," came the answer. Mrs. Fermi reported this response to another guest and asked him whether it was possible. "Do you think anything is impossible for Enrico?" was the guarded reply. Her efforts to find out from her husband whether he had sunk a Japanese admiral by some exotic remote control device were unavailing. Not until the war ended did Laura Fermi find out what had happened on that cold December day two and one-half years earlier.[84]

Fermi's triumph on the squash court had a liberating effect. It convinced the Americans that they no longer needed help from the British. And it started them on the path to Trinity, the first test of the bomb. "We were fairly sure . . . that we would be able to test the Fat Man . . . sometime around the middle of July," Groves wrote.[85]* The test site had to be flat and isolated, yet convenient to Los Alamos. The desert area selected was known as the Jornada del Muerto—the Journey of Death—a name given it four centuries earlier by the conquistadores. In 1945, it was part of the Army Air Corps' test range at Alamogordo. Oppenheimer puzzled colleagues by rechristening his eighteen-mile-wide and twenty-four-mile-long corner of it "Trinity," having privately invoked a sonnet by John Donne:

> Batter my heart, three person'd God; for, you
> As yet but knocke, breathe, shine, and seeke to mend;
> That I may rise, and stand, o'erthrow mee, and bend
> Your force, to breake, blowe, burn, and make me new . . .

Trinity was scheduled for 4:00 A.M. on July 16. At Los Alamos, the keen sense of impending climax was tempered by uncertainty and concern that the event would become an anticlimax. Some of this was expressed in a few lines of black parody:

*Little thought was given to testing Little Boy, the enriched uranium bomb; its simple gun method was judged very reliable, and in any case the available supply of U-235 was barely more than enough for the one such bomb intended for use against Japan.

From this crude lab that spawned a dud
Their necks to Truman's axe uncurled.
Lo, the embattled savants stood
And fired the flop heard around the world. [86]

Plans for the test were based on yields of 100 to 10,000 tons, although safety provisions were made for 20,000 tons. A betting pool on the yield was organized, and guesses ranged from zero to Edward Teller's high end estimate of 45,000 tons. Oppenheimer is said to have picked 200 tons, but he actually bet ten dollars against George Kistiakowsky's monthly salary that the device wouldn't work at all. The real number, as it turned out, was close to 19,000 tons, and Rabi won the pool, having picked 18,000 tons, mainly because it was all that was left when he chose.[87] (Rabi had been summoned by Groves, who wanted him there as a calming influence on Oppenheimer, who, predictably, was very tense. Rabi turned up at the desert site wearing a black suit and a homburg and carrying an umbrella.)[88]

Groves himself, along with Bush, Conant, Groves's chief of staff General Thomas Farrell, and some other VIPs, arrived on Sunday, July 15, the same day that Truman, Churchill, and Stalin were arriving in Potsdam, a Berlin suburb, for a Big Three conference. Truman and his advisers had delayed the start of the conference, feeling that a successful test of the new weapon would strengthen their position with Stalin at Potsdam.

Several hours before the countdown for Trinity, a storm arrived unexpectedly, creating pressure to postpone the test. Clear weather was essential for visual and photographic measurements, and rain or abrupt changes in wind direction just after the shot would create radioactive fallout hazards. But with Truman and Stimson awaiting word at Potsdam, Groves was reluctant to cancel. Groves and Oppenheimer consulted throughout the night. Fermi, along with several others, was very concerned about fallout, and he strongly urged Oppenheimer to postpone the test. As Groves later wrote, Fermi had already annoyed him by offering "to take wagers from his fellow scientists on whether the bomb would ignite the atmosphere, and if so, whether it would merely destroy New Mexico or destroy the world."[89]* "I took Oppenheimer into an office that had been set up for him in the base camp, where we could discuss matters quietly and calmly," Groves wrote. "The only other persons taking part in this conversation were some weather forecasters whom we called in. Since it was obvious that they were completely upset by the failure of the long-range predictions, I soon excused them. After that, it was necessary for me to make my own

*Fermi wasn't really worried about the atmosphere igniting, according to some colleagues, but had chosen a picturesque means of noting that no one could predict the actual effect of the test. A few others soberly took what he said at face value.

weather predictions—a field in which I had nothing more than very general knowledge."[90]

By 2:00 A.M., the weather was improving and the shot was rescheduled for 5:30. The rain stopped at 4:00. At 5:29:45 A.M. Mountain War Time, there flashed a burst of light that a young blind girl was reported to have seen from a distance of one hundred fifty miles. "Without a sound, the sun was shining," recalled Otto Frisch, codiscoverer of nuclear fission. "Or so it looked. The sand hills at the edge of the desert were shimmering in a very bright light, almost colourless and shapeless . . . after another ten seconds or so it had grown and dimmed into something more like a huge oil fire, with a structure that made it look a bit like a strawberry . . . the bang came minutes later, quite loud though I had plugged my ears, and followed by a long rumble like heavy traffic very far away. I can still hear it."[91]

Oppenheimer thought of a line from the Hindu scripture, the *Bhagavad-Gita:* "Now I am become Death, destroyer of worlds."

Exactly two hours after the explosion, Groves dispatched a coded report of the success to Stimson at Potsdam. Churchill, when informed, described Trinity as "a miracle of deliverance."

"The war is over," said General Farrell to Groves just after the explosion. "My reply was," Groves wrote, " 'Yes, after we drop two bombs on Japan.' "[92] Shortly before dawn on July 16, while Trinity was inaugurating the nuclear age, the uranium bomb—Little Boy—was loaded aboard the cruiser *Indianapolis* at San Francisco. The vessel was bound for Tinian, in the Mariana Islands in the Pacific Ocean, and arrived July 26.

Harry Truman has said that he "regarded the bomb as a military weapon and never had any doubt that it should be used."[93] The decision to drop it may have been an easy one, compared to the harder choices Truman confronted in his presidency—a time when he dealt with problems of an urgency and complexity that perhaps only Washington, Lincoln, and Roosevelt experienced. In any case, Truman never looked back, or, so far as we know, tried to inform himself about the exact circumstances in which the bomb was used, not once, but twice. Had he done so, he might have judged the step as more complicated than it seemed at the time. Around him he heard little disagreement that unless Japan promptly surrendered the weapon would be used. But from that proposition flowed some large questions that were never put before Truman. Would the bomb be used more than once? Against what targets? What, if any, limits would be put on its use? And if Japan's divided leaders failed to surrender even after the shock of Hiroshima and the impact of a Russian declaration of war, should they have been granted a respite in which to consider their plight before being struck a second time? Indeed, since the American invasion wasn't scheduled until November 1, why did use of the bomb acquire such urgency? Why the hurry?

The answer to the last question lies in Roosevelt's legacy to Truman, which included a commitment to the enemy's unconditional surrender and to ending the war as rapidly as possible with minimal loss of American life. According to Groves, Roosevelt told him that "if the European war was not over before we had our first bombs he wanted us to be ready to drop them on Germany."[94] If the bomb had been ready six months sooner, Rabi says, "Roosevelt would have had to use it against Berlin. It would have been criminal not to."

Truman's position should be seen in context. Mass terror bombing was a whirlwind already reaped by Hitler and starting to afflict Japan. Taking innocent life on a massive scale was being judged acceptable, even unremarkable. The raids against Dresden in mid-February 1944—history's most destructive one act—killed 135,000 people. In an attack on Tokyo, less than a month later, B-29 bombers set off a firestorm in which nearly sixteen square miles of the city all but vanished and over 80,000 lives were lost; another 40,000 were wounded. An atomic bomb was not expected to kill nearly so many. But estimates of American casualties in an invasion of the Japanese islands were frightening. "My clear recollection was a minimum of 400,000 upwards to one million," says Dean Rusk, former Secretary of State, who at the time was serving in the War Department. Briefly, a decision against using a bomb that was meant to spare hundreds of thousands of American lives, was most unlikely.

Nor would Congress have understood holding back a weapon on which $2 billion in concealed funds had been invested. James F. Byrnes, a political ally and confidant of Truman's, had long worried about Congress's reaction to the project, and he wasn't alone. "I have been responsible for spending two billions of dollars on this atomic venture," said Stimson. "Now that it is successful, I shall not be sent to . . . Fort Leavenworth."[95] Groves, however, was known to be the one who worried most. He had once been the subject of a congressional inquiry into alleged overspending; he emerged blameless from the experience but clearly didn't want to repeat it. Here is Groves replying to a question on using the bomb: "I said that they could not fail to use this bomb because if they didn't use it, they would immediately cast a lot of reflection on Mr. Roosevelt . . . why did you spend all this money and all this effort and then when you got it, why didn't you use it? Also, it would have come out sooner or later in a Congressional hearing, if nowhere else, just when we could have dropped the bomb if we didn't use it."[96]

In 1945, Groves had three laboratories working on two uranium enrichment methods. And at Hanford he was developing plutonium as well. Fiscal controls within the Manhattan Project were all but nonexistent, partly because of the tight security surrounding the work, partly because of its urgency. The congressional leadership was aware only of a supersecret bomb project, the funding for which had to be concealed. Clearly, Groves intended to vindicate the huge investment in developing two kinds of fission bombs by using both against Japan. Also, the engineer in Groves surely wanted to see how each would work. His writ ran far and wide. He reported to Army Chief of Staff George C. Marshall to the degree he reported to anyone, but Marshall gave him plenty of freedom. "He set the agenda, and he wasn't second-guessed," says Joseph Volpe.

On war-related matters, Truman at first relied on Stimson for political guidance and on Marshall for more strictly military counsel. As vice president, Truman had known nothing officially of the atomic bomb. As chairman of a Senate investigative committee, he had once been on the point of looking into activities at Oak Ridge and Hanford, when a visit from Stimson convinced him to leave in obscurity what his mentor called "the greatest project in the history of the world."[97] Not until April 25, nine days after becoming President, was Truman briefed on the bomb. Groves, not Marshall, accompanied Stimson to the Oval Office, and he did most of the talking. Truman learned then of the plan to test the implosion bomb in July and to have both weapon types ready in August.[98] Use of the new weapon against Japan was not at issue in the meeting and was taken for granted.[99]

On Truman's role, Groves said: "The initial decision and the primary responsibility were Mr. Truman's. *As far as I was concerned, his decision was one of non-interference—basically, a decision not to upset the existing plans.*" (emphasis added)[100] Groves once said that Truman in this situation "was like a little boy on a toboggan."[101]

On the day Stimson and Groves briefed Truman, Bush revived the issue of informing some other countries, notably the Soviet Union, before the bomb was dropped on Japan. Bush's prodding led to the creation of a so-called Interim Committee, which would develop policy for the atomic era until Congress could create a postwar agency for that purpose. The committee members were Stimson, George L. Harrison (a former chairman of the New York Federal Reserve), Bush, Conant, MIT president Karl Compton, Undersecretary of the Navy Ralph A. Bard, Assistant Secretary of State William L. Clayton, and James F. Byrnes, Truman's special representative. Although the group was set up to apply human intelligence and wisdom to managing what seemed a superhuman new technology, it devoted very little attention to the hard questions involving the use of the bomb against Japan. "The agenda in the early papers [minutes] contains no discussion of whether to use the bomb and where," says R. Gordon Arneson, who was then an army second lieutenant in Stimson's office; Arneson, who later became the State Department's senior adviser on nuclear issues, served as the Interim Committee's secretary and note taker. "Stimson didn't want advice," says Arneson. "The operation [bombing] was in train and no one wanted to stop it. As-soon-as-possible was the over-riding consideration. Probably no weapon in history went into operation so soon after being tested."[102]

On May 31 and June 1, more than three weeks after the Interim Committee first met, it did explicitly discuss using the bomb. Oppenheimer and Groves were invited to attend. One of two issues was whether to attempt several simultaneous strikes. Oppenheimer, according to Arneson's official notes, favored the idea, but Groves opposed it, partly because, as he said, "We would lose the advantage of gaining additional knowledge concerning the weapon at each successive bombing."[103] The other issue concerned the "types of targets and the effects to be produced." The committee recommended that "the bomb should be used against Japan as soon as possible; that it should be used on a war plant surrounded by workers' homes; and that it be used without prior warning."[104] But the committee then disavowed its own competence "to make a final decision on the matter of targets, this being a military decision."[105]

In effect, Truman's senior civilian advisers were isolating themselves from decisions involving the use of a novel weapon of mass destruction against civilian targets. Yes, they said, the weapon would be used, but questions of when and where were being delegated—essentially to Groves, a military bureaucrat with little background outside military construction and even less knowledge of the world.

He told Marshall sometime during the spring that it was time "to make plans for the bombing operation itself . . ." And he asked Marshall to designate some officer in operations planning with whom he could work. Marshall replied, according to Groves, " 'I don't like to bring too many people into this matter. Is there any reason why you can't take this over and do it yourself?' My, 'No, Sir, I will,' concluded the conversation, which constituted the only directive that I ever received or needed."[106]

The actual targets, Groves wrote, "should not have been previously damaged by air raids. It was also desirable that the first target be of such size that the damage would be confined within it, so that we could more definitely determine the power of the bomb."[107] In another revealing passage, Groves noted that he and Admiral William Purnell, his colleague and ally on the Military Policy Committee, "had often discussed the importance of having the second blow follow the first one quickly, so that the Japanese would not have time to recover their balance. It was Purnell who had first advanced the belief that two bombs would end the war, so I knew that with him and Farrell on the ground at Tinian, there would be no unnecessary delay in exploiting our first success."[108]

Identifying suitable targets that were not already being, or about to be, bombed to pieces was a challenge. The 20th Air Force was under a directive to bomb the following cities "with the prime purpose in mind of not leaving one stone lying on another": Tokyo, Yokohama, Nagoya, Osaka, Kyoto, Kobe, Yawata, and Nagasaki. Kyoto, along with the Emperor's palace, had been struck from the list by Stimson, who also drew a commitment that the air force would perform "only precision bombing."[109] But for Groves, Kyoto was the ideal target—"large enough to ensure that the damage from the bomb would run out within the city, which would give us a firm understanding of its destructive power."[110] The other targets for atomic bombs on the initial list were Hiroshima, Nigata, and the Kokura arsenal. Stimson and his wife had visited and knew Kyoto; they understood its symbolic importance as Japan's old capital, cultural heart and shrine of the Buddhist and Shinto religions. Stimson had no wish to make irreconcilable enemies of the Japanese. He vetoed Kyoto.

Groves never gave up easily. Hiroshima, he argued, wouldn't yield as much knowledge about the effects of the weapons as Kyoto. Kyoto had far more people and was located in a cup-shaped depression that would concentrate the effect of the blast. Unlike Hiroshima, it didn't have rivers which would inhibit incendiary effects. Groves persisted. At Potsdam, Stimson received a Groves-inspired cable from George Harrison: "All your local military advisers . . . definitely favor your pet city and would like to feel free to use it as first choice if those on the ride select it out of four possible spots in the light of local conditions at the time."[111] Stimson again said no, and took up the issue with Truman who backed him. On July 25, at Potsdam, Truman wrote in his diary: "This weapon is to be used against Japan between now and August 10th. I have told . . . Mr. Stimson to use it so that military objectives and soldiers and sailors are the target, not women and children."[112] This passage suggests that Truman had learned little or nothing about the thinking that lay behind the target selection.

Whether Stimson understood much more than Truman is far from clear. He saw the target list only because he took an initiative; General Nichols says it would not ordinarily have been sent to him. In sparing Kyoto, Stimson interfered with Groves and took an act of leadership; but this was the sole occasion on which he did rock Groves's boat. Strictly speaking, Stimson, Truman, and even Marshall were out of the "loop."

On June 12, a threat to the Groves operation popped up in the form of a report from a group of atomic scientists at the Manhattan District's Chicago lab, where Fermi had been when he produced the first controlled chain reaction. Known as the Franck Report for its chairman, James Franck, one of Oppenheimer's professors at Göttingen, the report called for abandoning secrecy and placing the bomb under international control; it also urged that the new weapon not be used against Japan. Instead, it proposed a demonstration "before the eyes of representatives of all the United Nations, on the desert or a barren island."[113]

Although the report was intended for Stimson, he never saw it. Franck and Compton took it themselves to his office, but, possibly because they didn't phone ahead for an appointment, they didn't see Stimson.

Four days later, Oppenheimer and other members of a scientific panel reviewed the Franck Report at Alamogordo, where they were preparing for Trinity. The demonstration idea drew little support; the panel members reported that they could "propose no technical demonstration likely to bring an end to the war . . . no acceptable alternative to direct military use . . ."[114] Rabi, who wasn't a member, later summarized the argument against organizing a demonstration for the Japanese: "Who would they send?" he asked. "And what would he report? You would have to tell him what instruments to bring, and where to stand, and what to measure. Otherwise it would look like a lot of pyrotechnics. It would take someone who understood the theory to realize what he was seeing . . . You would have to have built a model town to make a realistic demonstration. It would require a level of communications between us and the Japanese which was inconceivable in wartime."[115]

Oppenheimer saw nothing to be gained in a demonstration shot, and seems to have discouraged Teller from pushing the idea. "After the Nazis surrendered," says Teller, "Szilard sent me a petition to circulate in Los Alamos that we should not use the atomic bomb against the Japanese without first demonstrating the bomb. I thought this was highly reasonable. But Oppenheimer talked me out of it. And I felt relieved because I was not certain that I knew enough to make a recommendation in this regard. Today I am sorry that I backed away."[116]

A few insiders, including John McCloy, who was Assistant Secretary of War and a favorite of Stimson's, thought that the Japanese should see a demonstration before being struck. But the idea never had a broad following, and Groves, ever the adroit bureaucrat, moved quickly to isolate what support it did have.

An impassioned case against the bomb was made by John Winant, a senior diplomat who was ambassador to Britain. (It fell to him to obtain Churchill's formal approval of the plan to use the bomb against Japan; the terms of the Quebec Agreement required British concurrence.) So strong were his feelings that the bomb was inhumane that those whom he entreated—Stimson and Groves among them—worried about what he might do after it was used. Volpe was dispatched to London to restrain Winant. After Hiroshima, he recalls, "Winant was beside himself. He paced back and forth wringing his hands. He wanted to issue a statement. It was crazy. I was a first lieutenant—maybe a captain then—telling the ambassador he couldn't make a statement."

Sidetracking the plan to use the bomb was probably never in the cards. A convincing argument that Japan was being so badly hurt and depleted that its leaders were ready to surrender might have made a difference. But that argument was not being made convincingly. Instead, the prevailing attitude was that even the terrible fire bombings of the cities were having no apparent effect on Japanese morale and determination to go on fighting.

A most interesting dissent came from Eisenhower. During the Potsdam Conference, he and Stimson were dining together at his headquarters in Germany when, as Eisenhower recalled, "Stimson got this cable saying the bomb had been perfected and was ready to be dropped . . . Well, I listened, and I didn't volunteer anything because, after all, my war was over in Europe and it wasn't up to me. But I was getting more and more depressed just thinking about it. Then he asked for my opinion, so I told him I was against it on two counts. *First, the Japanese were ready to surrender and it wasn't necessary to hit them with that awful thing.* Second, I hated to see our country be the first to use such a weapon. Well . . . the old gentleman got furious. And I can see how he would. After all, it had been his responsibility to push for all the huge expenditure to develop the bomb, which of course he had a right to do, and *was* right to do. Still, it was an awful problem." (emphasis added)[117]

A climactic moment had already occurred in a meeting between Truman and his senior advisers on June 18. It was agreed that an invasion of the Japanese islands would begin on November 1. Marshall estimated casualties for the first thirty days of combat at 31,000. Truman asked Stimson whether an invasion by white men would cause the Japanese to close ranks. Stimson thought it would.[118]

Then, an awkward moment occurred when Admiral William D. Leahy, Truman's military adviser, objected to the requirement for Japan's unconditional surrender. Insisting on it, he said, would increase Japan's desperation, hence American casualties. But Truman had publicly committed himself to unconditional surrender. Given the bitterly anti-Japanese feeling in the country, changing course would have been very difficult, as Truman made clear.[119] Within the room, it was tacitly understood that unconditional surrender and the atomic bomb had acquired a one-to-one relationship.

The most astute and credible advocate of something less than unconditional surrender was Acting Secretary of State Joseph C. Grew, who had served as ambassador to Japan for ten years. Grew reckoned that the Japanese knew they were badly beaten, and by late spring were ready to yield, though not unconditionally. Retention of their imperial dynasty appeared to be one condition on which the Japanese couldn't budge.

The War Department, too, was uneasy about unconditional surrender, mainly because of a concern about Soviet intentions. At Yalta, Stalin had promised to invade Japan within three months of the end of the war in Europe. An American concession to the Japanese that ended the war quickly would deny him a chance to take part and thereby establish a foothold in Japan. Moreover, the Joint Chiefs of Staff and General Marshall felt that the Emperor's presence would help assure Japanese compliance with a cease-fire and occupation. "The present stand of the War Department," said an army planning document, "is that Japanese surrender is just possible and attractive enough to the U.S. to justify us in making any concession which might be attractive to the Japanese, so long as our realistic aims for peace in the Pacific are not adversely affected."[120]

At State, however, the line was hardening. In early July, Byrnes took over as secretary of a divided department. Grew's position was being opposed by Assistant Secretaries Archibald MacLeish and Dean Acheson. Japan's throne, they told Byrnes as he was leaving for Potsdam, is "anachronistic . . . perfectly adapted to the manipulation and use of . . . feudal-minded groups . . ."[121]

Over the next three weeks, Emperor Hirohito, a mysterious figure whose gentle nature was unknown to American officials, became the focus of a low-key struggle within Truman's entourage at Potsdam. Just before the conference, Stimson proposed a draft proclamation that would cover retention of the Emperor.

A few days later, he and Truman, along with Byrnes, were learning through intercepted messages between Japan and its ambassador in Moscow that retention of the Emperor was indeed a precondition to surrender. The Japanese were hoping that Moscow might agree to mediate.

On July 17, Stalin sealed his pledge to invade Japan by setting the date for August 15. "Fini Japs when that comes about," Truman noted in his diary for that day.[122] But a more important event—the successful Trinity test—had occurred the day before, and it sent American thinking off in another direction: The atomic bomb, not Russia's invasion, might now provide the missing incentive for Japan's capitulation. Support for the idea of conceding the Japanese their Emperor fell abruptly. Limiting the Soviet position in postwar Japan became the priority goal. And Byrnes, who never had been tempted by Grew's argument, set about drafting the Potsdam Declaration—the ultimatum to Japan—with some help from Truman and Churchill.[123] Only Stimson urged trying to induce surrender by warning the Japanese, either in the ultimatum or some private channel, of the two immense threats hanging over them—the atomic bomb and a Russian invasion. Truman said that he would take care of reassuring the Japanese about their Emperor, but he didn't do it.[124] And the ultimatum, because it contained no allusion whatsoever to the Emperor, made even more Herculean the task of those Japanese, in Tokyo, who were maneuvering to end the war.[125]

By then, the Americans had become reluctant even to admit the possibility of a Soviet presence in the area.[126] "I felt it was of great importance," Stimson wrote later in his diary, "to get the homeland into our hands before the Russians could put in any substantial claim to occupy and help rule it."[127] "I was extremely anxious to have the test carried off on schedule," said Groves of Trinity. "I knew the effect [it] would have on the issuance and wording of the Potsdam ultimatum."[128] Stalin didn't sign the ultimatum, which was issued on July 26, nor was he asked to. Japan rejected it.

Two days earlier, Truman very casually told Stalin that America had perfected a very powerful explosive. Stalin was just as casual, saying he hoped the Americans would make good use of the weapon against Japan.[129] Stalin's impassive reaction led Churchill and Byrnes, among others, to conclude that he hadn't grasped the importance of Truman's comment. But clearly he had, if only because Soviet agents—Fuchs among them—had kept him informed of America's bombs. Marshal Georgi Zhukov writes in his memoirs that "on returning to his quarters after this meeting, Stalin, in my presence, told Molotov about his conversation with Truman. The latter reacted immediately. 'Let them. We'll have to talk it over with Kurchatov and get him to speed things up.' "[130]

Five days after the ultimatum, one last message to the Japanese ambassador in Moscow was intercepted. "The battle situation has become acute," it said. "Since the loss of one day relative to this present matter may result in a thousand years of regret, it is requested that you immediately have a talk with Molotov."[131]

The Japanese were not to have much time to think about the ultimatum. Groves wanted to begin using the bomb three days later, but he was blocked by bad weather and Truman's strong feeling that he himself ought to have left Potsdam before the bomb was used. "Release when ready, but not sooner than 2 August," Truman cabled back.

On July 19, Groves alerted Oppenheimer: "It is necessary to drop the first Little Boy and the first Fat Man and probably a second one in accordance with our original plans. It may be that as many as three of the latter in their best present form may have to be dropped to conform with planned strategic operations."[132]

Using one atomic bomb to shorten the war was all but unavoidable; the step had acquired a relentless political logic. Dropping two bombs in rapid succession—without testing Japan's reaction to the first one—ought to have been a separate question but wasn't. "As far as I was concerned," Groves said, "there was no limit to the number of bombs that would be used. There was no debate ever on the matter of dropping a second bomb. The debate had all been on whether to use the atomic bomb . . . at all."[133] Groves was in control, although Truman may have believed otherwise. At Potsdam, he told Stimson he hoped only one bomb would be dropped.[134] Yet according to his memoirs, "an order was issued to General [Carl] Spaatz to continue operations [after Hiroshima] . . . unless otherwise instructed."[135] The order was never found. And as Leon Sigal explains in *Fighting to a Finish*, his authoritative book about ending the war in Japan, none was needed. Truman's absent order matched a directive drafted by Groves on July 24, and Groves made sure it was carried out as promptly as possible.[136]

On August 6, Little Boy was detonated over Hiroshima at an altitude of just under two thousand feet. Some days later, a Japanese newspaperman alighted from a train to find that the city's railway station—one of western Japan's largest—was no longer there. "There was a sweeping view, right to the mountains, north, south, and east—the city had vanished."[137] The blast and fire had destroyed over 62,000 of the metropolitan area's 90,000 buildings. Roughly 30 percent of the population—an estimated 71,000 people—died that day, and many more died later from injury and radiation.[138]

On August 8, the Soviet Union declared war against Japan and invaded Manchuria. Stalin had advanced the date of the move, doubtless out of concern that the shock of Hiroshima could end the war abruptly. Actually, the shock of Stalin's move against them is judged to have done more to deplete Japan's will to continue fighting than either of the two bombs. The immediate effect of the Hiroshima bomb was to isolate the city. Marshall, like most of his colleagues, had expected the Japanese to sue at once for peace. "What we did not take into account," he said long afterward, ". . . was that the destruction would be so complete that it would be an appreciable time before the actual facts of the case would get to Tokyo."[139] The Japanese army's Vice Chief of Staff, Torashiro Kawabe, noted that "since Tokyo was not directly affected by the bombing, the full force of the shock was not felt." And officials, he said, "had become accustomed to bombings" because of "frequent raids by B-29's."[140] "The city was cut off," says Gordon Arneson. "We didn't know they had not been able to react by the time of the second bomb."

On August 9, the day after the Soviet entry into the war, Fat Man was dropped on Nagasaki. Photo-reconnaissance pictures, according to Groves, showed 44 percent of the city destroyed. He and others have explained that because of bad weather, the bomb missed its aim point and thus caused less damage than had been expected. The Strategic Bombing Survey, Groves says, estimated 35,000 killed and 60,000 injured at Nagasaki.[141]

Among initiates, opinion on the Nagasaki bomb divides sharply. Many felt that a second bomb was needed to convince Japan's diehards that the first one was no fluke. Rabi, whose political judgment was respected by many colleagues, takes this view: "The idea of two sharp blows in succession was sound. The problem wasn't military. It was psychological. The Japanese people were thoroughly united. They were in a state of hysteria and needed a shock to bring them out of it. The Emperor finally intervened, something that had never happened. He did it to save his people from destruction." Rabi's colleague Hans Bethe disagrees: "I think it was necessary to drop one, but the second could have easily been avoided. I think Japan would have capitulated anyway. But by that time, the decision of using the second bomb was left to the field commander and field commanders use whatever they have."[142] Dean Rusk thinks the decision to use one bomb saved thousands of lives, but he feels differently about the second one. "After the war was over," he says, "we learned that Japan was closer to defeat than we had believed. My hunch is that the war would have ended the same way with only the Hiroshima bomb."[143]

Not much can be said with authority about Japan's decision to surrender except that the Emperor, who wanted to end hostilities, was shown later to have played the decisive role. Regrettably no senior figure in the American government, possibly excepting Grew, understood the Emperor's involvement. "This failure of understanding is itself understandable," writes McGeorge Bundy, "since there was no precedent whatever for such direct intervention [by the Emperor]."[144]

Ironically, the two atomic bombs were less effective than was this supposedly feudal imperial figure—a war criminal in Washington's eyes. "It is apparent," said the Strategic Bombing Survey, "that the effect of the atomic bombs on the confidence of the Japanese civilian population was remarkably localized. Outside of the target cities, it was subordinate to other demoralizing experiences."[145]

The second bomb never was an issue. Any doubts about the bombings were swept aside by a wave of relief and euphoria as the war ended. They were universally seen as having caused Japan's capitulation, thereby sparing many tens of thousands of American lives. However, some would now judge the second bomb as an example of what can happen when bureaucrats gain control of broad policy questions, as sometimes they do.

At Los Alamos, the regrets and second thoughts that some people developed came later. Laura Fermi's memoir conveys a flavor of the first reaction to the news of Hiroshima: "Genia Peierls, who always managed to learn what was going on ahead of the other wives, brought me the news on the morning of August 7th. It was around ten-thirty, and I was in my kitchen . . . I heard Genia run upstairs, her rapid steps imparting her agitation to the wooden staircase. 'Our stuff was dropped on Japan!' she shouted upon reaching our landing. 'Truman made announcement. It was transmitted ten minutes ago in Tech Area. Over paging system.' She stepped into my kitchen and stood there, her brown eyes aglow, her large hands spread out, palms upward, her red lips parted. 'Our stuff.' That is the phrase she used. Not even then, the morning after Hiroshima, did we, the wives, fully realize that Los Alamos was making atomic bombs."[146]

The Pueblo Indians were the first settlers of the canyons and mesas around Los Alamos, and they have lived there for at least a thousand years. For them, the news was disturbing. The Pueblo culture is as peaceful as any to be found. For man's most destructive contrivance to have been born on the ruins of ancestral Pueblo villages struck this people as cruelly ironic.

III

The End of Illusion

At Potsdam, Harry Truman made a diary entry that provided a sharp glimpse of his thinking: "It is a good thing that Hitler's crowd or Stalin's did not discover this atomic bomb."[1] For Stalin, the other party to the Big Three alignment, the weapon and the use that had been made of it spelled trouble. The unwillingness of Truman and Churchill to tell him about the bomb had alerted him to their supposed purpose. The explosions over Hiroshima and Nagasaki seemed to confirm it. Wrongly, though perhaps inevitably, he interpreted the atomic attacks on an enfeebled enemy as a message addressed to him: In the postwar realignment of power, an Anglo-American combine would seek preeminence through nuclear weapons. Shortly after returning from Potsdam, Stalin summoned Kurchatov (whom he was seeing daily) and others, including the People's Commissar of Munitions. "A single demand of you comrades," he reportedly said. "Provide us with atomic weapons in the shortest possible time. You know that Hiroshima has shaken the whole world. The balance has been destroyed. Provide the bomb—it will remove a great danger from us."[2]

Stalin also tried playing down the importance of atomic weapons. "I do not consider the atomic bomb as serious a force as some politicians are inclined to do," he said at one point. "Atomic bombs are meant to frighten those with weak nerves, but they cannot decide the fate of wars since [they] are quite insufficient for that."[3]

Telling Stalin about the bomb probably wouldn't have affected the Soviet Union's political aims or its gloomy estimate of the West's. Yet by not taking him into their confidence at any stage, Washington and London may have strengthened Moscow's paranoia and its resolve to match the

53

United States weapon for weapon while rejecting out of hand any reliable form of international control.

Truman's rendezvous with history coincided with a dispute with the Soviets over Poland arising from the Yalta agreements; these restored sovereign rights and self government to peoples in Eastern Europe whom the war had robbed of such rights. The Soviets had reneged and set up a puppet government in Poland. Since their military forces were in control of most of the region, there was little their wartime allies could do but protest. Ten days after becoming President, Truman met with Soviet Foreign Minister Vyacheslav M. Molotov and told him almost at once that the United States was getting tired of waiting for the Soviet Union to carry out agreements it had freely entered into. When Molotov interrupted, Truman said he wasn't interested in propaganda and dismissed him with an icy request to "transmit my views to Marshal Stalin." Charles E. Bohlen, who interpreted for both Roosevelt and Truman, described Truman's performance as "probably the first sharp words uttered during the war by an American President to a high Soviet official."[4] "I gave him the one-two, right to the jaw," said Truman.[5]

Among the most attentive monitors of the East-West scene was the community of atomic scientists, whose attitude toward their bomb was evolving. The success of Little Boy and Fat Man had produced some understandable exhilaration within the group that developed them. With the war over, atomic scientists had at first thought mainly about picking up their former lives. "Three fourths of the lab people were trying to get out as rapidly as possible," recalls Norris Bradbury, who replaced Oppenheimer as director at Los Alamos. "They were not concerned with issues. They were concerned with jobs and promotions at universities."[6] Oppenheimer himself left Los Alamos for Princeton's Institute for Advanced Study within twenty-four hours of the war's end. But then, the deepening chill in relations with the Soviets aroused concern about the new age, especially among those who had helped create it. They reckoned, as their leaders did not, that before long the Soviets, too, would have nuclear weapons. Many atomic scientists felt uneasy for other reasons; after having extended themselves in a crash program aimed at beating the Nazis to the punch, they became parties to the destruction of two cities that belonged to a different and rather battered enemy. Richard P. Feynman, among the greatest of the physicists at Los Alamos—"a magician," according to Hans Bethe—said later: "What happened to me—what happened to the rest of us is we started for a good reason, then you're working very hard to accomplish something, and it's pleasure, it's excitement. And you stop thinking you know; you just stop."[7]

A great many such people felt obliged by their recent past to exercise some influence over the future. But however novel the nuclear issues may have seemed to scientists, Washington took them in stride, because they were mainly jurisdictional—hence familiar. Was atomic energy to remain a military domain or would it slide toward civilian control? Within the Pentagon, maneuvering between military services for control of nuclear roles and missions had begun with the bombings, and a brisk pace was being set.

On the day Nagasaki was bombed, Truman promised Congress a plan for controlling atomic energy. A few weeks later, a bill was introduced in Congress which, in effect, would have left control of the entire American nuclear program in the experienced hands of General Leslie Groves. The May-Johnson bill, as it became known, provoked a savage battle between partisans of civilian and military control but seemed to satisfy President Truman. It didn't satisfy most scientists, however. "By then, the attitude at Los Alamos was let's pass something that gets it out of the hands of Groves," recalled William A. Higinbotham, the first director of the newly formed Federation of American Scientists.[8]

The lobby they erected was staggered when its natural leader and spokesman, J. Robert Oppenheimer, decided to support the May-Johnson bill. He told agitated colleagues to have patience and avoid interfering with the discussion about control of atomic energy.[9] I. I. Rabi, who knew him best, said that Oppenheimer's support of May-Johnson was an example of his arrogance. "He felt that by being inside it [the bill], he could control it. He was in a minority of one among the better-known physicists."[10]

Truman, believing that the May-Johnson bill would create a commission that was "virtually independent of executive control," abruptly switched sides.[11] In December, he told senior War Department officials, and Groves, that any new commission would be placed under civilian control. Brien McMahon, an ambitious freshman senator from Connecticut, offered a rival bill built around a commission composed of full-time civilians who would be subject to presidential authority. By January 1946, Truman had lost patience with the War Department's indifference to his views, and he declared his support for the McMahon bill.

The battle wasn't over. In Ottawa, a British physicist named Alan Nunn May was uncovered as a Soviet spy. Groves leaked the story to a newspaper columnist.[12] The ensuing public uproar coincided with the first postwar nuclear test. Abruptly, public support for a civilian commission fell off, as did prospects for even limited cooperation in the nuclear area with other governments. Truman took a noncommittal position. In March, McMahon arranged a small dinner during which he, Senator Arthur H. Vandenberg, the Republican leader in the Senate, and a few others invited the thinking of Eisenhower and Admiral Chester W. Nimitz, the Chief of Naval Operations. Both men stressed "their desire to establish civilian control to the last possible degree of national safety."[13] In April, Vandenberg offered a compromise that ended the struggle. The Atomic Energy Commission (AEC) would consist of five members—all civilians—appointed by the President and confirmed by the Senate. They would take advice from a military applications division. A military liaison committee, staffed by the services, would be able to review decisions of the commission and appeal these to the President. In short, the principle of civilian control was laid down, but the military would have a major role in production decisions—i.e., how many bombs to make—and the priorities of the overall atomic energy program. The McMahon bill was signed into law on August 1, 1946.

The battleground shifted to priorities. Bombs, it was more or less agreed, would not be treated as more important than so-called peaceful uses of the atom. "Half of our effort roughly was on weapons, half on everything else I could think of," says Norris Bradbury about early postwar work at Los Alamos.[14] And David E. Lilienthal, the first chairman of the AEC and former director of the Tennessee Valley Authority, held a strong pro-peaceful-uses bias. "Lilienthal was a great salesman," says Joseph Volpe, who was General Counsel of the AEC for several years. "He would make speeches holding a lump of coal in his hand and say something that size would keep a city of 100,000 warm for an entire winter."[15]

Society wanted to believe in a benign atom. The worry and insecurity arising from the bomb were partially offset in these early years by brave and romantic talk of a new, possibly divine age, rooted in a novel technology that could literally move mountains—a technology founded on universal mysteries that science had unraveled. Within days of the Nagasaki bombing, the atom began to be promoted as the answer to most problems. "We stand where Benjamin Franklin stood with his key and kite in relation to electricity," wrote novelist Philip Wylie in *Collier's* a few weeks after the war ended.[16] The public was informed that gasoline stations would soon be obsolete; just by tossing a pellet of enriched uranium the size of a small marble into the gas tank, a motorist would be able to drive for a year, if not for the life of the car. In November, *The New Yorker*'s cliché expert, Frank Sullivan, suggested that since tiny objects would now be performing so many services, the pea should be designated the official unit of measurement.[17] "Heat will be so plentiful that it will even be used to melt snow as it falls," declared Robert M. Hutchins, president of the University of Chicago. Atomic energy, according to economist Stuart Chase, would "revolutionize high-way construction (through controlled explosions that would fuse earth into lava, as at Alamogordo), air-condition cities in the tropics, and warm up polar housing for the comfort of man."[18] People talked about an atomic-powered airliner that would carry thousands of passengers.

Practical difficulties and pitfalls weren't being closely examined. The pellet of enriched uranium that was supposed to sustain an automobile was wholly useless because science never has discovered how to extract power from an ounce of uranium. Numerous advocates of nuclear gadgets were ignoring or minimizing radiation hazards. The costs, difficulties, and risks to public safety of building plants to generate nuclear energy—one of the feasible and promising uses of the atom—were not being thought through.

The enthusiasm for peaceful uses reached far into the scientific community, which tended to equate civilian control of atomic energy with high purpose, and military control not only with bombs but with overeagerness to use them. The heavy investment in peaceful uses did yield a few solid benefits, of which the most clearly promising seemed to be radioactive isotopes for medical purposes and for research in many areas. But nonsense and hyperbole about the atom-as-genie continued to mislead society for at least a decade. "A lot of people said things they wanted to believe," recalls Norris Bradbury.[19]

American exclusivity in atomic affairs—an instant first principle in Washington—was fantasy. Britain, too, knew all about nuclear fission, as did French scientists, a few of whom had been working on it longer than most. Scientists on all sides knew that the half-life of nuclear secrets and nuclear know-how would be brief. "We shall have atomic energy and many other things, too," Molotov told a party gathering in Moscow on November 7, 1945.[20]

Three days later, Clement Attlee, Britain's new Prime Minister, arrived in Washington hoping to rekindle cooperation on nuclear matters. Apart from wanting a partnership, Britain worried that protectionism would lead America back into isolationism; Britain saw itself then as policing half the world and wanted help with the job. Truman had delayed the meeting with Attlee as long as possible, and it did not go well. The British hoped to remove the restrictions on commercial exploitation of atomic energy to which Churchill had agreed at Quebec in 1943. Although Groves and Vannevar Bush—the experts on the American delegation—linked unacceptable conditions to Britain's proposal, Truman, Attlee, and Mackenzie

King, Canada's Prime Minister, expressed an interest in "full and effective cooperation in atomic matters." "We were allies and friends; it didn't seem necessary to tie everything up," Attlee said later.[21]

He was disabused a few weeks later when Truman refused outright to help Britain with a nuclear plant then under way. Since America had done so much for the British during the war, Congress saw no reason to gratify their aspirations for nuclear partnership.

The British continued pressing Washington to honor the wartime agreements of which Truman's people knew next to nothing. In fact, they were all unaware of the Hyde Park aide-mémoire which promised full collaboration. Unable to locate such a document in Roosevelt's files, the bewildered Americans were given a British photocopy. Groves considered it a forgery.*

Dean Acheson wrote about being disturbed for "some years to come" by the knowledge "that our government, having made an agreement from which it had gained immeasurably, was not keeping its word and performing its obligations . . . Grave consequences might follow upon keeping our word, but the idea of not keeping it was repulsive to me. The analogy of a nation to a person is not sound in all matters of moral conduct; in this case, however, it seemed to me pretty close."[22]

Not until mid-February 1946 was Acheson, who was then Undersecretary of State, told about the secret accord that had just been reached or any of the wartime understandings. Byrnes wanted him to help with amending the 1943 Quebec Agreement. Washington mainly wanted to water down a provision that forbade America or Britain to use nuclear weapons against another country "without the other's consent."† But Groves, according to Acheson, "threw a monkey wrench into the negotiating machinery" by sending Byrnes a letter which claimed that cooperation with Britain could be considered a military alliance and thus a violation of the United Nations charter which forbids secret agreements between member states.[23] And he reminded Byrnes that earlier Anglo-American accords had been kept secret from Congress and the American people. Another, more public arrangement, he warned, might have an adverse political effect at home.[24]

With this typically high-handed but effective ploy, Groves infuriated

---

*Years later, when the Roosevelt papers were being catalogued at Hyde Park, the aide-mémoire was spotted in a file on naval matters. Groves guessed that the paper was misfiled by a clerk who thought that Tube Alloys had something to do with ship boiler tubes (General Leslie R. Groves, *Now It Can Be Told: The Story of the Manhattan Project* [New York: Harper & Brothers, 1962], p. 402).

†Churchill's consent had been required before the bombing of Japan could go forward. He agreed on July 4, 1945.

Acheson, who told Lilienthal, according to the latter's diary for January 16, 1946, that "the War Department, and really one man in the War Department, General Groves, has, by the power of veto on the ground of 'military security,' really been determining and almost running foreign policy. He has entered into contracts involving other countries (Belgium and their Congo deposits of uranium, for example) without even the knowledge of the Department of State."[25]

The British, aware of what Groves was doing, pushed that much harder for movement on the secret November agreement. "It was quite impossible to fulfill the obligation of the arrangement," Acheson told a British group. "If a secret arrangement were carried out, it would blow the Administration out of the water." The British, he continued, "must just resign themselves to the fact that, although we made the agreement, we simply could not carry it out; that things like that happen in the [U.S.] government due to the loose way things are handled."[26] The Nunn May spy scandal had become an added burden for the British, whose security procedures were already judged insufficiently rigorous by some within Truman's entourage. In April, Attlee reminded Truman of what had been agreed to, only to be told that "the language 'full and effective cooperation' is very general."[27]

Attlee's exchange with Truman followed a decision by his government to build atomic weapons on its own. The bomb would impart cachet to a society which still saw itself as an imperial world power. Washington was thrown off by the decision; with the cold war speeding up and the administration expanding America's stockpile of bombs, the demand for natural uranium was rising. A British program would add to the pressure on the supply of ore, a large part of which came from the Belgian Congo; Britain's political access to this ore was at least as good and probably better than America's. But Washington felt that American needs could not be met unless Britain yielded its own share of the Congo ore.[28] Quite clearly, the parties had to negotiate; also, someone had to cover the congressional base, a thankless task that fell to Acheson, the only administration figure who was troubled by the display of bad faith toward the British or the peril of hiding basic information from Congress. In May 1947, he told Arthur Vandenberg and Bourke B. Hickenlooper, who were chairmen, respectively, of the Foreign Relations and Joint Atomic Energy committees, about the Quebec Agreement; its grant to either side of the right to veto the use of nuclear weapons was the most sensational of the concealed facts. These two stalwarts of the opposition party were appalled by the disclosure and by the discovery of their country's dependence on Britain for natural uranium ore.

These and other congressional leaders, as they, too, were briefed, demanded, rather illogically, that the Quebec Agreement be annulled in exchange for the financial aid to be granted to Britain under the just inaugurated Marshall Plan. Negotiations began, and the Quebec Agreement was "adjusted." Britain's right to veto use of the bomb was scrapped; Washington agreed to resume technical cooperation in various areas—none having to do with bomb design. The package deal, which was concluded early in 1948, was called a "Modus Vivendi" in order to protect it from the McMahon Act, which forbade formal agreements involving nuclear cooperation. As it turned out, Congress need not have worried about subterfuge, as the administration largely ignored both the letter and spirit of the Modus Vivendi.[29]

"The bitterest problem after I came in" was how George Kennan, the Director of the State Department's Policy Planning Staff from 1947 to 1950, described the British issue.[30] With the Modus Vivendi due to expire in 1949, an ugly situation grew worse. Acheson was deeply troubled. The only nuclear issue he ever seemed to care about or actually tried to influence was this one. Just after returning to government in January 1949—this time as Secretary of State—he found the British problem at the top of his agenda. The Berlin Blockade was under way, and there was pressure to exchange information with London about weapons. The Joint Atomic Energy Committee, which the McMahon Act had created, was sure to oppose any such move. Admiral Lewis Strauss, a determined and resourceful member of the AEC, was strongly opposed (as he would continue to be after becoming chairman in the Eisenhower years). It occurred to Acheson that Eisenhower, then president of Columbia University, might be able to help.

Eisenhower was on hand when Truman and some of his officials met informally at Blair House with key members of the Joint Committee; according to Acheson, he gave "an admirable statement of the need for the fullest confidence between the British and ourselves in the event of another global war . . . Our military fate and theirs [Eisenhower said] were so interlocked that it made no sense to exclude one weapon—which they would soon have anyway—from the scope of our full partnership."[31] Eisenhower also talked about how the situation, unless changed, could jeopardize the alliance.

A second meeting—this one with the full committee—was agreed to; Acheson hoped it would produce approval of some arrangement with the British. Six days later, the meeting was held, and, according to Acheson, it "was a failure just short of a disaster." He described it to Truman as a "shambles." Acheson, Lilienthal, and Eisenhower had been routed by the Republican members of the Joint Committee, especially Senators Vandenberg, Hickenlooper, and William Knowland (who would be Majority

Leader in a few years time). Eisenhower's performance seems to have been a memorable disappointment. [He] "had lost the fine evangelical fervor of the Blair House meeting," Acheson wrote, "when he had portrayed the importance of Anglo-American solidarity, and retreated into a simple soldier unacquainted with complexities."[32] And Volpe, who also attended both meetings, says, "Ike was very eloquent at Blair House and then let everyone down when time came to testify. It was an incredible performance. He folded completely before Vandenberg and Knowland. He was not about to get crosswise with them. McMahon sent Acheson a note saying, 'For God's sake, get him out of the chair.' "[33] Some who watched interpreted the radical shift in Eisenhower's attitude as meaning he had cast an eye to his political future and wanted to avoid antagonizing the Senate Republican leadership.

Acheson didn't meet again with the Joint Committee until October— just after, as he says, "the Russians had exploded an atomic device of their own and with it a good deal of the senatorial nonsense about our priceless heritage."[34] Sentiment on Capitol Hill on the British issue changed rather dramatically, if temporarily, and Whitehall's uppermost goal seemed to lie within reach. The official talks resumed and were proceeding smoothly, when, in Acheson's words, "a bomb exploded in London." It was the Klaus Fuchs affair; he was arrested on February 2, 1950, and charged with giving the Russians information he had acquired throughout most of the war and afterward. The incident confirmed the serious doubts about British security that were held in both the executive and legislative branches of government. Much to Acheson's regret, the talks with the British were indefinitely shelved. In 1951, the British asked Washington to test an atomic bomb for them. But the administration was by then so fearful of an adverse reaction in Congress that it wouldn't even risk seeking approval. "Statesmen are not architects, but gardeners dealing with materials as only nature can provide," Acheson said later.

Governments consider the activities of their enemies, or potential enemies, in "worst case" terms. Although the Anglo-American nuclear connection wasn't prospering, the Soviets thought it was. In the Truman-Attlee-King statement of November 1945, the Soviet press saw the formation of an "anti-Russian bloc" engaged in "atomic diplomacy."[35] Still, in January 1946, the U.S.S.R. voted with other members of the United Nations to set up a U.N. Atomic Energy Commission, at which point an agreement on international control seemed to beckon. But Acheson worried that the administration might not be up to making a sensible move in this direction. He complained to Lilienthal at this time about Truman and Byrnes having no knowledge or understanding of atomic matters.[36] Acheson was a realist. The enormity of the task of creating a mechanism for actually controlling the atom wasn't lost on him. Its implications pushed him to try.

Acheson persuaded Truman and Byrnes to set up a committee that would produce a plan aimed at controlling the atom without yielding America's "secret." The idea was to find a way of allowing the U.N. commission to keep the atom from blowing up the world, or part of it, while promoting its peaceful uses. Byrnes appointed Acheson to chair the committee, whose other members were Bush, Conant, White House scientific advisers, John McCloy, and, of course, General Groves, about whom Acheson continued to grumble. One of Acheson's assistants, a young lawyer named Herbert S. Marks, reckoned that the committee's only chance to succeed lay in having an expert board of consultants. Acheson agreed and named Lilienthal, whom Marks had once worked with, to chair such a board; his fellow advisers included Marks himself, Chester Barnard, the president of New Jersey Bell Telephone Company, and Robert Oppenheimer. There were others, but these were the key figures. Oppenheimer's experience and his aura allowed him to dominate the affair intellectually; moreover, he and Lilienthal were kindred spirits. Groves quickly found himself at odds with them. "Everybody genuflected," he complained. "Lilienthal got so bad he would consult Oppie on what tie to wear in the morning."[37] Acheson recalled that "the most stimulating and creative mind among us was Robert Oppenheimer's. On this task he was also at his most constructive and accommodating. Robert could be argumentative, sharp, and, on occasion, pedantic, but no such problem intruded here."[38]

What emerged became instantly known as the Acheson-Lilienthal Report, although its central feature was developed by Oppenheimer. In a radio talk, Acheson and Bush described the report as offering "a plan under which no nation would make atomic bombs or the materials for them. All dangerous activities would be carried on—not merely inspected—by a live, functioning, international Authority with a real purpose in the world and capable of attracting competent personnel." America's current monopoly, the report went on to say, "is *only temporary. It will not last.* We must use that advantage now to promote international security and to carry out our policy of building a lasting peace through international agreement."[39]

Acheson was abruptly disheartened by Byrnes, who said he "would recommend to the President that Bernard M. Baruch be appointed, as he [Byrnes] . . . somewhat unflatteringly put it, 'for the task of translating the various proposals stimulated by the Acheson-Lilienthal Report into a workable plan.' " Acheson protested; he didn't share the widely held view of Baruch—a seventy-five-year-old Wall Street speculator—as an institutionalized wise man and elder statesman. "My own experience," he wrote, "led me to believe that his reputation was without foundation in fact and entirely self-propagated."[40] Byrnes ignored him. He and Truman were then in a battle over the McMahon bill and worried that the Senate Special Committee might report a bill that would make it impossible for the United States to take part in any plan for controlling the atom. On March 16, Baruch was named American representative to the U.N. Atomic Energy Commission. As expected, the reaction on Capitol Hill was very favorable, but Lilienthal and the others were appalled. "When I read this news last night, I was quite sick," Lilienthal wrote in his diary. "We need a man who is young, vigorous, not vain . . . Baruch has none of these qualifications."[41] "That was the day I gave up hope," Oppenheimer said years later.[42]

In mid-May, Baruch and his own advisers began meeting with Acheson's people. The two groups wrangled bitterly. "This is the worst mistake I have ever made, but we can't fire him now," Byrnes candidly told the Acheson group.[43] Still, in most essentials, Baruch's plan resembled the Acheson-Lilienthal original. It envisaged a system for controlling the process by which either atomic weapons or nuclear energy for peaceful purposes would be produced. An International Atomic Development Authority would have jurisdiction over "all atomic energy activities potentially dangerous to world security." The United States would hand over to such an agency its stockpile of atomic weapons and its technical knowledge.

Baruch diverged mainly from Acheson-Lilienthal on how to deal with violators of the agreement. Any violator (i.e., the Soviet Union), he counseled, "should be subjected to swift and sure punishment; and in case of violation no one of the permanent members of the Security Council should be permitted to veto punitive action by the Council."[44] Truman and Byrnes agreed with him. There could be no veto on enforcement even though the United States and the Soviet Union, in framing the U.N. Charter, had insisted on being able to veto any international action against a great power. And, as McGeorge Bundy has written, "what would be meant by international action against a great power, or by 'swift and sure penalties' in so grave a case as illegal work on atomic bombs? War?"[45]

On June 14, 1946, Baruch unveiled his plan before the U.N. commission: "We are here to make a choice between the quick and the dead," he began portentously. "That is our business. We must elect world peace or world destruction."[46] The domestic reaction was overwhelmingly favorable.

Five days later, Andrei Gromyko, who had replaced Molotov as Soviet Foreign Minister, rejected the plan by counterproposing an international convention "prohibiting the production and employment of weapons based on the use of atomic energy."[47] Later on, according to the vague Soviet plan, nations could monitor the agreement by agreeing to some limited inspection of plants and other facilities. In July, Gromyko underlined his government's rejection by saying that the U.S.S.R. could not accept Baruch's proposals "either as a whole or in their separate parts."[48] In August, he buried the notion of international control—probably for good—saying that America's inspection proposal was not reconcilable with national sovereignty.[49]

The differences between Acheson-Lilienthal and Baruch never mattered. Neither plan had a chance. Although not yet visible, the competition in nuclear arms that Bohr had so gloomily anticipated years before was under way. Most of what Washington and Moscow did or said reinforced the one's darkest foreboding about the other. Moscow saw the Baruch plan as aimed at keeping the U.S.S.R. in an inferior position. In July, America exploded its second test on the Bikini atoll in the Pacific. This, *Pravda* said, was clear evidence that the U.S. aim was not to restrict atomic weapons but to perfect them.[50] Furthermore, the United States had demobilized its forces just after World War II ended, and already its atomic bomb was being perceived as the makeweight—the deterrent to a vast assault of Western Europe by the Red Army. American intelligence wasn't good and was greatly exaggerating Soviet military force and Moscow's intentions. Still, a try for international control had to be made. The most that can be said of the Acheson-Lilienthal-Baruch plan is that it did amount to a good, if futile, try. Reality lay in what Stalin had told Averell Harriman in October 1945: "We have decided to go our own way."[51] He knew then how impermanent the American monopoly would be. In just over a year, he had a functioning nuclear reactor.

George Kennan, a scholarly Cassandra who was then a diplomat assigned to the embassy in Moscow, had for two years been trying to disabuse those in Washington who thought the grand alliance could survive the war. On February 22, 1946, he dispatched a celebrated message, which became known as the "Long Telegram." Although the Russians, he said, didn't want to invade anybody—if only because they, too, had been ravaged by the war—they would, unless resisted, push outward by exploiting the vulnerabilities of Europe and Japan to political and ideological pressure. The Soviets, he predicted, would try to enlarge their power in Iran and

Turkey and might even try to acquire a port on the Persian Gulf or a base at Gibraltar. Kennan's telegram got Washington's attention, and General Marshall, the new Secretary of State, set up a policy planning staff with Kennan as its director.

Truman said he was "tired of babying the Soviets" and won bipartisan support for the so-called Truman Doctrine, which committed America to helping any society withstand aggression or coercion from the new imperialism.[52] Security would be collective; an assortment of small and middle-sized European states—still independent, but lacking economic or military power—would fall in behind American leadership. Meanwhile, the Soviets reacted to the threat from the West they professed to see—a familiar one, they intoned—by enlarging their zone of control. In February 1948, while Congress was debating the European Recovery Program, or Marshall Plan, Communists in Czechoslovakia seized power from a democratic government. In China, the Nationalist Army of Chiang Kai-shek appeared to be on the edge of defeat at the hands of Communist forces. Marshall, concerned, as always, about limited resources, advised against committing forces to China, as the Soviet threat to Europe was the greater concern. Korea, too, was worrisome, but far less so. The real problem lay in Germany—more precisely in Berlin.

Politics and geography made Berlin the gravest and most persistent source of tension in the nuclear age. Postwar Berlin, like Germany itself, was split into four zones controlled by the victors—Britain, France, the United States, and the Soviet Union—and located 110 miles inside Soviet-controlled East Germany.

Berlin tempted the Soviets because their rivals were at a strong disadvantage in protecting their access to the city. A failure to do so would be a blow to Western credibility (American especially) and West German confidence. By late March of 1948, continued bickering over German issues began to escalate. On April 1, General Lucius Clay, head of the American occupation forces, was notified by Soviet authorities that all Americans, military or civilian, en route to Berlin, would be checked by Soviet guards for identification. Clay asked Washington to approve a letter from him rejecting the Soviet move as a violation of American occupation rights. Truman approved his request. Then, on his own authority, Clay challenged the Soviet order by sending three trains into the Soviet zone with orders not to permit Soviet guards to board but not to shoot if they insisted on boarding. The Soviets boarded one train and sidetracked the other two. British military trains met with similar treatment.

On June 24, the city was sealed off by a total blockade. Truman had the choice of doing nothing, using force to assure access, or maintaining it by some less aggressive means. Doing nothing was excluded; to make the people in the Western zones dependent on the Soviets for food and fuel was unthinkable. Course two was strongly favored by General Clay and Robert D. Murphy, his State Department adviser. On June 26, they recommended in a telegram to Marshall that the U.S., Britain, and France take whatever measures would be necessary to open the surface routes to Berlin.[53] Clay specifically wanted authority to tell the Soviets that on a given date Washington would defy the blockade by sending either an armed convoy or an armed train to Berlin. He estimated the chances of either the convoy or train being met by force as very small.[54] "The plan," recalls Clark Clifford, who was Truman's special counsel at the time, "was to . . . arm the train with the most powerful fire power that had ever been assembled, notify the Soviets that the train was going to start from a certain location and that it was going to Berlin . . . if the Soviets stopped it, it would be construed as an act of war."[55]

Neither the Joint Chiefs of Staff nor the British or French supported Clay's proposal, and Truman rejected it. "The National Security Council did not share our confidence that the Russians were bluffing," wrote Murphy, who nearly resigned over the issue. "It has never seemed wise to me to base our own action on a bluff or to assume that the Russians are doing so," Acheson commented.[56]

Clay, again on his own initiative, had many weeks earlier begun using air force transports to carry supplies to personnel in the American sector of the city. Washington decided to answer the blockade by expanding this operation into a massive airlift; its scale would be sufficient to supply more than two million people with the food and coal they would need for an indefinite period of time. "We will supply the city as a beleaguered garrison," Marshall told the embassy in London on June 28.[57] The Soviets had the choice of attacking the airlift or not interfering with it. By late winter of 1949, Stalin had had enough of the blockade, and he set in motion a diplomacy aimed at ending it. On May 11–12, nearly a year after the blockade began, trucks and trains resumed the transit to Berlin. "It was a distinct and devastating public relations defeat for the Soviet Union," Clifford says.[58] And in a brief, lapidary comment, Acheson captured the import of this first Berlin crisis: "It shows the extreme sensitivity of Soviet authorities to developments in Germany and an almost equal lack of judgment in reacting to them."[59]

Two days after the blockade began, Truman approved the dispatch to Germany of two squadrons of B-29s, the same type of aircraft that had dropped the atomic bombs on Japan. In mid-July, two more squadrons were sent to bases in Lincolnshire, England, where American bombers had been based during the war. Although the aircraft were described in official news releases as "atomic capable," none of them had been modified to carry such weapons; but the Soviets may not have known that and obviously weren't supposed to. "I knew about the atomic strategic bombers based in England the moment they arrived," recalls Colonel General Nikolai Chervov, who is currently a member of the Soviet General Staff. "I was a student at the General Staff Academy . . . We were evaluating the U.S. nuclear potential and in particular those ninety atomic bombers with one or two bombs aboard. That meant approximately two hundred bombs, which was a real threat. Two hundred Hiroshimas."[60] Arneson says, "By sending the B-29s, we hoped to leave the impression that . . . they were armed with nuclear weapons, and that we were prepared to use them . . . [it was] psychological warfare."[61] There is no evidence to suggest that the ploy affected Stalin's calculations nor reason to assume that it might have.

Sifting their intelligence, the Russians may have concluded that the B-29s weren't nuclear capable; still, they couldn't be sure. The AEC had custody of atomic bombs, but Truman was under pressure to turn them over to the military. On July 15, the same day the B-29s left for Britain, Secretary of Defense James Forrestal asked Truman to transfer custody from the AEC to the Pentagon. Truman, according to Forrestal's diary, "wanted to go into this matter very carefully and he proposed to keep, in his own hands, the decision as to the use of the bomb, and did not propose 'to have some dashing lieutenant colonel decide when would be the proper time to drop one.' "[62] Three days later, after a meeting with senior advisers on the custody question, Truman told Forrestal—again, according to the latter's diary—that he wouldn't transfer custody, mainly for domestic political reasons but that after the election "it would be possible to take another look . . ."[63] A diary entry by Lilienthal about the meeting had Truman saying, "This is no time to be juggling an atom bomb around."[64]

Forrestal seems to have rated the prospect of war with the U.S.S.R. as higher than most of his other colleagues, and as Secretary of Defense his feelings on the custody issue were understandably strong. A Lilienthal diary entry for September 13 reads: "Their [Soviet] planes are in the air corridor today, and anything could happen . . . The President is being pushed hard by Forrestal to decide that atomic bombs will be used . . . The President has always been optimistic about peace. But he is blue now, mighty blue."[65] And General Kenneth D. Nichols, who had succeeded Groves as senior military expert on nuclear weapons, recalls Forrestal "pushing for preparation of a plan for using [atomic] bombs. Truman had ordered him to prepare a plan that excluded the use of nuclear weapons. But Forrestal persisted. He instructed the Chiefs to prepare a plan for use. Finally, there was a meeting of Forrestal and the Chiefs with Truman. Next day, he [Truman] approved a plan for use based on the idea it was the only way to stop an invasion of Europe."

The military chiefs were uncertain; atomic bombs were huge, unwieldy weapons for which suitable targets could scarcely be identified. These officers knew the weapons, of which they didn't have custody, were few in number, but most were unaware of just how few. "On June 30, 1948, there were fifty weapons in the stockpile," recalls Nichols. "Truman," he says, "never took any interest in the stockpile. Ike got a briefing every two months from me. We used to go for a walk, because Ike had decided that his own office was bugged."[66] (Nichols says it was bugged, but Eisenhower didn't know by whom. Eisenhower resigned as Army Chief of Staff in February 1948.) Admiral Leahy, Truman's senior military aide, noted that the U.S. didn't "have very much [in the stockpile] but still we could make plans to use what we have . . . I don't know what we could do but whatever we have we could use." And General Hoyt Vandenberg, the Air Force Chief of Staff, wasn't sure his service was even studying potential Soviet targets.[67]

Truman believed equally in presidential control of nuclear weapons and civilian custody of them. But Groves, who wasn't easily discouraged, maneuvered tirelessly to weaken the case for civilian control. He is believed to have been the source for a notorious leak about secret documents having been lost by or stolen from the AEC, which led Senator Hickenlooper, a favorite Groves leakee, to charge the AEC with incredible mismanagement. (The charge was later dropped.) Lilienthal countered by lobbying for the removal of his chief tormentor, Groves, as head of the Military Liaison Committee and the Armed Forces Special Weapons Project. Groves's zeal gradually overcame his judgment. He was increasingly seen as unreasonable and unmanageable, and by January 1948 his support system within the Pentagon and Congress had largely broken down. In late January 1948, Bush, Conant, and Oppenheimer met with the three service secretaries to decide how best to push him toward the exit. But just afterward, Groves preempted them by announcing his decision to retire from the army and enter private business.

If the nuclear age has produced an American bureaucratic colossus, Groves was perhaps it. His accomplishments may have matched his determination, which itself rested on an awesome sense that he knew best—that he alone had mastered the host of nuclear issues, political and technological. He considered many of those who disagreed with him as unreliable, if not suspect or even disloyal.

Groves was probably the first major figure within the nuclear culture to adopt an ultrahard anti-Soviet line; this he combined with a conviction that Soviet science would always lag well behind America's, whose security, he felt, must lie in doing whatever it took to preserve a long lead in advanced weapons over the enemy. If the line was not altogether original, it was one that Groves could argue with more force and credibility than most of his contemporaries; his anticommunism and sense of impending conflict with the Soviets had guided his thinking during the war and it suited the postwar mood, especially in Congress. It became a Washington commonplace that no one in government ever lost ground by taking the hard line—aligning himself with the worst-case view of Soviet intentions and the high-end estimate of Soviet military capabilities.

Truman's refusal to transfer custody of atomic weapons didn't mean that Groves had left the arena a loser. As much as anyone, he had already set in motion a process that would lead to military custody. "Civilian control had become a technicality," Volpe says. "As a practical matter, the military then had a good deal of custodial responsibility."[68] In 1946—probably in June—Groves and Air Force General Carl Spaatz secretly arranged with British Air Marshal Arthur W. Tedder to create storage sites for American nuclear weapons in Britain. Apparently, the fissionable cores of the bombs were not transferred in Truman's time. The British cabinet was not informed of the arrangement nor were most of the senior figures around Truman. Secretary of War Robert Patterson was told, and so was Eisenhower, the Army Chief of Staff. Who else knew isn't clear.[69]

Adjusting to the atomic bomb was hard for the military. Each service worried about threats to its conventional roles and missions from a device which they treated as an unwelcome parvenu. The Pacific war belonged to the navy, or so the navy thought, just as the war in Europe had belonged to the army. "Had we been willing to wait, the effective naval blockade would . . . have starved the Japanese into submission," said Admiral Ernest King, then the Chief of Naval Operations.[70] The airmen had wanted to bomb the Japanese into submission—but with conventional weapons. "Even without the atomic bomb and the Russian entry into the war, Japan would have surrendered in two weeks," said General Curtis LeMay, who had commanded the 20th Air Force and later became a controversial head of the Strategic Air Command. LeMay called the atomic bomb "the worst thing that ever happened" to the Army Air Forces.[71] And the army had, of course, reckoned on invading Japan to end the war.

In 1947, Congress reorganized the military by passing the National Security Act. It created the Department of Defense, headed by a civilian secretary, made a separate service of the air force, and institutionalized the Joint Chiefs of Staff. But the act did nothing to settle disputes between the services over their roles in the new age. The major quarrel over which service would possess and perhaps use the bomb pitted the air force against the navy. The navy recognized the air force claim but wanted a role for itself. This savage battle was waged in large part through leaks to the press.

For its time, the Truman administration was unusually leaky, partly because some of its senior figures feuded with a degree of hostility seen only occasionally since. Acheson feuded bitterly with Louis Johnson, who succeeded Forrestal at Defense. Johnson also feuded with David Lilienthal, who feuded as well with his fellow commissioner, Lewis Strauss. Shortly before his death in March 1987, Bromley Smith, a State Department diplomat who also served on the National Security Council staffs of Truman, Eisenhower, Kennedy, and Johnson, recalled a time when he was Acheson's special assistant for leaks to the press. His only function, he said, was to leak stories to the newspapers. He attended important policy meetings without anyone knowing why he was there. Nor did any of his colleagues ever discover who the actual source for numerous State-inspired disclosures really was. Acheson, Smith said, told him to operate wholly on his own and never questioned any of his leaked stories.[72]

Some leaks are aimed at gaining popular support for a major initiative. The Truman Doctrine, the Marshall Plan, and the North Atlantic Treaty Organization (NATO) were examples of this practice. Other leaks are intended to push one official's position and/or undermine someone else's; these are usually creative distortions of whatever is going on within the policy arena. A standard leak portrays some official's position on an issue in a light that will invite a presidential frown. Practiced leakers are less concerned with building themselves up than in damaging rival causes. Some reporters and columnists serve as regular outlets for some officials. The Lewis Strauss version of any major dispute within the AEC normally found its way into Arthur Krock's column in the *New York Times*.

Then as now, the incidence of disclosures involving nuclear weapons was remarkably—indeed, distressingly—high. By early 1949, the upstart air force was adroitly using the press to convince the public and Congress that a new strategic bomber, the B-36, would be the best way to deliver atomic bombs. In March, a spectacular leak of a presentation to the Joint Chiefs of Staff showed seventy strategic targets in the Soviet Union as lying within range of the B-36s. Carl Vinson, chairman of the House Armed Services Committee, demanded an explanation from W. Stuart Symington, the Secretary of the Air Force. Symington said the leak wasn't officially inspired.[73] The navy, too, saw itself bombing the Russian heartland—with planes launched from huge aircraft carriers. Plans to build some smaller ships were scrapped to make room in the navy's budget for the supercarrier. With the air force in full cry, and getting most of the new funds, the navy began to spread unfavorable reports about the B-36. Symington lodged an official complaint, and his ensuing correspondence was leaked to air force advantage.[74]

All this coincided with the departure of James Forrestal, a driven man who had become deeply disturbed and was losing touch with reality. He killed himself two months after resigning. His successor, Louis Johnson, a former national commander of the American Legion, was a shamelessly outrageous adventurer set on dominating not just the Pentagon but the national security apparatus of government. He had pledged to cut the defense budget by $1 billion, and in April he asked for and got Truman's approval to cancel construction of the first supercarrier, even though the keel had already been laid. Secretary of the Navy John L. Sullivan resigned in a rage. Johnson held the line on his unrealistically lean budget but not for long. The supercarrier program was merely delayed, not canceled. Events—milestones actually—in the cold war were about to bury Johnson's budget beneath new military requirements. The first of successive shocks was the Soviet atomic bomb. The second was escalation of a tense situation in Korea into war.

Feeling oppressed by crises at home and looming crises abroad, the Truman administration took immense comfort from its assumption that a Soviet bomb would not turn up and thereby make things worse. The foremost optimist was Truman himself, with Groves a close second. A Soviet bomb, according to Groves, lay twenty years or so away—if, indeed, there would be one at all. Truman was convinced that the Soviets would never have a bomb.* Even if their scientists overcame the natural barriers, Soviet industry would be unable to perform the supreme task of producing weapons-grade materials. In July 1949, Acheson told a meeting of senior

---

*A few people who knew him well say that years after he left office, Truman remained unconvinced that the Soviet Union had an authentic nuclear bomb.

officials and members of Congress that intelligence estimates pointed to a
Soviet bomb by mid-1951.[75] The estimate was apparently judged "soft" and
exaggerated.

By that summer, the air force had a long-range aerial detection system
for monitoring Soviet atomic activity. On September 3, an air sample taken
by a weather reconnaissance plane on a routine patrol from Japan to Alaska
showed a jump in radioactivity. When second and third samples taken by
the same aircraft showed dramatically rising increases, an alert from headquarters sent out other planes to collect samples. An ad hoc committee of
experts—Bush, Oppenheimer, Robert Bacher, and Admiral William Par-
sons—met to assess the data and determine whether a bomb had been
exploded or a nuclear reactor accident had occurred. The radioactivity,
they judged, could only have been produced by the explosion of a plutonium bomb.[76] Somewhere in northern Siberia, on August 29, the Soviet
Union had tested its first atomic bomb. The illusion of an American monopoly had lasted just four years and one month. On September 19, the
panel's findings were reported to Truman, who remained skeptical and
asked the members of the special committee to attest in individual statements their belief that the Russians had really done it. Truman didn't want
to make an official announcement, even though there was danger of a news
leak. He told Lilienthal that he wasn't sure the "Russians did actually have
a bomb." Lilienthal assured him it was a bomb.[77] Truman's advisers were
urging an announcement, and on September 23 he told the world: "We have
evidence that within recent weeks an atomic explosion occurred in the
U.S.S.R."

Official Washington didn't adjust easily. Arneson remembers a phone
call from Admiral Sidney Souers, Truman's national security adviser, who
said the fuss was probably caused by a reactor explosion, not a bomb. And
Louis Johnson, who for budgetary reasons wanted to play down the incident, tried planting a story that whatever Russia had tested, it wasn't a
bomb. Johnson had help from a few of his allies on Capitol Hill, one of
whom, Maine's Senator Owen Brewster, actually went public with this
line. So did Groves, who surmised that a reactor accident had occurred.[78]

Exactly how Washington—a city that is always awash in plans for
contingencies—could have turned so blind an eye to this one is rather
puzzling. Even before Hiroshima, Bush and Conant had estimated a Soviet
bomb within three to four years. Groves had taken issue with them
strongly.[79] In 1945, Hans Bethe had predicted in writing a Soviet bomb
within five years of the Trinity test. He and Leo Szilard, he says, often
discussed the matter and decided that Fuchs had saved the Soviet scientists
one year. Four to five years had been the estimate of most American experts,

who were always very conscious of their Soviet colleagues and prone to speculation about the sort of progress they might be making. When the public address system at Los Alamos announced the bombing of Hiroshima, some wag reacted by paging Pyotr Kapitza, the great Russian physicist.[80]

The act that created the Atomic Energy Commission also established a General Advisory Committee (GAC) to serve as its science advisory board. Oppenheimer was the first chairman of the GAC, which included Conant, Lilienthal, Rabi, Fermi, and Seaborg. Its executive secretary, John Manley, says he was "simply flabbergasted" by the Washington reaction to the Soviet test. In 1945, he said, "the scientists had predicted . . . that somewhere between '48 and '50, the Soviets would succeed in producing an atomic bomb. But there seemed to be absolutely no advance planning and anticipation of such an event . . . I found nothing really in State or Defense that indicated any preparation or any serious thought on this . . ."[81] Manley says the commission never once asked the GAC about when a Soviet bomb might appear.

Any one explanation for Washington's behavior would be clearer than the truth. Some people didn't consider the alternative to American monopoly, because they didn't want to. Their lapse was psychological; if they didn't plan for any such contingency, there wouldn't be one. A sufficient-unto-the-day-is-the-evil-thereof attitude comes naturally to big government. Others weren't prepared, either because they were unaware of what scientists had been saying or because it wasn't being said as explicitly as some surviving scientists of the era now recall it as being. Moreover, Oppenheimer, the one scientist who had regular access to senior officials and was known to subscribe to the five-year theory, wasn't calling a spade a spade.

"When will the Russians be able to build the bomb?" Truman asked him in 1946.

"I don't know," said Oppenheimer.

"I know," said Truman.

"When?"

"Never."[82]

"In SP [Policy Planning], we thought it would take them longer," recalls Paul Nitze, who replaced George Kennan as director of that office at the end of 1949. "SP was getting its technical guidance on the issue from Oppy. His advice was that it would take them longer, and we were therefore surprised when they did test the device."[83] Manley, who worked more closely with Oppenheimer and was very fond of him, says, "Oppy felt like the rest of us. The whole GAC took this [the Soviet bomb] in stride." Why then hadn't Oppenheimer reflected this GAC position in his dealings with policy people? "Oppy may have been doing something characteristic," Manley replied. "Telling the listener what he wanted to hear."[84]

Some time in 1946, the Soviet Union fission program was placed under the direct authority of Lavrenti Beria, the fearsome head of the secret police. A heavy veil of security concealed not just military research but work that in Washington would have been judged nonsensitive, hence unclassified.[85] American intelligence could learn little of value about Soviet progress in the nuclear realm. Washington may have discovered that Kapitza, the best-known and supposedly most creative of Russian nuclear physicists, had been put under house arrest; if so, the information might only have reinforced the optimistic view of a Soviet program that was no immediate threat.

A shocked Washington reacted to the cancellation of America's strategic advantage by resolving to restore it. A Soviet fission bomb would invite the "Super," as scientists called the fusion, or hydrogen, bomb (also known as the thermonuclear bomb). The fusion process, although more formidable than fission, wasn't new. In 1927, two young physicists at Göttingen—Fritz Houtermans, an Austrian, and Geoffrey Atkinson, an Englishman—began thinking about thermonuclear reactions in the sun and theorized that solar energy could be created through the fusion of lightweight atoms.[86] By the early 1930s, it was clear that by fusing certain isotopes such as deuterium or tritium, an explosion of unlimited scale could be produced. The essential distinction between fusion and fission also became clear: A fission bomb's yield is limited by natural boundaries. No such boundaries constrain a fusion bomb. By 1942, Edward Teller and a few others were working on fusion.

In October 1949, Truman was still unaware of a possible fusion bomb.[87] So intense was the secrecy on nuclear matters that no one, not even a sitting President, tried to know more than he absolutely needed to know. And if few people knew about fusion, absolutely no one knew how to make a fusion bomb. Teller argued strongly that far too little work was being done on fusion. "If the Los Alamos Laboratory had continued to function after Hiroshima with a full complement of such brilliant people as Oppenheimer, Fermi, and Bethe, I am convinced that someone would have had the same idea much sooner—and we would have had the hydrogen bomb in 1947 instead of 1952."[88]

"Teller disapproved of me because I couldn't make it [the Super] the

A-1 priority," says Norris Bradbury, who adds that the fusion bomb being worked on after 1946 required "great sophistication" in fission bombs. A fusion bomb must be triggered by a fission bomb. "Almost anyone could invent a device you could call a fusion bomb," says Bradbury, "but you'd have needed a freight train to deliver it."[89] "On the fusion bomb," says I. I. Rabi, "Teller made one proposal after another, and these were all shot down, some of them by Teller himself, some by other people."[90]

Within a few days of Truman's announcement on the Soviet bomb, Teller spoke with Ernest Lawrence, Director of the Berkeley Radiation Laboratory, and Luis Alvarez, another Nobel laureate—each of whom favored the Super—about a crash program. Lawrence then phoned Lewis Strauss, who the next day, October 7, sent a memo to his AEC colleagues calling for a "quantum jump" in planning for the Super. He meant, he said, "a commitment in talent and money comparable . . . to that which produced the first atomic bomb. That is the way to stay ahead."[91] A letter from Oppenheimer to Conant, written two weeks after the Strauss memo, portrayed the sharply rising political fortunes of the Super, plus the lingering doubts of many experts about its prospects as a real weapon: "Two experienced promoters have been at work, i.e., Ernest Lawrence, and Edward Teller . . . I am not sure the miserable thing will work, nor that it can be gotten to a target except by oxcart . . . What does worry me is that [it] appears to have caught the imagination both of the Congressional and of military people, as the answer to the problem posed by the Russian advance. It would be folly to oppose the exploration of this weapon. We have always known it had to be done, though it appears singularly proof against any form of experimental approach."[92]

The views of the GAC were not to be taken lightly. Starting with the apprehensive and enigmatic chairman, Oppenheimer, it was comprised of highly accomplished and respected figures. It had become the most influential source of guidance for the executive branch on nuclear policy.[93] The commission asked for a GAC opinion of the Super—whether if built it would be usable militarily and how it might compare with fission weapons. On October 29–30, committee members talked with Kennan, General Omar N. Bradley, then Chairman of the Joint Chiefs, and other scientists, including Hans Bethe, and members of the AEC itself. Bradley said there was "no choice but to build the Super," although any military advantages over fission bombs, he acknowledged, were "only psychological." Enrico Fermi gave an assessment of the prospects for a deliverable weapon and pronounced them little better than even. Oppenheimer asked each of the members to speak; then he stated his own view and summed up what he had heard: "There [is] a surprising unanimity—to me very surprising—that the United States ought not to take the initiative . . . in an all-out program. I am glad you feel this way, for if it had not come out this way, I would have had to resign as Chairman."[94]

The report concluded that the Super was probably feasible but so complicated and costly that it would penalize the fission bomb program, which the committee recommended expanding. A 500-kiloton atomic bomb was on the verge of being tested, and many insiders felt that it ought to satisfy any requirement for a bigger weapon. A sizable number of small and deliverable fission bombs seemed to make more sense than any behemoth. The only suitable targets for a Super, assuming one could be delivered, would be Moscow and Leningrad.

Rabi and Fermi issued a statement which, noting the absence of limits on the destructiveness of the Super, described it as "an evil thing considered in any light." They called for the President to declare publicly that developing such a weapon "was wrong on fundamental ethical principles."[95] For Fermi to take so strong a position on a policy issue surprised most of those who knew him well. ("Before he died, he said he wished he had been more political," says Bethe.)[96]

The other six members expressed their opposition in a slightly lower key: "We all hope that by one means or another, the development of these weapons can be avoided. We are all reluctant to see the United States take the initiative in precipitating this development . . . the extreme dangers . . . inherent in the proposal wholly outweigh any military advantage . . . a Super bomb might become a weapon of genocide."[97] "Conant spoke for most of the group," Rabi recalls, "in saying, 'the world is loused up enough.' "

Oppenheimer stayed on to confer with Acheson, who said later to Gordon Arneson: "I listened to Oppy for an hour and a half, and I didn't understand a thing he was saying. How can you expect a paranoid adversary to disarm by example?"[98]

"They argued for continued ignorance, and this I could not accept," says Teller of his adversaries.[99] Manley recalls Teller offering seriously to bet him that unless the Super were developed, he would be a Soviet political prisoner in the United States within five years.[100]

The battle within the administration that the GAC report could reasonably have been expected to set off never occurred. Rabi, still indignant, says Truman never even saw it. The balance of power was weighted heavily in favor of the advocates. David Lilienthal was strenuously opposed to the Super, but the AEC itself was split. He warned Truman that Brien McMahon, an avowed partisan of the Super, would try to "put on a blitz." "I don't blitz easily," Truman replied.[101] (He never liked McMahon and considered him overly ambitious.) But his own national security adviser, Admiral Souers, was another strong advocate of the Super and very close to Strauss. Souers had considerable influence with Truman. On November 18, Truman set up a special committee consisting of Acheson, Johnson, and Lilienthal to advise him on the Super. Within the Defense and State departments, the tide was beginning to run in its favor. According to General Nichols, whom McMahon drew on for guidance in this period, Bradley favored the Super, whereas Johnson was lukewarm. The air force, he says, favored it, "but less strongly than some." The other services, he says, were either lukewarm or indifferent. "They saw these weapons as threatening because the Air Force seemed to be the dominant player."[102]

Aside from the eternal Anglo-American problem, Acheson took a fairly neutral position on nuclear issues; he saw them, it seems, as being swept along by a tough political logic that he and his department could not affect. On request, Kennan drew up a long paper on the issue for Acheson. "I consider it to have been in its implications one of the most important, if not the most important, of all the documents I ever wrote in government," said Kennan in his memoirs. His paper argued that before proceeding with the new bomb, the government should make an effort to think through the option of "first use" of nuclear weapons. He expressed a strong aversion to this option, plus support for taking some risk in order to reach international agreement on controlling nuclear weapons. Kennan later wrote that while he couldn't remember Acheson's reaction, "I should think it was probably one of bewilderment and pity for my naiveté."[103] Arneson recalls Acheson summoning Kennan and saying, "George, if you persist in your view on this matter, you should resign from the foreign service; you should assume a monk's habit, carry a tin cup, and stand on the street corner and say 'the end of the world is nigh.' "[104]

Kennan had by then become counselor of the State Department, and was replaced as head of the Policy Planning Office by Paul Nitze, who, working with Arneson, became the key figure on nuclear issues. "Nitze," Acheson said, "was doubtful of the line of argument George Kennan had taken in his paper."[105]

By mid-November, the H-bomb story was beginning to leak; a Colorado senator, Edwin Johnson, had spoken about the weapon publicly. Lilienthal, its most influential adversary, was a burnt-out case; he had resigned and would leave soon. "He had seen himself as presiding over a vast domain of nuclear power," says Arneson, "but he ended saying he was a major contractor for the Defense Department. He was a tortured man."[106] Lilienthal's ally, Oppenheimer, cut a large figure in many places, but the White House wasn't one of them. He ill-advisedly once told Truman about feeling as if he had "blood on his hands." Truman told Acheson, "Don't you bring that fellow around here again . . . All he did was make the bomb. I'm the guy who fired it off."[107]

On November 23, Truman received a memorandum from Omar N. Bradley, a man whom he deeply respected, which made no military case for the Super but did say that for the Soviet Union to possess it, and the United States not to, "would be intolerable."[108] Two days later, Truman had a similar message from Strauss, a strong and persuasive figure: "Its [the Super's] unilateral renunciation by the United States could very easily result in its unilateral possession by the Soviet government."[109]

It didn't matter that a military use for the Super hadn't been identified or that its feasibility on technical grounds hadn't been established. What mattered was the likelihood of the Soviets adding insult to injury by moving up from the atomic to the hydrogen bomb. Their recent exploit dictated Truman's decision on the Super. And if the handwriting on the wall wasn't clear, it was made clear on January 27, 1950, when the Counselor of the British Embassy, Sir Derek Hoyar-Millar, appeared at the State Department to report that Klaus Fuchs had that day confessed to spying for the Soviet Union. His espionage covered American work on thermonuclear phenomena through the summer of 1946.[110]

Fuchs was a heavy offstage presence when, four days later, the members of Truman's special committee on the Super met in the old State-War-Navy Building. Acheson was in the chair. By then, he and Johnson, who didn't agree on much, had settled on the kind of recommendation to be made to Truman. For a time, Lilienthal argued unavailingly for taking a fresh look at the country's military posture, but then he gave up and agreed to support the Acheson-Johnson position. That done, the three men walked over to the White House and met briefly with Truman. After hearing some of Lilienthal's argument, Truman interrupted him and, according to Arneson's account, asked, " 'Can the Russians do it?'

"All heads nodded. 'Yes, they can.'

"Admiral Souers interjected, 'We don't have much time.'

" 'In that case,' Truman said, 'we have no choice. We'll go ahead.' "[111]
He then initialed the recommendations and approved a press statement.

The meeting had lasted just seven minutes—far too few, it can be argued, for Truman to have made one of the two most important decisions of the nuclear era.* Granted, he had little choice, at least based on what he knew. But he didn't know much; he wasn't aware that the military case for the weapon was nil or that even if the Russians started first down the new

---

*The first was F.D.R.'s decision to develop the atom bomb.

path, America's stockpile of fission bombs—a far more practical weapon—would sustain its nuclear advantage for a long time to come. Lilienthal had told him about the GAC report and described AEC views, but neither his staff nor Acheson nor anyone else had given Truman an options paper. "There were no papers done for the President," says Arneson. "No preparation at all really, except perhaps what individuals had been telling him privately."[112] Truman's advisers doubtless judged that he had no good option other than to go forward, and he clearly felt the same way.

A few weeks later, the Joint Chiefs, who had not before proposed a crash program, requested Truman to approve "all-out development of hydrogen bombs and means for their production and delivery." On March 10, Truman so ordered. His decision drew wide acclaim. The *New York Times* noted, "No Presidential announcement since Mr. Truman entered the White House seemed . . . to strike such an instant or general chord of nonpartisan congressional support."[113]

Ironically, the announcement came at a moment when the so-called classical Super, as conceived by Teller, was being written off by colleagues at Los Alamos. The basic math hadn't been done, and, it seemed, might not be doable. The key mathematician was Stanislaw Ulam, who didn't share Teller's passion for the Super. In February, Ulam pronounced the work being done on it a "fizzle." Then, abruptly, Ulam and Teller, who hadn't seen eye to eye, jointly produced a concept which Bethe described as "about as surprising as the discovery of fission had been to physicists in 1939."[114] "Ulam came into my office one afternoon and drew some pictures on the board," recalls Carson Mark. "He said these are more interesting than what we are doing. But Ulam wasn't thinking about the fusion bomb or making a connection between these pictures [calculations] and the fusion bomb. He went through the same exercise the next day with Teller, who instantly saw their relevance to the fusion bomb."[115]

The Ulam-Teller breakthrough remains highly classified but appears to rely on the use of two fission explosions to create the ultraefficient implosion required to ignite a Super.

Bethe and Mark had always opposed the Super, but the new approach, for which Teller accepted most of the credit, convinced them that it would work. "I used to say that Ulam was the father of the hydrogen bomb and Edward was the mother, because he carried the baby for quite a while," Bethe has observed.[116]

On May 8, the United States successfully tested the theory that a fission bomb could set off a thermonuclear reaction. Oppenheimer, who had once described Truman's fateful decision as the "Plague of Thebes," said later, "It is my judgment in these things that when you see something that is technically sweet you go ahead and do it and you argue about what to do about it only after you have had your technical success."[117] He added that if the Super had looked as promising in 1949 as it did in 1951, the GAC report would not have been the same.

In October 1952, Vannevar Bush urged that the United States forbear from testing a fusion bomb so long as the Soviets followed suit; each side, he said, would be free to carry out research up to the point of testing a device. Rabi and Fermi had earlier proposed halting the research itself, a step that could not have been verified. But a prohibition on testing could have been easily monitored by the same system that was already monitoring Soviet atomic tests. Bush made his proposal while serving on a panel of government-appointed experts—chaired by Oppenheimer—that was looking into arms control. The panel vetoed it.[118] Bush argued his case up as far as Acheson but got nowhere. He didn't even see Truman.[119] Arneson says that he and Nitze were not impressed with the argument for a testing moratorium. "Verification would be small comfort if we verified that they were ahead," he says. "We felt we couldn't allow them to get ahead."[120]

Almost certainly, Stalin's decision to develop a fusion bomb preceded Truman's. Kurchatov never allowed his lab associates to lie back and savor their success with the first Soviet atomic bomb. After a week's pause, he shifted his focus to a fusion program, which rapidly acquired top priority.[121] According to Bundy, "No one from Stalin to Sakharov appears to have harbored any doubt at any time that the right course of action was to get a Russian H-bomb just as fast as possible."[122] Whether the Soviets would have agreed to Bush's proposition is an intriguing imponderable. What is clear is that if ever there was a chance to block the deployment of fusion bombs, it lay in Bush's test ban—another of the options never put before Truman. The step was eventually taken (in a modified form)—but during the Kennedy era, when the horse had long since left the barn.

On November 1, three days before Eisenhower was elected President, the United States tested the first thermonuclear device—called "Mike"— at Eniwetok in the Marshall Islands. Its yield was 10.4 million tons TNT equivalent—a thousand times larger than Little Boy's.[123] The explosion dug a crater in the Pacific a mile long and 175 feet deep. An island called Eleugelab disappeared.

On August 8, 1953, just nine months later, Georgi Malenkov, Stalin's successor, proclaimed that "the United States no longer has a monopoly . . . of the hydrogen bomb."[124] Four days later, air samples were collected which showed traces of a Soviet bomb. The AEC pronounced it a "thermonuclear device," which it was, though barely. Its yield was smaller than the largest of the American fission bombs and only one twentieth the size of Mike. "The first Soviet test was in the spirit of *Potemkin*, which still lives," says Bethe.[125] He says the Soviets never tested that design again. The event had nonetheless the kind of impact on Washington that the first Soviet fission bomb had had. Lewis Strauss was opposed to even announcing it, Arneson recalls. "The idea of the Russians being abreast of us was mortifying," he says. "An actual insult."[126]

On March 1, 1954, the United States tested six versions of the Super, the first of which yielded 15 megatons. Unlike Mike, it was not a device, but a genuine, deliverable bomb.

On November 23, 1955, the Soviets tested their first true thermonuclear fusion device. It, too, was a genuine bomb and based on the same approach as America's. They had pulled even—technologically at least—and the nuclear arms race had escalated frighteningly. "Delicate balance of terror" was Churchill's indelible phrase. "Mankind," he said, "had been placed in a situation both measureless and laden with doom." Placed there, he might have added, by a quest for strategic advantage—the chimera of the nuclear age.

If the arms race had found its own mad momentum, the cold war ground on as before. The buzz word for American policy was "containment," a term synonymous with George Kennan, who wrote a seminal paper on coping with Soviet imperialism, a version of which, signed by "X," appeared, rather surprisingly, in the quarterly journal *Foreign Affairs* in July 1947. "The main element of any United States policy toward the Soviet Union must be that of a long-term, patient but firm and vigilant containment of Russian expansive tendencies," Kennan wrote. He has since reproached himself for the containment paper, because he thinks it was misunderstood. He felt, he says, "like one who has inadvertently loosened a large boulder from the top of a cliff . . ."[127] Kennan's strongly held views on the limits of Soviet power (discussed in the Long Telegram) didn't come through. Hence, the paper managed to nudge policy in directions Kennan says he deplored, giving it a strong military emphasis and applying containment globally rather than confining it to America, Europe, and Japan. Acheson described Kennan as a "horse who would come up to a fence and not take it."[128]

Washington didn't worry—not much anyway—about a massive onslaught against Western Europe. But Soviet pressure, it appeared, could be contained only by roughly equivalent military force, of which there had to be a large nuclear component. In July 1949, the Senate approved American membership in NATO—just the sort of entangling alliance Washington had normally avoided. America had tied itself to Europe. NATO remains a major part of the Truman legacy and was largely the creation of Acheson, the urbanely dominant and resourceful figure whose counsel Truman valued most. But most members of the Senate didn't understand what the treaty might require of the United States. Hard questions such as whether an attack on Paris would be treated the same as an attack on Chicago weren't being asked.[129] Whether the United States would respond in kind if an allied capital was struck with an atomic bomb is a question that European capitals have brooded over from the start.

American intelligence was estimating that by 1954 the Soviets would have two hundred atomic bombs, plus the intimidating capability of dropping several of them. Acheson asked Nitze to make a "comprehensive study of U.S. national security policy." Nitze's paper, another seminal document, was called NSC 68 (and remains widely known by that designation). It recommended a military buildup that would allow America to control land, sea, and sky. The United States, argued the paper, must be ready to confront Soviet force wherever it appears and must make no distinction between "peripheral and vital interests"; any place that tempted the Soviets would fall within the zone of American interests. No estimate was made of the cost of any such buildup; when Nitze showed Acheson a back of the envelope figure of $50 billion, Acheson told him to drop it.[130] Still the budgetary implications were frightening. Charles Murphy, Truman's chief domestic adviser, was "scared so much by the document that he didn't go to the office the next day, but just sat at home, reading the memorandum over and over."[131] Not long after seeing the document in April 1950, Truman told Louis Johnson that the "economy in defense policy was dead." He approved NSC 68, in principle, on April 28. In June, however, Truman told Arthur Krock that he still wanted to hold down spending on defense.[132] Quite clearly, a notion of security as far-reaching as prescribed by NSC 68 could not become actual policy before going through an exhaustive and protracted political process. What was to become of NSC 68 depended not so much on the document itself as on external events, notably the war in Korea. "Rearmament occurred not because of NSC 68, but because of Korea," recalls Lucius Battle, who served as Acheson's personal assistant.[133] Nitze agrees. "It [the war] translated a think piece into an operational document," he says.[134]

For the second time in nine months, a major event caught Washington by surprise and unprepared. On June 25, four days before North Korea invaded South Korea, Congress was told by Dean Rusk, then the Assistant

Secretary of State for Far Eastern Affairs, that "we see no present intention" of North Korea going to war. American intelligence had failed to discover that Kim Il-sung had already been to Moscow to seek Stalin's approval and support for the invasion.[135] "The North Koreans," recalled Nikita Khrushchev in his memoirs, "wanted to prod South Korea with the point of a bayonet. Kim Il-sung said that the first poke would touch off an internal explosion in South Korea and that the power of the people would prevail—that is, the power which ruled in North Korea." According to Khrushchev, Stalin "was worried that the Americans would jump in, but we were inclined to think that if the war were fought swiftly—and Kim Il-sung was sure that it could be won swiftly—then intervention by the USA could be avoided." Stalin then decided to ask Mao Tse-tung's opinion, Khrushchev said, and he "approved Kim Il-sung's suggestion . . ."[136]

On June 26, Douglas MacArthur, the Supreme Commander of U.S. Forces in the Pacific, cabled the President: "South Korean casualties as an index to fighting have not shown adequate resistance capabilities or the will to fight and our estimate is that a complete collapse is imminent."[137] At a meeting of senior officials called to discuss military options, Truman asked General Hoyt Vandenberg "if the United States could knock out Soviet [air] bases in the area." Vandenberg replied that it could be done with atomic bombs.[138]

But Vandenberg didn't favor using these weapons. None of the chiefs did, even after China entered the war in November 1950. Arneson recalls being sent to the Pentagon at a critical moment to find out from Bradley whether nuclear weapons might be used. Bradley, he says, replied, "Heavens no. Forget it." Like Vandenberg and others, Bradley felt that suitable targets didn't exist. The Joint Chiefs were also somewhat concerned that the Chinese move might have been a diversion preceding Soviet aggression in Europe.

"No one in the executive branch to my knowledge was pushing for use of nuclear weapons," says Nitze. He recalls working closely with General Herbert Bernard Loper, a deputy to Bradley and a member of the Military Liaison Committee. "We were persuaded," Nitze says, "that the stockpile was too small to have allowed nuclear weapons to be used to any decisive effect against China, North Korea, or the Soviets in the event they entered the war." Actually, there were a few officials in Washington, including Stuart Symington, then Chairman of the National Security Resources Board, who did strongly favor using atomic weapons against China. However, the only influential voice of that kind was MacArthur's. "He talked to his friends, and what he said came back to me and others," says Nitze. "He was saying that Washington didn't understand politics in the

Far East. We would be able to restore Chiang Kai-shek to the mainland only by defeating the Red Chinese armies, and that could be done only with nuclear weapons."[139]

"MacArthur urged all-out war against China," says Dean Rusk in his office at the University of Georgia in Athens, the community in which he has lived and taught since leaving the State Department. "Those of us who served in China knew you could mobilize millions of men to fight in China and never accomplish more than occupying coastal cities. All-out war would have required the mass destruction of Chinese cities. We would have worn the mark of Cain for generations to come. The political effect would have been devastating. Truman never spent an instant even thinking about it."[140]

In late November, the Chinese intervened in force at the Yalu River and swept MacArthur's troops into a rapid retreat down the peninsula. On November 30, Truman held a press conference in which he said, "We will take whatever steps are necessary to meet the military situation."

"Will that include the atomic bomb?" asked a reporter.

"That includes every weapon we have," Truman answered.

The reporter continued: "Mr. President . . . does that mean that there is active consideration of the use of the atomic bomb?"

"There has always been active consideration of its use," Truman said. "I don't want to see it used."[141]

Allied capitals, London especially, were deeply apprehensive, seeing in Truman's words a possible portent of World War III. A great debate erupted in the House of Commons; one hundred members of Attlee's Labour party signed a letter protesting the possible use of the bomb.[142] Attlee drew cheers by announcing that he would fly to Washington. A few days later, he arrived and got the reassurances he needed.* What he did not get was a commitment from Truman for consultation before an American decision to use atomic weapons; the wartime arrangements were null and void. Truman did, however, agree to keep the Prime Minister informed of "developments which might bring about a change in the situation."[143]

Had MacArthur—God's right-hand man, as Truman privately referred to him—won the argument on using atomic bombs, China might well have been provoked to fight on indefinitely and probably with far greater determination. In the summer of 1969, the Soviet leadership had to reckon with similar implications of a nuclear attack against the Chinese.

*"British documents reveal that Donald Maclean, a Soviet spy, was privy to information about Attlee's meeting with Truman in which the President made clear he had no intention of using the bomb" (Richard Betts, *Nuclear Blackmail and Nuclear Balance* [Washington, D.C.: Brookings Institution, 1987], pp. 35–36).

The analogy between pressure on Truman to use atomic weapons against China in 1950 and the Soviet position in 1969 is not a bad one.

Some Soviet officials say privately that agreeing to the Korean War was among the worst blunders their leadership has ever made. As in the Berlin Blockade, America successfully took on the forces of world revolution in far from ideal circumstances. Perhaps more important was the effect of Korea on cold war issues, especially German rearmament. Acheson and some others regarded the step as vital to Europe's security. Whether it could have been taken—whether the objections of Germany's old adversaries in Western Europe could have been overcome—without the Korean War is far from clear. By the fall of 1950, Europe was prepared to accept a rearmed West Germany.

Truman's presidency became one of the most admired of the century. No modern President confronted more hard decisions or made them in so crisis-ridden an environment. Moreover, besides standing the test of time, Truman's decisions were taken with what Stimson called a "promptness and snappiness" that enlivened the government. "When I saw him today, I had fourteen problems to take up . . . and got through them in less than fifteen minutes with a clear directive on every one of them," Joseph Grew once said (with perhaps some exaggeration).[144]

After beating Thomas E. Dewey in 1948—to everyone's surprise but his own—Truman seemed to be in open water. He owed nothing to anyone. He could—and did—appoint anybody he wished to appoint, including men for all seasons and administrations, like John McCloy. But a week is a long time in politics, as Harold Wilson once observed. Less than a year later, the administration was on the defensive, as an anti-Communist tide began to undermine the President and secretary of state who laid the foundation of contemporary American foreign policy. Truman and Acheson were the first cold warriors—in the large, nonpejorative sense of the term. But the Truman Doctrine, the Marshall Plan, NATO, Berlin, and Germany redux were being obscured by a popular perception of the Soviet menace running amuck at home and abroad. What was going well mattered less than what seemed to be going wrong. Alger Hiss, the man whom Acheson said he wouldn't turn his back on, was convicted of perjury in January 1950, a few days before Fuchs was unmasked. It appeared that because of spies and traitors, Russia had an atomic bomb. In China, the victory of the Communist forces was widely advertised as an administration failure. "Who lost China?" became a controlling question, as if China were America's to lose. The Republican right had tasted blood. Less than a month after Hiss's conviction, Senator Joseph R. McCarthy inaugurated his campaign against the State Department, which he accused of harboring Communists. "Dean Acheson's College of Cowardly Communist Containment" was a routine McCarthyesque portrayal of the department. Not long after the war in Korea began, Truman asked Averell Harriman to become a major foreign policy adviser and troubleshooter in the White House. "Help Dean," Truman said. "He's in trouble."[145]

A perverse irony was at work. Acheson's State Department was nobody's dovecote. The system of collective security with which Truman is justly identified was conceived and nurtured there. But domestic forces crippled State just when its influence within the government had reached an historic high and the White House's dependence on it was complete.

Truman and Acheson departed with little more than their dignity intact. But the security policy they left behind, although under heavy siege, remained defensible. Eisenhower's task was not to change course but to use his unequaled authority to stay on course. He understood the politics of his situation at least as well as anyone. Nuclear issues would test him—would shake his own assumptions—as nothing else could and become the source of his greatest frustration.

IV

The Enigmatic Presidency

The Eisenhower era aroused great expectations. Unlike any predecessor or successor, he arrived in the office a world figure and the first President since John Quincy Adams who had played a crucial role in the world's pivotal affairs. Eight years later, Eisenhower left the White House a depleted and enigmatic figure. "He was the most misunderstood of Presidents," said Bromley Smith, who worked with four of them.[1] Those who least understood Eisenhower were, in the main, people who watched him most carefully—other politicians, allied leaders, reporters. An abundance of documents, as well as diaries, memoirs and oral histories, makes clear what should have been clear from the start: Eisenhower was a superior political chief, more artful and intuitive by far than the numerous *têtes politiques* who derided him. He never was—as he seemed to many—the jejune, unindustrious ex-soldier who was a bit uncomfortable in mufti; photos of him leaning on his three-wood, or beaming at the badinage of wealthy golf and fishing companions, were deceptive. Yet he struck much of the Washington gallery as he struck Khrushchev when they met—as more led than leading.[2] Cloudy speech and scrambled syntax strengthened the impression of a well meaning but unremarkable man who, but for history's mysterious ways, would have lived out his life in the relative obscurity of army life.

Washington wondered whether Eisenhower had a political gift that would sustain him when the aura of "Ike," the supreme allied commander, had gone. He had always insisted that he wasn't political, and in 1948 told admirers that he would consider accepting the nomination of both parties, not just one of them.[3] With his geniality, simple tastes, and plainspokenness, he had little difficulty in persuading people that he was the Kansas farm boy he said he was.

Truman was the product of machine politics, Eisenhower of military statecraft. Truman was a conventionally partisan figure. Eisenhower and a large part of the party on which he descended were always an awkward fit. But their larger differences were stylistic. Where Truman stood on an issue (or a person) was rarely in doubt. Eisenhower's views on most issues, including the most far-reaching and controversial, were rarely clear. Artifice and ambiguity concealed them. "He never showed his hole card," says General Andrew Goodpaster, who served as Eisenhower's staff secretary and was closer to his thinking and key decisions during the White House years than anyone. Vice President Richard M. Nixon wrote that Eisenhower "was a far more complex and devious man than most people realized."[4]

Certainly Eisenhower's political style, whether natural or acquired from experience, was complex. During the 1930s, he was chief aide and speech writer for MacArthur, the army's "most politically manipulative general."[5] At one stage, he was the army's principal lobbyist on Capitol Hill. A few days after Pearl Harbor, General George C. Marshall, then Chief of Staff, transferred Eisenhower to the Planning Division of the War Department. There Eisenhower could compare Marshall's methods of operating at the upper reaches of power with MacArthur's. He would soon take on the intensely political job of commanding the coalition of allied forces in Europe. After the war, he was Chairman of the Joint Chiefs and then Supreme Allied Commander, Europe. By then, as his biographer, Stephen Ambrose, says, "Eisenhower knew Washington and its *modus operandi* at least as well as any of his predecessors, and far better than most."[6]

If Eisenhower exuded warmth, at another deeper level he was cold and distinctly unsentimental. A famous incident in Milwaukee during the 1952 campaign is instructive; there he let himself be talked into dropping from his speech a passage defending General George Marshall—his mentor and patron—against Senator Joseph McCarthy, who accused him, *inter alia*, of having lost China.* The risk, a modest one at most, of losing McCarthy's home state, was judged more important than setting the country straight on Marshall. Truman, a warmer-blooded political animal, would never have made any such tradeoff.†

---

*Marshall, said McCarthy, took part in "a conspiracy so immense and an infamy so black as to dwarf any previous such venture in the history of man" (Fred Greenstein, *The Hidden-Hand Presidency: Eisenhower as Leader* [New York: Basic Books, 1982], p. 160).

†During his short span as vice president, Truman shouldered the political risk of attending the funeral in Kansas City of Thomas (Boss) Pendergast, who, although he had served time in prison for tax evasion, remained the man whom Truman felt indebted to politically.

Paul Nitze was a Republican until 1952 and backed Eisenhower, he says, "until I got mad at him." First came the Milwaukee episode, then a campaign speech in which, he recalls, Eisenhower accused the Truman administration of having withdrawn American troops from Korea prematurely, thereby tempting the North Koreans to invade. Yet it was Eisenhower himself who had wanted to withdraw troops, according to Nitze. "I fought him tooth and nail on that while he was Army Chief of Staff," he recalls. "Acheson supported me. But Truman finally decided in Ike's favor." Nitze says he switched parties after the campaign.[7]

Whereas Truman preferred the company of his own kind and thrived on decision making, Eisenhower, despite his political gift, was uncomfortable with elected politicians and the routine decisions that presidents confront; he tended to let the system make some of these for him. But other decisions, notably those involving war and peace and nuclear arms, could not, he felt, be left to the system. He thought he knew at least as much about defense and its link to foreign policy as anyone anywhere. Like Truman and Acheson, he saw America's vital interests as lying in Europe, less so the Far East, which was the object of his party's greatest anxiety. He didn't have a similar interest in or feel for most other issues.

He distanced himself from Truman's policy mainly, it seems, to establish himself as an authentic Republican. His real differences lay with the Republican right, which was a force in foreign and defense policy that had somehow to be controlled. Since Eisenhower intended to sustain the Truman-Acheson line, he had to disguise his own views and intentions. "No one could sort out his exact motives in these defense matters," says Goodpaster. "He was an expert in finding reasons for not doing things."[8] He rejected pressure from advisers to take steps that would enlarge the risk of conflict. He might not say no categorically, but neither would he say yes. Occasionally, he would tie approval for such a step with support for it from congressional leaders or allies, already certain that the support wasn't there. The general who opposed using the atomic bomb against Hiroshima could, as President, occasionally talk about using it. Yet he never seriously considered doing so when the issue was actually posed. "He would float ideas in meetings that didn't reflect settled judgment," says Robert R. Bowie, who succeeded Nitze as head of the Policy Planning Staff. "Or he would sometimes take contradictory positions in the same meeting. He wanted to promote discussion."[9]

Eisenhower's goals, besides being blurry, were largely his own. They could be summarized as avoiding conflict and shrinking the federal budget. Most Republicans agreed about the budget but were equally determined to avoid yielding a single point of principle, let alone an inch of terrain, to the enemy. All around him Eisenhower heard that containment was too passive and should give way to the great task of "rolling back" world communism. His Joint Chiefs of Staff—a quartet for whom he had no great admiration—were bent on reorganizing the services around nuclear weapons and avoiding budgetary cuts. But since military spending absorbed about 70 percent of the total budget, the largest cuts would have to be made there.

For Eisenhower, a strong economy and a strong defense were sides of a coin. He was no latecomer to the cause of budgetary restraint. As army chief of staff, he had argued for holding the line on military spending. As President, gloomy estimates from the intelligence people about first a "bomber gap" with the Soviets, then a "missile gap," didn't impress him. His skepticism arose from experience with worst-case thinking, knowledge of the military culture, and his own perception of the limits of Soviet potential. "He knew that his interests and those of the services were in conflict," says Goodpaster, "because their interests lay in keeping alive the threat." In effect, Eisenhower's chief antagonists (aside from the dominant wing of his own party) seem to have been his chief military advisers and some hawkish Democrats like Stuart Symington. Goodpaster agrees and adds that "he would occasionally meet with the Chiefs and ask them to lift their sights and think about where our security really lies. He didn't get the response he wanted." The battleground throughout his tenure was the military budget. His natural allies were George Humphrey and Robert B. Anderson, a pair of fiscal conservatives who served him successively as Secretary of the Treasury. "He gave greatest weight to their views, because he shared them," says Goodpaster.[10]

As President, Eisenhower was both the foremost moderate and the foremost skeptic within his party and his administration. He knew that his regime coincided with a high point—possibly *the* high point—of American power. He also knew that vis-à-vis the Soviets he was holding the high cards. America, unlike Russia, had not been depleted by the war. America had a large stock of atomic bombs and, unlike its adversary, the means of delivering them at long range. Perhaps most important, American economic power dwarfed the Soviet Union's and probably then exceeded the rest of the world's.

A pure Eisenhower bias occasionally flashed through an utterance, never more clearly than in his farewell talk on January 17, 1961, when he warned the country to "guard against the acquisition of unwarranted influence . . . by the military-industrial complex."[11] In his memoirs, he wrote: "This was, at the end of my years in the White House, the most challenging message I could leave with the people of this country."[12] The reaction to the "military-industrial complex" speech, as it became known, was very favorable, not least because it came as an agreeable surprise. After eight years as President, Eisenhower had shared an anxiety that people didn't know he harbored but one they related to easily.

Nuclear arms were his main anxiety, however. Nuclear war, he thought, held no more attraction for the Soviet leadership than for him. Stalin had died a few weeks after Eisenhower's inauguration, and he felt certain that the new leadership in the Kremlin would be mainly interested in holding power, not squandering it in another even more destructive war.

At a time when thinking about the atom was still in its formative stage, Eisenhower was making it up as he went along. He was being tugged from opposite directions. The services had acquired custody of the weapons and been sanctioned to find ways of deploying and using them. A ton of TNT then cost seventeen hundred dollars. Fissionable material could produce the same explosion at a cost of twenty-three dollars.[13] Only by deploying nuclear weapons, it seemed, could the United States afford to meet its commitments, especially in Europe. But actually using the weapons except in the event of an all-out war in Europe was for Eisenhower close to unthinkable, even if he sometimes sounded otherwise. On October 30, 1953, he approved language as part of his Basic National Security Policy, which said: "In the event of hostilities, the United States will consider nuclear weapons to be as available for use as other munitions."[14] And in a news conference in March 1955, he said: "Now in any combat where these things can be used on strictly military targets and for strictly military purposes, I see no reasons why they shouldn't be used just exactly as you would use a bullet or anything else."[15]

Language of this kind was belied during moments of crisis when Eisenhower was at his most manipulative—sidetracking the question of using nuclear weapons and, above all, keeping his options open. He would allow neither the truculent rhetoric of fellow Republican leaders nor military argument to crowd him into a corner. He kept control. He seems to have judged the weapon and the talk about using it as constituting a deterrent to Soviet adventurism. The best way to prevent either a war in Europe or another debilitating Korea-style conflict would be to establish the nuclear threat. The inference was that conventional warfare had become all but unacceptable to the United States, which had the great advantage of possessing nuclear weapons; these would offset superior Soviet manpower. This concept, which might be called existential deterrence, became NATO doctrine and remains so. If the idea of using nuclear weapons in Europe is too horrifying to be credible, therein lies its merit, according to adherents; allied governments in Europe have been the most stubborn of these. Better a strategy that makes war unthinkable, they say, than one that relies on nonnuclear weapons and, hence, might make conflict in Europe less unthinkable.

In piecing together his version of deterrence, Eisenhower was being intuitive, not intellectual. Just as intuitively, he felt the need for initiatives that would make the nuclear environment less dangerous. Here again, he was treading unplowed ground. Nuclear arms control was even more notional than nuclear deterrence, but in some form it represented what Eisenhower was groping for. His efforts failed—victimized partly by bad luck but mainly by his own reluctance to push against the current. Eisenhower rarely met opposition head-on or stretched the political tolerances of his policies. The temporizing instinct that kept Eisenhower from defending Marshall (or taking on McCarthy) held him back from using his political weight to push the ideas that seem to have mattered most to him. He was always reluctant to put himself very far in front of his divided and fractious party. In the conclusion of his farewell address—the one in which he flagged the military-industrial complex—he said: "Disarmament . . . is a continuing imperative . . . Because this need is so sharp and apparent I confess that I lay down my official responsibilities in this field with a definite sense of disappointment."[16]

Eisenhower had first to cope with advice he was getting from other people who thought about nuclear weapons, among them Robert Oppenheimer, whose Disarmament Panel—the one for which Vannevar Bush had proposed a testing moratorium—had given Truman a report shortly before his departure. The document, which was among the first Eisenhower read, urged a diplomatic initiative with the Russians and more candor on nuclear matters; it noted that missiles would soon become as important as bombers, a prophecy that few, if any, of the people around Eisenhower took seriously but which greatly irritated the air force. Eisenhower, according to Robert Bowie, was strongly influenced by the report, discussed it with Oppenheimer a number of times, and encouraged him to write a public version, which resulted in the famous article in *Foreign Affairs* in which Oppenheimer likened the Americans and Russians to "two scorpions in a bottle, each capable of killing the other, but only at the risk of his own life."[17]*

Advocacy of a new and harder line dominated most of the advice, and Eisenhower reacted by taking a highly secret move aimed at neutralizing

*Oppenheimer was a gifted phrase-maker, but he borrowed the "scorpions in a bottle" image from Vannevar Bush.

the hard-liners and freeing his own hands. In early May, he and a few advisers met in the White House solarium and created separate task forces to examine three alternate policies toward the Soviet Union: continuing containment, rolling back communism by various means, and "drawing a line" between the Soviet bloc and the non-Communist world. The "solarium exercise," as the study became known, lasted several weeks and produced the recommendation Eisenhower wanted: continued containment. This outcome hadn't quite been left to chance. Eisenhower himself had picked the teams and had arranged for their conclusions to be put before a meeting of first-, second-, and third-tier government officials. After two hours or so, he said he would summarize. "He jumped up and spoke without notes for about forty-five minutes," Goodpaster recalls.[18] It was an impressive and convincing performance. George Kennan, the creator of the containment doctrine, had been asked to take part in the exercise. "The President showed an understanding as great, if not greater, than that of any of the other cabinet members who were there," he says.[19] (Secretary of State John Foster Dulles was among those present.) Eisenhower, by most accounts, dominated any meeting on national security issues.

Containment was fuzzed a bit and toughened but only rhetorically. A few slogans—"A Bigger Bang for a Buck," "A New Look," "Massive Retaliation"—clouded the situation. They were supposed to characterize a defense policy tailored for the nuclear era. The thinking that lay behind the bold phrases was not original to Eisenhower's people or even to the American military. In 1952, Britain's Chiefs of Staff had proposed a novel strategy based on reducing conventional forces and relying on long-range bombers equipped with atomic bombs. Unable to defend against such weapons, an aggressor would hesitate before taking a step that could invite dreadful retribution. Churchill had asked his chiefs to find a way of cutting defense costs in a time of economic crisis. None of the NATO governments, including America's, could then afford to fulfill military goals that they themselves had jointly approved at Lisbon in February. These unattainable goals were supposed to impress the Russians, whose strength had been greatly inflated by soft Western estimates and their own successful efforts to mislead American intelligence. Throughout the 1950s and early 1960s, the Soviets artfully concealed the shabbiness of their forces behind a contemporary version of Potemkin villages.

During the war, Harold Macmillan, who from 1957 to 1963 was Britain's Prime Minister, told his staff at Eisenhower's African headquarters: "We British must run this allied HQ as the Greek slaves ran the operations of the Emperor Claudius."[20] This attitude persisted; in the early years of NATO, the British military exercised considerable influence over American policy. During the summer of 1952, they tried but failed to tempt the American chiefs with their new strategy. The Americans resisted what they saw as a Churchill ploy to renege on his Lisbon commitments.[21] But the incoming Republicans, including Eisenhower, were more responsive. He had promised America "security and solvency."[22] Spending vast sums to deploy an army big enough to defend Europe and also fight brushfire wars in remote places struck him as unwise. The trendy view in defense circles was that the Russians would need only shoes to make their way to the English Channel. Eisenhower agreed that nuclear weapons were essential to Europe's defense. And Europe had to be defended. He was ready to use the threat of nuclear weapons to prevent the Communist bloc from nibbling at America by arranging proxy wars beyond Europe. But just how he would respond militarily in such situations, or against whom, was to remain unclear. The real point, he reckoned, was that nuclear weapons would allow him to contain communism yet spend less.

Eisenhower did cut the defense budget. And he went far beyond anything Truman might have said in endorsing nuclear options. But his words and deeds didn't match. "The only war he could envisage was a European war in which we would both use everything we had," says Goodpaster. A European war was most unlikely, however, and the crises that could be expected to pop up in more remote places didn't tempt Eisenhower and he would avoid being drawn in. "I'm going to do every-thing I can to keep us out of this," Goodpaster remembers him saying on one such occasion.[23]

He was under pressure from an influential group of Republican sena-tors to replace the Joint Chiefs of Staff, who were thought to favor a Europe-first policy. Eisenhower yielded; in May, he appointed Admiral Arthur Radford to replace General Omar N. Bradley, his great confederate, as chairman. General Matthew Ridgway, Admiral Robert Carney, and General Nathan Twining became, respectively, the Chiefs of Staff of the Army, Navy, and Air Force. The selection of Radford, an assertive figure with a bit of flash, went down especially well with the Senate's Asia buffs; his motto as a carrier admiral in the war against Japan had been "kill the bastards scientifically."[24] Radford was a strong advocate of air and sea power and was known to favor a tough line on China. He argued, not unreasonably, that the military couldn't lower defense spending until they were told which kind of war to prepare for and whether they would be allowed to wage it with nuclear weapons.[25]

On paper, he won the argument. In October, Eisenhower approved a new document (NSC 162/2), which, for planning purposes, removed the distinction between nuclear and conventional wars and between nuclear and nonnuclear weapons. In vain did General Ridgway and Secretary of the Navy Robert Anderson argue that tying security to nuclear weapons was a very dubious proposition, first, because it would seem to leave the country with no military option short of all-out war, and, second, because Soviet nuclear weapons would soon be able to neutralize America's. Congressional critics said, correctly, that the "New Look" was inspired by budgetary, not military, goals.

A document can describe policy but not execute it. Although nuclear weapons were being turned over to the military, Eisenhower, like Truman, reserved to himself the exclusive authority to use them. And while he might on occasion equate a nuclear bomb with an ordinary bullet, he more often dwelt on the inadmissible horror of nuclear warfare. What he gave the nuclear planners with one hand he took back with the other. No one knows precisely what he had in mind, because he didn't fully confide in anyone.

Adding to the confusion was the strident performance of Secretary of State John Foster Dulles, a potent figure who always seemed to be making foreign policy, even if he wasn't. In January 1954, Dulles made a public issue of defense policy by extolling a doctrine he called "massive retaliation." The administration, he told the Council on Foreign Relations, had decided "to depend primarily upon a great capacity to retaliate, instantly, by means and at places of our choosing"; the Pentagon, he said, could begin to plan accordingly. The cost of any alternative policy, he said, would be injuriously high. "If the enemy could pick his time and his place and his method of warfare—and if our policy was to remain the traditional one of meeting aggression by direct and local opposition—then we had to be ready to fight in the Arctic and the tropics, in Asia, in the Near East and in Europe; by sea, by land, and by air; by old weapons and by new weapons."

The reaction—at home and abroad—was strong and largely hostile. The phrase "massive retaliation," with which Dulles was to be forever identified, struck many people as menacing and jingoistic. The thinking that lay behind the words was judged dangerously simplistic; the United States, it suddenly seemed, stood ready to silence any serious provocation anywhere with nuclear weapons—to strike directly at Moscow or Peking—without reckoning on the Soviets responding in kind.

Neither Dulles nor Eisenhower had intended to convey the meaning that most people drew from the speech, which became the most controversial of the Eisenhower presidency. And they lost no time in edging away from massive retaliation. In a news conference in March, Eisenhower said, "All that the 'New Look' is is an attempt by intelligent people to keep abreast of the times; and if you want to call your today's clothes the 'new look' as compared to what Lincoln wore, all right, we are in the 'new look.' "[26] An article written for Dulles by Robert Bowie appeared in the April issue of *Foreign Affairs* and softened considerably the import of the January edict.

Eisenhower's relationship with Dulles added appreciably to the confusion about the President. They were an odd couple. Eisenhower's first choice for secretary of state, by some accounts, was John McCloy, but the party's Taft wing wouldn't accept McCloy.[27] At the time, Eisenhower told Canadian diplomat Lester Pearson that Dulles would be appointed but assured Pearson that he wouldn't be there long. Dulles had the respect of his peers. He knew the world, and most of his life seems to have been preparation for the job that various powerful Republicans were urging Eisenhower to give him. But there were many skeptics. A sanctimonious Christian moralist, Dulles struck numerous members of the foreign policy fraternity as not much of a diplomat. He had often guessed wrong,* and, more disconcerting, his views tended to shift, sometimes wildly, as he adjusted them to fashion and election returns.

Dulles wasn't Eisenhower's sort, and at first there was tension between them. A pedantic, sententious Dulles manner bored Eisenhower; aware of this, Dulles became diffident around him and tried too hard. Eisenhower edited any Dulles speech with care, often had to reel him in, and even to explain him. Toward the end of the first term, for example, Dulles gave an interview to *Life* which drew more flak than even his massive retaliation speech. "Of course we were brought to the verge of war," he said in reviewing administration decisions. "The ability to get to the verge without getting into war is the necessary art. If you cannot master it, you inevitably get into war. If you try to run away from it, if you are scared to go to the brink, you are lost . . . We walked to the brink and we looked it in the face." Dulles and "brinkmanship" became synonymous. "[He] doesn't stumble into booby traps, he digs them to size, studies them carefully, and then jumps," wrote James Reston in the *New York Times*.[28] The reaction from abroad was one of shock and even outrage.

With pressure building for Dulles to resign, Eisenhower came to his defense, calling him "the best Secretary of State I have ever known."[29] Still, Dulles impressed much of Washington as deceptive, ungenerous, and curiously partisan for someone who had functioned as a shadow secretary of state during the war and the Truman years. He treated the State Department like a fiefdom but did little to defend loyal subordinates against

---

*As late as November 1941, Dulles wrote: "Only hysteria entertains the idea that Germany, Italy, or Japan contemplates war upon us" (Richard Rovere, *The Eisenhower Years* [New York: Farrar, Straus & Cudahy, 1956], p. 58).

harassment and attack from the hard right. This side of Dulles seems not to have concerned his unsentimental chief.

To the surprise of advisers on both sides, they had become a team, and Eisenhower gradually acquired deep respect and even affection for Dulles. Dulles's craving for the limelight didn't bother the President. Neither did the dominant, though wholly mistaken impression of Dulles as the man in charge of foreign policy. "He got a sly amusement out of it," says Goodpaster. "Any time anyone got the credit for something he had done, he enjoyed it. 'I got that,' he said, 'from something Marshall said: "You can accomplish an awful lot if you don't care who gets credit for it." ' "[30] It was a deliberately chosen method of exercising leadership.

The exaggeration of Dulles's role also meant that he, not Eisenhower, would be blamed for various unpopular moves, a consideration not lost on the President. Allies and adversaries alike were fooled. The British and French actively disliked Dulles and worried about his seemingly unwholesome influence on Eisenhower. And Khrushchev wrote: "That vicious cur Dulles was always prowling around Eisenhower, snapping at him if he got out of line." But he also wrote: "I'll say this for him: Dulles knew how far he could push us, and he never pushed us too far."[31] Dulles was hardly the first trouble-prone, egocentric personality that Eisenhower had been saddled with by events. Ever the realist, he probably decided to make the best of the appointment and, in any case, rock no boats within his excitable party. That a situation which began as distasteful became a good one for Eisenhower was clear profit, as well as further evidence of his artfully disguised but remarkable gift for managing.

Dulles and Eisenhower shared the strong commitment of their predecessors to NATO and a rearmed West Germany anchored to it. On some alliance issues, the national security bureaucracy sometimes found the Dulles view sounder than that of Eisenhower, who, seeing the merit of the other's argument, would often yield to it. But Dulles never did acquire the moderate instinct that pushed Eisenhower toward arms control and some accommodation with Moscow. On nuclear issues in general, he lacked Eisenhower's acute sensitivity. Their divergence was most pronounced during moments of peak tension and crisis.

During his first term, Eisenhower confronted the question of using nuclear weapons three times, first in Korea. He was voted in partly because he seemed to stand a better chance of ending the war there on acceptable terms and had promised to do so. He said that he had a plan. It allegedly excluded both a continuation of the existing stalemate and launching an orthodox offensive. "To keep the attack from becoming overly costly, it was clear that we would have to use atomic weapons," he wrote. Letting the other side know that seemed to him to be the best way. ". . . We dropped the word, discreetly, of our intention," he said. "We felt quite sure it would reach Soviet and Chinese Communist ears."[32] Just what was said and to what effect is still unclear. A threat to drop atomic bombs on Chinese cities is supposed to have been passed to Peking through the Indian government in May. Dulles played a key role and felt strongly that the threat convinced the Chinese to conclude the war on reasonable terms. So did Vice President Nixon. "I'll tell you how Korea was ended," he told a secret caucus of southern Republicans. "We got in there and had this messy war on our hands. Eisenhower let the word go out . . . to the Chinese and North Koreans that he would not tolerate this continual ground war of attrition. And within a matter of months, they negotiated."[33] Eisenhower had also moved atomic weapons into Okinawa, where American bombers could launch strikes against China and Korea.[34]

In meetings held during the winter and spring of 1953, Eisenhower did occasionally wonder aloud about using nuclear weapons in Korea. Against enemy dugouts which honeycombed the hills, they might be cheaper than conventional munitions, he once observed. Another time, he noted that the Kaesŏng area might offer a good target for an atomic bomb. Dulles then remarked on the Soviet success in setting atomic weapons apart from all others in a special category. An effort should be made to break down that false distinction, he said. On another occasion, Eisenhower agreed that there weren't enough good targets for atomic weapons but said that, still, it might be worth using them if doing so would produce a large victory.[35]

The army demurred, questioning the usefulness of these weapons against military targets. In raising the question of using them at these moments, Eisenhower may have wanted to see how advisers, especially military advisers, would react. As always, however, his cards were visible to no one, the better to keep open his options. Sending a threat to the Chinese may have been among the ways he kept open the nuclear option. "The record is clear that the threat to Korea was conveyed," says Goodpaster. "Eisenhower did feel that it helped to end the war."[36]

A stronger case can be made that the threat, such as it was, had little to do with ending the war. "What was actually said to China was very vague and ambiguous," according to Dean Rusk, who says he read the record just after returning to government as secretary of state in 1961. "What has been claimed for that episode is quite an exaggeration."[37] Sherman Adams, Eisenhower's Chief of Staff, supports Rusk. "The threat was [never] as specific and as near to being carried out as Dulles intimated," he wrote.[38] In fact, when Dulles, in 1956, cited the Indian role, Prime Minister Jawaharlal Nehru flatly denied any involvement.[39] Adams also points out that allied opposition would have been a major barrier to escalation.

The relevant dates, as Bundy has observed, weaken the claim made for the threat. On returning from Stalin's funeral in late March, Chou En-lai, China's Premier, made his side's major concession by dropping the demand that all Chinese and North Korean prisoners of war be repatriated, by force if necessary. Chou's move occurred several weeks before China's leaders could have received the warning from Washington, and probably before they learned of the deployment of nuclear weapons in Okinawa.[40] Stalin's death, not the American threat, was probably the turning point in the truce negotiations; his successors scaled down the importance of the Korean conflict.[41] China, too, was paying a heavy price in Korea, and Eisenhower was a new force to reckon with. He was both a national hero just beginning his term and the head of a political party replete with jingoes and partisans of the exiled regime of Generalissimo Chiang Kai-shek on Formosa. As the war dragged on, they would inevitably add to the pressure on Eisenhower to end it by using every weapon at his disposal. Eisenhower, in turn, worried deeply about the threat from China to American forces in Asia. "What has really happened," wrote columnist Walter Lippmann, "is that both sides and all concerned have been held within a condition of mutual deterrent."[42]

Within six months of the armistice in Korea, America was nearing what Dulles would call the brink of war, this time in Indochina, where France's army controlled the major cities but was losing the countryside to the Vietnamese Communists. The French at home were losing their appetite for the struggle. The famous siege of Dien Bien Phu hadn't yet begun, although for a time in January 1954 the French forces deployed there had only six days' rations. Eisenhower told his security advisers, "There was just no sense in talking about United States forces replacing the French in Indochina . . . I can not tell you how bitterly opposed I am to such a course of action. This war in Indochina would absorb our troops by divisions."[43] But Eisenhower was willing to consider covert support for the French and wondered aloud about a group of adventurous pilots, without insignia, being sent out for an afternoon, or whether a capable Buddhist leader could be found to add fervor to the anti-Communist cause.[44]

On April 7, with the French garrison at Dien Bien Phu by now in a hopeless position, Eisenhower was asked at a news conference to comment on the strategic importance of Indochina. In a long and solemn response, he noted the "falling domino" principle. "You have a row of dominoes set up; you knock over the first one, and what will happen to the last one is the certainty that it will go over very quickly. So you could have a beginning of a disintegration that would have the most profound influences."[45] By then, Admiral Radford had reported the conclusion of an "advance study group" in the Pentagon: "Three tactical A-weapons, properly employed, would be sufficient to smash the Vietminh effort there."[46]

In Paris, the French military were counting on American military intervention, which alone could head off the loss of their colony. Radford, they felt, had promised aerial strikes against enemy positions.[47]* Administration rhetoric and private comment bore out at least guarded optimism on the French side. Briefly, Washington seemed ready for a showdown with Communist China, and Vietnam would be the battleground. But even as he talked about falling dominoes, Eisenhower had begun to distance himself from intervention. On April 5, he heard from Dulles that the French had conveyed to Ambassador Douglas Dillon in Paris their impression that "Operation Vulture"—an American plan to bomb the Vietnamese forces with conventional weapons—had been agreed to, and they hinted that they expected two or three atomic bombs to be used as well. Eisenhower instructed Dulles to have Dillon tell the French that they must have misunderstood Radford; that "such a move is impossible"; that without congressional support an air strike would be "completely unconstitutional and indefensible . . . We cannot engage in active war."[48]

Eisenhower knew that without commitments from allies, notably Britain, to take part in any intervention, the congressional leadership would not support American involvement. Radford himself was dispatched to London to see Churchill, who told him bluntly that if the British people had been unwilling to fight to save India for themselves, it was not likely that they would fight to save Indochina for the French.[49] With all this in view, Eisenhower attached precise conditions to American intervention: congressional approval (Dulles and Radford were instructed to consult the leadership), participation by Britain and other allies, and French agreement to independence for all of Indochina. "Without allies and associates," Eisenhower told his staff at one meeting, "the leader is just an adventurer, like

*Radford said later that General Paul Ely, the French Chief of Staff, hadn't understood that he, Radford, couldn't commit the U.S. government, and also that France would have to "internationalize" the war before America could become involved.

Genghis Khan."[50] But Eisenhower had no illusions about allies and associates; he knew that his conditions couldn't be met. He was operating, as he often did, by indirection—using other key players to block a course of action about which he had serious misgivings or had decided against.

Among the lingering impressions of this episode are General Ridgway's role and the lapses in communication between Washington and Paris. In his memoirs, Ridgway describes the alarm he felt when "individuals of great influence" began saying that Indochina was the place to "test the New Look." Convinced that intervention by air and naval forces would have to be followed by ground forces, he sent a team of army experts "to get the answers to a thousand questions that those who had so blithely recommended that we go to war there had never taken the trouble to ask. How deep was the water over the bar at Saigon? What were the harbor and dock facilities? Where could we store the tons of supplies we would need to support us there? How good was the road net—how could supplies be transported as the fighting forces moved inland, and in what tonnages? What of the climate? The rainfall? What tropical diseases would attack the combat soldier in that jungle land?" The answers, as Ridgway pungently described them, made an overwhelming case against intervention on the ground. "I lost no time," he writes, "in having the report passed on up the chain of command. It reached President Eisenhower. To a man of his military experience its implications were immediately clear. The idea of intervening was abandoned . . ."[51]

There can be little doubt of Eisenhower's profound concern about seeing Indochina fall to the Communists; the falling dominoes language fairly reflected his thinking. Ridgway's report, however, merely spelled out what Eisenhower intuitively knew. Ridgway was thus pushing on an open door.

Some months later, France's Foreign Minister, Georges Bidault, disclosed that during the critical days in April he had rejected an offer from Dulles to lend French forces a few atomic bombs. Dulles categorically denied Bidault's account and was supported by a French official, who said that Bidault had been "jittery [and] overwrought" and had misunderstood.[52] Still, Bidault was very experienced and nobody's fool; also, the French were aware that Washington's prointervention lobby, which included strong and resourceful figures in and out of the government, hadn't given up on saving Dien Bien Phu. In March, Senator Symington had raised with French Prime Minister René Pleven the question of using atomic bombs, and Pleven had noted "the lack of suitable targets."[53] On April 30, the national security planning board was still considering whether the "new weapons" could be used and whether "one new weapon could be loaned to France for this purpose. Could French airmen make a proper drop? Would the French government dare take [the] step?"⁵⁴ Radford's idea—by then strongly supported by General Nathan Twining—of using three tactical bombs to save the French garrison was still being discussed—with Dulles among others. However, in another meeting on April 30, Robert Cutler, Eisenhower's special assistant for national security, brought him a paper that discussed the ins and outs of using atomic bombs in Vietnam. After noting that the weapons probably couldn't be used unilaterally, Eisenhower turned on Cutler: "You boys must be crazy. We can't use those awful things against Asians for the second time in less than ten years. My God."⁵⁵

In reacting to what he thought, rightly or wrongly, was an offer from Dulles, Bidault was described as very upset, feeling "that the use of atomic bombs would have done no good tactically and would have lost all support for the West throughout Asia."⁵⁶ Bidault repeated the story in his memoirs. This was among the earliest in a long list of misunderstandings and disagreements with France on issues involving nuclear weapons. A few of them were to exercise a strong and, at times, controlling influence on American foreign policy.

France's Indochina war ended in July with agreement by Prime Minister Pierre Mendès-France to an independent but partitioned Vietnam—the setting for the larger conflict to come. A few weeks later, yet another crisis foamed up, this one in the Formosa Strait. The episode, which lasted eight months, put Eisenhower's manipulative gift to its stiffest test; the pressure on him to use nuclear weapons was heavier than at any other time in his presidency. The unlikely focus of the dispute, which pitted Communist China against the regime of Chiang Kai-shek on Formosa, was two small islands, Quemoy and Matsu; they were occupied by Chiang's forces but lay just a few miles off the Chinese coast, well within artillery range. In August, the mainland Chinese began a military buildup at a point opposite Formosa, just one hundred miles away, and in early September they began shelling Quemoy.

The Joint Chiefs all agreed that while the offshore islands were not essential to the defense of Formosa, the Chinese Nationalists couldn't hold them without American help. Only Ridgway opposed using American force to defend the offshore islands. He considered them wholly irrelevant, an opinion shared by most of the rest of the world, including America's closest allies. The other chiefs—Radford, Carney, and Twining—argued that losing the islands would deal a major psychological blow to the Chiang regime and sap its will to defend Formosa. They wanted prompt air strikes against the mainland. Dulles took a similar view. A visit to Chiang Kai-shek had convinced him of Communist China's determination to capture Formosa. "Foster agreed," wrote Eisenhower, "that the United States could not sit idly by and watch the Chinese on Quemoy and Matsu suffer a crushing defeat—a defeat which would lead to the loss of Formosa itself." And Dulles, again according to Eisenhower, told him that "if we defend Quemoy and Matsu, we'll have to use atomic weapons. They alone will be effective against mainland airfields."[57]

Eisenhower accepted the Dulles analysis. He, too, equated Formosa's security with Quemoy and Matsu. Both men felt that if Formosa were lost the other Asian dominoes, including Japan, would slowly but surely fall to the enemy. Eisenhower said as much in a letter to Churchill. Yet everything he did—every decision—indicates that he would not have gone to war for the offshore islands, let alone used atomic weapons against China. "Eisenhower never really envisaged fighting in the Formosa Strait," says Goodpaster.[58]

The country and the world, unable to read Eisenhower's mind, had reason to worry. Apparently, that was no accident. In a news conference on March 16, he was asked to comment on Dulles's remark that in the event of war in the Far East, "we would probably make use of some tactical small atomic weapons." Eisenhower's untypically straightforward reply included the memorable reflection about using atomic weapons "just exactly as you'd use a bullet or anything else."[59] In his memoirs, he explains: "I hoped this answer would have some effect in persuading the Chinese Communists of the strength of our determination."[60] Four days later, Dulles, who was clearly quite aroused, described the Chinese in a speech as "an acute and imminent threat . . . dizzy with success." He thought they were more dangerous than the Russians and compared their "aggressive fanaticism" with Hitler's.[61]

Most of the Senate's senior Republicans were urging the toughest possible line. "Either we can defend the United States in the Formosa Strait now or we can defend it later in San Francisco Bay," said Alexander Wiley, who was not among the most extreme of them. Elsewhere in Washington, as in other capitals, administration rhetoric seemed dangerously unreal. It ignored two key points: China wholly lacked the military means to capture Formosa, and Formosa was protected not by offshore islands but by one hundred miles of open sea and the presence of America's Seventh Fleet, which had been reinforced. "We seem to be drifting," said Dean Acheson, "either dazed or indifferent toward war with China, a war without friends or allies, and over issues which the Administration has not presented to the American people, and which are not worth a single American life."[62]

The pressure on Eisenhower was heavy but hard to evaluate. Its noisy, public flavor may, in his view, have encouraged restraint in Peking. But the downside was far from trivial. Allies like the British were mortified, and his own first priority—"free hands"—was threatened. On March 25, Admiral Carney told a group of reporters that he expected fighting over the offshore islands to begin on April 15 and that the President's military advisers had urged him to take preemptive action "to destroy China's industrial base and thus end its expansionist tendencies."[63] By then, Eisenhower's patience with his chiefs was fading fast. Ridgway had provoked him by testifying that thanks to the New Look, the army had become too small to defend Formosa. Eisenhower was angry enough to consider firing Ridgway, and Carney's ploy—an even greater irritant—had him muttering about taking charge of the Pentagon.*

Carney might have noted on his own behalf Eisenhower's own press conference statement and the unbuttoned comments of senior officials, especially Dulles, who spoke of "new and powerful weapons of precision which can utterly destroy military targets without endangering unrelated civilian centers . . . I imagine that if the United States became engaged in a major military activity anywhere in the world that those weapons would come into use."[64] This comment, especially the part about not endangering civilian centers, worried a few of Dulles's associates in the State Department, notably Robert Bowie, who asked the AEC and the CIA to work up an estimate of civilian casualties if atomic weapons were used against the military targets located near Quemoy and Matsu. The answer, Bowie says, was several million people. Just what Dulles made of this enlightening report wasn't wholly clear, but Bowie felt that he took the point.[65]

If somewhat isolated, Eisenhower was hardly a passive figure in this peculiar drama. A few days after the Carney indiscretion, he used his press secretary to inspire a lead for news stories which said: "The best political and military intelligence reaching the White House is that the Chinese Reds have not yet undertaken the kind of military and aviation buildup that would make an attack likely in the near future."[66] So much for the Radford-Carney line. Far more important, Eisenhower had already made two key moves to keep control of the situation. First, in January, he decided to involve Congress directly in whatever he decided to do. He took this step partly because he didn't want to edge the country toward war with China without having Congress with him. Second, and no less important, a congressional mandate, if adroitly handled, could help him control the war hawks in both branches of government. Specifically, he asked for and got a resolution from Congress that endorsed America's determination to fight

*In Eisenhower's presidency, unlike most others, the problem of Pentagon leaks wasn't severe. But his military people did tend to go public with their views, another troublesome tendency. Admiral Carney was not reappointed as Chief of Naval Operations after his two-year term expired.

for Formosa and gave the President discretionary authority to defend Quemoy and Matsu as well if he judged such action essential to Formosa's defense. Goodpaster recalls the handling of the Formosa resolution as vintage Eisenhower. Dulles had urged him, Goodpaster says, to have the language of the document commit the United States to defending Quemoy and Matsu along with Formosa. Eisenhower said no. He and he alone would decide on what, if anything, to do about the offshore islands.

His next key move was to send Goodpaster to Hawaii to ask the Commander in Chief of the Pacific Fleet, Admiral Felix Stump, for his assessment of whether Chiang Kai-shek could hold the offshore islands. Stump told Goodpaster that unless the Communists attacked within the next ten days, the Nationalists ought to be able to hold on without American help. From then on, Goodpaster reported, the other side "could overcome Nationalist opposition only by an all-out coordinated amphibious attack against Quemoy and Matsu, with artillery and air support."[67] Eisenhower didn't have to send his most trusted aide to Hawaii in order to have Stump's views. He could have asked the JCS to request them. But the chiefs, as he knew, were capable of putting the question to Stump in a fashion designed to fetch an answer they found congenial; Eisenhower knew the ways of bureaucracy as well as anyone. Goodpaster reckons that his report gave Eisenhower an argument for not intervening to help Quemoy and Matsu—the same purpose served by Ridgway's report on Vietnam nearly a year earlier.

Goodpaster's return coincided with the high point of public concern about intervention. Eisenhower had scheduled a press conference for March 23. Goodpaster and James Hagerty, the White House press secretary, wondered what he could say about the situation, and Hagerty asked him. "Don't worry, Jim," Eisenhower told him. "If that question comes up, I'll just confuse them." Of course it did come up, and he did confuse them: Could Eisenhower conceive of using nuclear weapons to deal with the Quemoy and Matsu problem? He replied by talking about human nature being the most unpredictable and unchanging factor in war. He added that "every war is going to astonish you in the way it occurred and in the way it is carried out."[68]

By late April, the Chinese had had enough of the tension and uncertainty. Chou En-lai announced that his people "didn't want war with the United States" and were "willing to strive for the liberation of Formosa by peaceful means as far as this is possible." The shelling of the offshore islands was halted. A few months later, talks between American and Chinese representatives began.

Europeans, said Eisenhower in a letter written in February to General

Alfred Gruenther, "consider America reckless, impulsive, and immature." He had asked Gruenther, who succeeded him as NATO commander (after a one-year intermediate tour by Ridgway) and was one of his closest and most trusted friends, to be an emissary to European governments during the Formosa crisis. Here at home, Eisenhower continued, he had to deal with "the truculent and the timid, the jingoists and the pacifists."[69] He could also have noted the pressure on him from the Joint Chiefs. "His independence of his military advisers has been in many ways remarkable," wrote Rovere, "and quite a few people feel that he has been able to get away with it only because he is a military man himself."[70]

In each of the crises in which the nuclear issue arose, Eisenhower used allies and Congress alike to suit his purposes. Fearful allied leaders, Churchill especially, balanced the partisans of intervention. So for the most part did the congressional leaders. Once consulted, most of them were usually more than content to leave the touchiest matters in Eisenhower's hands. After a discussion of all the implications of a given move over a quiet drink at the White House, he would usually be urged to take full responsibility. Only he as commander in chief was competent to make the decision, his auditors would say, giving him just what he wanted—their complicity and their proxies. An intriguing question is whether any of the allied leaders, especially those who, like Churchill, knew him well, understood that Eisenhower was consciously using them. The answer, though obviously not manifest, appears to be that they didn't. Other leaders never understood either his methods or his complete control of his foreign policy, according to Goodpaster.[71]

The President who reassured the boldest spirits with talk of falling dominoes repeatedly told his own inner circle that "you can't provide security with a Roman wall."[72] He meant that security must be supplied by people living within the area itself. The Eisenhower overview of security and nuclear weapons was captured by Stephen E. Ambrose: "He realized that unlimited nuclear war in the nuclear age was unimaginable, and limited war unwinnable. That was the most basic of his strategic insights."[73] In June 1954, when the question of a preventive nuclear strike against China arose, Eisenhower said to the chiefs, "There is no victory except through our imaginations."[74]

Eisenhower's aversion to nuclear war—limited or otherwise—was matched by an anxious but persistent effort to subdue the technology and its works. In August 1953, after the Soviet Union shocked Washington by testing a hydrogen bomb, he became even more determined to find a way of moderating the arms competition. He was already under public pressure, notably from the newspaper column of Joseph and Stewart Alsop, to strip away some of the secrecy about atomic weapons. Oppenheimer's report had, of course, pushed in that direction. Eisenhower rejected numerous drafts of a speech—"Operation Candor"—for being too gruesomely absorbed with human destruction, and eventually he produced his own idea. "Suppose," he said to Robert Cutler, "the United States and the Soviets were each to turn over to the United Nations for peaceful use, X kilograms of fissionable material."[75] A reluctant Lewis Strauss, Chairman of the AEC, drafted the proposal: A world authority composed largely of neutral countries would receive and store fissionable material, with specified amounts to be delivered each month, "independent of reliance upon . . . good faith or enforcement."[76] (The term "verifiable" was not yet in use.) And by October, the new project was in high gear.

Eisenhower was to offer the plan in a speech before the U.N. General Assembly. He decided first to show the draft to Churchill and French Prime Minister Joseph Laniel during a conference in Bermuda in early December. "I wanted to talk to Winston about it in detail, and to M. Laniel in general," he wrote.[77] (The distinction he drew, especially in nuclear matters, was not lost on the French. It reminded them of the Manhattan Project, from which they had felt excluded. Their resentment of preferential treatment accorded the British would only grow.)

The chances of "Atoms for Peace" gaining wide acceptance weren't good. Strauss and C. D. Jackson, a White House special assistant who wrote the various drafts, saw the speech mainly as propaganda, certainly not as a serious step toward disarmament. Eisenhower himself had once told Cutler that the "amount X [the fissile material to be stored] could be fixed at a figure which we could handle from our stockpile, but which it would be difficult for the Soviets to match."[78] But with exposure to the idea, Eisenhower had become deeply committed to it. "He put in a lot of work on the Atoms for Peace speech," says Goodpaster. "He saw it as a benchmark of his Presidency."[79]

From Bermuda, Dulles sent a coded message to Ambassador Charles Bohlen in Moscow instructing him to tell Soviet Foreign Minister Molotov that the President would be making a serious proposal at the U.N.—a proposal that would mean just what it said.[80] On December 8, Eisenhower stood before a world audience and set forth his plan for an International Atomic Energy Agency, which besides storing fissionable material would devise peaceful uses for it. To continue the atomic arms race, he said, "would be to confirm the hopeless finality that two atomic colossi are doomed malevolently to eye each other indefinitely across a trembling world."[81] The speech was passionately eloquent. At the end, "thirty-five hundred delegates began to cheer—even the Russians joined in—in an outburst of enthusiasm unprecedented in U.N. history."[82]

But the speech was the proposal's high point. After a rather warm response, the Soviets drew back, partly from concern that contributing material to a stockpile would only widen the American lead, even though Eisenhower had suggested contributions at a level of five American units to one Russian—a figure wide open to negotiation. The Soviets had been put on the defensive; as partly intended, the speech did score propaganda points. It was printed as a pamphlet in ten languages and distributed far and wide. Special briefings, magazine articles, and advertising were lavished on the print and broadcast media. Newspapers and radio stations throughout the world got Voice of America radio recordings. People heard broadcasts about nuclear devices to fight cancer, cut lumber, and power locomotives. Promotional films included *Atomic Greenhouse*, *Atomic Zoo*, and *Atom for the Doctor.*[83]

Larger purposes were also served. The speech led to the creation in 1957 of the International Atomic Energy Agency (IAEA)—an organization the world needed and one which has functioned well, within the limits of its resources. The speech also helped demystify the atom and remove some, though not enough, of the mindless secrecy about it that government had imposed. The speech warned the American people that nuclear weapons were no trump card and threatened both sides. Still, an important if modest opportunity was lost. Eisenhower had advanced a plan—the first of its kind—that imposed no unacceptable conditions to either side; nor did it require acceptance of a worldwide system of control and inspection. The idea flickered, then disappeared beneath the cold war's growing deposit of suspicion, secrecy, and competition in nuclear arms.

Not surprisingly, each side saw the other as committed to achieving a clear edge in nuclear weapons. By 1953, technology was busily enlarging the role of nuclear weapons in military planning. Atomic bombs were becoming smaller, down to 1,000 pounds from 10,000, with no penalty to yields. Besides aircraft, they could be used on surface-to-surface missiles (the Regulus and Honest John), long-range artillery shells, antisubmarine warfare depth charges, and atomic demolition land mines.

Each of the services was refashioning itself in a nuclear mold. Atomic bombs were being hung on the navy's carrier-based attack planes. The army was teaching itself to use nuclear weapons on the battlefield. But the air force had captured the dominant strategic role. It had the B-36 strategic bomber, the most potent weapons system the world had seen, yet one that would be supplemented and eventually replaced, starting in June 1955, by an even more advanced and reliable long-range bomber, the B-52. The air force also deployed nuclear-capable medium-range bombers and fighter aircraft. Still, America's advantage, although immense, wasn't large enough to satisfy key parts of the government, which saw the Soviets—uninhibited by the conventions of budgetary restraint—as fully capable of closing the gap and seizing a big lead.

The Soviets had a clear, though gloomy, picture of the military position of their adversary, an open society. "I used to take a pencil and compute the number of atomic shells, atomic bombs and launchers on the American side," General Chervov recalls. "And the sad fact was . . . that the U.S. nuclear superiority was absolute. Apart from that, the U.S. territory was at that time invulnerable."[94] He meant that while American bombers based at home or in Europe could strike Russia, the Soviet air force had nothing then with which to attack the United States. In that sense, the American advantage *was* absolute. But Washington was—and would remain—muddled about the forces of a wholly closed adversary society which concealed its strengths and, more significantly, its weaknesses. The dominant side of American intelligence began to convince itself that the balance of strategic advantage was swinging the wrong way.

American intelligence in the early 1950s was still in its formative stage. Surveillance of the Soviet Union—its priority task—wasn't possible. Most of today's ultrarefined techniques for monitoring Soviet military activities didn't exist. In any case, Allen Dulles, Eisenhower's CIA director, didn't like so-called technical intelligence, mainly because he didn't know anything about it. And he tended to leave military intelligence to the services themselves (which is what the National Security Act of 1947 had intended). Dulles, unlike his brother, was never much of a bureaucratic force but rather an old-fashioned spy-master who preferred HUMINT—trade argot for human intelligence. However, his agency's effort to establish a spy network in the Soviet Union had failed, and Eisenhower was pressing for information about Soviet military programs. He, like his intelligence advisers, felt that the United States was the priority target of Soviet strategic forces. In fact, Europe was their target, partly because the Soviet leaders wanted to put Europeans under as much pressure as possible, but also because they were not yet able to deploy weapons with enough range to reach the United States. For years, American intelligence exaggerated the Soviet threat to America and underestimated the threat from Soviet medium-range weapons to Western Europe.

The air force had the lead role in estimating Soviet bomber and missile

forces and was always prone to assign a far higher number to these than
was the CIA or the army and navy intelligence agencies. "The Air Force
was judged the least competent of the services," says John Huizinga, a
former director of the CIA's Board of National Estimates. "And it was very
hard to deal with Air Force assertions. You had to prove a negative, a
hopeless position to be in."[85]

In the May Day parade in 1954, the Soviets unveiled their first long-
range bomber—the M-4 Bison. It was considered a prototype and seemed
to portend a strategic bomber fleet that wouldn't be ready for deployment
before 1960. Then in July 1955, on Red Air Force Day, an American Embassy air attaché went to Tushino airport to watch Soviet military aircraft
fly by in review, and he was astonished to see twice as many Bisons as had
been observed earlier that year. The Soviets had actually duped him and
other Western observers. The ten Bisons which flew past the reviewing
stand made a wide circle, were joined by eight others, and then made
another pass.[86] The hoax—designed to conceal weakness—created the impression of a much larger long-range Soviet bomber force than actually
existed. The appearance of a second such bomber—the Tu-20 Bear—added
to Washington's anxieties. Talk of a bomber gap began. Air Force intelligence estimated the Russians would have six hundred to seven hundred
strategic bombers by mid-1959. The forecasts of the other intelligence agencies were lower, but these too overstated the case. Having been misled,
American intelligence began to mislead itself by exaggerating Soviet production capabilities. Another American military attaché, lying in a field
with binoculars, spotted the serial numbers on the tails of some Bison bombers. From these, Washington assumed that the airplanes were being produced in batches of ten, when in fact the real number was five. The Soviets,
says Goodpaster, just weren't exploiting capabilities attributed to them or
creating the new facilities American intelligence expected them to create.

Eisenhower never believed in the bomber gap. Long experience with
intelligence estimates had made a skeptic of him. He knew there was a fair
amount of hard information on Soviet testing programs but not much on
production and deployment. So any estimate drew on just one piece of the
puzzle. He might have been even more doubtful of the bomber gap had he
known of an air force study, called "Arctic Yoke," which minimized the
threat by citing the inadequacies of the forward airfields in Siberia on which
attacking Soviet bombers would rely. The study, according to a former
CIA official, concluded that few, if any, such planes would reach the United
States. But apparently Arctic Yoke was suppressed.

Whatever his feelings, Eisenhower couldn't ignore the bomber gap.

"*You're just wearing yourself out, Eldridge, splitting atoms at that old laboratory!*"

This cartoon suggests that atomic physics was a suitable topic for humorists as early as 1933.

(Drawing by Garrett Price; © 1933, 1961 The New Yorker Magazine, Inc.)

Niels Bohr (left), head of the
Institute for Theoretical Physics
in Copenhagen, and Max Planck
(right), a Nobel laureate at the
University of Berlin and creator
of the quantum theory, in Copenhagen, 1930. Bohr warned Roosevelt
and Churchill in 1944 about the
need to inform Stalin about the
atomic bomb and try to head off
a postwar nuclear arms race.

(AIP Niels Bohr Library)

Pyotr L. Kapitza, who worked
with Ernest Rutherford in the
early 1920s and '30s in Cambridge,
and later became Director of the
Institute of Physical Problems
in Moscow, was presumed to be
spearheading a Soviet atomic
bomb program. Kapitza, in fact,
opposed the bomb and was placed
under house arrest for the
duration of the war.

(AIP Niels Bohr Library)

In August 1939, the Soviet Union signed a nonaggression pact with Germany. Here Joseph Stalin shakes hands with German Foreign Minister Joachim von Ribbentrop.

(Keystone Photos)

Leo Szilard visited Einstein at his summer home in Peconic, Long Island, in 1939 to show him a draft of a letter to Roosevelt warning against the dangers of a German atomic bomb.

(G.W. Szilard/AIP Niels Bohr Library)

From left: Ernest O. Lawrence,
Arthur H. Compton, Vannevar Bush,
James B. Conant, Karl T. Compton,
and Alfred L. Loomis discuss
the cyclotron project at Berkeley,
March 29, 1940.

(Lawrence Radiation Laboratory/AIP
Niels Bohr Library)

From left: Drs. William G. Penney, Otto Frisch, and Rudolf E. Peierls pioneered the British nuclear program which anticipated the Manhattan Project. All three worked at Los Alamos during the war. Professor John D. Cockcroft (far right) went to Montreal to head up work on a heavy water reactor.

(London *Daily Telegraph*)

Enrico Fermi. In a graphite pile on a squash court at the University of Chicago, he produced the first controlled chain reaction. Rudolf Peierls wrote, "in Fermi's hands, problems that had been terrifyingly complicated for others often became very simple."

(Los Alamos Scientific Laboratory)

*Los Alamos: Some called it
a "Nobel Prize Winners Concentration Camp." It resembled
nothing so much as a frontier
town surrounded by armed guards
and barbed wire fences. The
streets were unpaved, and housing was a jumble of prefabs,
trailers, and apartment units.*

(Los Alamos Scientific Laboratory)

*In February 1943, Igor Kurchatov
was chosen to organize the Soviet
atomic bomb project because,
like Robert Oppenheimer, his
organizational gift matched his
scientific gift.*

(SOVFOTO)

*Scientists at Los Alamos met weekly
to exchange ideas and new insights.
Some credit the colloquia with
the speed of their progress on the
bomb. Scientists at the other "atom
cities" were forbidden such exchanges
by General Leslie R. Groves, and
sharing information between sites
was also not allowed. (From left,
second row: J. Robert Oppenheimer
in dark suit, Richard P. Feynman;
front: Norris Bradbury, John Manley,
Enrico Fermi, and J. M. B. Kellog)*

(Los Alamos Scientific Laboratory)

At Potsdam in July 1945, Truman and Churchill decided not to tell Stalin about the atomic bomb. But Stalin already knew about it. From left: Soviet Premier Joseph Stalin, President Harry S Truman, and Prime Minister Winston Churchill.

(AP/Wide World Photos)

J. Robert Oppenheimer, Director of Los Alamos, and General Leslie R. Groves, chief of the Manhattan Project, returned to the Trinity site. Here they are standing next to the remains of the tower at Point Zero.

(UPI/Bettmann Newsphotos)

*On August 6, 1945, Little Boy,
a uranium bomb, was dropped on
Hiroshima, Japan. This photograph
was taken on September 7, 1945.*

(UPI/Bettmann Newsphotos)

Top: Britain's Prime Minister, Clement Attlee (center), and Canada's Mackenzie King are greeted in Washington by President Truman on November 10, 1945. Attlee hoped to revive the nuclear cooperation that had existed during the war and which Roosevelt had guaranteed Churchill would continue after the war.

(AP/Wide World Photos)

Alsatian-born Hans Bethe left Germany in 1935 for Cornell University, where he has taught ever since. He arrived at Los Alamos in April 1943 and became the first head of the Theoretical Division. In 1945, he told the Senate Atomic Committee that European countries would be able to produce atomic bombs much more cheaply than the U.S. had.

(AP/Wide World Photos)

Senator Brien McMahon, Senator Arthur Vandenberg, and Major General Leslie R. Groves were the major players in the fight over who would control atomic energy. In the end, a compromise between the three produced the Atomic Energy Act on August 1, 1946.

(UPI/Bettmann Newsphotos)

"I suppose in a few years all this will be done by atomic power."

By late 1945, as this New Yorker
cartoon suggests, the atom was
being seen as a solution to earthly
problems, large and small.

(Drawing by Alain; © 1945, 1973
The New Yorker Magazine, Inc.)

Top left: *Andrei Gromyko has been one of the few continuities of the nuclear age. He served five general secretaries and dealt with six American presidents. This picture was taken when he was Soviet ambassador to the U.N. in early 1946.*

(AP/Wide World Photos)

Top right: *On September 23, 1949, President Truman announced that the Soviets had detonated an atomic bomb. Leo Szilard was one of the Los Alamos scientists who had warned that the Soviets would be able to match America's achievement within five years.*

(Argonne National Laboratory, Courtesy AIP Niels Bohr Library)

In 1949, the agreement allowing Anglo-American atomic cooperation was due to lapse. David E. Lilienthal, chairman of the Atomic Energy Commission, Secretary of Defense Louis A. Johnson, and Secretary of State Dean Acheson met on July 27 to discuss renewal.

(AP/Wide World Photos)

*A comment on the attempted
Soviet denial of Western rights
of access in Berlin.*

(Drawing by Alan Dunn; © 1949, 1977
The New Yorker Magazine, Inc.)

Herblock of the Washington
Post *comments on the first Soviet atomic explosion.*

(From the *Herblock Book*
[Boston: Beacon Press, 1952])

At the Geneva summit conference of 1955, President Eisenhower and Secretary of State John Foster Dulles confer, somewhat grimly it appears. Eisenhower did nothing to discourage the erroneous impression that instead of leading, he was being led.

(AP/Wide World Photos)

*Senator Stuart Symington and
Allen Dulles, Director of the
CIA, in April 1956. Symington
summoned Dulles because he felt
that CIA agents hadn't told their
boss that Russia had jumped ahead
of the U.S. in bomber strength.
Symington was wrong. Russia
lagged far behind.*

(UPI/Bettmann Newsphotos)

The air force estimate of the Soviet strategic bomber force was leaked to the press, and, in April 1956, Stuart Symington, who was chairman of a Senate subcommittee on air power, began to hold hearings on the issue. Admiral Radford, as well as witnesses from the army and navy, testified against the estimate, but in the end it fetched the air force budget an additional $928 million and Eisenhower was obliged to buy more B-52s than he wanted.[87] Ironically, the Soviet deception at Tushino, which had been designed to conceal an inferior position, helped to enlarge America's strategic advantage.

Eisenhower's skepticism didn't extend to the risk of surprise attack. The memory of Pearl Harbor continued to haunt the defense community. Although persuaded that Soviet leaders hoped to avoid war, Eisenhower couldn't be sure. Once they had a hydrogen bomb and the means to deliver it, the bare possibility of attack, he knew, could only grow and with it America's vulnerability to mass destruction. In planning a surprise attack, a closed society, he felt, would have an advantage denied an open society.[88] These reflections led Eisenhower to create a commission to look into surprise attack and find ways of avoiding it. The group was chaired by James R. Killian, who assembled a group of gifted and accomplished people. The ripple effect of their recommendations is still being felt; it produced a new stage in the superpower rivalry.

The report of this so-called Surprise Attack Panel, which was completed in 1955, concluded that two hundred bombs could defeat the United States; and a surprise attack, it appeared, would preclude the heavy retaliatory blow that would otherwise deter so horrendous a move.[89] In a few years, warned the report, the Soviets would be able to deliver their hydrogen bombs with long-range missiles. The report was an exhortation. America should capture the initiative—and not through sheer numbers of weapons but with superior technology. Recommendations included:

—Developing land- and sea-based versions of intermediate-range ballistic missiles (IRBMs)

—Dispersing America's strategic bombers and keeping some portion of them on continuing airborne alert

—Studying limited nuclear war as an alternative to massive retaliation and the New Look

—Examining the feasibility of destroying an incoming missile with
a defensive missile—a so-called antiballistic missile (ABM)

With this report, the scientists seized and held Eisenhower's attention.
Two of their proposals made a particularly deep impact. The first concerned long-range missiles, the second new methods of collecting intelligence and improving estimates. Top priority, said the report, should go to
developing intercontinental ballistic missiles—both land- and submarine-
based. Eisenhower fully agreed, even though he brooded about ICBMs and
the prospect of seeing them mated to hydrogen bombs. That such a destructive combination was feasible had been established by the calculations of
John von Neumann, the Budapest-born mathematician whom many of his
peers judged at least as brilliant and inventive as any of the prodigious
emigré scientists. Von Neumann functioned as a kind of superconsultant
to the Manhattan Project. His electronic computer, the ENIAC, performed
the calculations for the work at Los Alamos on the hydrogen bomb in the
early 1950s. He did math in his head which colleagues, including Fermi and
others, did with desk calculators or slide rules.[90] Von Neumann was an
unapologetic and committed atomic weaponeer in whom the creative impulse beat more strongly than in others. When he was put in charge of the
panel's Strategic Missile Evaluation Committee—the Teapot Committee
as it was code-named—he was already suffering from an incurable cancer.
His answer to the predictably large inaccuracies of the first-generation
ICBMs—Atlas and Titan—was to create a fission-fusion-fission bomb—a
weapon so dirty that if it missed the target, everything for miles around
would be destroyed.[91]

The ballistic missile age had clearly begun, but the scope of Soviet
activity was unclear. In appraising the chronic intelligence problem, Killian's panel urged more rapid development of satellites, but these were years
away, and the need for information that could be supplied only from
overhead photography couldn't wait. A system to bridge the gap would
have to be found—quickly. American radars in Turkey had identified tests
of short- and medium-range Soviet missiles at Kapustin Yar. And a Soviet
defector in Britain had conveyed hard information about missile research
being done in Russia by German rocket scientists. American intelligence
was also aware of parallel missile programs from which the German scientists were excluded. The need for precise data on Soviet missile development was urgent; the activity at Kapustin Yar was particularly worrisome.
(The information had not been shared with allies.) Since the air force,
according to General Twining, didn't have an aircraft that could photograph the installation, British intelligence was persuaded to do the job. A

stripped-down Royal Air Force *Night Intruder*, equipped with cameras and extra fuel tanks, overflew southwestern Russia but was nearly shot down en route and arrived in Iran full of holes. A spy, possibly H. A. R. (Kim) Philby, had tipped off Moscow about the flight. In one account, Robert Amory, then Deputy Director of the CIA, said, "The whole of Russia had been alerted to this thing and it damn near created a major international incident. But it never made the papers." The British were unwilling to repeat the experience.[92]

Clarence L. (Kelly) Johnson of Lockheed was consulted, and he provided the solution. Johnson, America's most celebrated airplane designer, ran a maximum-security "black program" plant in Burbank, California, which was known as the "skunk works." He quickly conceived a slow, unarmed spy plane—a jet-powered glider—that would fly over seventy thousand feet for up to four thousand miles, collecting information as it went. The air force dismissed the idea, but some of Killian's people instantly recognized it as a revolutionary approach to aerial reconnaissance. Without even waiting for his commission to make its recommendations, Killian went to see Eisenhower about Johnson's *Mosquito*, taking along a colleague, Edwin H. Land of Polaroid, who described the characteristics that would enable the airplane to fly above the reach of Soviet interceptors and surface-to-air missiles (SAMs). He also described a camera nearly as *outré* as the airplane—one that would take pictures of very high resolution from extreme altitudes. Eisenhower, according to Killian, asked "many hard questions" and then approved developing the system. "But he stipulated that it should be handled in an unconventional way so that it would not become entangled in the bureaucracy of the Defense Department or troubled by rivalries among the services."[93] The CIA, not the air force, was put in charge of the supersecret project. And so was born the U-2, a spy that became immensely useful to Eisenhower for a time and then dealt him the gravest injury of his presidency.

Eisenhower's confidence in and respect for the notables of the scientific community had grown, but so had his anxieties. Technology and cold war—the relentless tandem—pressed him to set in motion some strategic programs and to speed up others. As before, however, he felt strongly obliged to put some limits on the arms race. He was the first, though hardly the last, President to confront these contesting priorities—the first in a series to watch the nuclear arms buildup moving briskly at its own pace, the effort to bridle it laboring in place. The air force, which had a proprietary approach to strategic thought, reckoned that the New Look meant no less than devastating Soviet society in a first strike. "But even if you shoot first, you will probably die," argued Bernard Brodie, a pioneer nuclear strategist who felt that the hydrogen bomb excluded rational planning for war. "This [weapon] brings us a long way from the subtleties of a Clausewitz, a Jomini, or a Mahan," he wrote. "It brings us, in short, to the end of strategy as we have known it."[94]

Any first small step toward limiting arms would require a lessening of tension. Churchill had argued persistently for a Big Four summit, mainly for domestic political reasons. Anthony Eden, who replaced him in May 1955, favored meeting the new Soviet leadership, officially a troika: Nikita Khrushchev was the party chief, Nikolai Bulganin the head of government, and Marshal Georgi Zhukov, Eisenhower's wartime confederate, had become Minister of Defense, causing concern that the Red Army might be more influential. Was it a sign that "Russia was moving toward war?" Hagerty asked Eisenhower. Eisenhower said he doubted it. "If you're in the military," he said, "and you know more about these terrible destructive weapons, it tends to make you more pacifistic . . . [Besides,] they're not ready for war and they know it. They also know if they go to war, they're going to end up losing everything they have. That also tends to make people conservative."[95]

The political crisis over Quemoy and Matsu had frightened allies and much of Congress. By the spring of 1955, the call for peaceful coexistence was universal, and France's Prime Minister Edgar Faure had joined the British in pushing for a summit. So did Senator Walter George, an influential chairman of the Senate Foreign Relations Committee. For different reasons, Eisenhower and Dulles had opposed such a meeting. Eisenhower doubted that anything useful could be accomplished and wanted to avoid raising people's hopes only to see them flattened. Dulles worried, in the words of Charles Bohlen, "that the spectacle of Eisenhower shaking hands with Khrushchev would destroy the moral image of the United States, have a bad effect domestically, and tend to weaken the allies' will to stand up to communism."[96] And like many another foreign minister, Dulles disliked summits in principle, seeing them, not unreasonably, as hard to control and potentially mischievous.

Agreement by the Soviets to an Austrian peace treaty softened Eisenhower's objections to a summit, which then was scheduled for July in Geneva. Having lost the argument, Dulles hoped to restrict the meeting's agenda to such broad issues as a divided Germany and a captive Eastern Europe. The Soviets, he reasoned, would play to a world gallery as peace lovers while trying to divide the Western allies. But Nelson Rockefeller, who had succeeded C. D. Jackson as Eisenhower's special assistant, and a few others pressed for an initiative that would go down well and also be seen as a test of Soviet intentions. The upshot was "Open Skies," a proposal as appealing in its apparent nobility of purpose as Atoms for Peace.

The idea was to have the superpowers exchange charts showing the location of their military bases. Aircraft of each country would be allowed to fly over and photograph these installations. Reciprocal overflights would allay fears of surprise attack and thus reduce tension. At first, Dulles opposed the venture; Eisenhower had just appointed Harold Stassen, the former governor of Minnesota, as a Special Assistant on Disarmament. Dulles saw the involvement of presidential assistants as eroding his authority and bearing out his dimmest views of summitry. A collision between him and Stassen, an ambitious and determined man, seemed certain, and there were in fact several.

Eisenhower was very taken with the Open Skies idea. He even thought the idea might be negotiable. Goodpaster, Stassen, and Gruenther supported it, and gradually Eisenhower's more skeptical advisers, including Radford and Dulles, became converts. The idea had a reassuring heads-I-win, tails-you-lose quality. The open societies of the West would gain the intelligence they needed if Moscow accepted the idea, but would have a strong claim to the moral high ground if the Soviets rejected it. And reject it they were bound to, for secrecy was a habit. A society that found security in concealment and regarded the world outside with extreme suspicion was not likely to open its airspace. Bowie remembers thinking Open Skies "was a clever ploy but never in the least negotiable."[97]

Eisenhower described in his memoirs the highly favorable British and French reaction to the proposal, which he read aloud, and then that of Soviet Prime Minister Bulganin, who said it had real merit and would be studied sympathetically. "The tone of his talk seemed as encouraging as his words," wrote Eisenhower. A few minutes later, walking toward the bar with Khrushchev, he was disabused but enlightened. " 'I don't agree with the Chairman,' Khrushchev said, smiling—but there was no smile in his voice. I saw clearly then, for the first time, the identity of the real boss of the Soviet delegation." From then on, said Eisenhower, "I wasted no more time probing Mr. Bulganin; I devoted myself exclusively to an attempt to persuade Mr. Khrushchev of the merits of the Open Skies plan, but to no avail. He said the idea was nothing more than a bald espionage plot against the U.S.S.R."[98] Khrushchev was unwilling to reveal the weakness of Soviet defenses; also, the Soviet leadership was many years away from even partial recognition that security—theirs like everyone else's—relies on each side being able to see what the other is doing and assess its big weapon deployments. Few people on the American side saw matters in that light either.

Eisenhower may have been one of those who did. "In a selfish nationalistic sense, [Khrushchev was] partly right in the course he pursued," he wrote. "But in the same sense he was also partly wrong, for uncontrolled armaments might well lead in the long run to the destruction of his own country."[99]

Khrushchev's impressions of the first postwar summit are revealing: "We were encouraged," he wrote, "realizing now that our enemies probably feared us as much as we feared them . . . The Geneva meeting was an important breakthrough for us on the diplomatic front. We had established ourselves as able to hold our own in the international arena. Our success was confirmed by Eden's invitation for us to pay a state visit to Great Britain."[100] For his peers of the Politburo and for him, Khrushchev's voyage had literally been a trial run. He and they, as he said, were conscious of Stalin's repeated putdown: "You'll see, when I'm gone the imperialistic powers will wring your necks like chickens."[101]

Khrushchev took credit for giving missile development top priority. He further claims that his experience as a miner in the Donets Basin and as a supervisor of Moscow's metro construction led him to invent the missile silo. "I began trying to think of ways we could hide our missile sites from enemy reconnaissance," he wrote. "It occurred to me that since missiles are cylindrical, we could put them into sunken, covered shafts. I could see numerous advantages to this idea. To name just two: storing the rocket in a well would allow us to protect it against the weather; and second, in order to knock out a site, the enemy would not only have to find it—he'd have to score a direct hit."[102]

He may have inflated his own role. It would be difficult, however, to exaggerate America's reaction to the early Soviet exploits of missile and rocket technology. They provoked endless trouble for Eisenhower and anxiety in the country.

V

Mad Momentum

Ignorance and hyperbole fed America's anxiety. On October 4, 1957, the Soviets lofted into orbit the first man-made object—the *Sputnik*, or "fellow traveler" in Russian. The 184-pound satellite had no military importance. Technologically, it was crude and uninteresting, that is to specialists working in the embryonic American space program. But most of the world saw the accomplishment as a stunning first. The Soviets seemed to have taken control of outer space. "Listen now for the sound which forevermore separates the old from the new," said an NBC announcer. And the heavenly beep-beep was heard by millions. Eisenhower abruptly lost twenty-two points in the Gallup Poll.[1] A bit of Washington doggerel captured the flavor of the popular reaction:

> *Sputnik, Sputnik in the sky*
> *Emitting beeps as you go by,*
> *Have you room in your little bullnik*
> *For Ike and Dick and Foster Dullnik?*

"As it beeped in the sky, Sputnik created a crisis of confidence that swept the country like a windblown forest fire," wrote James Killian.[2] Senator Henry Jackson demanded a "National Week of Shame and Danger."[3] Eisenhower made matters worse by diminishing the event in a news conference five days afterward. *Sputnik*, he said, in what was perhaps his only major public relations gaffe as President, "does not raise my apprehensions . . . as far as security is concerned . . ."[4]

Sputnik did prove, Eisenhower conceded, "that they can hurl an object a considerable distance."[5] But that was the whole point. The significance of the exploit lay not with the satellite itself but with the huge SS-6 launcher that had boosted it into orbit. That kind of thrust would allow the SS-6 to dispatch a ballistic missile toward a target thousands of miles away. In August, the Soviets had achieved another major first by successfully launching a multistage ICBM at their Tyuratam testing range. "The United States," intoned Edward Teller on television, "had lost a battle more important and greater than Pearl Harbor." Asked what might be found on the moon, he said, "Russians."[6] Fears of a bomber gap were abruptly superseded and magnified by the appalling prospect of huge Soviet rockets threatening America from outer space. "The scientists were mortified," says Andrew Goodpaster. "Public opinion panicked. The era of long-range nuclear missiles was upon us. It was a new chapter and brought with it concerns about vulnerability and security."[7]

Sputnik provoked even broader worries: Scientific inquiry within an open and free society, it seemed, was less productive than the more focused and disciplined approach taken by a closed, authoritarian society. America must be falling behind in hard science and mathematics, the disciplines of the new age. The significance being accorded Soviet space exploits went beyond space itself. Democracy and free enterprise were abruptly seen as vulnerable in a way they hadn't been before *Sputnik.*

Eisenhower was never one to overreact. After meeting with Rabi, Killian, and a few other scientists he relied upon, he wisely decided against altering American research programs. He did create the Office of Special Assistant to the President for Science and Technology and named Killian to head it.

The pressure grew. *Sputnik* had revived what some called a "Pearl Harbor atmosphere." Eisenhower was swamped with advice, most of it pointing to more of everything—more space and missile research, more nuclear bombs, larger military forces, federal aid to colleges, and fallout shelters. On a less hortatory note, Rabi and a few others urged him to consider a nuclear test ban.

Although *Sputnik* didn't set off an East-West crisis or add to the risk of hostilities, it was as relentless as any problem Eisenhower had known. In November, he had a stroke, possibly caused by the stress of *Sputnik,* according to Dulles and Nixon.[8] He recovered in a few days. Then, in early December, the first test of America's space vehicle, the *Vanguard,* failed dramatically; the rocket and its three-and-one-half-pound satellite exploded on the launch pad. The event, following a successful launch of *Sputnik II,* which included an air-conditioned compartment containing a dog, "increased the hysteria and embarrassment in the United States and the ridicule abroad," wrote Killian. "Flopnik," "Kaputnik," and "Stayputnik" were among the derisive labels pinned to the American system, which was in fact a more advanced piece of hardware than the heroic *Sputnik*. Two weeks later, Eisenhower was victimized by a sensational press leak; an account of an ultrasensitive study on national security, known as the Gaither Report, was given to Chalmers Roberts of the Washington *Post*.

"The still top-secret Gaither Report portrays a United States in the gravest danger in its history," wrote Roberts.

"It pictures the Nation moving . . . to the status of a second-class power.

"It shows an America exposed to an almost immediate threat from the missile-bristling Soviet Union.

"It finds America's long-term prospect one of cataclysmic peril in the face of rocketing Soviet military might and of a powerful, growing Soviet economy and technology which will bring new political, propaganda, and psychological assaults on freedom all around the globe.

"Many of those who worked on the report, prominent figures in the Nation's business, financial, scientific, and educational communities, were appalled, even frightened, at what they discovered to be the state of the American military posture in comparison with that of the Soviet Union."[9]

The inspiration for the project was a proposal from within the government to spend $40 billion on a bomb shelter program. Killian asked H. Rowan Gaither, Jr., a lawyer and chairman of the Ford Foundation, to form an advisory group of experts. But what began as a modest study of civil defense needs mushroomed into a massive review of America's defense position. The project became "a caricature of government sprawl," recalls Spurgeon Keeny, who was a member and is now president of the Arms Control Association. "Some of the people wanted to go on a wartime footing. They worked themselves into a state of hysteria. It was the establishment gone wild."[10]

The quality and luster of the nearly one hundred people who prepared the Gaither Report guaranteed that it would in one way or another have a major impact. "It was like looking into the abyss and seeing Hell at the bottom," former defense secretary Robert Lovett is reported to have said on reading the report.[11]

Some of the report was useful. It stressed the need for a survivable nuclear deterrent, rightly citing the vulnerability of American strategic bombers and recommending the dispersal of the tightly bunched force. Less reasonably, it urged a program of building fallout shelters on an enormous scale. The twenty-nine-page document bristled with somber warnings, many of them wildly exaggerated: The Soviets had enough fissionable material for at least 1,500 nuclear weapons in 4,500 long- and short-range jet bombers, and 250 to 300 long-range submarines; they had an extensive air defense system. By 1959, the Soviets would be able to attack a defenseless America with long-range missiles, an area in which the report pronounced them ahead. The Gaither Committee recommended spending nearly $45 billion in extra funds over the following five years in both weapons and civil defense. Some members of the panel, sobered by the implications of the exercise, became converts to arms control.

In his memoirs, Eisenhower said the report was useful, acting "as a gadfly on any in the Administration given to complacency."[12] He was far less tolerant at the time, however. The authors got short shrift, according to Goodpaster. "Hell, these people come in here and they tell me things I've known all along," he quotes Eisenhower as saying. "I'm not going to dance at the end of the string of . . . people who try to give me . . . scare stories . . ."[13] Paul Nitze tends to agree; he played a major role in the project, although he says he wasn't, as many believed, the principal author. "Ike was supercilious," he recalls. "He didn't say yes and didn't say no. Dulles poured cold water on the report."[14]

Eisenhower was judged by some (including Goodpaster and Keeny) to be uncomfortable with crash programs. As a former military commander, he seems to have worried that the act of preparing for war, if carried very far, makes avoidance of war—of keeping under control the preparation—very difficult. He rejected the proposal for fallout shelters. "There was no defense," he noted, "except retaliation." Thus, fallout shelters "rank rather low in the list of priorities." And, "I can't understand the United States being quite as panicky . . ."[15]

He also said no to a crash program for nuclear weapons.* His instructions to the committee had been to recommend a course of action in the event of a nuclear war. Now, Eisenhower said, he realized he had asked the wrong question. "You can't have this kind of war," he told members. "There just aren't enough bulldozers to scrape the bodies off the streets."[16]

Eisenhower was seen by critics to have been slowed down by a major heart attack he had two months after the Geneva summit. Also, thanks to the Twenty-second Amendment, he had become the first President in American history to confront a legal requirement to relinquish the White House after his second term. With their mighty adversary an impending "lame duck" and possibly not what he was, Democrats scented opportunity. Chance had given them their issue—complacency—and chance would inflate it. Although wholly spurious, the issue acquired a life of its own and

*He did agree to a small increase in funding for missile programs.

helped the Democrats recapture the White House in 1960. American intelligence was an unwitting accomplice.

Intelligence collection techniques at the time were hardly primitive but don't bear comparison with the array of devices, as proficient as they are intrusive, by which various agencies monitor the Soviet Union today. Aerial reconnaissance of Russia had hardly begun when Eisenhower was beset by the missile crisis. The early U-2 flights were sporadic, their evidence inconclusive. Washington was getting some good intelligence by then, in part because Soviet communications were primitive and easy to "read." But this kind of intelligence wasn't of much help in judging whether certain facilities were being used to launch missiles or for other purposes. Anything that looked suspicious—a grain silo, a medieval tower—was judged a launch facility, often on the flimsiest evidence.

Actually, the intelligence was good enough to show a comfortable American lead in nuclear weapons. But analysts and various key officials were stressing not what the other side had currently deployed, but what it would be able to deploy in the near and middle run given the apparent scale of its production and development programs. And American intelligence had very little purchase on these. The practice of drawing up agreed interagency estimates of the threat was barely under way, and air force intelligence continued to dominate assessments of Soviet strategic potential. (Other intelligence agencies were a good deal more realistic.) The missile gap, like the bomber gap, was based on crude projections; the maximum number of units that the Soviets might conceivably be able to crank out within the factory space presumably available for the purpose would become a critical number.

Estimating was—still is—a highly inexact craft. An agreed NIE (National Intelligence Estimate) provides just a piece of a large puzzle. For example, just after Britain, France, and Israel invaded Egypt in November 1956, creating the Suez crisis, Khrushchev began to rattle his rockets and the British asked the CIA for an estimate of the threat to them from Soviet missiles. The two experts who were assigned to respond felt unable to do so—certainly not categorically. One of them was Howard Stoertz, a former member of the CIA's National Estimates staff. They knew the Soviets had developed medium-range missiles but didn't then know whether these were deployed and, if so, if they were within range of Paris and London.

Quite wrongly, American intelligence continued to identify the United States as the main target of the Soviet weapons, when in fact it was Europe. Nearly all of the bombers and missile systems then being built by the Soviets were of medium or intermediate range. Their two long-range bomber types—Bisons and Bears—were unsuited to intercontinental missions. The Bisons lacked the range for two-way missions against North America, and the Bears were overly vulnerable to air defense. The first Soviet ICBM, the SS-6, was a good launcher of *Sputniks* into space but far too primitive, hence unreliable, for military purposes.[17] Also, the Soviets gave first priority to destroying American nuclear weapons being deployed within easy reach of their European borders. "We were always underestimating their missiles and bombers that could hit Europe, and overestimating the longer range stuff," says Stoertz, who drafted the CIA's estimates of Soviet strategic forces.[18] In his memoirs, Khrushchev said, "What you have to remember is that when I faced the problem of disarmament, we lagged significantly behind the U.S. in both warheads and missiles, and the U.S. was out of range for our bombers. We could blast into dust America's allies in Europe and Asia, but America itself . . . was beyond our reach."[19]

Intelligence collection is a heavily veiled activity, but its product is leaked prodigiously. Often the leaks are aimed at pinning down inflated estimates of Soviet military strength (or in recent years, charges of Soviet cheating on arms control agreements). The evidence may be inconclusive or even point in another direction. Stories built around such disclosures tend to confuse and polarize discussion, and they often assist efforts in Moscow to exaggerate Soviet strength and hence conceal weaknesses. Khrushchev tirelessly inflated Soviet power. "We now have all the rockets we need," he liked to say. And he would compare Soviet missile production to "sausages coming out of a machine."[20]

According to the NIE for 1957, the Soviets would deploy 500 ICBMs by the end of 1960, 1,000 by the middle of 1961. These sobering numbers were promptly leaked. A leaked report on the American position showed a meager thirty ICBMs in 1960, seventy in 1961.[21] The seemingly huge gap aroused the darkest forebodings. "At the Pentagon, they shudder when they speak of the Gap, which means the years 1960, 1961, 1962 and 1963," wrote Joseph and Stewart Alsop in their column.[22]

Eisenhower was more than just skeptical; never for a moment was he persuaded of a missile gap. His years in Washington before the war, including the stint as the army's chief lobbyist on Capitol Hill, and his bigger jobs during and after the war had left him wise in the ways of bureaucracy and suspicious of intelligence estimates, especially those that seemed to suit the interests of one of the services, in this case the air force. In the Oval Office, Eisenhower railed against the "sanctimonious, hypocritical bastards" pushing the missile gap. "God help the nation when it has a President who doesn't know as much about the military as I do," he would say.[23]

Gradually, the intelligence began to support Eisenhower. U-2 flights were not turning up signs of any Soviet launching sites other than testing centers.[24] And some CIA analysts reckoned that the Soviet ICBM program was still in its larval stage. Although the case against the gap was there to be made, it wasn't made. The CIA began to hedge, but most of the other key players (aside from the army and navy) clung to the missile gap. Far easier to be a hider than a finder was a fashionable admonition. Hundreds of ICBMs might lie concealed beneath the arctic tundra.

Most of the witnesses who appeared before Lyndon Johnson's Preparedness Subcommittee argued the case for a missile gap. But the most persistent and febrile of the missile gap's loftier partisans was presidential candidate Stuart Symington. He warned a closed congressional hearing that the Soviet Union would have 3,000 ICBMs by the end of 1961, a number three times higher than the air force estimate.[25] And he went to the Oval Office to tell Eisenhower he was being too complacent.[26] Symington then warned Allen Dulles that the Soviet Union was conducting more ICBM tests than the CIA was actually reporting. His own agency was lying to him, Dulles was told. Ironically, most CIA analysts were fearful that their estimates were too high, and here was Symington accusing them of rigging an outrageously low figure. Goodpaster recalls being dispatched by Eisenhower to meet with Allen Dulles and Symington, who, he says, accused the intelligence people of covering up the truth and caving in to White House pressure. The CIA, Goodpaster added, wasn't much help because it didn't want to take the heat.[27]

The truth was that America's long lead in bombers was being matched in missiles. Three ICBMs were being developed: the Atlas and Titan liquid-fueled systems and the Minuteman, a solid-fueled missile which was far more advanced than anything in Soviet labs. Moreover, three American midrange systems were under way: the Thor and Jupiter land-based missiles, which were intended for deployment in Europe, plus Polaris, a solid-fueled system designed for the launch tubes of Polaris nuclear submarines. Polaris (like Minuteman) was a state-of-the-art weapon, whereas Thor and Jupiter were of the slow-reacting, less reliable liquid-fueled type. None of America's four liquid-fueled missiles was actually much good; at best, they were somewhat less bad—a bit less unreliable—than their Soviet counterparts. Eisenhower regarded the Thors and Jupiters as little better than junk. And while he was against deploying one long-range missile more than some absolute minimum number needed to deter Moscow, he was attracted to the Minuteman and Polaris systems. Minuteman would be deployed in underground silos, Polaris in submarines, which meant that each had the great advantage of being invulnerable. Because it wouldn't invite attack, such a weapon would have a so-called stabilizing effect. Curiously, the skewed estimates of a missile gap in Russia's favor normally didn't take into account these survivable American missiles that lay just ahead.

America's strategic arsenal nearly tripled during Eisenhower's second term. Most of the nuclear weapons were still gravity bombs, not missile warheads, and the American inventory contained not just a great many more bombers but vastly better ones. The truth about the missile gap was not to emerge on Eisenhower's watch. The CIA's first reconnaissance satellite, *Discoverer,* became available in the summer of 1960, but not for several months did it provide the broad coverage which revealed the infamous gap as myth and the American lead in nuclear weapons as overwhelming.

Their weapons gave Washington and Moscow a reason to talk to each other about ambiguous or provocative events. But communication with Moscow was erratic and rarely useful or even revealing. Today a hot-line agreement links the leaders by Teletype. At other more operational levels, however, reliable communication is still inhibited by the habit of deep mistrust, an eight-hour time difference between the capitals, and a fixed Soviet tendency to shut down the government on weekends and in August. Most serious has been the persistent inability of either side to see a tense, potentially dangerous situation from the other's point of view—to put itself, if only for caution's sake, in the other's shoes.

With the emergence of Khrushchev as absolute boss, there was more contact. A lively correspondence between him and Eisenhower began after the Geneva summit. Dulles was uncomfortable with the correspondence, feeling that Eisenhower tended to say more than he should. At State, Dulles restricted access to this "channel" to just one or two people, and in the White House only Goodpaster was involved. Khrushchev's natural style— ebullient, gregarious—created another less rarefied but perhaps more interesting channel; he began talking to Charles Bohlen, the American ambassador, and later to Llewellyn Thompson, who succeeded Bohlen in 1957. Both acquired access to Khrushchev that American ambassadors never had before or have had since with a Soviet party boss. Each was an experienced and widely respected Soviet specialist; each spoke fluent Russian. The improbable figure they dealt with was as tough and ruthless as he had to be. Khrushchev combined the soul of an achiever with an instinct for moderation, qualities that were offset by a reckless and impulsive streak that led to his eventual downfall. Bohlen described him as "coarse and vulgar . . . [He] enjoyed lying to make a story better or to score a point . . . On foreign affairs, [he] was a complete pragmatist, basing his decisions on the two cardinal rules of Soviet diplomacy—hold on to the Soviet system and avoid war."[28] For Macmillan, he was "a curious study . . . ruthless, but sentimental . . . a kind of mixture between Peter the Great and Lord Beaverbrook."[29] Eisenhower, says Goodpaster, "saw Khrushchev as quickminded, brilliant and earthy." (In high-level meetings, Khrushchev's language was always cleaned up by his interpreter.)[30]

Khrushchev struck two basic attitudes, which were very different and hard to reconcile. He would threaten and rattle his rockets, but his commitment to what he called "peaceful coexistence" and even to agreements on arms control was considered genuine by those who, like Bohlen and Thompson, understood him. It was the blustery threats, of course, that got the attention. At a Polish Embassy reception in Moscow in November 1956, Khrushchev, having had quite a lot to drink, issued his famous "we will bury you" threat to NATO ambassadors; it had a hollow ring for those who heard him, and most didn't take it seriously. The more genuine, or at least more realistic, Khrushchevian view of relations with the West emerged at the Twentieth Party Congress earlier that year when he broke with doctrine by announcing that war was no longer to be considered "fatalistically inevitable." Soviet nuclear weapons, he seemed to be saying, would head off the otherwise inevitable capitalist onslaught.[31] Although neither understood the other for a time (if ever), Khrushchev and Eisenhower felt much the same way about nuclear weapons and the need to control them, according to Goodpaster.

Still, it was the other Khrushchev who appeared to rock Eisenhower's second term with a procession of crises and minicrises. In less than three months in the latter part of 1958, he tested Eisenhower twice and in places where America's position was at best awkward. First came yet another crisis in the Formosa Strait, an episode in which Eisenhower saw Khrushchev's hand.

Chiang Kai-shek, according to Eisenhower, "helped complicate the problem. Ignoring our military advice, he had for many months been adding personnel to the Quemoy and Matsu garrisons, moving them forward, nearer the mainland."[32]* A third of Chiang's ground forces—100,000 troops—were deployed on the islands in August 1958, when the Chinese Communists abruptly began to shell them. The Communists were constructing new air bases and reinforcing garrisons near the islands. Eisenhower ordered American forces in the area to respond to a major assault

---

*After the first crisis over Quemoy and Matsu, Admiral Radford and a State Department official went to Taiwan, ostensibly to urge Chiang Kai-shek to evacuate them. Leon Sigal, in his *Fighting to a Finish*, cites Joseph Alsop as reporting that the American emissaries actually encouraged Chiang to continue building up the island garrison.

there with conventional arms, but he also told them to be ready to use atomic weapons, if necessary.[33]

The Chinese blockaded the islands, continued to bomb them heavily, and announced an imminent landing on Quemoy and the intention to liberate Taiwan.[34] Eisenhower added a fourth aircraft carrier to the Seventh Fleet, which was on station under his orders to escort Chiang's resupply vessels to the islands. He saw to it that these moves were leaked to the press and thus, as he said in his memoirs, "would not escape the notice of the Communists." On September 7, 1958, the first convoy was escorted from Taiwan to Quemoy.

The administration had concluded that only nuclear weapons could defeat an invasion of the islands. As before, the notion of using them to defend Quemoy and Matsu struck most concerned citizens, not to mention the world, as wholly irrational. Dulles nonetheless pressed for authority to use tactical atomic bombs against Chinese forces. Curiously, there then occurred a replay of the initiative taken in 1955 to disabuse him of the notion that using them against military targets adjacent to the islands need not cause large numbers of civilian deaths. C. Gerard Smith, who was close to Dulles and serving as director of the Policy Planning Staff in State, recalls him being "tempted by an activist group in the Pentagon that wanted to take out the artillery batteries at Amoy that were shelling the islands." Smith called in some weapons specialists from the Pentagon and asked them to estimate the civilian casualties any such limited nuclear strike would produce. "They estimated, I think, 186,000 civilian casualties," Smith says. "I never heard another word about it after that."[35]

It didn't matter, because Eisenhower, as before, never was prepared to approve even the limited strike, if only because of the risk of Soviet over-reaction. Khrushchev, in fact, promised to support China with nuclear weapons if America used them.[36] Still, Eisenhower was confident that the steps he had taken would deter the Communist bloc. "There is not going to be any appeasement," he said. And, "I believe there is not going to be any war."[37]

Both sides drew back. On September 6, Chou En-lai announced a four-day cease-fire and a resumption of ambassadorial talks on the situation. On September 30, Dulles told a press conference that the U.S. had "no legal commitment to defend Quemoy and Matsu" and that "if a . . . ceasefire could be arranged, it would be foolish to keep these large forces on these islands."[38] Another cease-fire was announced by the Communists in October, and they also said they would attack Chiang's convoys only on odd days of the month and allow them to resupply the islands on even-numbered days. "I wondered if we were in a Gilbert and Sullivan war," said Eisenhower.[39] The Chinese Communists gradually lost interest in the offshore islands.

Cuba aside, Khrushchev took his most reckless gambles in Berlin, because the pressure on him there was most acute. By September 1958, two million East Germans had gone; many thousands left each month and took refuge in West Berlin, which Khrushchev himself described as "a bone in his throat." West Berlin's phoenixlike revival and prosperity stood in brilliant contrast to the dreariness all around. East Germany, said Khrushchev, should have its capital free of "this state within a state."[40] He and others in the Kremlin probably worried most about the rearming of West Germany and the worst case—German nuclear weapons down the road.

On November 10, Khrushchev launched a protracted Berlin crisis with an ultimatum in the form of diplomatic notes in which he accused the three Western powers and West Germany of unlawfully occupying West Berlin and abusing their occupation rights. The postwar agreements on Germany were declared null and void and, with them, the right of Britain, France, and the United States to maintain troops in Berlin. The text of the note also seemed to say that if the Western powers didn't agree within six months to convert Berlin into a demilitarized city, Moscow would transfer to the East German government full sovereignty "on land, on water, and in the air."[41] Western access to Berlin across East German territory would thus be controlled by the East Germans instead of the Soviets.

Eisenhower never doubted that Khrushchev was bluffing. The Joint Chiefs wanted to use force—a full division—against any Soviet move to block the autobahn connecting West Germany to Berlin. Eisenhower and Dulles were opposed. Eisenhower observed that "one division was far too weak to fight its way through to Berlin and far more than necessary to be a mere 'show of force' or evidence of determination." He wanted to avoid forcing the Soviets into a corner—of having "to put up or shut up." A roadblock, he decided, could be dealt with by a probe with a much smaller unit.[42] In that event, Washington wanted advance approval from London and Paris to make a limited show of force on the autobahn. But the other capitals, while not disagreeing with the plan, insisted on withholding approval until the Soviets made a move.

In mid-November, Soviet troops held up three U.S. Army trucks outside Berlin for eight and a half hours. Khrushchev then delivered another formal note which warned: "Only madmen can go to the length of unleashing another world war over the preservation of privileges of occupiers in West Berlin."[43]

Eisenhower's position was difficult. Although Khrushchev was surely bluffing, his rashness had maneuvered the superpowers into a head-to-head confrontation. Berlin, he proclaimed, was a major source of tension and had to be stabilized by a more realistic arrangement. Was America ready to unleash thermonuclear war just to avoid de facto recognition of East Germany and keep inviolate Western access rights to a city located 110 miles from the Western frontier? For the first time, Eisenhower did have to contemplate nuclear war. Suppose Khrushchev raised the stakes after his famous six-month deadline expired in May by brushing aside a limited American show of force. What then? Eisenhower was ready to break relations, create another airlift, and then let matters take their course. "In this gamble," he told advisers, "we are not going to be betting white chips, building up the pot gradually and fearfully. Khrushchev should know that when we decide to act, our whole stack will be in the pot."[44]

Khrushchev must have reckoned that because of U-2 flights Washington saw Soviet military strength as falling far short of his shrill claims for it. In March 1959, he told Macmillan, who was visiting Moscow, that the May deadline on Berlin "was in no sense an ultimatum."[45] Still, after the deadline passed he continued to bluff, telling Averell Harriman, former ambassador to the Soviet Union, in June that "your generals talk of maintaining your position in Berlin with force. That is bluff. If you send in tanks, they will burn and make no mistake about it. If you want war, you can have it, and remember it will be your war. Our rockets will fly automatically . . ." And his colleagues echoed like a chorus, "Automatically."[46]

Fortunately, Kremlin bluster and Soviet deeds had little in common. By late spring, Eisenhower judged that Khrushchev was backing away from a showdown. The retreat was subtly done and with no loss of face (which suited Eisenhower), but it was a retreat. Khrushchev seemed ready even for serious bargaining in Geneva on a test ban treaty. Whether in spite of his Berlin gambit, or because of it, he now seemed bent on easing the situation. The question was how. Khrushchev clearly wanted a summit meeting; he had already invited Eisenhower to Moscow, promising him "heartfelt hospitality."[47] De Gaulle and West German Chancellor Konrad Adenauer were opposed to having a negotiation on so fundamental an issue as Berlin carried on over their heads. Eisenhower tended to feel the same way. Any such meeting, he felt, would contribute nothing unless preceded by serious progress at the ministerial level. He argued about it with Macmillan, who was looking ahead to fall elections and said he could not take his people into war without "trying the summit first."[48]

In July, Eisenhower made a move. He told Undersecretary of State Robert Murphy to inform a senior Soviet visitor named Frol Kozlov that a summit meeting was acceptable provided the foreign ministers, meeting in Geneva, made progress. At this point, fortune whimsically intervened.

Either Eisenhower didn't make himself clear or Murphy misunderstood, because in talking with Kozlov he didn't make the link. Khrushchev suddenly found himself invited to Washington—unconditionally. "I couldn't believe my eyes," he wrote. "We had no reason to expect such an invitation—not then, or ever for that matter."[49]

Eisenhower was no less surprised to discover that Khrushchev was coming. "To say that this news disturbed me is an understatement," he said.[50] The same was true of de Gaulle and Adenauer, who, Eisenhower noted, received the news "with consternation."[51] He abruptly decided to visit Bonn, Paris, and London to reassure his peers that neither concessions on Berlin nor any other separate deal would be made.

At home, the reaction was predictably polarized, with many people and their congressmen praising what they mistakenly saw as an Eisenhower initiative to break the stalemate and others horrified that the Butcher of Budapest was on his way to America. William F. Buckley, Jr., captured the spirit of the right by proposing to fill the Hudson with red dye to make it a "river of blood." The visit, he thought, "profanes the nation."[52]

Khrushchev's American odyssey consumed newsprint by the ton, and gave those who dealt with him at close range endless anecdotes on which to dine out. But on Berlin—the issue at hand—he and Eisenhower were not making progress. On a Sunday in late September, with time running out, they met at Camp David with their advisers, still far apart. The presence of Soviet Foreign Minister Andrei Gromyko may have cramped Khrushchev's style. Just before lunch, he and Eisenhower took a walk, accompanied only by Khrushchev's interpreter, Oleg Troyanovski. The breakthrough came abruptly. Khrushchev agreed to remove his ultimatum, and Eisenhower said he would recommend a Big Four summit conference and pay a visit himself to the Soviet Union. But after lunch, Khrushchev said he would not want his concession to appear in the joint communiqué. Eisenhower exploded, saying "this ends the whole affair. I will neither go to a summit nor to Russia."[53] Khrushchev then explained that he couldn't put out such a statement without first running it past his colleagues in Moscow. He asked Eisenhower to hold the communiqué until Tuesday morning. Eisenhower agreed. He and those around him guessed that Khrushchev had exceeded his brief. The incident showed Khrushchev's authority to be less than his studied flamboyance suggested.

For a time the air was filled with talk of the spirit of Camp David, which, it seemed, had pulled the world away from the brink. In fact, the Berlin problem was unresolved. Khrushchev had agreed to take it off the boil, but temporarily.

In maneuvering American support behind their interests, or trying to, Britain and France adopted divergent strategies. The British worked at sustaining their role as America's privileged ally, whereas the French, by and large, kept their distance and relied on the traditional diplomatic method. They reckoned that the special relationship Britain had built with the other and greater "Anglo-Saxon" power was actually a junior partnership and neither available to them nor desirable. An aversion to being *demandeur* runs deep in France. Best to drink from one's own glass while touching glasses all around, de Gaulle used to say. He agreed with Lord Palmerston, the nineteenth-century British statesman, that a nation doesn't have friends, only interests. Relations between the three countries were for years largely shaped by nuclear issues—by the determination in London and Paris to deploy nuclear weapons of their own, as distinct from relying entirely on America's. But each wanted American help; without it, the path to a nuclear deterrent would be longer, much more costly, and laden with uncertainty.

"Schizophrenic" best describes Washington's attitude toward assisting the British and French programs. The Eisenhower administration, like Truman's, tended to keep both at arm's length, even though Eisenhower himself fully understood and sympathized with Britain's interests. In 1950, the British began working on their own gaseous diffusion plant but got no help even though the technology had originated with them. The only Briton to gain access to the American plant at Oak Ridge in this period was Lord Portal, Marshal of the Royal Air Force. He was not shown much and later could report little except that he had needed a bicycle to travel from one end of the plant to the other.[54] In 1952, the British asked Washington if they could test a bomb at one of the American test sites in the Pacific. The Americans were standoffish and, in fact, tried to discourage the British, who then got permission from Australia to test their first atom bomb at Monte Bello Island; the date was October 3, 1952.

American support for France's program at this time was precluded, if only because their facilities were thought to be deeply penetrated by the Communist party. In 1956, Washington cut the price of enriched uranium sold abroad for industrial use, mainly to discourage France from building a plant for the production of fissile materials. Not long afterward, the problem of French security procedures had disappeared, and these were blessed by America's CIA and AEC.[55]

Oddly, the Suez crisis, which estranged London and Paris from Washington as nothing else before or since in the modern era, gave a mighty boost to the predilections of both for nuclear weapons. Eisenhower and Macmillan staged a post-Suez reconciliation in March 1957; this meeting and further conversations led to an agreement on exchanging nuclear technology and weapons design. Dulles knew that nothing less would persuade Macmillan to accept the restrictions of a test ban agreement that Eisenhower badly wanted. He went to the mat with Lewis Strauss, who fought the proposed new arrangement, and Eisenhower ruled in its favor; he had always wanted to restore the wartime nuclear cooperation promoted by Roosevelt and Churchill. In approving the agreement, Congress left little doubt that the sole beneficiary of the amended law would be Britain.

Suez divided Britain and forced Anthony Eden from office. But because Washington was judged to have betrayed its oldest allies, the affair united France, and strengthened the determination of its people to manage their own affairs. In May, the government put forward a new defense policy and pronounced the need for a "strategic reprisal weapon," meaning a nuclear weapon capable of striking the territory of a potential aggressor.[56]

Politically, France's bomb dates in a sense to a left-of-center icon: Pierre Mendès-France. As Prime Minister in 1955, Mendès tried but failed to promote world support for a test ban. He then acquiesced in a French program, giving two reasons: "One is nothing without the bomb in international negotiations . . . [the bomb] would be the main difference between France and Germany."[57] The Mendès-France government fell a few weeks later, and for a time the program's fortunes rose and fell as the revolving door of France's Fourth Republic briskly ushered successive governments in and out. But Suez and the prospect of a British bomb—an Anglo-American stew in French eyes—anchored the French program.

Anglo-Saxon exclusivity also provoked some remarkably foolish French overreaction. Early in 1958, Defense Minister Jacques Chaban-Delmas, a man for all seasons who still flourishes in French political life, was authorized to get some European backing for the program. His German opposite number, Franz Josef Strauss, then as now the political boss of Bavaria, was all too eager to play this game. The Italians, too, got involved, but less importantly. In February, Strauss accompanied Chaban-Delmas on a visit to the French nuclear site in the Sahara. There they agreed explicitly that German help would be paid for with technology covering nuclear warheads and delivery vehicles, along with conventional arms.[58] The so-called Strauss–Chaban-Delmas agreements were kept secret from other ministers in both governments and remained so for years to come.

The handful of French diplomats who did know of the initiative were appalled, aware of how strongly other powers—America, Russia, and Britain—would oppose any scheme that might create a German appetite for nuclear weapons. In 1954, West Germany formally disavowed the right to possess or develop them. In April, however, Strauss was interviewed by Richard Crossman, a prominent figure in Britain's Labour party, and said, "I can guarantee there will be no German nuclear weapons for three, four or even five years. But after that, if other nations—particularly the French—make their own H-bomb, Germany may well be sucked in, too."59*

Soviet space and rocket exploits caused some huddling together of NATO governments and a feeling among Europeans that the United States should share some of the responsibility for nuclear deterrence. Soviet midrange ballistic missile systems (MRBMs) were targeted against European cities, and Washington could hardly ignore the European pressure for involvement. By the end of 1957, Eisenhower and Dulles concluded that helping only the British wasn't enough. They offered to stockpile nuclear weapons in Europe under a "double-veto" system designed to guarantee continued American custody. This arrangement was supposed to assure continental allies that they had no need for nuclear weapons of their own. For those among them who agreed to accept launch sites on their territory, Washington also offered Thor and Jupiter missiles—again with the warheads remaining under American control. As a sweetener, Eisenhower proposed giving interested allies the data needed to build a nuclear submarine propulsion system—that is, if Congress concurred (a considerable if). Britain was in a special position, having already been assured of the submarine technology and having also agreed—as part of the deal—to accept Thor missiles. The Italians and Turks decided to take the missiles, but none of the other allies wanted these vulnerable, slow-reacting weapons, since they could invite a Soviet attack.

In Washington, the real issue was whether to help France become the world's fourth nuclear power; a rugged debate developed within the administration. John McCone, a passionate Francophile who had replaced Lewis Strauss as AEC chairman, wanted to sell enriched uranium to France. Major agencies, including State, were split. Since France was sure to have nuclear weapons one day, the argument was why not help and thereby spare her part of the huge investment in time and resources the task would require; in return, France would presumably play a stronger role in NATO and become more supportive of American policy. Other advocates, mainly

*Strauss later observed that Dulles himself told Adenauer that his country's action followed the standard legal phrase—*clausula rebus sic stantibus*—indicating that an agreement is in force only so long as the conditions under which it was made still apply.

in Defense, wanted to offset the heavy pressure on America's balance of payments arising from its NATO commitments.

Resistance was strong. America's duty, said some officials, was to discourage the spread of nuclear weapons, not help to spread them about—even to a close ally. Admittedly, the British horse was out of the barn but all the more reason to draw the line before the next aspirant.

Even more persuasive to many was the "German argument." "Never do for France what you are unwilling to do eventually for Germany," said Jean Monnet, the architect of the European Community, to numerous American officials (in successive administrations) who sought his sensible advice. France's political instability also seemed to argue against accelerating her entry into the nuclear fold.

Félix Gaillard, the last of the Fourth Republic's prime ministers, forced the issue by seeking approval to buy the guidance system for the Polaris missile system, the most tempting of America's new weapons. The United States was then developing a fleet of more than forty nuclear submarines, which, while submerged, would be capable of launching Polaris missiles with a range of more than 1,500 miles. In the end, Washington said no to Gaillard. His government, like its predecessors, was weak and no match for the furies let loose by the struggle for Algeria. These were about to extinguish the Fourth Republic and restore France's loftiest eminence, Charles de Gaulle.

De Gaulle's return to the helm meant that relations between Washington, London, and Paris would be directed by three worldly men and wartime confederates. As chief custodians of the alliance, they made an auspicious troika. Although Macmillan had not been nearly as grand a figure as the other two, they knew him to be shrewd and very capable; in fact, he was far more astute than Eden, his predecessor, and became Britain's ablest postwar Prime Minister before Margaret Thatcher.* He knew de Gaulle and Eisenhower very well—better even than either knew the other. But Macmillan uncharacteristically chose to believe what he wanted to believe about de Gaulle's intentions, a lapse for which he later paid dearly.[60]

Eisenhower had always found de Gaulle more sinned against than sinning during the war. Also, he was better able than most to see things from the French point of view. "In fairness to de Gaulle," he once told General Lauris Norstad, "we would react very much as [he] does if the shoe were on the other foot."[61] Most important, Eisenhower considered de Gaulle the strength of France.

---

*An American who tried to explain to Ike's staff the difference between Macmillan and Eden—two lookalike Britons—said, "Eden is the sheep striving to look like a man, Macmillan the man affecting to look like a sheep" (*The Economist*, January 3, 1987).

Eisenhower and Dulles knew that de Gaulle would press French claims and interests with greater force than any predecessor, and, in general, be a more persistent and demanding interlocutor. Just how much more demanding and difficult they would soon discover. But they may also have reckoned that ridding France of the Algerian incubus would keep him more or less fully occupied for some time.

If so, they were wrong. For de Gaulle, settling the Algerian issue would be a squalid prelude to a far more exalted task: ridding France of Anglo-American domination and molding the states of Western Europe into a French-led coalition *(un rassemblement des vieux pays autour de moi)*. He was uncomfortable as a member of the alliance system. Whatever its obvious advantages to France—and these he always relied on—he saw it as robbing individual members of their freedom of maneuver, if not their sovereignty itself. He rightly saw the system as dominated by America, with support from its special ally, Britain. De Gaulle's own preference was a restoration of a concert of powers, the system he understood better than any contemporary. Although a sworn enemy of what he called "bloc politics," de Gaulle began in September 1958 by proposing an inner Western leadership bloc of America, Britain, and France. It was not a notion that he himself took very seriously, since he knew in advance that Washington could not and would not give him a veto over the use of nuclear weapons anywhere in the world; this was a central and nonnegotiable feature of his proposal. None of it was in fact negotiable. But the predictable rejection of a so-called tri-directorate on purely French terms was used by de Gaulle to vindicate a policy aimed at blocking Anglo-American pursuits and freeing France's hands.

It was France's relative weakness vis-à-vis Germany that tugged hardest at de Gaulle's instinct. Like Mendès-France, de Gaulle saw nuclear weapons as becoming the eternal difference between France and Germany—as the means of securing French supremacy in Western Europe. In early September, he instructed a delighted Foreign Ministry to notify the West Germans—and Strauss personally—that France considered the so-called Strauss–Chaban-Delmas agreements to be null and void. Strauss sought unsuccessfully to see de Gaulle and appeal the decision. De Gaulle later told Adenauer that West Germany must never try to acquire atomic weapons.[62]

Eisenhower and Dulles wearied quickly of de Gaulle's insistence on playing a weak hand as if it were trump heavy. His tri-directorate initiative was especially vexing. At a NATO meeting in Paris in December, Dulles got a message from Eisenhower which mirrored their shared irritation. "It does seem that our friend should cease insisting upon attempting to control the whole world—of course, with partners—even before he had gotten France itself into good order."[63]

Although they had much the same view of de Gaulle, Eisenhower and Dulles didn't quite see eye to eye on whether to hasten his nuclear venture. Since de Gaulle would clearly acquire the bomb, Eisenhower saw no good reason not to help. "It seemed silly to him to make them waste money re-inventing the wheel," says Robert Bowie. Nor did Eisenhower have the sensitivity to the proliferation issue that was to give his successors greater pause. But on the issue of helping France, as on numerous others, his passivity—his disinclination to pit himself and his office against a political current—kept him from doing much about it, aside from talking to aides. For Dulles, the issue was French performance and reliability. De Gaulle would perhaps stabilize France but was likely to play a lone hand. The two met three times before Dulles died in May 1959. They had in common fifty or more years of experience in world politics, but otherwise they contrasted sharply. De Gaulle saw the world as an ensemble of nations; Dulles saw it as a system of two alliances, the one designed to check the malign purposes of the other.[64]

De Gaulle didn't tell his government to avoid seeking aid from America (or Britain). But he made clear that he would never pay a political price for any such help, and he told his people that while they were free to seek assistance, they were unlikely to succeed.[65] Perhaps because of Eisenhower's views, Dulles did little overtly to discourage aid to France; he knew he didn't have to. The strong protectionist bias of Congress's Joint Committee on Atomic Energy—the stiff political current which deterred Eisenhower—would do that for him.

In July 1958, Dulles offered France a submarine propulsion system. He worried that even this nonmilitary transfer might be vetoed by the Joint Committee. In any case, de Gaulle himself assured the veto by announcing in March 1959 that France's Mediterranean fleet was being withdrawn from NATO. It was both a purely symbolic and misleading gesture, as the fleet was French-controlled and in time of peace could be used as France saw fit. De Gaulle seemed to be saying that the fleet wouldn't be available to NATO in time of war—the only time it would be called on. The submarine deal thereupon collapsed. Under the amended atomic energy law, the President can provide assistance of this kind only by certifying that it would promote "the common defense and security." Whether the deal would have been approved but for de Gaulle's gesture was never clear. The Joint Committee took its guidance from Admiral Hyman Rickover, "father" of the nuclear submarine.* He and the committee took a highly protective view of submarine technology, which they knew was far ahead of the Soviet Union's.

A year later, in April 1960, de Gaulle was in Washington on a state visit, and Eisenhower told him that the next American Polaris submarine would be christened the *Lafayette*. And he presented his guest with a thirty-inch scale model of the boat. It had a cutaway cross section, showing the missile storage tubes, plus numerous interior features of the sub-marine.[66] On that improbable note, the Eisenhower-de Gaulle part of the nuclear-sharing saga ended. The next and far more episodic phase lay not far ahead. But as John F. Kennedy was to discover, de Gaulle was less interested in the nuclear aid France was being denied than in the aid being given to Britain.

It recently came to light that the first nuclear sharing, remarkably enough, was done by none other than France herself. Well before the U.S. said no to French requests for help and the Soviet Union backed off its agreement to help China, France had begun to give Israel the means of acquiring nuclear weapons. In 1955, a time when it was unclear that any French government would be politically up to building a nuclear bomb, David Ben-Gurion, Israel's "old lion," decided that the country he had helped bring into being must possess nuclear weapons in order to be sure of surviving. France was embroiled with Algeria's Arabs, who were sup-ported by Gamal Abdel Nasser, Israel's enemy and the Levantine Beelze-bub in French eyes. Ben-Gurion dispatched Shimon Peres to Paris as his emissary. France's nuclear program was much smaller then than Britain's and, of course, minuscule compared to America's. Still, it was big enough for Ben-Gurion's purpose. Soon after arriving, Peres was drawing support from senior political figures, well-placed military officers, and scientists working inside the Commissariat à l'Energie Atomique (CEA).[67]†

---

*So strong was Rickover's influence on Capitol Hill that when as captain he was passed over for promotion, his congressional partisans told the White House not to send up any more promotion lists until his name was included.

†The information on the French-Israeli connection was obtained primarily from conversation with a former French defense ministry official along with a book he and others regard as authen-tic: *Les Deux Bombes*, by Pierre Pean. I have also drawn on a lengthy article in the *Sunday Times* (London) for October 5, 1986. The article is based on interviews in London with Mordechai Vanunu, an Israeli nuclear technician who worked for nearly ten years within his country's nuclear weapons program. Vanunu was spirited out of Europe by Israeli intelligence and is now in prison.

The bond was strengthened by the Suez affair, which was orchestrated on the French side by Abel Thomas, an *éminence grise* and cabinet director to Maurice Bourgès-Maunoury, who served as defense minister and then Prime Minister. (Abel Thomas also had much to do with arranging the Strauss–Chaban-Delmas agreements.) Thomas and Bourgès-Maunoury were among a tiny circle of key people who not only furthered Israel's nuclear program but helped give it military direction. Another was Guy Mollet, a Fourth Republic stalwart and one of its longest-serving prime ministers. Peres drew close to them all; actually, his operational base for a time was the Matignon, residence and headquarters of French prime ministers. It is hard to see how, in these circumstances, this shadowy activity could have been carried on in immaculate secrecy, yet it was. Even de Gaulle was kept in the dark at first; some of his own people—died-in-the-wool Gaullists—were reluctant to break the conspiracy of silence by telling him. When he did learn of the extent of French involvement with Israel, de Gaulle exploded. He ordered a winding down of the activity. He was ignored, and Israel continued to receive the militarily critical elements from the cabal in France. "It was a conspiracy to keep de Gaulle in the dark," says a former French defense official. "He was furious. France, after all, was introducing nuclear weapons and the means of delivering them into the Middle East."[68] In 1961, a French ground-to-ground missile system, the Jericho, was also made available to Israel, apparently without de Gaulle's knowledge.

The high commissioner of the CEA during this period, Professor Francis Perrin, "father" of the French bomb, has now publicly reminisced about how France signed the contract to build Israel's reactor, including a secret underground plant that produced weapons-grade plutonium from which bombs were made. It had to be kept secret from the Americans, he said.[69] And it was. In 1960, an American U-2 aircraft photographed the French-built facility, which the Israelis said was a textiles plant, an explanation they clung to for some time.

The plant is located in the Negev desert, about nine miles from the town of Dimona. It was built between 1957 and 1964, and the number of nuclear weapons produced to date is now said to be about one hundred.*

During the time in which de Gaulle, Eisenhower, and Macmillan coincided, nuclear proliferation was not the issue. Washington was still trying to deal with the hard fact of Soviet bombs—and indeed missiles—

*This is the estimate of American nuclear physicists who have seen the information provided to the *Sunday Times* by Mordechai Vanunu. They were convinced of its authenticity. Intelligence agencies had tended to estimate the size of Israel's inventory as somewhere between twenty to forty weapons.

while also finding the right balance in its relations with allies of roughly equal weight: Britain, France, and Germany. They in turn were sorting out their roles. Britain and France had lost their global vocation. Nuclear weapons, they thought, could perhaps be a makeweight. The Germans, who couldn't have them, were adjusting to their anomalous role of Europe's economic giant and political dwarf. The spread of nuclear weapons became a vital issue, but slowly.

The missile gap, helped by Berlin, pushed Eisenhower into approving a larger buildup of nuclear weapons than he thought necessary or wise, but not large enough to appease his critics. Changing course, he knew, would require some form of restraint agreed to jointly in Washington and Moscow. A ban on nuclear tests emerged as a logical step. Completion of such an agreement before leaving office eventually became Eisenhower's loftiest goal. Americans who worried about radioactive fallout from tests, especially the lethal element known as strontium 90, supported him. So did State Department professionals; they liked the idea on the merits and because it responded to the worldwide anxiety about fallout.

In the places that mattered most, however, a test ban went against the grain. The Joint Chiefs of Staff and Secretary of Defense wanted improved nuclear weapons, which meant testing them. Scientists in the AEC's laboratories, who were engaged in developing a so-called clean bomb, argued against a test ban. Mainly for these reasons, the Joint Committee on Atomic Energy was strongly opposed.

Center stage was being held by Lewis Strauss, Chairman of the AEC, Dulles, and Harold Stassen, Special Assistant to the President on Disarmament. Stassen was a seasoned politician with a high profile, but he didn't stand a chance against the combined influence of Strauss and Dulles. He had been governor of Minnesota and a candidate for the GOP presidential nomination in 1948. Even by Washington standards, he was a conspicuously ambitious man. The rivalry between Dulles and Stassen was at times intense. Stassen was capable and resourceful, and his goals, in general, were shared by Eisenhower and were genuinely felt. But the banked political fire within pushed him on occasion to make ill-advised, if not foolish, gestures. In 1956, he threw himself in the path of Richard Nixon's certain renomination for vice president, weakening his own position.

Much the most resourceful of the naysayers was Strauss, who had influenced a number of issues, including Truman's H-bomb decision, and was viscerally opposed to a test ban. Strauss manipulated the President in a way that Dulles couldn't; Eisenhower had a solid grasp of foreign policy questions but was far less familiar with Strauss's subjects; on these, he was usually content to go along with "the system." The system was really Strauss, who excluded his fellow members of the AEC from the most sensitive matters.

Strauss was a self-made notable, a type Eisenhower admired excessively. At sixteen, he was a traveling shoe salesman, but by twenty he had become Herbert Hoover's right-hand man in the World War I Food Relief Administration. From there, he went to Wall Street and became a partner in an investment bank (after marrying the boss's daughter) and a millionaire. During the war, he served as Forrestal's assistant and before leaving the navy became an admiral. Strauss was a passionate and, many said, paranoid anti-Communist. He was also a man of considerable ability and charm.

Eisenhower extended Strauss's writ by making him his special adviser on atomic energy. "Strauss played Ike like a violin," says Eugene Zuckert, who was then a member of the AEC. "He was a very silky character."[70] Strauss managed to steer Eisenhower away from the test ban temptation at various decision points. He was helped for a time by Dulles, who tended to see the idea of arms control with the Soviets as ill advised, if not fanciful. They were a potent twosome, with Strauss deploying expert argument against a ban and Dulles able to cite hostility to the idea in London, Paris, and Bonn.

Each of the allies favored lowering tension and moderating the arms race, but each privately expressed strong objections to a test ban. The British and French, concerned with developing their own nuclear weapons, were understandably hostile to the idea. In Bonn, Konrad Adenauer, the granitic old Chancellor, saw arms control as a threat to his immediate goals: rearming West Germany and embedding it in NATO. Arms control, he argued, should await Soviet willingness to settle political issues.

Eisenhower tended to stand aside, perhaps to avoid having to commit himself before he had to. The politics swirling around the issue were fierce and intimidating. And he was deeply reluctant to push a test ban, whatever its appeal, over the objections of major allies. Khrushchev, too, appears to have been blown this way and that by the test ban issue. Self-imposed restrictions on improving nuclear weapons seemed even more unnatural in the 1950s than now. And the Soviet leadership, which had a clear view of its manifold weaknesses vis-à-vis the U.S., must have been at least as hesitant as Washington to accept a test ban. In both Washington and Moscow, support for the idea was closely linked to the rhythm of testing programs. As one side completed a series, its willingness to stop would rise, while its adversary would turn away from the idea until it too had conducted its next scheduled round of tests.

In August 1955, the Soviets held a series of hydrogen bomb tests and immediately began advocating a test ban. They might, warned the Pentagon, have "perfected warheads for future ballistic missiles."[71] And Washington was stung by the success of Moscow's proposal in shielding the Soviet Union from the rising hue and cry about fallout. Two months after the presidential elections, Washington countered by proposing a negotiated test ban coupled with an internationally supervised halt in production of nuclear weapons. The Soviets counterproposed an "immediate and unconditional halt to tests, without any inspection."[72] Neither side's proposal was remotely acceptable to the other. They seemed to be tacitly conspiring to avoid constraining the weapons competition.

In May, Eisenhower authorized Stassen to take to the London disarmament talks a "talking paper" that offered a moratorium on testing in return for eventual limitations on weapons production. But Stassen's reach continued to exceed his grasp, and he made a monumental gaffe. Eisenhower had told him to clear the paper with the British and French before discussing it with the Soviets. Instead, he showed it to the chief Soviet negotiator, Valerian Zorin, before the British and French had even been informed. Both allied governments were furious. (Macmillan's letter to Eisenhower is still recalled by some involved Americans. Britain had just exploded its first hydrogen bomb.)

In June, Zorin announced that his government would shelve its preference for a total ban in favor of a two- or three-year moratorium on testing, with supervision by an international agency stationed at various monitoring posts throughout the world, including on Russian territory.[73]

Publicly, Eisenhower held that it was necessary to continue testing, but privately he asked Strauss why more bombs were needed. In June, he met with Strauss, Teller, and Lawrence; Teller said that halting development of a clean bomb would be "a crime against humanity." Without disagreeing, Eisenhower observed that the United States ought not to "be crucified on a cross of atoms, so to speak." He never had been persuaded by the case for a clean bomb, yet he yielded to the Teller-Lawrence arguments and instructed Dulles to tell a press conference that America would accept a moratorium only if the Soviets agreed to a future cutoff in weapons manufacture.[74]

An agreement with the Russians to ban testing would be a leap to unfamiliar and possibly treacherous ground. Eisenhower was not then ready for the leap. Although disdainful of the argument for more weapons and convinced of the need for agreement with the Russians, he was unwilling to trust them or to pit his vast prestige against the heavyweight opponents of a test ban. As he dithered, opportunity slipped by.

Still the test ban was a hardier plant than it seemed to be. The pressure to do something—to break the relentless weapons cycle—was increasing at home and abroad. Furthermore, the United States was taking most of the blame for the stalemate. Obviously, any military agreement with the Soviet Union couldn't rely on trust and would have to be verifiable, as well as being otherwise acceptable. Only the test ban seemed to meet these conditions. By the spring of 1958, Eisenhower began relying more on James Killian, his science adviser, than on Strauss. Killian and some other scientists, including Hans Bethe and I. I. Rabi, were making him keenly aware that American nuclear weapons were more advanced than the other side's; a test ban would lock in these advantages. Strauss's influence had at last begun to decline, and he was headed for the exit. The President's Science Advisory Committee (PSAC) and its staff of experts were a more effective lobby than Stassen had ever been, and their task was made much easier by a shift in Dulles's attitude toward the test ban.

By this time, Dulles had not just switched sides, he had become the most effective of the advocates because, like his department, he was alarmed by the pernicious effect of the fallout issue on America's world position. (He still regarded arms control itself as nonsense.) For years, Strauss and his allies had trivialized fallout, and the government thereby lost its credibility on the issue. Although the danger was probably far less serious than portrayed by the shriller antinuclear elements, it was a source of genuine concern among scientists who saw some risk of genetic damage. Eisenhower at one point told Undersecretary of State Christian Herter that if atmospheric testing didn't stop soon, the "Northern Hemisphere might become uninhabitable."[75]

As always, the pivotal issue was verification. In April 1958, Hans Bethe reported to the NSC that atmospheric nuclear tests were fully detectable. Very small underground shots—in the one- to ten-kiloton range—were also detectable, he said. Dulles then drafted a letter to Khrushchev calling for "technical talks on a possible test ban inspection system."[76] Khrushchev quickly agreed. Over the summer, experts meeting in Geneva concluded that underground tests could be detected provided a network of seismic stations—as many as 160 to 170—could be created. (This was consistent with Bethe's report.)

Eisenhower was encouraged. He proposed negotiations and suspended American tests for one year. But now Khrushchev wavered; he worried, as he said in his memoirs, about international inspectors piercing the Soviet veil. "I agreed in principle to on-site inspection of the border regions and to airborne reconnaissance of our territory up to a certain distance inside our borders, but we couldn't allow the U.S. and its allies to send their inspectors criss-crossing around the Soviet Union. They would have discovered that we were in a relatively weak position, and that realization might have encouraged them to attack us."[77]

Although he was now fully prepared to take the leap, Eisenhower still worried about European opposition. In April, he told aides that "the thing hinged around our failure to get our principal allies, Britain and France, to agree to cessation of testing."[78] But the British did a sharp turnabout over the summer, largely because America's Atomic Energy Act was amended in their favor. Harold Macmillan, who had a more serious problem at home on the fallout issue than Eisenhower confronted, began abruptly to exhort Eisenhower on the test ban. By then, Eisenhower and Dulles had decided to ignore French objections, and German resistance had been disposed of in a joint Eisenhower-Adenauer declaration in which the U.S. promised to keep its forces in Germany and to seek an end to the country's division; Adenauer pledged in turn his country's continued buildup of forces in NATO.[79]

Around this same time—the summer of '58—scientists working with Teller devised "evasion scenarios," which purported to show how the Soviets could violate an agreement—continue testing—undetected. Immense underground cavities could be used to muffle the shock of an explosion, to cite one example. Testing on the back side of the moon—200,000 miles out in space—was among the more fanciful possibilities. Killian's people didn't take such notions seriously but knew they couldn't be put down by purely scientific argument. Alternatives to a comprehensive ban were considered, among them an agreement that would allow underground tests to continue since some of these were more difficult to monitor.

Negotiations began in Geneva on November 4. The Russians insisted that any control commission authorized to make on-site inspection would take decisions by unanimous vote, which meant they could veto any intrusive visits. They also said that control posts should be manned by nationals of the country in which they were located.[80] The Western side (America and Britain) wanted these stations manned by a combination of neutrals and people from one of the original parties to the agreement. And the West rejected the idea of a Soviet veto. The sides diverged as well on the number of on-site inspections to be allowed under an agreement.

As it became clear that tests of very small devices might go undetected, the focus shifted to an above-ground test ban. In April 1959, when talks resumed, Eisenhower proposed such an arrangement to Khrushchev. Eisenhower told his negotiator to drop the condition tying a test ban to nuclear disarmament, and Khrushchev in turn agreed to give up the veto. In Washington, opposition to agreement with the Russians was on the rise, even as prospects brightened. Khrushchev had encouraged opponents of agreement by renewing pressure on Berlin. But with the end of his presidency in sight, Eisenhower wouldn't be held back. He and Khrushchev continued to observe an informal moratorium on testing that began in 1958, and the negotiators continued to make fitful progress. By the spring of 1960, agreement lay well within reach. It was not to be. Abruptly, the high hopes of subduing the nuclear genie fell to grief on the wings of the U-2 aircraft flown by Francis Gary Powers.

Violating Soviet airspace with a manned aircraft had from the first made Eisenhower uncomfortable—more so it turned out than it did the handful of other senior officials who were involved with or knew about the program. The Kremlin was well aware of the overflights and could have judged them aggressive acts. The cargo could as well have been bombs as cameras. Eisenhower once said, "The Soviets . . . might misinterpret the overflight as being designed to start a nuclear war."[81] But there was no Soviet reaction; an admission that the country was unable to defend its airspace would have been far too embarrassing. Instead, the Soviets tried unavailingly to shoot down the high-flying intruders. Their embassy also complained, and Eisenhower occasionally put temporary holds on the program. Still, he wanted the intelligence; he needed progressively more and better information about Soviet weapons in order to make rational decisions about America's and hold off the patrons of the missile gap. He told none of them (or anyone else) about the U-2.* He ordered U-2 missions held to a minimum pending the arrival of reconnaissance satellites, but the need for some flights was urgent. And Khrushchev had not mentioned them at Camp David.

Eisenhower worried most about losing a U-2 and an ensuing uproar. Besides having Berlin to contend with, he was looking ahead to a four-power summit meeting and completion of the test ban treaty. A downed U-2 could gravely injure these prospects. He had always been assured by Allen Dulles that the gossamer craft was too fragile to survive even a glancing blow from Soviet air defenses. In any case, it was said to be

---

*Even if Eisenhower had been tempted to share the "take" from the U-2 program, he'd never have risked a leak that would have compromised governments like Pakistan's and Norway's from which the planes operated.

equipped with a self-destruct device.* Finally, although a U-2 pilot was no more likely to survive a mishap than his airplane, each had sworn to take his own life if he did; the paraphernalia of suicide were standard issue. The loss of a U-2 would amount to only that—the loss of an unmarked aircraft of untraceable provenance. Eisenhower was always dubious; his high regard for John Foster Dulles did not extend to his brother, whom he excluded from meetings that another CIA director might have attended.[82] When the U-2 was shot down, Eisenhower told Goodpaster that he would never again meet alone with Allen Dulles.[83]

Eisenhower and the other U-2 initiates debated whether to run the risk of staging another mission close to the four-power summit meeting that was to begin in Paris in mid-May. A last flight before the summit was scheduled to overfly Plesetsk, where the CIA had guessed correctly that the first operational Soviet ICBMs were located. Two other places wrongly believed by the air force to be launch sites would also be covered.[84] Reluctantly, Eisenhower approved the flight which took off from Peshawar in Pakistan on May 1—the U.S.S.R.'s hallowed May Day. The U-2 was shot down over Sverdlovsk, a large industrial city in the Ural Mountains. Captain Powers, the pilot, was captured alive and intact.

The incident became the *cause célèbre* that Eisenhower had always feared, but not right away. On May 3, NASA, the space agency, announced that one of its "Air Weather Service" planes was missing and presumed lost over southeastern Turkey. On May 5, the Soviets announced that an American reconnaissance aircraft had been shot down over their territory. Eisenhower was thereupon persuaded to approve a clarification of NASA's cover story which conceded that the pilot of the missing plane might have accidentally violated Soviet airspace. He did so only because Allen Dulles and others had convinced him that whatever happened, there would be no live pilot to bear witness. That evening, Khrushchev told a group of diplomats at a reception that he would have something "stupendous" to say the following day. And he did, introducing Powers to the world, along with a good deal of evidence that demolished the American cover story. But Khrushchev said he was willing to believe that Eisenhower hadn't approved the flight. The next day, the State Department acknowledged that spy flights "had probably been undertaken" but were justified by the Soviet refusal to accept America's Open Skies proposal of 1955. And in a press conference on May 11, Eisenhower discarded all pretense of not having known about the flights by taking full responsibility. "No one wants another Pearl Harbor," he said; aerial espionage was "a distasteful but vital necessity."

Until Eisenhower's statement, Khrushchev had scudded safely over

*It turned out that the device destroyed cameras and film, not the aircraft.

terrain strewn with traps. His forces had downed an intruder, he had exposed the imperialist's cover story for what it was, and he had let the President himself off the hook. Khrushchev had invested heavily in Eisenhower and could not afford to be let down. Besides lifting the ultimatum on Berlin and inviting his adversary to Russia, he had extolled his "statesmanship" and "desire for peace."[85] As Charles Bohlen was to say later, Khrushchev took the resumption of U-2 flights after Camp David as "almost a personal insult. More than that, I think it made him out a fool. He'd been telling . . . all the other leaders that Eisenhower was a good solid guy and you could trust him, and then—whambo—this plane comes over, and this shook a lot of Khrushchev's authority in the Soviet Union."[86]

At a reception in Moscow on May 9, Khrushchev took aside Ambassador Llewellyn Thompson and said, "This U-2 thing has put me in a terrible spot. You have to get me off it."[87] He may have thought, or hoped, that Eisenhower would apologize for the overflight, in which case the Paris summit might have remained on course and a test ban agreement completed. But Eisenhower's statement—his unwillingness perhaps to be seen as not fully in charge—stripped away Khrushchev's only line of defense from criticism and even ridicule from within. The two were caught in the same dilemma. Eisenhower felt he had to claim the right to violate Soviet airspace, Khrushchev to reject the claim and harden his position.

The summit, although not quite a nonevent, was a shambles. The Big Four met only once, an occasion dominated by Khrushchev's demand for an apology as a precondition to anything. Eisenhower refused, agreeing only to halt the U-2 flights. De Gaulle was a magisterial chairman, telling Khrushchev icily that a Soviet satellite, "launched just before you left Moscow to impress us, overflew the sky of France eighteen times without my permission. How do I know that you do not have cameras aboard which are taking pictures of my country?" A perhaps revealing moment occurred when Khrushchev softened his harangue and said, "Please understand that our internal politics require this [apology]. It is a matter of honor."[88] The reference to "internal politics" may have reflected the pressure he felt. Bohlen, who was there as note taker and said that Khrushchev's "anger and determination were real," felt that without an apology, Khrushchev was not authorized to take part in the conference. And he recalled that the Soviet leader stopped in East Berlin on his way back to Moscow and gave a "soothing speech, making it clear that he had no intention of heating up the Berlin issue."[89]

"Now there's really nothing left for me to do," said Eisenhower to George Kistiakowsky, his new science adviser, shortly after his return from Paris. Kistiakowsky recalled him as "an emotional, tragic figure."[90]

The unfinished test ban treaty seemed to be the major casualty of the U-2 affair, although a few officials felt that Khrushchev had used it as a pretext for avoiding an agreement he wasn't ready for. The various "what if" questions bandied about did not include, What if Powers had completed the flight? Raymond Garthoff recalls that he and others working on Soviet estimates at the CIA "were waiting with keen anticipation" for the arrival of the flight. "We were hoping for and expecting vindication of the 'low end' estimate [of Soviet ICBM strength]. We were assuming that the only launchers deployed were those we felt were at Plesetsk."[91] The Powers flight would have shown four ICBM launchers deployed at Plesetsk and nothing at the other places alleged by the air force to be launch sites. Thus, the evidence obtained from a completed flight could have strengthened Eisenhower's hand in the ebbing moments of his presidency.

His position then was somewhat anomalous and hardly enviable. He had urged restraint, but the stockpile of nuclear weapons was growing, most of it without coherent purpose. Develop now and worry later—a leitmotif of the nuclear age—was the attitude of those who continued to exaggerate the threat. Still, Eisenhower's defiance of the *Sputnik*/missile gap hysteria was an exceptional service and a cause of some distress to himself. "Never has a general been so hated as I am now in the Pentagon," he told Kistiakowsky a few months before leaving office.[92] His largest disappointment—the failure to restrict nuclear arms—was the other side of that coin; he was better—braver—at preventing foolish behavior than promoting sensible behavior.

With his prestige and sustained popularity, Eisenhower could have done more. Aside perhaps from de Gaulle, this seemingly open man was more enigmatic and hidden than any of the historic personalities he knew. He could, when he chose, confuse the country and the government about his intentions. And he was at his most enigmatic when doing what he did best—avoiding crises.

VI

Black Saturday

The contrast between the exiting, used-up President and his improbable successor, although vivid and even dramatic, was deceptive. Whatever their differences in age and experience, Eisenhower and Kennedy had more in common than either realized. Both were sensible and moderate. Each radiated a charm and vitality that enveloped those around them. Each understood the aloneness of the office and why an effective incumbent must avoid fully confiding in advisers. Each was absorbed by foreign and defense policy and not interested in most domestic issues, including civil rights. But each did have one domestic interest. Eisenhower's was the budget, which he was determined to balance; his commitment arose from the old adage that a sound economy and strong defense have a one-to-one relationship. Kennedy liked to tinker with fiscal and monetary matters, possibly because he understood them; he was the only President with an intellectual grasp of Keynesian economics. Eisenhower was always aware of the limitations of the office, and, while he had a less philosophical turn of mind and little feel for irony, he knew that sensible purpose was no match for fortune's whim.

These were still early days in the nuclear arms buildup. "What worried Eisenhower most wasn't what happened on his watch," says General Andrew Goodpaster. "He knew he could handle the military people. It was what would happen to another President—one who hadn't had his preparation or experience."[1] But Kennedy, too, became a skillful crisis manager and is now best remembered for his accomplishments in that role.

The day before his inauguration, Kennedy met with Eisenhower in the Oval Office. He was accompanied by Dean Rusk, designated Secretary of State, Robert McNamara, who would be Secretary of Defense, and Clark Clifford. Although the missile gap had been a campaign issue, neither man raised it, according to Rusk. Much of the conversation concerned Laos, the landlocked little kingdom that Eisenhower and Dulles had tried unavailingly to turn into an anti-Communist bulwark. Eisenhower, says Rusk, recommended putting troops into Laos and told Kennedy in a private aside that he would support him if he did so. But Rusk recalls Eisenhower also warning Kennedy that he would oppose him privately and publicly if anything was done about recognizing "Red China" or supporting its admission into the United Nations.[2]*

In a tumultuous first few months, Kennedy found crises everywhere except Europe, where the cold war was in a lull which the new administration hoped to prolong. In Moscow, Ambassador Llewellyn Thompson was instructed to look into the possibilities of a test ban and a meeting with Khrushchev. In early March, he saw Khrushchev, who said no to the test ban; he was already preparing to break the informal moratorium on testing that both sides had observed since 1958. Thompson could report agreement in principle on a Kennedy-Khrushchev meeting.

Robert McNamara and Roswell Gilpatric, the Deputy Secretary of Defense, quickly saw through the missile gap, to which Kennedy probably owed his election. On February 6, they held a "not for quotation or attribution backgrounder" to acquaint reporters with studies under way in their department. McNamara mistakenly assumed he was talking off the record, as well as not for attribution. The first question was about the missile gap; he said there were "no signs of a Soviet crash effort to build ICBM's" and that Russia and America had "about the same number of ICBM's at present—not a very large number."[3] "You couldn't hold the door locked," said McNamara. "They broke the damn door down."[4] Newspaper headlines that evening and the following morning, citing Kennedy's advisers, interred the missile gap. Kennedy was embarrassed and tried unsuccessfully to walk back the story, saying the study was incomplete. Everett Dirksen, Senate Republican leader, called him on February 7, asking for McNamara's resignation.[5] Over the next several months, the real state of the strategic balance gradually swam into focus.

Kennedy was eager to meet and, if possible, gain the confidence of his peers: Adenauer, de Gaulle, and Macmillan. And he wanted to have a firsthand impression of Khrushchev, the adversary. He met twice with Macmillan before seeing any of the others. A brief conference was held in

---

*Another Eisenhower imponderable: In reflective moments, he would occasionally cite the need to begin dealing with China as it was. He more than anyone could have influenced the national view of the issue. He never tried.

Key West toward the end of March, and the sole topic was the crisis in Laos. A week later, they met in Washington for formal talks, which didn't go well; Macmillan found his new interlocutor diffident and dependent on his advisers.[6] The singularly close relationship that developed later would not then have been predicted.

A few days later, Adenauer arrived in Washington for a visit that was even less successful. His test of any American was the strength of his commitment to West Germany, and neither Kennedy nor the members of his entourage tested well. (Neither, for that matter, did their predecessors, except for Dulles, whose memory Adenauer revered.) Adenauer never did feel comfortable with Kennedy, and de Gaulle, on whom the old man relied, fed these doubts.[7]

Khrushchev aside, de Gaulle interested Kennedy more than any of the others. It was arranged that he would visit Paris at the end of May, just a few days before meeting Khrushchev in Vienna. De Gaulle clearly liked Kennedy and a rapport was achieved, even though the views of the two men diverged on nearly everything except for Berlin, where, in general terms, they agreed to hold the line. Nuclear sharing was the large unuttered issue. De Gaulle wouldn't raise it, and Kennedy was not—not then certainly—ready to gratify French designs on American technology; the same was true of de Gaulle's celebrated proposal for a tri-directorate. The notion of Franco-British-American joint direction, wrote André Fontaine of *Le Monde,* was regarded in Washington as "chimeric."[8] In Paris, as elsewhere, the visit was seen as a glittering prelude to the serious business in Vienna.

Kennedy could not have picked a worse moment to take the measure of Khrushchev. The Bay of Pigs fiasco in Cuba and the President's sensible support for a neutral solution in Laos were misread in Moscow as evidence of weakness. "Khrushchev, I think, thought that mainly because of the Bay of Pigs, he was facing an incompetent Administration with weak leadership and felt he could take advantage of us," says McNamara.[9] Soviet intelligence would by then have collected some unflattering appraisals of Kennedy in London and, even more so, in Bonn. Yet no one around him argued against the meeting, according to Rusk.[10] Some of his White House entourage felt that Eisenhower had been too hard and unbending on Berlin, a sentiment not shared in the State Department.

For several days, the Soviet press had been preparing its readers for a thaw, not a crisis.[11] From Moscow, Thompson was forecasting a crisis over Berlin, probably in the fall. If so, ran the administration thinking, better to head it off than wait for it. None of the Americans in Vienna expected trouble there. To the contrary, they felt that Khrushchev would want to conclude the meeting on an upbeat note. And the first day of talks, for which there was no prepared agenda, didn't go badly, although Kennedy let himself be drawn into a pointless ideological debate of the sort that Khrushchev, the seasoned dialectician, thrived on. And Khrushchev took strong exception to Kennedy's repeated use of the word "miscalculate," which, in translation, sounded to him as if he couldn't calculate.

The morning after was very different. After some useless conversation about an inspected test ban, which Khrushchev seemed to equate with espionage, he braced Kennedy with the ultimatum that relaunched the Berlin crisis. Kennedy would have to sign an agreement confirming the two Germanies, or Khrushchev would conclude a separate treaty with East Germany no later than December, at which point the West's occupation rights in Berlin and access to the city would cease to exist. West Berlin could remain as before, except that its links with the outer world would be controlled by the East Germans. In no way would Moscow accept American rights in Berlin after the treaty. No further delay in making these new arrangements would be acceptable. And Rusk recalls Khrushchev saying that once these were in place, any attempt to interfere would lead to war. "In diplomacy you don't talk that way," Rusk says. "You talk about 'gravest possible consequences.' That's very rare, and it came as a surprise."[12]

Afterward, the two leaders met alone, with only interpreters, for a short time, but nothing was changed. Khrushchev later described Kennedy as looking "not only anxious, but deeply upset." He added that "the differences in our class positions had prevented us from coming to an agreement . . . Politics is a merciless business."[13]

Clearly, the miner's son from the Donets Basin—veteran party apparatchik, survivor, and strong man—saw before him a young, untried product of wealth and advantage. "Khrushchev could be very crude and tough in the way he talked, but there was quite a lot of difference between his threats and his actions," said Averell Harriman, who was there. "I don't think Kennedy fully understood that. It was the first time he'd seen Khrushchev and he was very much shocked, very much upset, shattered really, by this conversation in Vienna."[14]

"It was a good time to have a meeting with Kennedy," recalls Arkady Shevchenko, a Soviet defector who held several sensitive jobs, including special assistant to Andrei Gromyko. "However, the impression in the Foreign Ministry was that it went badly. Kennedy failed to deal with Nikita. That was dangerous. Nikita saw a weak man. He saw he could even intimidate him. Everyone was elated. It affected our inferiority complex about America. To find that an American President can be bullied and won't react in a strong way. This psychological effect was very important. They [the leadership] remembered Truman, a cold warrior, and Eisenhower, who was all smiles, but who, they knew, was a tough man." And what about Khrushchev's threat to make war? "That is a threat he used only to intimidate," Shevchenko said. "There was absolutely no intention of making war. It really surprises me that the Americans reacted that way. Soviet leaders don't necessarily look up to an American president. But they do respect what they call the correlation of forces. Khrushchev understood U.S. superiority."[15]

Everyone lost. The Americans, having arrived in Vienna more curious than apprehensive, left seized with the crisis they had hoped to avert. Their blustery foe had done what Kennedy had warned him against; he had miscalculated and thereby set the superpowers on a collision course. Later, he would pay dearly for having gambled and lost. Meanwhile, the seventeen months that linked the Vienna meeting to the end of the Cuban missile crisis in November 1962 became much the most dangerous of the entire cold war.

Among those on either side who were involved, there is a disagreement on just which crisis—Berlin or Cuba—carried the larger risk of war. Most, though not all, of the Americans agree with Rusk, who saw the Cuban confrontation—"two superpowers at each other's jugulars"—as the more dangerous. The Soviets, probably with few exceptions, would cite Berlin. Although most of them hoped to avoid a conflict in either place, the idea of going to war for Cuba, an island in what amounted to an American sea, seemed insane. In Berlin, they had a lot at stake and held the high cards, but not far away—along the frontier dividing Europe—lay the greatest confrontation of military force in peacetime history. Sparks from Berlin could have ignited a major conflict, a frightening prospect for Soviet generals. Colonel Oleg Penkovsky, who was then the West's best source of quality intelligence about his country's armed forces and leadership, was reporting exactly that. In his papers, which were smuggled out after his arrest in October 1962, Penkovsky cited leaders as realizing that "we are not ready for a major war" and generals as saying: "What in hell do we need this Berlin for? We have endured it for sixteen years; we can endure it a little more."[16]

Penkovsky was reporting serious weaknesses in the Soviet military position (nuclear and nonnuclear) and urging Washington to take stronger measures. You can afford to, he'd say. The rather hortatory quality of his reporting caused the CIA to discount some of it.[17] It didn't matter, however, because the unhappy Soviet ministers and generals he described had no choice but to go along with Khrushchev, who was then at the peak of his power. He was all but ignoring his Presidium* col-

*Today's Politburo was then called the Presidium.

leagues and listening mainly to his son-in-law, Aleksei Adzhubei, the editor in chief of *Izvestia.*

Whatever anxieties his recklessness caused colleagues, Khrushchev was clearly in charge. Eisenhower had called his bluff in Berlin, as Truman had Stalin's, but Kennedy couldn't assume that he was bluffing this time; the stakes were too high. Penkovsky was fearful, and so were the important figures whose views he disclosed. Returning home, Kennedy stopped off in London for a family christening but really to see Macmillan; it was then that their friendship—"Kennedy's closest personal relationship with a foreign leader," according to Arthur Schlesinger, Jr.—was born. Kennedy hadn't recovered from Khrushchev's verbal pounding (to which both Thompson and Bohlen felt he had overreacted). "The President was impressed and shocked," Macmillan later wrote. "It was rather like somebody meeting Napoleon . . . for the first time . . . For the first time in his life, [Kennedy] met a man wholly impervious to his charm."[18]

They agreed that any attempt at negotiation was premature and would be seen by Khrushchev as a sign of weakness. Back home, Kennedy asked for an estimate of how many Americans would die in a nuclear war. The answer was seventy million. He himself reckoned the chances of such an exchange at one in five.[19] "Kennedy was intelligent enough to know that a military clash would be senseless," wrote Khrushchev. "Therefore the United States and its Western allies had no choice but to swallow a bitter pill as we began to take certain unilateral steps. We decided . . . to lance the blister of West Berlin."[20]

Kennedy reacted to Vienna mainly by stepping up the military planning for several important contingencies. The one he expected, however, was a blockade. State Department professionals doubted that in the end Khrushchev would go that far. But Paul Nitze, who was then assistant secretary of defense and in charge of military contingency planning, says he "was sure the Soviets would do another blockade." They would, he says, "turn over the access routes to East Germans, who would then cut off access to the Western sectors of Berlin. The East Germans had more than enough forces for that. And if we attacked them, there was a big risk of the Soviets coming into it."[21]

Soviet leaders worry obsessively about Germany. They see West Germany as the potential leader of a hostile West European coalition bristling with nuclear weapons. They try and try again to isolate West Germany politically so as to control its behavior. Khrushchev didn't understand that American foreign policy in the nuclear age, if rooted anywhere, is rooted in the problem of the divided German people. Much of Washington's purpose has been to absorb their energies within a secure Western system—one sturdy enough to assure their country's stability and security.* Kennedy couldn't back away from the commitment to protect West Berlin and access to it. Any wavering on his part would have produced doubt and despair in Bonn and might have unhinged the Western Alliance. Equally vital was America's commitment to use force—nuclear weapons, if necessary—in Germany's defense. American guarantees were only as credible as the administration itself. Unlike John Foster Dulles, some of Kennedy's advisers considered Adenauer's need for constant reassurance as unreasonable, if not childish. He, in turn, worried that the Kennedy White House didn't understand the problem.

After the Vienna meeting, Rusk and Britain's Foreign Secretary, Alec Douglas-Home, had follow-up talks with Andrei Gromyko, their Soviet opposite number, whom Rusk recalls as being "very harsh. He, too, used the term 'war.' We said: 'If you want war, we can have one in five minutes.' Alec Home and I agreed to talk as long and repetitively as Gromyko did. We were in no rush to settle."[22]

In Washington, the administration was divided on just how tough it should be. Kennedy had called in Dean Acheson, Truman's formidable Secretary of State, and he was arguing forcibly that Khrushchev had started the crisis because he was convinced that nuclear war wouldn't occur. Washington must shake his complacency—must show that Berlin mattered more to America than to the Soviet Union; therefore, ran Acheson's argument, America had to take larger risks in protecting its rights than the Soviet Union might take in trying to suppress them.[23] Another faction wanted to mix military steps with an offer to negotiate. There was a large menu of options, starting, in the event of a blockade, with a limited probe of the autobahn. Another airlift was ruled out, partly because the other side could have disrupted allied traffic with electronic devices not available in 1948; also, the West Berlin airport didn't have adequate landing facilities for modern jet aircraft. Kennedy had decided to ask Congress to approve an increase in the draft and for standby authority to mobilize ready reserve and National Guard units. The emphasis was on enlarged nonnuclear forces. "But having mobilized, you had to demonstrate that you were serious," says Nitze. He describes four of the options: (1) a demonstration shot, or shots, of nuclear weapons, (2) "taking out" airfields in East Germany, Poland, and elsewhere in Eastern Europe, (3) sending a few divisions across the autobahn, (4) a counterblockade of the Soviet Union. "It was perfectly clear," says Nitze, "that the Soviets could defeat any of these options. If we had

*The appeal to France of cementing fraternal links with her old and most fearsome enemy arose from a similar purpose and largely explains the European Community.

used a demonstration weapon, they could shoot off six. Our few divisions couldn't do much against forty divisions. And what happens if you get a bloody nose? Do you go to nuclear war?"[24]

"Contingency plans are no more than that," says Dean Rusk dryly.[25] "In the White House, we didn't sign off on anything," says McGeorge Bundy, the National Security Adviser. "We didn't have to. Presidents don't sign off on a decision until they have to make it." Bundy recalls Kennedy asking Acheson, hardest of the hard-liners around him, when he would use nuclear weapons over Berlin. Acheson, Bundy says, answered very carefully: "Mr. President, that is a very important question. If I were you, I'd think about it very hard and tell no one what I'd decided." And, Bundy adds, "I never heard Kennedy say what he would do at the limit on Berlin."[26]

America's chief allies were even more cautious. Washington had minimal support for the idea of keeping open the autobahn, whatever happened. The British were skittish. De Gaulle, who never for a moment doubted that Khrushchev was bluffing, took the hardest line but committed himself even less militarily and still managed to promote Adenauer's concerns about the supposedly unreliable Anglo-Saxons. Franz Josef Strauss, Adenauer's Defense Minister, also took strong rhetorical positions, but he had long been fearful that Berlin might lead the Americans to use tactical nuclear weapons in a conflict that could destroy his country.[27] It was reminiscent of 1959 and the last conversation between Dulles, who was terminally ill, and Adenauer. "If the Soviets push this ultimatum on Berlin, we will go to nuclear war," said Dulles. *"Um Gottes willen nicht über Berlin,"* replied Adenauer—horrified. ("For God's sake, not over Berlin.")*

The new administration hadn't shaken down. It understood the Berlin problem, but only gradually was it acquiring the cohesion and confidence required to deal with it. There was confusion. Over the summer, Washington rattled the saber, trying to convince Moscow, as well as allied capitals, that America would, if necessary, use military force, without having convinced itself. Meanwhile, many people stockpiled food, detergent, etc.

Kennedy spent six weeks intensively reviewing his options. Besides enlarging American forces, he proposed mass construction of fallout shelters and food storage facilities.[28] The authorities made available blueprints for backyard and cellar shelters, and an instant cottage industry began flogging them (at prices ranging from $1,500 to $50,000).[29] Abruptly and for the first time, society took civil defense seriously.

*The source for this exchange is the American diplomat who was Dulles's note taker. A cynical although probably farfetched view of Adenauer's remark is that it reflected the abiding hostility of an old Rhinelander toward Prussians.

Kennedy's advisers split sharply on whether to soften a hardening line with a signal to Moscow that he was at least willing to discuss Berlin. Kennedy opted for the signal; he wanted to hold the initiative and, if possible, avoid a Soviet-sponsored peace conference.[30] Kennedy was impressed by recommendations for a rapid buildup of conventional forces in Central Europe. Those who urged this step included General Maxwell Taylor, who had become his military adviser, and General James Gavin; from Moscow, Llewellyn Thompson, to whom Kennedy listened carefully, was telling him that the Soviets would be impressed by significant low-key steps that did not alarm America's allies.[31]

On July 25, Kennedy unveiled his position in a starkly somber speech which described West Berlin as "the great testing place of Western courage and will, a focal point where our solemn commitments . . . and Soviet ambitions now meet in basic confrontation."[32] In Congress, the country, West Berlin, Bonn, and other allied capitals, the reaction was very favorable. A strong statement of American firmness had been awaited, and Kennedy didn't disappoint; his apparent willingness to negotiate an end to the crisis was noted, but the tougher passages seemed to constitute the real message and got most of the attention, not least from the other side. On July 26, the day after the speech, John McCloy got the first and purest Soviet reaction. He had been in Moscow for several days as Kennedy's emissary for talks on disarmament, and the day after the speech he found himself a guest of Khrushchev at his dacha on the Black Sea coast. There "the storm broke," said McCloy. The United States, said Khrushchev, had declared preliminary war on his country. Kennedy clearly intended to fight. Then Khrushchev, sounding perhaps a bit like King Lear, reasserted his intentions toward Berlin and his willingness to wage thermonuclear war if the West responded with force. He warned McCloy of a one-hundred-megaton Soviet "superbomb" that could be built and delivered by rocket on American territory. He expressed doubt that America and its allies actually would fight for West Berlin and urged a negotiated settlement.[33]

In July, more than 30,000 people left East Germany, a new high and more than double the monthly average in 1960. Walter Ulbricht, the party boss, began taking steps to restrict movement within the city; on August 2, the sixty to seventy thousand *Grenzganger*—commuters who lived in East Berlin but worked in one of the Western sectors—were brusquely served notice that the practice was no longer permitted.[34] Khrushchev's situation struck Kennedy as unbearable; he said as much to McCloy, who had just returned, predicting that Khrushchev would have to do something, perhaps build a wall.[35]

That week, Ulbricht began lobbying Khrushchev, who was in East

Berlin, for authority to seal off access to West Berlin with a "Chinese wall." On August 13, the infamous wall appeared. Although the human consequences were appalling and the world was shocked, most allied governments were relieved. Adenauer was involved in a political campaign and didn't even appear at the wall for a week.[36] No one knew how to respond—if at all. It was recognized that the East Germans would have to stop the outflow of their people, but Western intelligence hadn't anticipated a wall, as such, cutting off the three Western sectors of the city.[37]* It didn't matter. "When the wall went up, we saw it as a step they had to take to stem the hemorrhage," Rusk recalls. "We felt strongly about their treatment of their own people, but it wasn't an issue of going to war. Berlin itself constituted that issue."[38]

Kennedy had made clear his determination to fight, if necessary, for West Berlin and the access routes. The commitment didn't extend to the Eastern sector. A headline in the West German newspaper *Bild Zeitung* captured its readers' sense of helplessness, if not betrayal: KENNEDY IS SILENT, MACMILLAN IS OUT HUNTING, ADENAUER SNEERS AT BRANDT. (Willy Brandt was West Berlin's mayor and Adenauer's political rival.) "It's not a very nice solution, but . . . a hell of a lot better than a war," said Kennedy succinctly to Kenneth O'Donnell, his appointments secretary.[39]

A few of Kennedy's advisers urged him to send a regimental combat team across the autobahn to Berlin. The Soviets would see the troops as an earnest of his commitment. Kennedy was reluctant; General Taylor and the Joint Chiefs were opposed to the move. Robert Amory, then Deputy Director of Central Intelligence, recalls Taylor as saying, "That's a hell of a bad idea . . . any troops we have in Berlin will be casualties in the first six hours of fighting. We can't afford to give up five thousand good armed men . . . to that." On the 16th, Willy Brandt cabled Kennedy, deploring the feebleness of Western reaction and asking him to put more American troops in Berlin. "So with much hoopla," says Amory (who had urged the move), "that afternoon the combat team went in, and Vice President Lyndon Johnson flew [to Berlin] to make the commitment politically dramatic."[40] Kennedy felt obliged to act but also to avoid overreacting, since Khrushchev could easily fine-tune his own position by raising (or lowering) the pressure as he pleased. Kennedy was involving himself in the fine-tuning of the American position, so much so that within the State

*However, an "Eyes Only" telegram from Thompson to Rusk, dated March 16, warned that if the Soviet Union did postpone signing a separate peace treaty with East Germany, leaving West Berlin in peace, "we must at least expect [the] East Germans to seal off [the] Sector boundary in order to stop what they must consider [to be an] intolerable continuation of [the] refugee flow through Berlin."

Department he was considered the "Berlin desk officer." He often cleared telegrams before they went to Rusk for signature.[41]

As the inevitable war of nerves began, the East Germans warned Berliners to stay at least one hundred meters from the wall; furthermore, West Berliners would need travel permits to enter East Berlin. Foreigners, diplomats, and Western officials would be allowed to enter at just one of the various checkpoints.

A bad month ended on a distinctly grim note: The White House was shocked to discover that the Soviets were about to break the moratorium on atmospheric testing of nuclear weapons. There had been no forewarning from American intelligence (as there should have been), and Khrushchev had only just told McCloy that he would not resume testing unless the West did so. But he also noted pressure from Soviet scientists and military people to begin testing a huge new bomb.[42] On August 30, his spokesmen said that Soviet scientists had "worked out designs for creating a series of super-powerful nuclear bombs of 20, 30, 50, and 100 million tons of TNT; and powerful rockets . . . |to| lift and deliver such . . . bombs to any point on the globe . . ."[43] On September 1, the first of these behemoths was tested. Kennedy was deeply discouraged. The Soviets were thought to be trying to alter the balance of power, and he was now under heavy pressure to resume American testing. He had hopes that a treaty banning tests might still be possible, but on September 5, a day on which the Soviets tested their third big weapon, he announced his decision to resume testing underground.[44]

Three weeks later, McNamara was asked at a news conference if he might be intending to use nuclear weapons in connection with the Berlin crisis.

"Yes, I definitely do," he said. "We will use nuclear weapons whenever we feel it necessary to protect our vital interests. Our nuclear stockpile is several times that of the Soviet Union . . ."[45]

On September 19, General Lucius D. Clay returned to Berlin, this time as Kennedy's special representative. For Berliners, he was the stalwart of the blockade and airlift thirteen years earlier—American firmness incarnate. Kennedy sent him back to be a morale-sustaining presence and nothing more. If Khrushchev could break Berlin's morale, he would win; it was that simple. But Clay did not see himself in a passive role. Only by being aggressive, he felt—standing up to the other side at every opportunity— could he well and truly accomplish his mission. He had told Lyndon Johnson a month before that had he been in Berlin on August 13, American tanks would have rolled. (He later said that it was trucks, not tanks, he would have sent across.)[46]

In Washington, sending Clay was seen as a calculated risk. Harriman had once described him as a "natural-born tsar," so excitable that he "typically ran a temperature of 106 degrees."[47] For many others, he was quite simply a loose cannon. From the moment he arrived, Clay began pushing against what officials on all sides saw as the political tolerances of an exceedingly tense situation. Washington was in no mood for political gestures; Berlin was a powder train. Clay had no independent authority, being technically subordinate to local military and civilian officials, but he nonetheless made decisions in a proconsular fashion, often without checking with the White House or anyone else. His larger gestures captured the world's attention. Smaller ones went unnoticed in Washington, as, for example, asking army engineers to build a wall in the Grünewald, a forest in West Berlin, so that troops could practice knocking it down.[48]

One month after arriving, Clay produced the cold war's most public and haunting peril point. He chose a time when Kennedy had decided to lower the temperature in Berlin. On the night of October 22, Allan Lightner, the senior American civilian official in the city, was stopped by East German Vopos (police) at Checkpoint Charlie, an agreed crossing point for allied military personnel and civilians entering East Berlin and manned by American military police. Lightner and his wife were driving to a theater in East Berlin in their private car, a small Volkswagen; although it had official plates, American personnel normally used official cars when crossing into East Berlin. For whatever reason, a Vopo officer on the other side of the checkpoint halted the Lightners and asked to see their passports. They refused. American officials had been instructed not to deal with East German authorities; the West did not recognize East Berlin as being part of East Germany. American MPs, observing the incident, reported it to their provost marshal, who informed Clay. He ordered a platoon of infantrymen, four M-48 medium tanks, and two armored personnel carriers to Checkpoint Charlie. With the Vopos still blocking Lightner's passage (Mrs. Lightner had returned to the West Berlin side), two squads of American troops, their weapons at the ready, escorted the car through the checkpoint. The East Germans made no effort to stop them. The exercise was thereupon repeated, again without incident. Lightner said later, "If the East Germans had tried to stop us . . . say by shooting one of us, we would have had to kill all of them . . . All hell would have broken loose."[49]

Washington would never have approved this behavior had anyone bothered to check. In not reacting forcibly to the Wall, the allies were telling Khrushchev in effect: We won't make a fuss in East Berlin—your sector—but will stand fast in our sectors. (British officials were already allowing East Germans to check their passports.)

"Lightner went over there incognito," says David Klein, an ex-diplomat who was then dealing with Berlin as a member of Bundy's staff. "Sure, they challenged his rights, but normally he would have been expected to use a clearly marked vehicle. The concern was about Clay. No one in the White House was sure of being able to control what he did, or might do." Kennedy's position was awkward. Clay, his own emissary, had called asking for support for a show of military force if the East Germans continued pressing official personnel to show their papers. Kennedy needed him in Berlin. "We had to worry that Clay might even denounce Kennedy—do a MacArthur," says Klein.[50] Kennedy gave Clay the authority he asked for.[51]

Khrushchev dispatched a stalwart of his own, Marshal I. S. Konev, to take command of Soviet troops in Germany. "To use the language of chess," Khrushchev wrote, "the Americans had advanced a pawn, so we protected our position by moving a knight . . . He [Konev] reported that the Americans were getting ready to move in and destroy the border installations with infantry and bulldozers. We told Konev to station our tanks out of sight in the side streets and move them out to confront the Americans when they crossed the border."[52]

On Wednesday, October 25, two American officers in civilian clothes, driving a civilian Opel with official plates, crossed Checkpoint Charlie and were stopped by Vopos when they refused to show their passports. They turned around, picked up three jeeps full of soldiers, and passed through the checkpoint, this time without interference.

An hour later, ten M-48 tanks and three armored personnel carriers took up positions near the border. Each time a vehicle with official plates was stopped, the jeeps escorted it past the Vopos. On Thursday night, thirty-three Soviet tanks turned up and parked not far from the Brandenburg Gate—the first Soviet armor in East Berlin since 1953. On Friday, ten of these tanks descended the Friedrichstrasse and stopped about seventy-five yards from the American tanks, whose gun racks had been loaded and made ready for firing. For the first and only time in the cold war, American and Soviet tanks were nose to nose. Other governments and, indeed, the world watched and worried. Kennedy called Clay, who assured him there would be no shooting.[53] But Clay had created a situation of which none of the other personalities approved. The British were aroused. The State Department, along with General Lauris Norstad, the Supreme Allied Commander in Europe, saw the risks in this face-off as unjustified by any potential gain.

They felt no differently when the Soviet tanks withdrew on Saturday morning, sixteen hours after they had arrived. The flair and even daring of Clay's initiative lifted the city's sagging morale; in the broadest sense then, he was doing his job. The principle on which he had chosen to stand, however, was judged a distinctly minor one by his numerous critics. "It [the incident] did no permanent damage," says Martin Hillenbrand, who at the time headed the State Department's Office of German Affairs and was later ambassador in Bonn. "But it didn't affect Soviet policy."[54] Most diplomats felt that the situation could have set off an uprising in East Berlin or caused the Soviets to surround American tanks and escalate the tension; they hoped it wouldn't be repeated. Other governments had worried that Clay might actually knock down a section of wall. De Gaulle once told Adenauer, according to Bundy, that if the Americans had knocked it down, Berlin would have been lost.[55]

In Paris, General Norstad was in a fury about Clay's actions, which had exposed the U.S. to serious risks, among them having to back down before a much larger military force. Other soldiers, including General Maxwell Taylor, saw a danger of the American forces actually being destroyed. In Heidelberg, General Bruce Clarke was asked whether these units technically under his command (not Clay's) would have retreated if the Russians had used force against any of them in East Berlin. "I would hope so," said Clarke.[56]

Only Kennedy could have reined in Clay, who was outside both the military and the State Department chains of command. The order to Konev to withdraw his tanks came, of course, from Khrushchev: "I'm sure that within twenty minutes . . . the American tanks will pull back, too. They can't turn their tanks around and pull them back as long as our guns are pointing at them. They've gotten themselves into a difficult situation, and they don't know how to get out of it. They're looking for a way out, I'm sure. So let's give them one. We'll remove our tanks, and they'll follow our example."[57] He was right, except that he himself had created the theater that invited this sort of high drama. "I would say that in October 1961 the world was closer to the third world war than ever," says Valentin Falin, a senior Soviet functionary, ex-ambassador to Bonn, and now head of Novosti (a Soviet press agency). "Our tanks were then positioned in Berlin, combat ready, two hundred meters from American tanks. And, as an immediate participant of these events, let me assure you that if [the] Americans would follow the orders given to them—and the orders were to destroy the Berlin Wall—our tanks would then open fire."[58]

Like General Groves in 1945, Clay was operating largely on his own, leaving his principals the task of sorting out the implications and consequences. Looming over the affair were nuclear weapons. Several thousand of America's were by then in Europe—deployed in artillery battalions, aircraft squadrons, and integrated with other units. As for the long-range missile gap, much of the bureaucracy still kept faith with the myth, despite McNamara's February backgrounder. Over the summer of 1961, however, recovered film capsules of reconnaissance satellites made clear the still primitive state of the Soviet long-range missile program. Penkovsky, too, played a useful role, at least within the CIA. In May, according to Desmond Ball, "he is said to have delivered three installments of microfilm which contained the number of Soviet missiles deployed, highly technical information on the difficulties the Russians had encountered with the giant SS-6 ICBM, excerpts from the minutes of the top-level meetings at which it was decided to scrap the SS-6, and, finally, the admission from official records that the program was nearly a year behind schedule."[59] Penkovsky was toiling within a harsh CIA discipline. Robert Amory says that if his information had diverged from the overhead intelligence to an extent that might have marked him as a disinformation plant, "he would have been passed on to Jim Angleton's people."[60]*

By the fall, says Howard Stoertz, the overhead coverage seemed to eliminate most of the Soviet Union, aside from the eternally cloudy and hard to photograph Kola Peninsula, as being host to a sizable force of ICBMs. The inside joke, he says, "was that the peninsula would soon sink into the sea under the weight of all those ICBMs the Russians were supposed to have."[61]

On September 6, the CIA admitted that its current estimate of Soviet ICBM launchers was "probably too high."[62] The time to banish the gap formally had come. This was done a month later in a speech by Roswell Gilpatric, who explained to the Business Council at Hot Springs, Virginia, how American strategic forces were much stronger than Moscow's. A few days later, Khrushchev, aware that the actual gap favoring his adversary was growing, exploded a fifty-megaton weapon as a reminder of Soviet potential.

Khrushchev's misguided and, as it turned out, self-destructive adven-

*Angleton was the legendary head of the CIA's counterintelligence office.

turism meant that well over half of Kennedy's brief tenure, like Eisenhower's lengthy one, was agitated by a continuing East-West crisis. But in many other ways, the Kennedy experience was a break with the past, though a less sharp break than it was made to seem then. Novel management techniques were supposed to make sense of big weapons procurement, and the doctrine underlying deployment and any conceivable use of nuclear weapons became the focus of a fresh look by specialists who flocked to McNamara's Pentagon. They belonged in many cases to a priesthood bent on making an exact science of nuclear matters. Eisenhower's existential deterrence was banished; if nuclear warfare, or the threat thereof, couldn't be ruled out, a President mustn't confront the dilemma of having to yield in a crisis or destroy the other side's cities, thereby inviting the destruction of his own. He needed options—"a wider choice," Kennedy said, "than humiliation or all-out nuclear action." Also, the Soviet Union's development of long- and medium-range ballistic missiles threatened all NATO countries; Eisenhower's initial doctrine had been coupled with the so-called limited nuclear war concept. The idea was that short-range nuclear weapons would become an equalizer—the means by which NATO could overcome Moscow's heavy advantage in conventional forces. The Kennedy team continued to stockpile nuclear weapons in Europe, but the credibility of limited war there fell rapidly. The notion of confining these supposedly smaller nuclear weapons to the traditional battlefield in an area as densely inhabited as Western Europe was, on its face, preposterous. Using them, it seemed, would easily, if not inevitably, lead to general nuclear war. That, at least, is how it struck the Kennedy White House.

On arriving in office, Kennedy was presented with a war plan, described to him in a memo from Bundy as "dangerously rigid and, if continued without amendment, may leave you with very little choice as to how you face the moment of thermonuclear truth."[63] The plan was called SIOP-62, a coinage for its corpulent label—Single Integrated Operational Plan for Fiscal Year 1962. A SIOP is among the most sensitive and closely held of official documents; it identifies the Soviet and Chinese targets to be attacked, along with the type and number of weapons allotted to their destruction. SIOP-62 (like its predecessors) fancied releasing the entire American arsenal in one horrific spasm intended to eliminate all or most of the enemy's own nuclear forces. But Kennedy discovered while being briefed on SIOP-62 that, whatever happened, some portion of the admittedly inferior Soviet long-range force would survive to strike America.[64]

With McNamara as grand vizier for defense, the White House and the priesthood were pushing on an open door. "He abhors the thought that there is only one way of doing something; he is intensely interested in alternatives," wrote William W. Kaufmann, who closely advised McNamara (and a long line of his successors).[65] McNamara and Kennedy wanted to match the potential range of challenge with a correspondingly broad range of options. From a menu of alternate strategies, McNamara picked one called "flexible response"—"flexible" because, unlike the SIOPs, it recommended that if deterrence did fail, nuclear weapons should be used selectively. The initial targets would be enemy bomber and missile sites, of which there were, fortunately, not many. Other forces would be held in reserve if it should prove necessary to attack cities, but just the threat of such wanton destruction, it was felt, would encourage the other side to end the conflict on favorable terms. This strategy, like the others, relied then on the knowledge that America's long-range nuclear weapons were better and more numerous than Russia's. McNamara set about tailoring the forces to fit the strategy. America's deterrent would be built around survivable second-strike weapons. (Albert J. Wohlstetter, a pioneer nuclear strategist, recently said, "A force cannot deter an attack which it cannot survive."[66]) Being invulnerable (or nearly so), these would discourage, not invite, attack. Thus, McNamara recommended adding ten Polaris submarines to the number planned by Eisenhower and doubling the production capacity of the quick-reacting, silo-based Minuteman ICBMs. He increased the number of strategic bombers on ground alert status.

In the age of missiles, bombers struck some of the new people as all but obsolete. Bombers are, of course, slower to react, and their ability to penetrate Soviet air defenses is less certain. But in their slowness lies one of their advantages, they can be recalled. The bomber is reassuringly stable because it is so clearly a second-strike weapon. That aside, the air force clings to bombers with a devotion it will never feel for any missile system. And the affinity of one of the services for a weapons system is not to be taken lightly.

Some weapons didn't fit in, either because they were obsolete or vulnerable—hence unstable—or both. McNamara would balance the costs of improving the deterrent by ridding the strategic inventory of junk and canceling some new programs of which he was suspicious, which included an atomic-powered airplane and a highly controversial bomber, the B-70. Canceling the new bomber went down badly with the air force, especially its Strategic Air Command (SAC), which in the fifties and sixties tended to think of itself as a separate entity and to behave accordingly. (Curtis LeMay was the best known of its commanders—a legend, actually—but the most extreme example of SAC's truculent style was General Thomas S. Power, who succeeded LeMay in 1957.)

Both SAC and the parent air force strongly favored a nuclear-war-winning strategy—one that would allow the United States to strike first and shatter the other side's offense. "Counterforce," the insider's name for this prodigal approach, relied implicitly on the need to go first; going second would mean that many Soviet weapons on the target list would have already been launched against America. A preemptive strike under SIOP-62 amounted to releasing the entire force—then over 3,400 weapons—against targets in Russia, China, and Eastern Europe. Hundreds of millions would be destroyed. (China and East European countries would be struck even if they had no role in the conflict.)[67]

McNamara was having none of this nonsense. He wanted to draw the line somewhere—to avoid buying more weapons than were needed to support a deterrent strategy, with options built into it for the President. But what that meant—just where the line might be drawn—wasn't clear. "How much is enough?" was the question. In a celebrated commencement address at Ann Arbor in June 1962, McNamara said: "Principal military objectives in the event of nuclear war . . . should be the destruction of the enemy's military forces, not of his civilian population."[68] But not long afterward, he did a *volte-face* and began sizing the forces in a way that would allow each leg of the so-called triad—bombers, ICBMs, and submarine-launched ballistic missiles (SLBMs)—to destroy independently about 25 percent of the Soviet population and industry.* The emphasis thus moved from preemption to deterrence—"assured destruction" as it became known.

Exactly how McNamara's novel approach related to the SIOP was a source of discord, although less so than splits within the military over what forces a non-war-winning strategy would require. If McNamara thought that in the nuclear age less is more, or less is better, he had few takers within the services. The case of the much-admired Minuteman missile was illustrative and gave Kennedy a sharper sense of what he was up against. Everyone wanted a large role for Minuteman. LeMay, then the Air Force Chief of Staff, wanted to buy at least 2,400 of them. Power wanted 10,000 and was making his plans accordingly; he said as much in Kennedy's presence.[69] McNamara approved 1,200 units but told aides he expected the program to level off at 1,000, as it did. Curiously, he and Kennedy emerged from an exhaustive review with a program rather like Eisenhower's. Polaris and Minuteman were the chosen missiles of both administrations. Eisenhower

---

*An aide of McNamara's called the Ann Arbor speech an "aberration." "Bob," he said, "still wasn't thinking for himself. He was listening to his Whiz Kids and accepting too much of what they said at face value. In any case, he should have known there could be no such thing as primary retaliation against military targets after an enemy attack. If you're going to shoot at missiles, you're talking about first strike" (Henry L. Trewhitt, *McNamara: His Ordeal in the Pentagon* [New York: Harper & Row, 1971], p. 115).

had planned on 1,100 Minutemen, just 100 more than the number decided on by his successor. And Eisenhower had decided on 304 Polaris missiles on nineteen boats. Kennedy's initial recommendation was 464 missiles on twenty-nine boats. The similarity is the more striking, since Kennedy wasn't saddled with the fancied missile gap that had put Eisenhower under heavy pressure to do much more.

Adding to the confusion about flexible response was an obvious need to influence the procedure for controlling nuclear weapons. The Berlin crisis put the handwriting on the wall, and the ensuing Cuban psychodrama underlined it. America's command and control had been simplicity itself; the President alone held the authority for the weapons. A release order from him would send the entire force on its way, at which point command and control would cease to exist. But the fashion being created by McNamara and those around him insisted that any use of modern weapons must be measured and selective, a requirement that dictated a correspondingly refined system of command and control. An anomaly was emerging: The forces were being enlarged even before a means of managing them with adequate care had been set up. The question, simply put, was how to prevent a presidential release order from triggering SAC's spasm.

Ever the moth to Berlin's flame, Khrushchev tried in early 1962 to impose new restrictions on the air corridors to the city; certain altitudes and times of day would be reserved for his military aircraft. The allies ignored the restrictions. Soviet planes then began "buzzing" commercial aircraft and releasing strips of foil, a tactic aimed at confusing radars and hence a threat to safety.

Over the summer, the Soviets seemed to be changing course, if temporarily. In September, the Russian news agency TASS announced a postponement of the Berlin issue until after America's congressional elections in November.[70] By then Khrushchev had taken the last, greatest, and most ill advised of his gambles· He persuaded Cuba to accept deployment of Soviet ground-to-ground offensive missiles. Berlin and Cuba, Kennedy's *bêtes noires*, were becoming the same problem. Privately, the Soviets were suggesting a swap whereby they would give ground in Cuba if the Americans did the same in Berlin. Rusk told them, "You cannot support freedom in one place by surrendering freedom in another."[71]

In July, Soviet weapons and military units had begun arriving in Cuba.

In August, a U-2 aircraft spotted a surface-to-air missile (SAM) site being constructed. Two days later, Senator Kenneth B. Keating of New York claimed to have evidence of the presence of 1,200 Soviet troops in Cuba and of structures that appeared to foreshadow "a rocket installation."[72] The intelligence estimates judged the Soviet deployments as defensive, and Kennedy's advisers concurred. Although some analysts disagreed, Rusk says, "We thought they were mistaking SAM missiles for offensive missiles. The SAM looks like a hell of a missile."[73] Kennedy was worried. The good intentions of his campaign rhetoric included returning Cuba to the fold. As the fall elections approached, his distinct lack of progress became an issue. Keating stepped up the pressure, and his colleague, Indiana Senator Homer E. Capehart, called for an invasion of Cuba to remove the Soviet military presence.

Cuba was putting surveillance to its stiffest test. All the intrusive hardware—aircraft and satellites—relentlessly patrolled the skies over Cuba and the Soviet Union. Among other techniques relied on by the CIA was "crate-ology," a method of determining the contents of large crates carried on board Soviet ships known to be delivering arms. Specialists felt that the new technology allowed them to distinguish between crates carrying jet fighters and others carrying bombs.

There were endless reports of missile sitings, and, although routine, they added force to the charge that Kennedy was allowing Cuba to become a base from which Soviet weapons could threaten American cities and bases. Senator Everett Dirksen and Congressman Charles Halleck, the House Minority Leader, introduced a resolution to take military action against Cuba; it was watered down to demands for a blockade of the island. Deputy Secretary of State George Ball told Congress that the step would be an act of war.

On September 4, a critical date in the saga just beginning, Kennedy warned Moscow not to introduce offensive ground-to-ground missiles into Cuba. And the Soviet ambassador to Washington, Anatoly F. Dobrynin, came to see Attorney General Robert F. Kennedy earlier that day bearing an unusual private assurance from Khrushchev to the President that no ground-to-ground missiles or other offensive weapons would be sent to Cuba. He also volunteered his government's willingness to sign an atmospheric test ban under certain conditions.[74]

"When one sovereign deceives another, you get a crisis," says Harvard's Richard Neustadt, an astute monitor of presidential behavior. On Tuesday morning, October 16, Kennedy learned that Khrushchev had deceived him. CIA photo interpreters, examining the take from a U-2 overflight of western Cuba on the 14th, gave National Security Adviser

McGeorge Bundy the bad news. Launch sites were under way for 1,000-mile medium-range missiles (MRBMs) and 2,200-mile intermediate-range missiles (IRBMs).*

The surprise was complete. Cloudy weather had forced a lull in surveillance, and the sites had seemed to appear from nowhere. Soviet engineering techniques were more advanced than the CIA had reckoned them to be. Roberta Wohlstetter, who has examined both Pearl Harbor and the Cuban crisis, wrote, "The rapidity of the Russians' installation was in effect a logistical surprise comparable to the technological surprise at the time of Pearl Harbor."[75]

The reality sunk in during a briefing of a few senior officials later that morning. While offering public and private assurances about Cuba, Khrushchev had insinuated a huge amount of material and hardware there, enough for forty-two missiles (of a planned eighty), along with SAMs, MIG interceptors, and Ilyushin-28 light bombers, the latter carrying nuclear bombs. By deploying missiles within range of much of North America, Khrushchev was about to alter the political and strategic balance of power in a single stroke.

Inevitably, a lot of what happened over the ensuing thirteen days of the crisis has passed into legend. Kennedy and the Executive Committee of the NSC, or ExComm, as it became known, were widely judged to have managed the nuclear confrontation that perhaps had to happen once with restraint and moderation. Kennedy, we know, faced immense pressure to call Khrushchev's hand—to use his overwhelming air superiority to remove the missiles. And, of course, we know he chose instead to quarantine the island so as to give everyone time to consider the stakes and, in Khrushchev's case, find a way out.

The dozen regulars on ExComm observed immaculate secrecy; they met sometimes in the White House cabinet office but mainly in George Ball's conference room at the State Department. Not surprisingly, they disagreed sharply, sometimes acrimoniously, and most of them changed their minds on one issue or another, at one time or another. Kennedy's position was, of course, much the most complicated. The decisions would be his. Also, far more than any of the others, he had to see the affair not only as a crisis bearing unimaginable risks but as a threat to his party's control of Congress and, further along, to his presidency. The distance he had to travel over the famous thirteen days is perhaps best illustrated by remarks he made at the first meeting on the 16th. After some lively discussion of options, he named three for further consideration: "One would be

*The IRBMs were en route but never arrived.

just taking out these missiles. Number two would be take out all the airplanes. Number three is to invade." And, he added, as the group recessed, "We're certainly going to do Number One. We're going to take out these missiles."[76]

Robert Kennedy's performance was especially mercurial. Although widely portrayed as a moderate in the early ExComm meetings, the transcript shows that on October 16 he opposed an air strike because he considered it inadequate. He favored instead a full-scale invasion and even proposed fabricating an incident in order to justify the move.* And when he wrote his famous note—"I know now how Tojo felt when he was planning Pearl Harbor"—he may have meant, as one historian has observed, that "he really did understand how it felt to be contemplating a large-scale military attack, because that was precisely what he at this point wanted."[77] Not for some days did his dovish plumage appear.

A quarter century later, in March 1987, most of ExComm's veterans met with a dozen or so scholar-specialists of the affair, some with a lot of government experience, at Hawk's Cay in the Florida Keys, for a long weekend conference organized by the John F. Kennedy School of Government at Harvard. They were there to review what actually happened and what was learned. The meeting was remarkable, mainly for some intriguing revelations and insights which emerged and were wholly new to the ExComm veterans: Robert McNamara, McGeorge Bundy, George Ball, Douglas Dillon (Kennedy's Secretary of the Treasury), and Theodore Sorensen (special counsel to the President). Dean Rusk and Paul Nitze had planned to attend, but couldn't.† But a letter from Rusk, which was read to the conference by Bundy, produced its memorable moment.

Apart from reviewing fearsome uncertainties and Kennedy's options, the conferees wrestled with two large questions: Why did Khrushchev put the missiles into Cuba? Why did he take them out? Also, Rusk's letter put Kennedy's hitherto well-disguised position in a different light, forcing conferees to reconsider his intentions—the what might have been had the crisis lasted a day longer than it did.

The first of the surprises at Hawk's Cay was supplied by Sorensen in a comment about Kennedy warning Khrushchev not to put offensive mis-

---

*The transcript for October 16 (p. 27) shows that he suggested creating a pretext for an invasion by staging an action against the U.S. base at Guantánamo Bay, or by sinking a U.S. ship as was done in 1898 when the U.S. entered the Spanish-American War (Transcript, National Security Archives, Cuban Missile Crisis File).

†Other ExComm members not at Hawk's Cay include CIA Director John McCone, Deputy Undersecretary of State U. Alexis Johnson, Assistant Secretary of State for Latin America Edward Martin, and Deputy Secretary of Defense Roswell Gilpatric.

siles into Cuba. "I believe the President drew the line precisely where he thought the Soviets were not and would not be; that is to say, if we had known that the Soviets were putting 40 missiles in Cuba, we might . . . have drawn the line at 100, and said with great fanfare that we would absolutely not tolerate the presence of more than 100 missiles in Cuba. I say that believing very strongly that that would have been an act of prudence, not weakness. But I am suggesting that one reason the line was drawn at zero was because we simply thought the Soviets weren't going to deploy any there anyway."

In a conversation some months later, Sorensen said he spoke a bit loosely at Hawk's Cay and had meant to emphasize Kennedy's "reasonable certainty that he was stating something he felt reasonably sure they wouldn't do."[78] But the amended language doesn't remove the inference that Kennedy, had he known the Soviet missiles were en route, might have drawn a different line. Sorensen's comment may be the first clue to understanding Kennedy's own view of the crisis and what it would take to end it peacefully. No one, including Sorensen, knows exactly what Kennedy had in mind. He may have been thinking first of Berlin; hoping to avoid a major crisis there, he may have been prepared to take some political heat at home, as he surely would have if Soviet missiles had entered Cuba with impunity. Or Kennedy may have worried that Khrushchev would make a security treaty with Castro under which he would openly put missiles into Cuba just as the United States had put Jupiter missiles into Turkey.

In 1962, Soviet experts were sure that Khrushchev would never deploy nuclear weapons outside Russian boundaries. If he wouldn't deploy them in Warsaw Pact countries, why would he put them in Cuba? He probably did it, said Kennedy to Arthur Schlesinger, Jr., early in the crisis, to draw Russia and China closer together, to radically redefine the setting in which the Berlin problem could be reopened after the election, and to deal the United States a tremendous political blow.[79]

Kennedy's critics said that Khrushchev won, having succeeded in getting what he and Castro had wanted all along: an American non-invasion pledge. Few experienced people, Russian or American, would agree. Then as now, they saw two large and related motives lying behind Khrushchev's gamble. One was, as Kennedy said, Berlin. "We were told by a senior Russian," says Rusk, "that the idea was to get the missiles into Cuba and then revive the Berlin crisis with the Soviet position having more weight this time."[80]

The other motive was strategic. America's advantage was overwhelming—greater than it would ever be again. The ratio was roughly 5,000 deliverable American nuclear weapons to 300 Russian.* The ability of the Soviet force to reach targets in North America was rather suspect but couldn't be ruled out. At most, a Soviet first strike might have destroyed four to five hundred of America's weapons. But with missiles deployed in Cuba, the Soviets could have knocked out four fifths of the American arsenal. Although five hundred would have been left intact, the balance would nonetheless have changed. A planner on either side would have been impressed by Khrushchev's gambit.

Some experts feel that Khrushchev was driven by domestic pressures. The duel in Berlin had gone badly. Relations with China were sliding from bad to worse. His efforts to reform Soviet society were failing. Success in Cuba could clear the way for success in Berlin. Changing the strategic balance, about which the Soviet military were very uneasy as well as grumpy, could remove a possibly serious political liability in Moscow. Deploying medium-range missiles in Cuba was easier and much cheaper than trying to overhaul America in long-range bombers and missiles. "Khrushchev was shaking the tree," says Paul Nitze. "He could see all kinds of good things falling out."[81]

Khrushchev himself wrote, "It was during my visit to Bulgaria [May 1962] that I had the idea of installing missiles with nuclear warheads in Cuba without letting the United States find out they were there until it was too late to do anything about them . . . our missiles would have equalized what the West likes to call the 'the balance of power.' The Americans had surrounded our country with military bases and threatened us with nuclear weapons, and now they would learn just what it feels like to have enemy missiles pointing at you."[82] These words probably expressed what for Khrushchev was the driving consideration.

As for the risk, Khrushchev was still unconvinced that Kennedy could play poker with him. "Nikita wouldn't have deployed missiles in Cuba unless he thought Kennedy wouldn't act," says Arkady Shevchenko. "A few people warned him directly that the situation could lead to a blockade, and we would have no power to do anything. The nuclear option was excluded on all sides. The Soviet Union would not initiate a nuclear war. The option was explored, like all options, by the military, and rejected. Nikita ignored all this—because of his opinion of Kennedy. I once heard him myself in his office saying that Kennedy was a weak man. The Cuban crisis took him completely by surprise."[83]

Simply put, Khrushchev took a gamble he was not prepared to back

---

*Air force generals like Power and LeMay talked glibly then about taking out Russia's still puny arsenal in a first strike. At Hawk's Cay, McNamara conceded that Khrushchev, being aware of such talk, might have tried to discourage American notions of a first strike by putting missiles into Cuba.

up, because he didn't think he'd have to. "What was most dangerous in Berlin," says Shevchenko, "was the possibility of a minor episode producing a chain reaction. There were big unknowns. But any sensible American should have understood that the Soviet Union wouldn't fight for Cuba. Only if Nikita had been a madman would he have tried to go to war there. If the Americans thought he was a madman, they didn't understand him. And even with all his power, he could not have started a nuclear war. His order would not have been carried out."[84]

Khrushchev's lucidity was only one of ExComm's concerns, however. Another was the possibility of an unauthorized launch from Cuba. The "mad major" scenario haunted numerous senior officials because, as McNamara said, Washington had no control over its own nuclear weapons at this time. "We thought the Soviet officers might react the way NATO officers might have, and so we [his faction] were extremely reluctant to risk the air strike." And, he added revealingly, "I don't believe we ever discussed in ExComm how we would have responded to a nuclear weapon fired from Cuba."

On Wednesday, the 17th, the take from U-2 overflights showed that between sixteen and twenty-two missiles could be operational within a week. That same day, a message from Khrushchev was transmitted to Robert Kennedy through Georgi Bolshakov, a TASS correspondent in Washington whose earlier contacts with Robert Kennedy opened the so-called back channel between Washington and Moscow. Over the years, a great deal of sensitive business had been done through this channel. Khrushchev's message repeated the assurance that no missiles capable of striking America would be put in Cuba. "Bolshakov was more than just a minor official," said Sorensen at Hawk's Cay. "He was the channel between Kennedy and Khrushchev. When Bolshakov said there were no missiles, Kennedy believed him."

Quite probably, Bolshakov didn't know about the missiles. Khrushchev is thought to have kept most of his key people in the dark.[85] Gromyko came to see Kennedy on the afternoon of the 18th, just as the debate within ExComm was becoming intense and discordant. Kennedy elected not to confront him with his knowledge of the Soviet duplicity until he had decided what he was going to do about it. The focus of the conversation was Berlin, with Gromyko hinting that Soviet pressure would resume once the American elections on November 6 were out of the way. He also mentioned the possibility of another Kennedy-Khrushchev meeting.

Gromyko then assured Kennedy that Soviet assistance to Cuba was solely defensive. Kennedy reminded him of the earlier assurances from Khrushchev and Dobrynin to that effect and waited for him to set the record straight. When Gromyko didn't do so, Kennedy "sent for and read aloud his September warning against offensive missiles in Cuba. Gromyko 'must have wondered why I was reading it,' he said later. 'But he did not respond.' "[86]

Gromyko left Kennedy in high spirits, describing the meeting as "very useful."[87] But his assurance to Kennedy was seen as a conscious, bold-faced lie and, as such, became part of the legend. Aside from Gromyko himself, no one can say whether he lied. He wasn't a member of the Presidium or Khrushchev's small inner circle, and some American experts suspect that he didn't know about the missiles. Shevchenko doubts that either Gromyko or Dobrynin knew about them.[88] Curiously, Gromyko and Dobrynin— both highly skilled diplomats and both involved in misleading Kennedy— became the figures with whom Washington conducted most of its serious business with Moscow over the next quarter century.

Paul Nitze recalls ExComm's discussion during the first week as being "sophomoric—lots of morality issues raised."[89] The transcripts do show disarray, and that is hardly surprising. Some members saw themselves confronting risks on a scale defying instant comprehension and for which history offered no precedent. On Tuesday, the 16th, Kennedy expressed regret at having committed himself to act if the Soviets put offensive weapons into Cuba. "Last month I should have said that we don't care," he told ExComm. ". . . What difference does it make? They've got enough to blow us up now anyway."[90]

Others took a simpler and bolder view. Since the U.S. held all the military cards, Khrushchev's bold venture was a problem only to the degree Washington allowed it to become one by not swiftly excising the hostile missile presence. And if Castro was swept aside in the action, so much the better.

By Saturday the 20th, the members were looking mainly at two options: One was an air strike, the other a blockade. The initially strong bias toward the air strike had shifted, partly because of disagreement over whether the act should or should not be preceded by a warning to Cuba and the Soviets. Some felt that world opinion would turn against the United States if it launched a surprise attack. Others felt that a warning would defeat the purpose. The blockade drew little support at first. It would directly challenge the Soviet Union. More important, a blockade would take time—time during which the Soviet missiles could become operational. An air strike—at least, in theory—would remove them in a stroke and present Khrushchev with a *fait accompli.*[91]

Kennedy spent Friday in prearranged campaigning and then, having invented a cold, returned to Washington for the Saturday afternoon Ex-Comm meeting. McNamara had alerted four tactical air squadrons in case Kennedy decided on an air strike. Bundy presented the case for the air strike, McNamara for the blockade. By then, the blockade's major defect—the precious time it would expend—was being seen as a potential advantage; a nonviolent solution to the crisis might be found within that time. Gilpatric said, "Essentially, Mr. President, this is a choice between limited action and unlimited action; and most of us think that it's better to start with limited action."[92] A straw vote showed eleven members for the blockade, six for the air strike.[93]

"There isn't any good solution," said Kennedy. "Whichever plan I choose, the ones whose plans we're not taking are the lucky ones—they'll be able to say 'I told you so' in a week or two. But this one seems the least objectionable."[94] He meant the blockade.

Adlai Stevenson, the ambassador to the United Nations at the time, sat in on the meeting. He supported the blockade but recommended signaling the Soviets that in return for removing the missiles from Cuba the United States would be willing to withdraw its missiles from Turkey and Italy and give up its naval base at Guantánamo Bay.[95] Significantly, Kennedy seemed favorably disposed to a diplomatic approach, according to Nitze, who recalls that he himself, backed by Dillon and McCone, strongly opposed a trade and managed to silence the idea—temporarily.[96]

On Sunday morning, Kennedy, McNamara, Taylor, and a few others met with General Walter C. Sweeney, Jr., the Tactical Air Command Chief. He said that an attack from the air, even with as many as five hundred sorties, couldn't be expected to get all the missiles; thus the attack would have to be followed by an invasion so as to destroy any remaining missiles. Almost certainly, Kennedy privately ruled out an air attack at that moment, if he hadn't already done so.

Dean Acheson was dispatched the same day to inform de Gaulle. Kennedy himself was in daily touch with Harold Macmillan about the crisis and regularly saw Sir David Ormsby-Gore, who, besides being Britain's ambassador, was a friend from childhood. Adenauer would be briefed by Ambassador Walter Dowling. Finally, a coded text of a televised address Kennedy would give the next evening, with a cover letter, was sent to Khrushchev for delivery one hour before air time.[97]

Over the weekend, the armed forces began to prepare. Guantánamo was reinforced, the army's First Armored Division was redeployed to Georgia, two airborne divisions were alerted, and destroyers moved toward blockade positions in the Caribbean.

Washington was awash in rumors; a Berlin crisis seemed most likely. On Monday, the curtain parted. At 5:00, Kennedy briefed the congressional leadership. At 6:00, Rusk saw Dobrynin, who left the State Department looking ashen and shaken by some accounts. And then, Kennedy informed the world of the Soviet deception and made it starkly clear that a blockade was just one of several steps he might take to counter Khrushchev's move. Remarkably, neither Kennedy nor any member of ExComm was aware of a stunning event in Moscow that must have occurred shortly before his televised address. One man, Oleg Penkovsky, appears to have tried to start a war between the superpowers. What he actually did was revealed in October 1987—on the twenty-fifth anniversary of the missile crisis—by Raymond Garthoff, who had evaluated Penkovsky's reports, and, after leaving the CIA for State in 1961, kept up his contact with the handful of people who "handled" Penkovsky. One of these told him about this exceptional but wildly egocentric agent's parting gesture. Penkovsky had been under surveillance for some time and was arrested on October 22. The Soviets may have thought he had told Washington about the missiles. Penkovsky, wrote Garthoff, had been given a few coded telephonic signals "for use in emergencies, including one to be used if he was about to be arrested, and also one to be used in the ultimate contingency: imminent war. When he was being arrested, at his apartment, he had time to send a telephonic signal—but chose to use the signal for an imminent Soviet attack! . . . about to go down, he evidently decided to play Samson and bring the temple down on everyone else as well."[98]

Had Penkovsky sent such a message in normal circumstances, it would obviously not have been accepted at face value, but, as Garthoff noted, "October 22 . . . was not a normal day." His handlers, after considering their harsh options, decided to suppress Penkovsky's shocking signal. The CIA's senior people, including Director John McCone, were instantly informed of Penkovsky's arrest but not told about the message. However awesome the responsibility they took upon themselves, Penkovsky's handlers knew their man. In London on official business, he had asked his British handlers to introduce him to Queen Elizabeth, and he asked the Americans to arrange a meeting with Kennedy.[99] Like many another mole, Penkovsky had an exalted sense of his own importance.

American forces have been placed on a worldwide alert status on three occasions in the nuclear age. The alert puts them in a higher stage of readiness and is designed to emphasize to the other side the seriousness of the situation. The Soviets have never put their forces on any similar footing. Their concern with "Bonapartism" may exclude any such step. While Kennedy was making his speech, America's forces were moved up to an alert level known as DEFCON-3 (Defense Condition-3). All leaves were canceled and personnel recalled. ICBM launchers were prepared for firing, Polaris submarines hurried from their ports, the bombers were dispersed (many of them to civilian airports), and battle staffs went on round-the-clock duty.[100]

It was then decided to impress the Soviets with the ultrareadiness of SAC, and on Wednesday, the 24th, SAC was ordered to move to an even higher alert status known as DEFCON-2, the only time when American forces have ever been placed on this footing. But in relaying the order, General Power told his staff to "make a little mistake. Send a message in the clear."[101] Any such message would normally be encoded. Sending it "in the clear" amounted to telling Moscow that SAC's forces equipped to drop over 7,000 megatons of explosives—were now just one level below deployment for combat.[102] The Soviets, as Garthoff wrote, "must have been shocked suddenly to hear all the alert orders from Omaha and a steady stream of responses from bomber units reporting their attainment of alert posture, including nuclear-armed flights poised for attack on the Soviet Union."[103] Moscow, in short, got a message that Washington didn't know had been sent. During the crisis, other such "messages" of which Washington was also unaware were sent. Kennedy's control of his military was a good deal less than he had assumed it to be.

On Tuesday morning, Khrushchev's response to Kennedy—seething with indignant denials and accusations of "piracy"—arrived in Washington. It didn't get much attention. "We have won a considerable victory," said Rusk to George Ball. "You and I are still alive."[104]

Kennedy wrote back asking Khrushchev to avoid steps that would "make the situation more difficult to control than it is."[105] McCone informed ExComm that Soviet submarines were heading toward Cuba, and details of the naval blockade were discussed throughout the day. Recalling the events at Hawk's Cay, Abram Chayes, who had been the State Department's legal adviser, noted an irony: "When we sat down to draft a blockade proclamation, we didn't have any idea how to go about it; so we picked the last one off the shelf and used it as our template. Do you know which one that was? Cuba, 1898!"

The exact location of the missiles was, of course, known to ExComm. And the intelligence had detected vans of the kind that carry missile nose cones rumbling through Havana late at night. Missile storage facilities were being built. But the missile warheads had not been seen, and no one could say whether any had reached Cuba. Still, the assumption had to be that they were there. "The real issue," says Nitze, "was how much time you had before the warheads were mated with missiles."[106] "We never saw a warhead on a missile during that crisis," says Dean Rusk. "And we wanted to settle it before that changed. I don't know how many people had nuclear war in mind. I do know that John F. Kennedy and Dean Rusk had it in mind."[107]

The warheads never did reach Cuba. A special custodial unit of the Soviet Strategic Rocket Forces (SRF) was detected loading them into a large freighter, the *Poltava,* at Odessa. This was the first and only time that intelligence sources had spotted one of these units actually handling warheads.[108] The *Poltava* declared for a false destination (Algiers) and carried a false manifest, as it had done on earlier voyages when it carried missiles. This time, however, it was joined in the Atlantic by three Soviet submarines from the Northern Fleet. The ship was little more than two days from Cuba when the blockade began.[109]

It took effect on Wednesday morning—at 10:00. McNamara told Ex-Comm that the *Gagarin* and the *Komiles* were within range of the American ships; one or both would have to be halted sometime that morning. More bad news arrived: A Soviet sub was escorting the two ships.

At 10:25, John McCone reported that some of the Russian ships had stopped dead in the water. A few minutes later, the report was confirmed. Fourteen of the twenty Soviet ships had either stopped or turned back, the *Poltava* among them. At this point, Dean Rusk uttered the episode's memorable comment: "We are eyeball to eyeball, and I think the other fellow just blinked."[110]*

Later that day, U Thant, Secretary General of the United Nations, proposed suspending both the quarantine and further arms deliveries while the two sides negotiated. Khrushchev publicly welcomed the idea, but Kennedy rejected it. The Soviets, he said, had created a threat by putting missiles into Cuba which would have to be removed.

---

*Rusk himself thought nothing of the remark, which he says was drawn from a game he had played as a child in Georgia. "You sat close to each other," he said, "staring into one another's eyes, and the first one to blink lost." The remark was leaked, which, in the circumstances, angered Rusk, and also Kennedy. "I was mad as hell that some son-of-a-bitch would leak something like that at that time," said Rusk. "Early the next morning," he said, "I got a call from Kennedy, who told me to call in the reporter, find out who gave him the story, and fire the guy. So I called in the reporter and said, in effect, 'I haven't done this before—asked for a source—but I have to in this case. You make your living around this place and I suggest you tell me.' He did. I phoned Kennedy and said, 'I have the source, but I can't fire him. The reporter says you gave him the story at 4:00 yesterday afternoon.' Kennedy laughed and said, 'O.K., forget it' " (Conversation with Dean Rusk, November 10, 1986).

Within ExComm, discussion was centered on how long to rely on the pressure of the blockade. At what point would the air strike–invasion option be exercised? Except for General Taylor, the air strike advocates were not intimidated by the prospect of having to invade Cuba. "Invading the island was the last thing I thought we should do," said Taylor in an interview with Richard Neustadt. "Once you invade Cuba, what are you going to do with it? You gonna sit on it for eternity? You could have . . . guerrilla warfare against our occupying forces, and tie down a large part of your conventional strength."[111] Curiously, Taylor's aversion to invasion didn't weaken his support for an air strike, even though it was clear that the one would almost surely lead to the other.

On Thursday, the 25th, a Soviet ship, the *Bucharest*, crossed the barrier. Kennedy ordered U.S. warships not to stop and board the ship but rather to follow it. "We don't want to push him [Khrushchev] to a precipitous action," said Kennedy. "I don't want to put him in a corner from which he cannot escape."[112] That night, however, intelligence showed that work on the missile sites was speeding up. Would Khrushchev leave Kennedy a way out?

Kennedy stepped up the reconnaissance flights over Cuba. He ordered that all six Soviet submarines in the zone be "followed and harassed ."[113] (At one time or another they were forced to surface in the presence of U.S. warships.) Still, in his telephone conversation with Macmillan that day, he wondered whether a political solution could be offered—perhaps a trade of Soviet missiles for an international guarantee for Cuba against invasion.[114]

By Friday morning, ExComm's collective patience with restraint was fast declining. The missiles, it was feared, were on the verge of becoming operational. Equally likely and perhaps even more imminent was a major squeeze by Khrushchev on Berlin. But as the day wore on, the picture improved. Intelligence showed that all sixteen of the Soviet dry cargo ships—the five thought to be carrying missile equipment and the one with warheads—were returning to port. And at 9:30 that night, Khrushchev's celebrated "first" letter to Kennedy began coming over the Teletype. It was rambling, a bit confused, and remarkably personal; he had surely drafted it himself. But most important was the tone which, although occasionally menacing, seemed on balance conciliatory. He sounded like a man who wanted a way out. "Should war indeed break out," he warned, "it would not be in our power to contain or stop it, for such is the logic of war." And "Mr. President," he pleaded at one point, "you and I should not now pull on the ends of the rope in which you have tied a knot of war, because the harder you and I pull, the tighter this knot will become . . . Let us take measures for untying this knot." Toward the end came the famous hint that he would withdraw Soviet forces from Cuba in return for America's pledge not to invade. A few other Soviet signals reinforced the impression that Khrushchev was ready to make that kind of deal. Still, the situation was dicey and the letter clouded by its ragged, emotional style. "He gave us some concern because it . . . suggested that maybe the old man was losing his cool," said Rusk. "And we didn't like the thought that someone whose finger was on the nuclear trigger was losing his cool."[115] Still, the letter was cautiously judged a net plus. ExComm would meet the next morning to frame an answer.

Saturday, the 27th—"Black Saturday," as it was later called—was the first anniversary of the tank confrontation in the Friedrichstrasse. It began badly and got steadily worse. Early in the morning, the FBI reported that Soviet consulate personnel in New York, sensing American military action against Cuba—hence war—appeared to be preparing to destroy all sensitive documents. And a Soviet ship had broken away from others outside the quarantine line and was headed for Cuba.[116]

Just after ExComm sat down, Radio Moscow began broadcasting a second letter from Khrushchev to Kennedy. It bore no relation to the first. Khrushchev's agitated *cri de coeur* had been superseded, it seemed, by a tougher message with a committee-cleared imprint. The price was going up. Soviet missiles would come out of Cuba provided American missiles were withdrawn from Turkey. "It was like a bucket of ice in the face," said Douglas Dillon at Hawk's Cay.

Kennedy saw at once that a concrete, unavoidable issue was now squarely before him. He had probably expected it, even if the others had not. From the start, he had worried about the deployment of "soft," i.e., vulnerable, and obsolete American missiles in Europe, especially the Jupiters sold to Turkey and within easy range of Russian targets. After becoming President, he had instructed Rusk to take steps to remove the Turkish Jupiters. The Turks held fast. "They were very upset," Rusk said.[117] They argued the need for such missiles on NATO's southern flank. Later on, George Ball and Paul Nitze tried and failed to persuade the Turks to give up the missiles.

A part of the crisis mythology is that Kennedy, having told his people to get the Jupiters out of Turkey, was furious to find them still there. In fact, he was aware of the situation, but still he was furious. Khrushchev's second proposal had put him in a no-win position: Either he kept faith with Turkey, an ally, by sustaining a deployment of weapons that should never have been deployed at all, or he removed them under pressure, thereby inviting angry charges of betraying the Turks (and NATO), along with the political heat such charges would produce on the eve of an election.

"Have we gone to the Turkish government?" he asked that Saturday. "I've talked about it now for a week." When Rusk and Ball explained that it "would be an extremely unsettling business," Kennedy's answer was "Well, this is unsettling now, George, because he's got us in a pretty good spot, because most people will regard this as not an unreasonable proposal . . . I think we've got a very tough one here . . . because we wouldn't take the missiles out of Turkey, then maybe we'll have to invade or make a massive strike on Cuba which may lose Berlin. That's what concerns me."[118] The transcript of Black Saturday shows Kennedy time and again returning to the Jupiter issue, sometimes bitingly, while others tried to ignore it. He got very little support; many of ExComm's members remained opposed to a trade.

The Joint Chiefs, said General Taylor, recommended executing the air strike no later than Monday morning, the 29th, and making it part of the invasion plan.[119] At 4:00, Taylor reported that a U-2 had been shot down over Cuba by a Soviet SAM; the pilot was dead. The pressure for military action abruptly increased; ExComm had already decided to take out a SAM site if a U-2 were hit and to remove them all if a second aircraft were lost. The air strike and invasion seemed imminent. "There was a feeling that the noose was tightening on all of us . . . on mankind, and that the bridges to escape were crumbling," wrote Robert Kennedy.[120]

Equally bad was the next report: A U-2 had lost its navigational system and strayed over the Kola Peninsula. The instant anxiety was that the Soviets would see it as evidence of reconnaissance preceding a nuclear strike. McNamara was reported to have "turned absolutely white, and yelled, 'This means war with the Soviet Union.' "[121]

"By Saturday, the 27th, there was a clear majority in the ExComm in favor of taking military action," recalled Dillon at Hawk's Cay. "The expectation was a military confrontation by Tuesday and possibly tomorrow."

"I don't agree with Doug that we were all drifting toward an invasion," replied Sorensen. "That isn't to say that advocates of the quarantine weren't under pressure—we were, because the evidence was mounting that it hadn't worked . . . we were thinking that we had to come up with something."

McNamara disagreed with both, especially Dillon. "I believe we still could have done an awful lot more with the blockade. We could have continued to turn the screw for quite some time, and I believe that's what we would have done."

At some point during Black Saturday, Kennedy must have decided that ExComm had become a large part of his problem and that he would have to play a lone hand. He had known for several days that he would not attack Cuba. But he also knew, even if McNamara did not, that time had run out for the blockade; he could not "have continued to turn the screw for quite some time." The pressure to take direct action against the missiles and avoid the loss of another U-2 was too great. Kennedy knew the political heat, especially in Congress, from a continuing crisis would be intolerable. The thing had to be settled, and quickly.

By late afternoon, the ExComm meeting had become confused and rancorous. The issue was how to reply to Khrushchev's letter, especially his new terms. Robert Kennedy later wrote that it was he who suggested ignoring the second letter and replying instead to the more obliging message of the night before.[122] According to Bundy, however, "the notion of sticking to the Friday message was [Llewellyn] Thompson's. Others supported it, but the initiative and emphasis were mainly Thompson's."[123] The transcript supports Bundy. "I don't agree, Mr. President," said Thompson when Kennedy at one point expressed doubt about whether negotiation would work. Thompson then suggested dealing only with the first letter.[124] The President accepted the ploy, but the transcript shows him warning the others that if it didn't work, the Jupiter issue would have to be dealt with.[125] His letter to Khrushchev sidestepped it and ruled out negotiations unless the missiles were dismantled and work on the sites halted.

As ExComm's meeting broke up, Kennedy convened a smaller group in the Oval Office to discuss another message—to be conveyed orally to Dobrynin. "One part of the oral message," Bundy wrote, "was simple, stern and quickly decided . . . no Soviet missiles in Cuba, and no U.S. invasion. Otherwise further American action was unavoidable . . . The other part of the oral message was proposed by Dean Rusk: that we should tell Khrushchev that while there could be no deal over the Turkish missiles, the President was determined to get them out and would do so once the Cuban crisis was resolved. The proposal was quickly supported by the rest of us and approved by the President . . . No one could be sure it would work, but all of us believed it was worth a try."[126] In effect, Kennedy was giving Khrushchev an either/or proposal: Either accept my under-the-table trade or remove your missiles before I remove them.

Rusk, who had clearly been paying attention to Kennedy, still had another idea which he characteristically reserved for the President's ears alone. They talked tête-à-tête after the others had gone. What they decided *never* surfaced—was never known to anyone on ExComm—until the meeting at Hawk's Cay twenty-five years later. There, a letter from Rusk to the conference chairman was read aloud by Bundy to the surprised assemblage—people who, in most cases, thought they knew everything of importance about the missile crisis. Kennedy, wrote Rusk, had authorized him to call Andrew Cordier—a friend and former U.N. Deputy Secretary General—and give him a statement which would be made public by U Thant. The statement would propose the removal of both the Soviet missiles and the Jupiters. "Mr. Cordier was to put the statement in the hands of U Thant only after a further signal from us. That step was never taken and the statement I furnished to Mr. Cordier has never seen the light of day. So far as I know, Andrew Cordier and I were the only ones who knew of this particular step."

So here was Kennedy—the all-but-forgotten man at Hawk's Cay—preparing to do publicly what most of ExComm, according to the transcript of Black Saturday, was against doing even privately. Rusk's letter shows a President taking matters into his own hands—a political animal who had decided to take the intense political heat that a public trade of missiles would generate rather than the possibly greater heat that would build up if he failed to act at once. Kennedy, the chief executive, knew he held all the cards militarily, but he also knew that even though he could smash the Soviet Union in a nuclear war, one or more Soviet weapons would reach one or more American cities. He didn't see the missiles in Cuba as justifying even a small risk of war. Late on Black Saturday, he took the three steps designed to lower the risk. First, he deputized his brother to see Dobrynin that same evening and convey the two part message agreed to in the Oval Office by the small group. Second was the above-the-table missile trade that Rusk was told to arrange through U Thant if the under-the-table deal was rejected. And third, he ordered the Jupiters in Turkey made nonoperational in a fashion the Soviets could clearly see.

The long day ended on a deeply apprehensive note. After his brother returned to the White House to report on the meeting with Dobrynin, Kennedy ordered twenty-four troop carrier squadrons of the air force reserve to active duty. They would be essential to an invasion.[127]

"I'll never forget walking through the Rose Garden with Bob McNamara on Sunday morning," said Ball at Hawk's Cay. "It was such a beautiful morning, and it reminded me very strongly of the Georgia O'Keeffe painting of a rose growing through a skull." But by midmorning, the good news from Khrushchev had arrived. The gist of his message was that he had "given a new order to dismantle the arms which you described as offensive, and to crate and return them to the Soviet Union." "Khrushchev liked his own first letter enough to come back to it when it was offered," said Bundy. Thompson had been right the day before in saying, "The important thing for Khrushchev is to be able to say, 'I saved Cuba. I stopped an invasion,' and he can get away with this if he wants to . . ."[128] If Saturday, the 27th, was the cold war's best-remembered day for the members of ExComm, Sunday may have been that for the world. The worst was over.

For Kennedy and ExComm, the afterglow of struggle was darkened by the residue of Khrushchev's folly. Castro had never wanted the missiles, and, according to Khrushchev's memoirs, had to be persuaded to accept them.[129] But having accepted them, he was appalled by the idea of Khrushchev removing them under American pressure. On Sunday afternoon, Cuban forces surrounded the four Soviet missile bases and remained in place until Anastas Mikoyan arrived in Havana four days later. He came to persuade Castro to accept Khrushchev's deal with Kennedy.

The missiles were dismantled and crated, but over Castro's strong objections. American planes and ships monitored the outgoing cargo and the return passage of the Soviet boats—an exercise that convinced most experts that warheads for the Soviet missiles never had reached Cuba. The vans which carried nose cones were detected leaving Cuba, and the ship carrying them emitted no telltale radiation.[130] (A darker, though distinctly minority view, held that warheads may have come in and been left behind.)

The toughest issue turned on whether Soviet IL-28 bombers could remain in Cuba. On Sunday, Kennedy told ExComm that "we should not get hung up" on them. Then he changed his mind and a week later sent word to Khrushchev that the IL-28s had to go. Castro, predictably, was strongly opposed to letting them go, and ExComm was again embroiled in a tense debate, this time over airplanes. The blockade remained in place, with Bundy and McNamara urging that it be tightened and others wanting to harass the Cubans, mainly with surveillance. General Taylor, speaking for the Joint Chiefs, and Dillon recommended bombing the Cuban airfields.[131] Washington insisted that its no-invasion pledge was linked not just to the withdrawal of *all* offensive weapons but to its right to make on-site verification of their withdrawal.

On November 8, a covert action team blew up a Cuban industrial facility. The team was part of an operation called "Mongoose," in which Robert Kennedy was closely involved. Curiously, on the morning of October 16, shortly before ExComm's first meeting, R.F.K. had been arguing with John McCone, asking why more covert action wasn't being taken against Cuba. The plan was to send in ten Mongoose teams; three had been dispatched by late October when someone in Washington, aware that the timing for the activity couldn't be worse, sounded the alarm and the other teams were held back.[132]

What the Mongoose team did on November 8—two days after Kennedy's tough message on the IL-28s—was never mentioned by the Soviets, and most of ExComm was unaware of it. The effect of the incident isn't known. Khrushchev and Castro may have wondered whether a pledge from Kennedy to keep hands off Cuba would mean anything. Still, the incident may have inadvertently given Khrushchev added incentive to accommodate Kennedy, not Castro. But not until November 19 did Khrushchev manage to persuade Castro to give up the bombers, which, like the Soviet MIG aircraft and smaller arms, had been earmarked for transfer to Cuban ownership. The next day, Khrushchev assured Kennedy that the IL-28s would be gone within thirty days. Kennedy lifted the blockade that day, but he withheld the no-invasion pledge because Castro had refused to allow the United States to verify the removal of Soviet offensive arms. The best Khrushchev could get was an informal understanding that the United States wouldn't invade Cuba so long as no Soviet offensive arms were deployed there

The crisis was settled yet not completely disposed of. Its ghosts returned to agitate other presidencies, notably Jimmy Carter's.

The crisis pointed up the isolation of the presidency. An incumbent cannot easily share his priority concerns, let alone his responsibilities, with advisers. Kennedy, we know, didn't share some of his thinking with anyone, excepting Rusk. He shared his offer to Khrushchev of a private deal on the missiles with just a part of ExComm. Nitze says he knew nothing of it until Robert Kennedy's book, *Thirteen Days,* came out in 1969.[133] And no one, says Rusk—not Bundy, McNamara, or himself—ever told Lyndon Johnson about the trade, even though it probably settled the crisis.[134]

"We and the Soviets came out of Cuba more cautious and more thoughtful," says Rusk, who gives the credit to Kennedy. "There is an ancient Chinese proverb which says you should always leave your enemy an avenue of retreat.* Kennedy went to great pains not to drive Khrushchev into a corner."[135]

Other lessons of the crisis were canvassed at Hawk's Cay. Joseph Nye, the chairman and a Harvard political scientist, cited a few, including the "crystal ball effect" of nuclear diplomacy. "If the Kaiser, the Czar and the other leaders of Europe had been able to see in 1914 what the world was going to be like in 1918, there would have been no World War I. Nuclear weapons provide a powerful crystal ball." Leadership's inability to control events, if only because it can't control the various parts of the system, was

*"Build golden bridges behind your enemy" is a traditional rendering of the proverb.

borne in on everyone. General Power's decision to transmit the alert in the clear was one example. The violation of Soviet airspace by the U-2 on Black Saturday was another. Khrushchev, it now appears, was shocked to discover that one of his SAMs had shot down a U-2 on that hypertense day. His control of his volatile ally, Castro, was clearly tenuous. Suppose Kennedy and Khrushchev had both lost control. That prospect was among the most disturbing of the backward glances. Kennedy was remembered by Neustadt as saying, "Suppose he is in no better control of his government than I am of mine."

The crisis might actually have been a good thing, a few thought, because it quieted Berlin and broke ground for less tense U.S.-Soviet relations. But most conferees seemed to agree that in the post-Vietnam, post-Watergate environment, a President beset by crises would never have the time in which to make the considered decision that Kennedy had. Congress and the press are not what they were then. The *New York Times* found out about the Soviet missiles in Cuba, but was persuaded to sit on the story. Today, preemptive leaks from within an ExComm or from the congressional partisans of this or that option would sharply restrict a President's flexibility. "The most important part of crisis management," said Bundy, "is not to have a crisis, because there's no telling what will happen once you're in one."

McNamara then cited what he calls his law: "It is impossible to predict with high confidence what the effects of the use of military force will be because of the risks of accident, miscalculation, misperception, and inadvertence . . . it is the overwhelming lesson of the Cuban missile crisis. 'Managing' crises is the wrong term. You don't 'manage' them because you can't 'manage' them."

Eisenhower's law was much the same, and he stated it many times. For example, at a news conference in March 1954—a time when he was under pressure to intervene in Vietnam—he said, "There is only one thing I can tell you about war, and almost one only, and it is this: no war ever shows the characteristics that were expected; it is always different."

Khrushchev reaped a bitter harvest and would not recover. He had bet on Kennedy being irresolute, and lost that bet. In much of the Third World, he was seen to have let down the Cubans, hence the side. And, of course, he lost most heavily at home, because his bluff had been called.

In the aftermath of the crisis, its ripple effect was a lot more interesting than any lessons to be drawn from it. Berlin was taken off the boil—for good. And, it seemed, a less unstable environment just might lie ahead.

VII

On the Cusp

The balance of Kennedy's presidency was easier in one sense, less successful in another. He was enhanced by the crises which diminished Khrushchev, because he weathered them. But more intractable problems lay before him within the Western Alliance, notably with de Gaulle's France. De Gaulle was a more determined, resourceful, and worldly figure than any of his peers, Kennedy included. His passion was a global vocation that fitted his soaring vision of France. He summoned France's sense of past glory and great trials overcome by exemplary Frenchmen. Since he took no water in his wine, he never came close to creating the French-led coalition of states which was the only kind of Europe that suited his purpose. Yet he was the greatest tactician of his time and the master of *realpolitik*. World politics became a theater in which France's relative lack of power was obscured by the force and brilliance of de Gaulle's performance.

The dominant though tacit issue was whether America and Britain would assist, discourage, or ignore France's nuclear weapons program. The other question was whether the White House would continue to help Britain remain a modest nuclear power. Harold Macmillan was caught between his dependence on America and his strenuous efforts to make Britain part of Europe—to gain entry into the European Community, de Gaulle's chosen instrument for building his kind of Europe. De Gaulle calculated that Britain, another nuclear power, would challenge or dilute France's supremacy within the structure. Germany was the other threat. But French nuclear weapons would offset Germany's latent strength and constitute the enduring difference between the two old enemies.

Britain's relationship with America had entered a slow decline, reflecting Britain's declining world position. De Gaulle, had he chosen, could have become America's privileged partner—the European spokesman and interlocutor that Washington sought. However, any such role, it bears repeating, held no interest for him. Numerous State Department officials wished the British deterrent would disappear, and they strongly opposed abetting de Gaulle's plans.

Kennedy was leery of schemes intended to discourage either the British or French nuclear claims. Britain was unlikely to give up its deterrent with France about to acquire similar status. Also, while just as leery of doctrine and bold designs, Kennedy, like Macmillan, had attached himself to one—known alternately as "Atlantic partnership" and "twin pillars"—that ran counter to de Gaulle's. It amounted to promoting British membership in a politically cohesive European Community. Then as now, Europe was a collection of small and middle-sized states, no one of them capable of assuring its own well-being and each dependent for its security on American guarantees. A more closely knit structure of the sort envisaged by the Community's pioneers (mainly French) would gradually allow Europe to overcome centuries of strife and disunity and also do more for itself, thus lightening America's burden. De Gaulle's contempt for this notional scheme became legendary, even though it was no more implausible than his own. He and the Anglo-Saxons were on a collision course. He, alone, fully understood that; Washington and London didn't grasp the depth of his resolve, let alone anticipate its shattering effect on their plans.

On still another nuclear issue—this one doctrinal—Kennedy was having a hard time with de Gaulle and most other Europeans as well. America's stockpile of nuclear weapons in Europe was pyramiding. They were put there to help NATO defend itself against superior Soviet nonnuclear forces. Eisenhower had been uneasy with the buildup but did nothing about it. Kennedy and his advisers felt that a credible defense required strong nonnuclear as well as nuclear forces in Europe. They wanted a higher nuclear threshold. It was one thing to rely on nuclear weapons in the 1950s—when America had a near monopoly and faced little risk of retaliation (Khrushchev's bluster notwithstanding). It was quite another in the 1960s, with the Soviets in a position to respond in kind.

Europe's reaction was hardly enthusiastic. Having endured two devastating wars in a short span, Europeans were (and are) opposed to any strategy that might make war—nonnuclear or nuclear—less unlikely. They complained that Washington's new line signaled a retreat from the commitment to use America's strategic weapons in their defense. Lurking sensitivities were aroused. Why, asked Continentals, was Britain the sole beneficiary of America's nuclear largess? And why should they be asked to run the risk of turning Europe into a battlefield yet again but forgo possession of the weapons which would decide the outcome of a war? They were, they felt, being asked to risk everything so that America might remain a sanctuary.

In March 1962, General Maxwell Taylor returned from a trip convinced by talks in Paris that de Gaulle would be more of a team player on NATO issues if Washington lifted the embargo on aid to France's nuclear weapons program. Most of the Pentagon shared Taylor's view that continuation of the ban made no sense. Paul Nitze doubted that de Gaulle's cooperation was available at any price, but he felt it was essential to prove the point, so he, too, favored an initiative aimed at helping France in return for better cooperation from de Gaulle. A French military mission was invited to come to Washington with a "shopping list." The invitation was signed by Gilpatric and approved by McNamara but not cleared with the State Department.[1]

Predictably, the French list was a long one and the issue of what to do about it deeply divisive. Kennedy, like most of his senior officials excepting Rusk, had come to office pro-Gaullist. But by early 1962, he was deeply ambivalent about the general. The State Department, by then aware of the Pentagon's initiative, drew a bead on it. As in the past, it argued that Washington should not do for France what it would not be prepared to do eventually for Germany. Most of State's key officials were on balance against helping anyone's nuclear weapons program, including even Britain's. In mid-April, Kennedy ruled against the majority—the Pentagon and assorted other parts of the government—and decided not to help France. Although tempted at first to say yes—for the same reasons that had tempted Eisenhower—he accepted the conventional State Department argument that by helping France, he would not be helping himself; de Gaulle was unlikely to become a more obliging ally.

In the weeks that followed, matters became clearer still and much edgier. McNamara anathematized "weak national nuclear forces" in the commencement speech at Ann Arbor in which he unveiled America's "no cities" nuclear strategy. Such forces, he said, "are not likely to be sufficient to perform even the function of deterrence . . . [and] are dangerous, expensive, prone to obsolescence and lacking in credibility as a deterrent."[2] Any doubt about France being McNamara's target was removed a few days later when he issued a clarification excusing Britain from his broadside because its deterrent was coordinated with America's.

Kennedy and Macmillan underestimated de Gaulle, possibly because their attention was often elsewhere. The Cuban missile crisis, after obscuring other problems, changed everything. The cold war in its crudest and most unstable form was over. Overnight, Kennedy, not de Gaulle, was the undisputed leader of the West. His rising stock threatened Gaullist policy. To reverse the trend, de Gaulle would need a *coup de théâtre* of his own.

The virtuoso tactician easily maneuvered events toward this purpose. In November, while Kennedy's people were trying to get Khrushchev's IL-28s out of Cuba, another crisis erupted, this one oddly enough in Anglo-American relations. It began with Britain's discovery that Washington was about to cancel a missile called Skybolt, then being developed. Skybolt was a thousand-mile, two-stage ballistic missile designed for release from beneath the wing of a large airplane; it would allow bombers to stand off and attack an enemy well beyond the range of its air defenses. For the air force, Skybolt was the "Polaris of the sky." It would extend the life of America's B-52 force. For Britain, Skybolt was vastly more important and, indeed, vital; it alone could save a deterrent composed of 180 elderly bombers from obsolescence. Or so it seemed. In 1960, Eisenhower had agreed to sell Skybolt to Macmillan; in return he got an informal assurance that a naval base at Holy Loch, in Scotland, would be available to American nuclear submarines. In order to pay for Skybolt, the British canceled a missile of their own called Blue Streak. The decision was an act of faith in the "special relationship"; Britain's future as a nuclear power became dependent on a still-to-be-built American weapons system.

Macmillan's government was shocked, or pretended to be, by the cancellation, although it had received fair warning from the outgoing Eisenhower administration, as well as its successor, that Skybolt was in trouble. It was the most complex missile system yet undertaken by anyone; its costs and technical problems were expanding rapidly. McNamara finally concluded that Skybolt didn't justify all the expense and uncertainty; America didn't need it. But since Britain did, some parts of the Washington bureaucracy spotted clear profit in the missile's demise. Macmillan would have to withdraw Britain from the "top table," as he characterized the nuclear club.*

He was playing "Super Mac" (a Fleet Street label) to the hilt.† To succeed, he needed the acquiescence of Kennedy and de Gaulle. Only Kennedy could keep Britain's deterrent alive. Only de Gaulle stood between Britain and membership in the European Community—Macmillan's priority goal. As it happened, two meetings within two days of each other

---

*Britain angrily closed ranks. "Suez to Skybolt," said the Labour party's *Daily Herald.* "It has been a pretty rotten road."

†Macmillan was directing British foreign policy with great flair and sometimes accomplishing the unexpected. "Look fixedly in one direction, while moving the craft as smartly as possible in the other," he liked to say.

in December 1962 would settle both questions. First came Macmillan's talks with de Gaulle on the 15th and 16th at a château in the forest of Rambouillet. It was their third meeting in just over a year to discuss Britain's "European" bona fides and whether these justified admission into the Community of Six. Washington wanted Britain inside playing its old role of balancing unsteady Continentals, thereby becoming an even more useful American partner. Kennedy was optimistic; he would, he thought, know more when he saw Macmillan at Nassau on the 18th, but, meanwhile, he and his advisers were relying on deceptively bullish reports from the British and the French about the two earlier de Gaulle-Macmillan meetings.[3] In fact, de Gaulle had not tipped his hand, but it was hard for Washington to imagine that in the end he would block Macmillan's long and painfully negotiated bid.

De Gaulle's political position in December was much stronger than it had been during the earlier meetings. A month before, legislative elections had given him and his party a parliamentary majority, an event without precedent in French Republican history. The Algerian war had been set-tled, and his hands at last were entirely free. At Rambouillet, he gave Macmillan the bad news: Their two countries could cooperate but only bilaterally. There was no place for Britain in Europe. Macmillan eloquently and even emotionally put the case for Britain. At one point, he wept openly.[4] But de Gaulle was even more negative the following day. Macmil-lan left the château beaten, his foreign policy in ruins.

The communiqué disguised the abject failure of the meeting. Two days later, at Nassau, Kennedy expressed some concern about Brit-ain's European hopes. His advisers had warned him that another Anglo-American nuclear arrangement might give de Gaulle a pretext for vetoing Britain. Without telling Kennedy that he had just heard the veto pro-nounced, Macmillan said the two issues were not connected.[5] He had come to Nassau to obtain the Polaris missile system as a substitute for Skybolt; if possible, Britain's deterrent would be deployed beneath the waves. Most of Kennedy's advisers were opposed to selling Polaris, but they were over-ruled. Macmillan had been made politically vulnerable by the dark cloud hovering over Britain's deterrent. It had been put there by the Skybolt decision. His friend Kennedy would not accept the responsibility for bring-ing him down. Furthermore, unlike some of his advisers, Kennedy was unwilling to toss aside the special relationship, something he knew and understood, for the will-o'-the-wisp—a federal Europe.

With Macmillan's problem disposed of, the question became what to do about de Gaulle. Should Kennedy pacify, or try to pacify, the Elysée's great scold by offering him Polaris, too? Kennedy's thinking was strongly affected by a letter he received from Khrushchev at Nassau. "It seems to me, Mr. President, that [the] time has come now to put an end once and for all to nuclear tests, to draw a line through such tests."[6] The letter even opened the door to on-site inspection. Kennedy began to see the business of Nassau in a global context. In the letter's conciliatory tone, he scented the possibility of some improvement in great power relations. He had come to Nassau opposed on balance to retrieving the political fortunes of his friend, Macmillan. Still less had he been disposed to reopen the issue of helping de Gaulle. Changing course, however, just might fetch de Gaulle's acquiescence in a test ban treaty and perhaps even a more obliging Atlantic policy. And Khrushchev might, in turn, obtain China's signature on the treaty.[7] Macmillan was, of course, supportive, hoping for a reprieve from the verdict of Rambouillet.

In publicly offering the Polaris missile system to de Gaulle, Kennedy didn't seem to be risking much. Since France, unlike Britain, had neither the thermonuclear warheads for the missiles nor the submarine technology, de Gaulle was hardly likely to be tempted by an offer of a sub-launched missile. He would need much more. At Palm Beach, shortly after Nassau, Kennedy said to his old friend David Ormsby-Gore, "If de Gaulle accepts this deal—and I don't think he will—warheads lie at the end of the road—yours."[8] Kennedy meant that de Gaulle would require warheads and that he, Kennedy, was not going to take on the thankless task of seeking the Joint Atomic Energy Committee's approval of such a transaction.

Kennedy told Charles Bohlen, his ambassador to Paris, to open negotiations with de Gaulle at once. Bohlen's British colleague, Sir Pierson Dixon, got similar instructions from Macmillan. Each saw de Gaulle separately in early January and gave him to understand that he was being offered a good deal more than the unarmed Polaris missile system.[9] Accepting would have allowed de Gaulle to deploy a secure subsurface and fully modern nuclear force years sooner than planned and at a great saving in French resources. Accepting would have moved France into the *directoire à trois* with America and Britain that was supposed (wrongly) to be his loftiest goal. But the implicit price—being obliged to admit Britain into Europe and link his forces to those of the Anglo-Saxons—was too high. De Gaulle didn't want parity with Britain or a comparably special relationship with America. He wanted supremacy in Western Europe. In his memoirs, Macmillan records a comment a Gaullist minister made to Sir Christopher Soames, his Minister of Agriculture:

> Mon cher. C'est très simple. Maintenant, avec les six il y a cinq poules et un coq. Si vous joignez (avec des autres pays), il y aura peut-être

sept ou huit poules. Mais il y aura *deux* coqs. Alors—ce n'est pas aussi agréable.[10]*

On January 14, in one of his semiannual press conferences, de Gaulle produced the *coup de théâtre*. Britain was rejected. So was the Kennedy temptation—nuclear partnership. Occasionally, de Gaulle wrapped an event in myth, using the myth to justify a step he had already decided to take. A few days after the press conference, the myth appeared: The meeting in Nassau had provoked his veto of Britain's bid. By creating a new and stronger defensive link with the Americans, Macmillan, like British leaders before him, had shown that America mattered more to his country than Europe. Britain wasn't and couldn't be European. In early February, de Gaulle confirmed this version of events in a meeting with French parliamentarians.[11] But the British record of the Rambouillet meeting, which was transcribed and typed even before Macmillan left the château, clearly shows that de Gaulle, as noted, did say no to Macmillan there (two days before the Nassau meeting).†

Nuclear weapons were shaping relations between allies, just as they had between adversaries. In opposing the American emphasis on conventional forces, Europeans could reasonably argue that nuclear weapons, by their nature, were preventing war. But *these* were American and Soviet weapons—not British and French. At no time did British and French nuclear weapons promote the diplomatic ends of their governments; there is less to nuclear diplomacy than meets the eye. Rusk said that Khrushchev, in communicating with Kennedy, "never expressed serious concern about the British and French programs."[12] Nor can it be said that either of these small deterrents is really independent. A few of de Gaulle's generals conceived of a modest force of nuclear weapons as a detonator—a device which, at the limit, could trigger the American spasm. De Gaulle didn't discourage such thinking, but he was far too intelligent to take it seriously. In early 1962, a member of the Kennedy administration told French Defense Minister Pierre Messmer, who was objecting to joint targeting on the grounds that it would compromise French sovereignty, that if ever France should appear to contemplate the independent use of nuclear weapons against anybody, "we would not let you."‡

*"My dear. It's very simple. Now, with six members, there are five hens and a rooster. If you join (with the other countries), there will perhaps be seven or eight hens. But there will be *two* roosters. That isn't as agreeable."

†There is probably no reliable French record, because Prince Andronikov, de Gaulle's interpreter, took no notes.

‡The source for this comment was a senior member of the Kennedy administration, who did not explain how this injunction would be applied.

After de Gaulle put paid to Washington's grand design, Kennedy's skeptical instincts took tighter control. He didn't give up trying to strengthen the tie with the general, nor did he wholly abandon the design. But he did work harder at improving relations with his adversary, Khrushchev, and with another difficult and even more crucial ally, Konrad Adenauer. (His last meeting with Adenauer—in Washington, in November 1961—had not gone well, and it was agreed to burn the minutes of one of their conversations.) Kennedy began to give modest encouragement to a dubious scheme called the M.L.F., "multilateral (nuclear) force." It amounted to creating a fleet of surface ships armed with Polaris missiles and jointly owned and operated by several NATO members, each of which would have a veto over the use of the nuclear weapons. The M.L.F.'s purpose was to give the Germans a sense of participation in such matters. But since the missile warheads were to remain in American custody, not to mention decisions regarding their use, the M.L.F. would change nothing really; it was akin to taking clothes out of one closet and putting them in another. The project dated to the late Eisenhower period when the Defense Department, backed by some members of State, wanted to deploy ballistic missiles on barges and railroad cars in Western Europe. A variant of the idea was to offer ballistic missiles to several European countries, either for purchase or manufacture under American license. The navy was pushing its Polaris at the Europeans, with little regard to questions of control. (It had installed a small model of the Polaris system at NATO's former headquarters in Paris, and any curious delegate, by pushing a button, could witness a miniaturized missile takeoff.) And an air force colonel was simultaneously hawking the Minuteman, then hardly out of the design stage.[13]

The M.L.F. acquired considerable notoriety and some momentum. It survived Kennedy's skepticism but not Lyndon Johnson's, who shelved it—in December 1965—but not before it had divided and seriously weakened the government of Adenauer's successor, Ludwig Erhard, the M.L.F.'s only genuine supporter in Europe—and a reluctant one at that.

Khrushchev, like de Gaulle, was acutely aware that the White House sheltered the world's dominant political personality; he had the Cuban escapade to thank for that. But he may have reasoned that just as only the Americans and Russians could wage war, so could they—and they alone—place restrictions on nuclear weapons. Other nations could endorse any agreed superpower restrictions, but the negotiating process belonged to Washington and Moscow. Then as now, this distinction helped the Soviet Union by pointing up its status as the other superpower.

Kennedy was eager to have a test ban agreement. He and his advisers were more sensitive to the threat of nuclear proliferation than their predecessors had been. At a press conference in March 1962, Kennedy said: "Personally, I am haunted by the feeling that by 1970, unless we are successful, there may be ten nuclear powers instead of four, and by 1975, fifteen or twenty." In January 1963, not long after Khrushchev's unexpected letter arrived, he told his staff that the chief merit of a test ban would lie in discouraging other countries, especially China, from developing nuclear weapons.[14] Exactly why Kennedy thought an agreement between him and Khrushchev would inhibit China wasn't clear to many of his advisers, including Glenn T. Seaborg, the AEC Chairman.[15] Others in the Kennedy entourage saw the broad public concern with fallout as driving the President. One of them says, "The test ban deal was viewed cynically—as something that would quiet fears about strontium 90."

As before, the issue of how to verify a test ban—whether the Soviets in the end would permit intrusive inspections—appeared all but insurmountable. Tests in the atmosphere, space, or undersea could be monitored from afar but not so those conducted underground, which would require on-site inspection because explosions of very small nuclear weapons could, in theory, be concealed. Kennedy was not prepared to give up on a comprehensive ban. Khrushchev hinted that he was awaiting some new sign from Washington and Kennedy provided it. First, he proposed a new round of talks to be held in Moscow by senior figures. Then, in June, he made a speech at American University which Khrushchev described to Averell Harriman as "the best speech by any President since Roosevelt."[16] In it, Kennedy called for a reexamination of American attitudes toward the cold war and announced the upcoming talks in Moscow and a decision he had just made to suspend atmospheric testing of nuclear weapons. The State Department was caught "flat-footed," according to a former official there, having just one day's notice of the speech. The Soviet press reprinted the entire text, and Western broadcasts of the speech were heard unjammed by Soviet citizens, the first such event in fifteen years.

Kennedy chose Harriman as his emissary to Khrushchev, and someone from the Soviet Embassy said to Arthur Schlesinger, "As soon as I heard Harriman was going, I knew you were serious."[17] Since Britain, too, had a testing program and would be involved in any agreed ban, Macmillan sent an emissary, Lord Hailsham, to serve as a mediator between the superpowers.

Harriman's instructions, said one closely involved official, "were very simple: 'Just bring home the bacon.' " On arriving, he had to endure some

leg pulling from his whimsical host, who began by saying how glad he was
to see him, how he and his colleagues remembered Harriman's services
during the war. But then Khrushchev said, "We need to clear up a few
matters like Berlin and Cuba." The jokes out of the way, Harriman soon
found himself locked in serious negotiations with Gromyko. Kennedy
involved himself directly and was determined to avoid having the talks
jeopardized by leaks. Hence, he allowed just a few officials, notably Rusk,
Bundy, Thompson, and McNamara, to read Harriman's cables.

The bad news was that Khrushchev was unwilling even to consider
on-site inspections. The Americans were pressing for a comprehensive ban,
but Khrushchev wouldn't be drawn in. "The trouble with you," he said to
Harriman, "is you want to spy. That's your purpose . . . You're trying to
tell me that if there's a piece of cheese in the room and a mouse comes into
the room that the mouse won't go and take the cheese. You can't stop the
mouse from going for the cheese."[18] Khrushchev would consider a comprehensive test ban only if it were monitored by remote control—by so-called
black boxes. He proposed instead a limited ban—one that would halt testing
above ground but allow it to continue underground. Kennedy decided to
go along, given his negotiators' view that Khrushchev's stand on an inspected ban was nonnegotiable.* Not everyone around Kennedy saw the
comprehensive ban as out of reach. At one point, with the administration
insisting on a minimum of seven inspections, the Soviets informally agreed
to three. The American side thereupon suggested five. A serious effort to
compromise on four, according to some officials, might have produced
agreement on a comprehensive ban.

It took the Harriman team just twelve days to negotiate the less-
restrictive ban. Kennedy was preoccupied by France as well as China; he
wanted the signatures of both on the treaty. Three years earlier, in April
1960, de Gaulle had said that France would abandon its program only if
America, Russia, and Britain scrapped *their* nuclear weapons. (The first
French nuclear device had been detonated in the Sahara two months
before.)[19] Kennedy chose to replay the temptation of Nassau: In return for
signing, de Gaulle would get substantial nuclear assistance. "In effect, we
asked him what sort of nuclear cooperation he would require in order to
sign," said a senior member of the administration. For de Gaulle, a limited
test ban meant a total ban, since France hadn't yet begun to miniaturize her
nuclear weapons. Still, it's most unlikely he'd have signed, whatever the

---

*The step back from a comprehensive ban was greeted with relief in parts of the Pentagon and
the AEC. It was feared that a comprehensive test ban would cause American weapons laboratories
to close up shop, whereas their Soviet counterparts would continue creating new weapons as
before.

state of the French program. Kennedy's second offer was rejected as brusquely as the first and in the same fashion—during a press conference (on July 29), in which de Gaulle seemed to worry about the test ban as auguring "separate negotiations between the Anglo-Saxons and the Soviets . . . [on] other questions, notably European ones . . ."[20]

Besides trying to corral de Gaulle, Washington persisted in pressing Moscow to corral the Chinese. By then, however, Khrushchev knew there was nothing to be done. Back in the fall of 1957, he seems to have extracted China's acceptance of a test ban in return for nuclear assistance. But later, as he tried to build on his meeting with Eisenhower at Camp David, the split between communism's established church orthodox and the isolated church militant widened and poisoned relations. In June 1959, China demanded a sample atomic bomb and related production data. When Khrushchev refused, China announced on January 21, 1960, that it would not be bound by an "international agreement concerning disarmament."[21]

Describing the conversation about China in Moscow with Khrushchev, Carl Kaysen, Deputy NSC Adviser and a member of the Harriman team, said: "It was very rough. Khrushchev would say, 'I don't run a post office. If you want to talk to the Chinese, don't talk to me. Talk to the Chinese.' Even in 1963, we didn't understand the full extent of the split between them."[22]

A comprehensive ban would have frozen some important American advantages in weapons design—another reason perhaps for Khrushchev's rejection of it. Aside from silencing the fallout issue, the effect of the limited agreement was modest and lay in the eye of the beholder. "It should strongly inhibit the spread of nuclear weapons," the Senate Committee on Foreign Relations said in approving the agreement.[23] Perhaps. But American and Soviet test programs continued largely unaffected, except that they were forced underground and thereby sheltered from public pressure. And because it lacked the French and Chinese signatures, the limited agreement was unlikely to have much effect on the intentions of aspirant nuclear club members.

The test ban coincided with a time of remarkable transition. It was voted out of committee on the day of Martin Luther King's Freedom March on Washington, August 28, 1963. Pope John XXIII, a potent and much-beloved force for change, died while it was being negotiated. A few months later, in October, Adenauer and Macmillan resigned their offices within a few days of each other. Then, a few weeks later, Kennedy was gone—assassinated. "At heart, he was a European," said de Gaulle to the British ambassador on the morning after.[24] It was the highest tribute he could pay to the younger man whom he had liked, respected, and tilted against. He, de Gaulle, was again the West's, if not the world's, preeminent figure as the Johnson era began.

Johnson's horizon was far more limited than his star-crossed predecessor's. He was a power broker, with more than thirty years of Washington experience behind him. He manipulated men and institutions as well as Roosevelt, whom he identified with and would outperform in steering legislation through Congress largely unchanged. "He possessed all the strengths and liabilities" of the American political system, said one astute observer.[25] In sporting circles, Johnson would have been called a great natural talent —greater certainly than Kennedy. But he had little knowledge of the big world that lay beyond his sovereign writ. His immediate agenda was pushing Kennedy's domestic program through Congress and obtaining a mandate of his own at the ballot box. With that done—masterfully at that—he could look harder at the world beyond, particularly Vietnam.

Most of Kennedy's senior advisers on national security—Rusk, Bundy, and McNamara—were asked to stay on. ("I need your help more than Jack Kennedy did," Johnson told them before the funeral.)[26] They weren't sure about the man they were working for. Although intensely secretive, he tended as well to impulsiveness and robust indiscretion; one of those who stayed on described him in that sense as a "potential security risk."[27] (As noted, Johnson wasn't told about the trade that helped to settle the Cuban missile crisis.)

Johnson's mandate began just days after Khrushchev's ended. He was deposed as General Secretary on October 14, 1964, the victim of his earlier recklessness and excessive zeal. "Khrushchev was impressionistic," wrote Charles Bohlen, who knew him well. "World travels altered his views . . . If [he] had stayed in power, he might have been willing to explore paths toward détente that his cautious successors hesitated to tread."[28] Bohlen also knew Leonid Brezhnev, Khrushchev's successor, and considered him a typical crony/apparatchik and "third-rate party thug."[29]

Johnson kept faith for a time with Kennedy's foreign policy, but the past was becoming an unreliable guide. The tempo of change was rapid and not easily comprehended either in the White House or in Brezhnev's Kremlin. Among the swiftly converging events was China's explosion of its first nuclear device—on October 15, the day after Khrushchev's removal. The new Soviet leaders reacted nervously by trying to improve relations with China even though the break had been public and shrill. And they continued trying to erase the gap with American strategic forces. They made no effort to hide this intention. Just after the Cuban missile crisis, John McCloy was hosting Soviet Deputy Minister V. V. Kuznetsov at his house in Connecticut. "You Americans will never be able to do this to us again," Kuznetsov warned, after assuring McCloy that Moscow would observe the agreement to remove Soviet missiles and bombers from Cuba.[30]

Washington shared Moscow's China phobia. Kennedy began worrying aloud about a Chinese bomb early in 1961. And just after the Cuban missile crisis, he said to congressional leaders, "We've won a great victory. There is no threat anymore from Russia. The threat in the years ahead is China." He was, according to one account, "intrigued by arguments made . . . for knocking out the Chinese [atomic] installations."[31] The concern was that China, unlike Russia, didn't understand nuclear war; its leadership was alleged to think that China could survive what other countries would not survive. Thus, China, the argument continued, might use a nuclear weapon to provoke "catalytic" war. Khrushchev encouraged this notion; in conversations with Western visitors, he would cite China's irrational view of nuclear warfare.[32]

Johnson heard recommendations from some advisers to use nuclear weapons against China's embryonic atomic plants.[33] China had a diesel-powered submarine then with three launch tubes but no missiles for them. In 1964, serious consideration was given to "killing" this submarine. Nothing came of it, according to one ex-State Department official who says there was also discussion of having Rusk take up with Dobrynin the idea of joint steps to neutralize the Chinese nuclear threat. Such a discussion was in fact held, although Rusk doesn't recall it, nor does he recall seeing Dobrynin about it.[34] Johnson himself was less intimidated by a Chinese bomb than Kennedy.

His administration nonetheless inflated every minatory aspect of China's program: its scale, its worldwide political impact, the aggressive purpose it would serve. The alarmists were wrong on each count. The low-yield weapon China exploded in October 1964 had far less political effect than Washington expected. It did not foreshadow production of nuclear weapons on a meaningful scale, still less any sign that China might use or threaten to use what little it had.

Equally wide of the mark were the estimates about Soviet strategic programs at this time. As in the 1950s, when the intelligence community—then air force–dominated—inflated Soviet missile and bomber output, the tendency throughout most of the 1960s was to underestimate Soviet programs and misread the direction they would take. The low estimates were a course correction of sorts. The analysts were wary of inviting further public embarrassment by again exaggerating Soviet potential. And they mistakenly assumed that the other side's apparent commitment to ballistic missile defense (ABMs) would so deplete its economic resources that other programs would be scaled down. The most serious misjudgments of this kind were made between 1963 and 1967, a time when the Soviets were well along in an exuberant buildup of large ICBMs, especially the SS-9, which had vastly greater destructive potential than America's Minuteman system. The Soviets were making huge, land-based missiles their first priority instead of following the American lead, as American intelligence guessed they would, and building modern missile-carrying submarines and a new strategic bomber. Instead of shifting, as America had, to smaller, solid-fueled, quicker-reacting missile systems, the Soviets were clinging to their liquid-fueled, slow-reacting, less-reliable behemoths. The intelligence people hadn't yet understood that each side was improving the various parts of its nuclear forces at a pace quite different from the other; one side's pattern and rhythm of modernization was animated only in part by the other's programs. The emulation syndrome—what bureaucrats call "mirror imaging"—hadn't taken hold, although it would. Finally, experts thought that the Soviets, at most, were playing catch-up, not actually bent on deploying more land-based missile launchers than America, as indeed they were.

The strangest and least defensible buildup was being conducted by the Americans—in Europe. Any of the so-called conventional weapons that could be made in a nuclear version had years before been so configured and assigned for duty in Europe. Many of them were—are—preposterous in their nuclear roles and quite unusable. Atomic demolition mines (of which there were about 300 in the early 1980s) make no sense, if only because European governments are known to be unwilling to dig the necessary holes and tunnels for them prior to a crisis; later would be too late. About a third of the weapons in the stockpile were artillery shells with ranges of less than ten miles; they could only destroy what they were supposed to defend and hence were almost certainly unusable, too.[35]

Kennedy inherited a European-based stockpile of roughly 2,500 nuclear weapons. By the time McNamara called a halt in 1966, the figure had climbed to 7,200. And not until he had done so were European governments told the size of this massive arsenal they were hosting. McNamara blames what happened on "inertia." "We inherited a plan and built up to it," he says. "It was irrational. There was no military requirement for 7,000 of these weapons, or 6,000 or five, or four, or two thousand."[36] In allowing the stockpile to continue to grow unchecked, the administration was far afield from its strong declaratory emphasis on having nonnuclear options in Europe and raising the nuclear threshold.

In 1967, a year after the stockpile had leveled off and after five years of argument, NATO formally recognized that limited aggression should be dealt with on a limited scale; the McNamara Pentagon's ideas about flexibility and selective response found their way into NATO doctrine. Nonetheless, military planners continued to assume that Soviet aggression would promptly bring into play the equalizer—their tactical nuclear weapons. The Soviets deplore NATO doctrine, arguing that nuclear war cannot be limited, that any use of nuclear weapons would rapidly escalate. "It's impossible," says Valentin Falin, "to stop nuclear war once it's started or follow any rules in fighting it. The beginning of a nuclear exchange . . . means, in fact, the beginning of a full-scale nuclear war."[37]*

A number of former American officials would agree. In recent years, a few of them, including Bundy and McNamara, have argued that a defensive alliance should, after all, be able to defend itself and should be convinced that it can—that nuclear weapons don't represent usable military power but merely deter other nuclear weapons. These revisionists want the alliance to give up its declared willingness to be the first to use nuclear weapons in order to defend Europe against aggression. They provoked a lively argument over "no-first-use." European governments oppose abandoning the uncertainty in which NATO doctrine is wrapped, although they themselves would find agreeing on the use of nuclear weapons in the early stages of a conflict very difficult, perhaps impossible. Also, no one has ever devised a strategy for using NATO's tactical "Nukes," which means that the alliance has had a policy of no-first-use but can't say so.

Johnson was caught up in a national trauma—the war America didn't win. Yet he and the Soviet Union, Vietnam's arms supplier, were edging crablike toward a more cooperative relationship. They were in no hurry; Vietnam had made communication between Moscow and Washington more awkward than usual. But each side knew that the simplicity and clarity of the cold war were giving way to a more ambiguous set of considerations.

The White House and State Department were engaged in an arduous and occasionally acrimonious policy struggle over what to do. The NSC staff wanted to throw up a few bridges to the Eastern bloc. A major

*Despite their strong feelings on this matter, the Soviets must have a few limited nuclear options in their own planning inventory; it's hard to believe that one, or even two nuclear explosions, would provoke escalation on their part.

complication was General de Gaulle; he had extended diplomatic recognition to China as early as February 1964 and had been busily expanding his ties to the East. Early in 1966, he withdrew French forces from NATO. The State Department liked bridges, but worried that erecting any then would be misread as indifference to de Gaulle's policies and perhaps to the Soviet Union's support for North Vietnam. A speech by Johnson on October 7, 1966, settled the matter: "Our task," he said, "is to achieve a reconciliation with the East—a shift from the narrow concept of coexistence to the broader vision of peaceful engagement . . . We do not intend to let our differences on Vietnam or elsewhere ever prevent us from exploring all opportunities."[38]

Brezhnev affected disdain, declaring a week later that American officials entertained a "strange and persistent delusion" if they thought their relations with the Eastern bloc could improve despite the war in Vietnam.[39] But the Kremlin's ultracaution was set against its interest in confining China politically and modernizing the Soviet economy. Dealing with China argued for stability on the Western front. Improving the economy, not to mention competing with the West, would require access to Western commerce and technology. Most of Eastern Europe was alive to the prospect of expanding commerce westward. "Make the best deals you can, but don't fall in love," Moscow admonished its empire.

Besides building more missile launchers than Washington expected, Moscow was putting the latest of them in hardened silos, thereby creating a survivable second-strike force. The time of glib talk in SAC about being able to "get" all or most of the Soviet weapons in a first strike was clearly over.

The scale of the missile buildup, as it became a bit clearer, added to Washington's worries, chief of which was a Soviet antiballistic missile—ABM. An ABM system with the code name "Galosh" had been deployed around Moscow. And a high-performance air defense system—code-named "Tallinn" for the Estonian city—was being positioned around the country's perimeter. Washington was awash in controversy over whether Tallinn was no more than it seemed—a system designed to shoot down airplanes—or whether its larger role would be defense against incoming missiles. Some agencies, insisting on the worst case, forecast a nationwide Soviet defense from missile attack built around Tallinn. Anxious questions followed: Could American missiles, if launched in response to enemy attack, get through thickets of defensive missiles in any meaningful number? Or had the bedrock assumption about American forces—their assured ability to strike back in kind—been compromised?

As it turned out, intelligence estimates portraying Tallinn's darker purposes weren't borne out; the system was in fact no more than it seemed to be. As for the Galosh ABM deployed around Moscow, it was clearly a technically deplorable device and no threat to America's deterrent. Ironically though, Galosh, just by being there, planted the idea in Washington that the United States, too, had to have an ABM. If the Soviets could protect their cities, surely America could do no less, argued a passionate and resourceful ABM lobby. Also, an ABM system, said its partisans, would limit the damage of a nuclear attack and thus make one less likely to occur. The threat from China was invoked; construction of a large ballistic missile launch facility at Shuang-ch'eng Tzu had started in 1965. An ABM might be needed as a hedge against irrational Chinese leaders.

Numerous skeptics cited reasons for shunning the ABM: It wouldn't work because either side could swamp any missile defense simply by adding additional offensive missiles to its inventory. Thus, ABM deployment by the superpowers would only provoke another big cycle in the nuclear arms race. Moreover, if one side convinced itself its missile defense could limit damage, it might be tempted to launch a first strike. In short, a missile defense was increasingly seen not as advertised—an agent of stability, hence peace—but as a major source of instability, if not worse.

One strand of opinion identified good ABMs and bad ABMs. Deployed around cities, ABMs would be bad because they might arouse fears on the other side of a first strike. But placed around missile sites, ABMs would be good, because they would alert a potential aggressor to the increased "survivability" of the defended weapons. The somewhat metaphysical nature of the argument about defense was reminiscent of the theological disputes within the early church. And like those debates, this one has shown great staying power. (Ronald Reagan revived it most recently by proposing a largely space-based defense of America, popularly known as Star Wars.)

Agitating the ABM issue were parallel debates, one of which swirled around a force multiplier known as MIRV (for multiple independently targeted re-entry vehicle). As early as 1962, Polaris missiles had been equipped with a simpler variant—multiple re-entry vehicles (MRVs). Such warheads, like pellets from a shotgun, follow a single ballistic path and cannot be aimed at separate targets. But the more advanced MIRV system releases individual warheads at varying times and angles and can thus be assigned multiple targets. The technology is wondrous: The final stage of the missile is a bus which releases its payload of warheads one at a time by changing velocity and direction. The adjustments actually define the path of the warhead to its target.[40]

MIRV and ABM were sides of a coin. By equipping long-range missiles with multiple warheads, one side could overwhelm the other's ABM network (if there was one). Also, putting MIRVs on missiles already in place was much less expensive than buying entire new systems. Finally, it was instantly apparent that MIRVs, unlike ABMs, would actually work. But it was less apparent—at least at first—that MIRVs, like ABMs, would weaken stability. When sufficiently accurate, they would impart a first-strike capability against hardened enemy targets like missile silos. There were only two reasons for deploying MIRV: either to penetrate ABM defenses or to acquire the capacity to destroy some portion of the other side's missile forces, thereby limiting the damage to oneself in a nuclear conflict. Thus, if neither side had ABMs, there would be no obvious reason to deploy MIRV; the second reason for having it seemed irrelevant, since America had disavowed—at least, rhetorically—any intention of acquiring a first-strike option.

In 1962, McNamara could recommend sparing enemy cities and targeting instead its nuclear weapons, because there were very few of them. In January 1967, he took the opposite line, telling Congress: "I think we could all agree that if they struck first we are going to target our weapons against their society and destroy 120 million of them."[41] What had changed was the balance of forces. By 1967, the Soviets were well on the path to parity and their forces were less vulnerable. The superpowers were on the cusp between the first stage of their nuclear rivalry and the current stage. Put differently, the time when either side would allow the other to acquire an exploitable strategic advantage had passed, but the point was not easily or quickly grasped in either place.

McNamara was a partisan—an early one—of limiting strategic arms. But by 1967, his authority was being contested by the services and various grandees on Capitol Hill. The air force was pushing for a new strategic bomber and a new ICBM, larger than Minuteman. The navy wanted a fleet of missile-firing surface ships and more nuclear submarines and carriers. The army was lobbying for a heavy ABM defense of cities. Meanwhile, the war in Vietnam was draining resources. In MIRV, McNamara and his staff saw a providential restraint. It would do anything that the big-ticket missiles on the military's shopping list could do and do them far more cheaply. The air force and navy had argued that expanding Soviet industry had enlarged the target list—meaning more weapons were needed. MIRVs would satisfy the need without increasing the number of missiles.

In response, Washington took two contradictory steps: the first, a decision to deploy both MIRV and ABM systems; the second, a rather self-conscious experiment in serious arms control. Earlier experiments aimed at limiting production of weapons systems had foundered on the eternal on-site inspection clause, which was no more acceptable to the Americans insisting on it than to the Soviets. But the prospect of ABMs and big multiwarhead missiles caused experts to wonder if it might be possible to reach agreement limiting such devices without having to bell the on-site inspection cat. Reconnaissance satellites could monitor compliance with limits.

But in veering toward the still supersecret MIRV, Washington met itself coming back. It ought to have been clear from the first that MIRV would be a two-party game, yet little, if any, thought was given to what would happen when Moscow followed suit. The MIRV testing decision followed the deployment by the Soviets of the SS-9, a weapon of unimaginable destructive power—capable of delivering a vastly greater blow than the much smaller Minuteman. And the blow could be directed *against* Minuteman, the backbone of America's deterrent. A first principle of stable deterrence is that each side's forces should be invulnerable to attack so as to remove from both sides the incentive to strike first. A force of 300 SS-9s with six MIRVs each would, in theory, have been capable of destroying most of the Minutemen in their hardened silos. Compared to Minuteman, the SS-9 was a primitive system, yet its size and potential came to be seen as not just threatening but alarming. Some experts worried that during a crisis the Soviets might take out the Minuteman force in a bolt from the blue, even though America's sub-launched missiles and bombers would remain to destroy most of urban Russia. What would America's leadership do if the Kremlin bet against America's willingness to commit national suicide by avenging the loss of missiles scattered around sparsely inhabited parts of the country? The alternative would be to concede the argument so as to keep the larger part of society intact.

MIRV was a shining example of Washington's incurable tendency to exploit a technological lead. The "lead" invariably turns out to have been widely exaggerated. Sooner or later—usually sooner—the Soviet Union closes the gap and builds the same weapon. The balance of forces hasn't changed, but a weapon of greater versatility and destructive potential—a harder weapon to control—enters the superpower inventories. America, it bears repeating, had no need of MIRV. The decision to go forward with it was a self-inflicted wound that festered. Missile vulnerability became a continuity of this second stage of the nuclear age. It has skewed debate on national security, bedeviled every administration, and at times all but derailed the arms control process.

If bent on MIRV, McNamara was mortified by the ABM and determined not to deploy it. The issue mushroomed into the toughest battle of his tenure in the Pentagon. "At one point," he said, "almost everyone in the building was for ABM, except Cy Vance and me." (Vance was then Deputy Secretary of Defense.)[42] He estimated that defending cities against the Russians would cost $40 billion. At far less cost, he argued, Moscow could make a compensatory increase in its forces. The air force worried that defending Minuteman instead would damage prospects for new and larger offensive missiles. McNamara was not impressed by the missile defense option either; again, he felt it was something that could be easily overcome by Soviet offense. A third option was to deploy a so-called thin ABM system as a hedge against Chinese missiles and accidental launches from anywhere. But McNamara saw this as less a hedge against the Chinese than against the far more expensive and worrisome "thick" system being pushed by the Joint Chiefs and a few congressional barons who strongly favored missile defense and heeded Edward Teller, who told them in 1968: "You won't put any genie back into the bottle. All you can do is to create new genies, and hope that they will be better and more benevolent ones."[43]

Johnson fully shared McNamara's concern with exercising restraint and capping the arms race. But he would not sign on to McNamara's lonely campaign against the ABM. He respected the congressional partisans of the ABM and, more important, reasoned that their side would win. In a meeting at the LBJ ranch in December 1966, McNamara persuaded him to hold off the decision until the State Department had been able to explore with the Soviets the idea of talks on limiting strategic weapons, especially ABMs.[44] This compromise was as perishable as it looked. The Soviets were deeply reluctant to consider any limits on defense of the motherland. Washington pushed for talks between Johnson and Soviet Prime Minister Aleksei Kosygin, but the Soviets—busily narrowing the missile gap—played for time. The fencing continued until June, 1967, a month to remember. On the 5th, Israel launched the Six Day War against Egypt. Washington and Moscow wanted a cease-fire, and Kosygin told Johnson in a Teletyped conversation on their hot line that he would urge one; Johnson agreed to do the same. On Day Five, the cease-fire was agreed to, but the Israelis wanted more time in which to gain control of the Golan Heights on their frontier with Syria. Washington did not object. The Soviets were furious; Damascus lies within close range of the Golan Heights. Kosygin sent Johnson a tough message, perhaps the toughest of the cold war. "If you want war, you can have war" is how McNamara recalled its gist.[45] Johnson reacted by moving the Sixth Fleet closer to the Syrian coast. The hot-line conversation resumed, and in a few hours, the cease-fire was in place. But, as McNamara says, had it not been, "superpower military intervention in the region would have become a reality."[46]

Kosygin hadn't yet set a date for talks with Johnson. On the 17th, the Chinese exploded their first thermonuclear weapon. Richard Helms, the CIA Director, predicted that they would have ICBMs within five years. This prospect, an especially disturbing one in Moscow, seemed certain to strengthen Soviet determination to continue with missile defense. Still, Kosygin, after deciding to visit the U.N. General Assembly in New York, agreed at last to meet Johnson for talks on limiting weapons.

On the 23rd, they met in Glassboro, New Jersey, a small college town. The event was anticlimactic. Kosygin's hard line silenced what little hope there was that talks in the near term on limiting strategic arms might be possible. At one point, McNamara recalls, Johnson became "very frustrated . . . and said, 'Bob, for God's sake, you tell Kosygin what's wrong with their plan.' So I said, 'If you proceed with the antiballistic missile system deployment our response will not, should not be, to deploy a similar system. That would be a waste. I hope we don't do that. But our response will be to expand our offensive weapons in order that we may maintain that deterrent . . . It's not in our interest or your interest to do that. The way to stop that is for both of us to agree today that we will engage in talks leading to a treaty that will prohibit deployment of antiballistic missile systems' . . . He absolutely exploded. The blood rose into his face, his veins swelled, he pounded the table and he said—he could barely talk he was so emotional—he said, 'Defense is moral, offense is immoral!' And he believed it."[47]

Dean Rusk recalls Johnson dealing with Kosygin "in a go for broke fashion. He was saying, in effect, 'Just set a day and I'll have McNamara there in Moscow.' Kosygin's problem was that he didn't have . . . [any] authority to discuss limiting arms, least of all ABMs. He replied, in effect: 'How can you expect me to tell the Russian people they can't defend themselves against your rockets?' "[48] Kosygin struck Johnson as being obsessed with China; Johnson later reported that "every time Kosygin pressed me hard on something, I said what do you think the Chinese will do about that, and that upset him for twenty minutes and gave me time to recover my position."[49]

The failure at Glassboro meant that Johnson would approve missile defense. For McNamara—convinced that the least ABM system would be the least bad—this meant going forward with the anti-China system. "It was Congress-oriented, not China-oriented," he says now.[50] McNamara broke the news in a speech in San Francisco on September 18. Most of it amounted to a compelling case for restraint and a warning about the "mad momentum intrinsic to . . . all nuclear weaponry." He noted that uncertainties had inspired larger American forces than were needed, which in turn had pushed the Soviets to follow suit. "It is precisely this action-reaction phenomenon that fuels an arms race," he said. Then at the end, after explaining why deploying ABMs against Russia would be futile and even dangerous, he changed course and said that a modest deployment against a potential threat from China would be "prudent" and "relatively inexpensive."[51]

"The China issue was dragged in by the heels and became a make-weight for the decision," says Rusk.[52] No one was impressed, including the Soviets, who knew that a "thin" ABM defense of cities, whether called "anti-China" or "anti-Russia," would look much the same and have the same growth potential. Most sinologists were skeptical; they felt that China's bomb was not a serious threat and would discourage incautious or impulsive Chinese behavior, just as nuclear weapons have constrained the other club members.

"The Chinese are not completely crazy," said Senator Richard Russell, the imposing chairman of the Senate Armed Services Committee and an ABM stalwart. "They know they are not going to attack us with four or five missiles when they know we have the capability of virtually destroying the entire country . . . I don't like people to think that I am being kidded by this talk of defense against a Chinese nuclear attack."[53]

For the Soviets, a quantum leap in the arms race, as portended by parallel missile defenses, was an alarming prospect. Their primitive Galosh system had fetched no end of mischief. The Americans, operating from a wider and deeper technological base, could be counted on to build an ABM system that, who could say, might even work. And from this same awesome base another disturbing innovation—MIRV—abruptly surfaced. In mid-December, three months after McNamara's speech, the Pentagon lifted the veil on its solution to the Soviet ICBM buildup—a device for sending multiple, separately targeted warheads against an enemy. Within a few months, the Soviets were signaling an interest in arms control talks. Confirmation came in late June, when Gromyko announced the Kremlin's readiness to discuss limiting both offensive and defensive weapons.[54] Three days later, Johnson announced agreement to launch the process that quickly became known as SALT—Strategic Arms Limitation Talks.

Talking about talks was a lot easier than having them. In both capitals, there was heavy bureaucratic drag to overcome. Gromyko's statement limned the Kremlin's problem: "To the good-for-nothing theoreticians

HERBLOCK
©1957 THE WASHINGTON POST CO.

A comment on the first Soviet
Sputnik. *The sensational event*
occurred in October 1957.

(From *Herblock's Special for Today*
[New York: Simon & Schuster, 1958])

*"My, it's a big week for everybody! The Russians have the
Intercontinental Ballistic Missile, and we have the Edsel."*

*A cartoon in September 1957
captured a growing concern that
America might be concentrating
on the wrong things. Actually
the gap in missile and space technology was in America's favor.*

(Drawing by F. B. Modell; © 1957, 1985
The New Yorker Magazine, Inc.)

*Eisenhower and Khrushchev
meet during the latter's tour
of America in 1959.*

(UPI/Bettmann Newsphotos)

The West's big three, from right: President Dwight D. Eisenhower, Prime Minister Harold Macmillan, and President Charles de Gaulle leaving the Elysée Palace during the summit meeting in May 1960. The meeting was reduced to a shambles by Khrushchev's shrill protest of the U-2 incident.

(UPI/Bettmann Newsphotos)

Llewellyn E. Thompson, a career diplomat and one of the premier experts in Soviet affairs, appears with Nikita Khrushchev in September 1960. Thompson provided successive presidents with invaluable guidance.

(AP/Wide World Photos)

Top: The President and ex-
President in the spring of 1961.
Whatever their differences in age
and style, Eisenhower and
Kennedy had more in common
than either realized.

(John F. Kennedy Library)

Kennedy and Khrushchev during
their grim meeting in Vienna
in June 1961. The meeting was
premature. Kennedy wasn't ready
for it, and, more importantly,
his administration wasn't prepared for the Berlin crisis that
immediately followed.

(*Look* Magazine/John F. Kennedy
Library)

Ein München findet nicht mehr statt

„He he Mr. Chruschtschow – das sollte uns doch alles zum Verhandeln übrigbleiben!"

German: A Munich will happen no more. "He, he, Mr. Khrushchev—all of this was to be left for negotiating!" This cartoon from an influential German newspaper reflects West German doubts about the determination of the West's big three—America especially—to stand fast in Berlin.

(H. E. Kohler, *Frankfurter Allgemeine Zeitung,* September 13, 1961)

General Lucius D. Clay, Kennedy's special envoy to Berlin, arriving there on September 19, 1961, and being welcomed by Lord Mayor Willy Brandt. Clay was a reassuring presence to Berliners, but sometimes he operated outside the chain of command, a source of frequent concern in Washington.

(Keystone Photos)

"Later on, when we can afford it, we'd like to build a regular house, but right now we just want to borrow enough for a nice little fallout shelter."

This cartoon on October 21, 1961, portrays the anxiety set off by the Berlin crisis.

(Drawing by Stevenson; © 1961 The New Yorker Magazine, Inc.)

The famous, many would say infamous, meeting between President Kennedy and Soviet Foreign Minister Andrei Gromyko on October 18, 1962. Gromyko, who was accompanied by Soviet Ambassador Anatoly Dobrynin (center) and Vladimir Semenov (left), an aide, either didn't know that Soviet missiles had been put in Cuba, or, more likely, lied to Kennedy in denying their presence there.

(John F. Kennedy Library)

A facedown of American and Soviet tanks at Checkpoint Charlie in Berlin on October 27, 1961. For more than sixteen hours, American and Soviet tanks were nose to nose—the first and only such occasion in the cold war.

(AP/Wide World Photos)

October 1962: The Soviet freighter
Poltava *was carrying the warheads
for the Soviet missiles in Cuba.
The ship was one which halted
before the quarantine and then
returned home.*

(John F. Kennedy Library)

*Oleg Penkovsky, possibly the
most useful of all Western moles,
shown before the Soviet military
tribunal in Moscow that sen-
tenced him to death in May 1963.*

(Wide World Photos)

Kennedy with Secretary of
Defense Robert McNamara and
Secretary of State Dean Rusk
on the eve of their departure
for a NATO conference in
December 1962.

(Wide World Photos)

In a semiannual press conference
on January 14, 1963, de Gaulle
deals a shattering setback to
Britain's Prime Minister Macmillan and to Kennedy by saying no to Britain's bid to join
the European Community.
A major plank of Kennedy's
foreign policy had relied on British membership in an enlarged
community less dominated by
de Gaulle.

(UPI/Bettmann Newsphotos)

The Old Outlaw: (French title:
The Conquest of the East) "Hello,
old man Charly! Still determined
to shoot alone?" A famous French
cartoonist's burlesque of de Gaulle's
refusal to link the French
deterrent with U.S. and U.K.
nuclear forces. (Macmillan,
Adenauer, and Pompidou are
also shown.)

(Moi San, *Le Canard Enchaîné,* January 9,
1963/ARS NY, SPADEM, 1988)

Khrushchev greets Averell Harriman, the chief U.S. negotiator,
at the Kremlin during the last
round of talks on the nuclear
test ban, July 1963.

(UPI/Bettmann Newsphotos)

"*Aren't we fortunate to be living in a world that's
willing to ban nuclear testing!*"

*A tongue-in-cheek comment on
the limited test ban treaty which
the Senate approved in the
summer of 1963.*

(Drawing by Chon Day; © 1963
The New Yorker Magazine, Inc.)

Mushrooming Cloud

*China joins America and Russia
in the nuclear club.*

(From the *Herblock Gallery*
[New York: Simon & Schuster, 1968])

President Lyndon B. Johnson
and Defense Secretary Robert
McNamara shown at their meeting
at Glassboro with Aleksei Kosygin
in June 1967. Kosygin brusquely
rejected McNamara's cry from
the heart against ABMs, but not
long afterward Soviet policy
began to change.

(Y. R. Okamoto, LBJ Library)

President-elect Richard Nixon,
at the Pierre Hotel in New York
on December 2, 1968, is about
to announce that Henry Kissinger
(behind him) will be his national
security adviser.

(Neal Boenzi/NYT Pictures)

The American delegation early in the opening round of SALT talks, which began on November 17, 1969, in Helsinki, Finland. From left: Philip Farley, Llewellyn Thompson, Harold Brown, Paul Nitze, General Royal Allison, and seated, Gerard Smith, head of the delegation.

(UPI/Bettmann Newsphotos)

Henry Kissinger shown meeting secretly with Chou En-lai in Peking in July 1971.

(National Archives, Nixon project)

"You are getting sleepy, America . . ."

This 1973 cartoon portrayed a widening concern: While America slept, the Soviets would exploit détente by acquiring a strategic advantage.

(Tom Curtis, Milwaukee *Sentinel*, June 26, 1973)

This meeting with Brezhnev in Moscow and at Oreanda, where they are seen above, was the last hurrah for the beleaguered Nixon, whose triangular diplomacy had fostered a brief period of détente between the superpowers.

(National Archives, Nixon Project)

While Nixon and Brezhnev met alone in June 1974 in Oreanda, near Yalta, their advisers, Andrei Gromyko, Henry Kissinger, Anatoly Dobrynin, Alexander Haig, and Brent Scowcroft, waited beside the pool.

(National Archives, Nixon project)

who try to tell us . . . that disarmament is an illusion, we reply: 'By taking such a stand you fall into step with the most dyed-in-the-wool imperialist reaction [and] weaken the struggle against it.' "[55] "Theoreticians" meant Soviet military officers, whose journals were beginning to say that defense is a matter best left to military experts.[56]

Similarly, Washington's problems lay with the Joint Chiefs, who had to be fully involved with and acquiescent in any proposal to limit nuclear arms. By then, Johnson was a lame duck depleted by Vietnam and in no position to muscle an instrument of government as powerful as the chiefs, whose advantages included independent access to Congress. And Johnson, unlike his successor, had no interest in seeing optional draft proposals reflecting agency differences. He wanted to see—insisted on seeing—an *agreed* interagency position. Creating this *rara avis*—maneuvering a fragile paper through the trans-Potomac labyrinth—was a bureaucratic epic which began and ended in the Pentagon. In recent years, the Joint Chiefs have normally been a moderating influence on the often extremely "hawkish" tendencies of various parts of the bureaucracy, notably OSD (Office of the Secretary of Defense). But in 1968, OSD was something of a dovecote, many of whose key people were committed to nuclear arms control, and they had learned more about its ins and outs—what agreement would require—than colleagues in any other part of the government.

The chiefs were wary; an agreement with Russia to limit the weapons that mattered most was an alien concept. Aside from how to verify any such arrangement, the key issues were ABM limits and whether to ban the testing of MIRVs before that activity began. The air force and the navy were indifferent to ABM, but it was the army's piece of the strategic action. The army cared little about MIRV, but the air force and navy cared a lot. Each of the services would support the other's larger interests in this matter, which meant there was small chance for a proposal to set low limits on ABMs or to ban the testing of MIRVs. Most of the other principals were also opposed to banning or postponing MIRV tests before negotiations with the Soviets were under way.

A deadline for agreement between agencies was set for Wednesday, August 14, and on the 10th, with the suspense level peaking, agreement was pinned down. The chiefs, after meeting in "the tank" (their secure conference room) for nearly three days, emerged with a memorandum which endorsed most of what the other agencies had already agreed to.[57]

The price for the chiefs' support was exclusion of both a meaningful limit on ABM and a MIRV testing ban. Their position was: Don't limit technology, only numbers. And the proposal Johnson got called mainly for a freeze on long-range missiles at existing levels. Rather surprisingly, the chiefs did agree to forgo verification by on-site inspection. Instead, they would allow an agreement to be monitored with "high confidence"—as distinct from absolute certainty—which was the most overhead surveillance could guarantee.

Johnson approved the proposal, and talks were set to begin in Moscow or Leningrad on September 30. A joint announcement was prepared for release on August 21. But the day before, units of the Soviet and other Warsaw Pact armies invaded Czechoslovakia. Rusk telephoned Dobrynin that evening and informed him that everything was off. There would be no meeting.

Testing of "MIRVed" Poseidon and Minuteman missiles began on August 16, apparently to strengthen America's negotiating hand. And the Soviets, by chance, began testing the so-called SS-9 triplet—three warheads atop the world's largest missile—twelve days later.[58] The multiwarhead missile era was under way.

The Soviets may have wanted to usher in the SALT era while Johnson was still President. They had to wonder whether his successor would be someone less committed to arms control and inclined instead to recapture a commanding strategic lead by exploiting the MIRV and ABM technologies. The chances of heading off an American ABM would have been far better at the time of Glassboro when Johnson was less vulnerable and before his announcement that he would not again be a candidate for President. But the Soviets hadn't been ready then. Some of them will concede that their "education" began at Glassboro. Yuri Vorontsov, the Deputy Foreign Minister and chief arms control negotiator, once said regretfully: "It's too bad we waited so long. If only we had gone ahead with talks when McNamara was pressing for them. Don't think we weren't studying the problem. It was just too soon. We didn't think we were ready."[59]

VIII

The Back Channel

Foreign policy was Richard Nixon's vocation, as it was Eisenhower's and Kennedy's. In style and approach, however, he resembled neither. Each of them was secure within himself. Each of them was reflective and cautious. Nixon, although far less secure, was bolder. He fancied *realpolitik;* he was tempted by the opportunities open to a great power, more so than any predecessor. He could think conceptually, an attribute he appreciated in others. In a presidency full of surprises, Nixon would show that a Republican of his kind—one with authentic hard-line bona fides—could transact business with the Communist bloc that a rival with more moderate credentials wouldn't have attempted. The historic opening to China in February 1972 was his creation. It helped make possible the centerpiece arms control agreement—the treaty that all but banned ABMs—which was reached three months later in Moscow.

This peerless survivor of political disasters trusted very few people, none of them bureaucrats. He especially distrusted the foreign policy establishment. "From the outset of my administration . . . I planned to direct foreign policy from the White House," he wrote in his memoirs.[1] Henry Kissinger confirms this in relating what Nixon told him in their get-acquainted meeting at the Pierre Hotel in New York after the election: "He had very little confidence in the State Department. Its personnel had no loyalty to him . . . He was determined to run foreign policy from the White House . . . He felt it imperative to exclude the CIA from the formulation of policy; it was staffed by Ivy League liberals . . . They had always opposed him politically."[2]

There is usually a struggle, often bitter and protracted, for control of national security policy at the start of a new administration. Nixon's was an exception. Overnight, the National Security Council staff became the pacesetter—and a brisk pace it was—on security issues; the bureaucracy was kept busy chasing false hares, and department heads were put on a short leash. On his inaugural day, January 20, 1969, Nixon approved two memoranda, prepared by Kissinger, Assistant for National Security, which had the effect of creating a wholly new national security system—one that Kissinger, another conceptual thinker, would manage and that would give Nixon the control he craved.

Kissinger's power dwarfed that of any administration colleague or any predecessor in the job. He functioned as a kind of prime minister rather than a senior adviser. Before him, the grand panjandrums of foreign affairs in the cold war era had been secretaries of state. Acheson and Dulles were obvious examples. They didn't tolerate poaching, but neither of them would normally poach on the turf of others. McNamara's influence took him further into Dean Rusk's domain than any secretary of defense had been before, but the two got along nonetheless, and Rusk, the second-longest-serving secretary of state, not only outlasted McNamara but became Lyndon Johnson's closest adviser. Rusk was insular. His counsel was strictly reserved for the President, whether Kennedy or Johnson; he was intensely loyal to both. There was little difference between Rusk's private and public personalities. He was wooden with the press. He held late Friday afternoon sessions with the diplomatic press during which he said very little other than that he thought the North Vietnamese should stop bothering their neighbors. On most issues, however, he was hardheaded and pragmatic, and he left with the respect of the press and foreign diplomats alike. Sir Nicholas Henderson, a British diplomat who observed Rusk at close range and later became ambassador to Washington, wrote: "He was completely disinterested personally . . . He didn't try to score off anyone. He stated the US government's point of view with complete matter-of-factness. There were humanity and compassion and reason in what he said, but no heroics or emotion. If there was little sense of occasion and no attempt to dramatize anything, the temperature was always kept low, which is where it should be in international gatherings."[3]

Kissinger was the antithesis—as aggressive bureaucratically and as devious as Rusk had been unaggressive and straightforward. All these two had in common stylistically was a disinclination to confide in those around them, Kissinger even more so than Rusk. (In an interview with journalist Orianna Fallaci, Kissinger described himself as the lonesome cowboy riding into town.) He didn't arrive in Washington an unknown quantity. His reputation as a thinker and writer, notably on nuclear and alliance issues, was secure. As an occasional White House consultant, he was up to speed on various issues, Vietnam included. Still, no one, including colleagues at Harvard who thought he was in line for a lesser job, expected Kissinger (or anyone else) to take full possession of the national security turf. His *coup de main* on day one was, of course, partly Nixon's doing. Still, Washington's host of skeptics were very impressed, and the town lost no time in accepting Kissinger at his own robust self-valuation.

Kissinger relied on an ample operational gift, as well as his chief's antiagency bias, to neutralize competitors. Secretary of State William Rogers knew little of foreign affairs and would not have been a serious rival, even if Nixon had wanted to play them off. Rogers was among Nixon's closest confederates and had known him longer than most. But he didn't try to prevent the usurpation of his own functions, as Kissinger set about calling in ambassadors and briefing the press on policy matters. Rogers didn't like what was happening but knew that Nixon wouldn't intercede, if only because he loathed confrontation. Rogers was helpless.

Melvin Laird, the new Secretary of Defense, was different. Unlike Rogers, he knew his terrain well, having been for many years a key member of the Defense subcommittee of the House Appropriations Committee. "Laird was as close to Nixon as someone could get," says a former associate. "He thought he would be the key guy on strategic issues. Henry left him for dead."[4] Although he relentlessly undermined Laird, Kissinger respected him and didn't belittle him as he did most of the senior figures he worked with.

Kissinger dominated issues as perhaps no other policy maker has, partly through remarkable preparation. On the eve of any major meeting, he would absorb a bulky brief prepared by his staff, who would also have analyzed the positions of agency heads so that he always knew what to expect. His peers, in turn, would have done scarcely more than glance over the material and discuss it with aides during the brief ride to the White House. "It wasn't a fair fight," recalls one of Kissinger's former staff assistants.

Kissinger shared Nixon's distrust of bureaucracy, which, he knew, seeks instinctively to limit the options of leadership. And he did his considerable best to isolate bureaucracy from his purposes. His feel for Congress wasn't as good—less good than he thought—but during the years when he was riding high it didn't matter, if only because he understood the press and manipulated it as well—probably better—than any contemporary.

Press coverage of security issues was becoming steadily more competitive. Truman conducted press conferences around his desk in the Oval Office; photographers weren't present except at the end when the "still picture boys" were called in. There was plenty of leaking to the press, but less than in the 1970s and '80s. And there were fewer abusive leaks—one rival personality denigrating another—although, as noted, there was certainly some of that: Acheson and his bitter enemy, Secretary of Defense Louis Johnson, covertly assaulted one another in the press, as did Johnson and David Lilienthal, the first chairman of the AEC.

The war in Vietnam wrought a sharp change in how the national security apparatus used the press, and vice versa. There developed an even more symbiotic relationship between reporters and their sources. "The war turned a page into a new kind of journalism," recalls former Ambassador Robert McCloskey, who served as State Department spokesman for both Rusk and Kissinger.[5] Questions were raised, especially about the credibility of government, that had rarely been raised before and which divided the country. As the casualties grew heavier and the prospect of victory more remote, there began a conflict between the executive and legislative branches. This was a change. Politics had supposedly stopped at the water's edge after the Vandenberg Resolution, which blessed the Truman design for collective security. But the war allowed Congress to become more of a player in the national security process, thereby giving the press more to cover and write about. Congress was even emboldened to challenge the government not just on the war but on other security issues. An example was the debate over whether to deploy a missile defense around the country. Gradually, the conflict itself became the story. More exactly, controversy in Washington made a national security piece more accessible to the public, because controversy was a lot less complicated, hence easier to describe, than the complex issues lying at the heart of any such story.

Television news and coverage of the security issues grew together. Eisenhower's weekly news conferences weren't covered live by television; he was concerned with the print media. "We didn't even have television cameras in the White House then on a continuing basis," recalls Sander Vanocur, who covered it for NBC. His best stories, he says, were done for radio, not television.[6] Johnson thought he could use television news to promote the cause of the Vietnam War; the more he used it, however, the more onerous his course became. Kissinger's arrival coincided with both the bull market in national security stories and the coming of age of network news. Kissinger had no constituency outside the Oval Office (save for Nelson Rockefeller, who couldn't help him with Nixon's people), so he built one within the press corps. In the process, he made himself an instant celebrity and a few anonymous television reporters into household names. "He turned the use of the press by a public official into an art form," says McCloskey.[7]

The art form relied heavily on leaking, a practice that prospered in the Nixon-Kissinger-Ford era and then became routine. Those who complain most often and bitterly about leaks, especially on security issues, are sitting Presidents, although in recent years the White House has sometimes been the major source of them. Any one of a number of motives may inspire a leak. The technique is sometimes used to isolate an individual; he will be blamed for a leak that he had nothing to do with—blamed by the person or persons who inspired the leak. "The standards and rules of the game have changed," says George Vest, a highly respected diplomat who also served for a time as Kissinger's press spokesman at the State Department. "We have a knife-edged, vitriolic use of the press."[8] Gradually, the knife acquired a double edge. Over the five-year period in which Kissinger's stock was high—unrealistically high—he was largely immune to attack from any side. But when his stock slumped, as it was bound to, his opponents within the government, including a few who had learned from him, used the press against him. A handful of obscure second- and third-level figures who strongly opposed Kissinger's efforts to limit strategic arms and promote détente with Moscow took him on and beat him soundly.

Afterward, he put some distance between himself and the positions he had been pushing, and then he widened the distance, even managing at times to outflank his critics on the right. In fairness, Kissinger was hardly the first—only the most visible—Washington notable to make this course correction. A simple hard-line position is the natural sanctuary for a hard-pressed official bent on promoting the revival of his fortunes, however dim the prospects.

The chances are that Nixon and Kissinger will be as well remembered for their accomplishments as for the downside of their passage in power. In tandem, they did most to shape the curious political mold of this stage of the nuclear era. First, they launched détente and then set about trying—and failing—to institutionalize it. They left their successors with the option of trying either to advance the process or reverse it.

Even before Nixon's arrival, the Soviets alerted him to their lively interest in launching SALT. He and Kissinger were in no hurry. If the Soviets were so keen to begin this unnatural activity, let them pay something. On January 27, a week after his inauguration, Nixon told a news conference that the timing of the talks would be important; they should, he said, promote progress on "outstanding political problems." Abruptly, the term "linkage" was applied to the trendy notion that progress on SALT would require parallel progress on issues of special concern to Washington. Nixon was known to feel that little headway could be made in either Vietnam or the Middle East without some change in Soviet behavior, which he and Kissinger hoped to inspire. It was hardly surprising that Vietnam dominated their thinking. All else had to be secondary. Nixon's classical diplomacy—playing Moscow off against Peking—was aimed less at promoting an arms control agreement than in securing an exit from the war.

Kissinger and his staff wondered whether the Soviets actually would observe limits on their weapons. Or would they agree to limits which, being a closed society, they could then exploit by cheating. Other large questions loomed: Would limits on missile defense, about which the Soviets had done a *volte-face* sometime after Glassboro, be in America's interest? The threat to Minuteman—to "crisis stability," in the jargon—was being seen in a more sinister light, as the Soviets began testing immense SS-9 missiles with three warheads. Minuteman, it seemed, might have to be defended against a bolt from the blue. But would Congress approve going forward with city *and* missile defense? Nixon, like many another new President, wanted to cut the budget. The expansive ABM program he inherited was an obvious target. As for MIRV—that deceptively blameless answer to Soviet ABMs—serious people in both parties were beginning to have second thoughts, or outright doubts. Finally, the idea of the Soviets being able to protect their own missiles and threaten America's had escalated the debate among the brothers of the nuclear priesthood about strategic doctrine.

Like the early fathers of the church, they had split into contesting schools. The rather stronger of the two believed, like McNamara, that ballistic missile defense of cities was dangerous, even immoral, because it would undermine the opponent's confidence in his ability to destroy the defended cities in a second strike; in a crisis, therefore, he might be tempted to strike preemptively. This school argued that stability, an exalted goal in the nuclear age, relies on secure second-strike forces—on mutual assured destruction, or MAD, in the coinage of its detractors, whose faith lay in a more tempting but less persuasive doctrine known as "damage limitation." This school deplored as immoral the idea of renouncing the means to limit damage to one's own society. Thus, it would deploy offensive weapons capable of attacking the other side's missiles and bombers and also defend cities with ABMs. Its partisans were—are—in the main civilian members of the post-McNamara Defense Department and of various think tanks devoted to the arcana of nuclear strategy.

Nixon and Kissinger tried at first to maneuver between the antagonistic schools by declaring a need for "sufficiency." Just what the term meant was supposed to emerge from a cascade of analytical papers being generated by the Big Questions. Treating these as a whole would have been logical, but it wasn't feasible. The doctrinal dispute and the SS-9 threat were theological questions, whereas ABMs were agitating the country. They had nuclear warheads and were seen as undesirable neighbors by much of suburban America. A grass roots protest developed, most strongly around the fifteen metropolitan sites envisaged in the Johnson program known as Sentinel. Churches, unions, real estate developers, and peace groups worried aloud about cities becoming lightning rods. Congress was impressed by the outcry and by the case against ABMs being put forward by a long list of scientists and academic specialists. Slowly but steadily, the tide shifted against missile defense.

The administration wasn't disposed to yield, if only because the ABM could be the major bargaining chip in SALT. But it decided to put city defense on hold and adopt the more respectable argument of protecting Minuteman sites. The name of the program was changed from Sentinel to Safeguard. A long and acrimonious debate ensued. City defense, now unpopular, hadn't been abandoned by Nixon but merely reserved for a second stage. And the administration undermined its case for Safeguard by choosing to develop it with hardware designed for city defense instead of the simpler and cheaper components available for missile defense. The administration was trying to have it both ways. It won the argument only in the sense that the Senate eventually approved funding for Safeguard by one vote.[9] But the handwriting was on the wall. The thousands of pages of expert testimony against ABM, some of it exaggerated, left an indelible impression that missile defense, although a remarkable and even manageable technology, would be credible only so long as the adversary allowed it to be; and he wouldn't. Instead, at far less cost, he would always expand his offense and thereby overcome any conceivable defense.

Curiously, the collapse of the ABM's stock at home didn't cheapen its value as a bargaining chip in SALT. If the Soviets, unlike the American scientific community, took seriously the claims made for the American ABM, it was largely because of their respect for American technology; when Washington declares an intention to push back the state of the art in order to create a new weapon, Moscow doesn't tell itself not to worry. Instead, it usually tries to close the relevant technological gap—far enough, at least, to be able to build a comparable weapon. In the case of the ABMs, the Soviets had started earlier but lagged far behind in the critical computer technology. Their only good option was to use SALT to head off an American ABM.

Nixon and Kissinger worried about drifting into negotiation at a time when the United States wasn't building any new offensive missile systems or bombers that could be traded away. The ABM as a bargaining chip had to be seen in that light, they reckoned. There was little else to put on the table except for the wondrous MIRV, which the White House was loath to trade. It was the only new string to America's bow; it embodied a large, possibly insuperable, technological lead. Or so it seemed.

Almost no one in Congress knew what a MIRV was. In government, the talk about it was parochial and carried on by initiates. Laird began warning that the Soviet SS-9s, if MIRVed, could wipe out the Minuteman force. But his warning was used mainly to bolster the case for missile defense—for Safeguard. Another very different warning ought to have been made, but wasn't—at least not by any senior official. Only Glenn Kent, who was then a two-star general in charge of Air Force Studies and Analysis, argued that the Soviets, because they were building much heavier missiles than Minuteman, would one day be able to exploit MIRVs far more effectively than America could. In discussions of arms control proposals, Kent had been pressing this point for years; Nixon's advisers paid no more attention to it than their predecessors had.

The one political figure who opposed MIRV publicly was Edward Brooke, a freshman Republican senator from Massachusetts who had supported Nixon's rival, Nelson Rockefeller, for the 1968 nomination. During the campaign, Brooke met with Nixon, who told him that he would launch a negotiation aimed at restraining the Soviets and discouraging nuclear proliferation. He also said that the China question had to be addressed and settled. So Brooke, having been apprehensive about Nixon, was encouraged and campaigned vigorously for him.[10]

Even before the election, Brooke had decided to make an issue of MIRV. But opposition to ABM was the fashion, and at first his colleagues didn't want to complicate the debate by tossing in another big nuclear issue. On April 16, 1969, Brooke went to see Nixon about MIRV. Nixon was noncommittal. A week later, Brooke told a meeting of the American Newspaper Publishers Association that MIRV posed more serious risks than ABM and, if deployed, would make a strategic arms agreement unverifiable. His case was strong, and, lobbying hard, he lined up support for it in both houses of Congress, especially among members not yet identified with the ABM issue. On June 17, he and forty other senators sponsored a resolution calling for "a mutual suspension of MIRV flight tests."[11] They were on solid ground; only in the testing phase can intelligence distinguish single-warhead from multiwarhead missile launchers. Brooke's resolution was introduced in the House by one hundred members. The *Wall Street Journal,*

New York Times, Washington *Post,* Boston *Globe,* and many other newspapers endorsed the idea of a moratorium on MIRV testing.

Nixon was being told that MIRV deployments could begin in about a year. His staff argued that McNamara, by not building any new systems, had squandered America's leverage with the Soviets. MIRV, ran their argument, would restore it and should be deployed. He and Kissinger had already decided that putting limits on both ABM and MIRV would invite pressure from the Republican right wing and the Pentagon. And in his memoirs, Kissinger wrote: "To abandon ABM and MIRV together would thus not only have undercut the prospects for any SALT agreement but probably guaranteed Soviet strategic superiority for a decade."[12] Kissinger chose to miss the point: Brooke was proposing mutual, not unilateral, restraint.

His resolution was held up by the Senate Foreign Relations Committee. There the feeling was that Nixon wouldn't start to deploy MIRVs until he had tested the chances for mutual restraint in the SALT talks. Since these were likely to begin well before the year was out, nothing, it seemed, would be lost by waiting.

In a press conference on June 19, 1969, Nixon showed that he was ready to forget the harsh fate of the so-called Prague Spring and let SALT proceed. The talks, he guessed, could begin "sometime between July 31st and August 15th." But after having urged haste, Moscow now hesitated. The Soviets, too, were ready to start, said Gromyko on July 10, three weeks later, but he didn't set a date. Nixon was applying pressure of a kind the Soviets hadn't experienced. First was linkage. His willingness to start SALT, he'd said, was related to "other specific moves to reduce tension around the world."[13] Linkage irritated the Soviets but didn't threaten them as did Nixon's startling tendency to fish the Communist bloc's troubled waters. In early August, he visited Romania, the balkiest of Soviet satellites; the act, in Soviet eyes, was an unprecedented and calculated affront. Far worse was Nixon's apparent zest for exploiting the seething Sino-Soviet quarrel, which in March produced the first armed conflict between Communist powers; Russian and Chinese military units clashed twice on a disputed island in the Ussuri River, along the common border. Nixon began to scent opportunity.

Through the years, the press would periodically discover a new Nixon emerging from the carapace of the familiar Nixon—the "old" Nixon. The old Nixon had been one of those Republican stalwarts who saw the devil's own hand in any proposed softening of America's no-nonsense, nonrecognition of Red China policy. But writing in *Foreign Affairs* in October 1967, a new Nixon wrote: "We simply cannot afford to leave China forever outside the family of nations . . ."[14] China's escalating difficulties with Moscow could, it seemed, be turned to advantage. On April 22, Jacob Beam, the ambassador in Moscow, was instructed to assure Kosygin that the U.S. would not exploit these difficulties; the inference was that Washington could exploit them if it chose to. A month later, Gromyko gave Beam a message promising that the Soviet Union would not exploit America's troubles with China either.[15]

The Soviets were building up their forces—tanks, planes, and missiles—along the Chinese border, and in Washington, some sinologists warned of a "surgical" Soviet strike against China's nuclear production plant at Lanchow. In May, Nixon began probing the Chinese diplomatically, using intermediaries in France, Pakistan, and Romania to convey his interest in having talks. He saw an approach to China as an act he and he alone could perform. It would be, in the words of a former NSC staff member, "a single bold stroke accomplished not through elaborate technical agreements, but essentially through the strength of his presence."[16] The act, by perhaps lowering the pressure on China and increasing the pressure on Moscow, would strengthen Nixon's hand as he prepared to negotiate with the Soviets.

The Chinese were not yet ready for this game and didn't take the bait. Toward the end of the summer, the Soviets provoked new incidents on the Sinkiang border, and the fear of the surgical nuclear strike sharpened; an apparent crisis loomed for a moment and then faded. Arkady Shevchenko says the crisis was indeed more apparent than real: "Only Marshal [Andrei] Grechko [the Chief of Staff] seriously considered using nuclear weapons in 1969. No one above him did. The Politburo had to consider it, because he recommended it. But Brezhnev would never have allowed it to happen."[17] According to Shevchenko, whatever risk of a strike there may have been was silenced by a warning from Dobrynin that such an action against China would produce a "serious Soviet-American confrontation."[18]

Nixon and Kissinger continued to dangle SALT before the Soviets and bilateral talks before the Chinese. But the Soviets wanted first to show that stability within the Communist bloc was no less important to them than talks with the Americans. Not before they started parallel talks with the Chinese on the border issue could SALT begin. In September, the Chinese bent a bit. Kosygin went to Hanoi for the funeral of Ho Chi Minh and flew on from there to the airport at Peking, where he met China's Premier, Chou En-lai. Chou agreed to begin talks on the border issue on October 20. Perhaps coincidentally, perhaps not, Nixon met secretly with

Dobrynin that day. And five days later, on October 25, the world was told that SALT would begin on November 17 in Helsinki.[19]

On the eve of its debut, Nixon and Kissinger were no less wary of SALT. Soviet motives, although unclear, were suspect. So was the supposed goal of the talks: an agreement solemnizing parity, or equivalence as some called it, in strategic forces. Having grown accustomed to feeling itself comfortably ahead, would the country regard the pursuit of a chancier position as peculiar, even softheaded? Actually, the country was readier than perhaps it knew for some novel project that could take its mind off Vietnam and lower the tension. Nixon and Kissinger worried that the war might cause the country and Congress to weary of doing whatever was required to stay even with the Soviets in strategic arms.

The forces of the two sides were dissimilar and could not be compared glibly. They embodied the different technological attainments of the two countries and their different geographic positions. They still do. America comfortably deploys strategic weapons on land and sea, whereas the land is the natural strategic environment for the Soviets. When SALT began, they had 1,500 ICBMs, about five hundred more than America was deploying. But then as now, America had more and incomparably better strategic bombers. Then as now, the American ballistic missile submarines (SSBNs) were the more capable; they remain so, being quieter and hence harder to track. Also, unlike their Soviet counterparts, the American boats have easy access to the open seas and can remain on station for longer periods. In short, each side had advantages that were offset by the other's. And since each could inflict unacceptable damage on the other in a retaliatory strike, a state of parity had arrived. Neither side was going to allow the other to capture a meaningful advantage. Yet because of MIRV—the force multiplier—neither could be sure that the other wouldn't try. In a few months Washington would be deploying MIRVs, unless constrained by SALT; more than half of the 1,000 Minutemen were to be equipped with three such warheads. The Soviets would still have more ICBMs, but America would then be able to deliver many more weapons—that is unless the Soviets solved the technology and began stacking MIRVs like so much cordwood on their superbrutes, the SS-9 force. The administration worried that the Soviets, if only for political purposes, might create a first-strike threat to Minuteman, the backbone then of America's deterrent.

Although the threat dominated Washington's planning for SALT, it fell short of pushing the White House to the view that something should be done jointly about restricting MIRV. Instead, Washington would seek a numerical ceiling on long-range missiles. Since America wasn't building any more of these, a ceiling would have no effect on its position. But the Soviets would be affected; they were producing about two hundred fifty ICBMs and eight new submarines per year; the scale of the submarine program meant that as many as one hundred twenty-five or so new SLBMs were being built as well.[20] What Washington wanted most was a hold on the SS-9 program; that goal alone justified undertaking SALT. Gone from the White House rhetoric was the talk of linking progress in SALT to progress on contentious world issues.

Kissinger had, if anything, an even stronger hold on the SALT account than on the other topics of priority importance. A so-called Verification Panel which he chaired dealt with SALT-related issues. These emerged from a massive analytical process, itself directed by his staff. The head of the SALT delegation was C. Gerard Smith, Director of the Arms Control and Disarmament Agency (ACDA). Smith was highly qualified by experience, temper, and ability. He had been closely involved with nuclear matters for more than twenty years, first with the AEC and then with the State Department, where he had advised John Foster Dulles before becoming director of the Policy Planning Staff—one of the several jobs Paul Nitze had also held. Nitze, too, was a member of the SALT delegation; he represented the Department of Defense and by then had accumulated as much or more experience with the country's national security as any living American. Like Smith, he knew the ins and outs of nuclear weapons. But he was judged as more hard-line than Smith, who, like his agency, was thought by the White House to take an overly positive view of talks with the Russians. State and ACDA took a similar line on SALT. William Rogers was seen from the White House as lacking in rigor and skepticism. The White House brooded that the Soviets, while conceding little or nothing, would rely on SALT to widen public and congressional opposition to the Safeguard and MIRV programs.

Just before the delegation left for Helsinki, Nitze was called in by Nixon, whom he had known and gotten on with since Nixon's days as vice president. Nixon told Nitze that he didn't trust Rogers or Smith and suggested that he report directly to him. "I told him," Nitze says, "that you can't manage a delegation unless there is trust between its members. Nixon accepted that but said, 'Well, I've described the back channel communications available to you. If you see something going wrong, contact Kissinger, or me through Kissinger.' "[21]

The seven rounds of what became known as SALT I occupied thirty months, during which the venue of the talks alternated between Helsinki and Vienna. Secrecy was immaculate. The five hundred or so journalists who covered the early days of the opening round could say of the talks only that they were "businesslike."[22] (There were leaks, but from Washington.) The Soviets worried that Nixon would accept a ceiling in numbers of weapons systems only if they agreed to accept—to freeze—America's lead in the technology of multiple warheads. But then, as now, the Soviets saw large dividends to be gained from SALT. Formal parity in strategic weapons would point up the Soviet Union's status as the other superpower; SALT would confirm the lofty position of a state whose nonmilitary attributes were unimpressive. Also, better relations with the West could allow Moscow to cope more effectively with its China problem— perhaps even to prevent an anti-Soviet understanding between America and China.

The opening round, although exploratory, was long on surprise, starting with a spirited effort to neuter missile defense. The worry had been that Moscow, having noted fifty Senate votes against Safeguard, would give up nothing for a goal that Congress would eventually provide gratis. But the stunner fell when the talks turned to offensive weapons. Abruptly, the Soviets brought up forward-based systems (FBS)—their term for American aircraft deployed in Western Europe and on carriers in the Mediterranean and the Northeast Pacific. There were several hundred of these; they could, said the Soviets, strike the motherland and must therefore be treated just as if they were part of America's strategic forces and thus accountable in SALT. The Americans, appalled, rejected this proposition, arguing that the aircraft were tactical, not strategic. Many of them could, admittedly, attack Russia on one-way missions, but would be unable to return to base. Their role, quite clearly, was to counter an equivalent force of Soviet medium- and intermediate-range ballistic missiles targeted against America's European allies.

This Soviet demand became a constant of both SALT I and SALT II. Week in, week out, the American SALT delegates were told by Deputy Foreign Minister Vladimir Semenovich Semenov, the chief Soviet delegate, that the forward-based systems gave America a unilateral advantage. "No unilateral advantage" is allowed, Semenov invariably reminded the Americans at meetings. If twitted about the sameness of his script he would say, "Repetition is the mother of wisdom."

FBS was the issue that truly mattered to allied governments; they saw it as a test of America's grip on its own best interests. For Washington to bargain away assets bearing directly on Europe's security would have created a major rift within the alliance, thereby promoting a major Soviet purpose. In Washington, the FBS issue pointed up a dilemma: Increasingly, America confronted the twin requirements of upholding the strength and coherence of the Western Alliance while also assuring some degree of stability in East-West relations. With the Soviets planting the FBS issue squarely in the path to agreement, the tension between these requirements was clear.

Nixon had been under pressure from Rogers and Smith, as well as some congressional figures, to do something about MIRV in SALT. Rogers had publicly endorsed Brooke's resolution. But after flirting with the idea, Nixon told Smith that if the Soviets raised the issue of a moratorium, they should be informed it would be referred to him.[23] Neither side mentioned MIRV at Helsinki.

The Senate, still under the impression that Nixon would hold off on deploying MIRV until the talks had been given a chance, was thrown off stride on March 10, 1970, when Air Force Secretary Robert Seamans said that the first MIRVed Minuteman missiles would be deployed in June.[24] The reaction was swift; on March 24, Brooke's all-but-forgotten resolution proposing "an immediate suspension" of MIRV testing by both sides was reported out of the Foreign Relations Committee. On April 9, it passed the Senate. The vote was 72 to 6, a remarkably full-throated call for restraint.

Although the Senate's gesture had little effect on White House thinking, it showed that Washington had come face to face with the heart of the matter: In tandem, MIRV and ABM propelled the race for strategic advantage. Each system begot the other. Stop one and the case for the other disappeared. The main difference between them was that MIRVs would work and ABMs wouldn't—at least, not convincingly.

On the eve of the second round of SALT, the administration was reviewing various options, one of which proposed a ban on testing and deployment of MIRV. As drafted, the option provided for verification by each side's own national technical means, as distinct from intrusive means, i.e., on-site inspection. State, ACDA, and the larger part of the SALT bureaucracy strongly preferred this approach; monitoring the ban would not require on-site inspectors, and the Soviets would be certain to reject any proposal to have them. But the White House had the language broadened to include verification by on-site inspection. No one was altogether certain why Nixon and Kissinger took this step; it removed whatever possibility there might have been to sidetrack MIRV. In his memoirs, Kissinger assigns responsibility to the Pentagon.[25] Others, like Smith, while acknowledging the Joint Chiefs' distaste for restricting MIRVs, felt that Nixon and especially Kissinger wanted to appear to be doing something about MIRV without really doing anything.

Probably there was little, if any, chance of the Soviets agreeing to the proposal, which would have banned both testing and deployment while not preventing the U.S. from producing and stockpiling MIRVed missiles. The Soviets could have counterproposed a testing ban that didn't require on-site inspection. But they didn't. They were not then willing to be "frozen out," as the saying went, from any advanced technology.

Four years later, Kissinger was asked whether he was sorry the United States had gone ahead with MIRV in 1969. "Well, that's a good question," he said. "And I think that is the same question that people faced when the hydrogen bomb was developed . . . I would say in retrospect that I wish I had thought through the implications of a MIRVed world more thoughtfully in 1969 and in 1970 than I did."[26]

The term "technology creep" characterizes a cycle in which American innovation creates novel weapons or novel variants of existing weapons; these are matched by the Soviets, as they set about mastering the same technologies. From MIRV to Star Wars, the Americans have tried—unavailingly in every case—to use their broader technological base to acquire a lasting advantage, even when it was clear, as noted, that neither side would allow the other any such advantage. It isn't a case of successive administrations not learning the lesson of MIRV. They just ignored it.

The White House, beset by Vietnam, was still trying to add the China card to its hand. Early in 1970, a trap was baited. America would withdraw troops from Taiwan if the Chinese would host high-level talks in Peking.[27] But the American invasion of Cambodia in May closed off any Chinese interest. For months, Washington sent signals into an apparent vacuum. Then in October, Nixon began using the presidents of Pakistan and Romania to tell Peking that he now considered Taiwan "an internal problem" to be settled by the Chinese themselves and that talks could be held between high level officials (as distinct from ambassadorial officials). Diplomatic exchanges followed, and the usual stridency in the two sides' rhetoric about one another was muted. Also in October, Nixon told *Time* that "if there is anything I want to do before I die, it is to go to China."[28]

One wonders whether Kissinger informed the Chinese at this time about an amazing Soviet initiative in the SALT talks to create a de facto superpower alliance against other nuclear powers, notably China. In Helsinki, Semenov spoke with Smith about possible "provocative attacks by third nuclear powers." Months later, at a concert in Vienna, Semenov returned to the issue with a proposal that was formally presented three days later. On learning of plans for "provocative" action or attack, the United States and the U.S.S.R. would act jointly to prevent it, or, if it was too late for that, take joint punitive action against the guilty party. Apart from revealing the extent of Moscow's sinophobia, the affair had no effect. Washington rejected it immediately.[29]

In March, Pakistan's Yahya Khan, who by then was Nixon's emissary to Peking, launched a repressive war against secessionist East Pakistan. The United States stood nearly alone in not condemning this action. "We had few means to affect the situation," said Kissinger. "We had, moreover, every incentive to maintain Pakistan's goodwill. It was our crucial link to Peking; and Pakistan was one of China's closest allies."[30] The U.S. would continue to "tilt" toward Pakistan in its ensuing war with India in the fall.

On April 6, the Chinese invited the United States national table tennis team to an exhibition match in Peking; Prime Minister Chou En-lai received the team—the first representatives of the U.S. to visit the People's Republic of China. In May, it was arranged that Kissinger would make two visits to Peking—the first secret, the second public—and that Nixon would come later. "Each side," they agreed, "would be free to raise the issue of principal concern to it."[31]

In Peking, Kissinger presented his hosts with ultrasensitive intelligence on Soviet military activities that had been obtained by communications intercepts, high-resolution satellite photographs, and other sources. The material covered Soviet forces on the border with China.[32] This openhandedness fed suspicions among the handful of persons who were aware of Semenov's proposal to Smith that Kissinger did tell the Chinese about it.

In mid-July, the country and the world discovered that Nixon would visit China early in the following year. The stunned reaction contributed more than a little to the immense satisfaction that Nixon, rightly enough, took from his opening to China. It was his major moment, partly for its own sake and partly because of its heavy impact on Moscow, where lurking anxieties about a multipolar world were fully aroused. The Soviets would pay to keep the system bipolar; the world had to see that the superpower club was restricted to two members. The time of triangular diplomacy had begun, and a chief beneficiary was the SALT process.

Little or no progress had as yet been made. Limiting ABMs was the only shared interest. As the American side put up one proposal after another, a questionable negotiating tactic, the Soviets shot them down—mainly because each would have put a lid on offensive as well as defensive systems. Moscow was all for limiting the latter but not the former. Soviet thinking had come a long way since Kosygin chided Johnson at Glassboro about defense being moral and offense immoral. While offering no proposals themselves, the Soviets clung to a position that was as unspecific as it was inflexible. The American side saw them as being split into factions—as negotiating mainly with themselves. Moreover, the civilian members of the Soviet delegation, including Semenov himself, were kept woefully ignorant about their own weapons. Semenov didn't know the number of Soviet submarines deployed or under construction so Smith took him aside and told him.[33] One of the American delegates, Lieutenant General Royal B. Allison, once found himself being admonished by Colonel General Nikolai V. Ogarkov, a delegate and also the first Deputy Chief of Staff, that his Soviet civilian colleagues had no need to know about military matters. Ogarkov, a strong and stylish personality who later became Chief of Staff, then urged that the American side stop talking as specifically as it had been about Soviet weapons.[34]

The poky and unproductive style of the affair was for a time reminiscent of the Congress of Vienna in its formative stage. ("*Le Congrès danse mais il ne marche pas.*") The twice-weekly plenary meetings were routine affairs, largely taken up by Smith and Semenov reading prepared statements cleared at home. The special language of weaponry was a problem; the Soviet interpreters had no grasp of the actual meaning of what was being said, and very few of their American counterparts—only one really—ever did. The difficulty wasn't trivial, since it would eventually turn out that differences in the positions of the two sides were often in some part linguistic.[35] The Soviet civilians all seemed familiar with the Bible and were given to canonical utterances such as "we have just administered extreme unction to your proposal." An American military officer who was once reviewing the history of nuclear weapons said, "In the beginning, there was the long-range bomber." He was clearly serious, and the Soviet side rocked with laughter.

As 1971 began, the Soviets had deployed about 450 more ICBMs than the U.S. (counting some still under construction); they were building SLBMs at a rapid clip. And they had just concluded tests of multiple warheads for both the SS-9 and the more numerous SS-11s. The buildup was intimidating, its eventual scale an unknown. It did appear, though, that the SS-9 program had leveled off at 288 launchers, an encouraging sign. The bad news arrived in March. American intelligence saw some new holes—large enough to hold a missile at least as large as the SS-9—situated in the SS-9 fields. Other new holes began appearing in SS-11 fields. Their purpose was unclear, but the likely portents were ominous: MIRVed versions of existing missiles or new and more powerful missiles or both. On March 7,

Senator Henry Jackson declared on television, "The Russians are now in the process of deploying a new generation . . . of offensive systems . . . big or bigger than the SS-9s."[36] Although a Democrat, Jackson had been the first choice of Nixon and Laird for secretary of defense.* His looming offstage presence would crowd and eventually overshadow the onstage grandees.

Even before the new holes were spotted, the White House had ruled out yielding to pressure from its critics on Capitol Hill and in the press to make an ABM-only deal with the Soviets. Quite clearly, Moscow was more than ready for the deal, which could, it seemed, amount to as much as SALT would ever yield. "The best is the enemy of the good" was the gist of the argument for indulging Moscow's aversion to limiting offensive weapons. The contrary argument was that any chance to limit weapons of mass destruction would be gone once the administration played the ABM card.

With the pressure growing, Kissinger opened a back channel with Moscow, as he'd done with the Chinese. A back channel usually involved a senior personality on one side empowered to work on sensitive matters privately and independently of bureaucracy with some appropriate figure on the other side. In this case, the principals would be Kissinger and Dobrynin, who had already expressed an interest in secret talks.[37]

Tête-à-tête talks on SALT in Kissinger's office began in January 1971; he and Dobrynin had already isolated the pivotal issues: "simultaneity," i.e., Washington's determination to limit offense and defense at the same time, and Moscow's heavy pressure for a concession to their stand on forward-based systems. In May, the key breakthrough in the talks was made. The parties announced an agreement to agree: They would limit ABMs *and* take "certain measures with respect to the limitation of offensive strategic weapons."[38] What lay behind the event was the Twenty-fourth Soviet Party Congress in April, which strengthened the hand of Leonid Brezhnev, who by then had committed himself to having a quieter time with the West, i.e., a period of détente. Probably, Nixon's flirtation with China was pushing Brezhnev in this direction.

Dobrynin was promoted during the Congress to full membership in the Central Committee, and he returned from Moscow in late April with a new and wider negotiating brief. The Soviets had decided to grant the link between offense and defense. They were also ready to shelve FBS, at least until after a SALT I agreement had been reached. But the White House made a major concession in agreeing to freeze for the period of

---

*Jackson refused, mainly because acceptance, he judged, would harm his chances of one day being President.

agreement a three-to-two Soviet advantage in numbers of long-range missile systems. Washington had formally insisted on each side having "equal aggregates" of these weapons.[39]

Although the back-channel talks had broken the stalemate, Smith was far from pleased. First, he had been kept in the dark until one day before the May announcement. He was in good company; Laird hadn't been told either. "There was no need for me to tell Kissinger what I thought of his procedure in negotiating behind the back of all responsible Administration officials save the President," wrote Smith. "There were no building blocks, no analytical work, no strategic analysis in the agencies concerned. There were no Verification Panel or National Security Council discussions. There were no consultations with congressional committees or with allies. It was a one-man stand, a presidential aide against the resources of the Soviet leadership . . . Kissinger and the President went the Soviets one better. At least in the Soviet Union, the whole Politburo was consulted, on several occasions . . ."[40]

On reading the record of what had been agreed to, Smith judged it deficient on some points, one of them critical: SLBMs had been omitted from the freeze; construction of new ICBM silos would be halted, but Kissinger, for whatever reason, hadn't judged it essential to include SLBMs. Repairing this error—setting limits on SLBMs—became the thorniest issue and had to be settled at the summit. Kissinger himself correctly described the May understanding as "a milestone in confirming White House dominance of foreign affairs. For the first two years White House control had been confined to the formulation of policy; now it extended to its execution."[41] But the understanding was also, as even Smith said, a "turning point" in the negotiations.[42]

Thanks to Ronald Reagan, one of the lesser SALT issues was revived publicly—and polemically—in the mid-1980s under the popular heading "Star Wars." In 1972, its label was "Exotics," because it involved lasers, particle beams, and other directed-energy weapons. In the summer of 1971, State, the CIA, and the arms control agency proposed banning all futuristic ABMs, i.e., those which weren't really ballistic missiles and were based "on other physical principles." The Joint Chiefs opposed the ban. The White House felt that some research and development should be allowed since a total ban wouldn't be verifiable.

In the end, Washington decided to ban mobile exotics, whether based on land, sea, or in the air or space; no advanced development or testing of these would be permitted. But fixed land-based versions could be developed and tested, although not deployed. The loophole was created for land-based lasers, because Washington was taking a close look at them. The Soviets were at least as curious about lasers and were reluctant to forbear deploying them. At SALT, their military officers argued against restricting devices that didn't yet exist; the American military felt much the same way.[43] But in a rather unexpected and momentous breakthrough in January 1972, the front channel—Smith's delegation—got agreement from the Soviet side to ban everything except research and development of the fixed land-based exotics. Four months later, the parties solemnized this commitment to self-denial in two articles of the ABM Treaty and in an agreed statement that had the same legal force. The language of this ensemble is straightforward and seemingly unambiguous. Its exact meaning and intent were clear at the time to the Senate, as they are today to most interested lawyers. But a small cabal of Star Wars partisans arbitrarily reinterpreted the language affecting exotics in order to allow space-based testing of parts of a system that is generally thought to be as fanciful as it is dubious.

Apart from a strong aversion to inhibiting technological creep, the Pentagon in 1971 was unsure of what it wanted from SALT. With the war in Vietnam beginning to slow down, pressure to cut the defense budget was rising. The ABM's fall from fashion didn't bother the air force and navy, both of which saw it as drawing funds away from other big-ticket weapons they badly wanted. With its bombers and ICBMs, the air force controlled two legs of the triad of strategic forces. With SLBMs, the navy had the other leg. Not for some years had the budget for strategic weapons gone up, despite intermittent pressure from the air force for new systems to replace the ones then deployed. Nixon had actually cut strategic spending by $2 billion in fiscal year 1970.

Nixon knew that a SALT agreement—no longer a distant possibility— would require stout support from the air force and navy. And the lengthening wish list of both acquired larger significance in October when he announced that he would visit Moscow in the spring; a deadline for the SALT agreement had been set. Smith felt that in agreeing to a summit to be held in a presidential election year, Nixon was putting too much pressure on himself to reach agreement with the other side.[44]

Nixon was hardly indifferent to his situation. Just after the announcement, he complained in an NSC meeting about having no leverage. The Soviets, he observed, were grinding out new SS-9s and SLBMs, whereas the U.S. was merely improving Minuteman and Polaris. Leverage aside, Nixon also had to think of the ratification process, a time when the Senate, before approving a SALT agreement, would want to be sure that America wasn't falling behind. Nixon turned to Laird and Admiral Thomas Moorer, the Chairman of the Joint Chiefs, and asked what could be done quickly. They in turn put the question to the services. The air force was pushing for a new bomber, which became known as the B-1, but it was, at best, several years off. The air force could supply no answer to Nixon's question.

The navy had three answers, but could recommend only one: modifying Polaris submarines so as to equip them with more missile launch tubes. Another option was to build a new submarine and a new missile for it. But since the project might consume another nine years, the navy saw it as unresponsive to the supposed urgency of Nixon's situation.

What happened next is worth pausing over, because the answer Nixon received was not responsive to his question but did put American force planning onto a different and highly questionable path—one that is as controversial today as it was then. Several days after the navy had taken a position, Laird sent a memorandum to the White House recommending instead the new submarine project. "I was flabbergasted," recalls one NSC staff assistant. "It made no sense." Kissinger agreed that it made no sense and, on Nixon's behalf, sent Laird a letter directing him to review the decision, because it didn't respond to the request. Just before Christmas, Laird sent a reply in which he upheld his recommendation for the new submarine.

The apparent mystery concealed an especially savage bureaucratic battle involving some of the navy's—indeed, the Pentagon's—most illustrious personalities. The issue was an embryonic submarine, more accurately its size. Most of the navy's experts and key people, along with David Packard, the Deputy Secretary of Defense and an esteemed judge of hardware, favored a boat of fairly modest dimensions—a somewhat larger and improved variant of the Polaris boats. But Admiral Hyman Rickover, the fearsome pioneer of nuclear submarine technology, had something very different in mind: a boat he would wrap around a new reactor of unprecedented size. What he seemed to want was a monument to himself. He favored speed, and the new reactor would propel a new and correspondingly much larger vessel at a somewhat faster rate than missile-firing submarines normally travel. Because of his unexampled influence on Capitol Hill, Rickover won that battle, as he normally won most others. The new submarine, known as Trident, would be a genuine deepwater leviathan.

It would be equipped with a new missile whose longer range would enlarge the operating area from which boats could fire SLBMs at Russia by a factor of five—from roughly three million square nautical miles to fifteen million.[45] With so much more ocean in which to operate, the boats would be far more difficult for hostile attack submarines to find. Packard and others liked the longer-range missiles. It was Rickover's big boat they didn't like. Their preference was to have a larger number of smaller subs, instead of a few huge ones, so as to have more boats on station at any one time and thereby give Moscow's antisubmarine warfare units a bigger problem. Building Trident, its critics said, would be putting too many eggs in too few baskets.

Packard and others in the Pentagon wanted to defer any decision on a new boat until the 1980s. In the meantime, they proposed to equip existing submarines with the new longer-range missiles, an option known as EXPO, for "extended-range Poseidon." Although wholly sensible in military (and budgetary) terms, it was bitterly opposed by the navy, even by those who had lost the fight to Rickover on the Trident's size. Above all, the navy wanted a new boat, and sooner, not later.

Sometime after Christmas, Nixon met with Kissinger, Laird, Moorer, and Admiral Elmo Zumwalt, Chief of Naval Operations. Zumwalt, according to a member of Kissinger's NSC staff, had initially urged the Pentagon to adopt the modified Polaris option as the answer to Nixon's question. But now, "he fought and bled for the new boat option. What had happened in between was that Rickover went ballistic when he heard about this. He wanted his own power plant and boat and threatened to shoot down whatever else might be approved in its place—shoot it down, that is, on the Hill."[46] EXPO was dead. Trident was the only game in town. Nixon would presume to impress the Senate and America's allies, too, by adding nearly one and a quarter billion dollars to the budget for strategic arms. The larger part of the money would go to the Trident.

There remained the problem of somehow maneuvering the SLBMs into SALT. Having allowed the issue to go astray in the back channel, Kissinger used the back channel to settle it. Moscow, he knew, would agree to extend a ceiling on land-based missiles to include those deployed on submarines only if the White House agreed to freeze the heavy Soviet advantage in submarines (and launch tubes). But any such arrangement, he also knew, could arouse opposition in the Pentagon. In late April 1972, just a month before the summit meeting, Kissinger flew secretly to Moscow, where he sorted out the SLBM issue and narrowed differences on how to limit ABMs. Before going, he gave the Soviets a proposal on SLBMs, but one about which his administration colleagues knew nothing and which he arranged, through Dobrynin, to have Brezhnev offer him in Moscow.[47] In short, Kissinger invited the Soviets to present him with a proposal of his own devising that he could then take up with his colleagues on the Verification Panel in Washington. Even for Kissinger, this was sly and devious practice. And it worked. On April 28, just after his return from Moscow, the panel met. By then, it was clear that the navy wanted to speed up the Trident program, a costly and altogether questionable move; Trident already appeared to be the most expensive weapons system ever conceived. But a deal was there to be made. Admiral Moorer wanted White House backing for the speedup. Nixon and Kissinger wanted his support for an SLBM deal that would give the Soviet Union almost half again as many missile-carrying submarines as America. Tacitly, the deal was struck at the meeting. The decision to build Rickover's seagoing monument was a grave mistake. Bureaucratic self-interest had overwhelmed the national interest, not to mention common sense. The EXPO option did make sense and would today if it were available. In the winter of 1987–1988, as the Reagan administration tried to push along its own strategic arms negotiation with the Soviets, serious people worried that an agreement would leave the United States with too few missile-firing submarines—Trident submarines.

The way to the Soviet Summit was strewn with pitfalls," wrote Nixon.[48] He did not exaggerate. In both the front and back channels, the last exhausting weeks and days of the affair were surreal. The Soviets were shipping vast quantities of arms to the North Vietnamese, who, in March, crossed the demilitarized zone and launched a major invasion. American bombers stepped up the pace and on April 16 managed to hit four Soviet merchant ships in Haiphong harbor. The Soviets protested, although mildly. On May 8, with South Vietnam on the verge of giving up, Nixon decided to mine North Vietnam's coastal waters, which meant closing them to Soviet shipping. Kissinger and his staff, wrote Nixon, thought the step "would kill the summit."[49] A number of diplomats surmised, wrongly, that Nixon would prefer a cancellation to being seen in Moscow with Brezhnev just as the situation on the ground in Vietnam was going from bad to worse.

The pressure on Brezhnev was at least as heavy. By denying Haiphong to Soviet ships two weeks before the summit, Nixon had catalyzed the stiffest internal challenge to his authority that Brezhnev had ever faced.[50]

"Our ships were there, and the Americans dropped bombs on them," recalls *Izvestia*'s Alexander Bovin. "So Moscow faced a problem: to receive Nixon, or not to receive [him] . . . in such a circumstance."[51]

Three days before Nixon's scheduled arrival in Moscow, the issue was still being fought out. The signs of struggle surfaced with the demotion of a senior and powerful figure, Petr Shelest, during a special meeting of the Central Committee.[52] Shelest, an ultra-hard-liner, was replaced as party leader in the Ukraine by a Brezhnev hack, doubtless because he opposed making a SALT agreement with Nixon—perhaps at any time, but certainly then—and because he also opposed a nonaggression pact with West Germany, which was probably as important to Brezhnev as SALT. The pact was aimed at spreading Soviet political influence westward and improving access to European technology and commerce. In Bonn, the Bundestag hadn't yet ratified the treaty, and the outcome was far from certain. Cancellation of Nixon's visit might have tipped the balance against approval. It could also have cost Brezhnev the SALT agreement and his major moment with the Americans, which he saw as a prelude to others. He was feeling the pressure released by Nixon's triumphant ceremonial visit to China three months earlier and was determined to show, as he said later, that "Nixon went to Peking for banquets but to Moscow to do business."[53] The Soviets had also assumed that a superpower would not allow itself to lose a war. Thus Nixon, they reasoned, would deal with them from a position of even greater strength after he had polished off their allies in Hanoi. By then, he would appear awesome, in which case better to have an accommodation sooner, not later.

In his willingness to bargain against a summit deadline and, indeed, to come to Moscow with key issues still unresolved, Nixon showed himself as being at least as ardent as Brezhnev. Gone was the notion that a deal on SALT would require better Soviet behavior in various hot spots. Moscow's role in Vietnam's war spoke for itself. Also, not so long before the summit, the Soviets were seen by Nixon and Kissinger as egging on India in its war with Pakistan.* Nixon even considered canceling the meeting but decided against it, and Kissinger thought he was right.[54] Linkage is the stuff of brave rhetoric for those who wish, for whatever reason, to stand against an agreement without attacking it. Arms control, they argue, is a laudable enterprise but should not encourage Soviet steps to undermine peace and stability or be seen as excusing them. This argument became a continuity of superpower relations, however spongy its logic. An agreement, after all,

---

*"The Soviet Union, in other words, came close to giving Mrs. Gandhi a blank check," Kissinger wrote (Kissinger, *White House Years* [Boston: Little, Brown, 1979], p. 874).

is hardly a reward for good behavior but rather a set of goals that embody hardheaded assessments of the national interest.

On May 26, 1972, the ABM Treaty was signed. Each side surrendered any meaningful right to defend its society and territory against the other's nuclear weapons. That was the treaty's historic essence. And it remains so. The ABM Treaty is the backbone of today's arms control regime and, as such, is relied upon by the world. The text dealt mainly with verification. Eleven of sixteen articles were designed to prevent any circumvention of the agreement. And each side agreed to rely on its surveillance and detection systems to monitor the other's compliance not just with the treaty but with an interim five-year agreement that set the ceiling on long-range missile launchers. Also, both agreements forbade either side interfering with the other's surveillance systems or concealing those of its own activities which had to be monitored.

The interim accord on offensive missiles was controversial. Some experts deplored it for failing to slam on the brakes, as the ABM Treaty had done. Some political figures, notably Henry Jackson, saw the deal as one-sided, because it allowed the U.S.S.R. a large numerical advantage in missiles during the five-year span. Nixon and Kissinger could argue that a lid had been placed on the exuberant Soviet missile buildup, while American programs and plans were unaffected. Obtaining the link between offense and defense had not been easy, and some critics had not long before insisted on an ABM-only pact. In holding out for the link, Nixon and Kissinger could feel vindicated. Gradually, numerous partisans of arms control began to see the admittedly modest interim agreement as a first small step on the circuitous path toward limiting offensive arms.

Against the odds, the Moscow summit had actually taken place and produced agreement. The affair was, or seemed to be, an epiphany for détente. Brezhnev signed the agreements himself, thereby showing that SALT and détente enjoyed mighty patronage; protocol called for them to be signed by the powerless Soviet chief of state, who was then President Nikolai Podgorny.

The summit was the high point for détente, but also for Nixon and hence Kissinger. Less than a month later, on June 17, the office of the Democratic National Committee in the Watergate complex was broken into. The event seemed to be of little importance. Congress and the country overwhelmingly approved the SALT agreements. The opening to China was popular. The country sensed that its security and its interests abroad were being well looked after. Nixon was reelected by a huge margin. Not long afterward, his descent began.

Perhaps the first harbinger of trouble for détente appeared a full month before the summit, when the CIA discovered that the Russians were preparing to test a new ICBM, larger even than the SS-9. Clearly, the new holes in the SS-9 fields were intended for this latest behemoth, which presumably would be MIRVed and would replace the SS-9 force. Among the issues to be resolved was the size of new or improved missiles. Smith's delegation already knew that the Soviets had two new MIRV-capable missiles under development that were intended to replace the aging SS-11s—the mainstay of their deterrent.[55] The delegation hoped to prevent the Soviets from replacing their SS-11 force with an appreciably larger missile. But in Moscow, Brezhnev assured Nixon and Kissinger that "there was no need to change the dimensions of Soviet silos and that the Soviets had no intention of increasing the diameter of their missiles."[56] Two days later, the Americans learned from an intelligence intercept of a conversation between Brezhnev and a senior military official that the Soviets were planning sizable increases in the volume of their missiles.[57] Kissinger appears not to have grasped an important distinction between silo diameters and missile volume. The same silo—deepened somewhat, but unchanged in diameter—can house a significantly larger missile. Thus Brezhnev's assurance had little, if any, bearing on Soviet plans to replace existing missiles with bigger and better ones.[58] Yet thanks to the intelligence report, Kissinger was aware of actual Soviet intentions. Nonetheless, he later assured Congress that restraints on missile modernization agreed to in Moscow would head off heavier new missiles.[59] Within three years, the Soviets were deploying them and détente's downward slide had begun.

In the enduring sense, Nixon and Kissinger had exploited an opportunity to block ABMs, but they all but ignored the opportunity to kill MIRV.

IX

The Right Resurgent

s Watergate took over center stage and Nixon's agony began, his entourage couldn't quite believe what was happening. From the White House, it appeared that his deeds abroad and their high acceptance level at home would prove adequately redemptive. Early in 1974, Alexander Haig told William Hyland that the tide was turning in Nixon's favor. Haig had by then become Nixon's chief of staff; Hyland was among Kissinger's closest confederates. His strengths— Soviet affairs and SALT—were Kissinger's special interests. Hyland recently wrote, "Even allowing for Haig's natural exuberance, which in the NSC staff we knew so well, I was persuaded that he was right . . . in the middle level of the White House staff almost no one then thought Watergate would end in impeachment or resignation."[1]

But the big world—*le grand large,* as de Gaulle called it—was taking some distance from Nixon. And so, of course, were the country and Congress. Troubled now and on the defensive, Kissinger was trying to preserve détente. "Suicidal" was his typically morose characterization of the country's mood. "Four or five years of amassing capital in nickels and dimes is being squandered in thousand-dollar bills," he lamented to a friend.[2]

The hearings on Watergate began in May 1973, but Kissinger's immediate concern was Senator Henry Jackson, whose aversion to his works was becoming phobic. Jackson had sponsored amending the trade bill in language that denied Most Favored Nation (MFN) status to any Communist country restricting emigration. An exit tax was curtailing the outflow of Soviet Jews. Nixon and Kissinger had already agreed to extend MFN status to the Russians, who attached great symbolic importance to the step, even though it offered them little economically. Kissinger had been trying to link concessionary gestures to better Soviet cooperation on East-West matters, not least SALT. But now, here was Congress on the verge of using trade to lever changes in Soviet *domestic* policy. Jackson's amendment had seventy-two cosponsors, and Representative Charles Vanik introduced a similar version in the House.

Brezhnev was due to repay Nixon's visit by coming to Washington in June. On March 30, he sent Nixon a note saying, in effect, that the exit tax was none of Washington's business but would nonetheless be lifted. Jackson was unmoved. It wasn't enough, he told Nixon. Besides lifting the exit tax, the Soviets would have to guarantee permission for a fixed number of Soviet Jews to leave annually and would also have to ease emigration policies for other nationality groups. Jackson wasn't interested in compromise, said Kissinger.[3] He preferred having the issue.

Neither of the superpowers would be easily driven from the path toward better relations. In Moscow, two members of the Politburo were relieved of their duties allegedly for opposing Brezhnev's détente policy. East-West commercial contacts mushroomed. Political differences, large and small, were remitted to green baize tables. Negotiation was the fashion. The abuses arising from Germany's division were being moderated by a web of agreements. In Geneva, SALT II was under way. In Helsinki, the representatives of thirty-four European countries, plus America and Canada, were meeting in the Conference on Security and Cooperation in Europe, known as CSCE. Even Liechtenstein was there. So were Malta, San Marino, and the Vatican. Only Monaco and Andorra were missing from exploratory talks, whose purpose wasn't wholly clear. Moscow had pushed hard for them, hoping to gain acceptance of the status quo in Europe—mainly its division—that best suited Soviet policy. The NATO countries agreed to the Helsinki meeting provided the Soviet bloc came to Vienna for a somewhat smaller conference, one with a seemingly richer potential known as MBFR—for Mutual and Balanced Force Reductions. The idea was to reduce the forces deployed along the heavily guarded frontier in Central Europe. This "contact line," stretching 1,000 miles from the Baltic Sea to Czechoslovakia and festooned with minefields and automatic firing devices, separates West Germany from the Communist East. The rival forces on either side of the line totaled about one and one-half million men, 20,000 tanks, more than 5,000 aircraft, and 10,000 tactical nuclear warheads. It was and is the greatest array of force in peacetime history.

Actually, the Vienna talks and various other East-West projects were hostage to progress on strategic arms control—to building a second and larger SALT agreement around the modest five-year Interim Agreement. And in Geneva, SALT II was laboring. The Soviets were dragging their feet, and agencies in Washington were not within striking distance of an agreed American position. State still wanted to ban MIRV testing and deployment. Defense and the Joint Chiefs continued to be opposed, although not sure of what they wanted from SALT II. Congress had adopted a nonbinding resolution, sponsored by Jackson, which mandated the government to seek equality in weapons, although no one had spelled out just what the term meant. From parts of the Pentagon and Congress, there was some pressure to respond to Jackson by seeking an agreement based on "equal aggregates," i.e., equal numbers of nuclear delivery vehicles. Kissinger judged the various agency positions as nonnegotiable. "For the first time since I had come to government, I was bureaucratically isolated—and confronted with palpable absurdities," he wrote.[4]

Despite the Pentagon's strong aversion to limiting MIRVs, Kissinger wanted to raise the question with the Soviets, and for that he needed authority from Nixon. Philip Odeen, the senior NSC aide on defense at the time, recalls a staff meeting on the issue. Kissinger, he says, "went first to see Nixon to get his signature on a decision memorandum about going forward with a MIRV discussion. He couldn't get Nixon to focus on it. Nixon insisted instead on railing against everyone connected with Watergate. After an hour or so of this, Kissinger tried to return the conversation to the memorandum, and Nixon told him to sign it himself [meaning sign Nixon's name]. Kissinger said, 'I can't do that.' So Nixon then seized the paper and initialed it without even looking at it. This was a time when snap meetings of the NSC were called, practically at random, as part of an effort to let [Ron] Ziegler tell the world that Nixon was busily engaged with world problems in spite of it all. They'd spend an hour or so talking about some rather obscure issue which wasn't ready for decision. It was all designed to show that Nixon was on top of things. It was all too depressing."[5] Odeen resigned not long afterward.

The only guidance the beleaguered Nixon could offer his staff was that "we could never afford to be number two."[6] U. Alexis Johnson, a career diplomat who replaced Gerard Smith as head of the American delegation, was told to offer a "safe," i.e., nonnegotiable, proposal when he arrived in Geneva in March. Eventually, he was authorized to seek equal aggregates. The Soviets countered by reviving the issue of America's forward-based systems and proposing to fold them into a permanent version of the Interim Agreement. Each side rejected the other's position out of hand, and Johnson came home for new instructions. He didn't get them until Kissinger was on his way to Moscow to prepare for Brezhnev's scheduled arrival a few weeks later. Johnson was asked to hold back the new approach—a freeze on MIRVs—until Kissinger had taken it up with Brezhnev. Where the idea surfaced mattered little, since it amounted to freezing a unilateral American advantage. The Soviets, according to intelligence reports, were preparing to test new ICBMs that would carry MIRVs, and they would clearly reject any suggestion of a freeze even if they were accorded a reciprocal right to deploy more missile launchers overall than America. Brezhnev was fond of observing, correctly, that warheads, not missile launchers, kill people.

Watergate's ascending importance was borne in on Brezhnev when he arrived. The hearings, with John Dean in the witness chair, were postponed a week to avoid embarrassing Nixon.[7] The visit was of little or no lasting importance. It did produce an accord, called the Prevention of Nuclear War Agreement, the exact import of which was never clear. America's allies worried that it might be seen as a U.S. pledge not to use nuclear weapons in their defense, and Brezhnev encouraged this interpretation. The Chinese disliked it as well. In his memoirs, Kissinger said he doubted whether the agreement was worth the effort. "We gained a marginally useful text. But the result was too subtle; the negotiation too secret; the effort too protracted; the necessary explanations to allies and China too complex to have the desired impact."[8]

An agreement that breeds divergent interpretations, as this one did, only adds to the burden of leadership. Negotiators had struggled over the text of the Prevention of Nuclear War Agreement for nearly a year; it had taken that long to dull its anti-Chinese features. Brezhnev was far from satisfied with the final product; at San Clemente, he lectured Nixon about the nuclear threat from China and America's lack of sensitivity to it.[9]

The agreement was invoked only once—during the war between Israel, Egypt, and Syria that broke out in October, less than four months after it was signed. Nixon has since said that he considered using nuclear weapons when the Soviets threatened to intervene in this conflict;[10] but it is very unlikely that he did so. The accounts—written and otherwise—of insiders portray the Nixon of that hour as a man consumed by personal crisis, his sobriety in doubt, his presidency a shell beginning to crack.

On October 22, the Israelis, ignoring a cease-fire, surrounded Egypt's Third Army, thereby escalating the risk of a direct superpower confrontation. A new cease-fire was announced on the following day, but it, too, was violated. The Egyptians thereupon called on both Washington and Moscow to send troops to enforce the cease-fire. The Soviets were eager to oblige; the Americans were not. At 9:35 on the evening of October 24, Dobrynin read Kissinger, who by then was secretary of state as well as national security adviser, the text of a letter from Brezhnev: "I will say it straight that if you find it impossible to act jointly with us in this matter, we should be faced with the necessity urgently to consider the question of taking appropriate steps unilaterally."[11] The Kremlin had just stopped airlifting arms to Egypt, a decision that could have foreshadowed movement of troops to the area; Soviet airborne divisions had been put on alert, and eighty-five Soviet ships were in the Mediterranean. There were reports of one ship carrying radioactive cargo.

Kissinger judged the message from Brezhnev, which demanded "an immediate and clear reply," as "one of the most serious challenges to an American President by a Soviet leader."[12] Nixon has written that he was informed by Haig of the message and instructed him and Kissinger to convene a meeting, adding that "words were not making our point—we needed action, even the shock of a military alert."[13] In fact, Kissinger and Haig decided against waking up Nixon to tell him about the message from Brezhnev. He was, they thought, "too distraught to participate in the preliminary discussion."[14] He had been made "distraught" by the shocked and angry reaction to the famous "Saturday night massacre"—shorthand for Nixon's dismissal of Archibald Cox, the Watergate special prosecutor, a move which provoked the resignation of Attorney General Elliot Richardson and two of his associates. Kissinger describes Nixon that Wednesday evening as being "as agitated and emotional as I had ever heard him . . . He spoke of his political end, even his physical demise: 'They are doing it because of their desire to kill the President. And they may succeed. I may physically die.' "[15]

At 10:30, Kissinger convened a meeting of senior officials, notably Secretary of Defense James Schlesinger, Admiral Thomas Moorer, CIA Director William Colby, and three senior NSC staff members. An hour or so later, this group decided to place American forces on Defense Condition III, an alert status just short of full readiness for war. The order included SAC and the North American Defense Command, thus fully involving the nuclear forces.[16] An hour later, the 82nd Airborne Division prepared "for possible movement," and more aircraft carriers steamed toward the Eastern Mediterranean.[17] It was decided that Nixon's reply to Brezhnev—drafted within the meeting and not checked with Nixon—would be held up until Moscow could notice and think about the American military alert. The letter, according to Kissinger, rejected all of the Soviet demands and was "delivered to Dobrynin in Nixon's name" at 5:40 A.M. At about 8:00 A.M., Kissinger briefed Nixon on the night's events.[18]

The alert was headline news in that morning's papers and Kissinger was enraged—"shocked" he says in his memoirs. He had warned against leaks during the meeting the night before. Schlesinger recalls getting "an angry, very angry phone call from Dr. Kissinger, who said, 'It's all out. I've just heard on a radio broadcast that all of our forces have been put on alert. I thought you were going to keep this secret.' I said, 'There's no way that you can keep this secret when you put two million people around the world on alert.' "[19]*

Within the press, there was some suspicion that the larger purpose of the military alert—the first since the Cuban crisis—was to upstage Watergate. On the morning after the page one stories appeared, Nixon held a news conference and said, "It was a real crisis. It was the most difficult crisis we have had since the Cuban confrontation of 1962. But because we had had our initiative with the Soviet Union, because I had a basis of communication with Mr. Brezhnev, we not only avoided a confrontation but we moved a great step forward toward real peace in the Mideast. Now as long as I can carry out that kind of responsibility, I am going to continue to do this job."[20] But Kissinger had already told reporters on the previous afternoon that "the measures . . . we took and which the President ordered were precautionary in nature. We do not consider ourselves in a confrontation with the Soviet Union . . . We are not talking of a missile-crisis type situation . . . the Soviet Union has not yet taken any irrevocable action . . . We are not asking the Soviet Union to pull back from anything that it has done." Kissinger also indignantly rejected any link between the alert and the domestic crisis.[21] He quite clearly saw the alert as the most direct answer to Brezhnev's blustery message. Whether it affected the outcome was never clear.

In any case, the crisis was an overnight affair. Anwar Sadat, Egypt's President, abruptly withdrew his request for U.S. and Soviet troops and proposed instead an international peace-keeping force. Nixon attributed the quick end to détente: "Without détente, we might have had a major conflict in the Middle East. With détente, we avoided it."[22] Kissinger sought, as he later wrote, to "draw the Middle East into closer relations with us at the Soviets' expense . . ."[23] The United States, after years of being unable to influence most important capitals in the Middle East, abruptly became the dominant influence.

The huzzahs for détente were muted in other parts of Washington. Shortly after Brezhnev's visit, the Soviets began testing four new ICBMs. By August 1973, three of them—the SS-17s, SS-18s, and the SS-19s—had been successfully tested with MIRVs. The SS-18, in both MIRVed and single-warhead versions, would replace the SS-9 as the new superbrute.

*Kissinger and Schlesinger were well acquainted. They had been classmates at Harvard, where both graduated summa cum laude.

The SS-19s—most of them MIRVed too—would succeed the SS-11s as the mainstay of the Strategic Rocket Forces. A large part of Congress felt blind-sided by the new family of Soviet ICBMs, each of which was more powerful than its primitive antecedent; whether MIRVed or non-MIRVed, each could deliver a heavier blow, i.e., more megatonnage. A year earlier, just after the SALT I agreements, Kissinger, it may be recalled, had assured Congress that the understandings reached in Moscow would preclude new Soviet ICBMs of the "heavier" sort that had now arrived on the scene. He cited the "safeguard that no missile larger than the heaviest light missile that now exists can be substituted." But these words were contained in a unilateral American statement and offered no protection. He nonetheless indicated that the statement, combined with the restriction on increasing the size of the silos, provided "an adequate safeguard against a substantial substitution of heavy missiles for light missiles."[24] His chief tormentor, Henry Jackson, was hardly alone in judging these assurances as disingenuous.

Even more troublesome vis-à-vis Moscow was the administration's failure to obtain MFN status for Moscow. Kissinger's credibility as a negotiator was damaged. On December 11, the House passed the Trade Reform Act, incorporating the Jackson-Vanik amendment, by 319 to 80. Liberals and conservatives had joined in what Kissinger called "a rare convergence, like an eclipse of the sun" to prevent the expansion of trade relations between the superpowers.[25]

Kissinger had planned a visit to Moscow in late March 1974; he was starting to prepare another summit meeting there. Before leaving, he met twice with Jackson in an effort to settle their differences on Soviet emigration policies and the trade issues. Jackson indicated that if the Soviets issued 100,000 exit visas annually for Russian Jews he might withdraw his amendment to the trade bill then before the Senate. Kissinger remembers telling Jackson, "This is impossible, and it will lead to a confrontation, [and] he would say, 'Wouldn't it be nice to have a Secretary of State who doesn't take the Soviet point of view.' "[26]

Jackson's alter ego in these matters was a thirty-two-year-old staff assistant, Richard Perle, from whom much would be heard. Perle was is—a gifted and resourceful zealot and a hardball player of big-league quality. His pet peeves were Soviet emigration policies, arms control, and large Soviet ICBMs.*

Kissinger's own staff produced a proposal on SALT that he liked, and he gave it to Dobrynin in the back channel so that he could take it up with

*Some former officials who knew Jackson well say that he became more moderate and easier to deal with after Perle left him in 1981 to work in the Reagan administration.

Brezhnev in Moscow. The idea was to break the deadlock in SALT by proposing a ceiling on the so-called throw-weight of MIRVed ICBMs. "Throw-weight" is jargon for the usable weight of a missile system—the weight of its warheads and the mechanisms that target and release them. Throw-weight roughly determines the number of warheads of a given yield that a MIRVed missile system can carry. The Pentagon was very jumpy about the throw-weight of the new Soviet missiles, which greatly exceeded that of Minuteman and Poseidon. If the sides could agree on equal throw-weight for their MIRVed vehicles, the Americans would be left with many more of these than the Soviets. (This numerical advantage would somewhat offset the advantage to the Soviets of having ICBMs that could carry more warheads than their American counterparts.) In Moscow, the Soviets seemed fairly responsive, and for a moment the silhouette of a deal loomed. The Soviets, in return for conceding more MIRVed missile systems to the Americans, would be allowed a somewhat larger number of long-range nuclear delivery vehicles of all kinds. Brezhnev suggested 1,100 MIRVed vehicles for America, 1,000 for the Soviet Union. His offer wasn't acceptable; the Soviet number was too high, the disparity too little. Still, it was a start. Experience told Kissinger that having established the principle of disparity, he could improve on the numbers in later negotiation.[27] This time he was mistaken.

Back in Washington, he pushed for agreement to hold the Soviets to 850 MIRVed vehicles. Since at least 200 of these were likely to be submarine-launched weapons, the ceiling would leave the Soviets with 600 or so MIRVed ICBMs. Kissinger writes, "I now heard the astonishing proposition that this figure—which reduced the Soviet potential by several thousand warheads—was insignificant because even 600 ICBMs could threaten our Minuteman force . . . By now our domestic debate had turned liturgical. Slogans had become the weapons in a philosophical dispute over the nature of East-West relations."[28] On April 27, a day when he was to leave for Geneva and further talks with Andrei Gromyko, Kissinger chaired a major meeting on SALT of which he wrote: "In exasperation I said, 'What's all this I read about the throw-weight problem . . . If we want a bigger missile, why aren't we building one? Who's stopping us? I've certainly never heard of a proposal for a new ICBM since I've been here.' "[29] What he called "the galloping weakness of the President" invited attack on White House policy, although some critics within the administration, notably Schlesinger and Paul Nitze, were hostile strictly on the merits. It was the marriage of heavier Soviet missiles to MIRV technology that had created the predictable threat to Minuteman. Those like Senator Edward

Brooke, who had struggled unavailingly to hobble MIRV, had been rapidly vindicated. And Kissinger now was trying, just as unavailingly, to maneuver the horse back into the barn. Or switching the farmyard metaphor, a chicken of truly heroic size had come home to roost.

A fine irony underlay Kissinger's difficulties. America, too, had once built and deployed very large missiles similar to some of the Soviet missiles, but then Washington turned away from these and concentrated on smaller, more accurate systems with far better yield-to-weight ratios. Most people, as Kissinger so pointedly observed, thought it was the right choice. The Soviets had built heavy missiles, mainly because they couldn't build smaller ones; they lacked the technology for small on-board computers and miniaturized warheads. The greater throw-weight of their missiles tended to offset technological deficiencies, although not entirely. The better accuracy and presumed reliability of American systems was probably more important. From time to time, the Chairman of the Joint Chiefs was asked by a congressional committee whether he would rather fight a nuclear war with American or Soviet weapons. Invariably, the answer was—and remains—American weapons. In the spring of 1974, however, Jackson and his partisans were far more impressed with Soviet potential than reassured by America's advantages, which they judged at best as fleeting.

Kissinger took little encouragement from his meeting with Gromyko in Geneva. The Soviets wouldn't consider the proposal to limit them to 850 MIRVed missile systems. On the emigration issue, Kissinger suggested that 45,000 Russian Jews be allowed to leave annually. Gromyko was noncommittal but several days later agreed to that figure.

On June 3, only three weeks before the President's departure for Moscow, Schlesinger distanced himself from the Nixon-Kissinger SALT position in a letter to Jackson. Schlesinger and Nitze were both arguing against any agreement that allowed the Soviets more than two to three hundred MIRVed ICBMs.

On June 14, Nitze resigned from the SALT II delegation, citing the "depressing reality of the traumatic events now unfolding . . ."[30] Nitze says, "I felt that Nixon was too preoccupied with surviving and that in his effort to get an arms control agreement he might collapse under Soviet pressure."[31] "It was an amazing attack so short a time before Nixon's trip to Moscow," wrote Kissinger. "But it made dramatically clear that Nixon had no domestic base for any significant agreement in Moscow regardless of its content."[32]

At an NSC meeting five days before Nixon was to leave, Schlesinger proposed granting the U.S. nearly twice as many MIRVed ICBMs as the

Soviet Union. (The numbers were 660 for the U.S. and 360 for the Soviets.)
He also wanted equal aggregates, despite the built-in advantage to the
American side of his proposal, and he wanted to avoid any limit on multiwarhead SLBMs, where America was far ahead. Brezhnev had once turned
down a roughly similar proposal, as Kissinger pointed out, but Schlesinger
expressed confidence that Nixon would succeed where Kissinger had
failed: "You can be very persuasive—you have great forensic skills," he told
Nixon.[33] Kissinger complained, not unreasonably, that some of his opponents insisted on using SALT to solve all strategic problems. "The absence
of a SALT agreement," he wrote, "would not keep MIRVed Soviet missiles to below 300, nor would it ease the potential vulnerability of our
land-based force; in fact, by all projections it would lead to larger Soviet
MIRVed forces . . ."[34]

On June 24, the day before Nixon left, Jackson announced that he
would put forward new conditions regarding trade and emigration. He
didn't say what these would be, but the effect was to remove the topic from
the summit agenda, which was thinning out.[35]

The pivotal discussions were held at Brezhnev's Crimean residence on
the Black Sea. The White House called the place by its name—Oreanda—
but the nearest town was Yalta, site of the World War II conference that
many conservatives love to hate; thus, all news stories bore what from
Nixon's point of view was the worst of datelines. Dobrynin had told
Kissinger that widening the gap in allowable numbers of MIRVed vehicles
was possible. But it wasn't. The Soviets continued to see in the American
approach to MIRV a gambit aimed at freezing their inferiority.

At one point, Nixon met alone with Brezhnev and a Soviet interpreter
for three hours while their advisers awaited them nervously at poolside. He
said little to anyone about the discussion, except that China came up.
SALT, it seems, didn't. Kissinger says flatly that what Brezhnev proposed
to Nixon was an "unconditional treaty of non-aggression between the
United States and the Soviet Union." Any such agreement would have
appeared to be a green light for a Soviet attack on China.[36] According to
Hyland, who was there, "If Nixon took Brezhnev's bait on China there
would be a payoff in the SALT negotiations and Nixon's third summit
would be a success—a success that might just save the wounded president
from his impending impeachment."[37] Although seemingly tempted, Nixon
didn't take the bait.

The deal that Brezhnev had offered Kissinger in March was still available, but his numbers were even less acceptable in late June. The Pentagon
would not have supported any arrangement along those lines. Moreover,

Nixon, if he was to avoid impeachment by the Senate, would have to find thirty-four votes, most of them on the distinctly conservative side. Détente, it seemed, was being ground between the upper and nether millstones— between the increasing opposition to it in Washington and Moscow's reluctance to make a deal with Nixon that he could take home. Actually, the MIRV numbers on the table in Nixon's third and valedictory summit were better than those later agreed to by Gerald Ford, which became the basis of the SALT II Treaty—a more than respectable deal as judged by most sides.

By all accounts, Nixon cut a pathetic figure. He was in severe pain from an attack of phlebitis, and uncharacteristically out of touch with his briefing paper on SALT. He was clearly preoccupied with Watergate and said to have spent much of the time listening to White House tapes.[38] Kissinger and Haig fought constantly for control of their shattered chief.

Just before leaving Moscow at the end of the visit, Kissinger gave a news conference. He, too, showed the strain of the dreary encounter. Repeated questions about whether the Pentagon had blocked another SALT agreement led to an outburst: "What, in the name of God, is strategic superiority? What is the significance of it, politically, militarily, operationally, at these levels of numbers? What do you do with it?"[39] Kissinger had glimpsed the outline of a deal on SALT, but his principal was too enfeebled politically to pursue it. Anger and frustration provoked his *cri de coeur*, which he always regretted, not least because he made it in Moscow.

The prospects for SALT were not as dim as they seemed. Kissinger and Gromyko had avoided abject failure by agreeing to give themselves the option of trying to reach agreement eventually either on equal aggregates or on "offsetting asymmetries"—Potomac jargon for the notion of the U.S. having more MIRVed vehicles, the Soviets a slightly higher total force. And fortuitously, Nixon and Brezhnev decided to follow up this meeting with another one later in the year.

A few weeks later Nixon was gone. On August 9, Gerald R. Ford, just eight months after becoming Vice President, was sworn in as President.

Even before the swearing-in, Ford had asked Kissinger to stay on as both secretary of state and national security adviser. "Henry," he told him, "I need you. The country needs you . . . I'll do everything I can to work with you."[40] He describes meeting with Kissinger later on the inaugural day to discuss the state of the world: "The one bright spot I remember in our session that day was the possible chance to reach agreement with the Soviets during the strategic arms limitation talks . . ."[41]

Less than a week later, Ford had his first meeting with Dobrynin. The trade bill was still pending, and Dobrynin said his government could orally guarantee allowing 55,000 Jews to leave annually but would not put any such commitment in writing. Jackson was unmoved. "He was about to launch his Presidential campaign, and he was playing politics to the hilt," wrote Ford.[42] The Soviets were also smarting from an amendment to the Export-Import Bank bill that cut back their access to credits.

Before he could move on East-West issues, Ford had to resolve an especially awkward dilemma: whether to pardon Nixon or allow the judicial process to take its course. He decided that the country, depleted by Watergate, should be spared the sight of its former President being tried and perhaps punished for his misdeeds. Pardoning Nixon set off predictable charges that Ford and Nixon had secretly reached an agreement prior to the transfer of power. A small dark cloud hovered over Ford, and, rightly or wrongly, he felt that it never went away.

Although considered a novice in matters of national security, Ford actually knew a fair amount about them, having sat since 1953 on the House Defense Appropriations subcommittee; he had also been a member of the special subcommittee created to control funding for the CIA. As Vice President, he had been given weekly briefings by Kissinger and/or former Air Force General Brent Scowcroft, his deputy. He was keen to meet Brezhnev and get on with SALT. As usual, Kissinger would go to Moscow earlier to see what might be worked out. But first he wanted to launch a national debate on détente. He could hardly have chosen a worse time to try to arouse a society that had just seen a President forced from office and succeeded by a man who hadn't been elected to any national office. What clouded Kissinger's judgment may have been the lack of movement on SALT. Or it may have been Jackson and the mortification of having to tie American security goals to Soviet domestic policy. It may have been both of these, along with the decline in his stock that had begun a few months before.

The great debate was kicked off with a statement Kissinger delivered to the Senate Committee on Foreign Relations on September 19. He judged it his most important to that point. The statement stressed the benefits of arms control, trade, and normal relations with the Soviet Union, and warned against linking détente with "increasing pressure on the Soviets . . . [which] would be disastrous . . . We would not accept it from Moscow; Moscow will not accept it from us . . . We can not demand that the Soviet Union, in effect, suddenly reverse five decades of Soviet and centuries of

Russian history."[43] This statement drew little attention, although it was later used to support the contention that Kissinger had oversold détente.

The next day, Ford, armed with a Soviet assurance relayed by Dobrynin, to grant as many as fifty-five to sixty thousand Jewish exit visas, met with Jackson. A deal along those lines in which the Soviets would obtain an eighteen-month waiver on the Jackson-Vanik amendment was built into letters exchanged between the White House and Jackson; but one month later, just before Kissinger's arrival in Moscow, Jackson torpedoed the deal by telling reporters about the sixty thousand figure and calling it a "benchmark" which he said he thought would be increased.[44] There was no understanding of the sort, and the Soviets, who had been granting steadily more exit visas to Russian Jews, felt humiliated. Brezhnev had already deplored "demands . . . totally unconnected with the area of trade and economics and lying completely within the domestic competence of states . . ."[45]

The Soviets were appalled by the letters being made public and Kissinger's failure to discuss the content of Jackson's communication with them. Gromyko presented a formal letter of protest, which Kissinger, back in Washington, discussed with no one other than his staff until the Soviets, in an unusual show of temper, released it to the American press. Dobrynin warned that his government would reject the conditions placed on MFN in the trade bill if it became law and that the existing trade agreement between the two countries would be voided.[46] All that and more came to pass when Ford signed the trade bill a little later. Jewish emigration fell sharply (from an annual rate of 35,000 in 1973 to 13,000 in 1975). Brezhnev had been publicly embarrassed and, some thought, politically damaged. The chief casualty, of course, was détente. "From then on relations deteriorated rapidly," says Kissinger. "It was a sad period."[47]

It was bad, but not yet quite as bad as it seemed. Kissinger actually did rather well with SALT in Moscow, even though he found Brezhnev grumpy and mainly concerned with trade, the Middle East, and, as always, China.[48] As usual, Brezhnev had seen a proposal from Kissinger via Dobrynin. It was targeted at equal ceilings and limiting the Soviet heavy missile launchers to 250—none MIRVed. And it proposed a subceiling of 1,320 on MIRVed vehicles, a number amounting to 60 percent of the proposed overall ceiling—2,200. Brezhnev said he could accept either of two equal numbers—one for MIRVed vehicles, the other for the overall aggregate— or slightly disparate numbers. The latter approach meant that America would have the higher MIRV total, the Soviets the higher aggregate. Kissinger and his staff were encouraged. Brezhnev's numbers were close to theirs. He adamantly refused to cut his heavy missile force from 308 but did agree, as he eventually had in SALT I, to forgo compensation for American forward-based nuclear weapons and the British and French nuclear forces.[49]

Ford was encouraged by Kissinger's report—enough so that he decided on a meeting with Brezhnev in November, after he had completed a scheduled trip to Japan and South Korea. The Joint Chiefs blessed the package that Kissinger and Ford seemed on the verge of nailing down. But for Ford the bad news was that congressional elections at the time cost the Republicans four seats in the Senate, forty in the House.

On November 23, Ford flew from Tokyo to the Siberian coastal city of Vladivostok for what should have been his rendezvous with history. He could look ahead to 1976; he'd be seeking a mandate of his own then and be able to point to a broader and longer-lasting SALT agreement than the one Nixon had signed in '72, just a few months before his reelection. A Ford agreement, if achievable, would supersede Nixon's and erase its politically troublesome disparity in numbers of missile systems.* Although the visit to Vladivostok was to be partly a get-acquainted meeting, Kissinger's talks with Brezhnev a few weeks earlier had set the stage for just such a breakthrough.

It actually came on the first day, the 23rd. They were meeting in a health spa which Ford described as looking "like an abandoned YMCA camp in the Catskills." Brezhnev's mood, he said, was "ebullient." There was the customary badinage. "Kissinger is such a scoundrel," said Brezhnev to Ford. "It takes one to know one," replied Kissinger.[50] Ford and Brezhnev got on well from the start and seemed to enjoy each other (a good deal more so than was the case with Nixon and Brezhnev). Brezhnev asked Ford to halt production of the Trident submarine and cancel the B-1 bomber program. On the broader issues, he was more realistic and flexible. At one point, he grew impatient with advisers who persisted in sending him notes— cautionary ones, it seemed—so he expelled most of them from the room, at which point Ford dismissed most of his own entourage. Less conditionally than in Moscow, Brezhnev then offered Ford the choice between equal ceilings and offsetting asymmetries. And he restated his willingness to defer the issue of forward-based American systems. He continued to be unwilling to reduce his forces of heavy missiles beneath the existing number—308. The framework of what struck the Americans as a good deal was falling into place. Before agreeing, however, Brezhnev had to make a phone call and Ford a decision. Brezhnev's call was probably to Marshal Andrei Grechko in Moscow. The connection was poor, and Brezhnev had to shout. Helmut Sonnenfeldt, a member of Kissinger's staff who spoke Russian,

*SALT I had given the Soviets an advantage of six hundred or so launchers, although U.S. advantages in numbers of bombers and MIRVed missile systems continued to be offsetting.

chanced to overhear much of what Brezhnev was saying, which he recalls as being an argument for why the unfolding agreement was a good one for the U.S.S.R. Sonnenfeldt also remembers some conversation about the FBS issue, which may have been difficult for Brezhnev to let drop yet again.[51]

Rarely is either side given a choice of options, let alone attractive options. Although Ford had been granted such a choice, it was far from simple. In Geneva, his SALT delegation had pushed unsuccessfully for equal aggregates. Yet the "unequal" deal—the one that gave the Soviets the larger total, the Americans more MIRVed systems—was actually the more attractive of the two. The Jacksonian bloc, which had made an issue of disparate numbers, *might* respond more favorably to equality. But the unequal deal would have left the Soviets with fewer MIRVed missile launchers; fewer of these would have translated into less overall throw-weight and several fewer Soviet warheads. The equal ceiling was militarily meaningless, it was certain to be higher than the entire U.S. inventory; Washington wouldn't even build up to the ceiling, because no one, including the Joint Chiefs, could see any point in doing so.

At 1:00 A.M., Ford, Kissinger, and a handful of advisers, including Sonnenfeldt, Hyland, Jan Lodal (another NSC staff figure), and Scowcroft, broke away from the meeting and huddled in the cold outside so as not to be overheard. One by one, Ford polled them for their views on which option he should choose. The answers, by and large, were hedged, but it didn't really matter; everyone recognized that the decision was political and that only Ford could make it. With no hesitation he returned to the meeting inside and accepted Brezhnev's offer of equal ceilings. Each side's overall entitlement would be 2,400 long-range nuclear systems, of which no more than 1,320 could be MIRVed. An agreement built around these levels would last ten years.

Vladivostok became a major reference point for the nuclear age. Ford described himself as "euphoric" afterward, as "certain we would sign a SALT II accord" after "technicians had ironed out the few remaining problems." His strength was his knowledge of Congress, which "with a few exceptions," he predicted, "would probably endorse the new accord."[52] Hyland wrote: "He was under some pressure to prove himself a tough negotiator, one who would see through the traps and snares of détente. The main requirement was that he emerge with an arms control agreement that was 'equal,' interpreted to mean equality in every category of weapons. This rather simple-minded view of what was at stake badly limited Ford's maneuvering room. In the end he succeeded in reaching an agreement that was, in fact, equal in all respects. But in doing so a greater opportunity was missed, the chance to bargain for limits on those Soviet weapons that concerned us most, even if the trading resulted in an outcome that was not strictly equal."[53]

Choosing the wrong option didn't help Ford with the hard hats; they were unimpressed with the argument that the Vladivostok understanding had capped the nuclear arms race. Jackson said it was like "capping a mountain." Ford's choice at Vladivostok really didn't matter. What did matter was how he handled the political fallout from the encounter, along with related events, in a presidential election year. Here again, he had to choose between pushing a SALT II agreement to completion or turning away from Vladivostok and his most presidential moment. The decision he made may have cost him the presidency.

Ford and Brezhnev parted on warm terms and of one mind about SALT II: Each wanted and expected the shell of their understanding to be filled in with a formal agreement that could be signed at their next meeting. In Geneva, the tempo picked up instantly. "We stopped marking time after Vladivostok," recalls Jack Mendelsohn, who was then special assistant to Alexis Johnson on the American SALT II delegation. "Before that, we had been trying to badger them into freezing our advantages and accepting a permanent state of inferiority."[54]

Besides enlivening poky bureaucracies, a strong gesture, or commitment, from leaders does normally lead to full agreement. But the post-Vladivostok period was abnormal. The debate Kissinger had tried to launch in September was now under way, but not on the reasonable terms that he had sought. Détente's adversaries imparted a shrill and angry tone to the discussion, which then became polarized. Détente and SALT were grossly misrepresented. In turn, détente's defenders oversold it, thereby inviting an even more hostile polemic.

The controversy sharpened the appetites of two groups: ambitious officials and bureaucrats, reporters and editors. Both lots, as already noted, were finding stories about SALT and détente increasingly newsworthy as conflicts lying within them were exposed. The stronger claim of such stories to page one treatment, or prominent coverage by television news, gave government officials on the one hand and reporters and editors on the other an increasingly large stake in them.

Television's dominant role was reinforcing trends already under way, including a preference for conflict-based stories on foreign policy issues. (A focus on controversy was—is—especially helpful to reporters in covering nuclear arms control, which is complex, though less so than made to seem.) News editors and readers alike are easily drawn to public statements alleging a decline in America's military capabilities and warning of the related pitfalls of arms control treaties. Stories that show clashes over these matters between prominent political figures are equally tempting. Space limitations often challenge the ability of print journalists to deal adequately with the nuclear issue, but television news has a tougher problem. Ninety seconds is rarely enough time in which to do justice to the body of a story; inevitably, network news is swept up by controversial aspects, thereby enlarging them. Furthermore, television's trend away from hard news to softer, more personalized stories has strengthened the networks' preference for the confrontational story.

The process is circular. Because the best path to page one and a spot on television news may be paved with controversy, those who seek the exposure may want to promote controversy. And here the symbiosis tightens. Instead of being detached observers, media people become figures in their own right, because, as a practical matter, the enlargement of their role and status contributes to shaping, if not inviting, many of the stories they cover. The tendency was always there, notably in the interplay between prominent newspaper writers and their sources; but the heavy diet of conflict and the dominant role of television news built the tendency into a fact of daily life. For senior officials, the major near-term events to ponder are what will be reported on that day's evening news or in tomorrow's *New York Times* and Washington *Post*. The long term extends as far as the deadlines for *Time* and *Newsweek* (normally late on Saturday mornings). Among the harmful effects of all this can be the trivialization of an important story. It can be any story, but too often a story on a major nuclear issue—usually arms control–related—is trivialized by controversy, much of it contrived.

The heavy accent on controversy was confusing, as was the shrillness of the attack on détente and SALT. Americans became uncertain about what or how to think about arms control agreements with the Soviet Union. The people who seemed to know most about these disagreed sharply. For a long time, Americans had known only nuclear superiority; adjusting to a situation called parity was confusing, if not worrisome. Even the vocabulary was confusing. Most people still didn't know what the acronym MIRV stood for, let alone what a MIRV was. Détente is a French word and one with two very different meanings.* The critics charged that agreements reached thus far were all but worthless because the limits they

*The trigger of a gun is one, relaxation of tension the other.

set were so high as to mock the term "arms control." Advocates saw that argument as missing the point. The test of an agreement, they said, is not its scope; no single agreement could do more than settle a few of the issues. It can bound the overall problem, they said, not dispose of it and is really a step that makes possible the next step in a sequential process.

The critics argued that Moscow was using SALT to lull America into accepting a baneful change in the balance of power. And, the argument continued, if the Russians are for arms control there must be something wrong with it. The orthodox view was—is—that the Russian desire to negotiate is not a reason to oppose it; the criterion is, or should be, whether negotiation and agreement are in the national interest. Kissinger made the case for restraint often and well, on one occasion in an address to the American Legion: "Today, we, as well as the Soviet Union, must start from the premise that in the nuclear era an increase in certain categories of military power does not necessarily represent an increase of usable political strength . . . The overwhelming destructiveness of nuclear weapons makes it difficult to relate their use to specific political objectives and may indeed generate new political problems."[55]

Serious trouble began just after the Vladivostok meeting—provoked by two weapons systems that most people hadn't heard about. One was a new American cruise missile, called Tomahawk. The other was a new Soviet bomber, the TU-22M, designated Backfire by NATO and soon to become the world's best-known bomber.

Cruise missiles are like ballistic missiles in that both are unmanned and expendable. The resemblance ends there, however. Unlike ballistic missiles, cruise missiles have wings, are propelled by jet engines, and never leave the earth's atmosphere. They are subsonic, traveling at nearly five hundred miles an hour, or about as fast as airliners; this is only a fraction of the speed attained by ballistic missiles, which can reach targets thousands of miles away in less than half an hour. Compared with ballistic missiles, cruise missiles are small and cheap. The Tomahawk is a descendant of Hitler's V-1s—the unmanned terror weapons known as "buzz bombs," which struck at random against British cities in the latter part of the Second World War. After the war, both the Americans and the Russians developed variants of these primitive German cruise missiles. Each side advanced the state of the art, but not by much. The average "miss distance" of one of the early American cruise missiles, the Snark, was over a thousand miles. In the late 1950s and early '60s, America abandoned cruise missiles, seemingly for good, having found that ballistic missiles, besides being much faster, were far more accurate, far more reliable, and less complicated. The Russians reached the same conclusion, but since they tend to keep obsolete weapons in their inventory a good deal longer than the United States does, they hung on to the old cruise missiles, most of which were deployed at sea—mainly on attack submarines—as antiship weapons.

Although cruise missiles were abandoned by American weapons planners, they weren't forgotten. In the late 1960s, some technicians felt that progress in guidance and engine technology would eventually rehabilitate the weapon, even give it a major role. In the early 1970s, after showing revival signs and then floundering, the cruise missile acquired a formidable patron in Henry Kissinger, who urged the Defense Department to give it priority attention and support. At the time, Kissinger had no strongly held views on cruise missiles as weapons; he was neither for nor against them on the merits. But he did feel a need for some additional bargaining capital for the second round of SALT, which was just beginning. Although held in low esteem by the services, cruise missiles fitted nicely into what seemed at first a purely political strategy. America had, according to numerous officials and bureaucrats, a lead of ten or more years in cruise missile technology. A new guidance system known as "Tercom"—short for "terrain contour matching"—was supposed to lie well beyond Soviet technological capabilities. The necessarily small but powerful engine for a new generation of cruise missiles was said to be another all but insuperable obstacle to the Russians in the foreseeable future. "Keeping the Soviets awestruck by American technology" was how Schlesinger characterized the rationale for the new cruise missiles.[56] The "awestruck" Russians would acquire an incentive to negotiate acceptable limits on their MIRVed ballistic missile systems. Or so it seemed.

As a weapons program acquires standing, it creates constituencies within the government. And if the military case for the program has weaknesses, the various departments and offices with a vested interest in its future will build a better case. In the mid-1970s, a newly formed cruise missile lobby built a strong case for the new weapons. The argument rested on the proposition that whatever weapons the Soviets might develop in the decade ahead, the new American cruise missiles would allow the United States to keep pace and, at a minimum, maintain a healthy balance in strategic forces. But the expansive claims being made for the cruise missile clashed with the narrower, essentially tactical view of it as an asset to be sold off in SALT.

The struggle between these contesting viewpoints was joined just after the meeting at Vladivostok, which produced a serious misunderstanding about cruise missiles. According to the agreement, all air-to-surface missiles with a range greater than six hundred kilometers would fall within the ceiling on strategic weapons that the two leaders had approved. The American side, it seems, had intended that this restriction would apply only to ballistic missiles—and not to cruise missiles—launched from aerial platforms; however, the Americans failed to exempt cruise missiles during the meeting. A few days later, the administration gave the Russians an aide-mémoire that confirmed the main points agreed to at Vladivostok and the intention of signing a completed agreement in 1975. It, too, did not distinguish between ballistic and cruise missiles that might be dispatched from air to ground. (The relevant phrase was "air-to-surface missiles with a range not exceeding six hundred kilometers.") The Russians, however, took the position that the provision for a range of up to six hundred kilometers applied to both missiles types, and they proposed an outright ban on all sea- and ground-launched cruise missiles with ranges in excess of six hundred kilometers.

By this time, the Defense Department was contemplating the deployment of a great many—perhaps thousands—of long-range cruise missiles launched from airplanes; accepting the Soviet interpretation of the Vladivostok accord would have dimmed or eliminated that prospect. Nor was the reborn cruise missile lobby in Washington willing to accept a ban on long-range sea- and ground-launched versions of the system. Literally no one in government at that stage had even a remote interest in the ground-launched version, but to genuine partisans of cruise missiles, the sea-launched version, not the air-launched, was the future miracle weapon—small, versatile, cheap, and eminently concealable.

Washington's flirtation with a new generation of cruise missiles turned out to be troubling to the Soviet leaders. Their effort to ban two versions of the weapon and sharply restrict the third version became the priority goal of their negotiators. Quite possibly, the Russians were "awestruck" by the technology underlying the American programs. Unless these were neutralized in a SALT agreement, the Russians would feel strongly pressed to "mirror-image" the Americans; indeed, given the claims being made for cruise missiles by their American counterparts, Soviet military officials and bureaucrats were sure to insist on having similar programs. At this time, the Russians were occupied with several land-based missile programs, at least one new SLBM, and a missile-carrying submarine. Adding cruise missiles to the list would have meant placing yet another burden on a stagnant, overburdened economy. Soviet leaders apparently hoped that the disrepute into which the cruise missile had fallen would be permanent, partly because the weapon is just an unmanned airplane with stubby wings and any country capable of building an airplane could probably build a cruise missile, however crude. Such a weapon, the Russians know, wouldn't be accurate enough to threaten most military targets, but it might be good enough to hit one of their cities. Their aversion to cruise missiles became steadily more pronounced.

In Washington, partisans of arms control were equally opposed. New cruise missiles on either side seemed certain to create major uncertainties of a kind that the arms control process is supposed to discourage. Those deployed on ships and submarines would be very difficult to monitor—probably impossible. Because they are small and easy to conceal, there is no reliable way to count them. Because they are interchangeable—they can, for example, be fired from torpedo tubes and other dispensing mechanisms—there is no way to determine the actual armament of a given ship or submarine. Like other naval weapons, including torpedoes and depth charges, Tomahawk cruise missiles were supposed to be deployed on a wide variety of oceangoing platforms—submarines, cruisers, destroyers, and battleships that have been recommissioned mainly to carry the new weapons, thousands of them. And while there would be both nuclear and conventionally armed Tomahawks, it was always clear that distinguishing between the two wasn't possible. Also, unlike ballistic missiles, cruise missiles can be produced quickly and cheaply and can be stockpiled easily in large but inestimable numbers.

In Washington, Kissinger was discovering that efforts to reach a SALT II agreement in 1975 might come to grief on the issue of cruise missiles. "Henry sold cruise missiles to the Pentagon and then he couldn't buy them back" became the shorthand account of the state of play. His position was roughly this: He had no interest in seeing either sea- or ground-launched cruise missiles actually deployed, but he did want to keep open the possibility of deploying the air-launched version if it should be judged better suited to reaching targets in the Soviet Union than a manned bomber. And he was unwilling to give up any of the new cruise missiles without a matching concession from the Soviet Union. He was prepared to trade away the sea- and ground-launched cruise missiles, but he did intend to avoid restrictions on the air-launched version other than a range limit of about 2,500 kilometers. The services had very little interest in the ship- and ground-launched versions, but the cruise missile lobby—a covey of civilian bureaucrats—took the other view.

An even larger and more persistent dispute swirled around the Backfire bomber, although the issue itself wasn't very complicated: Was this new Soviet aircraft an intercontinental weapon and thus accountable in SALT? Or was it, as the Soviets (and most American experts) contended, a so-called medium bomber? At Vladivostok, Brezhnev categorically rejected the argument being put by some within the Pentagon that Backfire could reach American territory on one-way missions without refueling and should therefore be counted in SALT. Then, and over the next five years, the Soviets insisted that their airplane was not intended to be and never would be deployed as a strategic weapon—that whatever American experts thought about its capabilities, Soviet experts knew better, since it was their airplane. Actually, most American experts doubted that Backfire threatened the United States; on any extended long-range mission, it would have to fly at high altitudes and subsonic speeds—like an airliner and about as vulnerable as one. Backfire, it seemed, would be deployed for use against Western Europe, China, and naval ships. It would replace older Soviet medium bombers used for these purposes. Also, insisting on Backfire being covered by SALT would inevitably have pushed the Soviets to insist that the several hundred American longer-range nuclear weapons deployed in and around Europe be similarly dealt with.

Making an issue of Backfire, as Ford and Kissinger seemed to recognize, was pointless. At Vladivostok, they went along with Brezhnev, only to confront a squall back in Washington where a smallish group had convinced themselves that Backfire was a distinct threat. They were joined by a larger group of SALT baiters who saw through the issue but found it useful.

Ford's brief presidency was buffeted by difficulties he didn't create and by widening anxieties he could do little to affect. There was the strong inflationary pressure released by the war in Vietnam. The war and the manipulation of the energy market by the oil cartel deepened the country's perception of government no longer able to influence events in faraway places that bore on America's safety and well-being.

In Geneva, the shell of the Vladivostok understanding was being filled in, but fortune was looking askance at SALT and its patrons. In April 1975, Saigon fell to the North Vietnamese. The war had ended—badly.

On July 8, Ford announced that he would be a candidate for President the next year. A few days earlier, he had chosen not to see Aleksander Solzhenitsyn, who had been recently exiled from the U.S.S.R. and had sought a meeting with Ford through Jesse Helms, North Carolina's ultra-right-wing senator. According to Ford, both Kissinger and Brent Scowcroft advised against the meeting. In just a few weeks, Ford would be seeing Brezhnev in Helsinki. A meeting with Solzhenitsyn, it was felt, would go down badly in Moscow and might affect the talks.[57] Sonnenfeldt says there was another reason: "We thought we were within a day of getting both the Sakharovs out of the Soviet Union. We failed and lost on all counts. Avoiding Solzhenitsyn was very damaging."[58] George Will, the conservative columnist, described Ford's aides as "showing a flair for baseness that would have stood them in good stead with the previous Administration."[59]

On July 30, Ford had the first of two meetings with Brezhnev and Gromyko. It went badly. Brezhnev's declining health was becoming a factor, and the declining fortunes of détente heated the issues—the real and the unreal ones. Backfire, an unreal one, was flourishing in the Washington climate, and Ford had to deal with it; an argument over the airplane's range and capability became a shouting match, according to Sonnenfeldt, who says that each leader accused the other's staff of lying about Backfire.[60] Hyland described how bureaucrats on either side had involved Ford and Brezhnev in the arcana of flight profiles and other aspects of the issue which they could not be expected to master, and didn't. Ford, it turned out, had somehow acquired the impression of a threat involving hundreds of the new airplanes when actually only forty or so Backfires were then in service. Ford was "exasperated," said Hyland, to find "that nine months of haggling had been spent on fewer than fifty bombers."[61]

Their second meeting led nowhere, but it did clear the air; the parties left Helsinki with a better and more solemn appreciation of how far apart they were, how fragile a process détente was proving to be. Still, before they parted, Brezhnev took Ford aside and said he hoped he would run for the presidency and win. Hyland compared the two sides to "drowning men reaching out for each other's hand, lest they sink separately."[62]

At home, Ford was being pushed to the right by the dominant wing of his party; he went with the current, which meant that on SALT he would need further concessions. But Brezhnev had none to give. "Brezhnev had gotten little for détente," Hyland concluded; "the economic incentive had been taken away by a capricious Congress. At Vladivostok he had settled for the status quo, and the United States had then raised the ante. We were in for tough times . . ."[63]

Just after his return, on August 19, Ford warned Moscow against fishing troubled waters in Portugal. The Soviets were being careful not to interfere there and are believed to have told the Prime Minister, Vasco dos Santos Gonçalves, that they "had no interest in creating a confrontation with the United States over Portugal."[64] Moscow, in effect, turned its back on the last "Stalinist," i.e., hard-line, Communist party left in Western Europe.

Africa was different. There the Soviet Union and its more visceral antagonist, China, were in head-on competition. The Soviets correctly judged sub-Saharan Africa as outside the sphere of America's vital interests; they reckoned that Washington wouldn't seriously object to Soviet penetration of Portugal's former dependency—Angola—where, as in some other places, Moscow was intent on outmaneuvering the Chinese. At first, the Soviet calculation was borne out. Washington seemed to see the expanding Soviet involvement in this vulnerable but distant territory as within admissible bounds of competitive coexistence. Indeed, not until late October, several months after the big-power maneuvering in Angola was under way, did Kissinger take up the matter with Dobrynin.[65] As late as November, he was saying, "The United States has no national interest in Angola."[66] Nor did Washington seem to object to the MPLA (Popular Movement for the Liberation of Angola), although it drew support from Cuba, as well as Moscow.

By November's end, an abrupt rise in the number of Cuban troops in Angola forced the administration to object publicly and privately. "We have made clear that continuation of actions like those in Angola must threaten the entire web of Soviet-US relations," warned Kissinger. However, the words were hedged by an interesting comment on linkage: "As for the Strategic Arms Limitation Talks, we have never considered these to be a favor which we grant to the Soviet Union to be turned on and off according to the ebb and flow of our relations. The fact is that limiting the growth of nuclear arsenals is an overriding global problem that must be dealt with urgently for its own sake . . ."[67]

But the discordant effect of the so-called Angolan crisis was tilting the balance. Kissinger's voice had lost much of its resonance. The larger-than-life aspect had deserted him. Others were using the press at least as effectively, and much of what they contrived was aimed squarely at him. Opposition to his policies was becoming more cohesive and even organized. Critics on the far right joined others, like Jackson, who took a moderate line on most subjects but not on defense and détente, where their line was without nuance and rock hard. Elements within this bloc adopted tactics which, although hardly unknown to Washington, appalled those parts of the government in which foreign policy is usually developed. Creative distortions and outright lies about other people's views, not to mention government policy, were planted in outlets ranging from *Aviation Week*, a trade journal, to syndicated newspaper columns, including some of the most prominent.

A small but especially troublesome group—known to many as "the cabal"—consisted mainly of Richard Perle and one of his closest friends, a brash young man named John Lehman, who had strong right-wing political connections and for a time had served as an aide to Kissinger on congressional matters. In 1975, Lehman was deputy director of the arms control agency, a job for which he had needed Kissinger's intervention in order to overcome objections to him on the Senate Foreign Relations Committee. (Lehman became secretary of the navy in the Reagan era.) He was the Perle group's chief activist. Perle himself was judged its strategist.

One of their band was Major General Edward Rowny, a member of the SALT delegation representing the Joint Chiefs, who had named him to the job under pressure from Jackson's office. Inside the delegation, Rowny was thought to have transmitted the gist of what went on in members' meetings to Perle. At least once he took a call from Perle on a secure phone, which meant that the call had been placed from within the executive branch, probably the Pentagon, even though Perle was still working on Capitol Hill. Lehman was regarded within the government as the chief leaker. "The effect of Lehman's leaks was devastating," recalls Hyland, who chaired the SALT working groups. "I confronted him about this time [late 1975] and accused him to his face of handing this stuff over to Evans and Novak [the results of working group meetings].* He didn't deny it, but said he didn't do it directly all the time. He said he wasn't the only one."[68]

Kissinger could do little or nothing about the leaks from within the administration. Having once allowed the telephones of aides to be tapped, he was vulnerable and deterred from arranging surveillance. Ironically, the post-Watergate environment discouraged efforts to run a "tight ship."

Ford played directly into the hands of those who were undermining his foreign policy. On November 1, he fired Schlesinger and Colby. Nelson Rockefeller, who was then vice president, was told he would not be on the ticket when Ford ran for President. Kissinger lost his second hat—the national security adviser job—and was replaced by his loyal deputy, Brent Scowcroft. George Bush returned from the embassy in China to replace Colby at the CIA. And Donald Rumsfeld, who was then serving as Ford's chief of staff, took over the Defense Department. The press called it the "Halloween Massacre." At first Kissinger's hand was thought to lie behind these moves. He and Schlesinger had been rivals, and Schlesinger's removal from the board was the key maneuver. But Kissinger was actually a big loser in the shake-up. His pride was badly hurt, his access to Ford was cut back, and, most important, Schlesinger's departure actually weakened him. "Ford fired Jim at exactly the wrong time," recalls a veteran Kissinger associate. "We had just made our peace with him. He would not have been nearly the problem that Rumsfeld was.† Don had a different agenda. He wanted to turn around the Defense budget and be a real tough guy. He dedicated himself to that. He wanted to get his credentials in line. He engineered the Halloween massacre. He got Jim fired. He caused Bush to go to the CIA and himself to Defense." And why was Ford tempted to

*The reference is to the syndicated column of Rowland Evans and Robert Novak, a favorite outlet for the hard right.

†Schlesinger, unlike Rumsfeld, would have supported a SALT II treaty along the lines envisaged by Ford and Kissinger. He says so now.

fire Schlesinger? "Ford never got mad at anyone except Jim. Jim would sit there slouching and tending to lecture him, and you could see the red rising on Ford's neck." [69] (Schlesinger does have a professorial style and a tendency to lecture.)

For most of the then insiders, this account has a solid ring. "Rumsfeld maneuvered Bush into the CIA so Ford wouldn't make him Vice President," says one of them. Rumsfeld wanted that for himself. At least, that was the impression within much of the administration, although Rumsfeld himself contended that being sent to Defense cut him out, too. Another veteran of the NSC wars says, "Rumsfeld wanted to be secretary of defense in order to run for President. The jobs he had held—ambassador to NATO and White House chief of staff weren't stepping-stones." In his own memoir, Hyland refers to the Halloween massacre as a "disaster."

For Kissinger, the effect of the changes was abrupt. He and Ford traveled to the Far East in December, and from there Kissinger was planning a visit to Moscow to wrap up SALT II, or try to. This would mean obtaining a fig leaf on the Backfire issue and settling the cruise missile problem in a way that protected America's interest in deploying the air-launched version at extended ranges. "Henry wanted to get SALT by Christmas," recalls one of his associates. "But between Hong Kong and Jakarta, we got a cable from Rumsfeld asking how could he think about going to Moscow until there was an interagency framework for our SALT position. It was a monkey wrench. The trip was canceled."[70]

The worsening situation in Angola may have had something to do with it, but the larger reason seems to have been Rumsfeld's objection. On Saturday morning, December 6, readers of the Washington *Post* were told by Evans and Novak that "while President Ford prepared to be lectured in China on the dangers of détente, his national security bureaucracy was drafting top secret proposals for major concessions to Moscow in order to save a SALT II agreement at almost any cost. 'I think it's a disaster,'" they quoted one "outraged administration official" as saying. Their column described new options on Backfire and cruise missiles that would present Ford with "a stacked deck from which to choose a course bearing unalterable consequences for this country's future." Hyland and Sonnenfeldt were described as lobbying the new proposals through the bureaucracy in Kissinger's absence. Rumsfeld emerged from the column as both the "silent new boy" and key variable. His advice to Ford, said the piece, could determine whether Kissinger or his adversaries won the argument then raging over SALT.[71]

The column may have goaded Rumsfeld, as some people thought. Or it may have been pushing on an open door, as others thought. What did become clear is that Rumsfeld, a former congressman who had known Ford for some time, had the President's ear. Ford was taking advice from Rumsfeld on policy questions, which meant that he was taking political advice from him, because policy and presidential politics had converged.

Kissinger's Moscow trip was reset for late January. By then, the Soviet-Cuban–backed MPLA was winning in Angola. And Ronald Reagan had announced his presidential candidacy. Increasingly, Reagan was running against Kissinger, not Ford. Kissinger offered his resignation, but Ford wouldn't take it.

Kissinger complained about Angola to Dobrynin, who hinted that the Soviet military had created the situation with very little Politburo involvement. In Moscow, Kissinger raised the subject with Brezhnev, who had already been asked by the American press if he would discuss Angola with Kissinger. "If Kissinger wants to discuss Angola, let him discuss it with Sonnenfeldt," said Brezhnev. Kissinger got nowhere on the issue. "Brezhnev told us, in effect, to go to hell," says Sonnenfeldt.[72] The Kremlin's attitude was: We, too, are a superpower and must be expected to act like one.

The real business, of course, was SALT. Kissinger offered Brezhnev and Gromyko a proposal approved by the Pentagon. On the hardest issue, cruise missiles, the Soviets accepted one suggestion: The air-launched version would be allowed a range of 2,500 kilometers, as the Americans proposed, but any bombers equipped with these weapons would be treated like multiwarhead missile launchers and counted within the agreed ceiling on such systems—the Soviet position. Brezhnev didn't like much else of what he heard. He rejected a proposal to count all Backfire bombers produced after 1977 against the permitted aggregate, 2,400 vehicles. Nor would he agree that ship- and ground-launched cruise missiles could have ranges up to 2,500 kilometers. Kissinger then presented a fallback position that he had worked out with Ford, though not with the Pentagon. It didn't help much with Backfire, but it did narrow differences on the most contentious issue —cruise missiles deployed at sea.

In Washington, hard-liners doubted Kissinger's determination to battle for the right to deploy ground- or ship-launched cruise missiles at extended ranges, and they were right. The services, he knew, had no interest in the ground-launched versions (GLCMs, pronounced glickums), and the navy's interest in the SLCMs (the ship-launched version, pronounced slickums) was marginal. The air-launched option had to be protected, as everyone agreed. And that had been done; Brezhnev had gone along. The cruise missile lobby—a febrile group, by and large—was nonetheless unwilling to accept meaningful restrictions on SLCMs. Kissinger would have to be pulled back from the deal he was on the verge of making in Moscow. The spurious Backfire issue would help. So would the prospect of the New Hampshire primary, which was just a few weeks off.

Kissinger's adversaries wanted an NSC meeting to consider the package being worked out in Moscow. On January 21, the meeting was held; it went against him. Hyland was in Moscow with him and describes the news of the meeting and its outcome as a "bombshell." He says, "We thought we had a breakthrough and that the entire agreement could be worked out within a few months . . . At first Kissinger exploded, but then he became strangely resigned. I think he realized that this was the beginning of the end for him . . . In any case, we were finished—in practice and in theory."[73] The story of Kissinger's Moscow trip and of the "secret" NSC meeting that shot down his negotiations was promptly leaked to the press. One version had him violating his instructions and being reprimanded.[74]

"Under Kissinger and Ford," Reagan warned, "this nation has become Number Two in a world where it is dangerous—if not fatal—to be second best . . ."[75] It was effectively the end for SALT and even détente for the balance of Ford's presidency. Early in March he declared the word "détente" excluded from his political vocabulary. ("Peace through strength" became a campaign slogan.)

Ford's decision to turn away from the historic Vladivostok understanding may have been a serious political blunder, as many thought at the time. It was Rumsfeld, not Kissinger, whom he listened to and from whom he was taking advice. "He cost you the election," one of Ford's advisers remembers saying to him. Ford, he said, agreed. "It was the only time I ever heard him reveal this feeling."[76] Ford demurs: "I did differ with him [Rumsfeld] on this issue [SALT]. It was an honest difference of opinion. But the attitude in the Defense Department made it impossible to proceed in the environment of 1976. Rumsfeld and [Deputy Secretary of Defense] Clements were both hard-liners on SALT II. I think Don's attitude was substantive on the one hand, political on the other. He was strongly supported by John Lehman. I recall a memo from Lehman to Rumsfeld very much in opposition. But if I'd been elected in 1976, there's no question I could have gotten an agreement and gotten it ratified."[77]

He could have completed the SALT II agreement in the spring and then sought his party's nomination as President Ford—an achiever—rather than as candidate Ford, which, in effect, he became. His conservative credentials were hardly at issue; he was the most conservative President the country had seen since the Coolidge-Hoover era. Yet throughout the campaign, he continued to strive for the support of his party's right wing, even though it had no place else to go and even though it cost him votes in the country's political center. In a televised interview with NBC's John Chancellor on April 26, 1978, Ford said: "An American presidential election preempts an awful lot of time of an incumbent who's seeking to be elected in November. So, whether we like it or not, there is a hiatus that takes place in an election year as far as foreign policy is concerned. I don't think it's necessarily right—but that's the way the situation is, and we have to accept it."

Perhaps Ford did have the clearest view of his own position. Or perhaps he did misjudge the opposition to SALT by exaggerating its scope. Admittedly, the society is trendy and given to wild swings in attitude. The SALT I agreements were approved overwhelmingly, but SALT II was sure to have heavier going, even though Ford and Brezhnev had already removed the most vulnerable feature of the earlier agreement—the unequal ceilings on missile launchers. Briefly, it is far from obvious that Ford could have bulled his treaty through the Senate. But it's not obvious either that the country was as taken up by the SALT debate as Washington was. The instinct that drew public support for SALT I might in the end have sustained Ford's treaty and thus his presidency.

China was reemerging at this moment as a world power. It had been through the destructive Cultural Revolution and was negotiating a treaty of peace and friendship with Japan, resuming diplomatic relations with India, and replacing Moscow as a supplier of weapons to Egypt. China's rapprochement of sorts with its bitter enemy, the United States, was now the key variable in world politics. America had moved a long way from the view that in Vietnam it had been fighting Chinese surrogates in order to save Southeast Asia from communism. The Soviets, too, had hoped to improve their relations with China, especially after the death of Mao Tse-tung in September 1976. But the Chinese would neither forgive nor forget the unneighborly treatment they say they received from the other great Communist power. During each of the leadership changes following Mao's death, the line remained intensely anti-Soviet.

Equally steadfast was Moscow's resolve to make an arrangement with Washington that would translate into an anti-Chinese combine. Washington always said no, and a question arises. If Nixon and Kissinger, or Ford and Kissinger, had gone just partway with the Soviets would they, in turn, have moderated their behavior in Central Africa and granted concessions on SALT that would have helped Ford? Almost certainly, the answer is yes.

Yes is also the answer to the next question: Does America have more at stake in its relations with the other superpower than it has with a more open and congenial China? Still, neither Nixon nor Ford was willing to put relations with the U.S.S.R. ahead of relations with China, or even put them on the same footing.

"Leaders of men," de Gaulle wrote, "are remembered less for the usefulness of what they have achieved than for the sweep of their endeavors . . ."[78] Although disgraced, Nixon is remembered for the scope of his endeavors and, to a degree, for his achievements, too.

In backing away from the broader SALT agreement that lay within his grasp, Ford ignored the advantage of conservative presidents that Nixon exploited: their wider latitude in dealing with Communist powers. Kissinger knew the understanding in Vladivostok would become the broad base for further progress on SALT, if there was to be progress. And he might have sustained Ford's commitment to it had he himself not been diminished. Kissinger will be remembered as immensely accomplished—as the rare bird who, besides thinking big, got things done. He worked at a remarkable pace and dominated issues intellectually as few senior figures before or since. Part of his secret was in creating a staff of people who, besides being gifted and experienced, had good working relationships with colleagues in other offices and agencies. He became an act that others would try to emulate, with no great success. He didn't create the claw and fang method of doing business inside his part of the government, but he did much to create the environment in which the method came to flourish. He seems to have some regret, citing, for example, in his memoirs Schlesinger's resentment of the "not always tactful methods—to put it mildly—by which I operated. For example, until late in my term of office, I handled the SALT negotiations using my own staff and excluding representatives from the Department of Defense. This was both tactless and unwise; participation would have been educational for the Defense Department representative; . . . it would have made it easier to gain Defense Department support in NSC deliberations."[79]

The exact nature of his relationship with Nixon, however widely discussed then and later, is still unclear, at least in the sense of anyone knowing which of them was the inspiration for policy. Although each was a self-professed conceptualizer, Nixon's fingerprints are most clearly visible on the major initiative of his presidency, the opening to China. His piece in *Foreign Affairs* in 1967 foreshadowed not only the opening but also the triangular diplomacy that was used to put pressure on Moscow and elicit concessions in SALT. But it was Kissinger who understood the nature of linking Soviet behavior to other matters better perhaps than anyone. He didn't regard improved Soviet behavior as a precondition to a negotiation that promoted American interests. Instead, he saw negotiation partly as a means of levering more congenial Soviet behavior—of giving the Kremlin a vested interest in negotiation. He recalls that after Nixon's reelection, "he and I believed that we were in an unprecedentedly strong foreign policy position, almost unique. We were closer to both Moscow and Peking than they were to each other. We had a tremendous popular victory. We had ended the war in Vietnam . . . And I believe that without Watergate we would have had an extraordinary period of success with a strong Nixon and a still vital Brezhnev in power."[80]

Since leaving office, Kissinger has moved steadily to the right and routinely criticized the efforts of those who have tried to keep alive the process that absorbed him: limiting strategic arms and promoting détente.

X

The Real World

Incoming presidents are sobered—overwhelmed in some cases—by the responsibilities conferred on them by the nuclear weapons they command. They are briefed on the SIOP*—the target list and the weapons assigned to cover it. Looking for the first time at the options in the SIOP could be compared to taking a drink of water from a fire hose. Other briefings cover threats from the Soviet Union and from third countries, notably China and aspirant members of the nuclear club (plus unacknowledged members, like Israel). After being awed—at least by the SIOP briefing and the threat to the planet it starkly points up—the new President lets most of all this drift out of focus, except for the shrill domestic debate about the threat from the other superpower. Each President knows, or senses, that neither superpower is going to make a calculated nuclear strike against the other. But each perceives somewhat less remote threats of a nuclear weapon, or weapons, being used. Some new entrant in the nuclear club might use one. A misreading by either superpower of the other's actions could provoke a missile launch. In short, there are two ominous variables. One is the spread of nuclear weapons; the other is the vulnerability and unwieldiness of command and control structures. There is no easy, let alone obvious, solution to either problem. One of them—proliferation—is widely discussed. The other—how to reconcile the need to be able to use the weapons with the need to keep them under tight control—is kept obscure and ultrasensitive.

*Single Integrated Operation Plan. It identifies the Soviet bloc and Chinese targets to be attacked, along with the type and number of weapons allotted to their destruction.

The danger of nuclear weapons spreading is rooted in the Manhattan Project. The use of fissile material to make weapons led to the spread of the then novel nuclear technology, as did its later application to civil power programs. Nuclear weapons and nuclear power depend mainly on the same technology.

Eisenhower's justly admired Atoms for Peace program offered both a cover and a base for countries contriving to have at least the option of developing nuclear weapons. "Never in the history of mankind [was] so much information on modern technology, modern science . . . let loose to the public," recalls Raja Ramanna, a former Chairman of India's Atomic Energy Commission.[1] The scientists of a developing country like India, says Ramanna, saw atomic energy as "a new technology . . . that we should exploit . . . to make sure that we [would] not lose the second industrial revolution."[2]

Prime Minister Jawaharlal Nehru, a science graduate from Cambridge University, fully shared this view. Although he opposed nuclear weapons, he created the Indian Atomic Energy Commission and must have known that Homi Bhabha, its first chairman and an eminent physicist, was developing a highly sophisticated nuclear establishment that would provide the option of developing a bomb.

The pressure to adopt the option built dramatically after China defeated India in a battle over borders in the Himalayas during the winter of 1962–1963. But Nehru rejected a parliamentary petition to start a weapons program in March 1963. He died fourteen months later.

China, too, had a nuclear program; it drew at first on Soviet help, which, the Chinese felt strongly, was supposed to include a sample atomic bomb and the data concerning its manufacture.[3] It isn't likely that Moscow made so far-reaching a commitment. The annulment by the Soviets in 1959 of whatever they had promised was wickedly timed in the Chinese view; the crisis in the Formosa Strait during the previous summer had convinced them of the need to become an independent nuclear power—a status which the Soviets belatedly judged intolerable. "It is correct to say that some times there were attempts to prevent China from acquiring a nuclear capability," recalls Roland Timerbaev, a senior U.S.S.R. Foreign Ministry official.[4] Still, short of *force majeure,* there wasn't much the Soviets could do about it. The Chinese were determined. They had highly competent scientists, some of whom had been trained in Europe and America. Others had worked within sensitive areas of the Soviet weapons program.[5]

China's explosion of its first nuclear bomb in October 1964 traumatized the Indian establishment. Apart from a sudden sense of helplessness, Indians were impressed by the boost in China's prestige that followed the test shot. China had come "from a country which was considered as bankrupt . . . to a superpower, only because it had acquired nuclear weapons," says Subramanian Swamy, a Harvard-trained economist and former member of India's parliament.[6] Almost immediately, India's AEC was authorized to begin working on a nuclear device.

Exactly two years later, India's feeling of vulnerability rose again as China tested a nuclear-armed missile. By 1972, Prime Minister Indira Gandhi had apparently decided to go forward with a nuclear device.[7]

The year before, Pakistan was soundly thrashed by India and East Pakistan became the independent country of Bangladesh. Pakistan's Prime Minister, Zulfikar Ali Bhutto,* decided then to offset India's overwhelming military edge and impending nuclear capability by launching a nuclear program. Many years before, Bhutto had said, "If India builds the bomb, we will eat grass or leaves, even go hungry, but we will get one of our own."[8]

The dramatic improvement in U.S.-Chinese relations that followed Nixon's visit in 1972 probably hastened India's program. Domestic politics may also have pushed the project along. "There was a great feeling of gloom in the country," says Swamy. "And I also believed that [Mrs. Gandhi] knew that Pakistan was working feverishly on the bomb, and so she used the nuclear tests as a way of recovering some of her lost popularity, which it did momentarily."[9]

India's first test, in May 1974, shocked Pakistan and infuriated Canada. Under the terms of a Canadian sale of a heavy water reactor, India had pledged to use the reactor, and any plutonium it produced, for strictly peaceful purposes. No conditions for monitoring the pledge were attached to the arrangement.[10] Canada accused India of violating the peaceful uses constraint and suspended further assistance. India maintained that what it had conducted was a "peaceful nuclear explosion." Canada was unimpressed and not long afterward made the suspension official.

The test was directed by Ramanna, who even from a distance of four kilometers could see the ground rise up and fall back down. As he descended the platform, the aftershock nearly threw him off. "But what surprised us," he remembers now, "was there was a crow, dead, but completely unharmed physically. So the only explanation we could give was that the ground must have lifted so rapidly . . . the crow . . . had a heart attack."[11]

---

*Bhutto was hanged in 1979 by General Mohammad Zia ul-Haq, then Pakistan's President, on charges of conspiring to commit murder.

Although the motives for acquiring nuclear weapons vary from country to country, most aspirants want the political attributes they may confer: membership in a prestigious circle of nations, a claim to regional leadership, an offset to another's claim. Some countries may judge that proliferation is inevitable and do not want to be left behind, the more so if a neighbor is edging in that direction. Some governments deplore a two-tier world system based on a handful of states which have nuclear weapons and which try to discourage other states from having them. They may equate the discriminatory bias they perceive in such a system with imperialism and reject it just as vigorously. Other governments see nuclear weapons as a hedge against a future that is uncertain but probably hazardous.

The spread of these weapons is a multiple threat to the superpowers. The use or threatened use of a nuclear bomb in a local conflict could increase the danger of a confrontation between them. Progress toward a bomb by one state goads other aspirants and may inspire new ones. The United States, say, might have to intercede in a local conflict to block the use of nuclear weapons. Their spread could force the superpowers to develop defensive systems tailored to the threat from small nuclear powers. Proliferation increases the danger of catalyzed nuclear war—a strike from an ambiguous source aimed at provoking a superpower conflict. At the least, it poses a constant risk of accidental use of nuclear weapons since command and control in a country that has recently acquired the capability could be dangerously inadequate. Proliferation increases the risk of one state waging preventive nuclear war or striking preemptively against another country whose weapons are vulnerable. Closer to home, it could create the possibility of coercive threats to American cities (and/or those of allies) designed to oblige Washington to take, or not to take, a given course of action.

Fortunately, it isn't as easy to make a bomb as it has seemed, even though the technological know-how is hardly secret. John F. Kennedy's grim forecast of "fifteen or twenty nuclear powers" by 1975 wasn't borne out (although there may yet be that many by the year 2000). Some with potential are restrained from seeking the weapon for political reasons; the pressures created by new nuclear club members and/or coercive threats of terrorist groups pose even larger potential hazards to small and medium-size nations than to major powers. Some countries are restrained less by political pressures than by limits on their resources and their technological capabilities. But there are others who will struggle to overcome any obstacles to possess the bomb. Their behavior, some part of which they conceal or misrepresent, has always caused policy makers to take a somber, if not cynical view of the problem. "If I were Prime Minister of Japan or India—sitting next door to countries with nuclear capabilities, I might look at it differently," says Dean Rusk. "If you were Prime Minister of Japan, how much reliance would you put on U.S. protection if a threat from China or the Soviet Union developed?"[12]

Early efforts to encourage countries to use their nuclear power reactors for strictly peaceful purposes led to the creation of the International Atomic Energy Agency (IAEA) in 1957, one year after Canada sold India the reactor that caused the commotion. Eleven years later, the Non-Proliferation Treaty (NPT) was agreed to in Geneva. It had taken several years to negotiate, and most countries signed it. But those that didn't sign were the ones whose adherence mattered most, among them India, Pakistan, Israel, South Africa, Argentina, and Brazil. The treaty forbade the superpowers from doing what neither was likely to do: help others acquire a bomb. For the Soviets, its chief merit lay in yet another German disavowal of intent to acquire nuclear weapons.

Many countries—some of them signatories, others not—warned that unless the superpowers began whittling down their own arsenals of nuclear weapons and taking self-denying steps, such as halting tests, others could hardly be expected to exercise restraint. "Those who asked us to sign the nonproliferation treaty were themselves keeping atomic weapons," said India's Morarji Desai, a former Prime Minister.[13] In some capitals, a question arose: If nuclear weapons deterred war between America and Russia, why shouldn't they deter war between other rivals?

The NPT gave political, legal, and moral force to a party's commitment to nonnuclear status. But it carried no serious sanctions against violators; a signatory could exploit the treaty by using the benefits of nuclear cooperation that it offered to develop a bomb.

The latter 1970s—the era of Gerald Ford and Jimmy Carter—became a time of unusual tension and even discord between so-called nuclear have and have-not countries. The two administrations took different approaches to the proliferation issue. Ford's was subtler and relied more on quiet diplomacy. It reflected some of Kissinger's skepticism and his aversion to "overloading the circuit" in dealing with countries which in varying degrees feel that their security is linked with America's. "I agreed with Henry," says Ford. "If you are too tough on your allies you lose that relationship."[14] Carter's approach was more aggressive and direct. He made proliferation a campaign issue. The problem, or threat, was spreading, and two events in 1974 dramatized the inadequacy of America's approach to it: the world oil crisis and India's first nuclear test. Given the energy shortage, more countries than ever wanted nuclear technology. And more of them were becoming capable of supplying it.

Also in 1974, a CIA report on the subject said: "We believe that Israel has produced nuclear weapons. Our judgement is based on Israeli acquisition of large quantities of uranium, partly by clandestine means; the ambiguous nature of Israeli efforts in the field of uranium enrichment; and Israel's large investment in a costly missile system designed to accommodate nuclear warheads." The report went on to discuss aspirant club members and to note related dangers: "Governments anxious to acquire a token capability quickly are more likely to try to steal weapons than fissionable material . . . Terrorists might attempt theft of either weapons or fission able materials."[15]

The intelligence on Israel's program wasn't new. Dean Rusk recalls "telling Israel more than once that they would lose the U.S. and our nuclear umbrella if they introduced nuclear weapons and a threat to use them into the Middle East. But in the sixties, we got no cooperation at all from Israel when we sent people to look at that Dimona reactor."[16]

By 1975, the threat was multipolar. In East Asia, South Korea and Taiwan were seeking plants that separate plutonium from spent nuclear fuel; like Pakistan, each had arranged to buy such a facility from France.* The intelligence on South Africa was ominous and included a presumed *entente nucléaire* with Israel. In the Western Hemisphere, Brazil had arranged to purchase the complete fuel cycle—six to eight reactors, a reprocessing plant, and a uranium enrichment facility—from West Germany. Predictably, Argentina had resolved to stay roughly in step with Brazil and by 1974 had acquired heavy water reactors—the type that India had used to produce its plutonium.

In Washington, sentiment to cut back exports of relevant technology and equipment was rising within Congress and the bureaucracy. Kissinger vetoed a sharp American reaction to the Indian explosion, but he did authorize a study of how the U.S. could strengthen controls. Most nuclear suppliers had adopted export restrictions, but a buyer who wanted to avoid these could shop around. The French, who had never signed the NPT, took an especially relaxed view and did not always impose strict controls (whether their own or the so-called IAEA safeguards†) on the uses of

---

*The Taiwanese were also negotiating with Belgium.

†IAEA safeguards include inspections, inventories, and regular audits of sensitive materials to ensure that nuclear reactors are used for peaceful purposes only.

reactors and related items sold abroad. The Germans, too, tended to be somewhat permissive. With oil prices skyrocketing, nuclear power appeared to be heading into a massive growth cycle. (The prospects have turned out to be a lot less bright than they seemed in the mid-1970s.) And the competition in reactor sales was sharpening. The French and the Germans felt overmatched by the General Electric Company and Westinghouse, each of which held a major position within the market. Europeans felt that only by offering, in addition to reactors, other more sensitive parts of the fuel cycle—plutonium separation plants, for example—could they compete effectively.

The State Department study proposed a series of meetings of major suppliers with the goal of producing some controls that everyone, including France, could agree to observe. Agreement on all sides would, it seemed, stifle the tendency of some suppliers to be more permissive than others. Kissinger approved the idea of a suppliers conference. The French often disdain multilateral diplomacy, but eventually did agree to take part, although they insisted on secrecy and arrived skeptical.

The suppliers began meeting secretly in London in late 1974. To no one's great surprise, the Americans and Russians took the most restrictive approach; each was closer to the other in attitude than either was to any of the others. "The Russians were easy to deal with," recalls George Vest, the State Department diplomat who led Washington's interagency group. "Their attitude toward us was: we can take care of ours [our allies]. Can you take care of yours?"[17] The British, too, took a restrictive approach. The French for a time inclined toward laissez-faire. Bertrand Goldschmidt, their chief adviser and a scientist who had worked with Fermi in the early 1940s, typified France's attitude: The genie is out of the bottle and not much can be done. The French were then involved commercially with more worrisome countries—South Korea, Pakistan, and South Africa—than any of the other suppliers. But gradually they changed course and, in effect, agreed to join a consensus.

In London, no one talked about Israel and South Africa. "Israel was a given, not an issue," says Vest.[18] In Washington, the attitude toward Israel's clandestine program was strictly hands-off. Neither Congress nor the administration—any administration by this time—would press the Israelis for information, even though they were known to be fabricating nuclear weapons. The intelligence community was warned against giving information about Israel's program to other agencies.

In 1980, an Israeli engineer who had spent some time at the Massachusetts Institute of Technology and continued to visit Cambridge from time to time, let drop hints about Israel's association with South Africa in setting off a mysterious explosion in the South Atlantic that could have been a nuclear test. Some evidence, although by no means conclusive, pointed that way. A former senior government official, after learning of this conversation, says that he took up the matter with Admiral Stansfield Turner, Director of Central Intelligence, thinking that the CIA might wish to look into it. "We do not conduct espionage against Israel" was the reply.

Washington had been trying to persuade the South Africans to put under safeguards a uranium enrichment plant they had created. There were many bilateral talks, but they never went anywhere.

South Korea and Pakistan were first-priority agenda items in London. So was Brazil. The French, citing their commitments to South Korea and Pakistan, at first refused to withdraw from them. But under pressure from Washington, both South Korea and France agreed to inter that arrangement. On Pakistan, however, the French remained stubborn. And the Germans, defending their deal with Brazil, proved to be even more unyielding; their client was no less so. In 1975, Washington sent a mission to Bonn which tried to persuade the Germans not to proceed. The Germans, like the French, invoked their solemn commitment to a client. Also, they suspected that Washington was upset in part because German industry, not American, had won the contract with Brazil. This sale was particularly disturbing as it was much broader than the others; it involved more sophisticated technology, including a plutonium separation plant and help with a uranium enrichment facility based on a singular German design.

Ford was close to Helmut Schmidt, West Germany's Chancellor; they spoke on the telephone about once a week. Schmidt was even so unwise as to endorse Ford for reelection during the 1976 presidential campaign. German officials have said that Ford never raised the Brazilian matter with Schmidt. Kissinger didn't push either, which meant that efforts further down in the administration to affect the deal came to nothing.

Pakistan was another matter. Carter was making nonproliferation a campaign issue and had cited Pakistan as unreliable. In August 1976, Ford dispatched Kissinger to see Prime Minister Bhutto. He was bearing an offer to sell Pakistan one hundred A-7 Corsair jet aircraft if the deal with France was canceled. The sweetener didn't help. According to Agha Shahi, an adviser to Bhutto and later foreign minister, "Kissinger . . . exerted a considerable amount of pressure . . . on us to renege on the reprocessing plant agreement, which of course Prime Minister Bhutto refused to do."[19] Kissinger went from Islamabad to Paris, but didn't get very far with the French either.

Before Ford left office, the suppliers agreed in London on a set of guidelines which specified sensitive kinds of equipment and technology that could in the future be sold only if the buyer accepted suitably tight controls on their use. They also agreed on guidelines for the physical security of nuclear equipment and fuel, even though no two suppliers dealt with security in just the same way. Concern with terrorism helped produce agreement that each supplier, besides flogging his wares, would be transferring to clients his own security procedures as a condition of sale. And basic to these procedures was the need for security good enough to hold off a terrorist or paramilitary assault until reinforcements arrived. Some suppliers argued that material in transit, the time of greatest vulnerability, should have the least possible visibility, which obviously would mean having very little security. An opposing view held that material in transit should have high-visibility protection; that view prevailed, mainly because it fit the requirement of being able to hang on until help arrived.

The suppliers conference had been a success, thanks mainly to a low-key style, which matched the Ford administration's preference for quiet diplomacy. Carter raised the decibel level and gave proliferation a stronger emphasis, but his administration accomplished no more than Ford's. Indeed, had Ford been reelected, the more muted and traditional approach might have accomplished more.

Carter had pledged himself to heading off the German deal with Brazil. And two days after his inauguration, he dispatched Vice President Walter Mondale to Europe with the new administration's message about nuclear proliferation. In Brussels, only four days later, Mondale said that one of the "central themes" would be "stopping the sales of reprocessing plants such as those to Brazil and Pakistan."[20] In Bonn, he is said to have told Schmidt that Carter "was unalterably opposed to the transfer of the sensitive technologies to Brazil."[21] Schmidt stonily replied by noting his commitment to the NPT and the suppliers' guidelines, but he also restated his commitment to the agreement with Brazil. Carter's high-visibility, high-level initiative had the predictable effect of souring the atmosphere and further complicating intractable problems. Two weeks later, Warren Christopher, Deputy Secretary of State designate, was in Bonn, trying to persuade Schmidt to defer transferring the enrichment and reprocessing materials to Brazil until its reactors had been "safeguarded." Schmidt again said no. A U.S. mission to Brazil drew a cold, uncompromising reception; the Brazilians made their feelings clear by canceling a military cooperation agreement.

Secretary of State Cyrus Vance visited Schmidt in March; the Brazil deal was soft-pedaled. Carter may have begun to see that his imperious approach was getting nowhere and that the U.S.-West German relationship was more important than the transaction with Brazil. Senior officials, whether they like it or not, have to accept that nuclear nonproliferation is one of a number of competing priorities in relations with allies and other friendly countries and often not the first. Carter extended a three-year embargo on sensitive technology. He planned to cut off American aid to any country that detonated a "peaceful nuclear explosion." He wanted a voice in decisions involving an American client-country's other nuclear exchanges. And he wanted to be able to rule on whether a client-country could develop its own plutonium separation capability.[22] Each of these criteria was reasonable, if difficult to sustain, and each was justified by the performance of "threshold countries," i.e., aspirant members of the nuclear club.

An example is South Africa, which acquired its first reactor from the United States in 1965. In 1976, Prime Minister John Vorster told the world: "We are only interested in the peaceful applications of nuclear power. But we can enrich uranium and we have the capability. And we did not sign the Nuclear Non-Proliferation Treaty."[23] In August 1977, Soviet satellites detected preparations for what appeared to be a nuclear test in the Kalahari desert. Moscow alerted Washington, and American intelligence confirmed the Soviet report. At that point, the major Western powers—the U.S., Britain, France, and West Germany—applied pressure on South Africa to give up the test (in some cases threatening to break relations).

In the 1970s, Libya tried unsuccessfully to obtain nuclear help from China, Pakistan, the Soviet Union, and India (which has been unresponsive to requests for such assistance). In the 1980s, Libya has sought enrichment and reprocessing technologies—again unsuccessfully—from Belgium, Argentina, and Brazil.

In the mid-1970s, Pakistan received over $1 billion in aid from OPEC,* plus other Arab countries and Iran. The aid provoked unfounded speculation about an "Islamic bomb." More concretely, it gave Pakistan a reliable source of money and materials as Western sources, including France, dried up; in 1977, the French, reacting to pressure started by Ford and Kissinger and continued by Carter, suspended further assistance to Pakistan's plutonium separation project. According to Munir Kahn, Chairman of the Pakistan Atomic Energy Commission, "The Indian nuclear test had a strong negative impact on our program . . . because the supplier states thereafter reneged on existing agreements, cut off nuclear supplies even for our safeguarded nuclear facilities, and our program slowed down."[24]

Reagan's campaign rhetoric diverged from Carter's and was even more unrealistic. What other countries did about acquiring nuclear capabilities

*Organization of Petroleum Exporting Countries

was their own business, he declared. Fortunately, however, Reagan policy and Reagan rhetoric had nothing in common on this issue. His administration's handling of proliferation issues drew generally good marks from officials, who had worked this ground in the years before. "It was a very good reaffirmation of what had been built up," says one former official. Some of the problems now seem less immediate while others are neither more nor less onerous than before. The most serious near- and middle-term threat is an outright theft of nuclear material or a weapon by terrorists. Despite the efforts of the suppliers conference, the rigor of security procedures varies sharply from country to country.

Brazil's deal with West Germany gradually fell apart of its own weight. The Brazilians couldn't afford the reactors and never managed to make the German-designed enrichment technology work for them. The overall situation has improved, but Brazil and Argentina still refuse to sign the NPT, and in either country an immoderate regime could doubtless acquire the weapons option.

Israel remains in its special—all but unmentionable—status, determined to deny similar status to any of the other so-called confrontational states in the Middle East. In June 1981, Israeli bombers destroyed the Osiraq reactor in Iraq. It had already been the target of terrorist attacks, sponsored by Iran or Israel (or both), and it had been damaged once before in a bombing raid by Iranian aircraft. Israel professed to see the attack as necessary to nip in the bud an Iraqi nuclear weapons program. Prime Minister Menachem Begin noted underground working areas at Osiraq, the inference being that these concealed sinister pursuits. But there was nothing subsurface at Osiraq. Begin may have confused what he knew of Israel's Dimona reactor—and what goes on there underground—with the Iraqi reactor. Exactly what Iraq may have had in mind for the reactor, which was subject to safeguards, was never clear. Neither is it clear that Israel and South Africa have formed an *entente nucléaire*, but they probably have. ". . . my impression is that Israel and South Africa are cooperating today in . . . developing nuclear weapons," says Matityahu Peled, a retired general and a member of the opposition in the Knesset. "Of course, South Africa can offer Israel spaces which Israel doesn't have which are needed in second phases of developing weapons."[25]

Elsewhere, each of the threshold states could at this point cross over with little difficulty. Of these, India and Pakistan, with their history of exceptional communal violence, constitute the regional paradigm of what specialists have worried about for decades. Together they embody the major incentives that propel have-not countries toward have status. And they reflect the range of anxieties that cause have countries, especially the

United States and the Soviet Union, to discourage new entries into the nuclear club.

Returning to power in 1980, Indira Gandhi said that India would "not hesitate from carrying out nuclear explosions . . . or whatever is necessary in the national interest."[26] Both the United States and the Soviet Union were restricting further deliveries of nuclear fuel to India unless and until the regime accepted controls on *all* of its facilities—"full-scope safeguards," as they were called. Besides approving research on the design and manufacture of nuclear weapons, Mrs. Gandhi is said to have kept a test site in a state of readiness.[27]

Rajiv Gandhi, Indira's son, who succeeded his mother when she was assassinated, told Reagan in October 1987 that India's program was strictly its own "business" and "designed less to intimidate Pakistan than deter China."[28] Perhaps. But China's program has in recent years shown little momentum, whereas Pakistan's determined efforts to play in the same league are now thought to strike Indians as the more pernicious threat.

Although China is believed to have provided design information on nuclear weapons, Pakistan, like India, discovered self-help as the most reliable path to the option. In the mid-1970s, Pakistanis began collecting data and equipment for a uranium enrichment plant using ultra-high-speed centrifuges, a technology pioneered by the Dutch. Dr. A. Q. Khan, a metallurgist, acquired access to classified material in the Netherlands.[29] Using many private channels, Pakistanis managed to purchase equipment they needed for a plutonium separation plant at Rawalpindi and a uranium enrichment facility at Kahuta. "There's a great deal of ingenuity among . . . our people," says Shahi. "We went to all the little, small shops . . . and explained to them what we wanted . . . and by trial and error . . . developed this thing on an indigenous basis . . . so that is how we built it."[30] In September 1979, President Zia said Pakistan would complete the plutonium separation plant begun with French help on its own.

In 1979, Carter was obliged to suspend economic and military aid to Pakistan. He had little choice; Pakistan was in violation of an amendment, sponsored by Senator Stuart Symington, which bans aid to countries that buy or sell uranium enrichment and reprocessing equipment without attaching various safeguards. (The amendment was written in a fashion that exempts Israel from the penalty.) But in 1981, a year or so after the Soviet invasion of Afghanistan, Congress approved a request from Reagan to grant Pakistan a six-year waiver of the prohibition. Congress also voted a multi-billion-dollar aid package which allowed Pakistan to support Afghan rebel forces. Later, the Reagan administration tried without success to rein in Pakistan's nuclear program. By June 1986, the Soviets were worried enough to warn Zia that they could "not tolerate" Pakistan's nuclear capability.[31] Washington then warned Moscow to back off, thereby becoming the program's buffer. An American official said in November 1986 that Pakistan was only "two screwdriver turns" from having a fully assembled bomb.[32]

The waiver on the Symington amendment expired a year later. Congress left it to Reagan to determine whether Pakistan was really creating a weapons option and whether to renew the waiver on aid. Reagan, to no one's surprise, decided no and yes. The State Department guesses, probably correctly, that American aid acts as a restraint on Pakistan's more immoderate tendencies. If aid were cut off again, whether before or after the Soviets left Afghanistan, the Pakistanis might react by maneuvering themselves into a nuclear arms race with India. Not long before the waiver on the Symington amendment expired, a Pakistani diplomat in Islamabad said, "If Congress insists on its pound of flesh and stops the aid, they remove the only fig leaf that was stopping us going all the way and making a bomb. We'd no longer have any inhibitions."[33]

Subramanian Swamy estimates that India can "produce about 100 bombs a year of the range of twenty kilotons each . . . We have the capacity to produce intermediate range ballistic missiles which can go to China . . . and parts of the Soviet Union. And we have heavy bombers which can deliver weapons . . . It would take Indian physicists about three months to get going and producing not one bomb, but several bombs."[34]

Pakistan, too, can have a bomb in short order if its leadership should make the fateful decision. A part of the danger is that neither side is likely to be content with just one, or two, or three bombs. Specialists reckon they would accumulate quantities of fissile material and move toward stockpiles of fifteen to twenty bombs; thus the prospect of Indo-Pakistani relations being driven by a nuclear arms race is far from negligible. "If India goes nuclear, we will go nuclear," says General A. I. Akram, Director for Regional Studies in Islamabad. "And we know that if we go nuclear India will go nuclear. We'll actually cross the threshold together or not cross it at all."[35]

It doesn't have to happen. President Zia ul-Haq and Prime Minister Rajiv Gandhi pledged orally not to attack each other's nuclear installations. The pledge has yet to be put in writing, but given the region's surpassing volatility, leaders on either side understand the merit of restraint. What does or doesn't happen will depend in part on the superpowers. More often than not, the case for heading off proliferation is seen in Washington as having less weight than some competing priority. The continuing hypocrisy of both the White House and Congress with regard to Israel's program drains credibility from American rhetoric about proliferation. Moscow, too, preaches restraint but is loath to rock India's boat and blames the troubles in South Asia on Pakistan and its patron, the United States.

Perhaps the scope of the danger in South Asia will inspire a more coherent American approach, especially with Afghanistan largely settled. If so, the more venturesome leadership on display in Moscow, along with a more moderate style in Peking, might combine to make the exercise of restraint in New Delhi and Islamabad less difficult. Such is the hope, though not the likelihood.

Since Truman's day, presidents have tended to take for granted their control of nuclear weapons. After all, a decision to use them, or any other weapons, is supposed to rest solely with the Supreme Commander. The famous button is the metaphor for presidential control; it is actually a black briefcase with a combination lock under the handle and known among initiates as "the football." Even as metaphor the button is misleading. It suggests that if the awful, though remote, contingency should loom on the horizon, the President alone would decide whether to launch nuclear weapons or whether to wait a bit longer so as to be more certain of what was happening. The reality is that control of nuclear weapons, including release codes, has been diffused through the senior echelons of major military commands. In the worst case, a decision to launch need not necessarily come from the President, if only because he could be dead or out of touch with the command system. Or the pressure of events—the apparent lack of time, even a few minutes—in which to make a considered decision could maneuver his okay to send off nuclear weapons.

Truman did possess the authority over the weapons that he thought he had. And so did Eisenhower, at least until he began to deploy the weapons abroad in large numbers and field officers acquired de facto control over them. The war plan in those days, as noted earlier, provided for nothing less than the "spasm" response, sometimes called "the Doomsday Machine."

The supposed Eisenhower strategy of "massive retaliation" could not, in practice, have had much to do with retaliation, since an enemy strike would have wiped out command posts and communications systems. For many years, the country's early warning system—the North American Aerospace Defense Command, or NORAD—was housed in some highly vulnerable above-ground cinder-block buildings in Colorado. A few hand grenades could have knocked out the entire operation; but SAC opposed proposals to harden NORAD.[36] In that light, America's more plausible (or least implausible) option was to launch its nuclear forces on warning. So it must have seemed to a few air force figures, including General Curtis LeMay, SAC's Chief of Staff. In September 1957, LeMay briefed two visiting members of Eisenhower's Gaither Committee: Robert C. Sprague, an electronics manufacturer who had also served on the Killian panel, and Jerome Wiesner, who became Kennedy's science adviser and later president of MIT. Sprague noted a wall chart showing the response time of SAC's bombers; it seemed to suggest that none of them would get off the ground by the time Soviet bombers were picked up by the early warning network in Canada. Sprague and Wiesner each recalls LeMay affirming that view but adding: "I will know from my own intelligence whether or not the Russians are massing their planes . . . for a massive attack against the United States." And he said, "If I come to that conclusion, I'm going to knock the shit out of them before they get off the ground."

"General, that isn't national policy," Sprague remembers saying. "You know that." LeMay, he says, replied, "No, it's not national policy, but it's my policy."[37]

At the time, SAC's war plan wasn't tied in with the plans of the other services. In 1960, Secretary of Defense Thomas Gates ended SAC's autonomy by creating a joint strategic target planning staff.[38] But civilian leaders still could not acquire more than limited insight into the country's nuclear war plan and how it would work.

Kennedy and McNamara wanted to supplant the SAC spasm with a menu of options, a move that was far from being as simple as it appeared. They first decided to reduce vulnerability by creating alternative national command centers, a few of which were ships and aircraft.[39] But in 1963, McNamara told Congress that the command system was still vulnerable, especially SAC and the communications network.

Another problem lay with the bloated stockpile of nuclear weapons in Europe. American field officers had no authority to use those under their command without an appropriate order from the President. But as McNamara himself now says, "The conventional wisdom in the U.S. military then was that local commanders confronting an attack would use their nuclear weapons."[40] Washington had "zero" physical control over its nuclear weapons at this time, he also said recently. Still, the mad major scenario didn't trouble all senior officials. "I myself have never lost any sleep worrying that U.S. weapons might be used in some unauthorized way," says Dean Rusk.[41]

In June 1962, Kennedy created the National Military Command System. Until then, the President had not been directly involved in the details of warning and nuclear operations.[42] After the missile crisis in Cuba, the National Security Agency (NSA), which is charged with electronic and communications intelligence collection, began by passing the military chain of command and reporting directly to the White House; the adjustment somewhat strengthened the President's hand.

Most of what passes for central control today dates to the Kennedy era. A president's dominion is protected by a system built around coded procedures—electronic locks—which, in theory, no one else can control. The locks are known as PALs—for Permissive Action Links. They have remote-controlled digital codes which can be fed into a nuclear weapon's circuitry. A weapon cannot be armed and detonated until the PAL receives the correct code. The PALs were introduced in mid-1962; at first, they were only used with tactical weapons in Europe, not with the longer-range strategic weapons. The military didn't like them, worrying that these novel devices would hopelessly compromise readiness; the weapons, some thought, were being "locked up" by the Kennedy Administration."[43]

The so-called two-man rule was also introduced at this time. This required that each important action involving nuclear weapons be taken by two people with the same authority and training. Minuteman missile sites offer a good illustration. They are connected by underground cable to launch control centers. There are five such centers for each squadron—fifty missiles. The two-man rule requires a pair of officers in each underground command capsule to act jointly. Each has the combination to a double-padlocked safe containing the sealed authentication codes and two launch keys. Each of the two officers would separately decode and compare the codes in the launch order with those in the safe. If the codes match, the officers would then identify another digital group in the launch order just received; this group of eight digits is plugged into the PAL system and, in effect, arms the missiles. The next step would require the officers to turn dual keys that are located too far apart for either to turn by himself. And even then, nothing would happen immediately unless another two-man team in another launch center turned its keys too. Thus, four men, not two, are needed to launch Minuteman missiles.[44]

Each side wants to be confident that the other is exercising tight control over its nuclear weapons—tight enough to minimize the chance of accidental or unauthorized use. "We offered to share technology with the Soviets on accidental use," says Rusk. "PALs and so forth. We were very frank about that sort of thing."[45] The offer Rusk alludes to was made in December 1962, after the Cuban crisis. The Soviets declined it, saying that devices of the sort used by the Americans would be "unnecessary when nuclear weapons are commanded by the politically disciplined soldier of Marxist-Leninist heritage."[46]

The Soviet approach, although different, is no less careful than America's and, many experts would say, safer. Instead of relying on "hardware," the Soviets put control in separate organizations, no one of which can do much without an appropriate launch order from on high. Soviet leadership has always worried actively about "Bonapartism," and for many years the nuclear bombs and missile warheads were stored in depots guarded by the KGB. Some storage areas were located fifty miles or so from missile launch areas.[47] A few American experts believe that the KGB has acquired some, possibly all, of the custodial responsibility. They are certain that the Soviets, too, now use PALs as an additional precaution. Finally, political control of Soviet weapons is believed to lie strictly with the General Secretary, just as it does with the American President. "The Soviets have been more cautious than we, and the historic movement on both sides is toward greater caution," says James Schlesinger.[48]

The attitudes toward the weapons themselves vary sharply. Americans regard silo-based missile systems as the most unstable of them, because they are supposedly vulnerable to surprise attack. Ballistic missile submarines, because they are all but invulnerable, and long-range bombers are judged more stable. The Soviets, on the other hand, are uneasy with submarines and bombers because these are separable from the motherland, unlike missiles in silos which have the virtue of being fixed and thus continuously linked to command and control Soviet-style.

Diplomacy is an unchanging, inexact craft. Across the centuries, governments have routinely made decisions about other governments based on sketchy information and modest insights. The off-track bettor equipped with only the form sheet may be as well positioned for his wager as a big government confronting a set of policy options. America's strategic forces have been placed on an alert status at various moments of high tension, such as the Cuban missile crisis. The alert puts them in a higher readiness and is supposed to emphasize to the other side the seriousness of the situation. It could also cause the other side to assume the worst—that a preemptive strike was coming. The Soviets, as noted, have never put their forces on any such footing. The old fear of military adventurism and an extremely conservative deployment pattern would discourage strategic alerts; keeping many nuclear bombs and warheads a safe distance from their missile and bomber platforms is just one example of the leadership's caution. However, the net effect is to leave Soviet forces more vulnerable to attack than America's. Bombers are clustered on just a few airstrips. Soviet missile-

carrying submarines are easier to locate. Until recently, it took a lot longer
to make Soviet land-based missiles ready for launch than it did their American counterparts. Moreover, the units in charge of Soviet missile systems
do not possess the "unlock codes" that liberate the weapons from their PAL
devices.[49]

The real difference in the two approaches is that the Soviets seem to
require direct political involvement in the actual arming and firing of
nuclear weapons, whereas the American military, as a practical matter,
performs all these functions. Decisions made in the late 1940s and 1950s,
whatever their intent, set a pattern of inordinate military responsibility that
has continued

Uniformed military officers like to say, "We are part of the decision,
not part of the decision making." And most military people believe that to
be the case. But senior people in SAC and other commands have been made
part of the decision-making process by its very nature. And, as will be
shown, their role was enlarged by Carter and Reagan.

America's command system is bedeviled by a conflict which the
Soviets seem not to have, or if they have it, not to worry about. Being able
to use the weapons in the extreme case is, or seems, essential. But having
reliable political control over them is also essential, or would seem to be.
The issue is whether leadership can have it both ways: whether reliable
control means denying military people the flexibility they would need to
answer an attack before the command system broke down, with only chaos
and devastation left behind. The Soviets, as noted, accord first priority to
control, whereas Washington tries to reconcile the contesting priorities.

The weak link in the American deterrent, now as before, is the
"head"—the command and control system. Military communications, for
example, are not as secure or reliable as they should be. They rely mainly
on the commercial phone system, for which there may be no good alternative. "I think we would all like to be reassured that the Defense Department
does not rely on pay phones for its defense communications, or if it does,
that it has change," said Steven Weinberg, a Nobel laureate in physics, at
a conference on crisis management in 1983. After warning that "I may blow
your mind," Lieutenant General William Hillsman, then Director of the
Defense Communications Agency, said the "radars today are tied into
Cheyenne Mountain—NORAD—by telephone lines . . . we do not have
defense communications systems [for that purpose]. Everything we do here

in the United States that ties us together in terms of warning and deterrence is provided to us by the common carrier system, the private sector, the A.T.&T.s and the G.T.E.s."[50] Commercial lines constitute the President's main link to allied counterparts and America's nuclear-capable forces at home and abroad. Wherever he may be, his orders go through the White House switchboard to the Pentagon and from there to the military commands.

Talking to submarines poses special problems and those with missiles on board are not supposed to talk back. "The most serious deficiency in the Navy's strategic nuclear posture . . . is the lack of reliable, survivable communications at sea," said Thomas Haywood, the Chief of Naval Operations, in 1981. The problem seems to lie mainly with an airborne radio relay system for communicating with submarines after a nuclear attack. The system is called TACAMO, short for "take charge and move out." Its aerial platforms are unable to receive incoming messages while broadcasting, and since there are usually only two TACAMO planes aloft—one over the Atlantic and one over the Pacific—not all the submarines can be contacted in one broadcast. The navy has recently tried to divert hundreds of millions of dollars that were earmarked for improving the TACAMO system to support its exuberant shipbuilding program.[51]

There is an abundance of anecdotes and horror stories about communications lapses. The navy and the air force see upgrading communications links as wasting money; since nuclear war isn't likely to occur, the same money, they feel, is better spent on weapons. "A general who has worked at NORAD said that the problem with communications gear is that it's hard to get funding for things that 'aren't shiny and make a lot of noise and smoke,' " writes Daniel Ford.[52] The services have tried, sometimes successfully, to divert funds for improving communications into more congenial programs.

Not much was done about command and control between the Kennedy and Carter administrations. In 1974, the so-called Schlesinger Doctrine broadened the SIOP to include limited options; the idea was that these would more strongly discourage whatever aggressive designs the Soviets might have had on Western Europe. In theory, a more flexible strategy would demand a more flexible command system. But the system didn't actually change, and neither did the forces themselves. Kissinger wanted to allay fears (in Moscow and elsewhere) that the supposed shift would make nuclear war more likely; he and Schlesinger struck a deal whereby the declaratory shift would not affect the makeup of nuclear forces, only the manner in which some of them *might* be used. In practice, there was far less to the new line than met the eye.

The command system was rarely examined, let alone tested, and for years might have been a model for a sick joke. By the mid-1970s, the emergency procedures for the White House and the Pentagon had diverged. And that "just about guarantees that the President wouldn't even know the missiles were on their way until after they'd landed," wrote Bill Gulley, who had served as director of the White House Military Office.[53]

As the alert system was designed, a helicopter would carry the President to a "marry-up-point" with the emergency airborne command post, (NEACP, called "Kneecap") which communicates with SAC's airborne command center, "Looking Glass." The President and secretary of defense (or their successors) could send orders to Looking Glass which in turn could transmit a launch message to Minuteman launch control centers, bombers in flight, and (through TACAMO) submerged submarines.[54] The message would contain the digital group required to unlock the weapons.

What actually would happen if the President, Kneecap, and other national controls were destroyed is wholly unclear. Command of the strategic forces would probably shift to three commands—CINCSAC (Commander in Chief Strategic Air Command), CINCLANT (the Atlantic forces), and CINCPAC (the Pacific forces), each of which has an emergency airborne command post. But they would be unable to assess the damage, and if NORAD were destroyed, as seems likely, all three would be in the dark about what had happened. The war would be fought by three separate and uncoordinated commands—in effect, three sovereign powers.[55]

Carter was the first President to test the system to the point of going aloft in Kneecap. Zbigniew Brzezinski, his national security adviser, filled in for Carter in another exercise and reported that the helicopter took "roughly twice as long as it should have . . . [and was] almost shot down."[56] In one simulated exercise, the President was "killed" and no one knew who was in charge.[57]

Carter began by taking a strong interest in the command system and the SIOP—the first President to do so. He ended by approving some major alterations suggested mainly by Brzezinski, the latter's military assistant, General William Odom, and Harold Brown, the Secretary of Defense. Their concern with the inadequacy of the command system led to changes, most of which were aimed at supporting a broader strategy—one that envisaged the possibility of not just limited nuclear warfare but also protracted nuclear war. That Jimmy Carter—a certified dove and the most rhetorically committed nuclear disarmer among recent presidents—should have signed off on so dubious a proposition is irony of a kind peculiar to the Potomac Basin.

The changes, which stretched the already overstretched command system, were reflected in a celebrated document, called PD (Presidential Directive) 59, which emerged in July 1980. Its idea was that either superpower could use nuclear weapons "at levels ranging from tactical to the strategic, selectively at a large variety of targets over protracted periods of time." The words are Brzezinski's and are contained in a book he later wrote, *Game Plan: How to Conduct the U.S.-Soviet Contest*. For Paul Warnke, former chief arms control negotiator and head of ACDA, this basic premise of PD 59 was a "terminally bad joke."[58] The administration, wrote Brzezinski, wanted to "reduce the possibility that the U.S. could be coerced in time of crisis."[59] PD 59 and the dark warnings of related directives would help; he quotes one of them as referring to "a protracted nuclear conflict."[60] In short, if the Soviets did see limited nuclear war as an option, Brzezinski wanted them on notice that it would be a two-party game. And the prime targets, according to leaked stories, would be those "the Soviet leadership values most—its military forces and its own ability to maintain control after a war starts." Part of the new thinking was to strike the Soviet leaders in their bunkers.[61] PD 59 had introduced into the SIOP an explicit option for striking at the Soviet command structure. Earlier SIOPs hadn't made a point of avoiding "the head," but neither had they provided for decapitation. The new thinking assumed that the Soviets had targeted America at its weakest link—the command system. Emulation (if that's what it was) seemed only prudent. The incoming Reagan people liked PD 59, and they gave it a thrust of their own. They made decapitation a stouter option than before, even though it was—is—widely deplored by a legion of initiates. "You would want to communicate with the other side," says James Schlesinger. "The last thing you would want to do is remove the political brain. It is foolish to invest so much to accomplish something you should not want to accomplish."[62]

Carter invested rather heavily in modernizing the command structure; the idea was to offset vulnerability by adding redundant communication links. Reagan spent even more to the same end. One can applaud the redundancy but worry about side effects, including a loosening of central control of the command system. Just what the optimal degree of control may be lies in the eyes of the beholder. Tight control, it is argued, could paralyze the command system in an emergency. But the looser structure could deny the President control over his constitutional responsibilities at a time when the country and the world depended most heavily on his exercise of them. "The situation is loose," says a former senior adviser to Carter on these matters. "There are people up and down the line who can fire the weapons—not alone, but with some cooperation. But there is no conceivable alternative. The President can't handle this alone. We are talking about 25,000 weapons out there. Carter did tighten up, but he also introduced some flexibility, which amounted to substituting some agreed procedures where before there had been only fuzziness. In a crisis, no one knew before what would happen. This was an effort to at least remove some of the uncertainty. Also, a couple of dozen weapons would have put us [the command system] out of business. That was the real window of vulnerability. We started pumping money into doing something about that. Reagan has done even more."

Carter's specialists found some disturbing defects involving the Minuteman systems, which were, in theory, being constrained by PALs that had been installed in the 1960s. But instead of setting these at some number that would (in the extreme case) have to be dialed into a computer before the weapons could be armed, SAC had set the PALs at zero.[63] In short, SAC had nullified a major constraint on unauthorized use. Also, at one time, four young* officers in charge of any two launch control centers of a Minuteman squadron could have conspired to fire off up to fifty missiles. (The scenario is, of course, highly implausible.) The other three such centers of that particular squadron would have been powerless to stop them. This anomaly was removed in 1977 by the installation of an effective backup to the PALs.

Carter's people, like their predecessors and successors, discovered that missile systems on board submarines do not even have PALs, because the navy has successfully resisted them. The submerged boats can hardly be overrun by terrorists or other unauthorized personnel, and the introduction of PALs, the navy feels, would imply a lack of trust in the officers who have been carefully screened for this duty. (The air force, too, has resisted some constraints as being a veiled comment on the reliability of its people.) Yet the absence of PALs raises questions about whether a submarine commander could manage a missile launch on his own (another implausible scenario). The answer is that he couldn't on his own, but with help from as few as three or more of the crew (the number being dependent on their nimbleness and expertness) he could probably bring it off.

The apex of the command system consists of four nodes. The primary one is the Pentagon's National Command Center. Its alternate is located at Fort Ritchie, Maryland, and is where the Joint Chiefs go during an alert. The third is Kneecap. The fourth is a "black," i.e., supersecret, node which was created by Reagan and is probably a caravan of trucks. Its existence is unknown to most of the government. Carter created an emergency backup

---

*Most of the launch control officers are first lieutenants and captains, still in their twenties.

node in the form of three commands: SAC, CINCLANT, and CINCPAC. This meant, *inter alia*, turning over to the three commanders (and their designees) the release codes and other materials required to send out a message to execute the SIOP. Briefly, redundancy has been added to the command system, but the price, if that's the right word, has been a corresponding widening of control of the wherewithal to launch nuclear weapons.

The authentication codes themselves are produced by the National Security Agency and kept in plastic envelopes that snap open. The President's football doesn't contain these codes; they are held by the military, as are the PAL codes. The football does contain other codes by which he can identify himself as President. This he would have to do before his launch order could be accepted by any of the commands. In theory, a legal issue arises here. A President's identification codes should also be held by his potential successors, as designated by the Constitution and public law. But the high-pressure alert system, with its focus on prompt reaction, almost surely precludes deference to constitutional procedure.

The President, if he decided to release nuclear weapons, could pick a SIOP option, but could not involve himself in the coded execution message. The message would be "formatted" and sent by the National Military Command Center (if it still existed). It would consist of about thirty characters, including the digital release code. The message would be read and also sent out over Teletype. In a few minutes, it would reach launch control centers and bomber commands. Reaching submarines would take longer because of the lag in their communications. A Minuteman squadron could execute the order in three to four minutes. A submarine crew would probably need fifteen to twenty-five minutes.

The risk of nuclear weapons being taken over and misused is seen by experts as distinctly theoretical, not a cause for serious concern. Nor do most of them worry about a bolt from the blue aimed at the Minuteman force. What does worry closely informed people is the prospect of a crisis setting off an unintended nuclear war—a crisis in which each side had an incentive to strike first, because each had ascribed that intention to the other. The hair-trigger nature of the present command system isn't widely understood, even inside the government. Those otherwise antipodean presidents—Carter and Reagan—jointly evolved a system that relies on "prompt launch" (a successor designation to "launch on warning" and "launch under attack"). In trying to strengthen deterrence, Carter and Reagan added to the pressure to strike preemptively in a crisis. The pressure was always there, as General LeMay's early utterances make clear. The military, understandably, do not want the United States to absorb the first blow if it can be preempted by an American strike. A president who wished to exercise restraint in a crisis could find himself pitted against a system managed by general officers who controlled the hardware and the alert network. Some of what has been done to the system in the Reagan era isn't clear. What is clear to cognoscenti is that the machinery for allowing CINCSAC to launch on warning—a less euphemistic term than prompt launch—is smoother than it once was.[64]

A crisis would generate huge and confusing flows of information. The effect would be chaotic. Either side could be misled by radar blips and/or intelligence intercepts, or even reports from moles within the other's apparatus. False alarms cannot be excluded, if only because there have already been some which, had they occurred during a crisis or moment of high tension, could have made matters much worse.

Most of what passes for strategic doctrine in the nuclear age is abstraction, not reality. The rhetoric used to promote doctrinal refinements such as "limited nuclear war" or "protracted war" is mocked by their implausibility. In a speech unveiling PD 59, Harold Brown conceded that in his view, "What might start as a supposedly controlled, limited strike . . . would very likely . . . escalate to a full-scale nuclear war."[65] The command structure is too vulnerable to withstand an attack against it. Any nuclear exchange would quickly become uncontrollable. A legion of critics, including some who know better, have railed against what they call MAD—the doctrine of mutually assured destruction, which they say limits a President's options to retaliation against an aggressor's cities, thereby inviting the destruction of his own. Actually, the SIOP (as distinct from official rhetoric) has always included an array of options, some with only military targets. Reality lies in SAC's version of MAD—*massive* assured destruction. The idea is to be ready to deliver the heaviest possible blow against an adversary, if only because there may be time for only one blow. Therein, SAC feels, lies true deterrence, and SAC may well be right.

The concern must be that SAC is in too high a state of readiness. The boundary between prompt launch and preemption—going first—is very narrow. Suppose that during a serious crisis, it seemed on balance apparent that the other side was preparing to launch weapons. Would the U.S. wait for a reconnaissance satellite to spot the plumes of Soviet ICBMs lifting off, or would the argument for striking the other side first—destroying its command systems and a lot else—prevail? The answer is unclear. "It isn't a question of cold-blooded preemption, but rather being able to catch him in the act and getting there first," says John Steinbruner, director of Foreign Policy Studies at the Brookings Institution and an expert on command and control.[66]

The supposed theater for limited nuclear war, if it occurred, is Europe. The American nuclear weapons deployed there are stored in between fifty to one hundred specially designed facilities, all of which are known to the Soviet Union.[67] If attacking, the Soviets would obviously try to destroy these weapons in their storage sites. And although each is equipped with a PAL, it isn't likely, says one specialist, that "thousands of locked weapons" would be sent out "into the fog of war."[68] Yet once the weapons were released from their PALs, restoring centralized control over them, especially in the heat of battle, would be all but impossible.[69] If control cannot be restored, the war cannot be limited.

Here again, doctrine—in this case NATO's—is far afield from reality. Limited nuclear war in Europe, as elsewhere, is an oxymoron. Many ex-senior officials—McGeorge Bundy, Gerard Smith, George Ball, George Kennan, Cyrus Vance, and Henry Kissinger among them—deplore the fantasy on which the notion is built, although the latter two, unlike the others, are not ready to abandon the uncertainty it creates until the NATO countries have strengthened their conventional arms. "I originally favored the idea . . . of limited nuclear war," said Kissinger some years ago. "But even after twenty-five years of experience with the idea nobody has ever produced a model of limited nuclear war I could support or which made any sense."[70]

Limited nuclear war has very little appeal for the Soviets. Avoiding escalation, they feel, would not be possible. They, too, probably have some limited options in their war plan, but most specialists feel that uncontrolled escalation is what the Soviets fear most and would expect from any nuclear exchange.

Another major Soviet worry must be the command system, which is believed by some experts to be more vulnerable than America's because it is more centralized. If the top Soviet leaders were removed in a preemptive strike, the country's nuclear force might even be neutralized, another argument on either side for shooting first. "Use them [the weapons] or lose them" is the well-worn admonition. The superpowers seem to be aping an old American cliché—two gunfighters face to face in a deserted street, each fearful that the other will fire first.

In late April 1973, Elliot Richardson, then Secretary of Defense, held a staff meeting on the very day, as it happened, that he was asked by President Nixon to leave Defense and take over the Justice Department. The discussion at the meeting centered on NATO's defense doctrine, and the idea that a nuclear exchange could be limited to the battlefield was argued vigorously by a fairly senior civilian official. After a few minutes of this, General Creighton Abrams, the army's Chief of Staff, interrupted with an expletive, followed by the comment, "One mushroom cloud will be reported as one hundred, and that will probably be the end of the world." At that point, the discussion drifted off onto other topics.[71]

Insiders worry about senior officials having less knowledge of and control over the command system than they think they have. As a hedge against allowing nuclear war to break out more by chance than by design, Bruce Blair, an expert on command and control at the Brookings Institution (and a former Minuteman launch control officer), advocates what he calls a policy of "no immediate second use." Specifically, he recommends withholding authority to respond for at least twenty-four hours. He suggests that "nuclear decision-making should not be reduced to reflexes and brief drills, but should instead be regarded as a careful deliberative exercise of national leadership."[72]

This "fix" has been roundly criticized. It collides with articles of faith; deterrence, for example, is thought to depend on the certainty of prompt retribution. Also, in a serious enemy attack, it's unlikely that America's bombers and land-based missiles would survive for twenty-four hours. However, the missile-firing submarines already at sea would survive and be able to deliver close to four thousand warheads.

The idea of a twenty-four-hour hold, or some variant, is probably visionary. Still, the instability of the present system, with its dependence on prompt launch—whatever that means—highlights the need for a different policy—for one that stresses patience and stability. So far, no American President has seriously considered using nuclear weapons in a crisis (pace Richard Nixon). The ones who did confront the issue had plenty of time in which to decide, and it would be folly to allow the pressure of doctrinal thinking to limit some other President's time for reflection. For now, we have what some have called a "tradition of nonuse," not to mention a more benign East-West environment. Therein may lie the real protection against the vagaries of policy and fortune.

XI

The Inconstant Presidency

In choosing Jimmy Carter over Gerald Ford, the voters in 1976 selected a man who, running as an outsider, impressed them as refreshingly innocent of Washington connections and the ways of the city. The voters were right. Carter was something of an innocent, and it showed, not least in his management of East-West issues. He arrived with little sensitivity to what had gone on before. That in itself wasn't unusual. Most presidents do take an oddly proprietary approach to the superpower relationship—as if no predecessor had grappled seriously or imaginatively with it. This tendency is reinforced by the lack of continuity within the government. With any new President comes a new national security team, the members of which in most cases are keen to make their mark before returning to some university or law firm.

Carter had even less perspective on the past than most incoming presidents. From the first, he spoke and acted as if he knew best. Men like Paul Nitze who had devoted their careers to national security were dealt with cavalierly if their views diverged from Carter's. Not that Carter was under any obligation to adopt Nitze's views, which were at considerable variance with his own and those of most of his foreign policy team; but at a time when the Nitze viewpoint was prospering, it was foolish and self-injurious to deny any of its partisans a role. Insiders could have warned Carter, and did; but he wasn't listening.

Among the things Carter didn't understand was that in dealing with the Communist bloc a conservative Republican president had more latitude than a centrist Democrat who, if he is also an avowed disarmer, is sure to find the going heavy. Nor did he understand that lacking a track record, *inter alia,* he didn't have a solid base even within his own party. Like most leaders, Carter was a blend of pluses and minuses. His political gift fell short of the job. Like Nixon, he never made contact with Washington and remained something of a provincial—determined to show the town how to run the government.

His memoirs show belated recognition of the problem: "Having run deliberately and profitably as one who had never been part of the Washington scene, I was not particularly eager to change my attitude after becoming President. This proved to be a mistake . . . I realized the potential benefit to be derived from solid relationships with the Washington leaders who helped to shape public attitudes, but I thought that doing the best job possible in the White House would be enough to gain their support . . . I had not been in office a week before the top Democratic leaders in both Houses, Speaker Tip O'Neill and Majority Leader Robert Byrd, were complaining to the press that they were not adequately consulted. It seemed that Congress had an insatiable desire for consultation, which, despite all our efforts, we were never able to meet."[1]

Carter's approach to issues was moderate, his grasp of them impressive. He had a stubborn determination to do the right thing. What he mainly lacked were political judgment and steadiness. His sharp intelligence had no solid bottom to it. As President, Carter was over his head. His term was remarkably episodic. A procession of crises and minicrises—some self-inflicted—crowded him and his senior people. Although many, perhaps most of them, were not only capable but better qualified than their immediate predecessors, the chemistry at the upper reaches of the administration was very poor. For that, Carter and his National Security Adviser, Zbigniew Brzezinski, were largely to blame. The Carter White House was even more inept and overeager than it was unlucky. No other had managed to provoke Congress, allied governments, and the other superpower to the same extent at the same time. Put differently, Carter's foreign policy team was stronger at the fringes than in the middle. And by far the weakest point was the centerpiece: Carter himself. His presidency, like his pursuit of nuclear arms control, ended sadly, as a patch of truly bad luck added to the deposit of damage already done.

When Carter appeared, arms control had become fully respectable but not so nuclear disarmament, which struck some people as undesirable, others as utopian, and many as both. Carter's rhetoric had placed him with the disarmers. He made the first in a series of gaffes on the nuclear issue even before the inauguration. On January 12, 1977, he and a few of his senior appointees were being briefed at Blair House by the Joint Chiefs on nuclear matters, including the command system. Carter remarked at one point that he didn't intend to be cramped by doctrinal thinking. He then shocked the chiefs by saying he could envisage a strategic force of no more than two hundred SLBMs on either side. To propose a step that radical—cutting the number of delivery systems from nearly two thousand to two hundred— was later compared to asking a conference of international bankers to "solve the problem of poverty by dissolving their corporations and distributing their assets to the poor."[2] Predictably, the comment leaked, turning up in the Evans and Novak column under the headline NUCLEAR BLOCK-BUSTER. "Stunned speechless, General George Brown, chairman of the Joint Chiefs, stared at the man about to be his commander-in-chief" was among the breathless secondhand observations.

The event sent a frisson through the city. Carter and most of his people had little sense of the postelective politics of their situation, or they didn't care. They were aroused and ready for the fray. The intellectual candle-power of the national security team was high, but its political savvy, like Carter's, was in most cases low. An exception was Cyrus Vance, the new Secretary of State. He was an established and reassuring presence, having had a variety of Washington experience, including a tour as deputy secretary of defense under Johnson. Vance was not noted for his flair but for being sensible, moderate, and tested. The other key figures were Harold Brown, the Secretary of Defense, and Brzezinski. They, too, were known quantities. Brown, a physicist and prodigy, had logged roughly as much government service as Vance. His curriculum vitae included terms as secretary of the air force, director of defense research and engineering, and member of the SALT delegation; he thus arrived better equipped for his new job than anyone else who has ever held it. As expected, Brown proved to be very capable and had a huge appetite for the work. He was also cautious—overly so at times—and on critical issues sometimes politically unsure. Brown had been a better secretary of the air force than secretary of defense, although the Pentagon was run as well or better on his watch than at any other time.

Brzezinski had little direct government experience, but, like Kissinger, had been a prominent academic figure. Also like Kissinger, he was a natu-ralized citizen, a Polish emigré, and, his critics said, had a full measure of Polish Russophobia. Brzezinski was, in fact, a Soviet specialist. His strengths had always seemed to be a high articulation count and a consider-able tactical gift. He was less accomplished than such skillful predecessors as Bundy, Kissinger, his NSC role model, or General Andrew Goodpaster (who did the larger part of the job without the title), but he did have a fierce determination to dominate the policy process. Brzezinski became the first of the advisers to hire his own press spokesman. The NSC had come a long way since Truman asked Averell Harriman to join it in order to "help Dean—he's in trouble," a reference to Secretary of State Dean Acheson, who was under heavy attack from administration critics.[3] It has been no part of the purpose of recent NSC advisers to "help" the secretary of state. The contrary is more normally the case.

Brzezinski didn't succeed in dominating the policy process as Kissinger had, but he came close and did overshadow his rivals. Although Vance wasn't diffident, neither was he aggressive nor as "turf conscious" as his peers or as his staff and foreign diplomats thought he should have been. To have gone to the mat with Brzezinski would have been an unnatural act for Vance, but his unwillingness to do so weakened his position and the sensible approach he took to East-West relations. He probably should have gone to Carter after three months or so in the job and said: "Mr. President, it isn't working. You'll have to choose—Zbig or me." Carter liked and admired Brzezinski, but it's unlikely that he would have accepted the resignation of the secretary of state—not one as highly regarded as Vance—so early in his administration. Brzezinski's line was much harder than Vance's (or Carter's) and less tempered by experience. He seemed an odd choice for Carter, but it was an odd presidency.

Brzezinski's deputy was David Aaron, who had once served on Kissinger's NSC staff—on nuclear matters mainly—and then became Walter Mondale's chief foreign policy adviser. The Carter White House "didn't fully recognize how poisonous the atmosphere had become," Aaron recalls now. "We had to worry about Scoop [Jackson] and the Republicans. There was 'the Russians are coming' refrain. We were in for a rough time, and we were not aware of it."[4]

Carter's party was deeply divided. Jackson was riding even higher in the Senate and being strongly abetted by baronial fellow Democrats like Paul Nitze. A year before Carter's inauguration, *Foreign Affairs* carried an article by Nitze—a cry from the heart—which proclaimed nuclear superiority and "a war winning capability" as the Soviet goal. The article explained starkly why this goal lay within reach unless the U.S. set about improving its forces.[5] Owing to the author's experience and standing, it had unusual resonance.

In March, two months later, Nitze and Eugene Rostow, another Democrat and a former deputy secretary of state, decided to cochair a group called the Committee on the Present Danger. Twenty-six years earlier, in the same setting—Washington's Metropolitan Club—an earlier Committee on the Present Danger had formed to persuade Truman to increase defense spending and be tougher with the Soviets.[6] (After achieving success beyond their expectations, its members ended the association.) The new version—

a bipartisan list of highly visible men and women, many of whom had served alongside Nitze and Rostow at one time or another in senior jobs— was sure to be a factor as it set about alerting public opinion to the obscure peril.

Whether Carter thought his victory had blunted the assault on arms control and détente isn't clear. When asked during the campaign who his defense advisers were, he identified Nitze and Paul Warnke. The two had worked well together in the Pentagon under Johnson, but the views of the "two Pauls" (as they were known) were now far apart. Warnke was as prominent an advocate of SALT II and détente as Nitze was an antagonist. Anger and frustration goaded Nitze, according to some who knew him. He had been ignored by Kissinger in 1975, and he left government hostile and embittered. "Kissinger alienated Paul, and it came back to haunt us," says Roger Mollander, who was the NSC's chief SALT specialist in the Ford and Carter years. "I always thought Paul's attitude had roots in his feelings—almost a vindictiveness—about the shabby treatment he had got- ten from Kissinger. Paul had been a team player—always. He had delivered the Pentagon on the ABM Treaty. The [Joint] Chiefs knew and trusted him. He was 'of the Pentagon,' not just in the Pentagon like most other civilians. He was part of their 'us' in the us versus them. He was a formida- ble force, and could competently challenge the details of any position. That was one of the things that irritated Henry. He didn't want to take the time and often couldn't keep up with Paul on the details."[7] In 1976, Nitze contributed money to Carter's campaign, heard his advice rejected at a meeting of defense and foreign policy advisers in Plains, Georgia, did not receive a response to a paper on arms control that Carter had asked him to write, and, of course, wasn't offered a job.* Besides being opposed to Carter's thinking, Nitze was angry.

George Bush, a man with no previous intelligence experience, had replaced two professionals—Richard Helms and William Colby—as direc- tor of Central Intelligence. Hard-liners had drawn a bead on CIA National Intelligence Estimates dealing with the Soviet threat. Bush, a political animal, was sensitive to pressure. The President's Foreign Intelligence Advisory Board (PFIAB), a private group that monitors intelligence for the President, had been urging Ford to set up a rival team to do an independent threat assessment. Early in 1976, Bush yielded to the pressure that Colby had resisted and agreed to set up a "Team B" composed mainly of hard-liners from the right and far right to offset the alleged arms control bias of his own

*Others who attended the meeting in Plains felt that Carter found Nitze's extended comment tedious. It was not a successful meeting from any point of view.

analysts (and the rest of the intelligence community)—the "A team." (William Hyland, then Deputy Director of the NSC staff, encouraged Bush.) Team B drew up a competing estimate based on the same intelligence.[8] It reproached the in-house people for "not taking Soviet military power seriously enough."[9] The Soviets stood accused of wanting to disrupt ocean transport, the traffic of raw materials and fuel supplies; they were after "power on a global scale and strategic forces that would have a first strike 'war winning capability.' "[10]

Predictably, Team B's report was leaked shortly before the inauguration. Carter was furious, seeing the leak as aimed at manipulating him. Shortly before, he had met with members of the Committee on the Present Danger; the meeting had gone badly, and he may have blamed them for the leak.[11]

The debate was hardly new, each President since Johnson had confronted the issue of missile vulnerability. And it wasn't only the White House that underestimated the strength of the outcry. Years of worrying about whether one's own forces were vulnerable fed a swelling passion to make the other side's forces vulnerable. Nothing less than a nuclear war-winning strategy would do. A silly assertion about Soviet civil defense was the only new debating point. Looking over the abyss, strategy's Manicheans could see heavier Soviet missiles wiping out America's land-based forces with only submarines left to retaliate. But less accurate sub-launched missiles might be able to hit only cities which, thanks to the supposedly exuberant Soviet civil defense program, would have been largely emptied of their inhabitants. Among the hard-liners who took Soviet civil defense very seriously was T. K. Jones, who at the time was Nitze's chief "numbers cruncher." He and a colleague warned in an article in *Orbis* in the fall of 1978 that "to overpower the Soviet population defense would require a five-to-tenfold increase in the U.S. strategic arsenal." Jones later acquired some notoriety by telling the Los Angeles *Times* what he had been telling lecture audiences for some time: "Everyone's going to make it if there are enough shovels to go around. The idea is to dig a hole, and cover it over with a couple of doors and then throw three feet of dirt on top. It's the dirt that does it."[12]

Reality in the nuclear age is the stuff of trendy perceptions and often their victim. Gifted scientists and competent technicians are available to promote even the most farfetched argument. The argument may be vulnerable to ridicule but not to being deflated by facts; these are obscured by abstractions and unprovable assumptions. The notion of competent Soviet civil defense offers an example. Very little was actually known about the program, mainly, it appears, because there wasn't much to know. Jones and the other advocates were engaged in a self-deluding argument that drew far more respect than it deserved.

Over the years, the brotherhood of specialists, mostly civilians, who have made a calling of nuclear strategy has grown. They review all of the unknowns—unknowables really—that underlie the deployment of nuclear weapons and any conceivable use of them. They devise scenarios for protracted nuclear war and for limited nuclear war. (A comparison with medieval theologians is obvious, although the early fathers of the church didn't have applied mathematics to give texture to their creed.) Team B's technical consultants included Jones and Albert Wohlstetter, a brilliant logician and, as noted, pioneer nuclear strategist. Wohlstetter's early classified studies, including the first report on targeting (which revealed the vulnerabilities of SAC bombers to surprise attack), and his published writings were basic texts in a new literature. In the 1970s, he became the most visible (and credible) belittler of the CIA's estimates.

On the other side were those who, in varying degrees, favored a mix of second-strike forces which, on balance, they judged survivable. Most of them ridiculed the notion of a disarming first strike. "I have never believed in a bolt from the blue," says James Schlesinger, nobody's dove. "It was conceivable when we had just bombers located on fifty-odd airfields. But when we have 7,000 warheads on submarines, the idea that they might knock off 1,500 Minuteman warheads seems preposterous."[13]

If taken seriously, the first strike threat applied with greater force to the Soviet Union; roughly 75 percent of its strategic weapons were deployed in vulnerable silos, as distinct from just 25 percent of the American forces—a more balanced mix of ICBMs, SLBMs, and heavy bombers. Also, experts observed that for technical reasons missiles cannot be aimed at enemy targets with the same degree of confidence that is felt when they are launched on a testing range. Some experienced people warned that many of the weapons would not work as advertised and that a significant number on either side probably wouldn't work at all. "Perhaps the most dominant element in measuring nuclear forces against each other is the unknown and immeasurable element of the probability of major technical failure," notes Schlesinger. "It would tend to dominate any outcome."[14] The other risks an attacker would confront are, of course, enormous. The side attacked could empty its own silos if forewarned or use its surviving weapons to destroy the other. But common sense was no match for the minatory bolt from the blue; it had become the fashionable anxiety.

With the cold war less intense, the superpower rivalry was being shaped by tension between the buildup of nuclear arms and the stuttering, seemingly quixotic process aimed at curbing it. SALT, as Carter discovered, was becoming a lightning rod. The shrill debate turned on just how far to push negotiation as a way of heading off the Soviet threat as defined by hard-liners.

Soviet leaders probably have an easier time with arms control issues than Americans do. Full control is reserved to the Politburo, a body on which the armed forces are only occasionally represented. The debate in Moscow between the two sectors is rarely joined. And it's easier for Soviet leaders to see where their interest in arms control lies. A society that feels inferior to the West and intimidated by its past sees political and strategic advantage in the process; the point bears repeating. And a system that isn't working finds economic advantage in better relations with the West.

Like other nuclear issues, nuclear arms control is made to seem more complicated than it is. It is complicated, but no more so than, say, trade negotiations, and probably a lot less. Its vocabulary is forbidding, but what obscures the subject is dissonant voices. Compared to sorting out the problems of the Middle East and Central America, not to mention solving budget deficits, limiting nuclear arms is, or should be, relatively uncomplicated.

In striking contrast to civilian hard-liners was the changing attitude of the uniformed military in the 1970s. At first, the nuclear bomb was hard to fit into military planning. Then, the services began looking upon it as just another explosive device or weapon. "We've got nukes, so why not just use them and get it over with?" was the prevailing military view of crisis management in the 1950s and much of the 1960s. But the bias began to shift. Numerous officers who rose to higher ranks were exposed to a wider variety of experiences than their predecessors. Vietnam gave them a lot to think about. Several obtained graduate degrees from good universities. As civilian specialists lost their awe of nuclear weapons, uniformed colleagues acquired awe. Many were made uncomfortable by the glib manner in which the civilian priesthood discussed plans for using nuclear weapons in combat situations. Experienced military people were conscious of the lack of predictability, let alone control, in such situations. By and large, they rejected the notion that nuclear war can be controlled (just as Eisenhower rejected it in at least one news conference). A large segment of the uniformed military now doubts that nuclear weapons constitute a usable force and see them as strictly a deterrent—as discouraging the other side's use of nuclear weapons. The State Department aside, the government office most sympathetic to arms control in the 1980s had been the Joint Chiefs of Staff.

A president is easily turned away from an arms control agreement or understanding that he didn't negotiate himself. The temptation to do better is strong. But the negotiation isn't one that comes easily to big bureaucracies, which find the process workable only if sights are not set too high and if each agreement is seen as a step making possible the next step. The Vladivostok understanding was deplored by hard-liners as doing little or nothing about the supposed threat of a Soviet first strike. Bureaucracy's reply was that no one agreement could remove the threat. An accord could bound the threat, which could then be eroded further in later agreements.

Two days before Carter's inauguration, Brezhnev tried to reassure him about Soviet intentions. "The allegations that the Soviet Union . . . is trying to attain superiority in weapons in order to deal 'the first blow' are absurd and totally unfounded," he said in a foreign policy speech at Tula. "Détente is above all an overcoming of the 'cold war,' a transition to normal, equal relations between states."[15] The speech, Soviet diplomats said later, had been a major initiative aimed at the incoming administration, which, they complained, seemed not to have noticed it.

Soviet leaders would have preferred Ford to Carter. They prefer the known and predictable to the unknown. They loathe the discontinuity in American political life. For eight years, they had been dealing with Kissinger, a worldly figure with a rather European—hence familiar—approach. Carter struck them, as he did numerous foreign capitals, as naive and moralistic.

Still, with the American election at last out of the way, the Soviets expected to see agreement reached promptly on the Vladivostok understanding; for them it was a solemn event awaiting completion. Also, another accord could revive détente. Averell Harriman had been authorized to tell Brezhnev in September 1976 that Carter would sign a SALT II agreement based on the understanding.[16] But Carter's rhetoric, as in his inaugural address, about ridding the planet of nuclear arms, impressed the Soviets as having very little to do with Vladivostok. His pointed comments on the neuralgic issue of human rights in the U.S.S.R. troubled and provoked the Soviets. The relationship was off to a bad start and would not improve.

Carter himself told Ambassador Dobrynin on February 1 that he'd make a deal along the lines of the Vladivostok covenant.[17] He was well aware that Brezhnev had staked a great deal on the arrangements made with

Ford. But he wasn't keen simply to endorse an understanding made by Ford. Vance and Paul Warnke, who became director of the arms control agency and chief negotiator despite Jackson's strenuous opposition, favored a step-by-step approach, starting with Vladivostok. Others, including Brzezinski, Aaron, and Harold Brown, advocated trying for more. A good argument can always be made for a president trying to accomplish as much as possible in his first year, since his political position will never be stronger.

Vance was due to confer on SALT with Brezhnev and Gromyko in March. At a meeting of senior officials two weeks before, Warnke stressed the need to "get a handle" on the problem of the cruise missile "now, while we have control of the issue."[18] Carter's defense team was looking favorably on long-range cruise missiles—not just the air-launched version but also the sea- and ground-launched. Vance supported Warnke, but their colleagues were by then more concerned with how to improve the Vladivostok understanding, a notion that had rapidly gained favor with Carter. A new U.S. proposal, he decided, would require far deeper reductions across the board and lower limits on multiwarhead missile systems. New ICBMs, along with mobile versions, would be banned. But new cruise missiles would be permitted up to a range of 2,500 kilometers, although the Soviets for some time had insisted on holding the sea- and ground-launched version to 600 kilometers. Vance and Warnke were skeptical but didn't argue strongly against the revised approach, if only because they wrongly assumed that the Soviets would offer a counterproposal.

On the eve of Vance's departure, Carter upstaged the Soviets by offering the press a partial glimpse of what he would be carrying to Moscow.[19] Arriving on the 27th, Vance and his interagency party drew a frigid welcome, with Brezhnev attacking Carter's human rights policy and warning that interference by one side in another's internal affairs would block improved relations. He then turned the affair over to Gromyko, who rejected the new approach and offered no counterproposal. SALT was on the shelf. As Vance was leaving Moscow, Gromyko described the American initiative to a press conference as a "cheap and shady maneuver," seeking "unilateral advantages."[20] A senior British diplomat who was then in Moscow recalls, "When Cy Vance came with a proposal for deep cuts, the Soviets saw it as a propaganda move because Carter had already gone public. When they demarche and go public at the same time, it is mainly propaganda, and they assumed that's what the U.S. was doing. So you got Gromyko's press conference—repeated in the press and on TV for two days."

Carter probably surmised that the new approach could make a convert to SALT of Senator Henry Jackson, its most potent foe. Jackson and kindred spirits did applaud the proposal, but because of the world's high

hopes for the meeting, its abject failure was a shock. European allies, who
had been told to expect a somewhat altered version of the Vladivostok
accord, were alarmed, fearing that the new administration was rudderless
and without understanding of SALT or its importance. The verdict in most
places was harsh. "Too sudden, too public, too narrow and even too dis-
courteous," said George Kennan of Carter's first major move. "The Administration has made just about every mistake it could make in these
Moscow talks."[21] He spoke for the larger part of the foreign policy
community.

The administration was divided, hence confused, about where the
national interest lay vis-à-vis the other superpower. Carter's inexperience
was part of the problem, Brzezinski's role another part. National security
policy continued to be a growth industry, with the expanding role of the
NSC staff the most vivid and, to many, the most disturbing sign of the
trend. Brzezinski's agenda struck most insiders as different from Vance's or,
for that matter, Carter's. If Carter was reluctant to sign off on Ford's
agreement, Brzezinski was probably even more loath to certify the handiwork of Henry Kissinger, an old academic rival and a hard act to follow.
The first encounter with the Soviets fairly reflected the problem. A secretary of state, especially one as principled as Vance, is no match for a
resourceful NSC adviser with routine access to the President. The President may say no to him once or even twice, and then yield at the end of
the day. Access is critical; Brzezinski had it. Carter enlarged the problem
of divided advisers by changing course too often and allowing himself to
be seen as irresolute and inconstant. And, like Ford, he was victimized by
leaks, many of them coming from within the White House. The chief
source for these was Brzezinski, but Carter didn't seem to understand that.

Prospects for appreciably better relations between the superpowers
were dead. But SALT was a hardy plant. Even when relations dipped
sharply, neither the Carter administration nor the Kremlin lost sight of its
strong interest in SALT II. Over the weeks that followed his Moscow trip,
Vance had several meetings with Dobrynin. These so-called thinking-out-
loud talks were a variant of the Kissinger-Dobrynin back channel, and they
led to a three-tiered approach to SALT, of which the key element would
be a treaty lasting until 1985. It would cover reductions in the overall
number of systems and limit force multipliers such as multiwarhead missile
launchers. The second tier would be a three-year protocol to cover the
issues deemed not ready for longer-term settlement. These included first
and foremost the new cruise missiles and also mobile ICBMs and new types
of missile launchers. The third and less important tier would be a joint
statement of principles to govern SALT III. In May, Vance and Gromyko

"Isn't it great, dear? They'll have 1,320 missiles with MIRVs, and we'll have 1,320 missiles with MIRVs."

This cartoon reflects some skepticism about parity in nuclear warheads at these lofty levels.

(Drawing by Stevenson; © 1975
The New Yorker Magazine, Inc.)

*Gerald Ford's brightest hour as
President was here at Vladivostok
in November 1974. As he and Henry
Kissinger took leave of Leonid
Brezhnev, with whom they had just
concluded a major understanding on
SALT II, Ford pronounced himself
"euphoric." Behind them is Chief
of Staff Donald Rumsfeld.*

(TASS from SOVFOTO)

"So, you see, it's mainly a matter of timing and footwork."

*Some surmised that this cartoon
was inspired by the uphill struggle
in the midseventies to achieve
a second SALT agreement.*

(Drawing by Oldden; © 1974
The New Yorker Magazine, Inc.)

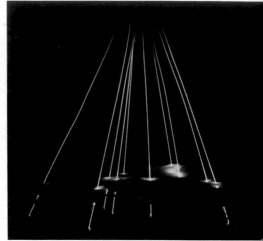

The controversial B1-B bomber:
President Jimmy Carter's decision
to cancel the B-1 harmed him, in
part, by reducing Senate support
for SALT II.

(Official U.S. Air Force Photo)

The "footprint" of the ten
reentry vehicles (MIRVs) aboard
an MX missile.

(Official U.S. Air Force Photo)

The Ohio, the first of the Trident submarines, awaits christening. Within the Pentagon and elsewhere, the Trident was judged by many to be far too large. They favored a smaller and cheaper design which would have allowed more boats to be deployed.

(AP/Wide World Photos)

A cruise missile breaks the surface of the water following a subsurface launch off the coast of California. The missile is, many think, the largest obstacle to continued progress in arms control and a source of instability.

(AP/Wide World Photos)

President Carter meeting with his deeply divided foreign policy advisers: Secretary of State Cyrus Vance (left) and National Security Adviser Zbigniew Brzezinski (right).

(UPI/Bettmann Newsphotos)

"He was reading an article about the neutron bomb. You know, the one that destroys people but not buildings."

The date of this cartoon (November 4, 1961) shows that the neutron bomb, which seemed so new and spooky in 1977, was based on technology that had been around for a long time.

(Drawing by Mulligan; © 1961
The New Yorker Magazine, Inc.)

The big four—Jimmy Carter, Helmut Schmidt, Valéry Giscard d'Estaing, and James Callaghan—meeting in an open but in Guadeloupe in January 1979. The secrecy surrounding the meeting, from which foreign ministers were excluded, was without modern precedent.

(AP/Wide World Photos)

Carter and Brezhnev exchange documents of SALT II Treaty in the Hofburg Palace. Carter withdrew the treaty from the Senate after the Soviet Union invaded Afghanistan in December 1979.

(AP/Wide World Photos)

This cartoon commented on the claim for SALT II as a step in a sequential process. Some officials envisaged future agreements as a series of protocols grafted onto this treaty.

(Drawing by Ed Fisher; © 1979
The New Yorker Magazine, Inc.)

ALL INCOMING
SOVIET MISSILES
OVER HERE
PLEASE

MX

NEVADA

THE ROCKIES

CHICAGO

THE WEST

MISSISSIPPI

CENTRAL PARK

THE ENVIRONMENT
MUST BE
PRESERVED!

A WESTERNER'S VIEW OF AN EASTERNER'S VIEW OF THE UNITED STATES.

Cartoonist Pat Oliphant, with a bow to Steinberg, comments on the so-called "sagebrush rebellion" against the plan to base huge MX missiles in Utah and Nevada.

(Pat Oliphant/Universal Press Syndicate, September 30, 1981)

Oleg Gordievsky, the defector from the KGB who performed exceptionally useful service for British intelligence prior to his formal defection. Gordievsky told the British early in the Reagan era about the KGB alerting its stations abroad to watch out for Western preparations for nuclear war.

(AP/Wide World Photos)

Defense Secretary Caspar Wein-
berger and David C. Jones,
Chairman of the Joint Chiefs,
during testimony on Capitol Hill
in October 1981. Jones supported
the SALT II agreement and
differed with Weinberger on most
issues. He retired in June 1982.

(AP/Wide World Photos)

Top right: Yuri Andropov, who
succeeded Leonid Brezhnev in
November 1982, anticipated at
least some of the reforms that
Mikhail Gorbachev is trying
to bring about.

(SOVFOTO)

Konstantin U. Chernenko re-
placed Yuri Andropov as General
Secretary of the Communist
party in February 1984.

(SOVFOTO)

President Ronald Reagan and
Soviet Ambassador Andrei Gromyko
stroll through the White House
colonnades. This meeting in Septem-
ber 1984 was Reagan's first
with a senior Soviet official.

(UPI/Bettmann Newsphotos)

President Reagan's grim farewell to General Secretary Mikhail Gorbachev after the failure of their meeting in Reykjavík in October 1986.

(AP/Wide World Photos)

Marshal Sergei Akhromeyev, chief of the General Staff of the Soviet armed forces, and a man whom American officials—civilian and military—like to work with.

(SOVFOTO)

*Secretary of State George Shultz
and Foreign Minister Eduard
Shevardnadze shortly before the
December 1987 summit. This was
a key relationship. These two
foreign ministers got on well
and found it easy to do business
together.*

(Diana Walker)

Reagan and Gorbachev shake hands after signing the treaty limiting intermediate-range nuclear weapons in Washington, D.C., in December 1987.

(UPI/Bettmann Newsphotos)

Gorbachev and Prime Minister Margaret Thatcher during their talks in Moscow in March 1987. Although poles apart, these fellow "revolutionaries" respect each other and enjoy arguing.

(Reuters/Bettmann Newsphotos)

"WELL, GOOD LUCK"

This Herblock cartoon in June
1988 makes the point that the final
Reagan-Gorbachev meeting was a
lesser event than Gorbachev's extraordinary special party conference
that came later in the month.

(© 1988 by Herblock
in the Washington *Post*)

met in Geneva and approved the three-tiered approach. They were edging SALT back onto the track it had jumped in early 1976 when Kissinger had been outdueled by his adversaries.

A few weeks later, Carter made a world-class political error. In a decision that surprised most of his defense advisers, he announced on June 30 that he was canceling production of the B-1 bomber, apple of the air force's eye and supposed replacement for the elderly B-52. The B-1 was among the most studied weapons systems of the nuclear age. It was derided by many, extolled by some. Critics questioned its ability to penetrate improving Soviet air defenses. Even if it could penetrate they doubted that, unlike the B-52, its useful life would be long enough to justify the costs of buying and deploying it. In the age of the missile, others argued, any new bomber is a pricey anachronism. The bomber leg of the strategic triad, they thought, should be removed altogether.

Heavy bombers are expensive, even compared with most other strategic weapons, and even more expensive to operate. But bombers offer advantages, not least their versatility. The weapons least likely to be used are nuclear bombs and warheads. Bombers, of course, can deliver conventional weapons in regional conflicts, an attribute that on occasion can be used to political advantage. More important, bombers, unlike missiles, could be recalled from a rendezvous with history. With so much stress on first-strike weapons, creating a new bomber—an unambiguously second-strike weapon—was regarded by many as a useful signal to send to the other side.

But even some bomber partisans opposed the B-1, arguing that cruise missiles launched from B-52s would stand a far better chance of reaching their targets. Other specialists recommended a mixed force—supersonic B-1s which could dash to their targets and B-52s which would loiter a thousand miles or more from targets at which they could launch their cargo of cruise missiles.

Carter had a menu of options, each of which bore political cost. Cancellation would cause the most trouble. The large B-1 constituency in Congress would be enraged, as would the air force, which had waited a long time for a new bomber. Others in Congress and beyond would not understand canceling America's largest strategic weapons program at a time when serious negotiations with the Russians lay just ahead. Still worse, to abort the program instead of trading it for Soviet concessions in Geneva seemed not just ill advised but foolish. Carter had campaigned against the B-1, but betting within the administration was that he would honor a classic Washington compromise—save money by slowing down the program and perhaps buying fewer planes. Harold Brown presented the options and expressed a personal preference for "not approving full-scale production of the B-1 but going forward with preliminary, small-scale production."[22] But Carter, the self-professed outsider, rejected compromise and so fulfilled his campaign pledge to cancel the program.

The decision was among the most self-injurious that he took. What Washington already suspected—that he didn't know what he was doing—seemed to have been borne out. Overnight he became not just the disarmer many judged him to be but a unilateral disarmer. The bipartisan coalition in the Senate on which the fate of a SALT II treaty would hang was instantly in jeopardy, as some members, mostly Republicans, began saying they would be unable to support any agreement with the Soviets made by Carter. "It was a terrible disappointment to me," says Gerald Ford more than a decade later. "My public support for the Carter approach to SALT disappeared."[23]

In Geneva some days later, the chief Soviet SALT negotiator, Vladimir Semenov, told Paul Warnke, his opposite number, that the American side should have waited "so that we could both have gotten credit."[24] Semenov meant that the two negotiators should have worked out a deal over the B-1, a possibility that no one in the White House even thought about. "That was our mistake," Brzezinski concedes. "Harriman was probably right." Averell Harriman, he says, told him that the B-1 should have been made part of the negotiation.[25] The Soviets, Warnke says, had inflated the airplane's significance. Gromyko had even argued in talks with Vance that under a SALT II ceiling the B-1 should have counted as two units.

Years later, some people guessed incorrectly that Carter had leap-frogged the B-1 in favor of the more modern Stealth bomber, about which little is known even now (the program is "black," i.e., ultrasecret) except that it's supposedly immune to radar detection. In June 1977, however, Stealth was barely a gleam in the eye, its exotic technology wholly unproved.

But Carter, it seems, was influenced by the argument for cruise missiles being able to do the same job more reliably than a high-performance bomber. Unlike Ford and his advisers, Carter disdained the more conservative mixed-force approach. Giving up on the B-1 meant plunging ahead with the Tomahawk cruise missile; both the air force and navy would deploy it.

Compared with ballistic missiles, the Tomahawk resembles a toy—eighteen feet long and only twenty-one inches in diameter. It weighs thirty-two hundred pounds. (The MX missile system weighs one hundred tons, is seventy feet long, and nearly eight feet in diameter.) Comparing cruise missiles with MIRVs is more significant. Both rely on very advanced technology; both are force multipliers; both can be destabilizing; both have enlarged the competition in nuclear weapons and created problems for arms control, mainly in the sea-launched version, or SLCM. The navy developed plans to deploy four thousand Tomahawk SLCMs, the majority of them armed with conventional warheads. Counting and keeping track of these could be impossible. Conversely, the air-launched version, or ALCM, can be reliably monitored just by multiplying the number of aerial platforms equipped to carry it by the number each such type of aircraft is capable of carrying. Airplanes carrying cruise missiles tend to be distinguishable from those which don't carry them and with a little effort can be made very distinguishable.

Cruise missiles were controversial, although the opposition to them was uncoordinated and barely visible. It came mainly from arms control advocates and the military services—two groups that are not infrequently on the same side of an issue, though as often as not for different reasons. Its numerous detractors doubted whether the Tomahawk would, or ever could, work as advertised. Its partisans, besides extolling the Tomahawk's economy and versatility, said that thanks to the miracle of Tercom—the "terrain-contour matching" guidance system—a once scandalously inaccurate weapon would be made "surgically accurate." Tercom consists of a computer and a radar altimeter and is supposed to allow the Tomahawk to fly safely at very low altitudes—normally between 100 and 400 feet—and to strike within 100 yards or so of targets lying 1,500 miles away. The system operates on the bold assumption that any location on the earth's land surface is uniquely defined by vertical contours, such as hills and trees, of the terrain. Stored within the computer are digital maps which display these contours at various places along the missile's preplanned flight path. By matching the ups and downs of the land over which it is flying with a stored map of the area, the missile, in theory, figures out exactly where it is and adjusts its course. The radar altimeter measures the missile's altitude by bouncing the signal off the terrain below. The missile, assuming everything works, can see and avoid the hills, tall trees, and other obstacles it encounters on the meandering, terrain-following path to the target. It must at all times be flying just high enough to avoid obstacles but low enough to avoid detection by enemy radar. But because they travel slowly, cruise missiles can be blown about and, being unpiloted, tend to wander and accumulate navigational errors. At distances of twenty to thirty miles—the range of many of the current antiship cruise missiles—the problem isn't normally a serious one. Over the considerably longer distances that the Tomahawk travels, Tercom must make many course corrections. The navy and air force worried that Tercom couldn't perform as intended except in ideal conditions. Moreover, Tercom relies on the contours of the earth's surface—

"terrain uniqueness" in the jargon of specialists. The flight path of cruise missiles attacking the U.S.S.R. would cover mainly flatlands, much of it as "terrain unique" as the Great Plains. "The Soviet Union is very flat," said James Schlesinger. "Cruise missiles would do well against the Matterhorn or the Empire State Building. A missile-silo cover lies eight inches off the ground. There is no relief around it. There is a lot of treeless tundra."[26]

The services also worried, with reason, that the new cruise missiles would compete for resources against programs they preferred. Bureaucracy likes to characterize projects that fare badly as "foot-shooting exercises." From a military point of view, rehabilitating the cruise missile was widely seen in much of the Pentagon as a foot-shooting exercise. The Soviets could be counted on to follow suit by developing their own second-generation cruise missiles. The irony was that even though the Soviets were reluctant to do so, they stood to gain more militarily. The benefits of antiship cruise missiles were clearly weighted on their side, mainly because they have more platforms of the right kind, while the United States deploys more targets of the right kind, notably aircraft carrier battle groups, of which the Soviets have none. Two former secretaries of defense—Schlesinger and Brown— feel that with both sides deploying the antiship cruise missiles, the advantage lies with the Soviet Union.[27] And when part of the Reagan Pentagon began building ships hand over fist, another part worried that America was creating targets for Soviet cruise missiles. They also worried about whether the sea- and air-launched Tomahawks would actually be able to reach targets in the U.S.S.R. Most Soviet urban-industrial complexes are in the interior of the country, while in the United States most such concentrations are on or near the coastlines. Thus, American cruise missiles must be able to travel much farther to their targets and overcome complex defenses.

Senior Soviet officials warned the Carter people against continuing with the cruise missile, especially the sea- and ground-launched versions. Since these could strike targets in Russia, the argument ran, deploying them would amount to a bald evasion of the limits agreed to in SALT. (The Soviets seemed to recognize that the air-launched version could be managed in SALT II.) They promised to follow suit, as indeed they did. (Today, from within the Pentagon comes the predictable warning that the U.S. must erect air defenses against the new Soviet cruise missile force, which American policy inspired.)

The Soviets could scarcely have been more impressed by the claims being made by the cruise missile lobby in Washington than allied capitals in Europe were. However tempting a small, cheap, seemingly competent weapon might be to a superpower, its appeal to lesser nuclear powers— Britain and France—struggling to maintain the credibility of their small deterrent forces would inevitably be far greater. Serious newspapers in Europe, especially Britain, began extolling the cruise missile as a "wonder weapon"—one that would "revolutionize" warfare. Carter's decision to cancel the B-1 bomber in favor of the ALCM seemed to confirm its wondrous qualities in European eyes. Yet by late 1977, Britain's military establishment had informally ruled out the possibility of rebuilding its aging deterrent forces around the cruise missile. The French, who hadn't been as strongly tempted as the British, reached the same conclusion. The weapon had failed to meet the rigorous standards of two countries that have limited resources and are disinclined to invest heavily in weapons that may perform well short of expectations.

As for the Germans and other nonnuclear members of NATO, their interest in American cruise missiles was mainly related to SALT. They worried that the Carter administration, about which they were already apprehensive, might give them up in SALT without a concession from Moscow that would reduce the threat to Western Europe from intermediate-range missiles; these were being upgraded by the introduction of an even more intimidating new system—mobile and MIRVed—called the SS-20. Europeans surmised that Washington might use the cruise missile, another weapon of intermediate range, as a chip with which to bargain away the threat from missiles targeted against America but not from those aimed at Europe.

Carter's relations with Europe's most potent figures—Helmut Schmidt, West Germany's Chancellor, and France's President Valéry Giscard d'Estaing—had begun badly. The two leaders were especially peeved and worried by what seemed an imperious and moralistic view of their civil nuclear policies. "Jimmy Carter came to the Summit having severely offended both [Schmidt and Giscard]," said David Owen, who was Britain's foreign secretary at the time. "His remarks were seen by the Germans and French as the expression of an American colonialism of a new and dangerous kind."[28] Carter's pronouncements on human rights abuses within the Soviet Union struck Europeans the same way and also worried them.

His relations with Giscard were never better than correct, and he couldn't get on with Schmidt, who considered himself, correctly, as the most gifted Western leader. Schmidt was also impulsive and censorious— as caustically judgmental in English as in German. Ford and Kissinger had made Schmidt feel that he was at least the coleader of the Western world, whereas the Carter people, he felt, were all but ignoring him. He would complain that they were playing with his chips and not even consulting him about SALT.

Americans who deal with foreigners, write Richard Neustadt and

Ernest May, "should 'place' them in *their* histories . . . Schmidt was only a half a dozen years older than Carter (and looked younger), but his political experience was incomparably wider. One of the ex-soldiers who made the German Socialist party pragmatic, nondoctrinaire, and able later to win support outside the working class, Schmidt had been a prominent figure in Germany since the early 1950s. His career had had ups and downs almost as sharp as Richard Nixon's. Schmidt's near oblivion had come in the late 1950s, a result of excessive passion in the losing cause of opposition to NATO nuclear weapons on German soil. He had recanted, had become a pragmatist in that sphere too, had written books which gave him high rank among 'defense intellectuals,' and had served a spell as German Defense Minister before becoming Chancellor. Carter and his staff should have been reminded of all that . . .

"But the failure in placement was mutual . . . Just a little reflection might have opened Schmidt's mind to the unpleasing truth that the new President probably knew little more about him than that he was a Socialist head of government with a frail majority, and possibly nothing about his country except that it used to be Nazi, now wasn't, but sold Americans too many cars. Schmidt might have expected to meet, as in fact he did, arrogance so innocent as not to recognize that *his* arrogance had some foundation. That Brzezinski was unlikely to orient Carter otherwise, Schmidt might have inferred from the barest glance at details. What was a Catholic Pole, son of a prewar diplomat—married to the niece of Czech President Beneš, victimized by Munich—likely to think or say about a German socialist born in the lower middle class and once a member of the Hitler youth?"[29]

Only with Britain's Prime Minister James Callaghan did Carter have genuine rapport. "Jim Callaghan had a wonderful handle on Carter," says Brzezinski. "Carter liked and admired him. It wasn't like Sadat, whom he looked on as an adored older brother. Callaghan was the uncle and knew how to play the role."[30] Neustadt and May write that "Callaghan managed to use Carter occasionally as the equivalent of an extra Labour Party whip."[31]

In late September, Vance and Gromyko met in Washington and began to fill in the three-tier framework they'd agreed to in May. This unexpectedly bullish news reinforced allied worries about Carter's intent. The attitude of most European leaders toward nuclear arms control was—is—volatile. They brood when the talks go badly and superpower relations nose dive, as was the case with Vance's failed visit to Moscow in March. But when the parties are moving briskly toward agreement, Europeans scent a deal that affects their security being made over their heads. Only rarely do they find a reassuring balance between too little and too much progress. All that is understandable, given Europe's dependence for its security on the guaranties of a country located in another hemisphere three thousand miles or so away and presided over by new faces every four years, or so it seems.

What Vance and Gromyko agreed to in principle was an overall ceiling of missile launchers and heavy bombers—2,250—and a subceiling on multiwarhead systems of 1,320.* Heavy bombers equipped with ALCMs would be counted within the latter entitlement, of which no more than 820 MIRVed ICBMs would be allowed. Although much else remained to be done, Vance described himself as "heartened and optimistic."[32] Carter himself was exhilarated enough to tell a Democratic party dinner in Iowa that a SALT agreement would be completed "within a few weeks." Vance and Warnke toned down that prediction to a few months.

Exactly a week after Carter's unguarded remark, Helmut Schmidt made a gesture, doubtless impulsively, that seemed to change everything. In a speech in London that he would like to have back, Schmidt called for a recognition of the need for parity in the nuclear and nonnuclear arms deployed by the two blocs. On the nuclear side, he wanted parity not just in strategic (intercontinental) weapons, but also in the lesser-range systems deployed in and around Europe. Americans called these "theater weapons," a term Schmidt loathed, feeling, understandably, that a missile launched from the U.S.S.R. at a European city was a strategic, not a theater weapon. If there was to be a negotiated parity in weapons that threaten America and Russia, he felt, then let there be parity in the "Euro-strategic" balance as well. Schmidt should have known better, especially since he was a bona fide expert on defense matters. The effect of parity in the nuclear forces deployed in Europe would be perverse: It would appear to remove the need for an American guarantee to use its longer-range nuclear forces in defense of Europe. The Soviet Union would be less deterred from threatening the continent.

However misguided, Schmidt's arrow did pierce Washington sensitivities and couldn't be ignored; something would have to be done about the nuclear balance in Europe, if only because Carter was already being seen as no pillar of strength in the role of the West's maximum leader. Even before Schmidt's London speech, fate had shoved onstage a wholly improbable issue that put him and Carter on a collision course. The question was whether to equip American artillery units in Europe with an enhanced radiation warhead (ERW)—so called because it was supposed to kill enemy

---

*The number 1,320 was agreed to at Vladivostok.

troops with increased radiation while reducing somewhat damage to property by suppressing blast and heat. Although never deployed, the technology had been on the shelf for many years and was better known as the "neutron bomb." Because the device was supposed to destroy people but spare property, initiates had mocked it as the "Republican bomb." (The Soviets called it the "capitalist bomb.") Actually, the weapon didn't produce much more radiation than the warheads it would replace, and its blast effect, if less than the others, was still very considerable. In short, the ERW was not very different from other nuclear weapons.

A series of articles by Walter Pincus in the Washington *Post* in the summer of 1977 described the neutron bomb and pointed to its impending deployment. Georgia's Senator Sam Nunn then pinpointed West Germany as the deployment site. The density of nuclear weapons located there far exceeded that of any other country. West Germany is carpeted with close to 3,500 weapons (American controlled). For years, Germans had suppressed anxieties created by the presence of all those nuclear weapons. But with reports of an infamous neutron bomb about to arrive, these anxieties shot to the surface. The reaction was visceral and emotional. "We were quite unprepared for the political storm that hit us only four and a half months after the inauguration," said Brzezinski.[33]

For Carter, the affair ballooned into "one of the most controversial and least understood issues [he] had to face . . ."[34] He postponed the decision about deploying the ERW. He and his advisers decided that if Europeans, i.e., Germans, wanted the neutron bomb, they would have to ask for it. But Schmidt wanted to avoid the political flak that would follow any move on his part to invite deployment. He hoped Washington would make the decision about whether to equip American artillery with a new American warhead. Schmidt also warned of trouble if West Germany was singled out as the only country in which the ERW was to be deployed. Germans are very touchy about what they call the "singularity" question.

In November, Carter sent a letter to Schmidt, drafted by Brzezinski, in which he spoke of delaying the decision if the Soviets chose not to deploy the SS-20. Since a Soviet turnabout was unlikely, the effect of the letter was to carry Carter closer to deployment than he wished to go. Schmidt remained noncommittal. Carter then telephoned him, and Schmidt, stressing the singularity issue, said the ERW would have to be located in at least one of the Benelux countries as well as the Federal Republic.[35]

In January, the administration told NATO that the U.S. would deploy the ERW in about two years unless the Soviets agreed to scuttle the SS-20. Over the next several weeks, Carter's people worked hard to obtain an allied consensus on deployment. They argued that he was committed and had mandated them to do this. Carter was being maneuvered into a position he didn't want to be in.

In late March, NATO was supposed at last to meet and issue an agreed statement of support for deployment. But just before the meeting, Carter instructed Vance to cancel it. Brzezinski now says, "Carter got snagged into it by Harold [Brown] and me. I didn't understand his position. I didn't understand that he wanted to abandon ERW. It was a failure of communication between the President and his closest advisers: Vance, Brown, and me. We thought we had his mandate. Had I realized he was dead set against deployment, we could have maneuvered to make Schmidt the fall guy. When I reported that we were ready to go ahead, he [Carter] was shocked and determined to go in the other direction. I should have read between the lines and understood [his position]. It would have been relatively easy to let Schmidt be the fall guy. He was the one who caused the trouble."[36]

Carter was between the rock and the hard place; his advisers were telling him that he was committed, but his European peers were unwilling to share the commitment except under conditions that made little sense. He decided to go ahead if the Germans and British would support him unequivocally.[37] Then while his emissary was en route to Bonn with this message, he changed his mind; he would not deploy the ERW. His decision was leaked, and news stories appeared on April 4, one day before Schmidt announced that Germany would support production of the ERW. On the 7th, Carter announced that he would "defer production of weapons with enhanced radiation effects."[38] As Vance has said, Carter also decided that he "would be influenced by what the Soviets did to show restraint in their conventional and nuclear arms programs."[39]

It was a proper debacle for which the blame fell partly, perhaps mainly, on Carter's advisers for having gotten the boss out on a limb. As for Carter, by confusing everyone—allies and advisers alike—with his abrupt reversals of position, he turned a sour situation into a full-blown alliance crisis, from which his standing there never fully recovered; the affair damaged him within Congress as well. Schmidt, too, paid a price for trying to have it both ways: avoiding responsibility for having deployment and not having it. The left wing of his party blamed him for acquiescing in the ERW, while the country's political right reproached him for Carter's decision to defer producing it.

When allies, Germans especially, worry aloud about American reliability, Washington reacts as if to a cattle prod, often overreacting. Carter's people responded to the dustup caused by ERW and Schmidt's London speech by exaggerating European concerns about the Soviet missiles pointed at their cities. Although allied governments wanted Washington to do something, most were not keen to have the new American cruise missiles on their soil as a makeweight to the SS-20s. Deploying such weapons in West Germany, where many or most of them would inevitably be based, would put Russian cities well within reach. Allied governments, as noted, wanted the midrange American systems—"gray-area" weapons, as they were being called—to be used in SALT to lessen the threat to them. There was no precedent for deploying the missiles in Germany, a move the Soviets were sure to judge deeply provocative. For them, the important facts of life in world politics include Germany's exclusion from the nuclear club. American missiles based in Germany and capable of striking the motherland wouldn't be quite as bad as German-owned missiles, but they would be perhaps the next worst thing. Bonn and other European capitals worried that any American deployment would badly skew East-West relations. The larger risks would be borne by West Germans, whose contacts with relatives and friends in East Germany, and trade with Eastern Europe, require a workable connection with Moscow.

Three distinct dramas were under way. One turned on the gray-area weapons about which Washington began secret bilateral talks with Bonn, Paris, and London. Off to the side were the SALT negotiators; they were making steady progress when their instructions from home allowed them to. But SALT was again becoming hostage to maneuvering by Washington and Moscow that now occupied center stage. Each side had begun making moves regarded by the other as opportunistic and even hostile. "Linkage" was still the shorthand term for the tendency of one side to slow down the negotiations until differences on other issues were deemed less acute.

As before, linkage was the most contrived of the barriers to progress. By 1978, it had also become the most unyielding. The Soviets must not be allowed to apply détente selectively, argued Brzezinski, the point of the spear on linkages. To gratify the Soviet quest for another treaty while the Kremlin was menacing pro-American societies in Africa struck the linkage enthusiasts as unrigorous and shortsighted.

Linkage pitted Brzezinski against Vance, who noted "growing public and Congressional concern about Soviet international behavior" but felt "that much of it arose from background press sessions held by staff members of the national security adviser and was self-inflicted."[40] Brzezinski saw "large international purposes" lying behind Soviet actions in the Horn of Africa. But Vance disagreed. These were not "part of a grand Soviet plan," he said, "but rather attempts to exploit targets of opportunity." Vance urged dealing with them in what he called the "local context in which they had their roots."[41] Brzezinski and like-minded members of Congress worried about a post-Vietnam hang-up that deterred Americans from defending their interests in the Third World.[42]

Actually, America was in better shape for coping with Soviet adventurism than it had been in the late sixties and early seventies, when the linkage argument surfaced: It was no longer bogged down in Vietnam. Domestic political pressure to reduce American troop strength in Europe had dissipated. Conversely, the Soviets were less well positioned to advance the dark purposes being ascribed to them. No longer were they the dominant external influence in the Middle East. That role belonged to the United States, thanks in part to the expulsion of the Soviets from Egypt, perhaps the heaviest of postwar blows to befall them. Their influence throughout most of the Mediterranean, like their naval presence, had declined. China was challenging them in Africa. But what was most worrisome to Brzezinski and others about Soviet activity in the Horn of Africa was its supposed effect on Egypt, Saudi Arabia, and the Sudan.[43]

By tempting ritual hard-liners on either side, the linkages notion infuses superpower exchanges with righteous indignation. Just as Carter's administration saw no connection between its line on human rights in the U.S.S.R. and SALT, the Soviets could see none between their role in Africa's Horn and the negotiations. The focus of the commotion in 1978 was the Ogaden, a desert waste of which most people in the administration hadn't heard, or if they had, couldn't locate. The Ogaden was disputed by Ethiopia, which had the jurisdictional claim, and Somalia's ruler, General Mohamed Siad Barre, who wanted it. He sniffed opportunity. Ethiopia's Emperor, Haile Selassie, was gone, and his successor, Lieutenant Colonel Mengistu Haile Mariam, was in Washington's bad books. Before invading the Ogaden, Siad Barre wanted a green light from Washington—an indication of support. When he mistakenly thought he had gotten one, he did invade, but his forces were routed by Ethiopia's army, strongly backed by the Soviets and their Cuban surrogates, and there was fear of Ethiopians crossing into Somalia. Brzezinski wanted to send an American carrier task force into the area, but the idea was opposed not only by Vance but by Harold Brown and General David C. Jones, Chairman of the Joint Chiefs. "All of them seem to me to be badly bitten by the Vietnam bug," Brzezinski wrote in his journal.[44] "It made no sense to attempt to bluff when we were not prepared to carry out the threat," said Vance. "In my judgment, the Horn of Africa was precisely such a case."[45]

In mid-February, Dobrynin assured Vance that neither Ethiopians nor

Cubans would cross into Somalia; Moscow had their assurances. The Somalis, although "increasingly desperate" in Vance's words, were refusing to withdraw from the Ogaden and appealing to Washington for help.[46] On March 1, Brzezinski said publicly that Soviet actions in the Horn would affect the SALT negotiations. The next day, Vance told a congressional committee that "there is no linkage between the SALT negotiations and the situation in Ethiopia."[47]

A week later, Siad Barre agreed to withdraw his forces and did so over the next few days. Vance judged it a "successful outcome." In linking the episode to SALT, "we were shooting ourself in the foot," he said.[48] But Brzezinski professed to feel that what had occurred in the Ogaden was the beginning of the end for SALT. "SALT lies buried in the sands of the Ogaden," he would write and often say.[49]*

The prophecy was a self-fulfilling one, according to his critics within the administration. The clash between rival foreign policy agendas was being felt, but not clearly seen. There was no disagreement over the broad goals—a SALT II treaty and normalizing relations with China—or how to achieve them. A return to triangular diplomacy was the obvious move. The two processes would be mutually reinforcing, as in the heyday of Nixon-Kissinger. It didn't turn out that way. Brzezinski was less concerned with playing off adversary powers than in cultivating one of them, China, at the expense of the other, the U.S.S.R. Perhaps he felt that only the pressure of an established and blossoming Sino-American link would fetch an acceptable SALT deal from the Soviets. Or he may have believed that such a link was simply more important. Or he may have thought of SALT as Vance's project and China as his own and hence the one to head the agenda; it may have been, and probably was, all of the above.

Add to the list the rising tension between Vance and Brzezinski. By early 1978, Vance knew that the State Department was losing out. Brzezinski held the high cards, and he was manipulating the system. His one-on-one sessions with Carter were skewing policy and weakening Vance's position. His background sessions with reporters were aimed at undermining Vance and sharpening their differences. He normally held these on Friday afternoons so as to "spin" the news magazines, which have Saturday closings. (In some periods, he leaked stories directly or through an aide on virtually a daily basis). He was very good at "spin control": He provided hard news, often misleading; he could be very personal about colleagues;

*David Owen, Britain's Foreign Secretary, characterized this Brzezinski view as "utter clap-trap. What happened in the Horn of Africa," he wrote, "was one of the best pieces of coordinated Western diplomacy we have yet seen" (*David Owen Personally Speaking to Kenneth Harris* [Weidenfeld & Nicolson, 1987], p. 119).

and he would put a story into a large context, which helped reporters. He discussed issues spilling out of world politics in bold brushstrokes. Vance, a lawyer, had a precise but unexciting and one-dimensional approach. Like Rusk, he had no gift, let alone taste, for spin control. He refused to build a firebreak against stories inspired by his rival, and more important, or worse, he forbade his aides at State from taking on the job. Vance never helped his own cause. Instead, he would carry his complaints to Carter, who would assure him that he had only one secretary of state—that he, Vance, was his number one adviser. Vance would return from a meeting with Carter and say to his advisers, "We're all in agreement. It's cleared up now." Of course, it wasn't. But Vance venerated the office of the presidency and would be temporarily reassured. In any case, he insisted on playing by the rules he had learned in an earlier era and refused to adjust to the bare-knuckled style of his rival.

The mercurial Carter probably meant what he said so reassuringly to Vance—at least when he said it—but he and his wife, Rosalynn, had known Brzezinski longer and better. Well before Jimmy Carter became his party's presidential candidate, or even well known, Brzezinski was tutoring the Carters in foreign policy. A strong personal link developed. "Brzezinski understood Carter's chemistry," recalls an official who watched at close range and concluded that Carter became dependent on Brzezinski even though their views often diverged. Moreover, Hamilton Jordan and Jody Powell, the White House staff members closest to Carter, were tacitly aligned with Brzezinski; because Carter was perceived as "soft," Brzezinski's harder line, they felt, would help politically. Many of the key decisions—not least the one to rescue the American hostages in Teheran—were made when Vance was out of town. It was not, as the secretary of state discovered, a level playing field.

Carter's erratic style enlarged Vance's problem; with less access to the Oval Office than Brzezinski, he was often blindsided. But even the White House staff could be thrown off stride by its impulsive leader. Brzezinski described a meeting in May 1978 with Hamilton Jordan, Carter's closest aide. "The impression has been created," he had Jordan saying, "that this Administration has pulled its act together. In fact, it's all a big accident, and who the hell knows whether the President will not veer in some direction tomorrow or the day after tomorrow."[50]

The Chinese were lecturing the administration about being soft on the Soviet Union, which was fretful about signs of improving Sino-American relations. Vance had been to China the previous summer, and since little had been accomplished then, there was pressure for another exploratory talk with the leadership. For months, Brzezinski had sought Carter's permission to make the trip. Vance opposed him, fearing, he said, "that such a highly publicized trip would bring into sharp relief the question of who spoke for the administration on foreign policy."[51] Vice President Walter Mondale wanted to go himself, and he, too, opposed Brzezinski's request. Carter overruled them and sent Brzezinski. The trip was very important to Brzezinski, he told Vance, and he asked Vance to understand his (Carter's) position.

Vance's concern was fully borne out; a trip that was to have been conducted in a low key became anything but. Brzezinski briefed the Chinese on American strategic policy and discussed steps for countering Soviet diplomacy that fitted Chinese thinking.[52] His visit was judged by some as a retaliation against Soviet activities in the Horn of Africa. At China's Great Wall, he called the Soviets "international marauders" and, by one account, "exuded receptivity to his hosts' suggestions that the U.S. and China make common cause against the 'polar bear.'"[53] On returning to Washington, he launched a major broadside against Moscow on the television program *Meet the Press*. Vance called him to complain about the remarks and repeated his complaints in a letter to Carter.[54]

In June, Carter put the China initiative on the closest possible hold. No more than a half-dozen people from State and the NSC staff were involved (plus Brown and Mondale). A special CIA channel was set up between the White House and the American Liaison Office in Peking. The normalization talks became one of the two best-kept secrets of the administration and proceeded briskly.* But progress on SALT—the other more visible half of the tandem—was anything but brisk. Washington's internal dispute over linkage was a drag on the process. Still, the expectation was that SALT could be settled before mid-December, the target date for completing talks with the Chinese.

As the end of the year approached, the two sets of talks were more or less in phase. Vance's stock had never been so high, mainly because of the Camp David accords, signed in September, which had put an end to the state of war between Egypt and Israel and for which he drew most of the credit. He was due to revisit the Middle East in early December and then travel to Geneva for talks on SALT with Andrei Gromyko starting on December 21. A half-dozen or so issues were still on the table; the idea was to settle these in Geneva and have Vance return with yet another major foreign policy success for the administration—a Christmas present for the country.

Before Vance left, a meeting was held with Carter in which it was

---

*The other was the operation aimed at rescuing the hostages in Iran.

agreed that the joint announcement of normalization would be made on January 1—after, not before, Vance and Gromyko had held their climactic talks on SALT. On December 4, the Chinese agreed to that date.[55] There was concern that to announce the start of a new era in Sino-American relations just before the meeting with Gromyko would be judged a hostile act by the Soviets, who might respond by sidetracking SALT. Several of Vance's advisers urged him to cancel his trip to the Middle East, arguing that to leave Washington with China and SALT both up in the air and Brzezinski capable of who knows what was just too risky.[56] Vance ignored this good advice. A few days after his departure, the last of the big tumblers fell into place in the China talks. On hearing the news, Brzezinski instantly informed Carter. "We agreed to move promptly with the public announcement," he writes, "and I called in the Chinese Ambassador to request that he pass the message to Deng [Xiao-ping], proposing that the announcement be made on Friday, December 15, and that Deng's visit be definitely scheduled for a fixed date in the latter part of January."[57] Given the risks to SALT, advancing the date of the joint announcement by two weeks made no sense, especially since the Chinese themselves had agreed to the January 1 date. Vance heard the news in a phone call from Carter. "I asked the President if it would be possible to hold up the announcement until January 1, as we had planned," he writes. "I thought it sensible to avoid this extra distraction in Geneva. It was certain to upset the Soviets. The President replied that he was concerned that the negotiations might become unraveled . . ."[58] Vance cut short his trip and flew home, arriving at the White House just before Carter's historic announcement.

A few days later, Vance was in Geneva for the meeting which, predictably, went badly. Once there, he was unable to obtain the authority he required to settle one of the thornier issues; Brzezinski and a few others blocked him. It didn't matter, however, because Gromyko's own instructions clearly ruled out an easy or prompt settlement of the issues; instead, he injected some new ones.

The television networks had been alerted that Carter might have a major statement to be broadcast live.[59] He didn't. The negotiations were on hold. A former aide to Vance—an admirer—says, "Cy allowed the event [the joint announcement] to occur. He failed to prepare the President on the connections between China and SALT. Carter had two alternative menus. Cy let him down by not fighting hard enough for his."[60] Vance paid the price. Among the effects, probably intended, of Brzezinski's strategic coup was the fall in Vance's stock to its pre–Camp David level. More important, linkage in the Brzezinski style had meant cementing the tie with China and dishing SALT. The events of December delayed the negotiations by five or six months. The treaty was not completed until June 1979. By then, a politically vulnerable document and an even more vulnerable administration were that much closer to the perils of the presidential election cycle.

The clock had become the enemy of the negotiations. A politically shrewder President—one more attuned to Washington rhythms—would have seen that further delay would be damaging. Had Carter begun by doing the expected—by cobbling together a "Republican" treaty from the Ford-Brezhnev understanding—he'd have been well positioned to take the next and bigger step that would have carried his own imprint; he could then have run for reelection as peacemaker par excellence. Carter knew that in yielding control of the Panama Canal, a brave decision, he used up a fair amount of political credit, especially with moderate Republicans. "My sense is that the Republican hierarchy has decided to go along with us on Panama and to fight us on SALT," he wrote in his journal.[61] Inevitably, the more sluggish pace of SALT played into the hands of opponents and pointed up the lurking question: Would two thirds of the Senate approve a treaty sent up by a president whose grasp of security matters was judged wanting?

Doubts of that sort about Carter began with his cancellation of the B-1 bomber (if not before). Among the other effects of this decision was the reawakened interest of the air force in a new missile system called MX (for Missile Experimental). Conceived as a successor to Minuteman, although much larger, the MX was encumbered by two difficulties. The first was the less than avid interest of the air force, which vastly preferred a new bomber to a new missile system. Second was finding a way of deploying the MX that didn't create more problems than it solved.

None of this mattered during Ford's time or the earlier part of Carter's. The MX was then a listless program. The air force wasn't pushing it, and knowledgeable elements of Congress, especially within the Senate Armed Services Committee, were unfriendly. Any new strategic weapon, they felt, had to be able to survive an attack; that was the first requirement. But the air force was still comfortable with putting missiles, whether new or old ones, in fixed silos. The air force doubted the Soviet ability to neutralize the Minuteman force in a first strike. Yet it, too, was interested in having a "silo buster"—a weapon that could do to Soviet silos what Soviet ICBMs could do to any Minuteman silos they managed to hit. The MX had been conceived as that weapon—as a device for waging limited nuclear war, i.e., destroying a major part of the enemy's strategic forces. The idea was to have three hundred MXs, each equipped with ten warheads and each capable of hitting a target 8,000 miles away with remarkable accuracy. These three thousand warheads would menace Soviet ICBMs, just as the latter could eventually menace their American counterparts. The effect would be to set both forces on a hair trigger, since in a crisis atmosphere each side would feel pressure to destroy the other's ICBMs before its own were blown away.

Creating this use-them-or-lose-them *Anschauung* was strongly opposed by members of Congress, officials, and bureaucrats. The pressure on the Soviets to hit first would be greater, since, as noted, so much more of their strategic power resides in vulnerable missile silos. In short, the MX, as envisaged, was deplored as an agent of instability. It posed the fundamental question: What is the purpose of nuclear weapons? To deter the other side's nuclear weapons? Or to limit the damage he can do by damaging him first? In a crisis, limiting damage to oneself would dictate shooting first. "Damage limitation" is another of the jargon phrases and more euphemistic than most. The damage from an attack by either side of the other's missile forces would hardly be limited, not to mention the devastation of the more general nuclear war that would ensue.

The executive branch was confused about where to put a new missile if there was to be one. Some of those who, like the air force, wanted to match the "hard-target kill" (silo-busting) capacity of Soviet missiles saw no reason to abandon the cheapest and easiest solution—fixed silos. Others worried mainly about vulnerability and thus opposed the silo option, but were hard-pressed to identify a basing scheme that did offer adequate protection for land-based missiles.

All this was mildly interesting but academic so long as the MX was becalmed. By early 1978, however, events began to budge it. The air force, after being denied its heart's desire—the B-1—was pushing for a new strategic weapon; although the MX struck airmen as a poor substitute, it was the only new program around. More important, the Soviets, as so often in the past, did the unexpected by testing a new guidance package on the SS-18, their heaviest missile, which imparted far greater accuracy—first-strike accuracy, or so it appeared. They had deployed just over 300 SS-18s, and these, if refitted with a cluster of ten, twelve, or fourteen new and more accurate warheads—the system could carry that many and more—would at last vindicate the persistently gloomy forecasts of Minuteman's impending vulnerability.

William Perry was then undersecretary of defense for research and engineering and justly regarded as one of the few star performers in the

Carter security entourage. The Soviet test, he says, "took the vulnerability issue from the back burner and moved it up to the front burner."[62] The expectation had been that the Soviets would not attain this kind of accuracy until they had a successor to the SS-18. The test, Perry says, suggested "that the threat [could be] on us in four or five years instead of ten or fifteen."[63] The Soviets also began testing their SS-19, another MIRVed system and the mainstay of their force, with the new guidance system.

It later turned out that the test results were misleading; the improvement in guidance was less than it had seemed, and the modified Soviet missiles would not possess first-strike accuracies. But the early tests, however misleading, set off alarms along the Potomac. A new bit of jargon—"the window of vulnerability"—popped up. It signified, as Perry recalls, "a time period after which the SS-18, with its accurate guidance, was deployed and before which we had an invulnerable ICBM deployed which could resist attack by it."[64] The MX became the great beneficiary of the window of vulnerability.

It benefited as well from Carter's problems. Some of his advisers felt that unless he allayed the doubts about him by building a new strategic weapon, the Senate might reject a SALT treaty. Vance says, "I had long felt, since the 1977 cancellation of the B-1 bomber, that ratification of the SALT II Treaty would be unlikely without a firm administration commitment to the MX program."[65] Put differently, the MX had at least as much to do with Washington politics as with military thinking. Yet since it existed only in a crude, unworkable design form, questions arose: Must a new missile be land-based? Or could it be a less vulnerable sub-launched system (SLBM)? And since both services wanted a new missile, why not create one that met both navy and air force preferences? That would mean a system small enough to be fired from existing launch tubes but large enough to give the air force its own silo buster.

The navy's candidate missile system was known alternately as the D-5 and Trident II. Its extended range—6,000 miles—would allow submarines to operate in a far larger area and thus be that much more difficult to locate. Also, unlike other SLBMs, the D-5 would be endowed with first-strike accuracy.

There ensued a lively debate. The idea of giving up on land-based missiles—and thereby denying the air force a strategic mission—wasn't seriously considered, although there was only one plausible reason not to do just that: the possibility—a small one—that submarines might one day be detectable, hence vulnerable, to antisubmarine warfare.

The other issue was whether to create a common missile, smaller than the original MX, or to have two new missiles. "My longest and toughest discussion with the President was on the issue of the D-5 and the MX," recalls Perry, who wanted to build the same missile for both services. "Half would have been air force blue, the other half navy blue, and we'd have saved a few billion dollars in the process."[66] Both the air force and navy opposed the common missile for their own different reasons, and so did Brzezinski. He and others felt that a new missile should be a big and distinctly land-based one—as big certainly as the Soviet SS-19. Brzezinski also cites the new targeting doctrine, PD 59, as a factor. "It posed a need," he says, "for such a weapon—one that could hit command bunkers, leadership centers, communication facilities and also population centers. MX in a survivable mode would be that sort of weapon."[67] But the navy's D-5 would also have been that sort of weapon. It would have had a similar (perhaps identical) warhead and similar accuracy, according to Perry. As then envisaged, the real difference was that the sub-launched missile was supposed to have six warheads, the larger missile ten. But the D-5, when deployed, will actually have eight warheads, and already appears to be a far better system than the troubled MX. "The D-5 removed the need for MX," says William Kaufmann, who has advised more secretaries of defense in these matters than anyone else.

Vance surprised people by supporting Brzezinski. His preoccupation was SALT, and he felt that the bigger weapon would be of more help on Capitol Hill, where the larger Soviet missiles were seen by some as locking America into an inferior position. The common missile aroused little, if any, congressional support. Some of the more hawkish members derided SLBMs as popguns, although even the smallest of their warheads contained three times the yield of the Nagasaki bomb.

Once Carter approved the big MX, it entered its rococo period—a time when numerous officials involved with defense buried themselves in the task of finding a way to deploy the MX which met criteria that seemed as contradictory as they were unbending. "Deceptive basing" was the catch-phrase. The Soviets must not be allowed to find the new missiles. Yet these would have to be visible for SALT purposes, which meant making sure the Soviets could count the number actually deployed. And whatever deceptive-basing method was chosen must not rob the MX of the silo-busting accuracy it would have in fixed silos. The problem generated hundreds of ideas. One that was in vogue for a time called for concealing each MX in a fifty-mile covered trench through which it would randomly travel; each trench would be separated by two or three miles from the next, which meant creating about two thousand miles of shielded trench. Apart from using up an inordinate amount of land, the method contained huge flaws that should have been instantly obvious: If attacked, it would propagate the blast effects it was supposed to resist, and enemy agents could plant sensory devices that would locate the missile's position.

Finding a home for the MX was ludicrous, because there was no sensible or acceptable home for it. At one point, there appeared a Pentagon chart illustrating the twenty-eight least-unpromising alternatives. Several of these were sea-based, including one called "Orca," which would have had missiles anchored offshore in capsules until a launch order arrived, at which point the capsule would float to the surface and fire. Another—the "Hydra"—had missiles floating unattended in the ocean until ordered to launch. Still another option was called "sandy silos." "On command," said the chart, "pressurized water fluidizes sand and capsule floats up. At surface, capsule opens and launches missile." One that appeared and then reappeared was known as "Pools." The missiles would have been randomly shuffled among 4,600 opaque-water pools covering an area of 5,000 square miles. The idea was ruled out, says the chart, "because of its heavy requirement for water in an arid area; water to fill the pools and replenish evaporation losses." Dirigibles, seaplanes, trucks, and commercial railroads were all considered, but, predictably, found to be unsuited to the improbable role. Discussion of most options was accompanied by snickering and giggling. Critics of land-based missiles felt vindicated; most considered mobile versions as fifth-rate submarines. "We were looking at it through technology blinders," says Perry, "and not seeing the political considerations."[68]

By the spring of 1979, hundreds of millions of dollars had been spent on the MX. Early in June, Carter complained that Brzezinski "was jamming a decision down his throat . . . namely . . . a new big missile and . . . a complicated trench system for basing . . ."[69]

Four days later, Carter announced his decision to go forward with the MX. The basing issue was postponed until after the summit meeting with Brezhnev later that month.

The basing scheme later settled on was one of several variants of the shell game under consideration. In this case, each of two hundred missiles, or peas, would be mounted on a huge 700,000-pound vehicle that would move at random between twenty-three shelters on its own private loop of roadway. At times, the missile and its launcher would be made visible, through ports in the roofs of the shelters, and thus could be seen by Soviet surveillance and meet SALT's verification requirements. The plan was to create a network of two hundred separate roadways and 4,600 shelters in remote parts of Utah and Nevada; roughly three thousand miles of special reinforced roadbed would be required.[70]

By most estimates, the basing scheme would have been the largest public works project ever undertaken. It confused the Congress, especially the Senate; some senators opposed the MX but supported SALT and hence agreed to acquiesce since, as some have said, the MX and SALT were a shotgun marriage. "I think that this [MX] is the kind of technological exotica that large organizations can get caught up in," said Senator Daniel Patrick Moynihan, the New York Democrat (and rather a hard-liner); "it's only when everyone else sees it that they look up and say: 'That's crazy.' "[71]

Paul Warnke recalls that shortly before he resigned as chief arms control negotiator and head of the arms control agency, Carter told him that he had to preserve the option but would never build the MX.[72] The Pentagon was estimating the cost of the system at $33 billion. The Congressional Budget Office's estimate was $60 billion. Other estimates were much higher. Carter's defense advisers, in George Santayana's terms, were redoubling their efforts while losing sight of their goals.

The MX, with its multiple shelters and its grid, would have to comply with thirty-three federal statutes, including numerous clean water and air laws and even the endangered species act.[73] Mountainous litigation could lie ahead.

> Put the weapons out to sea.
> Where the real estate is free,
> Far from you and me.

This Washington doggerel limned the problems of the MX, which, as Ronald Reagan would discover, were only beginning.

In just four weeks—early December 1978 to early January 1979—East-West relations and the affairs of the Western Alliance were blown far off course. First there was the reversal of SALT II's fortunes brought on by Brzezinski's China escapade. Next, in an even bolder gambit, he set in motion the process by which allied governments in Europe agreed to host American missiles capable of striking Russia. As in the China maneuvering, Vance was blindsided.

It began in October with a supersecret trip Brzezinski took to Europe. He had arranged to see James Callaghan, Giscard d'Estaing, and Helmut Schmidt. So well concealed was the Brzezinski presence that he might have been traveling incognito. To meet Callaghan, he had to travel to Blackpool, where the Labour party was having its annual conference. The town was swarming with press, but Brzezinski wasn't spotted.

The upshot was agreement to hold an informal midwinter meeting of the West's Big Four: Carter, Schmidt, Giscard, and Callaghan. Brzezinski wrote that Schmidt suggested the meeting.[74] In fact, the idea originated in the White House, as Callaghan's memoirs make clear, and probably with Brzezinski. "It was our initiative, but we acted as if it were Giscard's, because we knew the Italians would be pissed off" (at not being invited), he says. "It started with me. We needed to establish some sense of strategic direction after the ERW [neutron bomb] debacle."[75]

For different reasons, the prospect of a meeting suited them all. Callaghan and Schmidt wanted to promote the link between gray-area weapons and SALT. Also, as the meeting drew closer, the British scented an opportunity to take full advantage of Callaghan's close tie to Carter (over whom he still had unusual influence) to bid for a new American missile system to replace their aging force of Polaris SLBMs. They wanted the Trident SLBM, the newest and best of American strategic weapons. Overnight, the Trident would take on the significance to Britain that the ill-starred Skybolt had possessed in Harold Macmillan's day.

Giscard, too, had a stake in not just a meeting, but one that went well from Carter's viewpoint. Another of the best-kept secrets of the era was the substantial aid Washington was supplying to France's advanced nuclear weapons program. A process that had been denied de Gaulle started in the Ford-Giscard era and then grew significantly. In return, France was behaving more like an actual military ally than at times in the past, notably in the Gaullist years. Since the meeting was to be held in Guadeloupe— French territory—with Giscard as host, he intended it to go well. "Giscard reveled in it," says Brzezinski. "He saw himself as the intermediary between Carter and Schmidt."[76]

Domestic politics had a major role, as is usually the case with big departures in foreign policy. Carter and Schmidt were both looking ahead to elections in the fall of 1980. Carter would need European support for a SALT II treaty. And after the neutron bomb disaster, he needed to parry criticism at home as well as in Europe of his leadership of the Western Alliance.

The issue was what to do about the Soviet missiles targeted against European cities. To Carter's NSC staff, the answer lay in putting American missiles into the heart of Europe as an offset. "I was convinced by my staff . . . of the political necessity to deploy a European-based nuclear counter," says Brzezinski.[77] It would be just the sort of bold and improbable step that would fully respond to Schmidt's worries and Carter's need to cut a larger figure and disguise his weaknesses. The idea had been explored within the bureaucracy and in working-level discussions with allies. But it hadn't had high-level attention, let alone approval.

The meeting at Guadeloupe would fix that, and it was somehow arranged that the four leaders would not be distracted by whatever caveats or reservations their foreign ministers might have. This meeting's unique attribute would be the absence of ministers. The leaders would be accompanied by only their own senior security advisers—Brzezinski and his counterparts at Whitehall, the Elysée Palace, and the Federal Chancellory in Bonn. "Vance was very upset," recalls one of his advisers. "He felt for the first time that he was being excluded, even humiliated. He was as close as Vance could be to being emotionally upset. It was perhaps the first of the 'resignable' issues."[78]

Brzezinski confirms that the meeting in Guadeloupe produced the decision to put the American missiles into Europe.[79] "They never discussed the first question: Should we do this at all?" says David Aaron, who as deputy NSC adviser also played a major role. "They only discussed the mix of force options. Whether the weapons should be all U.S. And what the mix of GLCMs and Pershing II ballistic missiles should be . . ."[80] Schmidt went along with it, but his main concern was avoiding singularity.

Carter recalled applying pressure. "I pointed out that we must meet the Soviet threat on intermediate-range missiles . . . but that no European leader had been willing to accept on their soil our neutron weapons, ground-launched cruise missiles, or the Pershing II medium-range missiles."[81]

"The four of them sat in a bungalow very informally with no note takers," says Brzezinski. "I was called in once—during an SS-20 discussion—and I briefed them on the Pershings and GLCMs."[82]

What Schmidt and Callaghan had wanted was agreement that with SALT II signed and ratified, which they took for granted, the Soviet missiles aimed at them would be bargained away in SALT III. They had neither sought nor reckoned on a hardware solution to the SS-20 problem.

Yet they went along with the Americans. "Schmidt felt that SALT II would produce SALT III, and the need to deploy wouldn't arise," recalls Günther van Well, who at the time was state secretary in the West German Foreign Ministry and the most closely involved of Schmidt's diplomats. "And, like Carter, he must have been attracted at Guadeloupe to the idea of silencing the Christian Democrats [his political opposition], only to find that he had caused trouble within his own party."[83] Briefly, Schmidt was determined that if there was credit to be earned at home from this sort of response to the SS-20s, Carter wouldn't be the only beneficiary.

The SS-20 was a problem for Schmidt. It was more of a political than a military threat. The older Soviet missiles it had been designed to replace could destroy Europe as surely as the mobile, MIRVed SS-20 could. Specialists at State and Defense said the SS-20 would "only bounce the rubble," and before the neutron bomb affair (and, by and large, even afterward), neither agency saw much to be gained by spending $5 billion to put missiles into Europe; they would add nothing useful to the target coverage already provided by offshore American weapons, i.e., submarine-based missiles. But in Europe, Germany especially, the SS-20 was seen as particularly menacing and seemed to require a response of some kind. Schmidt, too, had an election to think about.

Callaghan was even less likely to question Carter than Schmidt. He and his advisers badly wanted the Trident, and their expectations weren't high. Britain's entire postwar experience with its mighty ally on nuclear matters had been dicey. There was the reneging on wartime agreements. And there was America's unnerving tendency to sell Britain a nuclear weapon system and then cancel it, as happened with Skybolt and then twice again. At Guadeloupe, Callaghan was looking ahead to a May election. He told Carter that if reelected he would probably ask to buy the Trident.[84] As they strolled along a beach, he added that his ministers hadn't reached a decision on what they wanted, but that he, Jim Callaghan, preferred the Trident. Carter thereupon told him that he would sell it to him and suggested that Callaghan put the request in writing.[85] (Callaghan hadn't lost his touch with Carter.)

Guadeloupe shook the State Department. Finding out exactly what went on and had been agreed to was difficult, even for Vance. "We never knew whether we saw all the messages being generated," says one of his former advisers. "Zbig had separate communications with Number Ten, the Elysée, and Schmidt's people . . ."[86] Brzezinski denies cutting out the State Department. Harold Brown says he didn't hear about the meeting until after it had happened. He doubts that he saw all the messages but says he did see some of them.[87]

In Washington, London, and Bonn, bureaucrats set about transmuting the outcome of Guadeloupe into agreed NATO policy. The cherished White House goal became an alliance blessing of a "two-track decision" to deploy the missiles while more or less simultaneously bargaining them away in Geneva. Washington was more than a little surprised by France's acquiescence, which would have been unthinkable in de Gaulle's day. But Giscard, it seemed, supported the project partly out of concern about a revival of German instability and, with it, the old tendency to play *cavalier seul* in Europe.

In Bonn, a major case of the jitters was being worked up by the prospective deployment. The lack of brio in SALT contributed. Over the spring and summer, the Germans tried unsuccessfully to defuse the situation. First they sought to bury the distinction between theater and strategic weapons by proposing that in the next negotiating round, both types be lumped together in a "single basket." The goal would be an agreed numerical ceiling covering both categories of weapons. But Carter's people had envisioned a quite different approach: separate ceilings worked out in roughly parallel negotiations. Bonn's single ceiling would have discouraged either superpower from devoting much of its entitlement to the less capable midrange weapons. Those America wanted to base in Europe had the serious defect of being far more vulnerable than the longer-range weapons deployed at sea and in North America. But Washington deplored and rejected the single basket, afraid that it would involve Europeans too closely in what seemed America's business: limiting strategic arms. ("We don't want them getting into our knickers" was the trans-Potomac line.) The Germans, aware of Washington's bias, argued again and again that any weapon threatening members of the alliance was ipso facto strategic. No one was making the other point: Longer-range Soviet weapons aimed at the U.S. could as easily be retargeted against Western Europe and thereby make nonsense of a separate agreement to limit those of lesser range.

For a time, the British supported the German single basket, but then abruptly switched sides, probably because they wanted to rock no boats in Washington with their Trident purchase agreement being worked out. And was there a link between the two-track decision and Trident? "The link was never explicit," says a closely involved British official. "People here [in London] were well aware of the lurking danger of repeating the history of the early sixties [a reference to Skybolt]. We had expected a very tough negotiation, but it turned out we were pushing on an open door."[88]

"It went so smoothly," recalls a British diplomat, also closely involved "Why? Why did we get such a good deal on Trident? With so little difficulty? Why was there no replay of the Skybolt-Polaris drama? Why did Jimmy Carter, who loathed nukes, want to spread Trident around? Why wasn't this used as an opportunity to drive us out of the nuclear business?"[89]

"We expected a lot of help from the British [on the two-track decision]," says Aaron. "And it wasn't necessary to link support for it and the Trident. The Brits were bending over backward to help. 'You want to deploy cruise missiles in Britain,' they said. 'Go ahead and do it.' "[90] According to Aaron, there was little resistance to approving Callaghan's request for the Trident. It was mainly a case of Washington not wanting France to be the only nuclear power in Europe.[91] Schmidt told Callaghan that he, too, held this view.[92]

Schmidt hadn't stopped trying to neuter the two-track approach. He proposed putting the new American missiles on some sea-based platform where they would be far less provocative (and also far less vulnerable). "As his troubles with his party group began, he started pushing the sea-based option," van Well says.[93] Brzezinski recalls Schmidt raising the sea-based alternative with him in Bonn, and says he reminded Schmidt that the U.S. already had submarine-based missiles covering targets of interest to NATO.[94] The White House was determined not to grant Schmidt what was then called a "safety net." For psychological reasons, the credibility of NATO's new nuclear force was supposed to rely on its proximity to Soviet SS-20s and airfields in Eastern Europe.

On one issue—German singularity—Schmidt would not compromise, and in the end he didn't have to. Somewhat surprisingly, the Italians elected to play host to American cruise missiles, doubtless feeling that the step would enlarge their role within the alliance. With great reluctance and under heavy pressure, the Belgians and Dutch also agreed to take part. In December 1979, NATO formally approved deployment of 464 ground-launch cruise missiles and 108 Pershing II ballistic missiles. About 200 of these would be based in West Germany, including all of the new Pershings, which could attack hardened military targets—command-and-control bunkers and missile silos—in the Soviet Union about six minutes after lift-off.

Over the years, Schmidt told several people, Paul Warnke among them, that he had never wanted the missiles. Instead, he said, he had wanted and expected a SALT agreement that would have removed any need to deploy them. The new enterprise was compared to an elephant mounted on a unicycle rushing downhill, with about as much control of its future.[95] The course it did travel was bizarre, as bizarre as the Reagan presidency, which it spanned.

The SALT II agreement, if ratified, would have buried the two-track decision (or at a minimum eliminated many of the missiles). It was signed at the Carter-Brezhnev summit (their only meeting) on June 18, 1979, an event the White House had expected many months sooner. There was little other business that could be done—not with Brezhnev, at least. "He was completely out of it," recalls Aaron. "Gromyko would grab his papers and do the talking. A wonderful moment came when Carter told Brezhnev he would name Tom Watson [Thomas J. Watson, Jr., ex-chairman of IBM] to be ambassador to Moscow. He extolled Watson as devoted to arms control, as a man of great wisdom and accomplishments, etc. He said

Watson knew all about high technology because of IBM. Finally, after what seemed nearly fifteen minutes of this, Brezhnev turned to Gromyko and said, 'If he wants to name a new ambassador, let him!' Brezhnev clearly thought Carter was asking his permission to name Watson."[96]

Five days after reaching the Senate, on June 22, the treaty was saddled with a serious handicap. Howard Baker, the leader of the Senate Republicans and a presidential candidate, told a news conference that he would oppose it. And he tied the credibility of his qualifications as a national leader to the role he would play in defeating the treaty. This was giving Republican moderates a harsh choice: Either reject their leader or reject a treaty that had been negotiated over six and one-half years by three administrations, two of them Republican.

Experienced Republican notables like Henry Kissinger and General Alexander Haig didn't help the situation. Kissinger told the Senate Armed Services Committee that he could support the treaty only "if it is accompanied by a vigorous expression of the Senate's view of the linkage between SALT and Soviet geopolitical conduct."[97] In tone and substance, Kissinger's heavily conditioned endorsement, like recent interviews he had given, clashed almost dramatically with the positions he took as Secretary of State. Haig's recommendation was "that the ratification of SALT II be held in abeyance" until a "firm, unambiguous demonstration of renewed strength and ability to lead" could be made.[98] (Their comments gave a foretaste of campaign rhetoric to come.)

As treaties go, SALT II was a very long and detailed one. But the core was uncomplicated, consisting of ceilings on numbers of weapons, restrictions on replacing or improving them, and a sweeping verification regime. All these provisions were mutually reinforcing. The ceilings held the Soviet Union well beneath its potential during the life of the agreement (which would expire in 1985). They closely resembled those worked out in Ford's time; actually, the larger part of the agreement was agreed to, or agreed to in principle, in the earlier period. Among the new articles was one that restricted new types of missile systems and numbers of warheads they could carry; it was widely judged the treaty's crucial element. A close second consisted of novel provisions for monitoring the agreement.

In hearings held over the summer, critics of the treaty didn't make a convincing case. The issue was really whether the country would be better off with or without the treaty. Without it, quite clearly, there could be a great many more nuclear weapons, more uncertainty, and probably less security. So despite Baker, the linkage lobby, and persistent attacks from Henry Jackson, the treaty seemed to have reached open water when the Senate recessed in August. Administration head counters were estimating eighty votes for it—thirteen more than required—when the roll in the Senate was finally called. It wasn't that the Senate had discovered a document of overwhelming merit. Or that SALT and détente were back in fashion; they weren't. It was more a case of having no good reason to vote against what was clearly a solid agreement of bipartisan provenance. Rarely, if ever, has the Senate gone against the President by rejecting a major treaty.*

In late August, the weakness of the SALT II Treaty's political moorings was made painfully clear by a remarkable event that seems no less so ten years later. It began with an intelligence goof. A training unit of Soviet troops—one that has been in Cuba nearly as long as Castro has been in power—was abruptly mislabeled an army combat brigade. By mid-August, the entire intelligence community had somehow convinced itself that the brigade was real. Brzezinski briefed Carter on August 14.[99] Vance wasn't informed until more than a week later. On August 28, the news began to seep into the government. Congressional leaders were informed, and all but one of them remained calm. The exception, Senator Frank Church, Chairman of the Foreign Relations Committee, was in an uphill battle for reelection against a hard-liner. Church was vulnerable on the Cuban issue; he had been to Havana in 1977, been photographed with Castro, and had commented favorably about him. He called a news conference and told reporters that the Soviets had placed a combat brigade of 3,000 or so men in Cuba. He wanted the President to "draw a line on Russian penetration of this hemisphere" and called for "the immediate withdrawal of all Russian combat troops from Cuba."[100] Church then suspended hearings on the SALT II Treaty and announced: "I see no likelihood that the Senate would ratify the SALT II treaty as long as Soviet combat troops remain stationed in Cuba."[101]

Had a so-called combat brigade actually been in Cuba, Church would have been borne out. Some would argue that he was borne out even though it wasn't there and nothing had changed. Their point is that SALT wasn't strong enough to survive many shock waves even if set off by events that turned out to be nonevents, as in this case.

Just how the government so thoroughly victimized itself was never clear. Such things happen, most people might say, because government is unmanageable and accident prone. "Appallingly, awareness of the Soviet ground force units had faded from the institutional memories of the intelligence agencies," said Vance. "It was a very costly lapse in memory."[102] He

---

*The League of Nations treaty was rejected after Woodrow Wilson urged Democrats to oppose it because of the amendments attached by Henry Cabot Lodge, the Republican senator from Massachusetts.

meant that SALT would be unable to stand up to any further Soviet provocation, whether the imaginary or all too real kind. Not many saw the affair as an artful ploy to weaken SALT, but the Soviets believed exactly that. One who may not have was Dobrynin, who had been in Moscow; both his parents were gravely ill, and he was irritated at having to return to Washington. He might understand how a mistake of this sort could occur, but he told Vance that he'd have trouble persuading Moscow.[103]

In October, McGeorge Bundy testified publicly that Kennedy had agreed in 1963 to the presence of a Soviet training brigade in Cuba.[104] The minicrisis faded quickly, but it nonetheless rekindled the energies of those who looked on East-West relations as an arm-wrestling exercise with the Soviet Union.

The swift pace of diplomatic life along the Potomac usually slows to a crawl during presidential election years. Incumbents are reluctant to expose their policies to unnecessary risks, and other governments tend to rest on their oars and await the outcome of America's interminable selection process. Even the chronic troublemakers will normally avoid provoking a sitting president in a campaign year, since there is always a reasonable chance that he'll be around for another four years. But this informal convention didn't protect the unlucky Carter. On November 4, the Ayatollah Khomeini's Revolutionary Guards seized the American Embassy in Teheran and made hostages of the staff. Carter himself was made hostage to a crisis more unyielding and irrational than most.

Barely a month later, on December 20, Soviet paratroopers invaded Afghanistan; other units arrived five days later. Carter called Brezhnev on the hot line and warned that "unless you draw back . . . this will inevitably jeopardize the course of United States–Soviet relations throughout the world." Brezhnev's reply—that his government had been asked to intervene—infuriated Carter. He felt betrayed.[105] A few hours later, he told a television reporter, "This action of the Soviets has made a more dramatic change in my own opinion of what the Soviets' ultimate goals are than anything they've done in the previous time I've been in office."[106] The comment played badly and turned into a political event. Carter sounded as naive as his critics had said he was. The incident isn't mentioned in his memoirs or those of Vance and Brzezinski.[107]

On January 3, 1980, Carter advised the Senate that further consideration of the SALT II Treaty would be inappropriate. Whether the Soviets had taken account of the effect of their action on SALT was never clear. Many experienced Americans felt that Carter had overreacted. "After all, the Soviets had been running Afghanistan for several years," says former CIA Director William Colby. "They didn't expect this heavy American reaction, and probably compared what they were doing in Afghanistan to what they did in Hungary in 1956—protecting their position within the sphere of what they regard as their vital interests."[108]

SALT was a casualty of extrinsic events such as the ill-timed Sino-U.S. announcement in December 1978. Brzezinski, as noted, blamed what befell the treaty on Soviet adventurism in the Horn of Africa. Others tended to see the phantom brigade as pivotal. It took precious time off the clock, as the interval between Senate ratification and the New Hampshire presidential primary (February 26) was seen to shrink. Perhaps more important, the brigade fiasco is thought to have convinced Soviet leaders that Washington was ready to scuttle SALT, and thus whatever happened in Afghanistan wouldn't matter much.

But SALT should never have been linked or otherwise affected by fighting in the Horn of Africa, or by the Iranian hostage crisis, or by the Soviet invasion of Afghanistan. In mirroring the rising violence in a volatile world, these and other unrelated events pointed up the need for something that drew the superpowers into a political process—i.e., SALT.

In recent years, Carter has told some former associates that he should have listened more to what Vance was telling him and less to Brzezinski. But he has also said that he should have paid closer attention to Brzezinski on various matters. The disarray of the Carter years now seems a bit tame when compared to the foreign policy babble that followed.

XII

The Abolitionist

Relief was the prevailing reaction of other governments to Reagan's triumph at the polls. Consistency and clarity would fill the void created by the inconsistency and uncertainty that had chafed friend and foe alike in the Carter years. Mark Palmer, a senior American diplomat, recalls having lunch the day after the election with a Soviet general. *Delovoy chelovyek*—"a man you can do business with"—was the Russian's opening comment. Soviets and West Europeans alike reckoned that Reagan's presidency would be a rerun of Nixon's. The truculent rhetoric could be ignored. It might take a bit longer, but Reagan and his people, like various predecessors, would rediscover the wheel, i.e., the continuities in American foreign policy. Foreign capitals didn't understand that Reagan and most of his national security entourage didn't believe in the wheel insofar as it represented the orthodox thinking that had shaped American foreign policy for twenty-odd years. They arrived with assumptions about the world that were different from those of all their predecessors, Republican and Democratic. This was especially true of relations with the Soviet Union. The clarity and coherence in foreign policy eventually did emerge but not until the last year of Reagan's presidency—after seven years of disharmony and chaos that exceeded any in modern memory.

Eisenhower arrived equipped by experience and capacity for the presidency. He was also a national hero and remained one. Reagan had none of these attributes. He was more isolated from the business of his office and less informed about issues than any postwar President. Yet he, too, became a national hero, as continuously popular as Eisenhower, and perhaps more so. Reagan's popularity was more intimidating than Eisenhower's. Until the Iran-scam affair in late 1986, he had a more indulgent press than any modern President, including Eisenhower who, because he confronted many more crises and difficulties than Reagan and made many more controversial decisions, drew far more criticism.

Good luck is part of the Reagan legend; he had more of that, too, than any modern President. The Washington *Post*'s Lou Cannon, who covered Reagan at the statehouse in Sacramento and later at the White House (and liked him), wrote in 1987: "In his Sacramento days, Reagan was sometimes called the 'great Rodini' for his wizardry at escaping political predicaments. He graduated to bring the 'teflon' president, a lucky man who found shamrocks in fields of dandelions and walked away from mistakes that would have sunk a lesser politician."[1] Reagan made many mistakes in the name of foreign policy, but none of them stuck, and he never had to confront a foreign policy crisis.

Reagan had many sides. There was the fantasist who confused illusion and make-believe with reality. In relating to victims of the Holocaust, he twice recalled having filmed concentration camps for the signal corps; he hadn't done so, but no one doubted that he believed what he was saying. He told of a World War II bomber pilot who went down with his stricken plane rather than leave behind a wounded gunner; it was apparently a screenplay he was remembering. It was another screenplay—*State of the Union*—he drew on when he uttered his famous caution at the meeting in Nashua, New Hampshire, during the 1980 primary campaign: "I'm paying for this microphone, Mr. Green."

Screenplays, unlike life, are linear and rarely complicated. The fantasist's exalted but uncomplicated view of America—"the city on the Hill" (a seventeenth-century term) he seemed to remember from another time—was a tonic. He was elected overwhelmingly by a society grown pessimistic and somewhat down on itself, in part because of events that were as perplexing as they were distressing: Vietnam and Watergate, credibility gaps and energy shortages. Leaders who had extolled détente and SALT turned away from them. What to believe? And instead of lifting the society's morale, Carter, the outsider, had further depressed it and then told people they were to blame for feeling anxious. Reagan will be remembered for having shored up morale and the office of the presidency; each of his predecessors as far back as Johnson had in one way or another weakened both. The fantasist, of course, converged with the entertainer and crowd pleaser—the best communicator since Roosevelt and clearly the best so far of the television era.

Years as president of the Screen Actors Guild created another side—

the pragmatic and shrewd negotiator. But when, in his midfifties, he took up politics, a struggle between the ideologue and the doer began. A former close associate—one who understands him better than most—saw it like this: "If you confronted Reagan with a victim of some cruel and unavoidable experience, he would be endlessly sympathetic and do whatever he could to help that person. If you told him there were actually 10,000 such unfortunates, with needs that could be met far more cheaply if dealt with as a bloc, you would lose him, because you would be talking program. Individual misfortune brought out the case worker. Misfortune on a grander scale brought out the ideologue. Which brings us to Gorbachev. Meeting the Soviet leader—an actual person—was an act of discovery and out popped not the ideologue who talked about 'evil empire' but the problem solver."[2]

In a time when power uses up chief executives remorselessly, this oldest of presidents was all but unaffected by the burden of office—at least during most of his passage—because he never fully shouldered it. Nor was it only his hands-off approach that was novel. Most modern leaders campaign on domestic issues—economic growth and welfare—and then, if elected, are plunged into foreign policy. Reagan campaigned in thundering terms against the foreign policies of his adversaries, whether Ford or Carter, but then all but ignored the subject—until he met Mikhail Gorbachev in November 1985. He left all that to others without creating a sensible decision-making apparatus. The net effect was endless skirmishing at both the cabinet and subcabinet levels, with no one, including Reagan, available to mediate remarkably shrill policy disputes between agencies.

Reagan extolled cabinet government, but during his first term the White House controlled domestic policy; it was then the best-managed White House staff operation Washington had seen for years. Instinct told the ideologue to let the gifted pragmatists around him, notably James Baker, his Chief of Staff, and Baker's deputy, Richard Darman, handle the key issues (outside foreign policy) and move the ball toward Reaganesque goals. "His image of cabinet governments clashed with his natural instinct about decision-making," recalls a former Reagan associate.[3]

Reagan said that he wanted the State Department, not a strong national security adviser, to manage foreign policy. As it turned out neither Secretary of State Alexander Haig nor the first National Security Adviser, Richard Allen, was a dominant influence on foreign policy. No one was. Reagan wasn't even sure what a national security adviser was supposed to do or what he wanted him to do. And he and Haig were an utter mismatch. In foreign policy, as well as some other areas, Reagan sought to resolve the conflict between his doctrinaire and pragmatic selves by having people of both types around him. As in Sacramento, he had decided against having one-on-one meetings with aides and officials. He wanted other people—both kinds—in the room, a style he brought to Washington and which Haig found more oppressive than others did. Haig couldn't adjust. He was used to giving and taking commands within hierarchical structures. He saw Reagan as the single authority but had no direct access to him. Like everyone else, he had to deal with a troika consisting of James Baker, Edwin Meese, and Michael Deaver; Deaver controlled access to the Oval Office, and Haig was rarely alone with Reagan; whoever else might be there would depend on the subject of the meeting.

"Haig couldn't deal with or even understand the reality of how Reagan operated," says a former official who observed them both. "He was in a constant state of psychological stress."[4] The White House staff was set on ousting Haig, who was not getting along with fellow cabinet members either. And since the NSC staff was weak, it couldn't perform its natural role of arbiter. The administration was a headless coalition, unified only by its rhetoric. The self-righteous hard line it proclaimed recalled the simpler era of the cold war when confrontation, as in Berlin, was a fact of life. Orthodox elements worried about what would happen when the nature of the Reagan presidency became apparent to other capitals. They were right to worry. Many other capitals experienced a sharp sense of disillusion. First and foremost of these was Moscow. The Reagan the Soviets had awaited—tough-talking but realistic—was abruptly seen as being dangerously unrealistic—as a man preparing to make war or assuming that war would come. The Soviets were frightened but took care not to show it.

Early in 1981, the KGB advised its stations in Western capitals that the United States was preparing to attack the Soviet Union. The stations were put on alert and told to report every scrap of information that might provide warning.[5] The order remained in force until the end of 1983. Washington didn't hear of it until much later—from information provided by Oleg Gordievsky, a senior KGB agent who became a British double agent and then defected in 1985.*

It wasn't any one event that alarmed Moscow but a pattern. Publicly, Haig called for "going to the source" of radical guerrilla forces and cited Cuba—and the Soviet Union—as responsible for the mess in Central Amer-

---

*Gordievsky was probably the most useful agent since Oleg Penkovsky. After becoming the KGB station chief in London, he was recalled to Moscow, apparently under suspicion, at which point Britain's secret intelligence service, MI6, arranged his "exfiltration" (the circumstances of which have never surfaced but are known to have been highly inventive).

ica.[6] Privately, says a senior American diplomat who was observing all this, Haig "was proposing steps—wild stuff—in the Caribbean [against Cuba and Nicaragua] that made moderates of Cap [Weinberger] and the President."[7]

Of doubtless greater concern was loose talk about nuclear war-winning capacity and limited nuclear options. In one way or another, all the senior figures—Reagan, Vice President George Bush, Haig, and Secretary of Defense Caspar Weinberger—helped create the impression of leaders for whom nuclear weapons held little awe.

The administration, said Weinberger in early budget hearings, would expand the country's capability for "deterring or prosecuting a global war with the Soviet Union."[8] Reagan's view was that the Soviets had long since concluded that a nuclear war was possible and winnable. Moreover, in news conferences Reagan inadvertently suggested that waging a limited nuclear war was possible.[9] And Bush, as a 1980 presidential candidate, had said that nuclear superiority didn't matter only "if you believe there is no such thing as a winner in a nuclear exchange . . . I don't believe that."[10]

Weinberger and Haig couldn't agree on whether NATO's contingency plans included firing a nuclear demonstration shot, and Reagan was unable to provide the answer.[11] Weinberger surprised everyone by saying, "Soviet missiles are now far more accurate than ours."[12] Aware that the reverse was still the case, the Soviets must have wondered what the administration had in mind.

Some of the specialists who entered the administration or acquired links to it could frankly envision a limited nuclear war or even protracted nuclear war. A State Department official who dealt with them said: "They work with what they call post-exchange scenarios, and some of these cover periods as long as five years. A scenario may assume eighty million dead on either side. The question is, Who is in a position to recover more quickly? The war never really stops; it goes on intermittently. One side gradually builds back its communications and its bomber runways. The other side destroys them again, with weapons fired from submarines that have remained on station, and so forth."[13]

Persistently shrill rhetoric had some effect. Soviet leaders, said Reagan in his first press conference, "reserve unto themselves the right to commit any crime, to lie, to cheat."[14] Anatoly Dobrynin, who as Soviet ambassador was then observing his sixth President, told Haig that this kind of comment would "cause great puzzlement in Moscow. I hope it will not continue."[15] It did continue.

The rhetoric was accompanied by an orgy of weapons procurement decisions. The SALT-related goals of limits based on parity were being set aside in favor of creating "margins of safety" that were supposed to restore some measure of superiority.

Communication between Washington and Moscow is rarely good, but not for a long time had it been as bad as in the early days of Reagan. He and his advisers had convinced themselves that the Soviets were testing America, although it was negotiation, access to technology, and trade they wanted. They were hardly inclined to confront America; there was Poland's Solidarity movement to deal with, not to mention Afghanistan, where the situation was going from bad to worse.

The British were not sharing either Gordievsky or the Gordievsky file with Washington, nor did they for some years. But some within Britain's intelligence community began asking American counterparts, in effect: Are you sure you aren't coming at them a bit too hard? As the British learned more from Gordievsky about the alert and Moscow's reaction to what the KGB stations were reporting, the warning got stronger. There seems to have been no doubt that Gordievsky was genuine (and very brave). He was also, according to one of the few Americans who interviewed him much later, "a very able guy."[16]

With instructions to overlook nothing, the KGB stations were logging the lights that burned in various offices of various government buildings to see whether key officials might be having prolonged meetings. Chauffeured official cars were monitored for the same reason. According to Gordievsky, his station even reported to Moscow on a blood drive held by the Greater London Council; it, too, might have been part of some larger and sinister purpose. Since KGB reporting is thought to be aimed at confirming views already held in Moscow—to bolster the current line—the British worried that the impact on Moscow of the bluster in Washington would be enlarged by the KGB itself. They had cause to worry. A major Hungarian official— shrewd, candid, and in a position to know—says that for their own self-serving reasons, elements within the KGB encouraged the view of Reagan as dangerous. And, he adds, the period of Soviet angst about Reagan lasted until he and Gorbachev met in Geneva in November 1985.[17]

On November 7, 1983, Grigory Romanov, who was the Communist party boss of Leningrad and Gorbachev's rival for the leadership, told a meeting in the Kremlin Palace of Congresses: "Comrades, the international situation at present is white hot, thoroughly white hot."[18]

And three months after his first meeting with Reagan, Gorbachev told the Twenty-seventh Communist Party Congress: "Never, perhaps, in the postwar decades has the situation in the world been as explosive . . . as in the first half of the '80s."[19] In an era when nuclear doctrine is labeled "prompt launch" (or "launch-on-warning"), the grotesque misreading on either side of the other's intentions during Reagan's first five years is worth sober reflection.

What the Soviets didn't understand (any more than the national security bureaucracy in Washington) was that Ronald Reagan wasn't an adventurer who saw nuclear arms as usable weapons; instead, he was an abolitionist—a far more convinced disarmer than Carter. Reagan was no admirer of arms control and its works. He wanted to have the advantage in nuclear weapons or else to rid the world of them. On this issue, he was a radical. At least twice in his first two years in the White House Reagan asked bureaucracy to give him a plan to eliminate nuclear weapons. Bureaucracy did not respond.[20] But Reagan had provided a clue to the path of his thinking during the 1980 campaign. "With all this great technology of ours, we . . . cannot stop any of the weapons that are coming at us. I don't think there's been a time in history when there wasn't a defense against some kind of thrust . . ."[21] Before very long, he would decide that technology could give America a security moat in outer space.

The administration was talking a tougher game than it was playing. Early in 1981, Reagan canceled the grain embargo against the Soviet Union that Carter had imposed after the invasion of Afghanistan. Reagan made this salute to the free-market system at a moment when the Soviets seemed to be on the verge of invading Poland and Haig was urging him to use the embargo as bargaining capital with Moscow.[22]

Reagan's letters to Brezhnev were not aggressive or even very critical. Moreover, unlike his speeches, they were oddly impersonal. Some were drafted within the bureaucracy, but others were largely Reagan's own work. Their message, according to one diplomat who saw them, was that "if the Soviets would just free up their system and let matters take their course, the two sides would be able to get together. The letters," he says, "were somewhat naive."[23] (For some reason, he adds, the letters were ordered destroyed, but the order was ignored within the State Department and the letters were preserved.)[24]*

Dobrynin's access to the White House had fallen off, and there was

*One is missing. It was written the night after Reagan was shot in March 1981. From his hospital bed, he composed by hand on a yellow legal pad an eight-page letter to Brezhnev, described as conveying the sentiments of one who has just had a brush with death (Hedrick Smith, *The Power Game: How Washington Works* [New York: Random House, 1988], pp. 304–5).

no other discreet channel to the Soviet leadership. Thus, most blunt messages were being delivered rhetorically, an obviously poor method of doing business with the other side. But in an administration that saw little serious business that needed doing, the breakdown in communications didn't seem to matter.

Among the first of the major foreign policy decisions was whether to observe the SALT agreements. On March 3, John Lehman, an *enfant terrible* of the Ford era and Reagan's first Secretary of the Navy, told reporters that America should not comply with either the SALT I or SALT II agreements. (The five-year Interim Agreement concluded by Nixon had technically expired, although both parties were continuing to observe it. And SALT II had, of course, never even been taken up on the Senate floor.)[25] To have a service secretary volunteering pronouncements of this kind infuriated the State Department; the compliance issue had not even been taken up within the hierarchy. The next day, State replied in a statement inspired by Haig that rejected Lehman's statements as "not authorized" or reflecting administration policy. "We will take no action that would undercut existing agreements so long as the Soviet Union exercises the same restraint."[26] On his own, Haig had laid down the policy. Only Reagan could have disowned it, but he typically chose to stay above the fray while his more hawkish advisers sputtered. In the foreign policy vacuum of Reagan's making, an aggressive senior figure—and Haig was that—could make policy just by being first to assert it.

Making it stick was another matter. Every administration since Lyndon Johnson's had been divided internally over various SALT issues but not on the desirability of the process. Reagan's was different. Only the State Department and the Joint Chiefs of Staff continued to favor SALT. State did so for political reasons. The chiefs, aware that America's strategic forces still held advantages over the Soviet Union's, wanted to sustain existing limits and prevent what was being called "breakout," i.e., a massive increase in Soviet forces. They didn't share the new administration's strong preference for scrubbing SALT and reestablishing American superiority in strategic forces. They preferred the relative certainties of parity to the uncertainties of a major new cycle of competition. "The chiefs were the most moderate force in town, even more so than State, which was being gutted," recalls a closely involved American diplomat. "People and jobs at State were being abolished. It was demoralizing—the lack of continuity."[27]

Weinberger and his staff were viscerally opposed to SALT. The NSC staff, to the degree it mattered, took its cues from Counselor to the President Edwin Meese, a hard-liner. And with William Casey at the helm, the CIA couldn't be supportive of SALT. The arms control agency's new leader was

Eugene Rostow, former cochairman of the Committee on the Present Danger and a full-throated critic of SALT II.

Thanks mainly to the Joint Chiefs, the line was held until early 1982, despite pressure from their adversaries, especially Weinberger. "His strength was Reagan's total confidence in and loyalty to him," recalls a former administration official. "Reagan paid attention when Cap was talking in a meeting, even when he talked at great length [as he often did], whereas with almost anyone else he would nod off after a couple of minutes."[28]

Weinberger's chief antagonist in these and other meetings was Air Force General David C. Jones, Chairman of the Joint Chiefs and the most knowledgeable of them on nuclear and arms control issues. A universally admired officer, Jones had been involved with nuclear strategy since 1949 and with SALT almost from the beginning. His disagreements with Weinberger in these and other meetings—on SALT II and many other issues— were blunt and often heated. Weinberger's alter ego and mentor in these matters was Richard Perle, who had helped Henry Jackson become the most feared of SALT-baiters. Perle was now an assistant secretary of defense. His contempt for the existing arms control regime matched anyone's. In knowledge of nuclear issues and operational skill, he was far ahead of most of the other new people, few of whom had much of either. Over the next several years, the Weinberger-Perle tandem more than held its own against arms control advocates who included the leaders of the other NATO governments and much the larger part of the foreign policy community.

Advocates understood that without the limits and restrictions of the SALT II Treaty, the superpowers would find themselves building more of everything. At best, they would be sustaining parity but with rising levels of unusable nuclear power. New and more versatile nuclear weapons would beget new uncertainties, hence instabilities. With the SALT II limits, each of the parties would have a reliable fix on what the other could deploy over a period of years. One of the treaty's articles limited each side's ICBMs to the maximum number of warheads with which it had been tested. But for this restriction, argued the advocates, the parties would victimize each other by launching a mindless "warhead-aimpoint" race.

Soviet cheating was basic to the case against the treaty. If past administrations hadn't detected cheating, it was because they believed what they wished to believe or because their estimates were insufficiently rigorous. Weinberger and the other hard-liners took for granted that the Soviets were cheating. "If the evidence was ambiguous, they judged it conclusive," recalls a former Joint Chief.[29] He and the other chiefs, along with the State Department, were made uneasy by this simplistic view. The job of monitoring Soviet military activities goes on with or without arms control agreements. But the verification provisions of the SALT agreements, their advocates argued, are immensely useful to an open society competing against an essentially closed society. By denying either side the right to conceal those of its activities covered by the agreement or to interfere with the other's surveillance systems, these and other provisions make a very hard task less hard and reduce uncertainties. For example, the intelligence community can distinguish between multiwarhead missile launchers and launchers of single-warhead missiles only in the testing phase; once the missiles are deployed in silos, it is all but impossible to tell whether they have one or several warheads. The Soviets tested and deployed their long-range missile systems in both single-warhead and multiwarhead versions. They reluctantly agreed in SALT II that any launcher that had ever contained a missile with more than one warhead would count against that side's entitlement to such systems.

The administration never did stop arguing with itself about SALT II. On May 13, Reagan told a press conference that the only parts of the agreement that were being observed were those that had "to do with the monitoring" (surveillance) of weapons. He was wrong, and quite clearly the compliance issue had to be resolved. In an NSC meeting a week later, Admiral Bobby Inman, the Deputy Director of the CIA and a distinguished professional, carefully explained to Reagan the advantages of the SALT II Treaty's verification provisions and the importance of the limits and restrictions it imposed.[30] Inman, Haig, and General Jones—the three military figures at the meeting, as Jones points out—argued for full compliance.[31] On May 30, Reagan announced publicly what the State Department had said more than a year earlier—that the U.S. would exercise restraint and not "undercut" SALT agreements so long as Moscow showed similar restraint. Weinberger, for one, had lost a round, but few decisions in the Reagan era were ever final—at least not those in the foreign policy domain. These were still early days in the battle over SALT II.

The struggle had thus far left a heavy deposit of bitterness. "We were exhausted by the fighting and all the blood being shed," recalls a diplomat who took part. "We were engaged in damage limitation. We couldn't do anything positive—take an initiative."[32] He and a handful of colleagues at State were trying to revive the arms control talks, which had been stalled since the Soviet invasion of Afghanistan. Allied governments were clamoring for negotiation. They had agreed to accept the new American missiles provided that talks aimed at removing the need to deploy all or most of them lay ahead. But when Carter withdrew SALT II from Senate consideration, the Europeans were stuck; without SALT II, there could be no

SALT III. The two-track decision was now on a single track heading toward trouble, perhaps big trouble. Everywhere in Western Europe (excepting France), the impending arrival of the new missiles had swelled the ranks of antinuclear groups. In some countries, middle-class people of all ages and political tendencies joined forces with the ritual disarmers and veteran demonstrators for a nuclear-free world. The churches joined the vanguard of a movement whose scale had no precedent. A rally in Bonn in October 1981 brought 250,000 people into the street; it was judged the largest gathering of Germans since John F. Kennedy's visit to Berlin in 1963.

The massive outcry was fed by an anxiety that 572 new missiles might tempt the superpowers to confine nuclear warfare to Europe and make sanctuaries of their own countries. A chicken had come home to roost. The tortuous path to NATO's two-track decision had begun with misguided concerns in Europe that Carter's SALT-negotiating strategy might make a battleground of the old continent yet again.

Soviet and European leaders were getting the same message: Washington didn't want to deal with Moscow at all. The Soviets would have preferred dealing with tough American demands to no dealing at all. In April, Weinberger told NATO defense ministers that "if the movement from cold war to détente is progress, then let me say we cannot afford much more progress."[33] Some of his aides were saying that America should not do business with the Soviets and couldn't depend on its allies. Genuine Reaganauts seemed to favor a Fortress America over the Western Alliance. In May, the administration wanted to drop references to détente from a NATO communiqué but was overridden by the Europeans.[34]

Helmut Schmidt was losing patience. On the evening of Reagan's inauguration he had met Cyrus Vance at Wiesbaden military airport. Vance, a private citizen then, had been asked by Carter to greet the American hostages whom Iran had just released from their long ordeal. Schmidt told Vance that he welcomed Reagan's arrival.[35] But within a year, Schmidt was complaining about the septuagenarians to the west and east of him. Brezhnev was in a steep physical decline, and worried Europeans felt they were seeing headless coalitions in both Moscow and Washington. Schmidt, for one, was unlikely to accept any of the new missiles on schedule unless and until a date for arms control talks had been set.

Despite some remarkable political success in the early going, the Reagan administration had by the summer begun to show a glint of that pale cast of frustration that all governments acquire. It arrived feeling duty-bound to improve the country's nuclear forces before taking part in talks to curb them. But Reagan's call to arms drew little public response and little applause in Congress. In defense spending, his administration's early reach somewhat exceeded its grasp. The inherited two-track decision vexed the new people, some of whom thought the missiles earmarked for Europe would be vulnerable, hence unstable. Others saw their financial cost as far exceeding any conceivable military benefit. But the political costs of whatever Reagan did seemed even heavier. He could hardly retreat from NATO's solemn decision to deploy the missiles—not with the Soviets trying to reverse it in typically heavy-handed fashion. But the costs of going forward were also heavy, given the surging antinuclear movement in Europe. Washington's reluctance to begin talks was feeding the pressure, not only in Europe but in America, where an antinuclear movement began to take hold in the winter of 1981–1982. Its focus was a proposal to freeze arsenals of nuclear weapons at current levels. By midwinter, the nuclear freeze was at the height of fashion, as numerous members of Congress discovered from constituent mail. Roman Catholic bishops condemned the reliance on nuclear weapons as a deterrent to aggression. And the navy began losing officers and seamen because, as James Watkins, Chief of Naval Operations, said, "Their serving in uniform was incompatible with the [bishops'] pastoral letter."[36]

The administration was on the defensive. It judged correctly that the nuclear freeze was trendy and probably lacked staying power. But the movement had captured the initiative, which elsewhere lay with the Soviets, who were clamoring for talks and staking a claim to the high ground. The administration could not avoid arranging talks—and fairly soon—about the intermediate, or midrange, systems deployed in Europe. And despite its deeper aversion to discussing the strategic, or long-range, weapons, there, too, events were forcing the decision.

In its first year, the administration managed to do almost nothing about SALT except change its name to START—for Strategic Arms Reduction Talks. The switch was more than a change of a letter in an acronym. Reagan and his advisers felt that only reductions—deep ones—justified the unnatural act of negotiations with the enemy on so vital a subject. Their predecessors had considered reductions as useful politically; they were easy for people to understand and thus gave credibility to the process. The logic of SALT—the quest for ceilings and subceilings, as well as restrictions on new and more modern weapons—was more complicated. But with each side deploying roughly 10,000 deliverable weapons, the size of the reductions hadn't seemed to matter as much as just obtaining limits on them, which at any level would reduce uncertainty and discourage pessimistic worst-case assumptions about what the other side could do over the span of the agreement. The restrictions on new weapons and on making existing ones more threatening would also promote stability, an exalted goal in the nuclear age.

Just setting a date for the talks was nearly as difficult as reaching the decision to have them. Haig met with Soviet Foreign Minister Gromyko in Geneva in late January 1982. They were supposed to announce jointly that strategic arms talks would begin March 30. The announcement wasn't made, largely because of two articles by Henry Kissinger that appeared on the Op-Ed page of the *New York Times* on January 17 and 18, just a few days before the Haig-Gromyko meeting. The articles deplored the reaction to the imposition of martial law in Poland and suppression of Solidarity as too little and too late. "How then can one explain the eagerness to continue all negotiations?" asked Kissinger. "How is one to explain a meeting between our Secretary of State and the Soviet Foreign Minister while martial law and concentration camps continue in Poland?" The articles reminded the administration of its early commitment to "linkage"; to not allowing the Russians to "insulate particular areas of negotiation—such as arms control—from their international conduct." The Kissinger pieces intimidated Haig; the joint announcement was postponed, and Gromyko was able to say that the United States still wasn't ready to set a date for talks, a comment Haig had to confirm.[37]

On May 9, Reagan told the graduating class of Eureka College, his alma mater, that the START team would be instructed to seek an agreement to reduce missile warheads, of which each side deployed about 7,500, by a third. The missiles that carry the warheads would have to be cut even more sharply. Pressure from the nuclear-freeze movement softened his tone, but the proposal, as Reagan outlined it, was hopelessly one-sided. Apart from hitting on a few goals, his administration had done very little; it was still deeply split on how to deal with the associated issues, of which there was a long list.

Any predecessor would have envied Reagan's freedom. Not since Richard Nixon's first term, when he journeyed to China and then concluded the SALT I agreements in Moscow, had any President's writ in East-West matters run as far as Reagan's clearly did. His popularity and strength within his own party were unshakable. And whereas Nixon, Ford, and Carter had to work hard at reassuring allied governments that SALT wouldn't weaken their links with the U.S., Reagan had no such problem. When he arrived, the link between security and arms control had become as clear to European governments as it had been to a succession of American presidents.

Reagan had an interesting choice. By keeping faith with his own strongly held views, he risked inviting difficulties at home and abroad. A change of course, as the Eureka speech seemed to some to foreshadow, would have offered him a sure claim to the role of the protector of stability and undoubted leader of the Western Alliance. In the bargain, his political base would have become that much stronger.

Reagan was not changing course. The Eureka speech was intended to contain the freeze movement and also deal with some of the pressure to have SALT II ratified. Sam Nunn, the Georgia Democrat who had become the most respected and influential member of the Senate on defense matters, was urging this step. Other figures in each party, even including the now studiously hawkish Kissinger on the Republican side, said they couldn't understand why it was unsafe to ratify an agreement that both sides were observing. Kissinger later said he could not understand the difference between the SALT process and the freeze proposal. The treaty, unlike the then more fashionable nuclear freeze proposal, would have reduced the Soviet arsenal by about ten percent as well as freezing it.

A restoration of SALT, with a commitment to serious bargaining, might have helped the defense budget. The more obvious military needs were not big-ticket strategic systems but improved conventional weapons and logistics, plus a more reliable supply of adequately trained manpower.

Nonetheless, Reagan's line hardened. Like every predecessor in the nuclear age, he was anxious to avoid the ultimate horror, or the risks thereof, and to improve relations between the superpowers. Like the others, he saw himself as custodian of the peace and as a bulwark against the worst. But the problem, he felt, was linear and uncomplicated: The forces of good were arrayed against the forces of evil. The former, he and his advisers felt, had rested on their oars in the 1970s, a prolonged lull which the latter exploited. The lopsided nature of Reagan's early START position reflected this view. In reproaching the nuclear freeze, Haig said in a speech on April 6: "A freeze at our current levels would perpetuate an unstable and unequal military balance. It would reward a decade of unilateral Soviet buildup and penalize the United States for a decade of unilateral restraint."

America could hardly be accused of neglecting its strategic forces in the era of Nixon, Ford, and Carter, a time when both superpowers accumulated the largest aggregation of destructive power the world has ever seen. The Soviets did spend more on big weapons. Being well behind technologically, they built entire new systems—three new land-based missiles, a new submarine, and new submarine-launched missile systems. America created the Trident submarine, the Trident missile system, and a long-range cruise missile. On either side, however, the buildup relied mainly on the force multiplier—the multiple warheads, or MIRVs. The

United States deployed fifty-five hundred new warheads in the 1970s, five hundred more than the Soviet Union.[38]

In the main, the administration was trying to close the window of vulnerability; Reagan had made a campaign issue of it. Carter's plan to scatter two hundred MX launchers in 4,600 shelters located on special roadways in remote parts of Utah and Nevada was fast fading. Local opposition—a sagebrush rebellion—was too strong and, besides the Mormon church and environmental groups, included Nevada's Senator Paul Laxalt, a Reagan intimate, and Utah's Jake Garn, another conservative and influential Republican senator. The ensuing litigation, quite clearly, would have submerged the legal resources of Utah and Nevada.

In early October 1981, the administration scrubbed the shell game approach and gave itself the option of putting MX missiles in silos. There was a hint that these would be protected by antiballistic missiles. But nothing had been decided. Weinberger favored deploying MX in large, specially designed airplanes. The MX basing problem hadn't become any less baffling. Leaving the silos unprotected would have amounted to a perhaps embarrassing admission that the window of vulnerability hadn't been there after all. But defending them would have provoked another debate over ABMs and reawakened anxieties of a rampant nuclear arms race.

Adding to the confusion was the declining credibility of the famous window. A heavy skepticism about it was becoming less muted, with serious people questioning or denying the existence of a first-strike threat. The editor of *Strategic Review*, a conservative and respected journal, wrote during the summer of 1981, "Nothing has been put forward which technologically supports the belief that we (or the Soviets) could, with any degree of confidence, expect to hit one silo at ICBM range, let alone 1,000 of them distributed over an area equal to one-third of the United States."[39] To the extent that a surprise attack actually was cause for concern, the MX missile system, especially if deployed in fixed silos, appeared to enlarge it by giving the other side a bonus for striking first. Also, the loose talk about being able to limit nuclear war was pointing up the proposition for what it is—a notion that would be merely frivolous if it were not so dangerous.

An argument that the MX wasn't needed had gathered strength. The U.S. was also developing a new version of the B-1 bomber, the more advanced Stealth bomber (still a black program), a cruise missile relying on the Stealth technology and the highly accurate submarine-launched Trident II missile system. The latter was a reminder (in Congress and beyond) that the sea is the best and most secure environment for nuclear weapons and that the United States, with its easy access to deep water, has obvious advantages in operating there. Putting an even larger proportion of the deterrent out to sea would have been a partial answer to the vulnerability problem. Bounding it with SALT II and a successor agreement would have been another partial answer. The best role for the MX, many felt, would have been as a bargaining chip in Geneva.

Less than a month after the Eureka speech, the Pentagon's five-year Defense Guidance appeared. "Nuclear conflict with the Soviet Union could be protracted," it said. And the U.S. "must prevail and be able to force the Soviet Union to seek the earliest termination of hostilities on terms favorable to the United States."[40] This and other documents showed that nothing had changed.

A few days later, in June 1982, General Jones retired as Chairman of the Joint Chiefs of Staff and warned that "it would be throwing money in a bottomless pit to try to prepare the United States for a long nuclear war with the Soviet Union."[41] A demonstration in favor of the nuclear freeze in New York's Central Park attracted 750,000 people, according to estimates of the police, who thought it might have been the largest (and most orderly) of any ever held in the park. But a proposal to freeze nuclear weapons died in the Senate Foreign Relations Committee about this time. And on August 6, the House of Representatives voted against an "immediate freeze" by 204 to 202.

The stormy and predictably brief passage of Al Haig ended a week later. On June 25, not long after Israel's invasion of Lebanon, Reagan accepted his resignation in a letter that Haig says he never wrote, although what seems to have happened is that his repeated offer to resign had at last been taken up.[42] He was replaced by George Shultz, who could hardly have been more different. Unlike Haig, he was a Reagan familiar. His strengths were caution and patience, whereas Haig was incautious and impatient. Haig had broad knowledge of the national security issues. Shultz hadn't been exposed to many of these, and had even avoided exposure to those involving big weapons and arms control. During his time as director of the Office of Management and Budget in the early 1970s, he had always shunned the subjects he was not at ease with. But unlike Haig, Shultz knew about running a big bureaucracy and dealing with key players other than just a president himself. Haig tried to dominate the foreign policy process by subduing the other players, as Kissinger, his mentor and then rival, had done. Shultz relied on the more indirect but traditional bureaucratic methods, such as forming alliances and coalitions with other agencies.

Other governments were relieved to see Shultz. He would be, they felt sure, a constructive and moderating influence, as on many issues he came to be. But in dealing with arms control, he had first to overcome his resistance to the subject and then adapt himself to the role of odd man out, which he generally was. Shultz moved for much of his tenure at what seemed a snail's pace and was judged a flop by diplomats, including many of his own. It's hard to see how he could have done otherwise. Within the interagency process, he and his department were bereft of allies. Shultz lacked support from even the arms control agency, which had been created to help a secretary of state. With an advocacy role, this agency, which has a smaller staff than the Battle Monuments Commission, normally allows the secretary of state to adopt the middle ground between contesting points of view within the government. But Shultz was well to the left of Reagan's arms control agency.

The Joint Chiefs of Staff, although still a moderate influence, were not much help either. For the first year or so, their unalloyed views were available to the White House. Then, the chiefs were gradually neutralized by Weinberger and Perle, especially after Jones retired. The NSC staff would obtain their views by sounding them out singly and privately. "The chiefs fell silent," recalls a senior American diplomat, "Perle was a master of intimidation."[43]

Shultz's chief adversary was Weinberger. Their struggle for control of policy—more interesting, more long-lasting, and more consequential than any other waged within the conflict-ridden administration—was a leitmotif of the Reagan era. Weinberger held the advantage. Both knew Reagan well, but Weinberger was closer to him and so were his views; in any case, he saw himself in an advocacy role—as Reagan's attorney for defense policy. Although Shultz could play the bureaucratic game, he wasn't as good at it as Weinberger, who excelled. The main asset Shultz brought to the struggle was patience.

They went back a long way. Weinberger had been Shultz's deputy for a time at the budget bureau. He took over the bureau when Shultz was named Secretary of the Treasury. Later, they worked together for the Bechtel Corporation, a mammoth construction firm based in San Francisco; Shultz was president, Weinberger the senior legal officer. Weinberger had wanted the State Department, but had to settle for Defense, a department whose affairs interested him less and which he never came close to mastering.* His job was raising the money for Reagan's defense buildup and resisting efforts to retard it. Stylistically, he and Shultz were opposites. Weinberger was blunt, outspoken, and even polemical. "He's the lightning rod for the administration," said a former aide.[44] Shultz was a plodder and

---

*His peers considered Weinberger less informed about and concerned with the business of his office than anyone who ever held it. The contrast with his immediate predecessor, Harold Brown, was striking.

said no more than he had to—less, actually, according to former aides. He would listen attentively to contesting arguments of his officials and when they had finished often say absolutely nothing. Within the State Department and foreign capitals, he was widely known as "the Buddha."

Shultz and Weinberger agreed on almost nothing. On East-West matters, Shultz was the moderate, Weinberger the hard-liner. But on various other issues, especially those which might have involved the use of military force in Central America, Lebanon, and Libya, Weinberger (and the Joint Chiefs) was dovish, Shultz hawkish.

While Shultz was taking over State, a few of the diplomats who had his ear urged him to take a less-cautious and laid-back approach in his appearances before Congress. They wanted him to put forward a rounded view of major issues, as Kissinger or Vance might have done. Shultz said no. "He would say, 'People who think they must have a strategy are wrong,' " one of these diplomats recalls. " 'The great managers are people who make decisions each day instinctively.' Shultz made an elaborate distinction between facts and theories. Was he too cautious? I don't know, but how many times can you go to the well and tell Ronald Reagan things that are very different from what he is hearing from all the others?"[45]

In the end, Shultz's patience overcame the odds; he simply wore down and outlasted Weinberger, who left his job a little more than a year before the end of Reagan's second term. The by-product of their duel—internal gridlock—lasted five and one-half years, a time when Reagan rarely left the sidelines. He delegated control of the East-West issues to Shultz and Weinberger. They in turn delegated operational responsibility for many of the issues to subcabinet-level subordinates, who became the key figures in that chapter of the arms control saga that covered the larger part of the Reagan era. The battles became fiercer than even those of the Nixon-Ford era, but only rarely were they joined at the senior level as in the past. Instead of being resolved in NSC meetings presided over by an informed president, the outcome was usually determined further down the line. It was a situation in which Weinberger's chief naysayer, Richard Perle, could flourish. He had allies on Capitol Hill and in the press. Hardball was his game. He had a better grasp of the nuclear weapons brief than most. His role as spoiler was ideally suited to the interagency chaos; blocking sensible proposals wasn't difficult. A competent naysayer could refuse to go along with key parts of a proposal or offer alternatives that were certain to be rejected by the other side.

Perle didn't confront much effective opposition after the Joint Chiefs had been tethered. His chief and perhaps most nimble adversary during Reagan's first term was Richard Burt, who came to the State Department from journalism in January 1981. Like Perle, Burt was a youngish defense intellectual; he knew his brief as well as Perle. However, unlike Perle, Burt didn't come with doctrinal baggage. What distinguished him was bureaucratic flair and an opportunistic style. Burt was Perle's opposite number in the interagency scrum, where his purpose was to hold his own. This meant keeping alive in some form the options favored by first Haig and then Shultz. "The two Richards," as many knew them, were Shultz-Weinberger surrogates.

The START talks in Washington had gotten under way in late June and were stuck fast. In its first fourteen months, the new administration had been unable even to decide what exactly ought to be reduced or limited. The NSC meetings on this and related issues were "wholly chaotic," says one participant. "Reagan seldom said anything that wasn't written on the card. He never weighed in. He was very passive. He wanted a consensus, and when it wasn't forged, he didn't lay down the law. Everyone went off in different directions. We'd leave a meeting and have no idea of what, if anything, had been decided."[46] In the end, Reagan surprised insiders by choosing the approach to START—limiting missile systems and warheads—favored by State and the Joint Chiefs; it had been bitterly opposed by Defense, which had insisted on forcing the Soviets to reduce their aggregate throw-weight to the American level. The actual proposal arising from this approach, however, was in no sense negotiable. Neither was Brezhnev's equally one-sided counterproposal, which was also made public. Washington and Moscow were returning to an earlier period when what passed for arms control policy was played to the galleries, with propaganda advantage the priority goal.

In September, Shultz had his first talk with Gromyko, a man he never liked or got on with. So troubled were relations that the question of a meeting between Brezhnev and Reagan didn't even arise. But Shultz took this occasion to deliver one of the few blunt private messages conveyed to the Soviets in this period. He warned Gromyko against putting MIG fighter aircraft in Nicaragua, a step that the Soviets had been preparing to take. (Haig had issued a similar warning early on.)

The administration had stepped up its attacks on the nuclear-freeze movement. In November, Reagan charged that foreign agents had been sent in "to help instigate . . . and keep such a movement going." Weinberger had made the same charge, adding that the movement was likely to "increase the dangers of war" by reducing the country's capacity to deter an attack.[47] Brezhnev accused Reagan of "threatening to push the world into the flames of nuclear war."[48] He was under pressure from his military chiefs to do more in response to the Reagan buildup. By then, he is said to have concluded that his détente-based Western policy was spent, if not moribund. It was hardly in worse shape than Brezhnev himself, who was a near invalid and scarcely able to work at all. He died on November 10, 1982, and was replaced by Yuri Andropov.

Although a more intellectually vigorous figure than his predecessor, Andropov, too, would be invalided on the job. He came already afflicted with a serious kidney disorder, and during much of his fifteen months as General Secretary he was regularly connected to a dialysis machine. Andropov was welcomed at home as a break with the past, and if he had lasted longer might have pursued reforms of the kind on which his protégé, Mikhail Gorbachev, seems to have staked everything. Despite his having recently been head of the KGB, Muscovites and perhaps a large part of the country thought, or perhaps hoped, that Andropov would improve the sclerotic Soviet system. Elsewhere, opinion was mixed. The tabloid reaction—TOP COP IS HEAD RED—reflected broad skepticism about prospects for much improvement on the East-West scene. In some capitals, however, the arrival of this interesting and seemingly businesslike figure appeared to augur well. But Andropov made no difference, if only because events would have ruled out any narrowing of the gulf between the superpowers on his brief watch. Andropov's year in power wasn't a rerun of Carter's last or Reagan's first two. It was even worse.

Deployment of the midrange American missiles in Germany and elsewhere in Europe was scheduled to begin later in 1983. European governments were anxious to see some progress in talks in Geneva that were supposed to settle the awesome problem that the impending deployment had created. The talks—known as INF (for intermediate-range nuclear forces)—had started in October 1981 and, like the parallel negotiation, START, had gotten nowhere. Brezhnev was winning the propaganda war on points when he died. Compared to the ambient jingoism of Washington, his line was comforting. It exploited trendy anxieties and looked toward nuclear-free zones, no first use, and an end to new weapons projects. But private messages from Brezhnev and particularly Gromyko to NATO governments contained crude threats aimed at coercing European leaders to walk back their decision to host the new missiles. Now Rome would be targeted if war broke out, Italy was told. Other capitals heard similar warnings. As often in the past, Moscow was overplaying a not very strong hand; the heavy pressure only reinforced the determination of NATO governments to do what they had agreed to do in December 1979. To have reneged—yielded to the pressure—would have been to grant the Soviets what diplomats call a *droit de regard*—an oversight—on allied decisions. Governments, especially Bonn's, would have been torn asunder politically, with some parties accusing the others of having put paid to NATO and the defense connection with America. There was a sense of being damned-if-we-do-damned-if-we-don't. Insecure governments confronted the prospect of massive demonstrations.

Almost but not quite lost in the fracas was the presumed purpose of the new missiles—to offset the Soviet SS-20s targeted against Western Europe, which had no similar weapons. Not to have one, the argument ran, would mean a break in the "continuum of deterrence"—NATO jargon for being able to meet aggression at any level without being wholly dependent on any one kind of weapon, including North American–based bombers and missile systems. The other part of the argument was political; the SS-20's larger purpose was said to be intimidation of Western Europe and thus could not be left unanswered. Dissenting voices included numerous authorities on Europe's security. The SS-20, they said, doesn't really enlarge the threat, because the Soviets could as easily obliterate European cities with their longer-range weapons or their older midrange systems. McGeorge Bundy made an eloquent case—a plea, really   against deployment: "With a single important exception, there is nothing the new warheads can do that cannot be done as well by other systems that we already have or plan to have . . . Nor does the location of the weapons make any difference from the American standpoint. Whether they are based in Germany, or at sea, or in Nebraska, there will always be the same awful magnitude in any Presidential decision to use these weapons against anyone, and in particular against the Soviet Union, whose leaders know as well as we do whose command would send them, and where to direct the reply . . . There is indeed one thing some of the new missiles can do that no other weapon can do, but it is something we should not want to be able to do. The Pershing II missiles . . . can reach Russia from Germany in five minutes, thus producing a new possibility of a super-sudden first strike—perhaps even on Moscow itself. That is too fast. We would not like it if a Soviet forward deployment of submarines should create a similar standing threat to Washington. It is not for us to be the ones who first put the decapitation of the great rival government on a hair trigger."[49]

Among those who had disapproved of the two-track decision was Paul Nitze, who, like many others, felt that, once made, the commitment to deployment had to be upheld.[50] Nitze's vigorous opposition to SALT II had fetched an offer from the Reagan people to run the INF talks. Whether his matchless experience with nuclear issues and long list of accomplishments also contributed to his selection is less clear. In picking Nitze, the new people didn't understand that they were getting an incurable problem solver. Outside government, an unnatural and uncomfortable setting for him, Nitze had been a resourceful blocker and naysayer. Back inside, he could be relied upon to be just as resourceful in finding ways to make agreement possible. Within the administration, probably only Perle, who had once worked for Nitze and understood his ways, was aware of his potential. Nitze was then a strikingly youthful seventy-four, the planes of his sculpted features unchanged by the years, the wiry frame no less fit for the more exacting ski slopes, quality tennis (singles), or weekly outings at his farm in Maryland. "My body does what I tell it to," he has said.[51] He left investment banking for Washington in 1940—summoned by James Forrestal, who had known him in New York. Except for the Carter years, Nitze always remained an insider, even during interludes spent outside government. He is a proud and many say vain man who is probably capable of a fair degree of self-deception, especially when he is not being used as he thinks he should be. Compared to most of the Reagan foreign policy entourage, Nitze not only had a track record, he was a star—a beacon for journalists and foreign diplomats and a reassuring face to their governments. He was virtually the only member of the group who knew anything about arms control negotiations and who, excepting Haig, also knew the defense brief. He may or may not have thought, as others did, that the INF job would be his last in government.

In mid-November 1981, twelve days before the INF negotiations began, Reagan astonished his own and other capitals by proposing to cancel deployment of *all* new midrange American missiles if Moscow would dismantle its SS-20s and the older systems these were replacing. As theater, his "zero option," as it was called, was a great success. In a stroke, he captured the high ground from Moscow and outflanked the peaceniks, unilateral disarmers, and the freeze movement. The proposal came on the eve of a rare Brezhnev visit to Bonn and seemed to offer the West Germans and other allies an intriguing out; the zero option would be instantly seen as meaning no deployments of the new missiles. However, experienced officials and diplomats were unimpressed, if not disheartened. Although the idea, they saw, would buy some time for beleaguered European governments, notably the West German, Belgian, and Dutch, it seemed otherwise divorced from reality. Why would the Soviets agree to dismantle hundreds of existing weapons in return for NATO agreeing to forgo a deployment of its own that key governments might end by refusing anyway? Briefly, the zero option was judged on many sides as wholly nonnegotiable; if clung to by Washington, it would mean no deal in Geneva, and no way out of NATO's predicament.

The origins of the idea are a bit unclear, having been traced by some to a Dutch peace movement, by others to Helmut Schmidt's Social Democratic party. A heavy irony runs through the odd history of the zero option. At first, the new administration disliked it. Then, after some months, Richard Perle began pushing the idea. He, of course, assumed that the advantages were wholly short term, the negotiability of a zero option equally zero, but that was doubtless part of its charm, given Perle's aversion to arms control. A brisk bureaucratic skirmish ensued, which pitted him against Richard Burt. State wanted to bargain with the Soviets instead of giving them a take-it-or-leave-it proposition. "State saw the zero option as trivializing the process," says a closely involved American diplomat.[52] The chiefs, too, preferred negotiation, but eventually fell in with the zero option, although convinced nothing would come of it. No one, in or out of government, could have envisaged a time when a dynamic and unconventional Soviet leader—Mikhail Gorbachev—would have the wit to take NATO up on the zero offer and then pocket the larger part of the credit for making it happen.

In Geneva, Nitze was on a short leash; his instructions gave him very little room to maneuver. But in periodic briefings of allied leaders, he had come under pressure, especially from Schmidt, to show progress. By the summer of 1982, Nitze was ready to do what seemed only natural and desirable: Make a deal. What he then produced was the most celebrated "What Might Have Been" of Reagan's first term. The Walk in the Woods, as the affair became known, has since passed into legend.

As negotiators will, he and his Soviet counterpart, a well-connected and high-flying Soviet diplomat, Yuli Kvitsinsky, had begun probing one another's instructed positions. Each man was saddled with an all-or-nothing brief. After a series of informal what-ifs—"what if my government offered to?" etc.— they met for lunch in mid-July at a restaurant above Geneva and then took the woodland stroll with which the occasion is identified. Nitze was free-lancing. He had no back channel in Washington on which to rely for guidance or support. Almost certainly, Kvitsinsky had a green light from someone in Moscow—a godfather who was probably Gromyko. Sitting on a log, the pair reached a startlingly simple and equitable understanding, which of course could have no status unless and until their leaders approved it. Had that occurred, each side would have been limited to no more than seventy-five of the weapons Nitze and Kvitsinsky were concerned with. The Soviets would have had to destroy their older midrange missile systems—380 in all—and more than half of the SS-20 force. They would have been left with just seventy-five SS-20s based within range of their targets in Western Europe. Another ninety would have been confined to an area well east of Novosibirsk, a city in southwestern Siberia.[53] With no midrange weapons yet deployed, America would have had nothing to dismantle. But the understanding did provide that America's entitlement could include no Pershing IIs; all seventy-five of its launchers would have to be drawn from the cruise missile component (originally set at 464). Being so much slower than ballistic missiles, the cruise missiles were seen by the Soviets as vastly less threatening. The Soviets weren't alone; many others saw the Pershings as destabilizing. Their capacity for destroying hardened targets just a few minutes after lift-off meant that in a crisis the Soviets could be struck without warning and would have to consider hitting these weapons before being hit by them. As the Jeremiah of crisis instability (missile vulnerability), Nitze, too, could have been expected to frown on the Pershings.

The Walk in the Woods was a very good deal—at least, as seen from allied capitals in Europe when they heard about it. It committed the Soviets to doing away with all but 20 percent of the midrange systems they had targeted against Western Europe. Also, they had dropped their long-standing claim for compensation in this class of weapons because of French and British nuclear weapons deployed against them. Nitze's deal would have vindicated the two-track decision and released European governments from their political torment.

The legend grew from what didn't happen after the Walk in the Woods. Allied governments didn't weigh in because they weren't told about it until too late. The State Department didn't work up a coherent position because it was leaderless; Shultz had just arrived and understood nothing of what had occurred. The President didn't receive the independent views of the chiefs, who on balance favored the Walk in the Woods, although the army was loath to give up the Pershing II. But the chiefs' conclusions were neutered by Perle and Weinberger before Reagan saw them. Perle played the key role; he attacked the understanding in a memorandum described by one official as "violent" in tone.[54] Weinberger didn't take a position at first, but he quickly fell in with Perle's opinion that the deal had to be rejected as one-sided—as allowing the Soviets to deploy the SS-20—a ballistic missile and MIRVed at that—whereas the U.S. was restricted to less-potent cruise missiles. Giving up the Pershings, the argument ran, meant giving up a weapon that could threaten the U.S.S.R. in the near term and thus help deterrence. Perle also worried that Nitze might have been set up; the Soviets, he surmised, would leak the understanding and then draw back from it. Schmidt could then have argued that since the

Americans were willing to give up the Pershings, why shouldn't his government do so?[55] The President decided against the deal and reaffirmed the zero option.

The Soviets, too, vetoed the deal, but after satisfying themselves that Nitze had no support for it in Washington, or for any deal that meant giving up the Pershing IIs. Kvitsinsky told Nitze that his government could not, for example, yield on the issue of French and British weapons. In any case, Washington drew the blame in Europe—for failing to see a good deal when its own man produced one and for failing to invite the views of allies on a matter that concerned them most directly.

In October 1982, Helmut Schmidt left the Bundeskanzleramt after eight years as Chancellor. If irascible, vain, and something of a scold, in his time he had been the most gifted and versatile of Western leaders; none could match his grasp of foreign, defense, and financial questions or his intellectual energy. He departed a spent figure as well as a casualty of the turbulence within his party set off by the two-track decision, for which he bore a large share of the responsibility. A few months after leaving, Schmidt defended his role in an interview with the Washington *Post* but added that he had always preferred countering the SS-20s with a sea-based deployment and that the popular outcry against the new missiles had vindicated him.[56] Like most Germans, Schmidt was very sensitive to the heavy concentration of nuclear weapons—other peoples' weapons—deployed in the Federal Republic. In and out of office, this angry man had a message for visiting American officials: You decided not to deploy missiles in Nevada and Utah over the objections of four million people. Well, sixty-two million Germans don't want missiles here either, but I agreed to take them.

Schmidt's reproach may have increased the administration's frustration over its inability to find a home for the MX, America's supposed answer to the window of vulnerability. By the end of 1982, Congress had seen thirty-four different basing schemes, the last of which was called "dense pack." The idea was to deploy the weapon in tightly bunched clusters; incoming Soviet warheads would, in theory, destroy each other—commit "fratricide"—instead of the target. There was some interest; dense pack would cost less than deceptive basing schemes, since only one silo per missile would be needed and the system would not be moved about. But the interest faded quickly. It was hard to explain how putting missiles closer together in fixed silos would remove the vulnerability problem. Apart from the ridicule the proposal attracted, whether fairly or unfairly, it would have violated a SALT II prohibition against building new fixed ICBM launchers or relocating existing ones. Reagan was on notice from Congress that further funds for the MX would be withheld until some sensible basing mode could be found.

Reagan was on the defensive. Aside from reviving the B-1 bomber program, his administration had done nothing but talk about restoring America's strategic edge. The much-deplored Carter crowd had at least put forward a plan for deploying the MX in a survivable mode. The legion of specialists who worried about missile vulnerability—including Reagan's natural constituency on these matters—was dismayed, even appalled by his inclination to put the MX in silos, where they would only strengthen any incentive the Soviets might have to strike first and hence enlarge the window of vulnerability. Furthermore, silo basing collided head-on with the notion dear to some Reaganauts that nuclear war is manageable and even winnable. How can you win if the other side destroys your best weapons?

Many of those in Congress who were on familiar terms with strategic issues saw no need for another land-based missile. A new SLBM, the Trident II, would be built, and the larger part of the Minuteman force was being improved. But a few of these same members thought the MX could be used to lever a more businesslike U.S. approach to the START talks in Geneva. Besides wanting the system for its own sake, the administration was arguing the need for it as a bargaining chip in the talks. Les Aspin, Chairman of the House Armed Services Committee, was pushing in this direction. He and a few House colleagues, notably Albert Gore and Norman Dicks, were urging the development of a much smaller and mobile single-warhead ICBM, which later became known as "Midgetman," although given its strong Capitol Hill patronage, some executive branch people called it "the Congress." Midgetman was popular not just on Capitol Hill but with experts like Paul Nitze because it offered stability. Being small, it could easily (though not cheaply) be made mobile. And with only one warhead, it wasn't a first-strike weapon or a tempting target. In any case, the MX had reached a dead end, and Reagan thus did what presidents often do when they are stymied: He created a commission and empowered it to find the answer.

The chairman of the bipartisan commission which began life on January 3, 1983, was Brent Scowcroft, a retired Air Force general and former NSC adviser to Gerald Ford. Respected on all sides for his moderate views and sensible approach to issues, Scowcroft was well suited to reconciling the views of a very glossy panel which included two former secretaries of state, Kissinger and Haig; four ex-secretaries of defense—Harold Brown,

James Schlesinger, Melvin Laird, and Donald Rumsfeld. Richard Helms and John McCone, both former CIA directors, were also there. Other key figures included William Perry, a veteran of the MX basing saga, and James Woolsey, a close friend of Aspin's and former undersecretary of the navy. Their report, which appeared three months later, had something for everyone: one hundred MX missiles for the administration, the Midgetman missile for its congressional partisans, and some changes in the administration's START position to mollify moderates on every side.

The report is best remembered for what it didn't do: solve the vulnerability problem. Indeed, the effect was to question the window of vulnerability. The one hundred MXs didn't require a survivable basing mode after all. Silos would do. American forces were described as adequate "even if the land-based missile force is vulnerable over the next decade." But the forces, added the report, should be designed to make the other side's equally vulnerable.[57] The document was interpreted by many people as either closing the notional window or implying that all along it had been *trompe l'oeil*. Put differently, America's deterrent wasn't broken and Reagan didn't fix it.

Among the least noticed and most significant comments concerned the Trident submarine. "A relatively few large submarines, each carrying on the order of two hundred warheads, presents a small number of valuable targets to the Soviets."[58] Here the commission echoed the counsel of Trident's opponents within the Pentagon in the early 1970s: Let's build a smaller submarine and have more of them.

Much of Congress reacted skeptically to the idea that Reagan would moderate his position in Geneva. Aspin, Gore, and others who had lent their support to the compromise were judged by many to have been taken in. The skepticism was justified. The administration adjusted its position slightly, but not enough to put the parties an inch closer to actual negotiation. It didn't matter. Reagan's focus had just shifted dramatically from offensive missiles to a space-based defense against them. Conceived as a legacy to the cause of keeping the planet intact, his scheme was unveiled in a nationally televised speech on March 23, two weeks prior to the release of the Scowcroft Commission's report. What Reagan and a tiny handful of others had in mind, it appeared, was an astrodome; inbound missiles would be destroyed by lasers, particle beams, and other directed-energy weapons deployed in space. Nuclear weapons, said Reagan, would be made "impotent and obsolete." "Wouldn't it be better to save lives than to avenge them?" asked the fantasist.[59]

"It was his Hollywood view," says one State Department figure who observed him closely. "If there is a problem, there must be a solution. His was either do away with them [the missiles] or create an umbrella."[60] Reagan said as much himself in a later speech at Glassboro, New Jersey, site of Lyndon Johnson's meeting with Soviet Premier Aleksei Kosygin in June 1967. He stood on its head the lecture Kosygin heard then from Robert McNamara about how trying to defend against nuclear weapons wouldn't work and would only beget many more of them. Reagan instead extolled a "shield that missiles could not penetrate—a shield that could protect us from nuclear missiles just as a roof protects a family from rain."[61]

Reagan had met Edward Teller in the autumn of 1966.* Teller had invited the new governor-elect of California to visit the Lawrence Livermore National Laboratory, about forty miles east of San Francisco. Reagan was briefed there on an upcoming test of a nuclear device designed to destroy incoming missiles in the air.[62] Teller was even then a true believer in the countercultural proposition that technology would allow a good defense to beat a good offense. Reagan, according to Teller, was deeply interested and asked several questions.[63] It's unlikely that he ever looked back; through the years he remained as convinced as Kosygin had been at Glassboro that defense is moral, offense immoral. The Soviet leadership, of course, changed its mind and pursued the ABM Treaty, which Ronald Reagan always opposed.

In the fall of 1980, a time when candidate Reagan was promising to upgrade the nation's offensive and defensive forces, Livermore successfully tested an "X-ray laser." Abruptly, the prospect of mounting such devices on orbiting satellites to kill hordes of incoming missiles swam into view.[64] Once inside the White House, Reagan was urged by Teller to develop a missile defense system. Teller had support from Joseph Coors, the brewery owner, and Karl R. Bendetsen, a former army undersecretary and later chairman of the Champion International Corporation; each backed a plan to create a separate agency for strategic defense.[65] This group drew support from Edwin Meese, the presidential counsellor, and William Clark, who had replaced Richard Allen as national security adviser.

Reagan was chafed by the futility of the search for an acceptable base for the MX; his frustration was keenly felt by various advisers, who were also acutely conscious of their expanding difficulties with Congress on the MX and other defense issues. Something new was needed—a way out of the impasse. As noted, Reagan had given the bureaucracy its chance—twice actually—to give him a plan for abolishing nuclear weapons altogether, and senior people, according to one veteran of the experience, "either laughed

---

*That same year, there appeared the Alfred Hitchcock movie *Torn Curtain*, which may have influenced Ronald Reagan's dream: "We will produce a defensive weapon that will make all offensive nuclear weapons obsolete—and thereby abolish the terror of nuclear warfare."

or did nothing. So when Edward Teller . . . [and others] pushed S.D.I. his way, he was ready for it. He wanted something. He doesn't like the idea of people living under the threat of nuclear annihilation. It collides with his upbeat, sunny view of life. S.D.I. probably could have been avoided if the system had provided an alternative. But it didn't, so he went elsewhere."[66] (S.D.I., of course, stands for Strategic Defense Initiative, the formal designation of Reagan's plan which became universally known as "Star Wars.")

Among those involved in the search for something new was Admiral James Watkins. General Jones's replacement as Chairman of the Joint Chiefs was Army General John W. Vessey, who knew rather little about strategic issues; Watkins did know something about them. He met twice with Teller and was impressed by the man and the case for strategic defense.

The chiefs were scheduled to take part in a meeting with Reagan on February 11 from which a solution to the MX basing problem was supposed to emerge. Watkins had been lobbying the other chiefs on strategic defense. After some discussion, Weinberger told Reagan that the chiefs had another approach—one that he himself could not then support.[67] In presenting the argument, Vessey must have echoed a Watkins comment: "We should protect the American people and our allies, not just avenge them." Watkins says, "The President was taken by the words to 'protect our people, not just avenge them.' And in fact, I believe he said, 'Don't lose those words.' "[68] The words, of course, weren't lost, and Reagan wasn't the first chief executive to feel that if a message plays well as a speech it will play well as policy. Each of the chiefs endorsed the idea of strategic defense, although they did not yet have a fix on what it would look like. But nothing, they assumed, would happen until the idea could be studied carefully within the government and worked out with the White House.[69]

State and Defense, not to mention America's allies, were blindsided by the unveiling of Star Wars. White House initiatives are invariably staffed out by appropriate agencies. But Shultz had only twenty-four hours' notice of this one. He was meeting in his office with a few aides when a copy of the speech arrived from the White House; Shultz was being informed, not asked to comment. "They were stunned, flabbergasted," recalled one of the aides.[70] Overnight, nuclear deterrence, the policy that had anchored peace for decades and defined relations between big governments, was out and defense of some radical kind was in. Weinberger was in Lisbon with Perle for a NATO meeting. They heard about the speech forty-eight hours before it was delivered. Working with others back in the Pentagon, Perle managed to delay it but only for twenty-four hours. Perle says, "It seemed unwise to me to launch a program of those dimensions without any advance preparation, without consultations with Congress, without consultations with our allies, without defining carefully the plan that we were going to pursue."[71] The Joint Chiefs, Watkins included, felt similarly. "What we had proposed was an aggressive learning experience," he says. "We wanted a research and development program that would allow the country to make a decision over the next several years on whether to do something about strategic defense. We couldn't know then whether it would be advisable to have space-based defense, ground-based defense or a mixture of the two."[72]

The private reactions of major allies ranged from abusively critical to angry. Washington was imposing a whole new strategy on them without warning, let alone consultation. The guarantor of Europe's security, it seemed, had opted for shielded insularity.

On sober second thought, however, matters appeared less grave. A notion as farfetched as Star Wars struck most competent scientists and technicians as being unlikely to get beyond square one. Washington and allied capitals relaxed. "Bureaucracy didn't take it seriously," recalls General Jones. "It was hard to get anyone to take the job of [S.D.I.] Program Manager. Abramson [General James Abramson, who took the job] had a terrible time. It took him a year to get a charter, two years to get it institutionalized. Bureaucracy took its cues from those signals."[73]

"For a year, most people didn't take S.D.I. seriously," says a closely involved British diplomat. "The papers on the subject were judged academic, certainly not operational stuff." As for public opinion, the idea of being defended, not just avenged, seemed wholly blameless. In fact, many people were confused, believing wrongly that the U.S. already had defenses against Soviet missiles; some of those who hadn't wanted ABMs around their cities and towns were sure that such systems existed elsewhere.

Although skeptical, some officials and many diplomats took a soberly cautious view. They knew that a seamless defense—the perfect astrodome—was fantasy, but a partial defense relying at least in part on space-based lasers and beam weapons might have some potential, although clearly not in the near term. Any such system, they reckoned, would emerge, if at all, in the next millennium. Also, in another year, there would be an election. Reagan would probably win it, but when next inaugurated—on January 20, 1985—he would be two weeks shy of his seventy-fourth birthday. Age could advance the start of his lame duck period. With bureaucracy dragging its feet on Star Wars and allied governments hostile, the idea seemed unlikely to survive the tenure of its lofty patron.

Only in Moscow was S.D.I. seen as deadly serious. Only the Soviets could have persuaded themselves of America's ineffable gift for squaring the circle technologically, so to speak. For them, Reagan's scheme was the devil's own mischief. Star Wars, if pursued, would bury the ABM treaty, by now a Russian icon. The treaty forbade testing and deployment of the systems on which Star Wars was based. Equally pernicious would be the effort needed to deny the Americans a unilateral advantage. The Soviets may have felt as if they were condemned to an endless and exhausting game of catch-up with a power holding higher cards. Actually, both sides had been working for many years on directed-energy weapons. Neither was then investing large sums, because throwing money at the forbidding array of technologies seemed premature, if not futile. But with the Americans mounting a full-bore attack on the whole lot, the danger of the existing technology gap widening irreparably had to be faced. Also, the Americans could talk about using directed-energy weapons in self-defense but might discover that they were better suited to an offensive mode. Finally, the Soviets, like America's allies, were comfortable with the status quo, i.e., nuclear deterrence.

In an interview with *Pravda* four days after Reagan's speech, Andropov conveyed the sense of Soviet shock. Space-based defense, he said, "would . . . open the floodgates of a runaway race of all types of strategic arms, both offensive and defensive. Such is the real purport, the seamy side, so to say, of Washington's 'defensive conception' . . . The Soviet Union will never be caught defenseless by any threat . . . Engaging in this is not just irresponsible, it is insane . . . Washington's actions are putting the entire world in jeopardy."[74]

Politically, the Soviets overreacted; in continuing to do so, they played into Reagan's hands by imparting a credibility to S.D.I. it would not otherwise have had. If the idea was so infeasible and, indeed, absurd, as a legion of scientists were saying, why then were the Soviets so stirred up and fearful? A Hungarian official with major foreign policy responsibilities thinks the Kremlin blundered; he partly blames the Soviet military, which, he says, "made S.D.I. seem credible and frightening in Moscow."[75]

"Within the Pentagon, many serious people saw S.D.I. as a serious diversion of resources," says an American diplomat. "It took several months for people like Weinberger and Perle to see its potential for mischief."[76]

Other agencies and other governments played for time in the hope that S.D.I. would in the long run be no more than a blip. But in Reagan's second term, it was the dominant superpower issue. It blocked a strategic arms agreement. It cast a heavy shadow over the Western Alliance. It reopened the debate on strategic defense which had seemed to end in 1972 with the ABM Treaty. The debate continues and, in one form or another, so will S.D.I.

XIII

Opportunity Lost

Reagan wasn't planning to extend the arms race into outer space. But the Soviets assumed, not unreasonably, that he would do just that. They were rattled, not only because they knew how ill-equipped they were to compete with America on a project so vast and technologically daunting but because other vulnerabilities were being exposed, above all their fragile leadership. Unlike Brezhnev in his last months, Andropov was an alert and lucid presence—when he actually was present—but the rapid rate of his decline must have been reminiscent of Brezhnev's final months. By the spring of 1983, it was clear to diplomats that Andropov wouldn't be around much longer and that the succession was uncertain. Although the chances of a younger and more vigorous figure—Gorbachev maybe—being picked weren't bad, the likelihood was that another ailing geriatric would follow Andropov.

Andropov had begun to question some of what passed for orthodox policy, including the inordinately heavy spending on strategic weapons. There was the dubious official practice of allowing each of two competing design teams to create the same strategic weapon rather than awarding the contract to one or the other of them. The military understood how stagnant the Soviet system and the economy had become; indeed, the only part of the system that functioned efficiently was the military, which lived within a virtually separate economy and had been running its own show since the post-Stalin era. Many of its leading figures, including Marshal Nikolai Ogarkov, the Chief of Staff, agreed with Andropov that priorities had to be shifted. Ogarkov opposed building more strategic weapons than the country needed, and he pushed for committing the same scientific and financial resources to other goals, including high-technology conventional weapons. Ogarkov's deputy and successor as chief of staff, Marshal Sergei Akhromeyev, is in the same mold; he has favorably impressed every American who has dealt with him. (According to Arthur Hartman, who was the American ambassador in Moscow at the time, most of the creative thinking within the military was being done then by Akhromeyev and a group around him.[1])

In Russian eyes, Reagan had introduced a massive complication. Besides the threat of an across-the-board American buildup, now there was the militarization of space to think about. "It sounds odd, but the Soviets think that if the Americans say they can do it, there must be something to it," says Hartman. "S.D.I. gave them a lot to think about: heavy pressure and huge expenditures. The pressure was unintended, but they felt it."[2] Andropov had promised to match the Americans "development for development" in creating new weapons.

Many Soviets, including Ogarkov and Akhromeyev, might have been tempted to use arms control as a device for lightening the load. But the Geneva talks were drenched in politics of a kind that had little to do with negotiation. The climate could hardly have been worse, and Reagan's red-baiting didn't help; he characterized the Soviet Union as "the focus of evil in the modern world" and as an "evil empire" in a speech delivered two weeks before the S.D.I. speech. (This speech, like the one on S.D.I., wasn't vetted by any government agency.)

Shultz and a few of the other cooler heads had been trying to restore amenities. A five-year agreement on grain sales to the U.S.S.R. was signed in late August. Negotiations for a cultural exchange agreement would be resumed. And Shultz was savoring a rare triumph over Weinberger and most of the rest of the government: Reagan had just agreed to end the embargo of American equipment to the Soviets for use in laying oil and gas pipelines. Renewing the habit of annual meetings between America's President and Andrei Gromyko seemed to be another sensible step. Gromyko invariably came to New York in September to address the opening session of the United Nations General Assembly and would then go to Washington and visit the Oval Office. The Afghanistan affair ended the practice; Carter didn't receive him in 1980, and Reagan hadn't done so either. Over the summer of 1983, tentative arrangements were made for Gromyko to call on Reagan during the next visit. Provided that nothing else went wrong, a meeting with so senior a Soviet official might end the squalid first phase of Reagan's relations with the Kremlin and inaugurate a more normal, or less bad, period. But on August 31, twenty days before Gromyko was due to arrive in New York, a Soviet fighter aircraft shot down Korean Air Lines

Flight 007, a Boeing 747 en route to Seoul with 269 people aboard. In the raucous aftermath, the governors of New York and New Jersey refused landing rights at any of their airports to the airplane bearing Gromyko and his delegation. Not for twenty years had Gromyko missed the opening of the U.N. General Assembly. The White House offered to let him land at a military field in a noncommercial aircraft, but he wasn't interested.

It wasn't the first such incident involving KAL. Five years before, one of its flights had lost its way and accidentally entered Soviet airspace near Murmansk. Flying at its cruising altitude and cruising speed, the airliner traveled several hundred miles, passing over two bomber bases, before being located by frantic Soviet defense units and forced to land. The incident was a deep and lasting humiliation for the responsible authorities; defense of the motherland is a sacred trust.

Even now, no one seems to know why Flight 007, with up-to-date avionics, could have strayed so far off course. The Soviets insisted, of course, that it was spying for the U.S., but many have examined that possibility and come away convinced that the KAL flight crew's mistake was an honest one.

The consequences of the Soviet pilot's actions were monstrous, but it, too, was later presumed to have been an honest mistake. His unit had wrongly identified the intruder as an American RC-135 reconnaissance aircraft. KAL 007's flight path had been similar to that used by these aircraft, which routinely loiter in airspace adjacent to Soviet coastlines, probing for electronic and communications data on air defenses; they also monitor Soviet ballistic missile tests. A test had been scheduled for August 31 but was canceled.

Communication within and between Soviet air defenses is electronically monitored around the clock by a network of regional stations operated by the U.S. National Security Agency using mostly military personnel. Three hours after KAL 007 left Anchorage, Alaska, one station picked up signals that the Soviets were tracking an unidentified airplane in the vicinity of the Kamchatka Peninsula. This information was not reported.[3] A few hours later, a Japan-based station overheard a Soviet pilot of an SU-15 interceptor shout *"Zapustkal,"* the past tense for having fired a missile.[4] For technical reasons, the report of this alarming intercept was delayed. Meanwhile, there were other reports of the Soviets conducting what seemed an unusually large training exercise for spotting intruders over Sakhalin Island. Some of the NSA stations nearest the scene were concerned that an RC-135—on a mission code-named "Cobra Ball"—had been the target of the air-to-air missile. But this aircraft was then reported to have returned safely to base.

Reports of the missing airliner were also coming in. By the evening of the 31st, Washington had begun connecting the missing KAL flight with the Soviet exercise.[5] The CIA and the DIA (Defense Intelligence Agency) cemented the connection by deciding that the SU-15 pilot had identified the intruder as a commercial airliner and cold-bloodedly shot it down. But air force intelligence officers declined to rush to that judgment. They knew that distinguishing the running lights of a Boeing 747 from those of an RC-135 was difficult. What had happened, they felt, was still unclear. This healthy caution was overwhelmed by the ballooning pressure within the administration to mislead itself by pinning a gross misdeed on the Soviets.

A key figure was Shultz, who because he had been doing what is normally expected of a foreign minister—trying to stay in contact with the other side—had made himself the Reagan team's odd man out; it was not an enviable position. In the KAL affair, the in-house voice of moderation on superpower matters became instead the unwitting agent of immoderation. Shultz was victimized by overeager senior staff people and sloppy intelligence.[6] Clearly furious, he appeared on national television in mid-morning of September 1 and gave what then became the official version: "The aircraft that shot the plane down was close enough for visual inspection of the aircraft." Angry rhetoric followed.

By then, intelligence officers in stations near the scene were convinced that the Soviet pilots hadn't knowingly shot down Flight 007. They were reported to have been "appalled" by Shultz's statement.[7] By the afternoon of the second day, air force intelligence confirmed the Soviet mistake. A Soviet pilot who had pursued the wayward Flight 007 over Kamchatka Peninsula had identified it as an RC-135. By then, however, the administration was locked on course. Reagan adopted an accusatory tone, and on September 5 proclaimed the worst case in a televised address: "There is no way a pilot could mistake this for anything other than a civilian airliner . . . this attack was not just against ourselves or the Republic of South Korea. This was the Soviet Union against the world . . ." He urged Congress to "ponder long and hard the Soviets' aggression" as it considered funding the MX missile system.[8]

A catastrophic accident had become part of the febrile competition between Washington and Moscow for the moral high ground. Moscow's version of events, first presented by Marshal Ogarkov, was that its Air Defense Force had been convinced that it was dealing with a reconnaissance airplane. Soviet authorities, no less arbitrary than the CIA and DIA, had then determined that Flight 007 had knowingly penetrated Russian airspace in an intelligence operation planned and directed by America.[9]

Name-calling continued through September, with each side clinging stubbornly to its version of the affair. It was, said Reagan on the 26th, a "timely reminder of just how different the Soviets' concept of truth and international cooperation is from that of the rest of the world. Evidence abounds that we cannot simply assume that agreements negotiated with the Soviet Union will be fulfilled."[10] Andropov delivered an answering broadside that managed to be equally explicit and even harsher.

Defense experts were more interested in the shabby performance of Soviet air defenses. For the second time in a few years, an airliner had penetrated Russian airspace and unintentionally eluded pursuit for some period of time. One wondered what bombers equipped with devices to avoid detection (and capable of supersonic speed) might be able to do. The question arose even more pointedly in May 1987, when Matthias Rust, a nineteen-year-old West German pilot, managed to fly undetected from Finland to Moscow and land his small aircraft in Red Square. The Soviets invest heavily in their air defenses, which in turn are a key factor in Western defense planning. Understandably perhaps, the planning ignores a salient point: Any system, however sophisticated, is no better than the people operating it.

In Geneva, Soviet negotiators were threatening to walk out of the talks on limiting intermediate-range nuclear forces if the new American missiles actually were deployed in Europe. Washington was unconcerned. The talks were going nowhere; the KAL incident had stiffened Moscow's resistance to concessions, or so it seemed. The only loser in a boycott would be the Soviet Union, which would be widely seen as a sulky bear retreating from its responsibilities back into its cave.

Some negotiators never stop trying. Paul Nitze and Yuli Kvitsinsky, the Walk in the Woods tandem, met on Saturday, November 12, in Geneva's Botanical Gardens. Kvitsinsky apparently proposed reductions of 572 weapons on either side, meaning the Americans would deploy none of their new weapons and the Soviets would reduce their own INF forces by that number.[11] The Soviets would also defer their claim to an allowance for British and French nuclear forces. The administration rejected the proposal and wouldn't make a counteroffer. Curiously, although many of its key figures, notably Weinberger and Perle, had at first been hostile to the INF deployments, they were now showing a marked preference for introducing the new missiles than for massively cutting back the Soviet forces targeted against Western Europe. Nitze pushed for deferring deployment. He was flatly turned down, with Weinberger urging that "we blow the whistle on this guy once and for all; we should come down on him like a ton of bricks."[12]

On November 22, the Bundestag in Bonn approved the deployment of the Pershing II missiles, the first nine of which arrived in West Germany the same day. On the following day, Kvitsinsky announced his government's withdrawal from the negotiations. Andropov then declared in a statement; "The Soviet Union considers it impossible to participate further in these talks."[13] Two weeks later, he began a boycott of the START talks as well. The Soviets had badly overplayed their hand. They needed the talks for both substantive and political reasons. But with threats to boycott and cruder threats to countries hosting the new missiles, the Soviets had painted themselves into a corner.

The chaos in Washington distracted European capitals from the mess Moscow had made of its affairs. The administration was still unequipped to make or abide by foreign policy decisions. The interagency process, such as it was, broke down constantly. The guerrilla warfare between agencies continued to be unremitting and savage. A laudable peace initiative in the Middle East collapsed almost at once. Then, an already controversial American military presence in Lebanon threw the government into turmoil when a single terrorist in a suicide truck laden with a ton of TNT crashed through a barrier in front of the marine barracks in Beirut and killed two hundred forty-one marines who were sleeping inside. The clear and inexcusable vulnerability of the barracks, reinforced by the strong feeling that the marines ought not even to have been in Beirut, would have become a major embarrassment for another President; but Ronald Reagan weathered it easily, partly, it seemed, by taking full responsibility and partly because of a distracting event: the successful invasion of the tiny island of Grenada two days later. In the same address he described the campaign in Grenada and the catastrophe in Lebanon. Much of public opinion associated itself with the President's sense of personal accomplishment and triumph in Grenada.

He inaugurated 1984, a campaign year, with a speech delivered on January 16 that many diplomats considered the most significant of his tenure in the White House. They thought, or perhaps hoped, that it would be a turning point. The message was that America's economy was recovering; its defenses were being rebuilt; its alliances were again solid. Reagan was now prepared to settle differences with the Soviets "peacefully and through negotiations." The new policy would be one of "credible deterrence, peaceful competition and constructive cooperation . . ."[14]

Aside from the flutter it caused within the *corps diplomatique,* the speech had curiously little resonance. Politicians and most other governments saw it as a curtain raiser of sorts on the presidential political campaign. The Soviets felt, or affected, disdain. Gromyko pronounced the speech a "hackneyed ploy" prompted by politics. And "it is deeds that are needed, not verbal exercises," he added.[15] If Western diplomats tended to give Reagan the benefit of the doubt, they worried about the absence of a policy, or even a design for one, that would give his words some tangible form. The smack of strong leadership wasn't there. Reagan might be making a course correction of his own, but he was still unwilling to break the interagency gridlock by intervening in the policy process. He craved consensus yet was still unwilling to forge it or even designate someone to do it for him. The State Department wanted to end the posturing on arms control that both sides had substituted for negotiation. Something new was needed. An obvious candidate would be a proposal to merge the INF and START negotiations. Running them on separate tracks never had made sense to many diplomats and specialists. Quite clearly, Washington couldn't reach its goal—a reduction of long-range Soviet missile systems—unless the Soviet goal—limits on the weapons of lesser range—was also satisfied. Moreover, an agreement in one forum but not the other could turn out to be highly undesirable; agreed limits on one category of weapons could be circumvented by expanding deployments of the other. Obviously, long-range Soviet missiles targeted against the U.S. could as easily be aimed at European cities, thus mocking an agreement reached in the INF basket. Lumping the not so different sorts of weapons into a single basket with the goal of an agreement putting both under one numerical ceiling had the merit of simplicity and seemed otherwise to make sense. Under any such agreement, the parties would doubtless allot most of their entitlements to the long-range weapons and minimize, if not eliminate, deployments of less capable midrange systems confronting each other at frighteningly short distances. The Germans, as noted, had once proposed this approach, and the British were tempted by it. "If the Americans wanted to merge the talks, there would have been no difficulty here [London]," says a British diplomat.[16] "The bigger the pie, the easier it becomes to lose sight of the small force." He meant that the issue of British and French forces probably wouldn't go away; in a single negotiation these weapons could be seen—and perhaps dealt with—as a small part of the entire East-West nuclear arsenal instead of as a large part of the nuclear forces deployed in Europe. Briefly, a single-basket approach could remove the political heat from the Euro-missile issue. It wasn't to be. The idea couldn't survive Washington's interagency process, and the Soviets never seemed interested in it themselves.

State's unavailing flirtation with the single basket in late 1983 coincided with Reagan's misadventure in Lebanon. The pressure on him to withdraw the marines had become overwhelming, and early in the campaign year he bowed to it. On February 7, Reagan announced the decision to begin the withdrawal. Three days later, Yuri Andropov, who hadn't been seen in public for 176 days, died. His successor would not be Mikhail Gorbachev, as some diplomats predicted, but Konstantin Ustinovich Chernenko, an unprepossessing figure who was best known for having been Brezhnev's chief crony for nearly thirty years; he also became Brezhnev's surrogate and legatee.

Selecting Chernenko meant undoing the brief Andropov experience and solemnizing a system as ossified as its leadership. Chernenko seemed little more than a caretaker—"a tremendously average man," commented one of his peers to Dusko Doder of the Washington *Post;* "an ideal number-two man," said another.[17]

Chernenko was seventy-two years old and rumored to be unwell. Among the British dignitaries attending Andropov's funeral was David Owen, a recent foreign secretary who had begun his career as a medical doctor. On meeting Chernenko, Owen saw a man enfeebled by emphysema. "He was short of breath and clearly wouldn't last long," Owen recalls.[18] He struck Washington as another pasteboard figure, likely to topple out of sight before any real business could be done with him. This perception was somewhat more apparent than real. Besides sustaining the downside of the Brezhnev legacy, Chernenko would uphold his patron's commitment to the quest for détente with the West. A resumption of direct contact between the superpowers was among his goals; these seemed clearer than Reagan's. People in Washington who complained about Reagan having no interlocutor in Moscow forgot that many capitals, not just Moscow, fretted that Washington, for practical purposes, had no one to speak authoritatively for Ronald Reagan, not even Ronald Reagan. The Soviet machine, with mostly elderly men operating it collegially, labored under Chernenko, as it had under Brezhnev. But it didn't break down.

With the marines leaving Lebanon, Washington's focus shifted to its superpower rival. A curious pas de deux began. Reagan wanted to create a visibly better prospect for arms control. The Soviets wanted to head off Star Wars. But with the forum in Geneva closed down and the habit of businesslike contact at the upper levels having lapsed years earlier, the parties were poorly positioned to give their priority interests a nudge. Shultz and Dobrynin began meeting confidentially during March. In June, Dobrynin presented a note from his government calling for "urgent measures" to prevent the militarization of space. Talks beginning in September in Vienna were proposed.

Besides banning weapons deployed in space against earthly targets, Moscow hoped to block other systems designed to destroy satellites. The use of antisatellite weapons, known as ASAT, was an alarming prospect for much of the defense and arms control community. Each side relies on its satellites to detect the other's missile launches. And each, the Americans especially, is heavily reliant upon them for military communications. If either worried during a crisis that it was about to be "blinded"—lose its reconnaissance satellites—the temptation to strike first would sharpen.

A new American ASAT system had entered the early testing stage; it was a small missile released unarmed from aircraft and designed to destroy a satellite by homing in and colliding with it. The device appeared to be a satellite killer that might actually work and hence was a threat to stability. Its advocates pointed to an existing Soviet ASAT as an argument for an American system. Opponents observed that America, too, had once deployed a similar device—about fourteen years earlier than the Soviet Union's appeared. The Soviet system, they argued, was very like the one America had abandoned—a primitive, low-altitude weapon and no threat to high-altitude satellites or to much else.[19]

The note that Dobrynin gave Shultz was made public in Moscow two hours later. Moscow had its answer that evening. The Americans were willing to meet in September on one condition: The Soviets would have to discuss a resumption of the talks in Geneva on long-range and midrange weapons. Replying just as promptly, the Soviets excluded any linkage between the Vienna meeting and the talks in Geneva that they were boycotting. Once again, the parties were playing to the galleries; this was express-lane tit for tat, with neither side willing to concede the initiative.

A moratorium on testing ASAT weapons had by then become a Soviet requirement. The administration wouldn't consider it, not seriously. Any such prohibition could have put a hold on Star Wars, since laser and beam weapons capable of destroying ICBMs on the ground or in the atmosphere could also be used to destroy orbiting reconnaissance satellites. The Pentagon saw in Moscow's outcry against ASAT a maneuver with Star Wars as its real target. People in Defense were no less skeptical of Star Wars, or S.D.I. as they called it, than before. But by then, according to a British diplomat, "Perle and others had begun to see S.D.I. as the great blocker [of arms control]. And for them, constraints on ASAT would have been the thin edge of the wedge—a transparent ploy for getting at S.D.I."[20]

Instead of posturing, the parties might have dropped their respective preconditions to a meeting and just met. They didn't. "Talks about talks about talks" was how a Western European diplomat characterized the affair. "We were talking about talking," said a Soviet diplomat, using oddly similar language.[21]

Heading into the election campaign, the administration was upbeat. It had come out of the crossfire of proposals and counterproposals in better shape than the Soviets. Its position impressed people as less rigid, hence more reasonable. Then, on September 10, the White House played a choice card. Andrei Andreyevich Gromyko had accepted an invitation to visit the Oval Office after a four-year absence. At seventy-five, Gromyko was one year Reagan's senior and had been closely involved in American affairs since 1939, first as a young diplomat, then as wartime ambassador to Washington (when Ronald Reagan's career in films was peaking), and finally as foreign minister, a job he had held since 1957. He had known every American President since Roosevelt.

The surprise was general. Why would Moscow oblige Ronald Reagan by accepting what seemed a politically inspired invitation? The polls were showing Reagan's only vulnerability as lying in his unbottomed hostility to the other superpower. Actually, the Soviets had no choice. Declining would have been a major blunder and caused the larger surprise. Washington could then have blamed Moscow for the continued heavy freeze that had settled over relations. Also, the visit would be an opportunity to make direct contact with Reagan himself and, in the bargain, show the world that the Soviets were not unwilling to meet their tormentor halfway. And, who could say, something might even come of it.

The idea for the meeting came from the State Department, not the White House. According to the Washington *Post*, it was strongly backed by Nancy Reagan; the White House Chief of Staff, James Baker; and the Deputy Chief of Staff, Michael Deaver.[22] The story was accurate, and so was the rumor beginning to seep out that Mrs. Reagan wanted her husband remembered for having lowered the risk of nuclear war. Only in 1984 had she begun to show an interest in his place in history, and he himself had been unconcerned with posterity's judgment or the demands of historiography. But Mrs. Reagan, once aroused, was determined. Most insiders thought her self-absorbed and acutely conscious of her own role. In relation to her husband, said one of them, she was as the moon is to the sun. And if, as seemed likely, the sun disappeared before the moon, she would want it to cast the brightest possible glow before fading out.[23] "She lobbied the president to soften his line on the Soviet Union," wrote Deaver.[24] Because of her support for the Gromyko visit—and Deaver's—the State Department was able to impose a degree of secrecy on it that was highly unusual in the Reagan era. State worried that administration hard hats would scuttle the visit by leaking word that Reagan's views of the Soviet Union and negotiating with them hadn't budged; any such story would have probably provoked a Soviet cancellation.[25]

The signals coming out of Moscow were mildly encouraging. Just before the visit, Gorbachev and Grigory Romanov, his supposed rival for the post-Chernenko leadership, made foreign policy speeches in which neither mentioned the need for American missiles to be withdrawn from Europe before talks could be resumed.[26] Still, expectations weren't high. With the new missiles being deployed in Europe, reviving the prostrate arms control process would require a huge effort, which might lead only to more talks about talks.

Although lacking summit pageantry, the meeting with Gromyko could have equivalent importance, at least as State saw it. He was perceived there as having become a czar of foreign policy and the source of Washington's difficulties. Other capitals demurred; they saw him as a dominant, though not controlling, figure. And they doubted that his line had become as extreme or hardline as State was saying it was. Gromyko's entire career had been largely spent in sorting out relations with America. He was at least as much the architect of the Soviet détente policy as anyone. The Third World held no interest for him; for example, it's doubtful that he ever visited sub-Saharan Africa. His life was his job, to which his approach was methodical and totally professional. "My personality doesn't interest me," he once told an interviewer.[27]

Gromyko's visit didn't appear to go well. The chemistry between him and Shultz had never been good; preliminary talks were sour, and then the line and tone of Gromyko's speech to the U.N. General Assembly angered Shultz, although most diplomats found it routine and no harder than usual.

The meeting with Reagan set no pulses throbbing. Gromyko clung to generalities and would not be drawn out on issues. He spoke at length about the push of technology and the problem of controlling arms before arms took control of men. Reagan showed little flexibility, although he did stray from his talking points by raising the question of merging the START and INF talks. Gromyko was unresponsive. Reagan commented apropos of nothing that he didn't eat children, and Gromyko solemnly replied that they weren't eaten in the Soviet Union either.[28] In planning the affair, State and the NSC staff had left a few minutes at the tail end of one session for Reagan to be alone with Gromyko; they wanted to give him a chance to discuss some issue one-on-one with a Soviet notable. One aide had the job of observing the pair through a peephole. He reported later that Reagan, once alone with Gromyko, disappeared into an adjoining bathroom. He emerged, and Gromyko followed suit. Gromyko reappeared, and the two then left the office and joined the others in the dining room, interrupting lively speculation about what they were talking about.[29]

If seemingly a nonevent, the meeting did nonetheless break the ice. It was, in fact, the first in a sequence of events that included four meetings between Reagan and Gorbachev. It put to rest much of the angst in Moscow about a Reagan thirsting to make war. Just after his smashing reelection, arrangements were made for Shultz and Gromyko to meet in Geneva in early January to discuss "a range of questions concerning nuclear and outer space arms."[30]

In December, Barry Goldwater announced, as chairman of the Senate's Armed Services Committee, that he would try to kill the MX missile system. "I'm not one of those freeze-the-nuke nuts, but I think we have enough," said this apostle of strong, state-of-the-art defenses.[31] And both Robert Dole, the Senate Majority Leader, and David Stockman, the budget director, were calling for big cuts in the Pentagon's budget requests.[32] Also in December, Reagan named Paul Nitze as special adviser to Shultz for the talks with Gromyko. And he hinted vaguely at a moratorium on testing of antisatellite weapons. The second term, it seemed, just might produce the kind of superpower accord that only a politically secure and usually lucky president could bring off. A whiff of change hung in the air.

Of change, drama, and surprise, there was to be a full portion. Still, some things change little, and slowly at that. The obstacles to an agreement on strategic arms were largely unaffected by the bustle of events and bizarre summit meetings.

Shortly after Reagan's reelection, John McCloy, then eighty-nine and the foreign policy community's chairman-laureate, sent him a letter with a copy to Shultz. He urged the President to negotiate an agreement with the Soviet Union. He didn't presume to tell the President what sort of agreement, although David Klein, who worked with McCloy, feels that he was thinking of an arms control treaty. McCloy wrote that in his own negotiations with the Soviets, he had always found someone on their side who thought about the problems as he himself did. He got back one note from Reagan thanking him for his advice and another from Shultz warmly thanking him for having raised the matter with the President *and* asking McCloy to let him know what sort of reply he got. McCloy was surprised that Shultz would ask a private citizen for that kind of information. A secretary of state, he felt, should know how his boss feels about negotiation with the other side.[33]

The epic superpower ascent toward arms control that would occupy the next four years began with the January talks in Geneva between Shultz and Gromyko. From them emerged the only workable compromise: Washington accepted the principle of "preventing an arms race in space" and agreed to address space-based defenses in formal talks, if these could be resumed. The Soviets agreed to resume them. The parties agreed on a three-basket approach that would cover strategic systems, midrange systems, and defensive systems, whether space- or ground-based. "We did not bang our fist on the table and did not even fling eyeglasses on the table," said the dour but sardonic Gromyko back in Moscow. And he warned portentously, "It is impossible to consider banning strategic weapons separately from the outer space issue."[34]

Ronald Reagan dealt with four Soviet general secretaries—as many as there had been prior to Brezhnev. The received wisdom within his entourage was that he could begin to deal seriously with the Soviets only when they, too, had a real leader, one who was physically whole and active. That case isn't persuasive; in its first term, the administration stubbornly refused to do much beyond striking an attitude of aloof hostility; it also tended to trace all or most of the world's ills to the Kremlin's door. The Walk in the Woods didn't fail because Brezhnev was declining, although that could have been a constraint on the Soviet side had the Americans taken up Nitze's initiative.

Not many expected that in the thaw to come Reagan would mortify his party's hard right and suppress some of the deeply held views he had carried with him to the White House. And no one expected a *Soviet* leader to catalyze this lively, occasionally hectic, period in superpower relations. But in policy and public relations terms, Moscow, not Washington, held the initiative during most of Reagan's second term. Washington reacted, often sluggishly. The form had been reversed.

In mid-December, a few weeks before the Geneva foreign ministers meeting, Mikhail Gorbachev visited London with his wife, Raisa. Soviet watchers took notice. His first visit to a major Western capital must have been planned and approved at senior party levels, thus reinforcing the impression of Gorbachev as Chernenko's likely successor. The second impression was of a visit that went remarkably well from Gorbachev's (and Moscow's) point of view. He and Prime Minister Margaret Thatcher, by then the West's elder statesperson, got on famously. After several hours of conversation—many more than scheduled—she described him as someone she could work with. A leadership change in Moscow was clearly not far off; Soviet television viewers could see already that Chernenko couldn't stand without assistance or speak for any length of time.

Toward the end of his life Konstantin Chernenko would open meetings of the Politburo and then yield the chair to Gorbachev. Gromyko and Viktor Grishin (who hoped to succeed Chernenko) objected, but their time was past.[35] Chernenko's funeral on March 13, 1985, was recalled by Celestine Bohlen, a Washington *Post* Moscow correspondent, as a time when "all the familiar and tedious rituals of death were speeded up, as if a movie had been put on fast forward. The dead leader did not even get front-page billing in *Pravda*. In another year, when the Soviet press began to call things by their own names, they would say that this was the end of the 'period of stagnation.' At that point, it became acceptable for Soviet officials—some of them today the most ardent spokesmen of the 'new thinking'—to concede publicly that they had been lying all those years."[36]

Washington sensed opportunity in the demise of Chernenko but was not prepared for Gorbachev. What Mrs. Thatcher and other Europeans saw in him squared not at all with the administration view, which held that all Soviet leaders are alike. If Gorbachev became a commanding figure with whom a dialogue was possible, so much the better. But the likely prospects were judged: (1) more stagnation by consensus; or (2) a fragmenting, or even a breakdown of central authority, as various baronial figures—each possessing great bureaucratic fiefdoms—struggled for power. Washington saw some of what Gorbachev saw: a Central Committee weakened by lack of leadership; major parts of the system—the KGB, the Foreign Ministry, the military—operating with more independence of party control than at any time in the past and often getting in each other's way. But like Gorbachev and others, these great satrapies knew that the system urgently needed major repairs. The KGB saw massive official corruption seeping into its own organization. The military saw spending on defense as having flattened out in 1977 and not increasing since. Gromyko was not nearly as accountable as he ought to have been for the country's external affairs, which were not in good order. Most important, the economy reflected the system: weak, inefficient, and overwhelmed by bureaucracy. Although hardly "an Upper Volta with rockets," as derisive critics portrayed it, the Soviet Union was held down by some of the same unyielding problems that afflict Third World economies

In Moscow, Gorbachev seemed the obvious solution. He had the necessary political talent and versatility. He was determined and willing to spill blood. He was the right age, fifty-four. And he clearly knew where he wanted to go, an aspect that wasn't understood in Washington. The Gorbachev takeover resembled to a degree the inauguration in Washington of a president who brings with him a new program and new faces, although they all belong to the same party as their predecessors.

Gorbachev was a regional figure. Instead of building his political career in Moscow, as so many other clever and ambitious young men do, he returned to Stavropol-krai, the territory in southern Russia in which he was born and raised, after taking a degree at Moscow State University. He entered the Komsomol (Communist Youth League), in which he rose rapidly and at some point acquired the patronage of Fedor Kulakov, one of the party's rising stars. While still in his thirties, he became a party manager for Stavropol-krai, which abruptly put him into contact with many senior party officials who regularly visit the spas at Mineral'nyye Vody—second only to the Black Sea as a holiday favorite of the *nomenklatura* (elite). Gorbachev made important connections—what Russians call *veze*—and these matter immensely in the Soviet system. State institutions that maintain sanatoriums there include the KGB, the Ministry of Defense, and the Committee for Atomic Energy. Some members of the Politburo and Central Committee have their own. Not surprisingly, local party appointments in Stavropol were cleared with various offices in Moscow.[37] Whatever Gorbachev had to do for the great and near great must have been done well. There isn't much hard information on that key period of his life. It is known, though, that besides Kulakov, who died in mysterious circumstances at the age of sixty, Gorbachev acquired there an even more powerful patron, Yuri Andropov. What seems to have attracted the austere Andropov was Gorbachev's rare incorruptibility.[38] Andropov and Mikhail Suslov, once the party's chief ideologist and second-ranking figure, are thought to have persuaded Brezhnev to appoint Gorbachev to fill the vacancy on the Central Committee left by Kulakov's death. His appointment was announced in November 1978. The thankless agriculture portfolio was part of the Kulakov legacy, but it did Gorbachev no harm. A year later, he became a candidate member of the Politburo and the following year, 1980, a full member. He was then forty-nine, eight years younger than the next youngest member, Grigory Romanov, and twenty-one years below the average age of his colleagues. In less than two years, Gorbachev's abundant talent, including a talent for survival, had made a deep impression on his peers, and his arrival at the top of the tree was judged a matter of time. It took five years, although he had control over much of the party well before taking charge.

The novel Gorbachev style included a vigorous interest in the press and its works that dated from the Stavropol period. The press more than amply returned his interest; the man and his purpose became the object of endless comment by professional Sovietologists and an abundance of instant experts. His affinity for the press was linked to an even more surprising flair for public relations. Even before Chernenko was officially dead, an ardent Gorbachev, often accompanied by his attractive wife, had become the willing quarry of camera crews and news photographers. He turned up in well-cut clothes that seemed to fit and upmarket felt hats. Raisa's high profile and higher style constituted another novelty. (It wasn't widely known that Andropov's wife, Tatyana, even existed until she attended his funeral.)[39]

Gorbachev is no closet social democrat, according to Western diplomats who have studied him. He is, they say, a modernizer and a reformer, coexisting with a conventional Marxist-Leninist. If Peter the Great had been a convinced Leninist, he'd have sounded like Gorbachev. "Socialism has not yet spread its wings as it should," he says. "We have vast potential which is as yet unused." And "It is a revolution without shots, but a deep and serious one."[40] According to Dimitri Simes, an emigré Russian scholar and practicing Sovietologist in Washington, "The people who were the most cynical and disillusioned when Gorbachev arrived were those who took Marxist-Leninism seriously."[41] Briefly, Gorbachev's assault on the party structure means no disrespect to the doctrine on which it is founded.

"There is often a huge misperception in the West of any new Soviet leader," says a senior British diplomat, another Sovietologist. "Gorbachev isn't making the Soviet Union more like us. He is making it less like what it was, or has been. His analysis of the Soviet economy and system corresponds to the Western view of them. His chances of surviving or succeeding—they are the same thing—are no better than fifty-fifty and maybe worse. He has to make life worse before he can make it better. There are no rewards for the sacrifices. The system and the Russian people have had a social contract: It says, 'Life here won't be as good as in the West and other places. There won't be a lot of material advantage. But you will have work and won't have to work very hard.' Gorbachev has busted half of that contract." One remembers the old Soviet joke: "They pretend to pay us and we pretend to work."

Diplomats warned that Gorbachev's openness and beguiling frankness were less attractive at home, where dirty linen isn't shown to outsiders. "There is a strong sense of we and they," says an American specialist. "It can be family versus nonfamily, or the Russian people against other peoples. One is either in the tent or outside the tent. Russians, especially young Russians, may be cynical and apolitical, but they are no less Russian than their elders."[42]

Most everyone within the tent, including the party bureaucracy, knows that something must be done about the economy. But the bureaucracy and some of Gorbachev's peers oppose his efforts to combine economic reform with social change. He regards the two as inseparable. Only if goods and information can be freely and easily exchanged can the whole dronish, parasitic structure be made productive; that is the Gorbachev view, which, as seen by his critics, puts glasnost and "democracy" ahead of party discipline and law and order. (Democracy in the sense Gorbachev favors it means more freedom of expression and some limited choice within the existing one-party system.) Gorbachev draws part of his strength from the absence of an alternative; his adversaries see no one else who might lift the country from its economic decline.

If the world beyond the Soviet bloc has grown accustomed to the Gorbachev style, the party bureaucracies of the bloc have not. At times recently, *Pravda* has been hard to find in the kiosks of some East European cities, notably Bucharest, where it may be judged to contain subversive material. Any official in some bloc countries would be jailed for talking about glasnost and democracy as Gorbachev has done. Bringing a society that is programmed to look ahead, not back, face to face with the Stalinist blight of its formative years shook the system and much of the society. Gorbachev has insisted on filling in what he calls the "blank pages" of Soviet history. But Russians living within and outside the party structure have had to ask: If Stalin was so awful, what is one supposed to think about his legacy—the system itself?

In Washington, the CIA had for some time prior to Gorbachev's arrival been bombarding Reagan with memos generated by William Casey about how the Soviet Union was falling apart. State regarded this material as inflated and aimed to please the addressee, as it did. "Reagan loved these summaries of CIA forecasts," recalls one American diplomat. "And then along came Gorbachev saying things that weren't very different. That affected Reagan's view of Gorbachev. He was saying what Reagan wanted to hear."[43]

The self-criticism—the departure from the routine practice of blaming foreign powers for what ails them—went down well in Washington. But all the novelty would stop at the water's edge, said the cautious and skeptical people who lay down the American line on Soviet foreign policy. At a party plenum in April 1985, Gorbachev set out an agenda that told a lot about his plans. Not all of it became public right away, but Washington was aware of what he said, including a warning that Soviet troops would have to withdraw—and soon—from Afghanistan. He even referred to the involvement there as a "bleeding wound."[44]

Washington was not convinced or even very impressed, and dismissed much of what Gorbachev has said and done as theater. A lot of it was indeed pure public relations; his chief adviser, Alexander Yakovlev, is the regime's grand vizier for press and propaganda, along with ideology. Nonetheless, running through the Gorbachev performance is a clear sense of the need for a period of calm on the foreign policy front in order to deal with the domestic front. Gromyko's sulky bear must not only rejoin the big world but also make a *bella figura*. This meant reviving the superpower connection *and* the competition with Washington for the moral high ground. Along the way, Gorbachev would say things that no one else in Moscow has said. At the Party Congress in February 1986, for example, he warned that the Soviet Union can be secure only if others are also secure. In the past, Soviet security was equated with the insecurity of others.

All of the above argued for resuming the arms control process. Doing so for domestic reasons, however, was probably more important. Arms control was hardly a substitute for economic reform, but that lay far ahead and a treaty with the U.S. might allow some redirection of resources. In shaping the next five-year plan, Gorbachev would have to control the military budget. His argument that unless the economy improved, the U.S.S.R. would become less capable of competing with the West—militarily or otherwise—had silenced the military but doubtless only temporarily. He and they, aware that the West was extending the technology gap, knew that the Soviet Union must cooperate with these countries rather than try to intimidate them. But another break in the dialogue with the U.S., they also knew, would dictate a hardening of the line at home, with renewed pressure to expand the military budget.

The wild card in all this was Star Wars, that reminder of the underdog's wearisome struggle to stay the course. In designing advanced gadgetry, the Soviets hold their own, but they have trouble producing it. An arms control agreement would buy Gorbachev some time in which to modernize production. But Star Wars was in the way. Reagan was committed to space defense as only he could be to idealized solutions, and the Soviet Union had been committed by Gorbachev's predecessors to stopping it, just as they had been committed to heading off the INF deployments. Actually, their campaign against S.D.I. allowed its American advocates, including Reagan, to point to Moscow's fulminations as evidence of the project's great potential. Gorbachev, and presumably Yakovlev, elected to soften the Soviet line. And very probably, Gorbachev used S.D.I. within the Politburo to strengthen his mandate to deal with the Americans on arms control and to modernize the economy. Still, the line on S.D.I. could change but not the bedrock Soviet resistance to it. Gorbachev complained to the Dutch Prime Minister that Reagan was using S.D.I. to wage economic warfare against him.[45]

Ronald Reagan had been induced by his advisers and his own illusions to embrace one of the more irresponsible platforms of modern times." The words were written not about Star Wars but Reaganomics—by David Stockman, Reagan's first budget director. "He had promised . . . to alter the laws of arithmetic," Stockman continued. "No program that had a name or line in the budget would be cut; no taxes would be raised. Yet the deficit was pronounced intolerable and it was pledged to be eliminated. This was the essence of the unreality . . . The White House's claim to be serious about cutting the budget had, in fact, become an institutionalized fantasy."[46]

Star Wars was another case of the fantasist chez Reagan overcoming a more realistic side. It became the largest of the obstacles to a strategic arms agreement with the Soviets, who were never likely to accept limits on their strategic offense so long as America planned to threaten that offense with a novel defense. In return for a small and probably meaningless concession on Star Wars, Reagan could at one time have had a strategic arms agreement of a scale that no predecessor would have ever tried for. But he must have sensed that a dream like Star Wars, once interrupted, cannot be resumed. To the end, he ignored the substance of progress in order to keep faith with its shadow.

Society was an accomplice. It wanted to believe. It saw the absurdity of Reaganomics, but credited its namesake with reviving the economy, uneasily excused the mammoth deficits that were piling up, and massively reaffirmed Reagan's mandate. His mythic shield against the unspeakable but unavoidable consequences of nuclear war met with undeserved tolerance and even approval. Among living creatures, says Hobbes, only man is granted "the privilege of absurdity."[47]

After being appalled at first by S.D.I., the Defense Department had officially rallied to it by the end of 1984. "An inspired vision," Weinberger commented.[48] The idea was to knock out attacking missiles before they reached the reentry, or terminal, stage. They are most vulnerable during the four minutes or so of the boost phase, when they are rising slowly and the emissions from their rocket plumes are easily detected. All of the warheads are still aboard the missile in this phase. Hitting it in the postboost, or midcourse, phase—after about twenty minutes—is far more difficult, though not impossible, say the advocates.

Star Wars weapons divide into three groups: lasers, which travel at the speed of light; particle beams, which go nearly as fast; and rocket-powered interceptors, which are slow.

A rash of studies by scientific groups, including the American Physical Society and the Congressional Office of Technology Assessment, threw heavy doubt on the concept. Besides being highly vulnerable to attack from the other side's beam weapons, the orbiting space stations would require inordinate amounts of nuclear power for "housekeeping," i.e., controlling altitude and receiving and transmitting information. No one could say how many lines of instruction the system might require, but ten million was judged a conservative estimate by some. (A shuttle launch, by comparison, requires about one hundred thousand lines.) And the computers would have to track the missile, the bus (the missile's final stage), and the warheads; they would have to distinguish warheads from decoys, coordinate satellites and weapons-firing devices, report on hits and misses, and also manage to survive countermeasures.[49]

Scientist advocates of Star Wars compared skeptical colleagues to those who doubted the Apollo program and the fission bomb. The skeptics rejected this analogy, arguing that putting people on the moon and splitting the atom were strictly scientific and engineering accomplishments, with only barriers to knowledge and understanding to be overcome. The unarmed moon, they said, has nothing in common with Russia, which deploys a wide assortment of nuclear weapons, many of which would be unaffected by a Star Wars defense.[50] Their point was that the other superpower, if planning an attack, would take steps to overcome a defense that would, of course, have to work as planned the first and only time it was used. There seemed to be a rich menu of measures that could be taken to neutralize Star Wars, the most basic of which would be swamping it with more warheads and also decoys. "Any defensive system can be overcome with proliferation and decoys, decoys, decoys, decoys," said Richard DeLauer in testimony before the House Armed Services Committee when he was undersecretary of defense for research and engineering in Weinberger's Pentagon.[51] Weapons experts like Ashton Carter, a Harvard physicist, noted that satellites cost much more than boosters. "We're going to go broke building satellites before they go broke building boosters," he said.[52]

Sir Geoffrey Howe, Britain's Foreign Secretary, asked whether Star Wars could be deployed "without generating dangerous uncertainty." He said, "There would be no advantage in creating a new Maginot Line of the twenty-first century, liable to be outflanked by relatively simpler and demonstrably cheaper countermeasures."[53] Star Wars was that rara avis which looked the same in London, Paris, and Bonn: The largest spending program ever proposed by any government would substitute an unworkable defense for nuclear deterrence. It could—probably would—demolish the ABM Treaty. Embassies in Washington warned that some of Reagan's people wanted to scrap the treaty because it forbade carrying out tests of various S.D.I. systems and subsystems. All Europeans regard the treaty as the backbone of the arms control regime. The British and French fear that without its heavy restriction on Soviet defenses, their own small missile forces might be unable to reach targets in the U.S.S.R. European leaders and their advisers were uniformly angry, not least those who had argued for having the new American missiles. "We regard nuclear deterrence as indispensable," said a French diplomat. "We cannot all go to the ends of the earth persuading Europeans that they should accept deployment of missiles, and then call them immoral and about to become obsolete . . . The Germans and the British share our precise concerns."[54]

Washington launched a multifront campaign to overcome the resistance of its major allies to S.D.I. Offering them a share of the research activity in what salesmen were calling the "third industrial revolution" was one tactic. Another amounted to what British diplomats called "show and tell." America must proceed with S.D.I., ran the argument, in order to overhaul the Soviets in a vital area of technology. Diplomats and officials were shown pictures of Russian laboratories behind whose doors advanced development work was supposed to be going on. The pictures were unconvincing. "The show and tell rubbish was shown to successive diplomats arriving in Washington and to successive ministers of defense," said a British diplomat. "There were private briefings of the Prime Minister by [NSC adviser] Bud McFarlane."[55] One of his colleagues added, "There was an effort to show the Soviets as being ahead. It was very dishonest. The subject is complicated. Comparing the two programs is comparing apples and oranges. The U.S. stuff is more advanced, but will it work? The Soviet technology is older, hence presumably more manageable. But will it necessarily work any better? Who knows? Space defense requires computers and heavy lift. The U.S. is way ahead in computers and will stay ahead. They are ahead in lift."[56]

Not much is known about the Soviets' research in laser and beam weapons except that, like the Americans, they have been at it for decades. Both programs date to the late 1950s. Each is thought to be still in the early stages, held in check by huge technological barriers. But scientists, by and large, feel that the lead, if there is one, lies with America, given its stronger technological base.

By early 1985, it was clear that only Ronald Reagan and a coterie of true believers could take a Star Wars defense seriously. Several others, including those who were lobbying Congress and other governments most intensely, saw it as a surrogate for something they did believe in: land-based nuclear defense. Most were veterans of the embittered debate on ABMs in the late 1960s and early '70s. They intended to win a replay, with Reagan's vision and determination clearing the way. Gradually, advocacy of Star Wars separated the faithful few who echoed the President's line about a defense that would eliminate missiles from those who adopted the more modest contention that Star Wars would strengthen deterrence by complicating Soviet planning for a first strike. An American diplomat compared the selling of Star Wars to a televised light-beer commercial. "Some people say it's less filling, others that it tastes great."[57]

A hardy perennial of the Reagan era was the issue of whether to continue observing the SALT II Treaty. The case for ending the practice of informal compliance rested largely on charges of Soviet cheating. As before, only State and the Joint Chiefs plumped for the treaty. They wanted the cheating issue dealt with at a special forum created by the SALT I agreements for just that purpose, a strategy that had always worked well in the past. Defense, notably Weinberger and Perle, still preferred having the issue—using it to score debating points. Between 1981 and 1985, the alignment of agencies on the issue didn't change, and neither did the arguments.

Most of the supposed violations were seen as spurious by disinterested experts. A few fell into a gray area, and one was genuine. It concerned a large phased-array radar which the Soviets built near Krasnoyarsk in central Siberia in the early 1970s, about the time the ABM Treaty was signed. The treaty provides that radars of this type must be located on the periphery of the two countries, not inland, where they could be used to track incoming missiles. The station at Krasnoyarsk is one of a network of 12. Unlike the other 11 all built on the periphery—its inland location violates the treaty. The radar's purpose, according to the Soviets, is to track space vehicles, a function allowed by the treaty. The CIA concluded that the radar actually filled a gap in the Soviet early warning system through which missiles from America's Trident submarines might travel.[58] Members of the Supreme Soviet have said privately that building the Krasnoyarsk radar was a blunder. They add that not for many years was the government aware of what the military was doing at Krasnoyarsk.[59] Construction at the site was halted when it was still two years or so from completion. (It will probably have to come down if there is to be a strategic arms agreement.)

Predictably, the cheating issue provoked another test of strength over SALT II compliance. Reagan was due to render his decision on the matter on June 10. NATO ministers, meeting in Estoril, Portugal, a few days earlier, took issue with the American hard line on Soviet violations. Their concern was not so much with the charges as with the resolve of Reagan's hard-liners to cite these as cause for dismantling the SALT regime. Shultz shared the allies' concern. He transmitted their view in a strong message to Reagan. On June 5, the Senate voted ninety to five for a resolution urging the President to continue observing the treaty. Prime Minister Margaret Thatcher, whom Shultz saw on his way back to Washington, weighed in with a typically explicit message urging full compliance.[60] But the Joint Chiefs, who split with Weinberger over the issue, tilted the balance once more. They came down in favor of sustaining the limits on Soviet systems in part to avoid having to spend money on new strategic weapons that would be better spent on conventional arms. Reagan surprised most of his own advisers by agreeing yet again to comply with the unratified treaty that he had often characterized as "fatally flawed."[61]

By then a Reagan-Gorbachev summit was in the offing. The advocate was Shultz. "At first, it was difficult. Only a handful of people at State were pushing it," recalls an American diplomat who aided Shultz. "Nancy Reagan and Mike Deaver were very helpful. But Cap [Weinberger], Meese, and Casey were Mau-Mauing the enterprise. Reagan himself seemed most interested in finding out whether Gorbachev believed in God."[62] He added—and others agree—that Reagan was very eager to meet Gorbachev and, unlike some of his entourage, not at all worried about being eclipsed by the younger and more dynamic figure—the man who had dazzled Margaret Thatcher and others with his flair and grasp of complicated issues. Reagan insisted on arrangements that would allow plenty of time for private conversation with Gorbachev.

The Soviets were eager to meet. Gorbachev emerged as a keen summiteer. A meeting with Reagan was good theater, good politics at home, and a good reminder to the world of who the other superpower was, especially when it was being run by a man so strikingly different from each of his predecessors.

The awkward variable was Star Wars. The Soviets insisted that the meeting, scheduled for Geneva in November, would have to be more than a fireside get-together, as the American side seemed to prefer. They wanted to make some progress on nuclear issues; predictably, they stressed the need to head off an arms race in space. Unwisely, they said the meeting would be a failure unless there were movement toward their position.

Less than three weeks before the meeting, Reagan repeated a bizarre offer to provide his space shield to other nations, including the Soviet Union. A week before the meeting, he clarified his position: "I don't mean we'll give it to them. They're going to have to pay for it—but at cost. But we would make this defensive weapon available."[63] Reagan had high confidence in the one-on-one meeting with the other fellow as a device to clear away difficulties and misunderstandings. He seemed to think that once Gorbachev saw the beauty of the Star Wars concept, his resistance to it would vanish. He actually told Gorbachev during the meeting that it would be dangerous if just one side were to deploy a space defense.[64]

"All that money thrown at unattainable goals will hit some other, different targets," said a prominent French business figure around this time. "And these will give America commercial advantages vis-à-vis everyone else."[65] Gorbachev, too, was more concerned about spin-off from Star Wars than a fanciful space shield. Yet another technology gap in offensive weapons loomed ahead, and Gorbachev put this problem to Reagan, who assured him that S.D.I. was a purely defensive program.[66] Gorbachev wasn't convinced. But according to Ambassador Arthur Hartman, who sat in on the meeting, "Gorbachev decided that Reagan meant what he said at Geneva. He did want to rid the world of nuclear weapons, and he was deadly serious about S.D.I. Gorbachev's idea was to persuade Reagan to take the one [abolition] without the other [Star Wars]. He seems to have decided at Geneva that he could bring it off."[67]

In five hours of conversation with his rival, Gorbachev discovered a man whose immense goodwill on nuclear issues was matched by a remarkable ignorance of them. As Hartman suggests, Gorbachev must have reckoned that he could exploit his discovery. Everyone left Geneva satisfied, the Americans because their man had emerged intact from five hours of conversation with a formidable rival. They had gotten the "photo ops" they came for at no cost; indeed, Reagan seemed to have emerged the winner on points because nothing had been conceded. The Soviets, after creating expectations of an American concession on space warfare, departed empty-handed. What's more, Gorbachev had agreed to a follow-up meeting in 1986 in Washington.

Further east, the outcome looked quite different. "The Geneva meeting was crucially important," says a member of the Hungarian Central Committee. "It persuaded Gorbachev that agreement with Reagan was possible. Many Soviets had disagreed with that analysis."[68] An American diplomat who was there agrees: "The most important effect was the Soviet leaders being able to satisfy themselves that Gorbachev could get on with Reagan."[69] Gorbachev might have observed that relations had improved considerably since the time of the KGB's all-points alert about Ronald

Reagan, nuclear bully boy. The summit communiqué said that "nuclear war cannot be won and must never be fought."[70]

But the statement ducked the S.D.I. issue. Neither side had really understood the other. Gorbachev either didn't notice or underestimated Reagan's stubbornness—his unshakable faith in an idea whose time he felt had come. Gorbachev could perhaps be excused for having had some skepticism about a program estimated to cost between $200 and $300 billion and for which there was no consensus in Washington or the Western Alliance. In turn, Reagan and various advisers didn't understand that Gorbachev probably couldn't come to Washington unless and until some kind of compromise on limiting arms, notably those earmarked for outer space, had been worked out. Two very different men had restored the dialogue and imparted momentum to it. Yet diplomatically, they had set themselves on a collision course.

Washington basked in a warm summit afterglow. The arms control talks would resume in January. Gorbachev appeared to want an agreement with Ronald Reagan, partly because he was the only president available to deal with and partly because Reagan was very secure politically. An agreement with him was unlikely to encounter the political squalls that had victimized the SALT II Treaty.

The summit boosted George Shultz's stock to an all-time high, and Weinberger appeared to have been a heavy loser. He didn't go to Geneva but tried to sabotage the meeting by leaking a letter on the very day Reagan arrived, urging him to avoid any of the steps that might lead to negotiation.[71] But things were rarely as they seemed in Reagan's Washington. Having banked the political returns from the summit, the administration did nothing about following it up. Mrs. Thatcher sent Reagan a message early in the new year urging him to do something about arms control while there was time remaining to him. She didn't get an answer, and nothing was done.[72]

Instead, Gorbachev took the initiative and the spotlight. He was not to relinquish them. On January 15, he called for abolition, in stages, of *all* nuclear weapons by the year 2000. He proposed starting with a 50 percent cut in the long-range systems over a five- to eight-year period. He wanted to end the arms race in space before it began and to ban any further testing of nuclear weapons. Most astonishing, he ambushed NATO capitals with a proposal to dismantle all the Soviet and American midrange weapons deployed in the European theater. The famous zero option—handiwork of hard-liners, nonnegotiability its charm—had been embraced by this alarmingly original Soviet leader. He even suggested that the reduction and dismantling of the nuclear arms could be intrusively verified by on-site inspection.

Although thrown well offstride, most of official Washington saw the initiative as pure theater. But Pentagon hard-liners were worried, perhaps for the first time. Gorbachev, they felt, had gone over the heads of Reagan's entourage and addressed himself to a serious abolitionist. "Gorbachev soured the atmosphere with the January 15 speech and then a procession of initiatives, mostly aimed at the gallery," recalls an American diplomat. "Reagan was the only exception. He liked the January 15 speech. His comment was. 'Why did it take so long?' It was only Gorbachev's timetable that put him off. Both of them had crazy timetables."[73]

Over the next several weeks, Gorbachev did make several proposals, none of them serious and some frivolous. But he was setting a fast pace, and Washington could think of little to do or say other than to push for a date for the next summit. Moscow rejected a February date; the Twenty-seventh Congress of the Soviet Communist Party was being held then. Washington had pressed for an early summer meeting, but the Soviets held back. The sides had very different priorities. Reagan was keen to give Gorbachev a tour by helicopter of some American towns, villages, and marinas so he could see for himself how different the systems were—how much better off the American workingman and his family were. But Gorbachev wanted— probably needed—to have something to sign at the next meeting. Politically, he was in no position to take part in another idle pageant.

In its central aspect, the situation was surreal. Lying behind Gorbachev's showboating was an absolute need to avoid a new cycle of competition in arms at the high end of technology. For all the proud talk, his system could barely compete at the middle level. But the Reagan administration, for all its talk about standing tall, was still unable to decide on a new strategic missile, nor was it any closer to agreement about what it might want to extract from a serious negotiation. Instead, Reagan had set about trying to implant his innocent dream of a space shield into the national psyche via the mashed potato circuit; the off-year congressional elections lay some months ahead. Nothing less than a radically altered superpower relationship would do. Star Wars would be the guarantor of a world freed from the nuclear terror.

At some point, however, the program's unreality would take its inevitable toll, and that point precisely coincided with the start of Gorbachev's exuberant nuclear diplomacy. The services had no fondness for Star Wars and, faced with cuts in military spending, their support for exotic new hardware was tepid. Both the Senate and House did make heavy cuts in the program. Members felt more secure in denying the President's pet project, partly because of three successive failures of American space vehicles. The first was the loss of the *Challenger* space shuttle in January. In April, a Titan 34-D rocket and its ultrasecret payload exploded just after lift-off, and two weeks later, a Delta rocket carrying a weather satellite disintegrated after little more than a minute of flight. If the space program's basic hardware couldn't be relied on, what was one to think about the endlessly more complex Star Wars technologies? If experts couldn't debug the shuttle, how could they debug Star Wars? The even more worrisome disaster at Chernobyl, site of the Soviet nuclear reactor explosion on April 26, added to the rising skepticism about advanced technology in general. The term "technological hubris" came into vogue.

Chernobyl shook every European capital. Its radioactive fallout affected all their countries, as did the questions it raised about nuclear power. But even more upsetting were moves being made by Gorbachev and Reagan that Europe's leaders could do little about. In appropriating the zero option for midrange systems, Gorbachev had put himself in a heads-I-win, tails-you-lose position. He didn't need the SS-20s and its older siblings. Some small portion of his longer-range systems, of which there was a healthy surplus, could cover the same targets. But with this all but painless gesture, he might rid Europe of the American missiles capable of striking Russia. And by agreeing to what was generally seen as a one-sided, if not cynical, offer by Washington, he would bank most of the credit from any deal that was made. But if there were no deal—if NATO reneged on its own proposal—Gorbachev would be credited with having gone the limit in trying for agreement and his rivals would bear the blame for failure. His gambit had put the West Germans, British, and other hosts of the new missiles in an awkward spot. Having taken intense heat for accepting the deployments, they were deeply reluctant to walk back that decision and reopen the matter. They had convinced themselves and a large part of public opinion that the missiles would tighten the link between Europe and the guarantor of its security. Removing them might turn out to be as politically dicey as introducing them had been.

Even more distressing was a bare-knuckled assault on the entire SALT regime being mounted by the Weinberger faction. SALT II compliance was again in their sights and, more alarmingly, so was the ABM Treaty, which specifically banned a space-based defense, and, as normally interpreted, ruled out not just deployment but also development testing of the directed-energy weapons on which Star Wars was supposed to hinge. Only laboratory research would be allowed, because that cannot be monitored. Some months after Reagan's reelection, a handful of Star Wars partisans began searching for a way around the treaty's high walls. Richard Perle and Fred C. Iklé, Undersecretary of Defense for Policy, asked a young New York lawyer named Philip H. Kunsberg to determine whether the treaty actually meant what everybody said it did. Some months later, Kunsberg, who had no relevant experience, produced a "radically revised interpretation of the ABM Treaty."[74] His report was referred to the State Department's newly arrived legal adviser, former judge Abraham D. Sofaer; the general counsel of the arms control agency, Thomas Graham, Jr.; and the Office of the General Counsel of the Department of Defense. After a cursory review of the negotiating record and a talk with Nitze, Sofaer concluded that the treaty did allow testing and development of defense systems based on new technologies but not their deployment. He reported as much to Shultz and Nitze on October 3, the same day that six former secretaries of defense restated their support for the ABM Treaty and advised the parties to "avoid action that erodes [it]."[75]* Sofaer had been told by a member of his staff that Graham and John McNeill, assistant general counsel for Defense, had both rejected the case for reinterpretation. The staff member also took that position. Sofaer did not report their views to Shultz and McFarlane.[76]

Three days later, Robert C. (Bud) McFarlane, the National Security Adviser, repeated the revisionist Sofaer line on *Meet the Press*.[77] The televised comment was pronounced official policy by the White House spokesman two days later. Shultz was as surprised and unprepared as he had been when Reagan unveiled Star Wars in March 1983. Mrs. Thatcher and West Germany Chancellor Helmut Kohl were also surprised and promptly questioned the move in messages to Reagan.[78]

Although the issue isolated Shultz within the government, he managed to fashion a compromise: The administration would continue to observe the narrow—that is, the literal and restrictive interpretation while reserving the right to apply the broader, more permissive version when it chose to. As Georgia's Senator Sam Nunn and others pointed out, this was saying that a treaty could be explained to the Senate as meaning one thing, but then, if some future president found himself inconvenienced, it could be reinterpreted. There was no place or precedent for any such executive branch edict, said Nunn.[79] If the administration didn't like the ABM Treaty, he said, abrogating it would be more honorable than twisting its

*They were Harold Brown, Clark Clifford, Melvin Laird, Robert McNamara, Elliot Richardson, and James Schlesinger.

meaning.[80] Some past presidents had discarded treaties they didn't like. But the Reagan administration was unlikely to inflame relations with allies and adversary alike by disowning the ABM Treaty.

Reagan was just as annoyed at most allied leaders in Europe as they were at him in May 1986, the moment he chose to change course on SALT II compliance. Except for Mrs. Thatcher, none of them had supported his decision in April to bomb Libya as a means of discouraging terrorism. Nor, as noted, did allied ministers support the administration's sweeping view of Soviet cheating. So as Shultz tried yet again to head off a Reagan decision to break away from SALT II, the European card he liked to play was worth much less. Even more important was the altered role of the Joint Chiefs in this discussion. When General David Jones and General John Vessey had been chairmen, the chiefs had backed State's position on SALT II compliance. The views of the new chairman, Admiral William J. Crowe, Jr., were more neutral. Crowe was asked to comment on SALT II, but fellow chiefs were not asked. And they were not involved in meetings on SALT II. "You don't meet because someone doesn't want to hear your answer," says Admiral James Watkins, who was still Chief of Naval Operations and accustomed to being heard on these subjects.[81]

The decision to scrap SALT II was announced May 27. Mrs. Thatcher, who had been warned a few days earlier, was deeply embarrassed as well as disappointed. Her cooperation with and support for the Libyan bombing had, she thought, earned her the credit she needed to nudge the decision her way. The fuss made in Britain of the Libyan affair had just begun to die down when Reagan dropped this second shoe. Denis Healey, the shadow foreign secretary, said it was the worst moment in Anglo-American relations since the Suez crisis.[82]

On May 29, just two days after Reagan's announcement, the Soviets put forward a proposal in Geneva that was not only serious and lacking in fanfare but drew mainly on State Department thinking. When serious and businesslike in the past, they had dropped their ritual demand to include forward-based American weapons within any agreed limits on long-range systems. Now they dropped it again. In other ways, the positions of the parties were close. Each had proposed cutting by half the inventories of long-range weapons. Much the hardest issue turned on Star Wars. It wasn't negotiable, according to Reagan. It had to be negotiable, according to the Soviets; unless limits could be put on defense, they said, there would be no limits on offense. They proposed reaffirming the commitment to the ABM Treaty, as interpreted by both sides since it was signed in 1972. They wanted a nonwithdrawal pledge of fifteen to twenty years but would clearly settle for less.

Gorbachev had made another move from which he couldn't lose. His proposal struck Western diplomats as reflecting the contours of the only possible deal. A link between offense and defense had to be there. In June, the Soviets began adding substance to the contours. "This was hard to deal with because it contained mainly our own ideas," says an American diplomat.[83] But Washington was still preoccupied with trying to extract a date for the summit from the Soviets, who continued to demur. Gorbachev's aggressive diplomacy in Western Europe was beginning to prosper, and his emissaries noted plausibly that he could hardly be expected to visit Washington at a time when the Americans were making their plans to breach the SALT II limits.

Reagan's letters to Gorbachev continued to reflect his sunny confidence that the other man could be persuaded to see the light on space defense. A letter from Gorbachev in late June may have begun to disabuse him; it made clear that some give in his position on space defense was required. There ensued an epic struggle over Reagan's reply. The issue was whether to concede a link between offense and defense by agreeing to a period of nonwithdrawal from the ABM Treaty, as the Soviets had proposed. Such a step would meet their condition, provided it was also agreed that the treaty would be interpreted as narrowly as in the past. The Reagan letter, which was sent on July 25, was studiously ambiguous. He seemed to be moving in Gorbachev's direction without actually doing so. The glass could be seen as half full or half empty. Although quite general, the letter did put forth the daring suggestion that *all* ballistic missiles could eventually be done away with. This notion originated with Perle. Like the zero INF option—also his idea—it was judged nonnegotiable, hence harmless. For that reason, the Joint Chiefs approved its inclusion in the letter to Moscow, just as they had once approved the zero option.

A major breakthrough seemed to be within reach but for one large unknown, Ronald Reagan. There for the taking lay an agreement of the kind that he and like-minded advisers had always said they wanted: one based not on limits pegged at upper levels but on massive reductions of strategic missiles and warheads. In return, he'd have to accept some constraint on the testing of various Star Wars components for a period of years, ten perhaps. But those items were not likely to be ready for testing within that period. So what, if anything, would be lost by granting this one concession? Unless he did grant it, warned some advisers, Gorbachev might cancel the Washington summit. Those who knew Reagan best doubted that he would allow the vision to be trifled with. Its opponents were legion. Any constraint, once accepted, could be the beginning of the end for Star Wars. Thus, the full weight of superpower relations, not to mention progress in nuclear arms control, seemed to hinge on whether one side could arbitrarily reinterpret the most important compact to which both were party.

Both sides tried behaving as if their problem would settle itself. In August and September, an American delegation led by Paul Nitze (known within the bureaucracy as "Snow White and the Seven Dwarfs") held talks with Soviet counterparts in Moscow and Washington. They covered all points on the arms control agenda as preparation for a meeting in New York between Shultz and Eduard Shevardnadze, Gorbachev's Foreign Minister. Shevardnadze surprised Shultz by agreeing that all the issues, including even human rights, were on the table. And his side, he said, wanted to carry on these wide-ranging talks methodically and without preconditions. This was just what Washington wanted to hear, and a meeting between Reagan and Shevardnadze was arranged for September 19.[84]

Shevardnadze brought to the Oval Office a letter from Gorbachev proposing a minisummit—a base camp meeting in London or Reykjavík. Quite clearly, Gorbachev had concluded that given the chaos in Washington, any progress on arms control could be made only with Reagan himself. But since Reagan continued to withhold the concession he needed on Star Wars testing—the treaty commitment issue—Gorbachev was unwilling to take part in another summit, least of all on Reagan's turf. He might have been unable to obtain the authority he needed from the Politburo to go to Washington unless something had been nailed down ahead of time. And the something would have to cover the space defense issue.

Reagan was attracted to the proposal. A two-day meeting in Reykjavík was scheduled for October 11 and 12—an agreeably short time before the midterm elections. *Both* sides were keen to show progress. An understanding or framework agreement on INF—the least difficult issue—probably lay just ahead; that, at least, was Washington's assumption. The Soviets encouraged this sanguine Washington view by expressing a willingness to liberate INF from Gorbachev's iron precondition: Progress on any one front would be linked to progress on all fronts. "Everyone expected a meeting aimed at promoting an INF deal," recalls a former administration official.[85] But did the Americans mislead themselves? Were they aware that once the meeting began, Gorbachev would link everything to Star Wars? A U.S. diplomat says, "They told us more or less there would be no precondition. They said, in effect: 'We will have new things to say in every area and of course S.D.I. is very important.' "[86]

What occurred at Reykjavík defied comprehension. There can have been no stranger meeting between leaders of big powers—whether allied or adversary—in modern memory. During fifteen hours of conversation, Reagan and Gorbachev came very close to agreement on eliminating most, if not all, of their nuclear weapons. Two high rollers were matching idealized visions and raising each other. They reached a higher and more rarefied place than anyone had been, and then fell off the cliff.

Reagan and a small entourage arrived expecting a curtain raiser to the main event in Washington. It was apparent that Gorbachev had something else in mind. His delegation, starting with Alexander Yakovlev, was top-heavy with specialists in propaganda and public relations. Just before the start of the first meeting—a private chat between the two leaders—Gorbachev waved a distinctly heavy brief at Reagan, as if to suggest that he had brought quite a lot to talk about. And he had. "We were hoist on our own petard," says an American official who was there. "We had been saying that we wanted to talk about everything."[87] But, in fact, the American side was unprepared to talk about much other than INF. Reagan, according to an aide, "opened on human rights, and then said the purpose here is to prepare for the Washington meeting. He asked for ideas on dates, and noted that this [encounter] was a pre-meeting."[88]

Shultz and Shevardnadze joined the discussion after an hour or so, and Gorbachev, reading from a short paper, declared that space defense was on the table and closely linked to the other main agenda items, including INF. His proposals were sweeping and included a 50 percent cut in strategic arms, elimination of all midrange systems in Europe, and new negotiations to ban nuclear testing.[89] He was ready to meet some long-standing American requirements: a cut in heavy Soviet missile systems and no allowance for British and French weapons. But he also proposed a period of nonwithdrawal lasting ten years from the ABM Treaty and restricting Star Wars research and testing to the laboratory.

Meetings of experts followed and, at Shultz's suggestion, continued through the entire night. The key discussions were between Nitze and Marshal Sergei Akhromeyev, who is, says Nitze, "a pleasure to do business with."[90] Akhromeyev could quite clearly act for Gorbachev, whereas there was no military figure on the American side who could speak for the Joint Chiefs.

A Sunday morning meeting, the last on the schedule, went smoothly for a time, with the parties building on a framework that Nitze and Akhromeyev had worked out. Then, predictably, space defense reared up and halted progress. The meeting adjourned, with Reagan and Gorbachev agreeing to reconvene at 3:00 P.M. But first, Shultz and Shevardnadze would meet with a few senior aides to see if something could be accomplished. The only issue, said Shevardnadze, was whether Reagan would commit himself on nonwithdrawal from the ABM Treaty, as strictly interpreted. While he spoke, Perle and Colonel Robert B. Linhard, the NSC staff's chief arms control expert, scribbled some lines on a piece of paper which was passed to Shultz, who, after noting that the suggestion it contained had no official status, read from it. The stunning crux of the language drew on the offer contained in Reagan's letter of July 25 to eliminate all ballistic missiles. But whereas the letter had been silent on the timetable for reaching this lofty goal, the Perle-Linhard paper proposed ten years. Fifty percent of all nuclear weapons would be cut in the first five-year period, during which both sides would remain faithful to the ABM Treaty. Adherence to the treaty would continue for another five years, during which the parties would dismantle the rest of their ballistic missiles, keeping only what remained of their bomber and cruise missile forces. But at the end of the ten-year period, with all ballistic missiles gone, either side would be free to deploy an antimissile defense as insurance against cheating, accidents, or missiles belonging to others.

Over the next four hours, the parties thrashed about with this radical approach. It presented a problem for the Soviets. Their strength lay in ballistic missiles, and these would be gone. America held an advantage in bombers and cruise missiles, many of which would remain. So Gorbachev counterproposed eliminating not just most, but all nuclear weapons during the ten-year period. Reagan, by most accounts, responded favorably. "All nuclear weapons? Well, Mikhail, that's exactly what I've been talking about all along . . . get rid of all nuclear weapons. That's always been my goal."

"Then why don't we agree on it?" Gorbachev asked.

"We should," Reagan said. "That's what I've been trying to tell you."[91]*

The exchange is cited by Donald Regan, who left with Reagan just after the meeting broke up. Afterward, Moscow and Washington would disagree on whether Reagan did agree to abolish nuclear weapons in ten years. The Soviets said he did, the Americans that he did not—only that he saw abolition as the eventual goal. Yet in a postsummit discussion with members of Congress, Reagan left the impression that he and Gorbachev had agreed on abolition. Moreover, by one account, the then national security adviser, Vice Admiral John M. Poindexter, warned Reagan that " 'we've got to clear up this business about you agreeing to get rid of all nuclear weapons.'

" 'But, John,' replied Reagan, 'I did agree to that.'

" 'No,' persisted Poindexter, 'you couldn't have.'

" 'John,' said the President, 'I was there, and I did.' "[92]

---

*The quotation marks are mine. Donald Regan says that "out of deference to the office and the man," he hasn't quoted the President directly. He does, however, quote Gorbachev.

It is, of course, clear why the near thing abruptly collapsed. Gorbachev shattered the magic moment by tying it to acceptance of a ban on Star Wars research and testing outside the laboratory (and a recommitment to the ABM Treaty). By then, the word "laboratory" provoked Reagan as few others. Testing confined to a laboratory, he thought, would kill space defense. He was not aware—and Gorbachev may not have been either—that the ABM Treaty, as normally interpreted, does permit a good deal of the sort of developmental testing that was at issue. "Laboratory, laboratory, laboratory," Regan cites the President as saying gloomily in the car as they left the meeting.[93] Probably no one of the four people in the room did understand what the treaty did and did not allow. (For example, it does allow testing beyond the laboratory of certain novel technologies and devices but not of deployable systems or their components.) Nitze, Perle, and Linhard could have explained the ins and outs. But no one of them was in the room. Nor was Akhromeyev. This absence of expertise during such a conversation helped explain the fiasco.

Most American diplomats doubted that Gorbachev could have acted any differently. He had arrived, they guessed, with a brief that had been cleared with the Politburo and allowed no give on Star Wars. But it appears that he didn't share his intentions with most of those who accompanied him. "His people were saying before the meeting that they didn't expect him to be overly tough on S.D.I.," says one of the Americans who was there. "They were saying it could be worked out."[94] And Paul Nitze recalls that after the meeting broke up and the Soviet side was leaving, Akhromeyev put his arm around his shoulder and said, "This was not my fault." Even he may not have been fully informed of the constraints on Gorbachev.

One is left wondering whether the outcome would have been different if Gorbachev had known more about the ABM Treaty. Two days later, Yuri Dubinin, the Soviet Ambassador in Washington, was instructed to tell the State Department that a laboratory (as applied to Star Wars research) didn't refer only to an enclosure, but could also mean a testing range. A month later, the Soviets were saying that laboratories could exist in space and some Star Wars–related research conducted in them. "They were clearly falling off the tough position they took in Reykjavík," says an American diplomat who took part. "That could mean Gorbachev goofed there or that Reagan broke up the meeting before Gorbachev could make whatever concessions on S.D.I. he brought with him."[95]

Many wondered why no one on the American side—unprepared and in way over its head—didn't suggest a few weeks' pause in which to digest all that had been accomplished. A pause would have allowed the White House to consult the Joint Chiefs, allied governments, and Congress on an impending accord of colossal scope. Without a word to anyone, Reagan had almost turned the Western security system upside down. Allied leaders judged the what-might-have-been as constituting a near abandonment of the American commitment to defend Europe. "Reykjavík shook her rigid," says David Owen of Mrs. Thatcher's reaction.[96] Other European leaders, the Joint Chiefs, and key congressional personalities were equally shaken. A nuclear-free world was hard to envisage. Being able to verify any such millennial development was harder still to envisage. And even if the West could adjust to the idea, there was great doubt that the Soviets could, given their profound sense of being encircled by enemies. No one questioned Reagan's serious intent, but there was great skepticism about Gorbachev. All parties were confused, not least the Soviets, who had trouble finding a common line to take on Reykjavík. In the following week, Gorbachev said one thing and two of his officials something else on the issue of whether an INF accord was linked to space defense.

The lasting importance of Reykjavík had little to do with the confusion and outcries that followed, or with its lesson about the hazards of improvisation at the summit. The meeting showed Gorbachev that serious business could be done with Ronald Reagan, the most intensely anti-Soviet of American presidents. On both days, Gorbachev repeatedly sought reassurance from Reagan that the latter really meant what he said about being willing to withdraw the Pershing and cruise missiles from Europe. It was as if he couldn't quite believe it. Also, much of what was agreed to at Reykjavík couldn't be walked back and was later put into agreed language by the delegations in Geneva. But even more important was the effect of Reykjavík on relations between the superpowers. Nineteen eighty-six had been a year of persistent tension and flare-ups between them. The irony of Reykjavík—on its face a horrendous failure—is that not long afterward a less shrill and seemingly less mistrustful dialogue between Washington and Moscow was under way; relations became less tense and more predictable.

Reykjavík was too bold for the world," says George Shultz. "It jarred people to think about no nuclear weapons. But we made more headway on limiting them there than in any two-day history of man."[97]

At first, he and Reagan clung to abolition as a not so distant goal. But the reaction to Reykjavík in Washington and Europe disabused them. British and French forces would not be part of any such romantic stuff, as Shultz for a moment seemed to think they might be. Mrs. Thatcher and

French President François Mitterrand, after a brief huddle, set the administration straight. Nuclear deterrence was not to be trifled with; Europe was unwilling to re-create the system that produced two devastating wars in a quarter century. Typically, Mrs. Thatcher came to Washington to deliver the verdict on Reykjavík herself. In the wake of her visit and tough messages from other places, the notion of eliminating ballistic missiles was banished. But NATO did bless the plan to reduce the long-range versions by half.

At about this time, Ronald Reagan's luck began to change. For six years, his exceptional popularity and credibility had made the White House the center of political gravity. The Reagan agenda was America's agenda, and neither anxious allies nor political opponents could do much about it. But as Harold Wilson, twice Prime Minister of Britain, once said, "A week is a long time in politics." A National Security Council staff run amuck and trying to arrange an arms-for-hostages swap with Iran dealt its chief the heaviest blow of his political career. Nothing would ever be quite the same for Reagan, and large questions arose. Would a beleaguered White House create a constitutional crisis in the middle of a presidential crisis by seeming to scuttle the ABM Treaty? To insist on reinterpreting the treaty was judged the same as scuttling it. On February 6, 1987, Senator Sam Nunn, a potential presidential candidate, warned Reagan that his position would create a "constitutional confrontation of profound dimensions. Such a decision would also very likely be taken on Capitol Hill as the end of arms control under your Administration."[98] Rather surprisingly, Chancellor Kohl, a cautious man, sent Reagan a letter at this time urging him not to apply the broad interpretation to the treaty. He never got an answer.[99]

The Soviets were at least as confused as anyone else about how to react. At long last they had made what seemed productive contact with this American President who, although a self-professed enemy, could deliver on his commitments. But after Iran-scam, could he still deliver? There was doubt. For months, the Soviets had been alternately delinking and relinking a zero INF accord and their well-worn edict on fidelity to the narrowly interpreted ABM Treaty. Among the questions for Gorbachev was whether to harden his position in the light of his rival's sudden vulnerability or soften it so as to make it easier for Reagan to reach an agreement they both wanted. On February 27, former Senate Majority Leader Howard Baker was appointed to succeed Donald Regan as chief of the sorely troubled White House staff. In Washington, Baker was a reassuring presence. The next day, Gorbachev delinked INF for good from the other issues.

Gorbachev, it bears repeating, wanted better relations with the West in order to concentrate on his domestic agenda. In Margaret Thatcher he found a kindred spirit. Although poles apart doctrinally, each of them was—is—determined to change the ways of an unproductive social and economic system. She, too, equates the task of modernizing a society with revolutionizing it. In March, she visited Moscow for two days and had eleven hours of conversation with Gorbachev on the first day alone. At one point, he spoke without interruption for one and one-half hours about glasnost and perestroika. "He really lights up when he talks about internal change," says a senior British official. "He exudes power and energy like no one I've ever seen. They sat at a small round table," he continues. "At times—especially intense moments—their faces were no more than nine inches apart. There were frequent clashes, like thunder squalls."[100]

Mrs. Thatcher adopted the practice of sending lengthy messages to Gorbachev after her visits to Washington. And, not surprisingly, she lectured Reagan, Shultz, and other senior officials in Washington about why the Gorbachev revolution was in everyone's best interest and should be encouraged. Her argument, simply put, was that contented Russians would be easier to deal with than discontented ones. The Western side, she felt, would have less difficulty with a reasonably well-off Soviet society than one that felt deprived and insular but was also very strong militarily. Gorbachev could have had no more ardent or persistent advocate than this otherwise sworn enemy of socialism in all its forms.

Reagan's interest in an arms control agreement had grown as his domestic problems worsened. Indeed, each side wanted a good summit meeting in Washington before the end of the year. With INF no longer linked to larger problems, Washington and Moscow gave it top priority. Although inherently simpler than START, INF had its own hazards. There were numerous allied sensitivities and concerns. Every move at Geneva had to be coordinated with London, Bonn, and Paris. Verification was thorny. Long before Reykjavík, a few hard-liners had demanded on-site inspection. Given the Soviet "record of cheating," said Weinberger, "you have to have the ability to do what bank examiners do."[101] In March, American negotiators proposed that each side be present to witness the destruction of both the missiles and the launchers. They called for "perimeter and portal monitoring" of missile production sites. And they asked for the right to make spur-of-the-moment challenge inspections—any time, any place.

The Soviets accepted and raised the ante. In April, they called for "on-site inspection of U.S. and third-country facilities," thus folding American allies into the drama.[102] Then, in May, Yuri Vorontsov, Deputy Foreign Minister, noted that "according to the U.S. proposal . . . inspectors will be sent only to the gates of the enterprises. We propose that they should also be granted access inside the enterprise."[103]

Abruptly, the administration became the victim of its own posturing. Unlike START, an INF agreement didn't really require intrusive on-site verification. "No one even understood what 'any time, any place' meant," says a German expert. "None of this was thought through."[104]

"The Soviets backed us into a corner," says an American expert who agrees. "We had talked about intrusiveness—continually—and they took us up on it, saying, in effect, 'Absolutely. Right on. Any time. Any place.' We backpedaled. When it dawned on us that 'any place' included some highly sensitive installations, we drew back."[105]

"The Soviet verification package was essentially the same as ours," says a closely involved American diplomat. "But they played the hand in a way that let us choke on our own vomit."[106]

The issue created deep splits within the administration and unhappiness in allied capitals. There was the frightening prospect of roving Soviet teams popping in and out of ultrasensitive installations having little or nothing to do with the agreement. Abusing the right to go any place, any time, they might, for example, insist on being shown Fort Meade, home of code-breaking and code-making technology, or advanced nuclear weapons bases. Several experts had argued that on-site inspection imparts a false sense of security. One side, they noted, can always hide what it chooses from the other's inspectors. Such people felt more comfortable with satellite surveillance.

Once again, the administration had made a sweeping proposal aimed at complicating life for the Soviets, only to have them complicate life by accepting it. "Gorbachev bought challenge inspection just the way he bought the zero option," says an American diplomat.[107] The administration was taken off the hook by the negotiation itself. By early summer, the parties had agreed to "zero" not only the midrange missiles with ranges up to 3,000 miles, but also some of the shorter-range systems, capable of traveling about 500 miles. Abolishing this entire class of weapons simplified verification, since detection of a single missile system would constitute a violation. Somewhat less rigorous verification arrangements for INF were in place by mid-September. On-site inspections could still be made on demand but only at specified locations.[108]

By autumn, INF was the only game in town, mainly because it was doable. A START agreement—larger, more complex, and far more controversial—seemed well beyond the capacity of a spent and troubled administration. Moreover, the Star Wars/ABM Treaty issue blocked the way.

However, Gorbachev was probably using INF to isolate Washington's hard right on arms control, perhaps to make it difficult for naysayers to oppose the process. And with relations between Moscow and Washington by now less tense and far more businesslike, Washington began to feel a sense of missed opportunity. But with SALT II on the shelf and START sliding toward the next administration, diplomats wondered what Reagan's successor could or would do on curbing strategic arms. They wondered if INF's importance would be exaggerated, perhaps by both sides, and thereby blur START.

INF was a step, but a small one. There was far less to the self-congratulatory boast about abolishing an entire class of weapons than met the eye. The weapons amounted to less than 4 percent of the aggregate nuclear strength of the superpowers, i.e., 50,000 weapons. Since either side could and, of course, would be covering the targets assigned to weapons headed for the discard, the agreement had little practical effect. It did set some useful precedents, starting with an intrusive and otherwise formidable verification system. And it could mean, as Lord Carrington, NATO's former Secretary General, suggested, that "Europe will become a much less nuclear place."[109] But numerous members of the defense and foreign policy communities were indifferent to INF, just as they had been indifferent, or opposed, to the two-track decision in 1979. The new missiles, they felt, had little military importance and politically would do more harm than good. These same people later felt that removing them in an agreement that ignored the longer-range weapons also made little sense. "I thought INF was a case of misplaced priorities," says House Armed Services Committee Chairman Les Aspin. "To reach into the whole arsenal and pluck one little band of missiles to deal with was strange. The other side can easily circumvent with the long-range stuff. And the agreement leaves out the most dangerous and destabilizing weapons—the short-range nuclear artillery. The pressure in a conflict is on them first—to use them or lose them. The rational move would have been to start with those and not deal with the intermediate-range weapons except as a package [with the long-range systems]."[110]

Not until late October were the dates for the Washington summit—December 7 through 10—agreed to. By mid-November, the administration's attitude toward what could be done in the time left to Reagan shifted. Abruptly, administration people began thinking that a sweeping START agreement could actually be reached—perhaps in time for the follow-up summit in Moscow. Gorbachev was known to want one, and Reagan was presumed to remain attracted to the larger agreement. Had the situation been scripted in Beverly Hills, the much deplored meeting at Reykjavík would have become prelude to an occasion of truly historic measure. Agreement in Moscow would be a fittingly happy ending to the more or less unclouded Reagan presidency.

Weinberger left the Pentagon in mid-November; Perle was already gone. Frank Carlucci, a seasoned and widely respected figure, had replaced Weinberger. And Lieutenant General Colin L. Powell succeeded Carlucci as national security adviser, having been his deputy. For the first time in the Reagan era, the secretaries of state and defense, along with the national security adviser, were all on the same page, as bureaucrats say. The three began meeting without aides or note takers each morning at 7:00 A.M., and continued to do so. Maneuvering START issues through the machine would require a decision-making process that worked; there now seemed to be one.

As the system changed and the tone improved, some problems became less intimidating; one of these was Star Wars. The issue of interpreting the ABM Treaty was being taken out of Reagan's hands. In September, Congress passed the military spending bill in a form that denied funds for tests of Star Wars components that violated the restrictive interpretation of the treaty. Nor would funds be available for the purchase of equipment used for any such future testing. This step was worked out by Congressman Aspin and Senator Nunn with Carlucci and Howard Baker. Predictably, Star Wars itself was changing. The visionary space shield was giving way to the far more modest concept of ground-based defense, notably against accidental missile launches. Star Wars had seemed a more appropriate label than S.D.I. for a system designed to create orbiting battle stations which, inevitably, would be countered by similar Soviet battle stations. But now the administration's designation, S.D.I., seemed appropriate.

Gorbachev had by then been convinced by people like Andrei Sakharov and Roald Sagdeyev, director of the Soviet space institute and his guru in these matters, that S.D.I. was not the threat it had seemed; he probably also understood that time was running out on Reagan's scheme. And he knew that the harder he pounded away at S.D.I., even privately, the more certain Reagan would be of the soundness of his own position. The dream was not to be frittered away even for a strategic arms accord.

The Washington summit would be the first treaty-signing ceremony since Carter and Brezhnev met in Vienna in June 1979 to sign SALT II. The contrast then was striking—Brezhnev, old and infirm, couldn't speak extemporaneously and read from a script. Carter, younger and energetic, had hoped for a robust, far-reaching discussion. This time the contrast in style and age was just as arresting, but worrisome. Gorbachev's penchant for the bold, unpredictable initiative might take in Reagan, now in the twilight of his presidency, as it had at Reykjavík.

They signed the INF Treaty on Tuesday, December 8, 1987. It identified thirty or so facilities in the West as subject to inspection and eighty-odd in the Eastern bloc.[111]

The heavy-duty labor on START was performed by Nitze and Akhromeyev, who had worked together productively for some time. At Reykjavík, the parties had agreed to heavy cuts on warheads—down to 6,000. The other critical numbers required of a START agreement fell into place in Washington: no more than 1,600 delivery systems on either side and each side's ballistic force limited to 4,900 warheads, of which no more than 1,540 could be deployed on heavy land-based missile systems. The effect of this restriction would limit the Soviet SS-18 force to 154 units, since the weapon had been deployed with ten warheads.

The harder problem was still S.D.I. On Wednesday morning, the 9th, Reagan restated his commitment to a space shield. Gorbachev replied: "Mr. President, do what you think you have to do. And if in the end you think you have a system you want to deploy, go ahead and deploy. Who am I to tell you what to do? I think you're wasting your money. I don't think it will work. But if that's what you want to do, go ahead."[112]

Not before the final hour of the meetings did Nitze and Akhromeyev manage to hit on acceptable communiqué language for the S.D.I.-ABM puzzler, and then it was unclear what they had done. The delegations in Geneva were instructed "to work out an agreement that would commit the sides to observe the ABM Treaty, as signed in 1972, while conducting their research, development, and testing as required, which are permitted by the ABM Treaty, and not to withdraw from the ABM Treaty, for a specified period of time."[113]* "We had postponed our quarrels," said Gennadi Gerasimov, the Soviet spokesman, of this ambiguous mouthful.[114] No one disagreed.

Unlike Reykjavík, the Washington summit had been professionally run and very businesslike. It seemed an ideal prologue to a more dramatic last encounter between Reagan and Gorbachev in Moscow. Expectations arose. Despite appearances, however, the meeting hadn't produced what bureaucrats want from summits: the political energy to settle big issues. "It

---

*The key element in this language is the comma before the "which," an arduously worked out concession to the American side. The Soviets (along with some allied governments) opposed the comma. The Americans felt it would promote a broad interpretation of the treaty by separating the phrase preceding it, which seemed to permit a full range of testing and development, from the rest of the passage.

was anticlimactic—mainly grunt work on details of the issues," says a British diplomat.[115]

Shultz became more cautious after the meeting. He was seen correctly now as the administration's dominant figure, but his power was still limited. Around the time of the summit, he tried and failed to secure the job of director of the arms control agency for Nitze, his chief adviser in these matters. He wrote a memorandum to Reagan urging the appointment. The hard right successfully opposed Nitze, arguing that he was too soft.*

Bullish talk of a START agreement persisted. Senior officials like Nitze noted privately that the issues, although difficult, could be disposed of in time for the spring summit. Some professionals took comfort from the knowledge that the larger part of the INF Treaty had been negotiated in the two months prior to signature. Surely if both Reagan and Gorbachev wanted this monument to their four meetings they could crack heads together and make the agreement happen. Appearances were deceptive. START wasn't just a lot more complicated than INF. It covered the weapons that the parties cared most about—weapons which in a comparative sense were the crown jewels, whereas INF's modest array of midrange systems was a rhinestone bracelet. Neither side pushed with enthusiasm, and the Americans were as unable to reach decisions internally as they had been in the chaotic heyday of Weinberger and Perle. "If they [the Soviets] came to us and said, 'You write it, we'll sign it,' we still couldn't do it," said a senior official.[116]

Nor had Reagan become a factor. Between the Washington and Moscow summits, he put no pressure on the system to produce an agreement. The Joint Chiefs were especially sensitive to his noninvolvement. Although not opposed to the deep reductions that had been agreed to, they doubted their value. The chiefs like limits and don't think the levels at which they are set matter much—not with both arsenals being as large as they are. What most worried the chiefs in the interlude between the two summits was the lack of consensus within the government on the weapons that would remain *after* the heavy cuts were made. Unless the forces left behind were survivable, a START agreement would create the sort of instabilities that arms control is supposed to discourage. Perversely, the most survivable strategic weapons are by and large the most expensive. The chiefs wondered what could be done—what new hardware purchased—to guarantee survivability. And how would Congress feel about providing the money in light of a major agreement that was supposed to lessen the burden?

Ronald Reagan affected the chiefs' behavior simply by being a by-

*There is an irony here. Early in 1977, Nitze opposed Paul Warnke's appointment to the same job for essentially the same reason.

stander. "If you are a service chief, you worry about decisions controlling your budget, the role and missions of the service, and the next twenty to thirty years of your future," commented one official. "And you think of some bureaucrat waving all that in front of a president who won't understand it, but may sign it anyway."[117] Put differently, the services, especially the air force and navy, which have the dominant strategic roles, were unwilling to make decisions until they knew whose ox would be gored in the budgetary process.

In the recent past, says Frank Carlucci, the chiefs "hadn't been as deeply involved but are now meeting every morning at 8:00 A.M. on arms control. They are becoming an arms control body."[118] But damage limitation was their game; they were making clear an aversion to reaching a START agreement, at least on Reagan's watch. They did so, for example, by expressing reluctance to take part in various studies, because the studies would churn up the decisions to be taken. Also, the chiefs had not yet recovered from the shock of Reykjavík. They didn't exclude the possibility that in a one-on-one conversation in Moscow, Gorbachev might say, "Let's just get rid of all these things," and Reagan might reply, "That's always been my dream."

The Soviet position was harder to read. If Washington had pushed, Moscow would probably have gone along. But aware that a START agreement couldn't be ratified in the little time remaining to Reagan, the Soviets may have been less eager for agreement than before; almost certainly, they'd have been more reluctant than before to make concessions to a lame duck president. They may have asked themselves what would be lost by waiting for Reagan's successor. Most of what had been agreed to in START, notably the 50 percent cuts, was presumably safe—unlikely to be canceled by either George Bush or Michael Dukakis. And either of these two, the Soviets may have concluded, would be less committed than Reagan to space defense. Apropos, the Soviets could see a tightening American defense budget and a Congress ill-disposed to funding research for space defense. No longer were the Soviets pressing on the S.D.I./ABM front. They were content to live with the ambiguities of the Washington summit communiqué, perhaps because Congress wouldn't sanction any step that violated the treaty.

On the other two key issues, the Soviets also had the more defensible arguments. One was mobile missiles. The American position—unrealistic and unsustainable—was banning them, even though mobility and survivability are thought to have a one-to-one relationship. The Soviets deploy mobile ICBMs.

Much the more important and more divisive issue, however, turned on what to do about sea-launched cruise missiles. For years, the Americans had insisted on leaving them outside the numerical ceiling of any agreement. The Soviets insisted on including SLCMs and proposed a limit of 400 units. On this issue their heels were dug in, partly perhaps because they were still behind in the cruise missile technology, though not much; the CIA thinks they may have as many as 1,500 nuclear-armed SLCMs in the 1990s.[119] The Soviets argued that allowing SLCMs to run free outside START would be a major circumvention of the agreement. Their position was obviously correct, as well as sensible. Modern SLCMs are yet another example of the American tendency to adopt some new device mainly because technology has made it available to Washington, but not to Moscow (at least, not yet). MIRV is the most celebrated such example. But a respectable case could be made for MIRVs in the feverish era of the great ABM debate. There is no case for the SLCMs. They are the devil's mischief—small, cheap, fungible, and impossible to count or otherwise keep track of. Distinguishing between nuclear and conventionally armed SLCMs is just as impossible. They mock the term "arms control." As part of an agreement, they couldn't be monitored unless inspectors on either side were permitted to board the other's submarines and surface ships to verify compliance. The Soviets proposed this step. The Americans rejected it, the navy being understandably horrified by the idea of Soviet technicians examining the innards of America's more advanced submarines.

Virtually no one, however, doubts that the Soviets stand to gain the most militarily from nuclear-armed SLCMs. "We're the ones who are vulnerable to a nuclear SLCM attack," says Les Aspin. "We have the coastal cities."[120]* SLCM is one cat that should never have been let out of the bag.

Verification in general was even tougher to deal with in Washington than Geneva. It was, and is, the point at which all the major difficulties converge. It wasn't only that SLCMs couldn't be monitored in a way acceptable to the Americans. The INF experience left agencies, especially the Joint Chiefs, deeply fearful of permitting intrusive verification of America's strategic assets. "INF gave us an unbelievable amount of new stuff to deal with," says Aspin. "And START, well, we can't even absorb it intellectually. It's a different world."[121]

A Catch-22 was tossed into the process by INF. After approving it, the Senate would hardly agree to a much broader and controversial agreement on START unless Soviet compliance could be monitored intrusively. Yet some officials wonder whether it would be possible to maneuver agreement through the system that would give adversary inspectors the kind of access

*He meant that the targets for American SLCMs lie far inland; they would have to overcome heavy Soviet defenses and the attrition rate would be high.

the Senate would require of similar Soviet facilities. The chiefs and others feel as if the Soviets stand to gain more from intrusive verification because there is more sensitive technology to find out about in America than in Russia. "Verification has proved to be more complex than we thought it would be," Carlucci says dryly. "The flip side of the coin is its application to us. The more we think about it, the more difficult it becomes. We have people working around the clock on it. We don't need the any time, any place. We can have agreement without being totally intrusive."[122] Perhaps. But the signs are that the Soviets will not budge from their stand on SLCMs, with all that it may portend for ultrarigorous verification.

Less than three months after the Washington summit, Reagan said— "the time is too limited" for completion of a strategic arms agreement before the spring meeting in Moscow.[123] Just afterward, a key State Department figure, speaking on "deep background," said this was "a conscious effort (inspired by State) to lower public expectations so that a summit would not be judged a failure if there was no START agreement."[124] He and others were still talking as if the problems were manageable, agreement achievable. They were whistling in the dark. There was little active support for a START agreement elsewhere in the government.

"The real problem is that we have no consensus in the system," Aspin said shortly before the Moscow summit.[125] A State Department official agreed: "We can't make decisions about future force structures unless we have consensus. We don't. Congress has to be part of it. We must have Sam Nunn, Les Aspin, and the leadership on board. Otherwise it won't work. Everyone knows that after Reagan it will be tougher to get money for weapons programs."[126] He meant that unless both branches could agree on what to deploy and what was affordable, the system would still hold back on a strategic arms agreement.

Reagan's arms control position was inadvertent. He got to it one step at a time, with little, if any, forethought about where he was headed. And it is the inadvertence that the Joint Chiefs and other parts of the system deplored. At each stage, they felt a need to know what would happen next— whether any thought had been given to the country's defenses. The irony is that a president who, besides being hostile to arms control, was bent on rebuilding America's defenses, embarked on a grandiose disarmament scheme often without considering its military effects.

Reagan and Gorbachev tried to do too much too soon. In playing at one-upmanship with the major transaction that lay before them, they over-strained the tolerances of their systems—at least, America's. In arms control, the best is usually the enemy of the good. Before and after the Moscow summit, a few serious people wondered whether a strategic arms accord could be obtained even by Reagan's successor. They also wondered whether something that used to be called SALT, which relied on a more gradual approach than Reagan's, could be revived. Still others reckoned that the focus would shift from nuclear to conventional arms control, where much larger budgetary savings could be made.

Gorbachev's senior advisers are astute observers of the American scene. Yet he and they may have miscalculated by deciding to await Reagan's successor before pressing for a START agreement. Had they pressed Reagan before the Moscow summit, the Americans just might have mustered the energy and discipline to have met them halfway. Reagan still possessed a mystique that neither of his possible successors would have. Like Eisenhower, he left the White House nearly as popular as when he arrived. Perhaps more important, Gorbachev may have overlooked the advantage of having a Republican president's signature on an arms control agreement. There will always be a bloc of right-wing senators who will oppose any such treaty, whether signed by a Republican or Democratic president. But the hostile bloc will be larger if the President is a Democrat. In the spring of 1988, neither Michael Dukakis *nor* George Bush could have been expected to have an easy time with the Senate's right wing.

Reagan and Gorbachev got what they wanted from their last meeting: a powerful media event. In Moscow, they may have turned a page to a new era in superpower relations even if little actual business was done. Not since the heyday of the Nixon-Brezhnev connection did prospects seem so bright. (But Reagan was attacking détente in those days and might not have been impressed had the Bolshoi orchestra played "The Star Spangled Banner" for Nixon as it did for him.) Still, for Gorbachev, the real function of the Moscow summit was to strengthen himself within the Soviet Communist party as he prepared for a more important event—a special conference of the party which began a month later and was the first of its kind since July 1941. Another successful summit, observed Arthur Hartman, would make it "harder for those who want to oppose him."[127]

Before and after Reagan came to Moscow, Gorbachev made the hard news. Margaret Thatcher had once told him that Afghanistan would be a test of his differentness.[128] And Washington had put him under pressure to withdraw his troops; other things, it seemed, might even be linked to the step. In early April, Gorbachev announced that the troops would be withdrawn, starting on May 15. Some days later, as the summit began, Soviet officials were describing the decision to invade as an appalling mistake, even "a crime."[129]

For some time, Gorbachev had been playing to the *narod* (ordinary people) against the party apparat. A part of his purpose was to expose more of what goes on in party councils. In the weeks preceding the Moscow summit, he took steps to let Russians know that he was being opposed from even within the Politburo, where opposition isn't supposed to exist, but of course always does, although hidden from view. In speaking to newspaper editors on May 10, he used the word *sumiatitsa*, which means turmoil, to characterize his troubles.[130] Coming from the country's maximum leader, the term sounded very odd. How much of all this was tactical—a campaign to generate support by arousing concern—was unclear. Gorbachev did confront passive political resistance from much of the party bureaucracy, and he couldn't claim progress on the economic front. He stood accused of trying to go too far too fast. It was hardly surprising that Viktor Chebrikov, head of the KGB, sided with Gorbachev's political rival, Yegor Ligachev. But as resistance widened and with the summit only a week away, Gorbachev abruptly escalated the pressure on the system. He maneuvered a package of proposals—the most radical yet—through the Central Committee for which he would seek support at the special party conference. He was asking the party to accept limits on its power by:

—Limiting party interference with government offices and institutions

—Restricting party officials to two five-year terms. Politburo members and the General Secretary would be subject to the measure

—Allowing the Central Committee to select members by secret ballot. The provision was partly aimed at allowing Gorbachev to arrange the removal of his opponents

—Providing legal guarantees: "Everything is permissible unless prohibited by law"

—Rehabilitating victims of the Stalin purges

—Strengthening legislative bodies[131]

On May 26, the Supreme Soviet granted citizens the legal right to form cooperatives outside the state sector.[132]

Four days before, Hungary's Communist party concluded its own special conference by voting out János Kádár, the leader who had ruled for thirty-two years and presided over Hungary's transition to the more open economy and permissive style known as "Gulash communism." Károly Grósz, the man who ousted Kádár, is exactly Gorbachev's age and reputedly just as determined. He has promoted two prominent liberals to the Politburo, one of them a Social Democrat, and the other a man who when asked what sort of democracy he wanted said: "A democracy without adjectives."[133] The changes within Hungary's party were a sharp reminder to its Soviet comrades of the myriad ways in which glasnost could threaten Moscow's control over restive dominions. Violent demonstrations in Armenia and Azerbaijan were another.

Gorbachev's own special conference accomplished much of what he asked of it. Although he failed to maneuver personnel changes within the party, he emerged with his grip on the tiller more secure and his writ appreciably wider. The affair seemed to have buried sixty years of stifling political conformism in Soviet politics. Party leaders clashed openly. Delegates bluntly deplored the bureaucracy's dead hand in their affairs. Gorbachev wanted the party bureaucracy held as scapegoat for the continuing failure to make economic progress. That happened. He intended the conference to condemn the experience of the past twenty-five years, including the past three, and the conference gave him that much and more. Then, in October, he did manage to impose major personnel changes.

His larger purpose was—is—to carry the party beyond a point of no return politically. The conference was a step in that direction—a long one perhaps, but still just a step. If further steps succeed, he can be relied on to attempt the even more difficult step: transforming the system that has paralyzed the Soviet economy and taking it, too, beyond a point of no return.

In orchestrating the party conference, Gorbachev was helped by being able to show that he had transformed the superpower relationship which, when he took over, was close to its nadir. In the bargain, he could say that the threat of war was less and the strategic balance more reliable. As for not having obtained a strategic arms agreement with Reagan, he could also point out that the importance of the Soviet Union's relationship with the United States transcends any one agreement, or even arms control itself. Not unreasonably, he could argue that what he and Reagan accomplished has isolated the American hard right on arms control. No longer will it be able to make the standard three-point argument against agreements: (1) they aren't verifiable; (2) the Soviets will violate them; (3) no agreement can be made so long as the Soviets remain in Afghanistan.

As the Reagan era ebbed, the initiative in East-West affairs lay even more securely with Gorbachev, which is where it had been for nearly three years. The page in bilateral relations had been turned, but at some levels the superpower competition and rivalry would continue. Gorbachev would use his high profile abroad to strengthen his claims at home where he had set in motion the revolution that had to come. He could become a modern version of Peter the Great, or he could be remembered as another of the reformist czars who, despite good intentions, brought on further harshness and stagnation. Gorbachev is, and for some time may remain, the scene's great variable. Upon the outcome of his bold and exhilarating venture will depend the course of one superpower, along with a lot else.

Epilogue

"T he unleashed power of the atom changed everything, save our modes of thinking," said Albert Einstein.[1] Premonitory events—the ravaging of Dresden, the fire bombing of Tokyo—conditioned Western capitals for the use of nuclear weapons; the mass destruction of innocents, if they were subjects of totalitarian aggressors, was legitimized.

The awesome significance of the nuclear weapon is all too seldom reflected in the effort of governments—any government—to deal with it. In Washington, the policies which shaped much of what has gone on have in the main been very conventional, meaning they arose, as usual, from individual and departmental self-interest. To have expected more might have been excusable, but, for many reasons, unrealistic. There is first the tendency of officials, including presidents, to become weather vanes—to move with the flow of fashion. Some officials create the fashion. Others are ideologues and fully capable of conspiring against the declared goals of the President they serve. Ford's was a notable example of a presidency which was harmed from within. So, too, would Reagan's have been harmed had the chaos within his foreign policy apparatus been less complete, or his goals on nuclear issues less fanciful.

How any one President does with these issues depends less on the adversary than on how well he can sell his policies within his own administration, especially the defense establishment, and Congress. And as Congress is more and more an anarchy of competing parts, the sales are that much more difficult to make. Starting with Truman, Presidents have taken many, possibly most, of their key decisions on superpower issues in response to pressure from within the government. Truman's decision to go forward

413

with the hydrogen bomb came after no more than seven minutes of discussion with advisers, if only because he reckoned, probably correctly, that he had no choice. Eisenhower's was a "hidden-hand Presidency,"[*] because he felt it had to be. He had to show the ascendant right wing of his party that he was responsive to its militant anticommunism, which meant concealing or disguising much of what he actually did. Kennedy was unwilling to rock General Lucius Clay's boat during the Berlin crisis for fear that Clay would turn on him. And one year later, on Black Saturday, Kennedy made decisions to settle the Cuban missile crisis in private out of concern for the reaction within his administration (as well as Congress). Eisenhower would have appreciated Kennedy's position. Lyndon Johnson tried to launch the SALT talks *after* the elections in 1968, having been obliged to scuttle plans to begin them when Soviet bloc forces invaded Czechoslovakia in August of that year. And Nixon visited Leonid Brezhnev in July 1974, wanting to make a deal that might restore some semblance of authority and credibility to his presidency, yet unable to accept a good trade because it wasn't quite good enough to have survived the wind then prevailing in Washington. The same wind intimidated Ford and caused him to turn away from what would have been his only lasting achievement—his chance to be more than a footnote. Jimmy Carter withdrew SALT II—as much Ford's treaty as his—from the Senate floor for mainly the same reason.

Truman, Eisenhower, and Kennedy were wholly secure within themselves and with the job. Each had intuitively good judgment on most basic issues. None among the first five of their successors possessed all of these attributes. As president, each had one or more obvious strengths, but each was also flawed or deficient in one way or another. Of course, Truman, Eisenhower, and Kennedy had to cope with actual confrontations and are best remembered for those trying moments. The nuclear issues confronting their successors turned largely on less straightforward but more contentious questions such as how to stay ahead of or even with Soviet strategic power. They had to reconcile the pressure to exploit technology's creep with pressure to exercise restraint. And in one way or another, each had the legacy of Vietnam to deal with.

Roosevelt and Truman dealt only with Stalin. Their divergent approaches reflected the difference between wartime allies and cold war adversaries—and to some extent the differences between the prenuclear and nuclear ages. Eisenhower and Kennedy had to cope with Nikita Khrushchev, the boldest and most volatile of Soviet leaders. He was succeeded by Leonid Brezhnev, who smothered what remained of Khrushchev's re-

[*]Fred Greenstein, *The Hidden-Hand Presidency: Eisenhower as Leader* (New York: Basic Books, 1982).

formist impulse and encouraged the system's unhealthiest tendencies—indolence, cronyism, and corruption. Yet Brezhnev—a crude, jumped-up apparatchik—signed SALT agreements with two of the five American presidents he dealt with and for a decade or more was the patron of détente in Moscow. Gorbachev, the most versatile and dynamic of Soviet leaders, dealt for nearly four years with Ronald Reagan, a man who knew less than his predecessors about East-West issues and who delegated far more responsibility than any of them did.

Reagan's easy passage notwithstanding, presidents can afford to delegate only so much responsibility in the nuclear age. Admiral Hyman Rickover and Generals Lucius Clay and Leslie Groves illustrated—each in a different way—the pitfalls of allowing strong, subcabinet people to operate quasi-autonomously in pursuit of private agendas, which in Rickover's case produced a monument to himself, the Trident submarine. Clay was outside the chain of command in October 1961, and at moments Groves might just as well have been.

In 1945, Truman allowed a few people down the line, notably Groves, to have an all but free hand with operations of surpassing sensitivity. But in 1948, as the first Berlin crisis began, Truman took control. In his own more subtle, indirect fashion, Eisenhower, too, managed the numerous near crises of his episodic presidency. JFK learned from his Berlin crisis that he had to keep control *and* his own counsel. He did so in the Cuban crisis.

Truman was just right for his time, a threshold whose abrupt challenges called for bold initiatives of the sort that this courageous, resolute, and rather uncomplicated man never shrank from. Whether he'd have done as well at some later and more complex stage in the nuclear age is not clear.

Eisenhower was the most astute of the nuclear age presidents in dealing with security issues, partly because he understood them and the bureaucratic politics surrounding them. He also knew more about the presidency when he acquired the office than the others did, and he knew far more about the ways of executive government. He was constantly tugged by the pressures of the cold war and by baseless fears of a bomber gap and a missile gap. A lasting irony of Eisenhower's presidency is that even though he saw through the alarmist and self-serving assertions about America's defenses, the biggest buildup of nuclear weapons was approved on his watch. It is equally true that the buildup of weapons, and certainly delivery systems, would have been bigger still had anyone else been President then.

Eisenhower isn't likely to be ranked among the great presidents as Truman already is by many historians. Although well equipped to deal with the conflicts and confrontations of the 1950s, Eisenhower might have chalked up more conspicuous and tangible successes in the 1980s, a time when East-West accommodation was well within reach. But his presidency did offer an example of why it might be desirable to elect to the office someone who has nothing to prove. Kennedy had everything to prove and was rightfully concerned about his paper-thin majority over Nixon.

Eisenhower didn't let on that he was fully in charge. Kennedy left no doubt that he was in charge, even though he was tentative and unsure in the early part of his administration. Kennedy probably had the quickest and subtlest mind of any recent President, although his immediate successors— Lyndon Johnson and Richard Nixon—were not far behind and much more complicated than either he or Eisenhower had been. Kennedy's mistrust of bureaucracy probably matched Eisenhower's and was far more obvious. But like Truman, Johnson, and Ford, he understood Congress better than the sprawling executive branch. Nixon's experience as vice president aroused his loathing of the foreign policy bureaucracy. Carter and those he brought with him to the White House knew little of either branch. They did know about the Georgia county unit system, an exacting political environment but very different from Washington's. Carter learned an immense amount about national security problems, but not enough about managing them politically. Reagan was, of course, far less directly involved with these than any predecessor had been. He governed like a plebiscitary monarch.

The effect of nuclear weapons on relations between adversaries— America and Russia, Russia and China—is without precedent. The same may be said of their effect on relations between allied countries, as, for example, the United States and the old nation-states of Western Europe, France, and Britain, not to mention the relations of each with Europe's most potent society, West Germany. The nuclear weapon, as distinct from traditional considerations, has defined these relationships and set the history of our time on its curious course—a course that was to avoid another great war, if only because of the common fear of crossing the nuclear threshold. Not much of lasting importance in world politics has been unconnected to the bomb. The cold war in relations between de Gaulle's France and Washington in the 1960s makes the point; at the heart of the quarrel lay the reasons for the French weapons program and America's attitude toward it. Certain of the decisions that led to the larger American involvement in

Vietnam were influenced by the crisis in faraway Berlin, where the Western position was judged to depend on American willingness to hang tough on *all* fronts, even if that meant accepting the possibility of using nuclear weapons.

Many American experts deplore the tacit understanding that each superpower holds the other's society hostage to its nuclear weapons. There must be a better way, they think, to manage the genie, but they haven't found one. Their alternatives to pure deterrence, however dressed up in doctrinal jargon, all amount to some kind of nuclear-war-winning scheme.

Still, the role of deterrence can be exaggerated or misunderstood. The long peace between the great powers which nuclear weapons have done so much to foster would obviously count for nothing if deterrence should fail. Simply because deterrence has worked so far is not reason enough to assume that the command and control system on either side will perform just as it ought to in the event of an inadvertant launch or even the appearance of one during a crisis. Improvements in the accuracy, yield, and versatility of nuclear weapons are prejudicial to presidential calm and deliberation in a crisis. So, too, are some of the newer radars and other detection and tracking systems. These disgorge information by the yard and at a speed that adds heavily to the pressure on commanders in tense or critical moments. The commander of NORAD (North American Air Defense Command) would in some presumed crises have only three minutes in which to authenticate reports of a Soviet missile attack. In that event, the President would have no more than four minutes in which to make his fateful decision. That was the amount of time available to the captain of the USS *Vincennes*, which mistakenly shot down an Iranian Airbus over the Persian Gulf in the summer of 1988. A president could be similarly victimized by a fallible detection system or a misreading of its report by fallible people. Briefly, peace and security cannot be taken for granted. The uncertainties arising from vulnerable command systems and the spread of nuclear weapons argue against doing so. So does the occasional mismatch of ordinary people, however well-trained, with the increasingly complex and sophisticated hardware they are asked to master but can be overwhelmed by.

Moreover, the long peace hasn't relied solely on deterrence. NATO has remained intact for longer than any comparable alliance of consenting sovereign societies. The European Community is a bold and novel experiment by member states aimed at overcoming centuries of strife and disunity, not to mention two civil wars in this century. Germany, the chief aggressor in these wars, is anchored to these Western institutions. The alliance has its unsteady moments, and the Community still lacks the solidarity envisaged by its prophets, but each of these improbable entities has done its part to create a new and more stable order in which the long peace has taken root.

Lastly, the protection against nuclear war also draws upon the lengthening tradition of nonuse of the weapon. Less uncertain relations and better communications between the superpowers can discourage miscalculation and overreaction.

During much of the nuclear age, the United States overreacted, usually by enlarging or misreading the threat posed by Soviet forces or exaggerating the capacity of the Soviet Union to achieve its rhetorical ends. In the great power game, America's is the hand that most people would prefer to play. It is the leader of a system whose economic and political strength dwarfs that of the rival bloc, a system held together by something larger and more durable than intimidation. Ironically, the United States persistently reinforced the Soviet Union's claims by exaggerating its military attributes and even suggesting that these had put the Western system at a strategic disadvantage. The irony in all this has many edges. The Soviets were, of course, painfully aware that they weren't nine feet tall, despite Washington's gloomy assertions that they were. They probably put the darkest—most threatening—interpretation on Washington's inflated assessments of their power. Misestimates are mischievous. They will never convince the Soviet Union that the strategic balance of power is weighted in its favor, but Americans and their allies might think so, at which point sensible policy becomes harder to make.

Nuclear weapons aside, Soviet adventurism and intimidation of other societies have done as much as anything to shape superpower relations. Moscow should have known that an unnatural process like arms control wouldn't prosper if Washington saw its interests, even nonvital ones, threatened in various parts of the world. The inflated linkage issue sank SALT II and perfectly suited the purposes of cold warriors. Predictably, Soviet-inspired experiments in Third World countries have failed badly. The unlucky clients have been mainly African societies: Angola, Ethiopia, and Mozambique. None of the three regimes has ever controlled all of the countryside or been able to survive without outside military help. Other African societies that experimented or flirted with the Soviet model discarded it and their Soviet advisers. Afghanistan became an analogue to Vietnam. By the time Reagan and Gorbachev met in mid-1988, Soviet officials and diplomats were complaining to Americans about being overextended and overexposed in Third World hot spots. The Soviet press carried stories about how operations in regional conflicts had harmed other, more important national interests. His country, says Shevardnadze, must "limit and reduce rivalry, eliminate confrontational features in relations with other states, and suppress conflict and crisis situations."[2]

For various reasons, Moscow is not obsessed with China now. The Chinese, too, have become more inward looking and more concerned with their own reforms. Their dealings with Washington no longer arouse Kremlin fears of an anti-Soviet conspiracy, as was the case in the 1970s. And China has been reassured by a number of Soviet moves, including the withdrawal of forces from Afghanistan, agreement to dismantle all SS-20 missile systems, including those deployed against China and Japan, and Moscow's willingness to encourage a Vietnamese withdrawal from Cambodia.

Mikhail Gorbachev is changing, perhaps revolutionizing, the system of which he may be the most brilliant product. His main problem is that Russians are uncomfortable with choices. They prefer security to freedom if forced to choose. In return for security—jobs, housing, education—they have been willing accomplices of the bloated bureaucracy that manages their lives. Russians, said Aleksander Herzen, inventor of the "glasnost" concept, "are indifferent to individual freedom, liberty of speech; the masses love authority. They are still blinded by the arrogant glitter of power, they are offended by those who stand alone . . ."[3]

Their concern for personal security is matched by a common concern for external security. A society that has been invaded six times over the past hundred and eighty years and that, as it constantly reminds the world, lost twenty million people in its most recent war, plans conservatively and worries inordinately, if not obsessively, about security and the sanctity of its borders. Gorbachev is trying to change this thinking by playing down the well-worn threat from old enemies. It is a high-wire act.

Whether Soviet society, on balance, will side with him and against the impacted apparat he is trying to upend isn't clear. It *is* clear, though, that Gorbachev must at some point show some progress on the economic front. For that, he will have to keep tight control of military spending, which in turn means controlling what bureaucrats call the "threat assessment." How his military people assess the threat will depend to a large extent on relations with Washington and possibly on prospects for controlling arms, nuclear and nonnuclear. An agreement on strategic nuclear arms would help politically but wouldn't save much money. An agreement to reduce conventional weapons would help politically and *would* save money. With strategic arms control in trouble in Washington, it's possible that the INF Treaty will have been the curtain raiser not on a START treaty but on a vastly complicated conventional arms negotiation involving all NATO and Warsaw Pact members and their arms. Gorbachev's target in any set of negotiations will be Western technology. He requires access to it, and he must constrain technology creep if he is to constrain military spending. He needs a prolonged détente.

Within the Soviet system a major debate is under way about whether the armed forces should move to a less offensive and more defensive posture in Europe. The issue pits part of the civilian bureaucracy against part of the military bureaucracy, and it divides the latter; there is a conservative faction that prefers to leave things unchanged and another group that, like its civilian colleagues, wants Soviet forces to be seen as less threatening. Perhaps glasnost in Eastern Europe, with the prospect of fundamental change, will push Moscow toward a more defensive force posture. It seems already clear that most East European military forces wouldn't fight seriously, unless attacked.

So much depends on Gorbachev's staying power and, indeed, survival. Despite the astonishing candor and openness of his ruling style, much is unclear and perhaps, as he sees it, must remain so. Early in 1988, Yegor Ligachev tried to restrain or perhaps even displace him and may have come close to succeeding—just how close is also unclear, as is the alignment of forces for and against Gorbachev at any given moment.

Gorbachev and Marshal Sergei Akhromeyev are people with whom Westerners can do business; Margaret Thatcher said as much about Gorbachev after meeting him, and no one disagrees. The reflexive paranoia that had been common to Soviet leadership since Stalin is being effaced by Gorbachev. George Shultz and Eduard Shevardnadze quickly developed a relationship very like that between two Western foreign ministers who got on together. They wrote to each other frequently and called each other by their first names. When meeting, they plowed through crowded agendas just as ministers of allied governments normally do.

The bilateral relationship being worked out should be more important than arms control itself, assuming, of course, that Gorbachev survives. Indeed, it may become possible to accomplish some of the goals of the arms control process without the process itself, at least as we know it. Bureaucracy has a hard time with arms control, and so does Congress. So did the

Lateran Council of Pope Innocent II, which in 1139 banned the use of the crossbow against Christians and was ignored. A more predictably business-like relationship between Washington and Moscow might allow each side to tailor its nuclear arms policies in a fashion that avoided provoking the other. The parties might exchange lists of the items of the greatest concern to them. A president might find it easier to challenge his opposite number in the Kremlin to take a constructive step that he would match in some appropriate way. Rather than reaching for formal agreement—always an elusive goal—it might be possible to constrain another cycle in the arms race through the acquisition and budgetary processes.

Still, against the odds, nuclear arms control did prosper for a time and might well again. Implicitly, it has lain close to the heart of East-West affairs since the Eisenhower era, perhaps even the late Truman. It has survived immense difficulties. It is attacked from the right and the left, neither of which understands what the process is intended to do. It wasn't created to reduce the numbers of weapons, except secondarily. Its purpose was—is— to make more remote the risk of nuclear war by reducing uncertainties and promoting stability. It is a political process. The left and right both favor massive reductions and deplore what they see as a tendency of arms control to stimulate the competition in strategic arms. There is far less to this contention than meets the eye. Without the ABM Treaty—the centerpiece agreement—there would be many more strategic weapons of all kinds. Without SALT II, the Soviets could have deployed a much larger force of their most threatening weapons—MIRVed ICBMs—than they did. And without some steady show of restraint, the superpowers will find it even harder to curb the traffic by other countries in weapons of mass destruction.

Ever since Roosevelt and Churchill rejected Niels Bohr's anxious counsel to tell the Soviets about the Manhattan Project, technological creep—the monkey-see, monkey-do syndrome—has been setting the tone and pace of the arms race. America has been the innovator, Russia the emulator. "You've got it. We must have it, too" is the normal Soviet attitude. America's is: "We have it. You don't. We won't give it up." For a time the American desire to open a lead in advanced technology was understandable, especially given the pressures of the cold war and the massive Soviet conventional forces being used to intimidate Western Europe. But as time wore on and the reality of the Soviet will and capac-ity to narrow and even close these gaps became clear, Washington was not just kidding itself; it was taking steps that threatened its own national security.

In creating novel weapons systems, little, if any, thought was ever given to what the United States was trying to accomplish—to whether and, if so, how some new device was consistent with the country's broad political and strategic goals in the world. Questions such as what kind of strategic weapons are desirable and which ones are undesirable weren't seriously asked (except in the case of ABMs). MIRV, as noted, is often cited as the paradigm. But nuclear-armed sea-launched cruise missiles are at least as hard to deal with. Unlike MIRVs, they appear to defy the methods of arms control—that is, unless the navy changes its mind about allowing Soviet inspectors to examine American submarines. The SLCM is more than another foot-shooting exercise, more than just another "weapon that isn't needed responding to a threat that doesn't exist"—a characterization that has been applied to some other systems. As both sides deploy SLCMs, negotiated limits on nuclear arms will lose their meaning, as will the arms control process itself, unless governments take strong self-denying action—and soon.

Regional issues will also test a changed superpower relationship. In the past, Moscow and Washington have tried with other suppliers to limit the spread of nuclear weapons. The problem is still there and is made more serious by sales of missile systems to countries which in some cases—Iran and Iraq—routinely bombarded one another with them. Israel, a nuclear weapons state, has tested a longer-range version of France's Jericho missile, which appears to be capable of reaching Russian territory. Pakistan, a so-called near-nuclear state, has test-fired a missile capable of carrying a nuclear weapon. The system is believed to have been made with help from China. It may be capable of striking New Delhi or Bombay and resembles some older Soviet missiles of a type sold to Iraq and Syria. The Soviets have now transferred an improved version of one of these systems to Syria. With material supplied by a West German equipment firm, Iraq has developed and used chemical weapons. Other Middle Eastern countries are now capable of equipping their missiles with toxic chemicals at the front end. China has supplied Saudi Arabia with a midrange ballistic missile that Israel, ironically, helped to design and develop. The missile can travel 1,600 miles and is believed capable of carrying nuclear and nonnuclear warheads. Briefly, weapons of mass destruction will increasingly become available on the open market unless steps are taken to discourage sales. Washington is talking with allies about precisely that. But the more serious problem lies with a growing second tier of suppliers, such as India, China, Israel, North Korea, and Brazil. Neither the United States, which has given missile technology to Israel, nor the Soviet Union has clean hands. It is too late for them to lead by example; they must devise an approach that will restrain the new arms merchants and their clients, most of whom are truculent or confrontational.

National security policy had been a growth industry, with the special aura of the nuclear issue promoting the larger part of the growth in recent presidencies. The expanding role of the National Security Council staff is the most vivid—some would say disturbing—example of the trend. Harry Truman, who created the NSC, kept it on a short leash, partly by limiting the writ and size of its staff; in his day, it varied in size from four to five anonymous souls. The work attracts strong and gifted personalities, and the intensity of the struggle to dominate policy has grown as the structure has grown. The lasting damage to Reagan was done by a rogue NSC staff that was answerable to no one and ran secret operations outside the interagency process. The arena for the process is one in which subcabinet-level people, like their betters, can make names for themselves, thereby enlarging the opportunities that may await them outside government. The competition is bare-knuckled and the victim, increasingly, is public policy.

Excepting Eisenhower and perhaps Nixon, incoming American presidents have known little of the larger foreign policy issues that absorbed so much of their energies. Not much can be done about the presidential selection process, nor, it seems, about the way presidents choose key advisers in this area. According to a recent study on the problem of communication between the superpowers, few of the twenty-nine people who have served in the past quarter century as secretaries of state or defense, national security advisers, or CIA directors had had direct experience with the Soviet Union.[4] The situation is no better at the levels just below. American presidents once relied upon and were greatly helped by Soviet specialists within the foreign service, notably George Kennan, Charles Bohlen, and Llewellyn Thompson. Thompson was surely the most useful of all the American public servants who have advised presidents and secretaries of state on issues affecting the superpower relationship.

Today such people are not available. The expertise lies with the Soviets. It is no longer a level playing field. Before leaving Washington in April 1986, Soviet Ambassador Anatoly Dobrynin was for twenty-five years the channel between six presidents and five general secretaries. Georgi Kornienko, who assisted Dobrynin at the Central Committee, was for a time his deputy in Washington and then spent twenty years in the Soviet Foreign Ministry specializing in American and East-West affairs. Kornienko's successors in Washington were first Yuri Vorontsov, who served for eleven years, and then Aleksander Bessmertnykh, who was there for twelve. As deputy foreign ministers they are still heavily involved in superpower issues. Within the American foreign service, there are no comparable figures. And there is equally little American expertise in German affairs, even though the most sensitive and complex of America's allied relationships is with West Germany, a country to which the Soviets also devote a large pool of expertise. American diplomats have little incentive to acquire such knowledge, since it is rarely drawn upon by inexperienced policy makers, who tend to control matters within a tight little circle.

Helmut Schmidt has written that in East-West relations, "worst case scenarios reign."[5] This tendency to assume the worst is most pronounced, hence worrisome, during crises. At a technical level, communication between Washington and Moscow has improved and contacts between various kinds of specialists on either side have multiplied. But the larger communication problem—comprehending one another's motives and attitudes—has been largely unaffected by the change, especially on the American side. In a crisis, it is critically important for both the President and the General Secretary to have a reliable and immediately recognizable back channel. Both Averell Harriman and Anatoly Dobrynin served long and well in this role. The KGB resident in Washington, Alexander Fomin, and ABC reporter John Scali—the two men who got Khrushchev's message to Kennedy during the Cuban missile crisis—were not clearly identified with either government and only by chance did the message reach the addressee. For most of the 1980s, there was no reliable channel between Washington and Moscow.

Since Vietnam, national security policy has been dominated by the contesting pressure to build more and better arms and to control these arms. In the upper reaches of government, reputations are made on this dual issue. Henry Kissinger is an example. Another is Paul Nitze, who for nearly a half century has worked on a wide variety of security issues but is identified now with arms control. Jurisdiction lies with multiple interests: the State and Defense departments, the NSC staff, the Joint Chiefs of Staff, the arms control agency, and the Central Intelligence Agency. To these may be added individual players—a powerful member of Congress, a commanding figure outside government, even a columnist or reporter serving as the outlet for a practiced leaker. People try to interpret an administration's policies and decisions in the light of reason and rational alternatives, but only occasionally does big government make major decisions on that basis. And it rarely makes them for one reason alone. Multiple considerations, not necessarily connected to one another, usually lurk behind any one decision. The self-deception of leadership can be critical. Power breeds self-deception, one of the least examined and least understood of statecraft's phenomena.

The more power a leader, or his *éminence grise,* acquires, the more prone he becomes to self-deception—to concealing his motives even from himself. Yet in any internal clash on an East-West issue, it may be only the President who will articulate the adversary's point of view or stake in the situation, because other officials are reluctant to risk doing so. Thus, Soviet capabilities often translate into Soviet intentions. On arms control, the advocacy side is usually at a disadvantage, with its back to the wall as it tries to prove it isn't naive or unrealistic about the Russians.

From the mid-1950s to the early '60s, Washington exaggerated Soviet capabilities, alarming itself and the country with its talk first of a nonexistent bomber gap, then of a nonexistent missile gap with the Soviet Union. From the early to midsixties, Washington underestimated Soviet strategic force planning. Over the next five years, it misread the direction of Soviet plans and overreacted to the infant Chinese program. The various agencies that make up what is called the intelligence community can—often do—clash over how to interpret the data they share (or are supposed to share). The Central Intelligence Agency is usually less prone to worst-case analysis than the Defense Intelligence Agency. The intelligence agencies of individual military services also tend to be somewhat less ritually hard line than the DIA. It is on Soviet military capabilities that the CIA and DIA probably disagree most often. Sometimes there is pressure to adjust estimates of Soviet force planning to fit a policy line; these are usually painful episodes.

On any East-West issue there are usually two schools of thought. One tends to see the Soviet Union as changeless—relentlessly determined to expand its influence and power at America's expense. Such people see the Soviet system as a particularly nasty expression of imperial Russia, its nuclear weapons a menacing force that allows an otherwise second-rate society to deal with the United States on equal terms. The other group tends to see Soviet motives as more "nationalist" than expansionist, as more defensive than offensive. The record suggests that both sides are partly right. It also suggests that the softer line is rarely a good one to be identified with—not if one is pursuing a career in politics or government.

Nuclear issues have never been exposed to the same degree of public scrutiny as other issues. If they had been, topics like protracted nuclear war or limited nuclear war would have been lost in ridicule. By now, society should have acquired a more consistent view of nuclear weapons, as distinct from a feeling—at times shaky—that neither side is likely to use one in anger. The issue is unlike any other which involves public opinion. In the case of an unpopular Asian war, or a tax bill, trade legislation, or wage and price controls, public opinion must be carefully considered by prudent leadership. But on the nuclear issue, a politically secure leader—a Reagan or a Nixon at the height of his credibility—can do largely as he pleases. A weak leader—a Nixon as he was at his second Moscow meeting with Brezhnev—will find the going heavy, not because public opinion has shifted in any fundamental sense but because it doesn't really know what it thinks, and can therefore be blown about by those whose voices carry most strongly at any one time. The public is further confused by the tendency of many officials to push their own positions and/or undermine someone else's with leaks, many of which are creative distortions of whatever is going on within the clamorous arena of East-West policy.

Presidents haven't helped much. The White House hasn't been a bully pulpit for discussion of the nuclear issue, mainly because presidents, whether hard- or soft-liners, are not comfortable with it. The issue has no constituency, and it has a forbidding quality that discourages not only presidents but the political system generally.

Decisions in the nuclear age have often involved too few people, and too many of them are narrowly focused specialists—brothers of the nuclear priesthood and the inspiration for notions of limited nuclear war and competent civil defense. These are examples of the priesthood's tendency to reify, a term which the dictionary defines as treating an abstraction as if it had concrete or material existence. In creating nuclear war scenarios over the years, many of the brothers have reified that which is unknown and cannot be known about nuclear war unless there is one. Their thinking, too, is typically self-deceptive and as distant from reality as that of opposing generals in the First World War, which caused the slaughter of hundreds of thousands of young soldiers. The priesthood hasn't yet affected behavior, but the danger is that it could. The worst effects of its notions so far have been on the debate, or what passed for debate. Instead of a sober and balanced discussion of nuclear issues, society has been confused, hence victimized, by shrill and polarized debate, the terms of which are often as arbitrary as they are absurd.

A world with adversary powers deploying nuclear arms, along with other societies, some unstable, bent on acquiring the weapons is uncertain, and dangerous enough. To say that it is even more menacing than it is carries the risk of self-fulfilling prophecy. So does the corollary proposition that nuclear war can be won. Even with a large enough second-strike capacity to destroy the Soviet Union many times over, American policy was captive in the 1970s and most of the 1980s—and to a degree still is— to the Pearl Harbor psychology: by fear of a bolt from the blue.

Perhaps the Gorbachev agenda does foreshadow a quieter time. If so, nuclear issues could become less contentious—less overdrawn by the passions and worst case estimates of zealots. Washington may be able to worry less about the Soviets and concentrate on tangible problems such as Third World debt and trade policy, not to mention the Middle East and the spread of weapons of mass destruction there and elsewhere. The superpowers could and should have reordered their priority concerns years ago. Yet even now, as the need for a different and more realistic view of national security is widely perceived and accepted, the nuclear age continues, as it began, in a bog of official and bureaucratic discord. Government still cannot decide what or how to think about the superpower competition in nuclear arms. "We had the experience but missed the meaning," wrote T. S. Eliot.[6] The question before the house is whether, in a time of rival superpowers, government can base nuclear policy on sensible and balanced estimates of the threat. With great difficulty and perhaps not at all would thus far seem to be the answer.

Notes

I

1. Cabell Phillips, *From the Crash to the Blitz: 1929–1939* (New York: Macmillan, 1969), p. 173.
2. Henry L. Stimson and McGeorge Bundy, *On Active Service in Peace and War* (New York: Harper & Brothers, 1947), pp. 309, 316.
3. Phillips, p. 548.
4. William Langer and S. Everett Gleason, *The Challenge to Isolationism: 1937–40* (New York: Harper & Brothers, 1952), p. 182.
5. Robert Jungk, *Brighter than a Thousand Suns: A Personal History of the Atomic Scientists* (New York: Harcourt, Brace, 1958), p. 46.
6. Bernard J. O'Keefe, *Nuclear Hostages* (Boston: Houghton Mifflin, 1983), pp. 9–10.
7. Richard Rhodes, *The Making of the Atomic Bomb* (New York: Simon and Schuster, 1986), p. 84.
8. Rudolf Peierls, *Bird of Passage: Recollections of a Physicist* (Princeton, N.J.: Princeton University Press, 1985), p. 19.
9. Jungk, p. 32.
10. Alice Kimball Smith and Charles Weiner, eds., *Robert Oppenheimer: Letters and Recollections* (Cambridge, Mass.: Harvard University Press, 1985), p. 100.
11. Jungk, p. 38.
12. Rhodes, p. 54.
13. Peierls, p. 56.
14. Jungk, p. 50.
15. Ibid., p. 60.
16. Peierls, p. 95.
17. Jungk, p. 57.
18. Conversation with John Manley, December 30, 1986.
19. Jungk, p. 49.
20. Rhodes, p. 228.
21. Spencer R. Weart and Gertrud Weiss Szilard, eds., *Leo Szilard: His Version of the Facts*, vol. II (Cambridge, Mass.: MIT Press, 1978), p. 17.
22. Bertrand Goldschmidt, *The Atomic Complex: A Worldwide Political History of Nuclear Energy* (La Grange Park, Ill.: American Nuclear Society, 1982), p. 9.
23. Margaret Gowing, *Britain and Atomic Energy, 1939–45* (London: Macmillan, 1964), p. 33.
24. Jungk, p. 25.
25. Albert Speer, *Inside the Third Reich* (New York: Macmillan, 1970), p. 366.
26. Ibid., pp. 226–27.
27. Conversation with I. I. Rabi, November 12, 1986.
28. *Washington Dispatches, 1941–45: Weekly Political Reports from the British Embassy*, H. G. Nicholas, ed. (London: Weidenfeld & Nicolson, 1981), p. 599.
29. Raymond Garthoff, *Soviet Military Policy: A Historical Analysis* (New York: Praeger, 1968), p. 180.

II

1. Margaret Gowing, *Britain and Atomic Energy, 1939–45* (London: Macmillan, 1964), p. 39.
2. Ronald W. Clark, *The Greatest Power on Earth* (New York: Harper & Row, 1980), p. 62.

3. Otto Frisch, "Nuclear Fission," *Annual Reports on the Progress of Chemistry for 1939* (The Chemical Society, 1940). Cited in Gowing, p. 40.

4. Gowing, p. 40.

5. Peter Pringle and James Spigelman, *The Nuclear Barons* (New York: Holt, Rinehart and Winston, 1981), p. 13.

6. Rudolf Peierls, *Bird of Passage: Recollections of a Physicist* (Princeton, N.J.: Princeton University Press, 1985), pp. 153–54.

7. Ibid, p. 154.

8. Ibid.

9. Ibid., p. 155.

10. Ibid., p. 156, and Gowing, p. 45.

11. Robert Jungk, *Brighter than a Thousand Suns: A Personal History of the Atomic Scientists* (New York: Harcourt, Brace, 1958), p. 109.

12. Peierls, p. 160.

13. Gowing, p. 210.

14. Jungk, p. 109.

15. Peierls, p. 163.

16. Ibid., pp. 157–58.

17. Bertrand Goldschmidt, *The Atomic Complex: A Worldwide Political History of Nuclear Energy* (La Grange Park, Ill.: American Nuclear Society, 1982), p. 31.

18. Richard Rhodes, *The Making of the Atomic Bomb* (New York: Simon and Schuster, 1986), p. 280.

19. Ibid., p. 307.

20. Ibid., p. 314.

21. Ibid., p. 315.

22. Ibid.

23. McGeorge Bundy, *Danger and Survival* (New York: Random House, 1988), p. 39.

24. Conversation with I. I. Rabi, November 12, 1986.

25. Conversation with John Manley, December 30, 1986.

26. Rhodes, p. 338.

27. James B. Conant, *My Several Lives* (New York: Harper & Row, 1970), p. 277.

28. Rhodes, p. 362.

29. Ibid., p. 366.

30. James B. Conant, *A History of the Development of an Atomic Bomb*, unpublished ms., OSRD S-1, Bush-Conant file folder 5, National Archives, Washington, D.C., 1943. Cited in Rhodes, p. 369.

31. Richard G. Hewlett and Oscar E. Anderson, Jr., *The New World: 1939–46, vol. I, A History of the United States Atomic Energy Commission* (University Park: Pennsylvania State University Press, 1962), p. 46.

32. Ibid., p. 259.

33. Gowing, p. 123.

34. Hewlett and Anderson, p. 261.

35. Ibid., p. 82.

36. Pringle and Spigelman, p. 19.

37. Ibid., p. 16.

38. Bertrand Goldschmidt, The *Atomic Adventure* (New York: Pergamon, 1964), p. 35.

39. Goldschmidt, *The Atomic Complex*, p. 54.

40. Rhodes, p. 277.

41. Goldschmidt, *The Atomic Complex*, p. 55.

42. Peter Goodchild, *J. Robert Oppenheimer: Shatterer of Worlds* (New York: Fromm, 1985), p. 103.

43. Pringle and Spigelman, p. 17.

44. Jungk, p. 119.

45. Rhodes, p. 451.

46. Los Alamos Scientific Laboratory, *Los Alamos: Beginning of an Era.* Reprinted by the Los Alamos Historical Society, New Mexico, 1986, p. 12.

47. John Purcell, *The Best Kept Secret: The Story of the Atomic Bomb* (New York: Vanguard, 1963), p. 161.

48. Conversation with General Kenneth D. Nichols, December 12, 1986.

49. Conversation with William Higinbotham, January 12, 1987.

50. Laura Fermi, "That Was the Manhattan District: A Domestic View— II," *The New Yorker*, July 31, 1954, p. 51.

51. Jungk, p. 118.

52. Pringle and Spigelman, p. 20.

53. Bundy, p. 56.

54. WGBH taped interview with General Kenneth D. Nichols, Tape #A01034, Pt. 2, p. 11.

55. Rhodes, p. 445.

56. Conversation with I. I. Rabi, November 12, 1986.

57. Jeremy Bernstein, "Physicist—I," *The New Yorker*, October 13, 1975, p. 84.

58. Dean Acheson, *Present at the Creation* (New York: Norton, 1969), p. 164.

59. Leslie R. Groves, *Now It Can Be Told: The Story of the Manhattan Project* (New York: Harper & Brothers, 1962), pp. 61, 62, 63.

60. Ibid., p. 63.

61. Rhodes, p. 570.

62. Ibid.

63. Rhodes, pp. 500–1.

64. Jungk, pp. 30–31.

65. I. N. Golovin, *I. V. Kurchatov: A Socialist-Realist Biography of the Soviet Nuclear Scientist*, trans. William H. Dougherty (Bloomington, In.: Selbstverlag Press, 1968). Appendix.

66. Rhodes, p. 525.

67. Gowing, p. 439.

68. Rhodes, pp. 529, 530.

69. Groves, pp. 135–36.

70. Gowing, pp. 357–58.

71. Ibid., p. 447.

72. Conversation with Joseph Volpe, November 25, 1986.

73. Rhodes, p. 523.

74. Ibid., p. 539.

75. Ibid., p. 543.

76. Peierls, p. 200.

77. Gowing, p. 264.

78. Peierls, pp. 199–200.

79. Jungk, pp. 270–71.

80. Rhodes, pp. 206–7.

81. Peierls, p. 86.

82. Rhodes, pp. 231–32.

83. Spencer R. Weart and Gertrud Weiss Szilard, eds., *Leo Szilard: His Version of the Facts*, vol. II (Cambridge, Mass.: MIT Press, 1978), p. 146.

84. Laura Fermi, "That Was the Manhattan District: A Domestic View," *The New Yorker*, July 24, 1954, pp. 38, 39.

85. Groves, p. 288.

86. Los Alamos Scientific Laboratory, p. 44.

87. Ibid.

88. Goodchild, pp. 150–51.

89. Groves, pp. 296–97.

90. Ibid., p. 292.

91. Goodchild, pp. 161–62.

92. Groves, p. 298.

93. Harry S Truman, *Memoirs, vol. I, Year of Decisions* (Garden City, N.Y.: Doubleday, 1955), p. 419.

94. Groves, p. 184.

95. Rhodes, p. 686.

96. Len Giovannitti and Fred Freed, *The Decision to Drop the Bomb* (New York: Coward-McCann, 1965), p. 322. Cited in Leon V. Sigal, *Fighting to a Finish* (Ithaca, N.Y.: Cornell University Press, 1988), p. 221.

97. Truman, p. 10.

98. Bundy, p. 59.

99. Ibid.

100. Groves, p. 265.

101. Fletcher Knebel and Charles W. Bailey, "The Fight Over the A-Bomb," *Look*, August 13, 1963.

102. Conversation with Gordon Arneson, December 11, 1986.

103. Notes of the Interim Committee Meeting, Thursday, May 31, 1945, p. 14.

104. Notes of the Interim Committee Meeting, Friday, June 1, 1945, pp. 9–10.

105. Ibid., p. 10.

106. Groves, pp. 266–67.

107. Ibid., p. 267.

108. Ibid., p. 342.

109. Sigal, p. 194.

110. Groves, p. 273.

111. Foreign Relations of the United States (hereafter FRUS), The Conference of Berlin, vol. II, p. 1372 (Washington, D.C.: GPO, 1960).

112. Robert H. Ferrell, ed., *Off the Record. The Private Papers of Harry S Truman* (New York: Harper & Row, 1980), p. 55.

113. Alice Kimball Smith, *A Peril and a Hope* (University of Chicago Press, 1965). Appendix B, p. 567.

114. Goodchild, p. 144.

115. Robert Donovan, *Conflict and Crisis: The Presidency of Harry S Truman, 1945–1948* (New York: Norton, 1977), p. 66.

116. WGBH interview with Edward Teller, Tape E 00001, pp. 5–6

117. "Ike on Ike," *Newsweek*, November 11, 1963, p. 108.

118. Donovan, p. 70.
119. Ibid.
120. Ray S. Cline, *Washington Command Post: Observations Command Post* (Washington, D.C.: GPO, 1951), pp. 345–46. Cited by Sigal, p. 124.
121. FRUS, The Conference of Berlin, vol. I, The Potsdam Conference (1945), p. 896.
122. Ferrell, p. 53.
123. Sigal, p. 130.
124. Ibid., p. 140.
125. Ibid., p. 130.
126. Bundy, p. 88.
127. Henry L. Stimson, diary, August 10, 1945.
128. Groves, p. 292.
129. Donovan, p. 93.
130. Georgi Zhukov, *The Memoirs of Marshal Zhukov*, trans. Novosti (New York: Delacorte, 1971), p. 675.
131. Lewis L. Strauss, *Men and Decisions* (Garden City, N.Y.: Doubleday, 1962), p. 189.
132. Groves to Oppenheimer, July 19, 1945. Cited in Knebel and Bailey, "The Fight Over the A-Bomb," p. 23, and *Look,* August 13, 1963.
133. Lansing Lamont, *Day of Trinity* (New York: Atheneum, 1965), p. 304.
134. George M. Elsey note, undated, from the 1945–46 folders, in the papers of George M. Elsey, from the Atomic Energy Folders, Harry S Truman Library, Independence Mo., cited in Donovan, p. 98.
135. Truman, *Years of Decisions,* p. 423.
136. Sigal, p. 215.
137. William L. Laurence, *Dawn Over Zero* (New York: Knopf, 1953), p. 252.
138. U.S. Strategic Bombing Survey (Pacific), *The Effects of Atomic Bombs on Hiroshima and Nagasaki* (Washington, D.C.: GPO, 1946), p. 9. Cited in Sigal, p. 224.
139. Rhodes, pp. 736–37.
140. Torashiro Kawabe, in Statements of Japanese Officials, vol. II, no. 52608, p. 97. U.S. Army in typescript, cited in Sigal, p. 226.
141. Groves, p. 346.
142. WGBH interview with Hans Bethe, Tape #B01006, p. 4.
143. Conversation with Dean Rusk, November 10, 1986.
144. Bundy, p. 85.
145. U.S. Strategic Bombing Survey (Pacific), p. 22.
146. Laura Fermi, "That Was the Manhattan District, A Domestic View—II," *The New Yorker,* July 31, 1954, p. 51.

III

1. Robert Ferrell, ed., *Off the Record: The Private Papers of Harry S Truman* (New York: Harper & Row, 1980), p. 56.
2. David Holloway, *The Soviet Union and the Arms Race* (New Haven, Conn.: Yale University Press, 1986), p. 20. Quoted by A. Lavrent'yeva in "Stroiteli novogo mira," *V mire knig,* 1970, no. 9, p. 4.
3. Ibid., p. 27, citing *Pravda,* September 25, 1946.
4. Charles E. Bohlen, *Witness to History, 1929–1969* (New York: Norton, 1973), p. 213.
5. Robert Donovan, *Conflict and Crisis: The Presidency of Harry S Truman, 1945–1948* (New York: Norton, 1977), p. 42, citing the Journal of Joseph E. Davies, Library of Congress, Joseph E. Davies Papers, Washington, D.C., Box 16, April 30, 1945.
6. Conversation with Norris Bradbury, January 4, 1987.
7. "Richard Feynman Dead at 69; Leading Theoretical Physicist," *New York Times,* February 17, 1988.
8. Conversation with William Higinbotham, January 21, 1987.
9. Robert Jungk, *Brighter than a Thousand Suns: A Personal History of the Atomic Scientists* (New York: Harcourt, Brace, 1958), p. 232.
10. Conversation with I. I. Rabi, November 12, 1986.
11. Richard G. Hewlett and Oscar E. An-

derson, Jr., *The New World: 1939–46,* vol. I, *A History of the United States Atomic Energy Commission* (University Park: Pennsylvania State University Press, 1962), p. 438.

12. Gregg Herken, *The Winning Weapon: The Atomic Bomb in the Cold War, 1945–1950* (New York: Knopf, 1980), p. 133.

13. Hewlett and Anderson, pp. 505–6.

14. Conversation with Norris Bradbury, January 4, 1987.

15. Conversation with Joseph Volpe, November 11, 1986.

16. Cited in Paul Boyer, *By the Bomb's Early Light* (New York: Pantheon, 1985), p. 113. Philip Wylie, "Deliverance or Doom?" *Collier's,* September 29, 1945, p. 19.

17. Frank Sullivan, "Cliché Expert Testifies on the Atom," *The New Yorker,* November 17, 1945, pp. 27–29.

18. Boyer, p. 113.

19. Conversation with Norris Bradbury, January 4, 1987.

20. Hewlett and Anderson, p. 461.

21. Herken, p. 63.

22. Dean Acheson, *Present at the Creation* (New York: Norton, 1969), p. 164.

23. Ibid., p. 166.

24. Herken, p. 145.

25. David E. Lilienthal, *The Journals of David E. Lilienthal,* vol. II, *The Atomic Energy Years* (New York: Harper & Row, 1964), p. 10.

26. Ibid., p. 26.

27. Hewlett and Anderson, p. 480.

28. Bertrand Goldschmidt, *The Atomic Complex: A Worldwide Political History of Nuclear Energy* (La Grange Park, Ill.: American Nuclear Society, 1982), p. 96.

29. Ibid., pp. 96–97.

30. Nuel Pharr Davis, *Lawrence and Oppenheimer* (New York: Fawcett, 1968), p. 281.

31. Acheson, p. 316.

32. Ibid., p. 319.

33. Conversation with Joseph Volpe, November 25, 1986.

34. Acheson, p. 320.

35. Herken, p. 66, citing the *New York Times* of November 12, 19, 1945.

36. Lilienthal, p. 10.

37. Peter Goodchild, *J. Robert Oppenheimer: Shatterer of Worlds* (New York: Fromm, 1985), p. 178.

38. Acheson, p. 153.

39. Ibid., pp. 153–54.

40. Ibid., p. 154.

41. Lilienthal, p. 30.

42. Goodchild, p. 180.

43. Peter Pringle and James Spigelman, *The Nuclear Barons* (New York: Holt, Rinehart and Winston, 1981), p. 52.

44. Chalmers M. Roberts, *The Nuclear Years: The Arms Race and Arms Control* (New York: Praeger, 1970), p. 16.

45. Bundy, p. 163.

46. Pringle and Spigelman, p. 54.

47. Roberts, p. 19.

48. Bundy, p. 165.

49. Roberts, p. 20.

50. Pringle and Spigelman, p. 55.

51. Roberts, p. 18.

52. Harry S Truman, *Memoirs,* vol. I, *Year of Decisions* (Garden City, N.Y.: Doubleday, 1955), p. 552.

53. Donovan, p. 367.

54. Acheson, p. 262.

55. WGBH interview with Clark Clifford, Tape #B2FSF2, p. 7.

56. Acheson, p. 262.

57. Donovan, p. 367.

58. WGBH interview with Clark Clifford, Tape #B2FSF2, p. 8.

59. Acheson, p. 274.

60. WGBH interview with Nikolai Chervov, Tape #32, p. 5.

61. WGBH interview with Gordon Arneson, Tape #A02019, Pt. 1, pp. 5, 6.

62. Walter Millis, ed., *The Forrestal Diaries* (New York: Viking, 1951), p. 458.

63. Ibid., p. 461.

64. Lilienthal, vol. II, p. 391.

65. Ibid., p. 406.

66. Conversation with General Kenneth D. Nichols, December 12, 1986.

67. Richard Betts, *Nuclear Blackmail and Nuclear Balance* (Washington, D.C.: Brookings Institution, 1987), p. 24.

68. Conversation with Joseph Volpe, November 25, 1986.

69. Conversations with former British and American officials.

70. Ernest J. King and Walter M. White-hill, *Fleet Admiral King: A Naval Record* (New York: Norton, 1952), p. 621.

71. Sigal, p. 178, citing the *New York Times,* September 21, 1945.

72. Conversation with Bromley Smith, October, 23, 1986.

73. Paul Y. Hammond, "Super Carriers and B-36 Bombers," in *American Civil-Military Decisions: A Book of Case Studies,* ed. Harold Stein (Tuscaloosa: University of Alabama Press, 1963), p. 491.

74. Ibid., pp. 488–89.

75. FRUS, vol. II, p. 491.

76. Goldschmidt, p. 88.

77. Lilienthal, p. 571.

78. Herken, p. 302, citing the *New York Times,* September 25, 1949.

79. Lansing Lamont, *Day of Trinity* (New York: Atheneum, 1965), p. 104.

80. Conversation with Hans Bethe, April 22, 1987.

81. WGBH interview with John Manley, Tape #B02016, p. 13.

82. Pringle and Spigelman, p. 43.

83. Conversation with Paul Nitze, December 18, 1986.

84. Conversation with John Manley, December 30, 1986.

85. Herbert York, *The Advisors: Oppenheimer, Teller and the Superbomb* (San Francisco: W. H. Freeman, 1976), p. 40.

86. Jungk, pp. 27–28.

87. Bundy, p. 200.

88. York, pp. 27-28, citing *The Legacy of Hiroshima,* p. 50.

89. Conversation with Norris Bradbury, January 4, 1987.

90. Conversation with I. I. Rabi, November 12, 1986.

91. Goodchild, p. 197.

92. Ibid., p. 199.

93. Bundy, p. 206.

94. Goodchild, p. 200.

95. York, p. 158.

96. Conversation with Hans Bethe, April 22, 1987.

97. York, pp. 155–56, 157.

98. WGBH interview with Arneson, Tape #A02019, Pt. 1, p. 13.

99. WGBH interview with Edward Teller, Tape #E00002, p. 3.

100. Conversation with John Manley, December 30, 1986.

101. Pringle and Spigelman, p. 98.

102. Conversation with General Kenneth D. Nichols, December 12, 1986.

103. George F. Kennan, *Memoirs, 1925–1950* (Boston: Little, Brown, 1967), pp. 472, 474, and Acheson, p. 347.

104. WGBH interview with Arneson, Tape #A02020, Pt. 2, pp. 2–3.

105. Acheson, p. 347.

106. Conversation with Gordon Arneson, December 11, 1986.

107. Pringle and Spigelman, p. 95.

108. Richard Hewlett and Francis Duncan, *The Atomic Shield, 1947–1952, vol. II, A History of the United States Atomic Energy Commission* (University Park: Pennsylvania State University Press, 1969), p. 395.

109. Bundy, p. 210.

110. Gordon Arneson, "The H-Bomb Decision," *Foreign Service Journal* (June 1969), Part II, p. 26.

111. Arneson, "The H-Bomb Decision," *Foreign Service Journal* (May 1969), Part I, p. 27.

112. Conversation with Gordon Arneson, December 11, 1986.

113. York, p. 70.

114. Richard Rhodes, *The Making of the Atomic Bomb* (New York: Simon and Schuster, 1986), pp. 771, 773.

115. Conversation with Carson Mark, January 3, 1987.

116. Rhodes, p. 773.

117. Jungk, p. 296.

118. Roberts, p. 27.

119. McGeorge Bundy, "The H-Bomb: The Missed Chance," *New York Review of Books,* May 13, 1982, p. 19.

120. Conversation with Gordon Arneson, December 11, 1986.

121. I. N. Golovin, *I. V. Kurchatov: A Socialist-Realist Biography of the Soviet Nuclear Scientist,* trans. William H. Dougherty (Bloomington, In.: Selbstverlag Press, 1968), pp. 64–65.

122. Bundy, p. 197.

123. Rhodes, p. 777.

124. Jungk, p. 305.
125. Conversation with Hans Bethe, April 22, 1987.
126. Conversation with Gordon Arneson, December 11, 1986.
127. Kennan, p. 356.
128. Walter Isaacson and Evan Thomas, *The Wise Men* (New York: Simon and Schuster, 1986), p. 450.
129. Ibid.
130. Ibid., pp. 490, 499.
131. Fred Kaplan, *The Wizards of Armageddon* (New York: Simon and Schuster, 1983), p. 140.
132. Isaacson and Thomas, p. 504.
133. Conversation with Lucius Battle, May 18, 1987.
134. Conversation with Paul Nitze, December 2, 1986.
135. Isaacson and Thomas, p. 506.
136. Nikita S. Khrushchev, *Khrushchev Remembers*, ed. and trans. Strobe Talbott (Boston: Little, Brown, 1970), pp. 367–68.
137. Harry S Truman, *Memoirs*, vol. II, *Years of Trial and Hope* (Garden City, N.Y.: Doubleday, 1956), p. 337.
138. Robert Donovan, *The Tumultuous Years: The Presidency of Harry S Truman* (New York: Norton, 1982), p. 198.
139. Conversation with Paul Nitze, December 2, 1986.
140. Conversation with Dean Rusk, November 10, 1986.
141. Truman, *Years of Trial and Hope*, p. 395.
142. Betts, p. 34.
143. Hewlett and Duncan, p. 533.
144. Donovan, *Conflict and Crisis*, p. 20.
145. Donovan, *The Tumultuous Years*, p. 261.

IV

1. Conversation with Bromley Smith, October 23, 1986.
2. Nikita S. Khrushchev, *Khrushchev Remembers*, ed. and trans. Strobe Talbott (Boston: Little, Brown, 1970), p. 397.
3. Richard Rovere, "Letter from Washington," *The New Yorker*, November 6, 1952. In *Affairs of State, 1950–1956, The Eisenhower Years* (New York: Farrar, Straus & Cudahy, 1956), p. 50.
4. Richard M. Nixon, *Six Crises* (Garden City, N.Y.: Doubleday, 1962), p. 161.
5. Fred Greenstein, *The Hidden-Hand Presidency: Eisenhower as Leader* (New York: Basic Books, 1982), p. 11.
6. Stephen Ambrose, *Eisenhower*, vol. II, *The President* (New York: Simon and Schuster, 1984), p. 18.
7. Conversation with Paul Nitze, May 5, 1987.
8. Conversation with General Andrew Goodpaster, November 5, 1986.
9. Conversation with Robert R. Bowie, May 27, 1987.
10. Conversation with General Goodpaster, November 5, 1986.
11. Dwight D. Eisenhower, *Public Papers of the Presidents of the United States* (hereafter PPOP), *1960–1961* (Washington, D.C.: Government Printing Office, 1961), p. 1038.
12. Dwight D. Eisenhower, *The White House Years: Waging Peace, 1956–1961* (Garden City, N.Y.: Doubleday, 1965), p. 616.
13. FRUS, 1952–1954, vol. II, p. 854.
14. Ibid., p. 593.
15. Eisenhower, PPOP, 1955 (Washington, D.C.: GPO, 1959), p. 332.
16. Eisenhower, PPOP, 1960–1961, p. 1039.
17. J. Robert Oppenheimer, "Atomic Weapons and American Policy," *Foreign Affairs* 31, no. 4 (July 1953), p. 529.
18. Conversation with General Goodpaster, November 5, 1986.
19. Telephone conversation with George Kennan, May 12, 1987.
20. *The Economist*, January 3, 1987, p. 40.
21. Lawrence Freedman, *The Evolution of Nuclear Strategy* (New York: St. Martin's Press, 1983), p. 80.
22. Warner R. Schilling, Paul Y. Hammond, and Glenn H. Snyder, *Strategy, Politics and Defense Budgets* (New

York: Columbia University Press, 1966), p. 389.

23. Conversation with General Goodpaster, November 5, 1986.

24. Townsend Hoopes, *The Devil and John Foster Dulles* (Boston: Little, Brown, 1973), p. 194.

25. Schilling, Hammond, and Snyder, p. 427.

26. Eisenhower, PPOP, 1954 (Washington, D.C.: GPO, 1954), p. 330.

27. Hoopes, pp. 135–36.

28. Hoopes, p. 311, citing the *New York Times,* January 15, 1956.

29. Hoopes, p. 311.

30. Conversation with General Goodpaster, November 5, 1986.

31. Khrushchev, p. 398.

32. Dwight D. Eisenhower, *The White House Years: Mandate for Change, 1953–1956* (Garden City, N.Y.: Doubleday, 1963), pp. 180, 181.

33. Edward Friedman, "Nuclear Blackmail and the End of the Korean War," *Modern China* (January 1975), p. 76.

34. Conversation with former senior government official.

35. FRUS, 1952–1954, vol. XV, pp. 1014, 770, 826.

36. Conversation with General Goodpaster, November 5, 1986.

37. Conversation with Dean Rusk, November 10, 1986.

38. Sherman Adams, *First-Hand Account* (New York: Harper & Brothers, 1961), p. 118.

39. Hoopes, p. 310.

40. Bundy, p. 238.

41. Friedman, p. 87.

42. Robert Donovan, *Eisenhower: The Inside Story* (New York: Harper & Brothers, 1956), p. 119.

43. FRUS, 1952–1954, vol. XIII, Indochina, p. 949.

44. Ibid, pp. 953, 1014.

45. Eisenhower, PPOP, 1954, p. 383.

46. FRUS, 1952–1954, vol. XIII, Indochina, p. 1271.

47. Hoopes, p. 208.

48. Ambrose, p. 179.

49. Richard M. Nixon, *RN: The Memoirs of Richard Nixon* (New York: Grosset & Dunlap, 1978), p. 152.

50. Stanley Karnow, *Vietnam: A History* (New York: Viking, 1983), p. 197.

51. Matthew B. Ridgway, *Soldier: The Memoirs of Matthew B. Ridgway* (New York: Harper & Brothers, 1956), pp. 276–77.

52. FRUS, 1952–1954, vol. XIII, Indochina, p. 1933.

53. Ibid., p. 1096.

54. Ibid., p. 1447.

55. Ambrose, p. 184, citing interview with Dwight D. Eisenhower.

56. FRUS, 1952–1954, vol. XIII, p. 1927.

57. Eisenhower, *Mandate for Change,* pp. 463, 476–77.

58. Conversation with General Goodpaster, November 5, 1986.

59. Eisenhower, PPOP, 1955, p. 332.

60. Eisenhower, *Mandate for Change,* p. 477.

61. Ambrose, p. 240.

62. Hoopes, p. 450.

63. Ibid., p. 280. Also Ambrose, p. 240.

64. Hoopes, pp. 277–78, citing the *New York Times,* March 13, 1954.

65. Conversation with Robert R. Bowie, June 17, 1987.

66. Hoopes, p. 281.

67. Eisenhower, *Mandate for Change,* p. 477.

68. Ibid., p. 478.

69. Fred Greenstein, p. 21.

70. Richard Rovere, "Letter from Washington," *The New Yorker,* February 17, 1955. In *Affairs of State, 1950–1956, The Eisenhower Years,* p. 249.

71. Conversation with General Goodpaster, November 5, 1986.

72. Conversation with General Goodpaster, June 18, 1987.

73. Ambrose, p. 107.

74. Ibid., p. 206.

75. FRUS, 1952–1954, vol. II, p. 1213.

76. Donovan, p. 187.

77. Eisenhower, *Mandate for Change,* p. 251.

78. FRUS, 1952–1954, vol. II, p. 1213.

79. Conversation with General Goodpaster, November 5, 1986.

80. Donovan, p. 183.

81. Eisenhower, PPOP, 1953, p. 817.

82. Ambrose, p. 149.

83. Peter Pringle and James Spigelman, *The Nuclear Barons* (New York: Holt, Rinehart and Winston, 1981), pp. 123–24.

84. WGBH interview with General Chervov, Tape #32, pp. 6, 3.

85. Conversation with John Huizinga, June 2, 1987.

86. William E. Burrows, *Deep Black: Space Espionage and National Security* (New York: Random House, 1986), p. 68.

87. John Prados, *The Soviet Estimate: U.S. Intelligence Analysis and Russian Military Strength* (New York: Dial Press, 1982), p. 44.

88. James R. Killian, Jr., *Sputnik, Scientists and Eisenhower: A Memoir of the First Special Assistant to the President for Science and Technology* (Cambridge, Mass.: MIT Press, 1977), p. 68.

89. Charles A. Appleby, Jr., "Eisenhower and Arms Control, 1953–1961: A Balance of Risks" (Ph.D. diss., Johns Hopkins University, 1987), p. 3.

90. Robert Jungk, *Brighter than a Thousand Suns: A Personal History of the Atomic Scientists* (New York: Harcourt, Brace, 1958), p. 292.

91. Ibid., p. 307.

92. Michael R. Beschloss, *MayDay: Eisenhower, Khrushchev and the U-2 Affair* (New York: Harper & Row, 1986), pp. 78–79.

93. Killian, p. 82.

94. Bernard Brodie, "Strategy Hits a Dead End," *Harper's* (October 1955), pp. 33–37.

95. Ambrose, p. 248, citing Hagerty diary, February 8, 1955.

96. Charles E. Bohlen, *Witness to History, 1929–1969* (New York: Norton, 1973), p. 378.

97. Conversation with Robert R. Bowie, May 27, 1987.

98. Eisenhower, *Mandate for Change*, p. 521.

99. Ibid., p. 522.

100. Khrushchev, p. 400.

101. Ibid., p. 392.

102. Ibid., p. 48.

V

1. Michael R. Beschloss, *MayDay: Eisenhower, Khrushchev and the U-2 Affair* (New York: Harper & Row, 1986), p. 148.

2. James R. Killian, Jr., *Sputnik, Scientists and Eisenhower: A Memoir of the First Special Assistant to the President for Science and Technology* (Cambridge, Mass.: MIT Press, 1977), p. 7.

3. Beschloss, p. 148.

4. Eisenhower, PPOP, 1957 (Washington, D.C.: GPO, 1958), p. 730.

5. Ibid., p. 721.

6. Killian, p. 8.

7. Conversation with General Andrew Goodpaster, November 5, 1986.

8. Beschloss, p. 149.

9. Killian, p. 98.

10. Conversation with Spurgeon Keeny, July 9, 1987.

11. Albert Wohlestetter, "Rivals, But No Race," *Foreign Policy*, Fall 1974, p. 85.

12. Dwight D. Eisenhower, *The White House Years: Waging Peace, 1956–1961* (Garden City, N.Y.: Doubleday, 1965), p. 223.

13. WGBH interview with General Andrew Goodpaster, Tape #603027, p. 1.

14. Conversation with Paul Nitze, May 15, 1987.

15. Stephen E. Ambrose, *Eisenhower*, vol. II, *The President* (New York: Simon and Schuster, 1984), p. 434.

16. Gregg Herken, *Counsels of War* (New York: Knopf, 1985), p. 116.

17. David Holloway, *The Soviet Union and the Arms Race* (New Haven, Conn.: Yale University Press, 1986), pp. 66–67.

18. Conversation with Howard Stoertz, June 23, 1987.

19. Nikita Khrushchev, *Khrushchev Remembers: The Last Testament* (Boston: Little, Brown, 1970), p. 411.

20. WGBH, *The Nuclear Age*, "A Bigger Bang for a Buck."

21. Desmund Bau, *Politics and Force Levels:*

The Strategic Missile Program of the Kennedy Administration (Berkeley: University of California Press, 1980), p. 7, and Lawrence Freedman, *U.S. Intelligence and the Soviet Strategic Threat* (Princeton, N.J.: Princeton University Press, 1986), p. 75.

22. Beschloss, p. 150.
23. Ibid., pp. 153–54, 155.
24. Freedman, p. 70.
25. William E. Burrows, *Deep Black: Space Espionage and National Security* (New York: Random House, 1986), p. 100.
26. Beschloss, p. 153.
27. Conversation with General Goodpaster, June 3, 1987.
28. Charles E. Bohlen, *Witness to History, 1929–1969* (New York: Norton, 1973), p. 497.
29. Harold Macmillan, *Riding the Storm: 1956–1959* (New York: Harper & Row, 1971), p. 634.
30. Conversation with General Goodpaster, June 16, 1987.
31. Holloway, p. 32.
32. Eisenhower, *Waging Peace*, p. 293.
33. Morton H. Halperin, *Nuclear Fallacy: Dispelling the Myth of Nuclear Strategy* (New York: Ballinger, 1987), p. 34.
34. Eisenhower, *Waging Peace*, p. 694.
35. Conversation with C. Gerard Smith, May 20, 1987.
36. Holloway, p. 84.
37. Eisenhower, *Waging Peace*, p. 301.
38. Townsend Hoopes, *The Devil and John Foster Dulles* (Boston: Little, Brown, 1973), p. 452.
39. Eisenhower, *Waging Peace*, p. 304.
40. Ibid., p. 330.
41. Hans Speier, *Divided Berlin: The Anatomy of Soviet Political Blackmail* (New York: Praeger, 1961), pp. 10–11.
42. Eisenhower, *Waging Peace*, pp. 340–41.
43. Hoopes, p. 466.
44. Ambrose, p. 503.
45. Eisenhower, *Waging Peace*, p. 353.
46. Arnold Horelick and Myron Rush, *Strategic Power and Soviet Foreign Policy* (Chicago: University of Chicago Press, 1966), p. 120.
47. Ambrose, p. 504.
48. Eisenhower, *Waging Peace*, p. 354.

49. Khrushchev, *Khrushchev Remembers: The Last Testament*, p. 369.
50. Eisenhower, *Waging Peace*, p. 407.
51. Ibid., p. 413.
52. Beschloss, p. 184.
53. Eisenhower, *Waging Peace*, p. 447.
54. John Newhouse, *De Gaulle and the Anglo-Saxons* (New York: Viking, 1970), p. 14.
55. Ibid., p. 12.
56. Ibid., pp. 15–16.
57. *L'Aventure de la Bombe*, meeting organized at Arc et Senans, Université de Franche-Comté and the Institut Charles de Gaulle, September 27, 28, and 29, 1984 (Paris: Plon), p. 81.
58. Conversations with various French officials at various times.
59. *Daily Mirror* (London), April 2, 1958.
60. Newhouse, p. 74.
61. Ambrose, p. 539.
62. Newhouse, p. 66.
63. Ambrose, p. 502.
64. Newhouse, p. 57.
65. Ibid., p. 59.
66. New York *Herald Tribune* (Paris Edition), April 27, 1960.
67. *Les Deux Bombes* by Pierre Pean (Paris: Fayard, 1982), and *The Sunday Times* (London), October 5, 1986.
68. Conversation with former French official, August 1987.
69. *The Sunday Times* (London), October 12, 1986.
70. Conversation with Eugene Zuckert, July 3, 1987.
71. Ambrose, p. 267.
72. Ibid., p. 401.
73. Macmillan, p. 306.
74. Robert A. Divine, *Blowing on the Wind: The Nuclear Test Ban Debate* (New York: Oxford University Press, 1978) p. 149, and Ambrose, p. 404.
75. Ambrose, p. 523.
76. Divine, p. 207.
77. Khrushchev, *Khrushchev Remembers: The Last Testament*, p. 536.
78. Divine, p. 210.
79. Charles A. Appleby, Jr., "Eisenhower and Arms Control, 1953–1961: A Balance of Risks" (Ph.D. diss., Johns Hopkins University, 1987), p. 69.

80. Glenn T. Seaborg, *Kennedy, Khru-shchev and the Test Ban* (Berkeley: University of California Press, 1981), p. 16.

81. Beschloss, p. 151.

82. Ambrose, pp. 509–10.

83. Beschloss, p. 272.

84. Conversation with Raymond Garthoff, former member of the CIA's National Estimates staff, June 22, 1987.

85. Beschloss, p. 239.

86. Beschloss, p. 239, citing the Columbia University Oral History Project.

87. Beschloss, p. 257.

88. Ibid., pp. 287–89.

89. Bohlen, p. 470.

90. George Kistiakowsky in an interview with Carl Sagan in 1982; "Confessions of a Weaponeer," NOVA, 1986.

91. Conversation with Raymond Garthoff, June 22, 1987.

92. Kistiakowsky-Sagan interview.

VI

1. Conversation with General Andrew Goodpaster, June 16, 1987.

2. Conversation with Dean Rusk, November 10, 1986.

3. Desmond Ball, *Politics and Force Levels: The Strategic Missile Program of the Kennedy Administration* (Berkeley: University of California Press, 1980), pp. 90–91.

4. WGBH interview with Robert McNamara, Tape E05041, p. 3.

5. Conversation with Robert McNamara, September 19, 1987.

6. John Newhouse, *De Gaulle and the Anglo-Saxons* (New York: Viking, 1970), pp. 122–23.

7. Ibid., p. 124.

8. *Le Monde*, April 4, 1961.

9. Conversation with Robert McNamara, September 19, 1987.

10. Conversation with Dean Rusk, November 10, 1986.

11. *Le Monde*, May 31, 1961.

12. Conversation with Dean Rusk, November 10, 1986.

13. Nikita Khrushchev, *Khrushchev Remembers: The Last Testament* (Boston: Little, Brown, 1970), p. 499.

14. Glenn T. Seaborg, *Kennedy, Khru-shchev and the Test Ban* (Berkeley: University of California Press, 1981), p. 67.

15. Conversation with Arkady Shevchenko, November 11, 1986.

16. Oleg Penkovsky, *The Penkovsky Papers* (Garden City, N.Y.: Doubleday, 1965), p. 207.

17. Conversation with a former CIA official.

18. Harold Macmillan, *Pointing the Way: 1959–1961* (New York: Macmillan, 1972), pp. 357, 400.

19. Honoré M. Catudal, *Kennedy and the Berlin Wall Crisis: A Case Study in US Decision Making* (Berlin: Berlin Verlag, 1980), p. 123, citing William E. Leuchtenburg, "President Kennedy and the End of the Postwar World," in Aida DiPace Donald, *John F. Kennedy and the New Frontier* (New York: Hill and Wang, 1966), p. 133.

20. Khrushchev, *Khrushchev Remembers: The Last Testament*, p. 504.

21. Conversation with Paul Nitze, May 15, 1987.

22. Conversation with Dean Rusk, November 10, 1986.

23. Jack M. Schick, *The Berlin Crisis: 1958–1962* (Philadelphia: University of Pennsylvania Press, 1971), p. 148.

24. Conversation with Paul Nitze, May 15, 1987.

25. Conversation with Dean Rusk, November 10, 1986.

26. Conversation with McGeorge Bundy, September 22, 1987.

27. Newhouse, pp. 90, 135, 139.

28. Catudal, p. 181.

29. Norman Gelb, *The Berlin Wall: Kennedy, Khrushchev, and a Showdown in the Heart of Europe* (New York: Times Books, 1986), p. 244.

30. Catudal, p. 183.

31. Ibid., p. 178.

32. Theodore Sorensen, *Kennedy* (New York: Harper & Row, 1965), p. 592.

33. Catudal, pp. 197–98.

34. Ibid., p. 205.
35. Ibid., p. 200, citing interview with Walt Rostow, North Germany Television Network, August 12, 1976.
36. Newhouse, p. 140.
37. Catudal, pp. 239–41.
38. Conversation with Dean Rusk, November 10, 1986.
39. Gelb, p. 213.
40. Oral History interview of Robert Amory by William W. Moss; John F. Kennedy Library, pp. 32–33.
41. Catudal, p. 152.
42. Seaborg, p. 74.
43. United States Arms Control and Disarmament Agency, *Documents on Disarmament, 1961* (Washington, D.C.: Government Printing Office, 1962), p. 347.
44. Seaborg, p. 88.
45. WGBH, *The Nuclear Age,* "The Education of Robert McNamara," 1987.
46. Gelb, p. 248.
47. Walter Isaacson and Evan Thomas, *The Wise Men* (New York: Simon and Schuster, 1986), p. 456.
48. Gelb, p. 248; Catudal, p. 133; and conversations with retired diplomats and officials.
49. Gelb, p. 252.
50. Conversation with David Klein, September 22, 1987.
51. Gelb, p. 254.
52. Khrushchev, *Khrushchev Remembers: The Last Testament,* pp. 504–5, 507.
53. Gelb, p. 256.
54. Conversation with Martin Hillenbrand, September 14, 1987.
55. Conversation with McGeorge Bundy, September 22, 1987.
56. Gelb, p. 257, citing Catudal interview with Clarke.
57. Khrushchev, *Khrushchev Remembers: The Last Testament,* p. 507.
58. WGBH interview with Valentin Falin, Tape #89, side A, pp. 1–2.
59. Ball, p. 103.
60. Conversation with Robert Amory, September 25, 1987.
61. Conversation with Howard Stoertz, June 23, 1987.
62. John Prados, *The Soviet Estimate: U.S. Intelligence Analysis and Russian Military Strength* (New York: Dial Press, 1982), p. 118, citing CIA, "Current Status of Soviet and Satellite Military Forces and Indications of Military Intentions," September 6, 1961.
63. Scott D. Sagan, "SIOP-62: The Nuclear War Plan Briefing to President Kennedy," *International Security* 12, no. 1 (summer 1987), p. 23, citing covering note on Kissinger memo on Berlin, National Security Files, Box 81, Germany-Berlin-General, JFK Library.
64. Ibid., p. 22.
65. William W. Kaufmann, *The McNamara Strategy* (New York: Harper & Row, 1964), p. 49.
66. WGBH interview with Albert Wohlstetter, Tape #E05011, p. 3.
67. Fred Kaplan, The *Wizards of Armageddon* (New York: Simon and Schuster, 1983), p. 269.
68. Kaufmann, p. 116.
69. WGBH interview with Robert McNamara, Tape #E05043, p. 7.
70. Gelb, p. 271.
71. Schick, pp. 210–11.
72. Robert A. Divine, ed., *The Cuban Missile Crisis* (New York: Quadrangle Books, 1971), pp. 7–8.
73. Conversation with Dean Rusk, November 10, 1986.
74. Robert F. Kennedy, *Thirteen Days: A Memoir of the Cuban Missile Crisis* (New York: Norton, 1971), pp. 23.
75. Arthur Schlesinger, Jr., *A Thousand Days* (New York: Fawcett Premier Books, 1971), p. 732.
76. Richard E. Neustadt and Ernest R. May, *Thinking in Time: The Uses of History for Decision Makers* (New York: The Free Press, 1986), p. 5, citing JFK Library recordings of excerpts of early ExComm meetings.
77. Marc Trachtenberg, "White House Tapes and Minutes of the Cuban Missile Crisis," *International Security* 10, no. 1 (summer 1985), p. 167.
78. Conversation with Theodore Sorensen, October 2, 1987.

79. Schlesinger, p. 742.
80. Conversation with Dean Rusk, November 10, 1986.
81. Conversation with Paul Nitze, October 7, 1987.
82. Khrushchev, *Khrushchev Remembers: The Last Testament*, pp. 493–94.
83. Conversation with Arkady Shevchenko, November 11, 1986.
84. Ibid.
85. Graham T. Allison, *Essence of Decision: Explaining the Cuban Missile Crisis* (Boston: Little, Brown, 1971), p. 135.
86. Sorensen, pp. 690–91.
87. Elie Abel, *The Cuban Missile Crisis* (New York: Bantam, 1966), p. 63.
88. Arkady N. Shevchenko, *Breaking with Moscow* (New York: Knopf, 1985), p. 154.
89. Conversation with Paul Nitze, October 7, 1987.
90. Transcript of October 16, 1961, ExComm Meeting, p. 15, National Security Archives, Cuban Missile Crisis File, Washington, D.C.
91. Sorensen, p. 687.
92. Ibid., p. 694.
93. Schlesinger, p. 739.
94. Sorensen, p. 694.
95. Kennedy, p. 27.
96. Conversation with Paul Nitze, October 7, 1987.
97. Abel, p. 91.
98. Raymond L. Garthoff, *Reflections on the Cuban Missile Crisis* (Washington, D.C.: Brookings Institution, 1987), pp. 40–41.
99. Ibid.
100. Richard Betts, *Nuclear Blackmail and Nuclear Balance* (Washington, D.C.: Brookings Institution, 1987), p. 118.
101. Scott D. Sagan, "Nuclear Alerts and Crisis Management," *International Security* 9, no. 4 (spring 1985), pp. 108, n 22.
102. Betts, p. 118.
103. Garthoff, p. 38.
104. Abel, p. 110.
105. Kennedy, p. 38.
106. Conversation with Paul Nitze, October 7, 1987.
107. Conversation with Dean Rusk, September 28, 1987.
108. Conversation with former intelligence official.
109. Garthoff, p. 22.
110. Conversation with Dean Rusk, September 28, 1986.
111. Taylor interview with Richard Neustadt, June 28, 1983, pp. 2, 3 (transcript).
112. Kennedy, p. 55.
113. Ibid.
114. Harold Macmillan, *At the End of the Day: 1961–1963* (New York: Harper & Row, 1973), pp. 210–11.
115. WGBH interview with Dean Rusk, Tape #D04080, p. 15.
116. Roger Hilsman, *To Move a Nation* (Garden City, N.Y.: Doubleday, 1967), p. 220.
117. Conversation with Dean Rusk, November 10, 1986.
118. McGeorge Bundy and James Blight, "Eleventh Hour of the Cuban Missile Crisis, October 27, 1962: Transcripts of the Meetings of ExComm," *International Security* (winter 1987–88), pp. 37, 55.
119. Ibid., p. 63.
120. Kennedy, p. 75.
121. Sagan, "Nuclear Alerts and Crisis Management," p. 118.
122. Kennedy, pp. 79–80.
123. Conversation with McGeorge Bundy, September 22, 1987.
124. Bundy and Blight, p. 59.
125. Ibid., p. 91.
126. Bundy, pp. 428–429.
127. Kennedy, p. 87.
128. Bundy and Blight, p. 59.
129. Khrushchev, *Khrushchev Remembers: The Last Testament*, p. 511.
130. Garthoff, p. 75, n. 20.
131. Ibid., p. 71.
132. Ibid., pp. 78–79.
133. Conversation with Paul Nitze, October 7, 1987.
134. Conversation with Dean Rusk, September 28, 1987.
135. Conversation with Dean Rusk, November 10, 1986.

VII

1. John Newhouse, *De Gaulle and the Anglo-Saxons* (New York: Viking, 1970), pp. 155–56.
2. William W. Kaufmann, *The McNamara Strategy* (New York: Harper & Row, 1964), p. 116–17.
3. Newhouse, p. 181.
4. Ibid., p. 211.
5. Ibid., pp. 217–18.
6. Arthur Schlesinger, Jr., *A Thousand Days* (New York: Fawcett Premier Books, 1965), p. 818.
7. Newhouse, p. 223.
8. Conversation with the late Lord Harlech, formerly Sir David Ormsby-Gore, late 1967.
9. Newhouse, pp. 225–26.
10. Harold Macmillan, *At the End of the Day: 1961–1963* (New York: Harper & Row, 1973), p. 365.
11. Newhouse, pp. 210–11.
12. Conversation with Dean Rusk, November 10, 1986.
13. Newhouse, p. 114.
14. Glenn T. Seaborg, *Kennedy, Khrushchev and the Test Ban* (Berkeley: University of California Press, 1981), p. 188.
15. Ibid., p. 181.
16. Theodore Sorensen, *Kennedy* (New York: Harper & Row, 1965), pp. 729–30, 733.
17. Schlesinger, p. 824.
18. Seaborg, p. 241.
19. Ibid., p. 23.
20. Newhouse, pp. 245–46.
21. Morton Halperin, *Sino-Soviet Relations and Arms Control* (Cambridge, Mass.: MIT Press, 1967), pp. 141, 143.
22. Conversation with Carl Kaysen, November 5, 1987.
23. "Report by Senate Foreign Relations Committee on the Test Ban Treaty, September 3, 1963," in *Documents on Disarmament 1963* (Washington, D.C.: Arms Control and Disarmament Agency, 1964), p. 453.
24. André Fontaine, *History of the Cold War from the October Revolution to the Korean War* (London: Secker and Warburg, 1968), p. 463.
25. Philip Geyelin, *Lyndon B. Johnson and the World* (New York: Praeger, 1966), p. 9.
26. Charles Roberts, *LBJ's Inner Circle* (New York: Delacorte, 1965), p. 37.
27. Conversation with former member of Johnson's NSC.
28. Charles Bohlen, *Witness to History, 1929–1969* (New York: Norton, 1973), p. 498.
29. Conversation with Charles Bohlen, October 1964.
30. Bohlen, p. 496.
31. Chalmers Roberts, *First Rough Draft* (New York: Praeger, 1973), pp. 217, 218.
32. Morton Halperin, *China and the Bomb* (New York: Praeger, 1965), p. 28.
33. Geyelin, p. 54.
34. Conversation with Dean Rusk, November 9, 1987.
35. Leon V. Sigal, "No First Use and NATO's Nuclear Posture," *Alliance Security: NATO and the No-First-Use Question* (Washington, D.C.: Brookings Institution, 1983), p. 111.
36. Conversation with Robert McNamara, November 12, 1987.
37. WGBH interview with Valentin Falin, Tape #655000, p. 8.
38. United States Arms Control and Disarmament Agency, *Documents on Disarmament, 1966* (Washington, D.C.: Government Printing Office, 1967), pp. 652–53.
39. Thomas W. Wolfe, *Soviet Power and Europe, 1945–1970* (Baltimore: Johns Hopkins Press, 1970), p. 266.
40. John Newhouse, "Annals of Diplomacy: SALT—The Labyrinth," *The New Yorker*, May 5, 1973, p. 54.
41. Testimony before combined session of the Senate Committee on the Armed

Services and Senate Committee on Appropriations, January 25, 1967 (Washington, D.C.: GPO, 1969).

42. John Newhouse, "Annals of Diplomacy: SALT—A Weapon in Search of a Role," *The New Yorker*, May 12, 1973, p. 94.

43. Richard Rhodes, "Edward Teller's Terrors," p. 70 (unpublished ms).

44. Newhouse, *The New Yorker*, May 12, 1973, pp. 102–3.

45. Robert S. McNamara, *Blundering into Disaster: Surviving the First Century of the Nuclear Age* (New York: Pantheon, 1986), p. 13.

46. Ibid.

47. WGBH interview with Robert McNamara, Tape #F05045, pp. 2–4.

48. Newhouse, *The New Yorker*, May 12, 1973, p. 110.

49. Roberts, first rough draft, pp. 244–45.

50. Conversation with Robert McNamara, November 12, 1987.

51. Newhouse, *The New Yorker*, May 12, 1973, p. 112.

52. Ibid., p. 102.

53. I. F. Stone, *Polemics and Prophecies, 1967–1970* (New York: Random House, 1970), p. 158.

54. Chalmers Roberts, *The Nuclear Years* (New York: Praeger, 1970), pp. 91–92.

55. *Pravda*, June 28, 1968.

56. John Newhouse, "Annals of Diplomacy: SALT—A Simple, Clear Proposal," *The New Yorker*, May 19, 1973, p. 89.

57. Ibid., pp. 98–99.

58. Ibid., p. 100.

59. Conversation with Yuri Vorontsov, autumn 1971.

VIII

1. Richard M. Nixon, *RN. The Memoirs of Richard Nixon* (New York: Grosset & Dunlap, 1978), p. 340.

2. Henry Kissinger, *White House Years* (Boston: Little, Brown, 1979), p. 11.

3. Nicholas Henderson, *The Private Office* (London: Weidenfeld & Nicolson, 1984), p. 61.

4. Conversation with senior administration official, November 25, 1987.

5. Conversation with Robert McCloskey, February 9, 1987.

6. Conversation with Sander Vanocur, January 8, 1987.

7. Conversation with Robert McCloskey, February 9, 1987.

8. Conversation with George Vest, October 6, 1986.

9. John Newhouse, "Annals of Diplomacy: SALT—A Simple, Clear Proposal," *The New Yorker*, May 19, 1973, p. 109.

10. Conversation with Alton Frye, then Brooke's staff director and now vice president of the Council on Foreign Relations, October 3, 1986.

11. Alton Frye, *A Responsible Congress: The Politics of National Security* (New York: McGraw-Hill, 1975), p. 60.

12. Kissinger, p. 212.

13. Newhouse, *The New Yorker*, May 19, 1973, p. 112.

14. Richard M. Nixon, "Asia after Vietnam," *Foreign Affairs* (October 1967): 121

15. Kissinger, p. 173.

16. Roger Morris, *Uncertain Greatness: Henry Kissinger and American Foreign Policy* (New York: Harper & Row, 1977), p. 204.

17. Conversation with Arkady Shevchenko, November 11, 1986.

18. Arkady N. Shevchenko, *Breaking with Moscow* (New York: Knopf, 1985), p. 166.

19. Newhouse, *The New Yorker*, May 19, 1973, p. 114.

20. John Newhouse, "Annals of Diplomacy: SALT—The Back Channel," *The New Yorker*, May 26, 1973, p. 78.

21. Conversation with Paul Nitze, May 15, 1987.

22. Newhouse, *The New Yorker*, May 26, 1973, p. 84.

23. C. Gerard Smith, *Doubletalk: The Story of SALT I* (Garden City, N.Y.: Doubleday, 1980), p. 166.

24. Frye, p. 71.
25. Kissinger, p. 540.
26. Smith, p. 177.
27. Raymond Garthoff, *Détente and Confrontation* (Washington, D.C.: Brookings Institution, 1985), pp. 223–24.
28. Ibid., p. 227, citing *Time*, October 5, 1970.
29. Newhouse, *The New Yorker*, May 26, 1973, p. 94.
30. Kissinger, p. 853.
31. Ibid., p. 725.
32. Garthoff, p. 233. Garthoff cites Seymour Hersh, *The Price of Power* (New York: Summit, 1983), and says, "I have been able independently to confirm this fact with intelligence officials who subsequently learned of the disclosures."
33. John Newhouse, "Annals of Diplomacy: SALT—At the Summit," *The New Yorker*, June 2, 1973, p. 80.
34. Newhouse, *The New Yorker*, May 26, 1973, p. 96.
35. Conversation with an American participant.
36. John Newhouse, *Cold Dawn* (New York: Holt, Rinehart & Winston, 1973), p. 202.
37. William G. Hyland, *Mortal Rivals: Superpower Relations from Nixon to Reagan* (New York: Random House, 1987), p. 27.
38. Richard Nixon's radio and television statement of May 20, 1971. Cited in Newhouse, *The New Yorker*, May 26, 1973, p. 109.
39. Ibid., p. 110.
40. Smith, pp. 224, 225, 234.
41. Kissinger, p. 822.
42. Smith, p. 225.
43. Ibid., p. 265.
44. Ibid., p. 319.
45. Barry Carter and John Steinbruner, "Trident," reprint from *Commission of the Organization of the Government for the Conduct of Foreign Policy* 4 (June 1975), "Appendix K: Adequacy of Current Organization: Defense and Arms Control," p. 175.
46. Conversation with former Defense Department official, December 8, 1987.
47. Conversation with Henry Kissinger, June 1973.
48. Nixon, p. 586.
49. Ibid., p. 603.
50. Newhouse, *The New Yorker*, June 2, 1973, p. 88.
51. WGBH interview with Alexander Bovin, Tape #679000, p. 5.
52. Newhouse, *The New Yorker*, June 2, 1973, p. 88.
53. Kissinger, p. 836.
54. Ibid., p. 903.
55. Garthoff, p. 169 n. 98.
56. Kissinger, p. 1220.
57. Garthoff, p. 173.
58. Ibid., p. 171 n. 102.
59. Ibid., p. 173.

IX

1. William G. Hyland, *Mortal Rivals: Superpower Relations from Nixon to Reagan* (New York: Random House, 1987), p. 70.
2. Henry Kissinger, *Years of Upheaval* (Boston: Little, Brown, 1982), p. 125.
3. Ibid., p. 987.
4. Ibid., p. 265.
5. Conversation with Philip Odeen, February 10, 1987.
6. Kissinger, *Upheaval*, p. 268.
7. Hyland, p. 68.
8. Kissinger, *Upheaval*, p. 286.
9. Hyland, p. 63.
10. "What the President Saw: A Nation Coming into Its Own," *Time*, July 29, 1985, p. 53.
11. Kissinger, *Upheaval*, p. 583.
12. Ibid., pp. 583–84.
13. Richard Nixon, *RN: The Memoirs of Richard Nixon* (New York: Grosset & Dunlap, 1978), p. 938.
14. Kissinger, *Upheaval*, p. 585.
15. Ibid., p. 581.
16. Raymond Garthoff, *Détente and Confrontation* (Washington, D.C.: Brookings Institution, 1985), p. 379.
17. Richard Betts, *Nuclear Blackmail and Nuclear Balance* (Washington, D.C.: Brookings Institution, 1987), p. 124.

18. Kissinger, *Upheaval*, pp. 591, 593.

19. CBS News, Walter Cronkite interview with James Schlesinger, 1985, for "Hiroshima," p. 24 of transcript.

20. Richard Nixon, PPOP, 1973 (Washington, D.C.: GPO, 1975), p. 900.

21. "Secretary Kissinger's Press Conference of October 25," *Department of State Bulletin*, Volume 69 (Washington, D.C.: Government Printing Office, November 12, 1973), pp. 588, 592, 591, 590.

22. Nixon, PPOP, 1973 (Washington, D.C.: GPO, 1975), p. 902.

23. Kissinger, *Upheaval*, p. 594.

24. Garthoff, p. 173, citing "Question and Answer Session after a Briefing by Dr. Henry Kissinger," p. 10.

25. Nixon, *RN*, p. 875.

26. WGBH interview with Henry Kissinger, Tape AO7020, p. 9.

27. Kissinger, *Upheaval*, p. 1024.

28. Ibid., pp. 1026–27.

29. Ibid., p. 1027.

30. Ibid., p. 1152.

31. Conversation with Paul Nitze, January 6, 1988.

32. Kissinger, *Upheaval*, p. 1152.

33. Ibid., p. 1158.

34. Ibid., p. 1155.

35. Ibid., p. 1151.

36. Ibid., 1173.

37. Hyland, p. 65.

38. Richard Valeriani, *Travels with Henry* (Boston: Houghton Mifflin, 1979), pp. 141–42.

39. Hyland, p. 72.

40. Gerald Ford, *A Time to Heal* (New York: Harper & Row and the Reader's Digest Association, 1979), p. 30.

41. Ibid., p. 33.

42. Ibid., p. 139.

43. "Statement by the Honorable Henry A. Kissinger, Secretary of State before the Senate Foreign Relations Committee," #366, September 19, 1974, pp. 15, 17.

44. Paula Stern, *Water's Edge: Domestic Politics and the Making of American Foreign Policy* (Westport, Conn.: Greenwood Press, 1979), p. 164.

45. Ibid., p. 165.

46. Garthoff, p. 460.

47. WGBH interview with Kissinger, Tape AO7020, p. 9.

48. Hyland, p. 88.

49. Garthoff, p. 444.

50. Ford, p. 214.

51. Conversation with Helmut Sonnenfeldt, December 21, 1987.

52. Ford, pp. 218–19.

53. Hyland, p. 79.

54. Conversation with Jack Mendelsohn, January 11, 1988.

55. Hyland, pp. 72–73, citing Kissinger address to American Legion, August 20, 1974.

56. Conversation with James Schlesinger, February 5, 1988.

57. Ford, pp. 297–98.

58. Conversation with Helmut Sonnenfeldt, December 21, 1987.

59. George Will, "Solzhenitsyn and the President," Washington *Post*, July 11, 1975.

60. Conversation with Helmut Sonnenfeldt, December 21, 1987.

61. Hyland, p. 124.

62. Ibid., p. 125.

63. Ibid., p. 127.

64. Garthoff, p. 487, citing Tad Szulc, *Foreign Policy*, no. 21 (winter 1975–1976), pp. 9, 44.

65. Ibid., p. 522.

66. Ibid., p. 520, citing "Questions and Answers Following the Secretary's Pittsburgh Address," November 11, 1975, *Department of State Bulletin*: 73 (December 1, 1975), p. 768.

67. Ibid., pp. 523–24, citing *Department of State Bulletin*: 74 (February 16, 1976), p. 180.

68. Conversation with William Hyland, October 16, 1986.

69. Conversation with former White House NSC official, winter 1988.

70. Conversation with former NSC staff member, winter 1988.

71. Rowland Evans and Robert Novak, "New Concessions for a SALT Accord," Washington *Post*, December 6, 1975.

72. Conversation with Helmut Sonnenfeldt, December 21, 1987.

73. Hyland, p. 161.
74. Ibid., p. 162.
75. Ford, p. 373.
76. Conversation with former Ford associate, January 1988.
77. Conversation with Gerald Ford, January 26, 1988.
78. Charles de Gaulle, *The Edge of the Sword* (London: Faber and Faber, 1961), p. 61. Originally published in France in 1932 under the title *Le Fil de l'Epée*.
79. Kissinger, *Upheaval*, p. 1154.
80. WGBH interview with Kissinger, Tape #AO7020, p. 6, Tape #AO7019, p. 14.

X

1. WGBH interview with Raja Ramanna, Tape #009068, pp. 6–7.
2. Ibid., p. 2.
3. *Xin Hua*, August 15, 1963, and September 1, 1963.
4. WGBH interview with Roland Timerbaev, Tape #B09009, p. 4.
5. *A Secret Journey: The Story of the Birth of China's 1st Atomic Bomb*; compiled by Shenjian (4377/0494, Chapter of the Ministry of Nuclear Industry), p. 27.
6. WGBH interview with Subramanian Swamy, Tape #009062, p. 3.
7. Leonard S. Spector, *Nuclear Proliferation Today* (New York: Vintage, 1984), p. 33.
8. Peter Pringle and James Spigelman, *The Nuclear Barons* (New York: Holt, Rinehart and Winston, 1981), p. 388.
9. WGBH interview with Subramanian Swamy, Tape #009063, p. 1.
10. Spector, p. 24.
11. WGBH interview with Raja Ramanna, Tape #009070, pp. 3–4.
12. Conversation with Dean Rusk, November 10, 1986.
13. WGBH interview with Morarji Desai, Tape #009066, p. 2.
14. Conversation with Gerald Ford, January 26, 1988.
15. CIA, "Prospects for Further Proliferation of Nuclear Weapons," sanitized copy, paragraphs 3, 13, 14, September 4, 1974.
16. Conversation with Dean Rusk, November 10, 1986.
17. Conversation with George Vest, February 1, 1987.
18. Ibid.
19. WGBH interview with Agha Shahi, Tape #009048, p. 11.
20. William H. Courtney, "Brazil and Argentina: Strategies for American Diplomacy," in *Nonproliferation and U.S. Foreign Policy*, ed. Joseph A. Yager (Washington, D.C.: Brookings Institution, 1980), p. 380, citing Bernard Weinraub, *New York Times*, January 25, 1977.
21. Ibid., p. 381.
22. Michael Nacht, "Controlling Nuclear Proliferation," in *The Eagle Entangled: U.S. Foreign Policy in a Complex World* (New York: Longman, 1979), ed. K. Oye, D. Rothchild, and R. Lizber, p. 157.
23. Richard K. Betts, "A Diplomatic Bomb? South Africa's Nuclear Potential," in Yager, ed., *Nonproliferation and U.S. Foreign Policy*, p. 284, citing *Newsweek*, May 17, 1976, p. 53.
24. WGBH interview with Munir Khan, Tape #009052, 1987, p. 5.
25. WGBH interview with Matityahu Peled, Tape #209035, p. 8.
26. Leonard S. Spector, *Going Nuclear* (New York: Ballinger, 1987), p. 77.
27. Ibid., p. 77, n. 10.
28. Washington *Post* editorial, "Second Best," October 21, 1987.
29. Spector, *Going Nuclear*, p. 103.
30. WGBH interview with Agha Shahi, Tape #009049, p. 2.
31. Bob Woodward, "Pakistani A-Bomb Reported Near," Washington *Post*, November 4, 1986.
32. Ibid.

33. Philip Revzin, "Nuclear Project Bedevils Aid for Pakistan," *Wall Street Journal,* December 8, 1987.

34. WGBH interview with Subramanian Swamy, Tape #009064, pp. 15–16.

35. WGBH interview with General A. I. Akram, Tape #009057, p. 1.

36. Paul Bracken, *The Command and Control of Nuclear Forces* (New Haven, Conn.: Yale University Press, 1983), p. 187.

37. WGBH interview with Robert Sprague, Tape #C03005, p. 4.

38. Bruce G. Blair, *Strategic Command and Control: Redefining the Nuclear Threat* (Washington, D.C.: Brookings Institution, 1985), p. 70.

39. Alain C. Enthoven and K. Wayne Smith, *How Much Is Enough? Shaping the Defense Program, 1961–1969* (New York: Harper & Row, 1971), p. 169.

40. Conversation with Robert McNamara, September 19, 1987.

41. Conversation with Dean Rusk, November 10, 1986.

42. Bracken, p. 26.

43. Donald R. Cotter, "Peacetime Operations: Safety and Security," in *Managing Nuclear Operations,* ed. Ashton B. Carter, John D. Steinbruner, and Charles A. Zeart (Washington, D.C.: Brookings Institution, 1987), p. 49.

44. Conversation with Bruce Blair, October 20, 1987.

45. Conversation with Dean Rusk, November 10, 1986.

46. Stephen M. Meyer, "Soviet Perspectives on the Paths to Nuclear War," in *Hawks, Doves and Owls: An Agenda for Avoiding Nuclear War,* ed. Graham T. Allison, Albert Carnesale, and Joseph S. Nye, Jr. (New York: Norton, 1985), pp. 191–92.

47. Ibid., p. 188.

48. Conversation with James Schlesinger, February 5, 1988.

49. Bruce Blair, *Nuclear Postures of the Superpowers* (Washington, D.C.: Brookings Institution, 1989), ms.

50. Daniel Ford, "A Reporter at Large Part I (U.S. Command and Control)," *The New Yorker,* April 1, 1985, pp. 54–57.

51. Daniel Ford, *The Button: America's Nuclear Warning System—Does It Work?* (New York: Simon and Schuster, 1985), p. 196.

52. Ibid., p. 177.

53. Bill Gulley, with Mary Ellen Reese, *Breaking Cover* (New York: Simon and Schuster, 1980), p. 179.

54. Bruce Blair and Kurt Gottfried, ed., *Crisis Stability and Nuclear War* (New York: Oxford University Press, 1988), p. 15.

55. Conversation with Bruce Blair, October 20, 1987.

56. Zbigniew Brzezinski, *Power and Principle* (New York: Farrar, Straus and Giroux, 1985), p. 15.

57. Thomas Powers, "Choosing a Strategy for World War III," *The Atlantic Monthly* (November 1982), p. 95.

58. Paul Warnke, "The World According to Brzezinski," *The Washington Monthly* (July/August 1986), p. 52.

59. Zbigniew Brzezinski, *Game Plan, How to Conduct the U.S.-Soviet Contest* (Boston: Atlantic Monthly Press, 1986), pp. 160–61.

60. Ibid., p. 161.

61. Lawrence Freedman, *The Evolution of Nuclear Strategy* (New York: St. Martin's Press, 1982), p. 393, citing Richard Burt, "US Stresses Limited Nuclear War In Sharp Shift on Military Strategy," *International Herald Tribune,* August 7, 1980.

62. Conversation with James Schlesinger, February 5, 1988.

63. Conversation with Bruce Blair, October 20, 1987.

64. Conversation with Bruce Blair, November 23, 1987.

65. Harold Brown, Remarks at Naval War College, Newport, Rhode Island, August 20, 1980.

66. Conversation with John Steinbruner, February 24, 1988.

67. Morton H. Halperin, *Nuclear Fallacy: Dispelling the Myth of Nuclear Strategy*

(New York: Ballinger, 1987), pp. 93, 103–4.

68. Bracken, pp. 168–69.

69. Halperin, p. 106.

70. John Newhouse, "A Reporter at Large

—Arms and Orthodoxy," *The New Yorker,* June 7, 1982, p. 96.

71. Ibid., p. 100.

72. Blair, *Strategic Command and Control,* pp. 288–89.

XI

1. Jimmy Carter, *Keeping Faith: Memoirs of a President* (New York: Bantam, 1982), pp. 126, 71.

2. Thomas Powers, "Choosing a Strategy for World War III," *The Atlantic Monthly* (November 1982), p. 84.

3. Robert Donovan, *The Tumultuous Years: The Presidency of Harry S Truman* (New York: Norton, 1982), p. 261.

4. Conversation with David Aaron, December 28, 1987.

5. Paul Nitze, "Assuring Strategic Stability in an Era of Détente," *Foreign Affairs* 54, no. 2 (January 1976), p. 207.

6. Gregg Herken, *Counsels of War* (New York: Knopf, 1985), p. 274.

7. Conversation with Roger Mollander, January 4, 1988.

8. William G. Hyland, *Mortal Rivals: Superpower Relations from Nixon to Reagan* (New York: Random House, 1987), p. 85; John Prados, *The Soviet Estimate: U.S. Intelligence Analysis and Russian Military Strength* (New York: Dial, 1982), p. 250.

9. Prados, p. 250.

10. Ibid., p. 252.

11. Herken, p. 281.

12. John Newhouse, "A Reporter at Large —Arms and Orthodoxy," *The New Yorker,* June 7, 1982, p. 92, citing "U.S. Could Survive in Administration's View," Los Angeles *Times,* January 16, 1982.

13. Conversation with James Schlesinger, February 5, 1988.

14. James Schlesinger, "Statement before the U.S. Senate Committee on Foreign Relations," April 30, 1982, p. 3.

15. Prados, p. 269; Raymond Garthoff, *Détente and Confrontation* (Washington, D.C.: Brookings Institution, 1985), p. 585.

16. Strobe Talbott, *Endgame: The Inside Story of SALT II* (New York: Harper & Row, 1979), p. 39.

17. Richard E. Neustadt and Ernest R. May, *Thinking in Time: The Uses of History for Decision Makers* (New York: The Free Press, 1986), p. 116.

18. Talbott, p. 57.

19. Neustadt and May, p. 119.

20. Talbott, p. 74.

21. Hyland, p. 215.

22. Conversation with Harold Brown, April 1, 1988.

23. Conversation with Gerald Ford, January 26, 1988.

24. Conversation with Paul Warnke, September 26, 1986.

25. Conversation with Zbigniew Brzezinski, March 1, 1988.

26. Conversation with James Schlesinger, February 5, 1988.

27. Conversations with James Schlesinger and Harold Brown, February 5, 1988.

28. Kenneth Harris, *David Owen Personally Speaking to Kenneth Harris* (London: Weidenfeld & Nicolson, 1987), p. 122.

29. Neustadt and May, pp. 186–87, 189.

30. Conversation with Zbigniew Brzezinski, March 1, 1988.

31. Neustadt and May, p. 189.

32. Cyrus Vance, *Hard Choices: Critical Years in America's Foreign Policy* (New York: Simon and Schuster, 1983), p. 61.

33. Zbigniew Brzezinski, *Power and Principle* (New York: Farrar, Straus and Giroux, 1985), p. 301.

34. Carter, p. 225.

35. Conversation with Zbigniew Brzezinski, March 1, 1988.

36. Ibid.

37. Brzezinski, p. 304.

38. Garthoff, p. 852.

39. Vance, p. 95.

40. Ibid., p. 84.

41. Ibid.
42. Brzezinski, p. 183.
43. Ibid., p. 178.
44. Ibid., p. 183.
45. Vance, p. 85.
46. Ibid., p. 87.
47. Brzezinski, p. 185.
48. Vance, p. 88.
49. Brzezinski, p. 189.
50. Ibid., p. 222.
51. Vance, p. 114.
52. Garthoff, p. 599.
53. Talbott, p. 153.
54. Brzezinski, p. 221.
55. Garthoff, p. 708.
56. Conversation with former State Department officials.
57. Brzezinski, pp. 230-31.
58. Vance, pp. 109-10.
59. Talbott, p. 244.
60. Conversation with former State Department official, March 1988.
61. Carter, p. 224.
62. WGBH interview with William Perry, Tape #A12139, p. 8.
63. Ibid., p. 9.
64. Ibid., Tape #A12143, pp. 3-4.
65. Vance, p. 365.
66. Conversation with William Perry, March 2, 1988.
67. Conversation with Zbigniew Brzezinski, March 1, 1988.
68. Conversation with William Perry, March 2, 1988.
69. Brzezinski, p. 334.
70. John Newhouse, "Reflections," *The New Yorker*, December 17, 1979, p. 142.
71. Robert G. Kaiser, "Stiff Opposition to MX Plan Emerges," Washington *Post*, November 6, 1979.
72. Conversation with Paul Warnke, March 30, 1988.
73. Kaiser, Number 6, 1979.
74. Brzezinski, p. 304.
75. Conversation with Zbigniew Brzezinski, March 1, 1988.
76. Ibid.
77. Brzezinski, p. 308.
78. Conversation with former State Department official, March 1988.
79. Conversation with Zbigniew Brzezinski, March 31, 1988.
80. Conversation with David Aaron, December 28, 1987.
81. Carter, p. 235.
82. Conversation with Zbigniew Brzezinski, March 1, 1988.
83. Conversation with Günther van Well, October 27, 1987.
84. Conversation with David Owen, former foreign secretary, August 4, 1987.
85. *Sunday Times* (London), "Insight," December 9, 1987, p. 14.
86. Conversation with former Vance adviser, March 1988.
87. Conversation with Harold Brown, April 1, 1988.
88. Conversation with British defense official, August 4, 1987.
89. Conversation with British diplomat, August 5, 1987.
90. Conversation with David Aaron, December 28, 1987.
91. Ibid.
92. James Callaghan, *Time and Change* (London: Collins, 1987), p. 555.
93. Conversation with Günther van Well, October 27, 1987.
94. Conversation with Zbigniew Brzezinski, March 1, 1988.
95. John Newhouse, *The New Yorker*, June 7, 1982, p. 62.
96. Conversation with David Aaron, December 28, 1987.
97. John Newhouse, *The New Yorker*, December 17, 1979, p. 159.
98. "Military Implications of the Treaty on the Limitation of Strategic Offensive Arms and Protocol Thereto," *Hearing before the Committee on Armed Services United States Senate*, Part I, (Washington, D.C.: GPO, 1979) p. 356.
99. Brzezinski, p. 347.
100. Garthoff, pp. 828-29.
101. Talbott, *Endgame* (New York: Harper Torchbooks, 1980), p. 285.
102. Vance, p. 362.
103. Conversation with former State Department official, April 1988.
104. David D. Newsom, *The Soviet Brigade in Cuba: A Study in Political Diplomacy* (Bloomington: Indiana University Press, 1987), p. 49.

105. Garthoff, pp. 949.
106. Ibid., p. 950, citing the *New York Times*, January 1, 1980.
107. Ibid.
108. Conversation with William Colby, March 14, 1988.

XII

1. Lou Cannon, "Why Reagan Is Finally Winning in Foreign Policy," Washington *Post*, August 10, 1987.
2. Conversation with former Reagan administration official, April 1988.
3. Conversation with former Reagan administration official, April 1988.
4. Conversation with former Reagan administration official, April 1988.
5. Murray Marder, "Defector Told of Soviet Alert: KGB Station Reportedly Warned U.S. Would Attack," Washington *Post*, August 8, 1986.
6. Ibid.
7. Conversation with American diplomat, July 1987.
8. Robert Scheer, *With Enough Shovels: Reagan, Bush and Nuclear War* (New York: Random House, 1982), pp. 5–6.
9. Laurence Barrett, *Gambling with History: Reagan in the White House* (New York: Penguin, 1984), p. 308.
10. Scheer, p. 29.
11. John Newhouse, "A Reporter at Large —Arms and Orthodoxy," *The New Yorker*, June 7, 1982, p. 92.
12. Ibid., p. 93.
13. Ibid., p. 90.
14. Ronald Reagan, PPOP, 1981 (Washington, D.C.: Government Printing Office, 1982), p. 57.
15. Alexander M. Haig, Jr., *Caveat: Realism, Reagan, and Foreign Policy* (New York: Macmillan, 1984), p. 103.
16. Conversation with Soviet specialist, July 1987.
17. Conversation with official of Hungarian Central Committee, July 30, 1987.
18. Marder, August 8, 1986.
19. Ibid.
20. Conversations with senior American diplomats.
21. Scheer, p. 104.
22. Garry Wills, *Reagan's America: Innocents at Home* (Garden City, N.Y.: Doubleday, 1987), p. 345.
23. Conversation with senior diplomat.
24. Conversation with Soviet specialist, July 1987.
25. Hedrick Smith, *The Power Game: How Washington Works* (New York: Random House, 1988), pp. 576–77.
26. Ibid., pp. 577–78.
27. Conversation with American diplomat, July 1987.
28. Conversation with former administration official, April 1988.
29. Conversation with former member of the Joint Chiefs.
30. Strobe Talbott, *Deadly Gambits: The Reagan Administration and the Stalemate in Nuclear Arms* (New York: Knopf, 1984), p. 274.
31. Conversation with General David C. Jones, April 21, 1988.
32. Conversation with senior diplomat, July 1987.
33. Raymond Garthoff, *Détente and Confrontation* (Washington, D.C.: Brookings Institution, 1985), p. 1030, citing *Time*, April 27, 1981, p. 27.
34. Ibid., p. 1030.
35. Conversation with Benjamin Read, former Undersecretary of State, who accompanied Vance on this mission.
36. WGBH interview with James Watkins, Tape #11036, p. 48.
37. Newhouse, *The New Yorker*, June 7, 1982, pp. 49–50.
38. Ibid., p. 86.
39. A. G. B. Metcalf, "Missile Accuracy—the Need to Know," *Strategic Review* 9, no. 3 (summer 1981), p. 5.
40. Robert Dallek, *Ronald Reagan: The Politics of Symbolism* (Cambridge, Mass.: Harvard University Press, 1984), p. 156, citing the *New York Times*, May 30, 1982.
41. Scheer, p. 9, citing "Preparing for a Long Nuclear War Is Waste of Funds, General Jones Says," Washington *Post*, June 19, 1982.

42. Haig, pp. 312–14.
43. Conversation with senior diplomat, July 1987.
44. "Cap Weinberger Under Siege," *Newsweek*, May 23, 1983, p. 21.
45. Conversation with senior American diplomat, July 1987.
46. Conversation with former NSC member.
47. Reagan, PPOP, 1982, p. 1454, and Dallek, p. 157.
48. Barrett, p. 324.
49. McGeorge Bundy, October 1982, in Newhouse, *The New Yorker*, June 7, 1982, pp. 70–71.
50. Talbott, p. 53.
51. Strobe Talbott, "Arms and the Man," *Time*, December 21, 1987, p. 76.
52. Conversation with American diplomat, August 1987.
53. John Newhouse, "A Reporter at Large —Arms and Allies," *The New Yorker*, February 28, 1983, p. 70.
54. Ibid.
55. Conversations with American and European diplomats.
56. "Helmut Schmidt on Those Missiles," Washington *Post*, February 13, 1983.
57. Robert S. Dudney, "How MX Will Transform Nuclear Strategy," *U.S. News & World Report*, April 25, 1983, p. 23.
58. Hearing on Strategic Programs, House Committee on Armed Services, April 20, 1983 (Washington, D.C.: U.S. Government Printing Office, 1983), p. 45.
59. Ronald Reagan, PPOP, 1983, vol. I (Washington, D.C.: Government Printing Office, 1984), pp. 443, 442.
60. Conversation with American diplomat.
61. David Hoffman, "Spin Control: The Dizziness Following Reykjavík," Washington *Post*, November 2, 1986.
62. James Chace and Caleb Carr, *America Invulnerable: The Quest for Absolute Security from 1812 to Star Wars* (New York: Summit Books, 1988), p. 294.
63. Ibid., p. 295.
64. Ibid., p. 312.
65. Smith, p. 605.
66. John Newhouse, "The Diplomatic Round—Summiteering," *The New Yorker*, September 8, 1986, p. 50.
67. Smith, p. 607.
68. WGBH interview with Admiral James Watkins, Tape #11035, pp. 32, 38.
69. Smith, pp. 608–9.
70. John Newhouse, "The Diplomatic Round—Test," *The New Yorker*, July 22, 1985, p. 41.
71. WGBH interview with Richard Perle, Tape #11064, p. 18.
72. Conversation with Admiral James Watkins, May 5, 1988.
73. Conversation with General David Jones, April 21, 1988.
74. *Pravda*, March 27, 1983, in Foreign Broadcast Information Service Report, p. A3.
75. Conversation with official of Hungarian Central Committee, July 30, 1987.
76. Conversation with American diplomat, July 30, 1987.

XIII

1. Conversation with Arthur Hartman, April 28, 1988.
2. Ibid.
3. Seymour M. Hersh, *"The Target Is Destroyed": What Really Happened to Flight 007 and What America Knew About It* (New York: Random House, 1986), p. 45.
4. Ibid., p. 61.
5. Ibid., p. 70.
6. Ibid., pp. 100–2.
7. Ibid., p. 104.
8. Ronald Reagan, *Public Papers of the Presidents of the United States, 1983*, vol. II (Washington, D.C.: Government Printing Office, 1985), pp. 1228, 1229.
9. Hersh, p. 171.
10. Reagan, *Public Papers of the Presidents, 1983*, p. 1352.
11. Strobe Talbott, *Deadly Gambits: The Reagan Administration and the Stalemate in Nuclear Arms Control* (N.Y.: Knopf, 1984) p. 202.
12. Ibid., pp. 203–4.

13. Foreign Broadcast Information Service —Daily Report, Volume 3, November 25, 1983, p. AA2.

14. *Weekly Compilation of Presidential Documents*, vol. 20, nos. 1–25 (Washington, D.C.: National Archives, 1984), p. 44.

15. Talbott, p. 345.

16. Conversation with British diplomat, August 4, 1987.

17. Dusko Doder, *Shadows and Whispers: Power Politics Inside the Kremlin from Brezhnev to Gorbachev* (New York: Random House, 1986), p. 210.

18. Conversation with David Owen, May 9, 1988.

19. John Newhouse, "The Diplomatic Round—Talks about Talks," *The New Yorker*, December 31, 1984, p. 40.

20. Conversation with British diplomat, August 4, 1987.

21. Newhouse, *The New Yorker*, December 31, 1984, p. 43.

22. Lou Cannon and David Hoffman, "Soviet's Visit Set in Secrecy," Washington *Post*, September 30, 1984.

23. Conversation with former administration official, April 7, 1988.

24. Michael Deaver, *Behind the Scenes* (New York: Morrow, 1987), p. 39.

25. Newhouse, *The New Yorker*, December 31, 1984, p. 47.

26. Ibid., p. 46.

27. "The Gromyko Method: His Negotiating Technique Combines Guile with 'nyet,'" *Newsweek*, October 1, 1984, p. 27.

28. Newhouse, *The New Yorker*, December 31, 1984, p. 48.

29. Conversation with senior American diplomat, July 1987.

30. "Endnotes," *Department of State Bulletin:* 85, no. 2094 (January 1985), p. 74.

31. *The Economist*, December 15, 1984, p. 23.

32. Ibid.

33. Conversation with David Klein, September 22, 1987.

34. "Excerpts from Interview by Gromyko on Arms Talks," *New York Times*, January 13, 1985.

35. Seweryn Bialer, *The Soviet Paradox:* *External Expansion, Internal Decline* (New York: Knopf, 1986), p. 115.

36. Celestine Bohlen, "Moscow Diary: Watching the Birth Pangs of Glasnost," Washington *Post*, May 8, 1988.

37. Zhores A. Medvedev, *Gorbachev* (New York: Norton, 1986), p. 57.

38. Dusko Doder, "Power in the Kremlin," Washington *Post*, July 30, 1985.

39. *Time*, January 4, 1988, p. 31.

40. Flora Lewis, "The East Is Moving," *New York Times*, October 2, 1987.

41. Conversation with Dimitri Simes, September 23, 1987.

42. Conversation with American diplomat, May 13, 1988.

43. Conversation with senior U.S. diplomat, May 10, 1988.

44. Conversation with State Department specialist, May 13, 1988.

45. Conversation with senior Swedish official after Dutch and Swedish ministerial talks.

46. David A. Stockman, *The Triumph of Politics: Why the Reagan Revolution Failed* (New York: Harper & Row, 1986), p. 380.

47. Thomas Hobbes, *Leviathan*, Part I, Chapter 5, 1651.

48. Newhouse, *The New Yorker*, December 31, 1984, p. 40.

49. John Connell, *The New Maginot Line* (London: Secker and Warburg, 1986), pp. 194–95.

50. John Newhouse, "The Diplomatic Round—Test," *The New Yorker*, July 22, 1985, p. 42.

51. John Newhouse, *The New Yorker*, December 31, 1984, pp. 40–41.

52. WGBH interview with Ashton Carter, Tape #11005, p. 26.

53. Newhouse, *The New Yorker*, July 22, 1985, p. 44.

54. Ibid., p. 38.

55. Conversation with British diplomat, August 3, 1987.

56. Conversation with British diplomat, August 4, 1987.

57. Newhouse, *The New Yorker*, July 22, 1985, p. 42.

58. "The Crisis at Krasnoyarsk," *New York Times* editorial, March 23, 1985.

59. David Aaron, "Verification: Will It Work?" *The New York Times Magazine*, October 11, 1987, p. 122.

60. Newhouse, *The New Yorker*, July 22, 1985, p. 52.

61. Ibid., p. 52.

62. Conversation with American diplomat, May 10, 1988.

63. *Weekly Compilation of Presidential Documents*, vol. 21, nos. 27–52, (Washington, D.C.: National Archives, 1985), p. 1387.

64. Conversation with American diplomat who took part in the summit, May 21, 1988.

65. John Newhouse, "The Diplomatic Round—Summiteering," *The New Yorker*, September 8, 1986, p. 51.

66. Ibid.

67. Conversation with Arthur Hartman, April 28, 1988.

68. Conversation with Hungarian official.

69. Conversation with American diplomat

70. *Weekly Compilation of Presidential Documents*, vol. 21, nos. 27–52, (Washington, D.C.: National Archives, 1985), p. 1422.

71. Raymond L. Garthoff, *Policy Versus the Law: The Reinterpretation of the ABM Treaty* (Washington, D.C.: Brookings Institution, 1987), pp. 10–11.

72. Newhouse, *The New Yorker*, September 8, 1986, p. 44.

73. Conversation with American diplomat, July 30, 1987.

74. Garthoff, p. 7.

75. Ibid., p. 9.

76. Ibid., p. 8, n. 7.

77. "Mr. McFarlane's Interview on 'Meet the Press,'" *Department of State Bulletin*, 85, no. 2105 (December 1985), p. 33.

78. Garthoff, p. 3.

79. Newhouse, *The New Yorker*, September 8, 1986, p. 60.

80. Neil A. Lewis, "Of Discarded Treaties and the ABM Furor," *New York Times*, March 17, 1987.

81. Conversation with Admiral James Watkins, May 5, 1988.

82. Newhouse, *The New Yorker*, September 8, 1986, p. 59.

83. Conversation with American diplomat, November 18, 1986.

84. Conversation with American diplomat, November 17, 1986.

85. Conversation with former administration official, November 21, 1986.

86. Conversation with American diplomat who took part in Reykjavík meeting.

87. Conversation with American diplomat who attended the meeting.

88. Conversation with senior administration official, May 9, 1987.

89. Don Oberdorfer, "At Reykjavík Soviets Were Prepared and U.S. Improvised," Washington *Post*, February 16, 1987.

90. Conversation with Paul Nitze, February 14, 1987.

91. Donald Regan, *For the Record: From Wall Street to Washington* (New York: Harcourt Brace Jovanovich, 1988), p. 350.

92. Jane Mayer and Doyle McManus, *Landslide: The Unmaking of the President, 1984–1988* (Boston: Houghton Mifflin Co., 1988), p. 283.

93. Ibid., p. 352.

94. Conversation with American diplomat who took part in Reykjavík meeting, May 16, 1988.

95. Conversation with American diplomat, May 21, 1988.

96. Conversation with David Owen, August 4, 1987.

97. Conversation with George Shultz, November 13, 1987.

98. Michael R. Gordon, "Reagan Is Warned by Senator Nunn over ABM Treaty," *New York Times*, February 7, 1987.

99. Conversation with German diplomat, May 14, 1987.

100. Conversation with British official, August 7, 1987.

101. Weinberger on NBC's *Meet the Press*, cited in Jack Mendelsohn, "INF Verification: A Guide for the Perplexed," *Arms Control Today* (September 1987), pp. 25–26.

102. "INF Background and Negotiating History," *Arms Control Association Background Paper* (January 1988), p. 7.

103. Mendelsohn, p. 26.
104. Conversation with German diplomat, May 24, 1988.
105. Conversation with American specialist, December 22, 1987.
106. Conversation with American diplomat, September 8, 1987.
107. Conversation with American diplomat, May 20, 1988.
108. Michael R. Gordon, "Negotiating the Arms Treaty: Verification Issue Proved Thorny," *New York Times*, January 1, 1988.
109. Flora Lewis, "Rating 'Double Zero,' " *New York Times*, September 22, 1987.
110. Conversation with Les Aspin, May 17, 1988.
111. "Locations of Sites Named in Arms Agreement," *New York Times*, December 11, 1987.
112. "The Spirit of Washington," *Time*, December 21, 1987, p. 19.
113. *Weekly Compilation of Presidential Documents* (Washington, D.C.: National Archives, 1987), p. 1495.
114. *Time*, December 21, 1987, p. 21.
115. Conversation with British diplomat, May 12, 1988.
116. Conversation with State Department official, May 16, 1988.
117. Conversation with State Department official, May 20, 1988.
118. Conversation with Frank Carlucci, May 23, 1988.
119. Michèle Flournoy, "A Rocky START," *Arms Control Today* (October 1987), p. 13.
120. Conversation with Les Aspin, May 17, 1988.
121. Ibid.
122. Conversation with Frank Carlucci, May 23, 1988.
123. Lou Cannon, "Reagan: No Pact by Moscow Summit," Washington *Post*, February 26, 1988.
124. Conversation with State Department official, March 12, 1988.
125. Conversation with Les Aspin, May 17, 1988.
126. Conversation with State Department official, May 20, 1988.
127. Frederick Kempe and Peter Gumbel, "Reagan Aims to Give Soviet Chief a Boost in Meeting at Summit," *Wall Street Journal*, May 27, 1988.
128. Conversation with senior British diplomat, August 5, 1987.
129. Robert Kaiser, "Leaders Team Up Against Cold War Dragon," Washington *Post*, June 3, 1988.
130. "Turmoil, Panic, Even a New Party," *The Economist*, May 14–20, 1988, p. 50.
131. Michael Dobbs, "Soviets Offer Curbs on Party's Power: Sweeping Proposal Backs Gorbachev," Washington *Post*, May 27, 1988.
132. Michael Dobbs, "Legislators Weigh in on Cooperatives Law," Washington *Post*, May 27, 1988.
133. "Round Two in Hungary," *The Economist*, May 28–June 3, 1988, p. 47.

Epilogue

1. Ralph E. Lapp, "The Einstein Letter That Started It All," *New York Times Magazine*, August 2, 1984, p. 54.
2. FBIS, October 27, 1987, p. 52.
3. Aleksander Herzen, *From the Other Shore*, cited by Isaiah Berlin in *Russian Thinkers* (New York: Viking, 1978), p. 88.
4. Panel Report of the National Academy of Public Administration, "Strengthening the U.S.-Soviet Communications Process to Reduce the Risks of Misunderstandings and Conflicts" (Washington, D.C.: National Academy of Public Administration, April 1987), p. 5.
5. Helmut Schmidt, *A Grand Strategy for the West* (New Haven, Conn.: Yale University Press, 1985), p. 151, cited in the Panel Report of the National Academy of Public Administration, p. 1.
6. T. S. Eliot, *Four Quartets* (New York: Harcourt Brace & Jovanovich, 1943), p. 39.

Selected Bibliography

Adams, Sherman. *Firsthand Report: The Story of the Eisenhower Administration.* New York: Harper & Brothers, 1961.

Allison, Graham T. *Essence of Decision: Explaining the Cuba Missile Crisis.* Boston: Little, Brown, 1971.

Allison, Graham T.; Carnesale, Albert; and Nye, Joseph S., Jr. *Hawks, Doves, and Owls: An Agenda for Avoiding Nuclear War.* New York: Norton, 1985.

Alsop, Joseph and Stewart. *We Accuse! The Story of the Miscarriage of American Justice in the Case of J. Robert Oppenheimer.* New York: Simon and Schuster, 1954.

Ambrose, Stephen E. *Eisenhower, the President, Volume II.* New York: Simon and Schuster, 1984.

American Physical Society. *Report to the American Physical Society of the Study Group on Science and Technology of Directed Energy Weapons.* New York: The American Physical Society, 1987.

Arms Control Association. *Star Wars Quotes.* Washington, D.C.: Arms Control Association, 1986.

Barrett, Laurence I. *Gambling with History: Reagan in the White House.* New York: Penguin Books, 1984.

Bechhoefer, Bernard G. *Postwar Negotiations for Arms Control.* Washington, D.C.: Brookings Institution, 1961.

Berman, Robert P., and Baker, John C. *Soviet Strategic Forces: Requirements and Responses.* Washington, D.C.: Brookings Institution, 1982.

Bernstein, Barton J., ed. *The Atomic Bomb: The Critical Issues.* Boston: Little, Brown, 1976.

Beschloss, Michael R. *May-Day: Eisenhower, Khrushchev and the U-2 Affair.* New York: Harper & Row, 1986.

Betts, Richard K. *Nuclear Blackmail and Nuclear Balance.* Washington, D.C.: Brookings Institution, 1987.

Bialer, Seweryn. *The Soviet Paradox: External Expansion, Internal Decline.* New York: Knopf, 1986.

Blair, Bruce G. *Strategic Command and Control: Redefining the Nuclear Threat.* Washington, D.C.: Brookings Institution, 1985.

Bottome, Edgar M. *The Missile Gap: A Study of the Formation of Military and Political Policy.* Rutherford, N.J.: Fairleigh Dickinson University Press, 1971.

Brooks, Charles G., ed. *Best Editorial Cartoons of the Year—1981 Edition.* Los Angeles: Pelican Publishing Company, 1981.

Bundy, McGeorge. *Danger and Survival.* New York: Random House, 1988.

Burrows, William E. *Deep Black: Space Espionage and National Security.* New York: Random House, 1986.

Carter, Jimmy. *The Presidential Campaign, 1976,* vol. 1, parts 1 & 2. Washington, D.C.: Government Printing Office, 1978.

———. *Public Papers of the Presidents of the United States: 1977,* Book I & II. Washington, D.C.: Government Printing Office, 1978.

Chace, James, and Carr, Caleb. *America Invulnerable: The Quest for Absolute Security from 1812 to Star Wars.* New York: Summit Books, 1988.

Clark, Ronald W. *The Greatest Power on Earth: The International Race for Nuclear Supremacy.* New York: Harper & Row, 1980.

Committee on International Security and

Arms Control National Academy of Sciences. *Nuclear Arms Control: Background and Issues.* Washington, D.C.: National Academy Press, 1985.

Compton, Arthur Holly. *Atomic Quest—A Personal Narrative.* New York: Oxford University Press, 1956.

Council on Foreign Relations, Inc., in cooperation with the Centre for European Policy Studies. *Blocking the Spread of Nuclear Weapons: American and European Perspectives.* 1986.

Dallek, Robert. *Ronald Reagan: The Politics of Symbolism.* Cambridge, Mass.: Harvard University Press, 1984.

Dallin, Alexander. *Black Box: KAL 007 and the Superpowers.* Berkeley: University of California Press, 1985.

Davis, Nuel Pharr. *Lawrence and Oppenheimer.* New York: Fawcett World Library, 1968.

Deaver, Michael, with Herskowitz, Mickey. *Behind the Scenes: In which the author talks about Ronald Reagan and Nancy Reagan . . . and himself.* New York: Morrow, 1987.

Department of State. *Foreign Relations of the United States 1952–1954: General Economic and Political Matters.* vol. I, parts 1 and 2. Washington, D.C.: Government Printing Office, 1983.

———. *FRUS 1952–1954: National Security Affairs,* vol. II, parts 1 and 2. Washington, D.C.: Government Printing Office, 1984.

———. *FRUS 1952–1954: Indochina.* vol. XIII, parts 1 and 2. Washington, D.C.: Government Printing Office, 1982.

———. *FRUS 1952–1954: Korea,* vol. XV, parts 1 and 2. Washington, D.C.: Government Printing Office, 1984.

Department of State. *Department of State Bulletin,* vol. 84, nos. 2087–2093. June–December 1984. Washington D.C.: Government Printing Office, 1984.

———. *Department of State Bulletin,* vol. 85, nos. 2094–2105. January–December 1985. Washington D.C.: Government Printing Office, 1985.

Dietz, David. *Atomic Science, Bombs and Power.* New York: Dodd, Mead, 1958.

Divine, Robert. *Blowing on the Wind: The Nuclear Test Ban Debate, 1954–1960.* New York: Oxford University Press, 1978.

Donovan, Robert J. *Eisenhower: The Inside Story.* New York: Harper & Brothers, 1956.

———. *Conflict and Crisis: The Presidency of Harry S. Truman: 1945–48.* New York: Norton, 1977.

———. *Tumultuous Years: The Presidency of Harry S. Truman: 1949–53.* New York: Norton, 1982.

Dunn, Lewis A. *Controlling the Bomb: Nuclear Proliferation in the 1980s.* New Haven, Conn.: Yale University Press, 1982.

Eisenhower, Dwight D. *The White House Years: Mandate for Change, 1953–1956.* New York: Doubleday, 1963.

———. *The White House Years: Waging Peace, 1956–1961.* New York: Doubleday, 1965.

———. *Public Papers of the Presidents of the United States: 1953–1961.* Washington D.C.: Government Printing Office, 1954–1962.

Feis, Herbert. *Japan Subdued—The Atomic Bomb and the End of the War in the Pacific.* Princeton, N.J.: Princeton University Press, 1961.

Ferrell, Robert H., ed. *Off the Record: The Private Papers of Harry S. Truman.* New York: Harper & Row, 1980.

———, ed. *The Diary of James C. Hagerty— Eisenhower in Mid-Course, 1954–1955.* Bloomington: Indiana University Press, 1983.

Feynman, Richard. *Surely You're Joking, Mr. Feynman!.* New York: Norton, 1985.

Ford, Daniel. *The Cult of the Atom: The Secret Papers of the Atomic Energy Commission.* New York: Simon and Schuster, 1982.

———. *The Button: The Pentagon's Strategic Command and Control System.* New York: Simon and Schuster, 1985.

Ford, Gerald. *A Time to Heal: The Autobiography of Gerald R. Ford.* New York: Harper & Row, 1979.

Freedman, Lawrence. *The Evolution of Nuclear Strategy.* New York: St. Martin's Press, 1983.

———. *U.S. Intelligence and the Soviet Strategic Threat.* Princeton, N.J.: Princeton University Press, 1986.

Garthoff, Raymond L. *Soviet Military Policy: A Historical Analysis.* New York: Praeger, 1966.

———. *Détente and Confrontation: American-Soviet Relations from Nixon to Reagan.* Washington, D.C.: Brookings Institution, 1985.

———. *Policy Versus the Law: The Reinterpretation of the ABM Treaty.* Washington, D.C.: Brookings Institution, 1987.

Goldschmidt, Bertrand. *The Atomic Adventure.* New York: Macmillan, 1964.

———. *The Atomic Complex: A Worldwide Political History of Nuclear Energy.* LaGrange Park, Ill.: American Nuclear Society, 1980.

Golovin, I. N. *I. V. Kurchatov: A Socialist-Realist Biography of the Soviet Nuclear Scientist.* Translated by William H. Dougherty. Bloomington, IN: Selbstverlag Press, 1968.

Goodchild, Peter. *J. Robert Oppenheimer: Shatterer of Worlds.* New York: Fromm International, 1985.

Gowing, Margaret. *Britain and Atomic Energy: 1939–1945.* London: Macmillan, 1964.

Greenstein, Fred I. *The Hidden-Hand Presidency: Eisenhower as Leader.* New York: Basic Books, 1982.

Groves, Leslie R. *Now It Can Be Told.* New York: Harper & Row, 1962.

Gulley, Bill, with Reese, Mary Ellen. *Breaking Cover.* New York: Simon and Schuster, 1980.

Halle, Louis J. *The Cold War as History.* New York: Harper & Row, 1967.

Halperin, Morton H. *China and the Bomb.* New York: Praeger, 1965.

———, ed. *Sino-Soviet Relations and Arms Control.* Cambridge, Mass.: MIT Press, 1967.

———. *Nuclear Fallacy: Dispelling the Myth of Nuclear Strategy.* New York: Harper & Row, 1987.

Hammond, Paul. "Super Carriers and B-36 Bombers," in *American Civil-Military Decisions: A Book of Case Studies.* Edited by Harold Stein. University: University of Alabama Press.

Herken, Gregg. *The Winning Weapon: The Atomic Bomb in the Cold War: 1945–1950.* New York: Knopf, 1980.

———. *Counsels of War.* New York: Knopf, 1985.

Hersh, Seymour M. *The Price of Power: Kissinger in the Nixon White House.* New York: Summit Books, 1983.

———. *"The Target Is Destroyed": What Really Happened to Flight 007 and What America Knew about It.* New York: Random House, 1986.

Hewlett, Richard G., and Anderson, Oscar E., Jr. *The New World, 1939–1946, Volume I: A History of the United States Atomic Energy Commission.* University Park: Pennsylvania State University Press, 1962.

Hewlett, Richard G., and Duncan, Francis. *Atomic Shield, 1947–1952, Volume II: A History of the United States Atomic Energy Commission.* University Park: Pennsylvania State University Press, 1969.

———. *Nuclear Navy, 1946–62.* Chicago: University of Chicago Press, 1974.

Holloway, David. *The Soviet Union and the Arms Race.* New Haven, Conn.: Yale University Press, 1983.

Hoopes, Townsend. *The Devil and John Foster Dulles.* Boston: Little, Brown, 1973.

Hyland, William G. *Mortal Rivals: Superpower Relations from Nixon to Reagan.* New York: Random House, 1987.

Jenkins, Roy. *Truman.* New York: Harper & Row, 1986.

Johnson, Lyndon B. *The Vantage Point: Perspectives on the Presidency, 1963–1969.* New York: Holt, Rinehart, & Winston, 1971.

Johnson, U. Alexis, with McAllister, Jef Olivarius. *The Right Hand of Power.* Englewood Cliffs, N.J.: Prentice-Hall, 1984.

Jungk, Robert. *Brighter Than a Thousand Suns: A Personal History of the Atomic Scientists.* San Diego: Harcourt Brace Jovanovich, 1958.

Kalb, Marvin and Bernard. *Kissinger.* Boston: Little, Brown, 1974.

Kennan, George F. *Russia and the West Under Lenin and Stalin.* Boston: Little, Brown, 1960.

———. *Memoirs, 1925–1950.* Boston: Little, Brown, 1967.

———. *Memoirs, 1950–1963.* Boston: Little, Brown, 1972.

———. *The Nuclear Delusion: Soviet-Ameri-*

can Relations in the Atomic Age. New York: Pantheon, 1982.

Killian, James R., Jr. *Sputnik, Scientists, and Eisenhower: A Memoir of the First Special Assistant to the President for Science and Technology.* Cambridge, Mass.: MIT Press, 1977.

Kistiakowsky, George B. *A Scientist at the White House: The Private Diary of President Eisenhower's Special Assistant for Science and Technology.* Cambridge, Mass.: Harvard University Press, 1976.

Knebel, Fletcher and Bailey, Charles W. *No High Ground.* Westport, Conn.: Greenwood Press, 1960.

Kunetka, James. *Oppenheimer: The Years of Risk.* Englewood Cliffs, N.J.: Prentice-Hall, 1982.

Lamont, Lansing. *Day of Trinity.* New York: Atheneum, 1965.

Lang, Daniel. *Early Tales of the Atomic Age.* New York: Doubleday, 1948.

Lapp, Ralph E. *The New Force: The Story of Atoms and People.* New York: Harper & Brothers, 1953.

Laurence, William L. *Dawn Over Zero—The Story of the Atomic Bomb.* New York: Knopf, 1953.

Long, Franklin A.; Hafner, Donald; and Boutwell, Jeffrey, eds. *Weapons in Space.* New York: Norton, 1986.

McMahan, Jeff. *Reagan and the World: Imperial Policy in the New Cold War.* New York: Monthly Review Press, 1985.

Macmillan, Harold. *Riding the Storm, 1956–1959.* New York: Harper & Row, 1971.

———. *Pointing the Way, 1959–1961.* London: MacMillan, 1973.

———. *At the End of the Day, 1961–1963.* New York: Harper & Row, 1973.

MacKenzie, Norman and Jeanne. *H. G. Wells.* New York: Simon and Schuster, Touchstone Books, 1973.

Mancall, Mark. *China at the Center: 300 Years of Foreign Policy.* New York: The Free Press, 1984.

Mayer, Jane and McManus, Doyle, *Landslide; The Unmaking of the President 1984–1988,* Boston, Houghton Mifflin, 1988.

Medvedev, Zhores A. *Gorbachev.* New York: Norton, 1986.

Millis, Walter, ed., with the collaboration of E. S. Duffield. *The Forrestal Diaries.* New York: Viking, 1951.

Morris, Roger. *Uncertain Greatness: Henry Kissinger and American Foreign Policy.* New York: Harper & Row, 1977.

National Archives and Records Service. *Weekly Compilation of Presidential Documents, January 2, 1984–June 15, 1984,* vol. 20, nos. 1–25. Washington, D.C.: National Archives and Records Service, 1984.

———. *Weekly Compilation of Presidential Documents, 1985,* vol. 21, nos. 1–52. Washington, D.C.: National Archives and Records Service, 1985.

Newhouse, John. *De Gaulle and the Anglo-Saxons.* New York: Viking, 1970.

———. *Cold Dawn: The Story of SALT.* New York: Holt, Rinehart, & Winston, 1973.

Nicholas, H. G., ed. *Washington Dispatches 1941–1945: Weekly Political Reports from the British Embassy.* London: Weidenfeld & Nicolson, 1981.

Nixon, Richard M. *Six Crises.* New York: Doubleday, 1962.

———. *Public Papers of the Presidents of the United States: 1973.* Washington, D.C.: Government Printing Office, 1975.

———. *The Memoirs of Richard Nixon.* New York: Grosset & Dunlap, 1978.

Nye, Joseph S., Jr. *Nuclear Ethics.* New York: The Free Press, 1986.

O'Keefe, Bernard J. *Nuclear Hostages.* Boston: Houghton Mifflin, 1983.

Osgood, Robert E. *NATO: The Entangling Alliance.* Chicago: University of Chicago Press, 1962.

Oye, Kenneth A.; Rothchild, Donald; and Lieber, Robert J., eds. *Eagle Entangled: U.S. Foreign Policy in a Complex World.* New York: Longman, 1979.

Peierls, Rudolf. *Bird of Passage: Recollections of a Physicist.* Princeton, N.J.: Princeton University Press, 1985.

Phillips, Cabell. *From the Crash to the Blitz: 1929–1939.* London: Macmillan, 1969.

Powers, Thomas. *Thinking about the Next War.* New York: Knopf, 1982.

Pringle, Peter, and Spigelman, James. *The Nuclear Barons.* New York: Holt, Rinehart, & Winston, 1981.

Purcell, John. *The Best Kept Secret: The Story of the Atomic Bomb.* New York: Vanguard, 1963.

Quandt, William B. *Decade of Decisions: American Foreign Policy Toward the Arab-Israeli Conflict, 1967–1976.* Berkeley: University of California Press, 1977.

Reagan, Ronald. *Public Papers of the Presidents of the United States: 1981.* Washington, D.C.: Government Printing Office, 1982.

———. *Public Papers of the Presidents of the United States: 1982,* Book I & II. Washington, D.C.: Government Printing Office, 1983.

Rhodes, Richard. *The Making of the Atomic Bomb.* New York: Simon and Schuster, 1986.

Roberts, Chalmers M. *The Nuclear Years; The Arms Race and Arms Control, 1945–1970.* New York: Praeger, 1970.

Rovere, Richard H. *Affairs of State: The Eisenhower Years.* New York: Farrar, Straus, & Cudahy, 1956.

Scheinman, Lawrence. *Atomic Energy Policy in France under the Fourth Republic.* Princeton, N.J.: Princeton University Press, 1965.

Schick, Jack M. *The Berlin Crisis, 1958–1962.* Philadelphia: University of Pennsylvania Press, 1971.

Schilling, Warner R.; Hammond, Paul Y.; and Snyder, Glenn H. *Strategy, Politics, and Defense Budgets.* New York: Columbia University Press, 1962.

Schwartz, David N. *NATO's Nuclear Dilemmas.* Washington, D.C.: Brookings Institution, 1983.

Sherwin, Martin J. *A World Destroyed: The Atomic Bomb and the Grand Alliance.* New York: Knopf, 1975.

Shevchenko, Arkady N. *Breaking with Moscow.* New York: Knopf, 1985.

Sigal, Leon V. *Fighting to a Finish: The Politics of War Termination in the United States and Japan, 1945.* Ithaca, N.Y.: Cornell University Press, 1988.

Smith, Alice Kimball. *A Peril and a Hope: The Scientists' Movement in America: 1945–47.* Chicago: University of Chicago Press, 1965.

Smith, Alice Kimball, and Weiner, Charles, eds. *Robert Oppenheimer: Letters and Recollections.* Cambridge, Mass.: Harvard University Press, 1980.

Smith, Hedrick. *The Power Game: How Washington Works.* New York: Random House, 1988.

Spector, Leonard S. *Nuclear Proliferation Today: The Spread of Nuclear Weapons, 1984.* New York: Vintage, 1984.

———. *Going Nuclear: The Spread of Nuclear Weapons, 1986–1987.* Boston: Ballinger, 1987.

Speier, Hans. *Divided Berlin: The Anatomy of Soviet Political Blackmail.* New York: Praeger, 1961.

Steele, Jonathan, and Abraham, Eric. *Andropov in Power: From Komsomol to Kremlin.* New York: Doubleday, Anchor Press, 1984.

Stern, Paula. *Water's Edge: Domestic Politics and the Making of American Foreign Policy.* Westport, Conn.: Greenwood Press, 1979.

Stern, Philip M., and Green, Harold P. *The Oppenheimer Case: Security on Trial.* New York: Harper & Row, 1969.

Stimson, Henry L., and Bundy, McGeorge. *On Active Service in Peace and War.* New York: Harper & Brothers, 1947.

Stockman, David A. *The Triumph of Politics: Why the Reagan Revolution Failed.* New York: Harper & Row, 1986.

Stokely, James. *The New World of the Atom.* New York: Ives Washburn, 1957.

Szulc, Tad. *The Illusion of Peace: Foreign Policy in the Nixon Years.* New York: Viking, 1978.

Talbott, Strobe, edited with introduction, commentary, and notes by Edward Crankshaw. *Khrushchev Remembers.* Boston: Little, Brown, 1970.

———. *Khrushchev Remembers: The Last Testament.* Boston: Little, Brown, 1974.

———. *Endgame: The Inside Story of SALT II.* New York: Harper & Row, Harper Torchbooks, 1979, 1980.

———. *Deadly Gambits: The Reagan Administration and the Stalemate in Nuclear Arms Control.* New York: Knopf, 1984.

———. *The Russians and Reagan.* A Council on Foreign Relations Book. New York: Vintage, 1984.

Terrill, Ross. *800,000,000: The Real China.* Boston: Little, Brown, 1972.

Truman, Harry S. *Years of Decision, Volume I.* New York: Doubleday, 1955.

———. *Years of Trial and Hope, Volume II.* New York: Doubleday, 1956.

Truman, Margaret. *Bess W. Truman.* New York: Macmillan, 1986.

U.S. Congress, Office of Technology Assessment. *Ballistic Missile Defense Technologies,* OTA-ISC-254. Washington, D.C.: Government Printing Office, September 1985.

U.S. Strategic Bombing Survey. "The Effects of Atomic Bombs on Hiroshima and Nagasaki." Washington, D.C.: Government Printing Office, 1946.

Weart, Spencer R., and Szilard, Gertrud

Weiss, eds. *Leo Szilard: His Version of the Fact: Selected Recollections and Correspondence, Volume II.* Cambridge, Mass.: MIT Press, 1978.

Wells, H. G. *The World Set Free—A Story of Mankind.* London: Macmillan, 1914.

Yager, Joseph A., ed. *Nonproliferation and U.S. Foreign Policy.* Washington D.C.: Brookings Institution, 1980.

York, Herbert. *The Advisors: Oppenheimer, Teller and the Superbomb.* San Francisco: W.H. Freeman, 1976.

———. *Race to Oblivion: A Participant's View of the Arms Race.* New York: Simon and Schuster, 1970.

Zhukov, G. K. *The Memoirs of Marshal Zhukov.* Translated by Novosti. New York: Delacorte Press, 1971.

Articles

Arneson, Gordon. "The H-Bomb Decision." *Foreign Service Journal* (May 1969): 27–29.

———. "The H-Bomb Decision, Part II." *Foreign Service Journal* (June 1969): 24–27, 43.

Ball, Desmond. "Targeting for Strategic Deterrence." *Adelphi Papers,* no. 185 (Summer 1983), International Institute for Strategic Studies, London.

Beatty, Jack. "In Harm's Way." *The Atlantic* (May 1987): 37–53.

Bialer, Seweryn, and Afferica, Joan. "The Genesis of Gorbachev's World." *Foreign Affairs, America and the World 1985* 64, no. 3 (1986): 605–44, Council on Foreign Relations, New York.

Blechman, Barry M., and Hart, Douglas M. "The Political Utility of Nuclear Weapons: The 1973 Middle East Crisis." *International Security* 7, no. 1 (Summer 1982): 132–56.

Bundy, McGeorge. "The H-Bomb: The Missed Chance." *The New York Review of Books* (May 13, 1982): 13–22.

———, transcriber, and Blight, James G., ed. "October 27, 1962: Transcripts of the Meetings of the ExComm." *International Security* 12, no. 3 (Winter 1987–1988): 30–92.

Chang, Gordon H. "To the Nuclear Brink: Eisenhower, Dulles, and the Quemoy-Matsu Crisis." *International Security* 12, no. 4 (Spring 1988): 96–122.

Davis, Lynn. "Limited Nuclear Options: Deterrence and the New American Doctrine." *Adelphi Papers,* no. 121 (Winter 1975/76), International Institute for Strategic Studies, London.

Flournoy, Michele A. "A Rocky START." *Arms Control Today* 17, no. 8 (October 1987): 7–13. Arms Control Association, Washington, D.C.

Friedman, Edward. "Nuclear Blackmail and the End of the Korean War." *Modern China* 1, no. 1, (January 1975): 75–91.

Garthoff, Raymond L. "Postmortem on INF Talks." *Bulletin of the Atomic Scientists,* 40, no. 10 (December, 1984): 7–10.

———. "Did Khrushchev Bluff in Cuba? No." *Bulletin of the Atomic Scientists* 44, no. 6 (July/August, 1988): 40–43.

Halperin, Morton. "Chinese Nuclear Strategy: The Early Post Detonation Period." *Adelphi Papers,* no. 18, (May 1965), Institute for Strategic Studies, London.

Horelick, Arnold L. "The Cuban Missile Crisis: An Analysis of Soviet Calculations and Behavior." *World Politics* XVI, no. 3 (April, 1964): 363–89.

Hough, Jerry F. "Gorbachev's Strategy." *Foreign Affairs* 64, no. 1 (Fall 1985): 33–55, Council on Foreign Relations, New York.

Jones, Rodney W. "Nuclear Proliferation: Islam, the Bomb and South Asia." *The Washington Papers* 9, no. 82 (1981), Sage Publications, California.

Mandelbaum, Michael. "The Luck of the President." *Foreign Affairs, America and the World 1985* 64, no. 3 (1986): 393–412, Council on Foreign Relations, New York.

Mendelsohn, Jack. "INF Verification: A Guide for the Perplexed." *Arms Control Today* 17, no. 7 (September 1987): 15–19, Arms Control Association, Washington, D.C.

Powers, Thomas. "Choosing a Strategy for World War III." *The Atlantic Monthly* (November 1982): 82–110.

———. "What Is It About? Neither Superpower Can Explain a Competition that Threatens Mutual Annihilation." *The Atlantic* (January 1984): 35–55.

———. "Is Nuclear War Impossible?" *The Atlantic* (November 1984): 53–64.

Sagan, Scott D. "Nuclear Alerts and Crisis Management." *International Security* 9, no. 4 (Spring 1985): 99–139.

Sigal, Leon V. "Bureaucratic Politics and Tactical Use of Committees: The Interim Committee and the Decision to Drop the Bomb." *Polity* 3 (Spring 1978): 326–64.

———. "The Reagan Compromise on ABM." *Bulletin of the Atomic Scientists* 44, no. 3 (April 1988): 10–15.

Trachtenberg, Marc. "The Influence of Nuclear Weapons in the Cuban Missile Crisis." *International Security* 10, no. 1 (Summer, 1985): 137–163.

U.S. Senate. Committee on Armed Services. *Military Implications of the Treaty on the Limitation of Strategic Offensive Arms and Protocol Thereto (Salt II Treaty).* Parts I and II. Washington, D.C.: Government Printing Office, 1979.

———. *Nominations of Harold Brown and Charles W. Duncan, Jr* Jan. 11, 1977. Washington, D.C.: Government Printing Office, 1977.

Welch, David A., and Blight, James G. "The Eleventh Hour of the Cuban Missile Crisis: An Introduction to the ExComm Transcripts." *International Security* 12, no. 3 (Winter 1987/1988): 5–29.

Wells, Samuel F., Jr. "Origins of Massive Retaliation." *Political Science Quarterly* 96, no. 1 (Spring 1981): 31–52, Academy of Political Science, Columbia University, New York.

Index

463

A Note About the Author

John Newhouse is a staff writer for *The New Yorker* and the author of several books—most recently *The Sporty Game* (1982). He is also a Guest Scholar at the Brookings Institution in Washington, D.C. In the mid- to late 1970s, he served first as Counselor and then as an Assistant Director of the Arms Control and Disarmament Agency. Earlier, he was a staff member of the Senate Committee on Foreign Relations (1959–1964). He is a member of the Council on Foreign Relations and the International Institute for Strategic Studies.

A Note on the Type

This book was set in a digitized version of Janson. The hot-metal version of Janson was a recutting made direct from type cast from matrices long thought to have been made by the Dutchman Anton Janson, who was a practicing type founder in Leipzig during the years 1668–1687. However, it has been conclusively demonstrated that these types are actually the work of Nicholas Kis (1650–1702), a Hungarian, who most probably learned his trade from the master Dutch type founder Dirk Voskens. The type is an excellent example of the influential and sturdy Dutch types that prevailed in England up to the time William Caslon (1692–1766) developed his own incomparable designs from them.

Composed by The Haddon Craftsmen, Inc.,
Scranton, Pennsylvania

Designed by Anthea Lingeman